HUMAN SEXUALITY 90/91

Fifteenth Edition

Editor

Ollie Pocs
Illinois State University

Ollie Pocs is a professor in the Department of Sociology, Anthropology, and Social Work at Illinois State University. He received his B.A. and M.A. in sociology from the University of Illinois, and a Ph.D. in family studies from Purdue University. His primary areas of interest are marriage and family, human sexuality and sexuality education, sex roles, and counseling/therapy. He has published several books and articles in these areas.

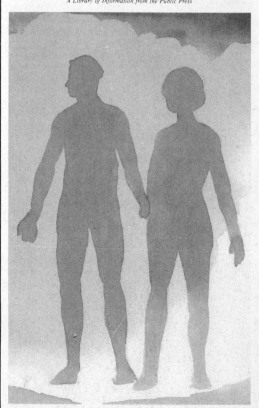

A Library of Information from the Public Press

Cover illustration by Mike Eagle

The Dushkin Publishing Group, Inc.
Sluice Dock, Guilford, Connecticut 06437

The Annual Editions Series

Annual Editions is a series of over fifty volumes designed to provide the reader with convenient, low-cost access to a wide range of current, carefully selected articles from some of the most important magazines, newspapers, and journals published today. Annual Editions are updated on an annual basis through a continuous monitoring of over 200 periodical sources. All Annual Editions have a number of features designed to make them particularly useful, including topic guides, annotated tables of contents, unit overviews, and indexes. For the teacher using Annual Editions in the classroom, an Instructor's Resource Guide with test questions is available for each volume.

VOLUMES AVAILABLE

Africa
Aging
American Government
American History, Pre-Civil War
American History, Post-Civil War
Anthropology
Biology
Business and Management
Business Ethics
Canadian Politics
China
Comparative Politics
Computers in Education
Computers in Business
Computers in Society
Criminal Justice
Drugs, Society, and Behavior
Early Childhood Education
Economics
Educating Exceptional Children
Education
Educational Psychology
Environment
Geography
Global Issues
Health
Human Development

Human Resources
Human Sexuality
Latin America
Macroeconomics
Marketing
Marriage and Family
Middle East and the Islamic World
Money and Banking
Nutrition
Personal Growth and Behavior
Psychology
Public Administration
Social Problems
Sociology
Soviet Union and Eastern Europe
State and Local Government
Third World
Urban Society
Violence and Terrorism
Western Civilization, Pre-Reformation
Western Civilization, Post-Reformation
Western Europe
World History, Pre-Modern
World History, Modern
World Politics

Library of Congress Cataloging in Publication Data
Main entry under title: Annual Editions: Human sexuality. 1990/91.
1. Sexual behavior—Addresses, essays, lectures—Periodicals. 2. Sexual hygiene—Addresses, essays, lectures—Periodicals. 3. Sex education—Addresses, essays, lectures—Periodicals. 4. Human relations—Addresses, essays, lectures—Periodicals. I. Pocs, Ollie, comp. II. Title: Human sexuality.
ISBN 0-87967-849-6   155.3′05   75-20756

Fifteenth Edition

Manufactured by The Banta Company, Harrisonburg, Virginia 22801

To the Reader

In publishing ANNUAL EDITIONS we recognize the enormous role played by the magazines, newspapers, and journals of the *public press* in providing current, first-rate educational information in a broad spectrum of interest areas. Within the articles, the best scientists, practitioners, researchers, and commentators draw issues into new perspective as accepted theories and viewpoints are called into account by new events, recent discoveries change old facts, and fresh debate breaks out over important controversies.

Many of the articles resulting from this enormous editorial effort are appropriate for students, researchers, and professionals seeking accurate, current material to help bridge the gap between principles and theories and the real world. These articles, however, become more useful for study when those of lasting value are carefully *collected, organized, indexed,* and *reproduced* in a *low-cost format,* which provides easy and permanent access when the material is needed. That is the role played by *Annual Editions.* Under the direction of each volume's *Editor,* who is an expert in the subject area, and with the guidance of an *Advisory Board,* we seek each year to provide in each ANNUAL EDITION a current, well-balanced, carefully selected collection of the best of the public press for your study and enjoyment. We think you'll find this volume useful, and we hope you'll take a moment to let us know what you think.

Sex lies at the root of life, and we can never learn to reverence life until we know how to understand sex.

—*Havelock Ellis*

The above quote by one of the first sexologists highlights the objective of this book. Learning about sex is a lifelong process that can occur informally and formally. With knowledge comes the understanding that we are all born sexual, and that sex, per se, is neither good nor bad, beautiful nor ugly, moral nor immoral.

While we are all born with basic sexual interests, drives, and desires, human sexuality is a dynamic and complex force that involves psychological and sociocultural dimensions in addition to the physiological ones. Sexuality includes an individual's whole body and personality. We are not born with a fully developed body or mind, but instead grow and learn; so it is with respect to our sexuality. Sexuality is learned. We learn what "appropriate" sexual behavior is, how to express it, when to do so, and under what circumstances. We also learn sexual feelings: positive feelings such as acceptance of sexuality, or negative and repressive feelings such as guilt and shame.

Sexuality, which affects human life so basically and powerfully, has, until recently, received little attention in scientific research, and even less attention within higher education communities. Yet our contemporary social environment is expanding its sexual and social horizons toward greater freedom for the individual, especially for women and for people who deviate from societal norms: those who are somehow handicapped and those who make less common sexual or relationship choices. Without proper understanding, this expansion in sexual freedom can lead to new forms of sexual bondage as easily as to increased joy and pleasure. The celebration of sexuality today is most likely found somewhere between the traditional, rigid, repressive morality that is our sociosexual heritage, and a new performance-oriented, irresponsible, self-seeking mentality.

In trying to understand sexuality, our goal is to seek a joyful acceptance of being sexual, and to express this awareness in the most considerate way for ourselves and our sexual partners, while at the same time taking personal and social consequences into account. This anthology is aimed at helping all of us achieve this goal.

The articles selected for this edition cover a wide range of important topics and were written primarily by professionals for a nonprofessional audience. In them, health educators, psychologists, sociologists, sexologists, and sex therapists writing for professional journals and popular magazines present their views on how and why sexual attitudes and behaviors are developed, maintained, and changed. This edition of *Annual Editions: Human Sexuality* is organized into six sections. *Sexuality and Society* notes historical and cross-cultural views, and analyzes our constantly changing society and sexuality. *Sexual Biology and Health* explains the responses of the human body and new concerns with sexual hygiene. *Reproduction* discusses some recent trends related to pregnancy and childbearing, and deals with reproductive topics including conception, contraception, and abortion. *Interpersonal Relationships* provides suggestions for establishing and maintaining intimate, responsible, quality relationships. *Sexuality Through the Life Cycle* looks at what happens sexually throughout one's lifetime, from childhood to the later years. Finally, *Old/New Sexual Concerns* deals with such topics as sexual orientation, sexual abuse and violence, and AIDS.

The articles in this anthology have been carefully reviewed and selected for their quality, currency, and interest. They present a variety of viewpoints. Some you will agree with, some you will not, but you will learn from all of them.

Appreciation and a thank you go to Susan Bunting for her work and expertise. We feel that *Human Sexuality 90/91* is one of the most useful and up-to-date books available. Please let us know what you think. Return the article rating form on the last page of this book with your suggestions and comments. Any book can be improved. This one will continue to be—annually.

Ollie Pocs

Ollie Pocs
Editor

Contents

Unit 1

Sexuality and Society

Eight selections consider sexuality from historical and cross-cultural perspectives, and examine today's changing attitudes toward human sexual interaction.

To the Reader   iv
Topic Guide   2
Overview   4

A. HISTORICAL AND CROSS-CULTURAL PERSPECTIVES

1. **Why We Need Limits,** Jean Bethke Elshtain, *Utne Reader,* September/October 1988.   6
   The author ponders the benefits and problems of **sexual freedom**, viewing limit-setting not as a return to the **repression of the past** but as a way to return meaning and maximize **equality** in sexual relationships.

2. **Beware of Setting Limits,** Judith Levine, *Utne Reader,* September/October 1988.   9
   The author warns that we must continue to fight for **sexual liberation** and **sex education** in order to mount a unified and effective attack on AIDS and to counteract the current growing **anti-sex hysteria**.

3. **The Politics of Child Sexual Abuse: Notes From American History,** Linda Gordon, *Feminist Review,* January 1988.   12
   The author cites evidence that the presence or absence of a feminist movement at different points in history has had a profound impact on the perception of and response to the problem of **child sexual abuse**. She also examines **current issues** relating to this problem, and looks at the **politics** of prevention.

4. **Sex in China,** Fang Fu Ruan and Vern L. Bullough, *Medical Aspects of Human Sexuality,* July 1989.   17
   For more than 30 years very restrictive policies have existed in **China** regarding **sexual information and behavior**. The '80s have brought some new openness, according to this article. Read about the kinds of questions Chinese men and women are now asking and receiving answers to in their media.

5. **AIDS News, Highlights: Fifth International AIDS Conference: Montreal, June 4-9,** Patricia Kloser, *Medical Aspects of Human Sexuality,* August 1989.   21
   Although AIDS is in the news daily, separating fact from fear and myth is still not an easy task. This article summarizes the **data and trends shared at the prestigious 5th International AIDS Conference** held in June of 1989 in Montreal.

B. CHANGING SOCIETY/CHANGING SEXUALITY

6. **The Chemistry of Love,** John Poppy, *Esquire,* May 1989.   24
   Chemicals known as **neuropeptides** may be the link between the **mind and body** that explains why scientists are agreeing with your grandmother's wisdom that happy feelings and thoughts lead to healthy bodies. But did your grandmother say touch also contributes to health? This article does.

7. **What Keeps Women "in Their Place"?** Anthony Layng, *USA Today Magazine (Society for the Advancement of Education),* May 1989.   28
   In spite of nearly two decades of activism directed at realizing **equality between the sexes**, inequality is still very evident. Dr. Layng, a professor of anthropology, examines the beliefs and customs of developed and tribal societies, and of men and women, that contribute to this disparity.

8. **The American Man in Transition,** Michael Segell, *American Health,* January/February 1989.   32
   A new American Health/Gallup survey has found that both men and women believe **men need to change**. Read about this **masculine ideal** and a range of issues and reactions associated with it.

The concepts in bold italics are developed in the article. For further expansion please refer to the Topic Guide, the Index, and the Glossary.

Unit 2

Sexual Biology and Health

Eleven selections examine the biological aspects of human sexuality and emphasize the importance of understanding sexual hygiene.

The concepts in bold italics are developed in the article. For further expansion please refer to the Topic Guide, the Index, and the Glossary.

Unit 3

Reproduction

Eleven articles discuss the roles of both males and females in pregnancy and childbirth, and consider the influences of the latest birth control methods and practices on individuals and society as a whole.

Unit 4

Interpersonal Relationships

Seven selections examine the dynamics of establishing
sexual relationships and the need to make these
relationships responsible and effective.

Unit 5

Sexuality Through the Life Cycle

Eight articles consider human sexuality as an important element throughout the life cycle. Topics include sexuality and its relationship to children's feelings about themselves, responsible adolescent sexuality, sex in and out of marriage, and sex in old age.

The concepts in bold italics are developed in the article. For further expansion please refer to the Topic Guide, the Index, and the Glossary.

Unit 6

Old/New Sexual Concerns

Fourteen selections discuss ongoing sexual concerns: sexual orientation, sexual harassment and violence, and the growing concern over AIDS.

The concepts in bold italics are developed in the article. For further expansion please refer to the Topic Guide, the Index, and the Glossary.

The concepts in bold italics are developed in the article. For further expansion please refer to the Topic Guide, the Index, and the Glossary.

Topic Guide

This topic guide suggests how the selections in this book relate to topics of traditional concern to human sexuality students and professionals. It is very useful in locating articles which relate to each other for reading and research. The guide is arranged alphabetically according to topic. Articles may, of course, treat topics that do not appear in the topic guide. In turn, entries in the topic guide do not necessarily constitute a comprehensive listing of all the contents of each selection.

TOPIC AREA	TREATED AS AN ISSUE IN:	TOPIC AREA	TREATED AS AN ISSUE IN:
Abortion	20. The Case for National Action 21. His Sexuality, Her Reproductive Rights 29. Voting in Curbs and Confusion 30. Abortion: Right or Wrong?	Health	5. AIDS News 6. The Chemistry of Love 11. Chemistry of Sexual Desire Yields Its Elusive Secrets 12. Is Orgasm Essential? 13. Contagious Fortune 14. STDs—Sexually Transmitted Diseases 15. UTI's 16. The Healthy Male 17. Infertility 18. Demystifying Menopause 19. Sharp Rise in Rare Sex-Related Diseases 22. Yes, You Can 26. Vasectomy Update 39. Double Vision 44. What Doctors and Others Need to Know
Abuse, Sexual	3. The Politics of Child Sexual Abuse 38. Sex in Childhood 50. Shattered Innocence 51. Sexual Harassment, '80s-Style 53. Male Rape: The Hidden Crime		
Acquired Immune Deficiency Syndrome	2. Beware of Setting Limits 5. AIDS News 13. Contagious Fortune 19. Sharp Rise in Rare Sex-Related Diseases 25. Kids and Contraceptives 35. Sexual Pursuit 37. I Love You, But Can I Ask a Question? 54. Patient Guide: How to Use a Condom 55. Can You Rely on Condoms? 56. AIDS and the College Student 57. Helping Schools to Cope With AIDS 58. Flirting With AIDS	Homosexuality	46. Straight or Gay? 47. Gay and Lesbian Adolescents 48. The Impact of Homophobia 49. Homosexuality: Who and Why?
		Incest	3. The Politics of Child Sexual Abuse 7. What Keeps Women "in Their Place"? 38. Sex in Childhood 50. Shattered Innocence
		Infertility	17. Infertility
Adolescents/ Teenagers	20. The Case for National Action 25. Kids and Contraceptives 29. Voting in Curbs and Confusion 40. What College Students Want to Know About Sex 41. Masturbatory Behavior in College Youth 47. Gay and Lesbian Adolescents 48. The Impact of Homophobia	Intimacy, Sexual	6. The Chemistry of Love 8. The American Man in Transition 9. Close Encounters 10. The Power of Touch 11. Chemistry of Sexual Desire Yields Its Elusive Secrets 31. Barriers in the Initiation 33. How Do You Build Intimacy in an Age of Divorce? 35. Sexual Pursuit 42. Sex: Better After 35 43. Good Sex Makes Good Marriages
Aging	42. Sex: Better After 35 43. Good Sex Makes Good Marriages 44. What Doctors and Others Need to Know 45. Love, Sex, and Aging		
Attitudes/Values	2. Beware of Setting Limits 4. Sex in China 6. The Chemistry of Love 7. What Keeps Women "in Their Place"? 8. The American Man in Transition 22. His Sexuality, Her Reproductive Rights 23. Saying No to Motherhood 30. Abortion: Right or Wrong? 32. Study Defines Major Sources of Conflict Between Sexes 35. Sexual Pursuit 39. Double Vision	Love	6. The Chemistry of Love 8. The American Man in Transition 32. Study Defines Major Sources of Conflict Between Sexes 33. How Do You Build Intimacy in an Age of Divorce? 35. Sexual Pursuit
		Men	8. The American Man in Transition 16. The Healthy Male 21. His Sexuality, Her Reproductive Rights 26. Vasectomy Update 31. Barriers in the Initiation 32. Study Defines Major Sources of Conflict Between Sexes 41. Masturbatory Behavior in College Youth 42. Sex: Better After 35 44. What Doctors and Others Need to Know 46. Straight or Gay? 47. Gay and Lesbian Adolescents 48. The Impact of Homophobia 53. Male Rape: The Hidden Crime
Birth Control/ Contraception	24. The Crisis in Contraception 25. Kids and Contraceptives 26. Vasectomy Update 27. Pill Politics 28. A Failed Revolution		
Childbirth	7. What Keeps Women "in Their Place"? 20. The Case for National Action 21. His Sexuality, Her Reproductive Rights 23. Saying No to Motherhood		
Children	3. The Politics of Child Sexual Abuse 7. What Keeps Women "in Their Place"? 9. Close Encounters 25. Kids and Contraceptives 38. Sex in Childhood 46. Straight or Gay?		

TOPIC AREA	TREATED AS AN ISSUE IN:	TOPIC AREA	TREATED AS AN ISSUE IN:
Myths/Misinformation	4. Sex in China 18. Demystifying Menopause 22. Yes, You Can 30. Abortion: Right or Wrong? 44. What Doctors and Others Need to Know 51. Sexual Harassment, '80s-Style 53. Male Rape: The Hidden Crime	**Sex Education**	2. Beware of Setting Limits 20. The Case for National Action 31. Barriers in the Initiation 38. Sex in Childhood 40. What College Students Want to Know About Sex 57. Helping Schools to Cope With AIDS
Parents	17. Infertility 46. Straight or Gay? 47. Gay and Lesbian Adolescents 48. The Impact of Homophobia	**Sexual Dysfunction**	11. Chemistry of Sexual Desire Yields Its Elusive Secrets 15. UTI's 16. The Healthy Male 35. Sexual Pursuit 36. Not Tonight, Dear 42. Sex: Better After 35 43. Good Sex Makes Good Marriages 44. What Doctors and Others Need to Know
Politics of Sex/ Sexuality	2. Beware of Setting Limits 3. The Politics of Child Sexual Abuse 4. Sex in China 7. What Keeps Women "in Their Place"? 20. The Case for National Action 21. His Sexuality, Her Reproductive Rights 27. Pill Politics 30. Abortion: Right or Wrong? 51. Sexual Harassment, '80s-Style 53. Male Rape: The Hidden Crime 57. Helping Schools to Cope with AIDS	**Technology**	6. The Chemistry of Love 11. Chemistry of Sexual Desire Yields Its Elusive Secrets 15. UTI's 24. The Crisis in Contraception 27. Pill Politics 28. A Failed Revolution 29. Voting in Curbs and Confusion 59. The Emerging Strategy to Contain AIDS
Pornography	2. Beware of Setting Limits 7. What Keeps Women "in Their Place"? 51. Sexual Harassment, '80s-Style	**Therapy/Counseling**	10. The Power of Touch 31. Barriers in the Initiation 33. How Do You Build Intimacy in an Age of Divorce? 37. I Love You, But Can I Ask a Question? 39. Double Vision 47. Gay and Lesbian Adolescents 53. Male Rape: The Hidden Crime
Pregnancy	20. The Case for National Action 21. His Sexuality, Her Reproductive Rights 22. Yes, You Can 25. Kids and Contraceptives 27. Pill Politics 29. Voting in Curbs and Confusion	**Women**	3. The Politics of Child Sexual Abuse 7. What Keeps Women "in Their Place"? 15. UTI's 17. Infertility 18. Demystifying Menopause 21. His Sexuality, Her Reproductive Rights 23. Saying No to Motherhood 27. Pill Politics 28. A Failed Revolution 32. Study Defines Major Sources of Conflict Between Sexes 35. Sexual Pursuit 39. Double Vision 47. Gay and Lesbian Adolescents 48. The Impact of Homophobia 51. Sexual Harassment, '80s-Style
Relationships	1. Why We Need Limits 6. The Chemistry of Love 8. The American Man in Transition 31. Barriers in the Initiation 32. Study Defines Major Sources of Conflict Between Sexes 33. How Do You Build Intimacy in an Age of Divorce? 34. Major Mergers 35. Sexual Pursuit 36. Not Tonight, Dear 42. Sex: Better After 35 43. Good Sex Makes Good Marriages 44. What Doctors and Others Need to Know		
Research	5. AIDS News 6. The Chemistry of Love 11. Chemistry of Sexual Desire Yields Its Elusive Secrets 24. The Crisis in Contraception 27. Pill Politics 31. Barriers in the Initiation 32. Study Defines Major Sources of Conflict Between Sexes 39. Double Vision 41. Masturbatory Behavior in College Youth 46. Straight or Gay? 49. Homosexuality: Who and Why? 50. Shattered Innocence 51. Sexual Harassment, '80s-Style 55. Can You Rely on Condoms? 58. Flirting With AIDS 59. The Emerging Strategy to Contain AIDS		

Sexuality and Society

- Historical and Cross-Cultural Perspectives (Articles 1-5)
- Changing Society/Changing Sexuality (Articles 6-8)

People of different civilizations in different historical periods have engaged in a variety of modes of sexual expression and behavior. Despite this cultural and historical diversity, one important principle should be kept in mind: Sexual awareness, attitudes, and behaviors are learned within sociocultural contexts that define appropriate sexuality for society's members. Our sexual attitudes and behaviors are in large measure social and cultural phenomena.

For several centuries, Western civilization has been characterized by an "anti-sex ethic" which has normatively limited sexual behavior to the confines of monogamous pair bonds (marriages) for the sole purpose of procreation. Today, changes in our social environment—the widespread availability of effective contraception, the liberation of women from the home and kitchen, and the reconsideration of democratic values of "individual freedom" and the "pursuit of happiness"—are strengthening our concept of ourselves as sexual beings and posing a challenge to the "anti-sex ethic" that has traditionally served to orient sexuality.

As a rule, social change is not easily accomplished. Sociologists generally acknowledge that changes in the social environment are accompanied by the presence of interest groups that offer competing versions of what "is" or "should be" appropriate social behavior. The contemporary sociocultural changes with respect to sexuality are highly illustrative of such social dynamics. Many of the articles in this section document changes in the social environment and the beliefs of different groups about what are or should be our social policies regarding sexuality. The articles also illustrate the diversity of beliefs regarding what was beneficial or detrimental about the past, and what needs to be preserved or changed for a better future.

The fact that human sexuality is primarily a learned behavior can be both a blessing and a curse. The learning process enables humans to achieve a range of sexual expression and meaning that far exceeds their biological programming. Unfortunately, however, our society's lingering "anti-sex ethic" tends to foreclose constructive learning experiences and contexts, often driving learning underground. What is needed for the future is high-quality, pervasive sex education to counteract the locker room, commercial sex, and the trial-and-error contexts in which most individuals in our society acquire misinformation, anxiety, and fear—as opposed to knowledge, reassurance, and comfort—about themselves as sexual people.

A view of the past illustrates the connectedness of our values and perceptions of sexuality with other socio-political events and beliefs. A cross-cultural view illustrates common human patterns and needs with respect to sexuality and other interpersonal issues. Several of the articles in this section describe and examine patterns of change in political, economic, medical, and educational spheres with patterns in family and intimate relationships, sex roles, sexual behavior, and sexual abuse. Although the authors may not agree on the desirability of the changes they describe nor advocate the same future directions, they do emphasize the necessity for people to have information and awareness about a wide range of sexual topics. They also share another belief: we as individuals and as a world society have a vital interest in the translation of social consciousness and sexuality into a meaningful and rewarding awareness and expression for all of society's members.

The first subsection, *Historical and Cross-Cultural Perspectives*, contains five very powerful commentaries on past and present sexual behavior, sexual abuse, and sexual health in the United States and the world. Each author cites problems and outcomes associated with misinformation and lack of access to accurate or complete information about sexuality. Each calls for increased awareness and advocacy so that tomorrow will bring more positive sexual experiences for individuals and will improve sexual health in the era of AIDS.

The second subsection, *Changing Society/Changing Sexuality*, contains three articles that address changes in our personal and society's view of sexuality, femaleness, maleness, and relationships between the sexes. The first article, "The Chemistry of Love," addresses the link between mind and body related to sexuality and sexual functioning. The second and third articles focus on changes, or lack of them, in our views and treatment of the two genders. "What Keeps Women 'in Their Place'?" ponders the discrepancy between our words and actions with respect to equality of the sexes. "The American Man in Transition" identifies the changes men and women believe men (and our ideas about them) need to make as we enter the last decade of the twentieth century.

Looking Ahead: Challenge Questions

Do you believe the pendulum has swung too far toward a "pro-sex ethic"?

What evidence do you see of continuing "anti-sex hysteria"?

Will more openness about sex and sex education improve or harm sexual relationships?

What surprised you about the questions asked by the Chinese people about sex?

How do you expect our views of men and women to have changed by the year 2000?

Which changes in sex roles predicted by the authors in this section do you see as positive? Negative?

Why we need limits

JEAN BETHKE ELSHTAIN

 Robin Williams is on stage at a comedy club in San Francisco, improvising on whatever the audience cries out. "Safe sex," one man shouts. Williams responds, "Safe sex? Are we interested in having sex in a safe? *No.* Can you masturbate and be safe? How do you know where your hand's been?" The laughter seems to be both hearty and nervous.

New slogans like "safe sex" and new verbs like "to condomize" are meant to reassure, but mostly they remind us that sex isn't what it used to be. I believe that sex was *never* what it "used to be," according to the claims of sexual revolutionaries in their most utopian, politically innocent, and morally insouciant expressions. Here I want to explore whether it is possible to construct an understanding of sexuality that is generous in its approach to diverse forms of sexual expression but that insists, simultaneously, on an ethic of limits.

If we came of age in the 1960s, we were told that sexual revolution presaged the total transformation of society; and that all the evils in the world—from imperialism to racism, militarism to environmental decay—could be traced to repressed, patriarchal standards of sexuality. Suppressed libidinal energy, once it flowed freely, would automatically result in an anti-authoritarian ethic of liberty and justice for all. The cause of pleasure became at one with the cause of justice—every horny kid's wish and justification. By making love, one was striking a blow against making war.

But does not anonymous lovemaking, free from constraints, mimic rather than challenge the anonymous killing of war? There was a dark underside to all of this from the start. Since that time, many young women, including my daughters, now in their 20s, have told me something like this: "The sexual revolution probably opened up some things. A positive aspect might have been fighting the double standard—so women could fool around the way men had and get away with it too. But it wasn't ever 'free.' We were pressured more than ever to be sexually liberated *by* men and then were accused of being uptight and puritanical if we didn't want sex or wanted more than sex."

"My whole peer group, men and women both, are confused about what relationships are supposed to be," a 26-year-old woman recently told me. "All the women are working on, well, I guess I would call it the spiritual aspects of sexuality. They don't want sex for its own sake anymore and they think, and I agree, that a lot of sexual revolution stuff set up a standard where women got to act like predatory men. I'm sick of it. Now, with AIDS, we're not having sex at all—and still finding it hard to achieve a decent relationship."

That the generation of those now in their 20s finds having and sustaining a relationship a burden of nearly overwhelming scope speaks both to the turmoil and promise of our humanity. It also signifies a *particular* sign of these times: the inevitable, collective letdown from the false promises of sexual revolutionaries.

How did sex become so important to us in the late 20th century that we created a culture of narcissism embracing sexuality as the definition of human essence? Sex both defines us and sep-

From *Utne Reader*, September/October 1988, pp. 52–55. Excerpt from *Tikkun*, March/April 1988. Tikkun, 5100 Leona Street, Oakland, CA 94619. Reprinted by permission of *Tikkun* and the author.

There was a dark underside to the sexual revolution from the start.

arates us from one another. Each sexualized self now belongs to one of a rapidly expanding set of categories: Not just heterosexual or homosexual, we are now sadomasochistic, or one of many brands of fetishists, or vanilla or butch lesbians or whatever. Each of us speaks "the truth" about him or herself—the sexual truth. We cannot cross the great divide to understand

anybody else. As for sexual morality, it too has been fashioned by the self alone, tailored to the individual's desire for pleasure. The loneliness of the long-distance sexualist. Whatever happened to dreams of community?

Slowly more and more folks have realized that it isn't so simple after all. What about violent pornography? What about people's responsibilities to one another? What about the dubious fruits of unbridled sexual predation? Is a language available to discuss these questions or are we doomed to fall back into the usual "thou shalt nots"? Pro-sex or anti-sex: two sides of the same coin. But most of us are neither pro nor anti, as these terms are usually construed. Instead, we are troubled—troubled by the moral vacuousness of

Erotic experimentation: Should we set limits?

I want to keep the best of the sexual revolution. The new freedom to talk openly about erotic matters is a blessed thing. A few straightforward words can sometimes clear up misunderstandings that would have produced a lifetime of guilt and shame in the devastating silence of times past. I want information on erotic feelings and actions, anatomy and physiology, venereal diseases and disorders, and birth control and abortion made available to people young and old in a form appropriate for their age. And I hope that all sex education would place the mechanical and medical aspects of the subject in the larger context of erotic love and creativity.

As for pornography, I don't want my children or anyone else introduced to erotic activity through X-rated material. Some sex reformers argue that filmed pornography is educational and therapeutic, since it demonstrates a variety of sexual techniques and allays guilt. All I've ever learned from hard-core pornography is that sex is impersonal, mechanical, and generally exploitative of women. Even if pornography is good medicine for certain adults, it still makes a distorted and grotesque erotic introduction for young people.

As bad as most pornography is, state censorship is even worse. I want to live in a society that does what it reasonably can to protect children from pornography but renounces all sexual censorship for adults. I'd like to be able to see truly erotic films and read truly erotic books, in which physical joining is presented in a context of care, mystery, and surprise. Prohibition won't encourage such erotica. A transformation of erotic attitudes, starting at birth, will.

I see our increasing tolerance of diverse sexual preferences as a sign of social health. Each relationship must stand, not in terms of the sexual preference involved, but on its own particular qualities. I want to live in a society in which there is no bias against homosexuality, bisexuality, or any other non-exploitative, non-proselytizing erotic preference.

The women's movement is, for me, the most

radical and potentially most transforming movement of our times. There are many arguments for sexual equality, but none more compelling and immediate than the erotic. At best, making love involves a rich, complex, and powerful exchange of information: verbal, expressive, sensory, emotional, and, ultimately, moral. Its intensity lies in mutuality. In any relationship where one of the partners is treated as an inferior, the exchange is truncated, the act of love corrupted. A meeting of equals, however, holds nearly infinite possibilities. Trusting one another, we can trust the moment, whatever comes.

I am deeply grateful for the many new freedoms and perspectives of the sexual revolution. However, I think we have taken some wrong turns—wherever we have split sex from love, creation, and the rest of life, wherever we have trivialized and depersonalized the act of love itself. These misappropriations of freedom, far more than any attacks from the so-called Moral Right, now threaten our recent gains.

Perhaps most insidious is a pervasive, covert prescription that we had better have an active, diverse sex life and that we had better start young and continue old. If anything in human life should be voluntary and spontaneous, erotic activity should. And yet over the past two decades, people have forced themselves, with sinking hearts and aching guts, to try anal sex, mechanical sex aids, premarital sex, group sex, spouse swapping—not because they really *wanted* to, but because they thought they *should*.

I'm not arguing against erotic experimentation, but against the obligatory freedom that involves a precarious alliance of the genitals and brain without the assent of the heart and guts. There is a touch of insanity in smiling blandly at sexual practices that damage the body, demean the individual, or depersonalize and trivialize life.

—George Leonard

Excerpted with permission from the book Adventures in Monogamy *(1988). Jeremy P. Tarcher, Los Angeles, $8.95.*

an earlier vision of sexual liberation, troubled by the moral censoriousness of current demands to return to ancient *diktats*.

The AIDS crisis has crystallized ruminations that had already begun to take shape. It provides a most fearful and intemperate opportunity to celebrate God's righteous wrath in the suffering of other human beings; but it also gives all religious groups the chance to respond with compassion, as exemplified in the recent statement from the National Conference of Catholic Bishops. It calls AIDS a human illness, not God's judgment, and proclaims that "discrimination or violence directed against persons with AIDS is unjust and immoral." It makes even more urgent the work of those in the homosexual community who promulgate an ethic of responsibility and care instead of promiscuity; and it prompts heterosexuals to rethink whether the sexual liberation standard was from its inception the generalization of a norm of adolescent male sexuality writ large onto the wider social fabric.

We are moving toward a vision of sexuality that is both mysterious and powerful. For instance, feminists who are mothers are pointing out that maternal sexuality coexists complicatedly with male/female

People in their 20s find having and sustaining a relationship to be a burden of nearly overwhelming scope.

sexuality. Sue Miller's book *The Good Mother* (Harper & Row, 1986) unearths this conundrum with great sensitivity and power, highlighting, for example, the strangeness of the mother's breast simultaneously as an object of male desire and fantasy and a source of loving nourishment to an infant. Perhaps sexuality is the giving to another who can respond in an equal, intimate way. We cannot return to the good old days

The body is a site of meaning and purpose.

when men were men and women were women and homosexuals stayed in closets. Nor do I and others, long skeptical of how sexual liberation got billed on the social marquee, want such a return. We have struggled too long to carve out more equitable relations between men and women. We have seen too much pain inflicted upon our homosexual brothers and sisters because they *are* who they are. A politics of limits, of which sexuality is one feature, respects a zone of privacy where what goes on between people is nobody's business but their own and those who love them.

But this is the beginning, not the end, of reflection. The fact is that *every way of life* is built upon notions of morality; that *every way of life* creates barriers to action in certain areas, most especially, in the words of the philosopher Stuart Hampshire, "the taking of human life, sexual functions, family duties and obligations, and the administration of justice." What ought those constraints be in a world that can no longer rely upon, and agree upon automatically, traditional limits? Without a set of moral rules and prohibitions, no *human* society could exist. For our time a workable view of sexuality is one that recognizes that all conflict between our sexual and social selves cannot be eliminated—an impossible task—but might grow less destructive; that our sexual identities are not the rock-bottom "truth" about ourselves but, instead, one feature of our complex selves; and that homosexuals and heterosexuals can come to accept one another as finite beings who, for a brief time, are compelled to live out their mortal existences in one another's company. Unlike abstract plans of a society to come, confronting sexuality *today* is a series of concrete imperatives, threaded through and through with ideas and deeds that link us to other human beings in the present and in the past.

Beware of setting limits

JUDITH LEVINE

 In the past decade we've witnessed *sex the question* transformed into *sex the problem*. The problem of teenage pregnancy has become the problem of teenage sex, so we try to teach abstinence instead of contraception in the schools and convince ourselves that teenagers have sex only because of peer pressure. AIDS is perceived not as a horrible disease of the body, but as the wasting away of the morals of the body politic. The cure is to contain not the virus, but non-conventional, non-monogamous sex.

In response to all this, the political left says nothing. In fact, it consistently puts sex at the bottom of its agenda of social issues or sometimes demonstrates downright anti-sex and anti-pleasure biases. In the 1980s, ever more squeamish about appearing unserious, the left distances itself from popular culture (which is all about fun) and from pro-sex feminists, gays, and other erotic minorities for whom sexual freedom is a fundamental struggle. This is more than an abstract problem: According to the Centers for Disease Control, in the 1990s AIDS may kill more Americans annually than were lost during the entire Vietnam War, yet no left group makes the epidemic a central issue.

Meanwhile, many other once open-minded people dismiss the sexual revolution as a childish flight of caprice, and even though they don't see AIDS as the scourge of God, they use the disease as a justification for endorsing certain kinds of sex and relationships and censuring others. These "liberals" find in AIDS the silver lining of newly "meaningful," committed sex. Even from the gay community a pious monogamy emanates—*vis* the mass marriage ceremony at the gay and lesbian march on Washington.

All this distresses me mightily, because, like Emma Goldman, who didn't want a revolution she couldn't dance to, I don't want one I can't fuck to. I consider pleasure a revolutionary goal. And I still endorse the commitment of the sexual revolution and the early women's movement to forging new personal alliances, new forms of love and friendship—includ-

While death is all around us, let us nurture pleasure—for pleasure is life.

ing sexual ones. Though never a smash-monogamy zealot, I believe in destabilizing traditional sexual setups and struggling, as we did in the 1960s and '70s, with the emotions that go with such a cultural upheaval.

At the risk of sounding "nostalgic"—or, in the age of AIDS, either frivolous or crazy—I contend that we can't change society if we don't challenge the sexual hegemony of the nuclear family and resist its enforcement of adult heterosexual monogamy. Supporting "alternative" families or giving lip service to gay rights isn't enough; we must militantly stand up for everybody whose sexuality falls outside "acceptable" bourgeois arrangements—even far outside of them.

But you can't do this without asking fundamental questions about sex. Questions like, is monogamy better? (My answer: not necessarily.) What's wrong with kids having sex? (Often, nothing.) Why is it worse to pay for sex than to pay for someone to listen to your intimate problems or care for your infant? (You tell me.) You can't ask those questions if you whisk sexuality to the bottom of the list of "serious issues," far below peace, or child care, or even AIDS.

Indeed, AIDS should have us thinking harder than ever about how to preserve pleasure in our lives. If the disease limits our options, at the very least we don't have to be sanctimonious about it! I may currently like having sex with only one person, but I don't like feeling I'd better sleep with him exclusively from now on, or death will us part. Fear of death is about as felicitous a motivation for monogamy as fear of impoverishment is for staying married.

We shouldn't be looking for meaning in sex at all, but rather trying to strip implicit meaning from

From *Utne Reader*, September/October 1988, pp. 56–63. Excerpt from *Tikkun*, March/April 1988. Tikkun, 5100 Leona Street, Oakland, CA 94619. Reprinted by permission of *Tikkun* and the author.

sex. I don't mean pushing for casual sex, but instead allowing a separation of sex from commitment and then, by conscious decision only, rejoining the two. This would not only emancipate women to make the choices men have always made about what sex means in a given relationship, it would enhance the possibility for stronger alliances, both passionate and emotional.

Our task today is not to pine away in nostalgia, but neither is it to disavow the sexual liberation we fought for in the past decades. We need to keep pleasure alive as a vital part of the progressive political vision at the same time as we confront AIDS, which vanquishes pleasure more powerfully than any repression the right or the left could ever dream up. We must help our children feel that sex is good in an era when sex can bring death, and learn how to relate sexually to each other when new relationships are short-circuited, and old ones sustained, by fear.

The first priority (and it's sickening that this doesn't go without saying) must be a unified fight against AIDS. We must demand government funds for research, medical treatment, and education, and oppose repressive policies on testing, employment, housing, and schooling. And since AIDS is becoming a disease of the poor and drug-addicted, we must redouble our efforts to eradicate poverty.

We have no choice but to teach children safe sex, but we must avoid hysteria, too. If a boy is gay, he is at high risk, but politicized awareness of his identity is

The anti-sex hysteria presents a great challenge to us as lovers.

The changing face of lesbian sex

Before AIDS ever surfaced, sex for women was anything but safe. Sexual abuse, the risk of unwanted pregnancy, the uncertain status of abortion, and the threat of rape all conspired to create an atmosphere of sexual vulnerability. Far from being something new, women's quest for safe sex has been a constant. From our mothers' warnings against "going too far" to the feminist insistence that, at best, we are all "sexual survivors," risk and desire are braided together in female sexuality. So women are old hands at calculating the pleasure/danger equation. But we don't all come up with the same answers.

For those of us who spent 10 or 15 years puzzling through the sexual implications of feminism and the lesbian continuum, eroticism itself was in danger of becoming a forbidden fruit. Pleasure *was* danger: Sexual attraction was deemed objectification and therefore exploitation, drugs and alcohol were agents of substance abuse, and sexist rock 'n' roll was to be replaced by healing women's music. The community's focus on safety shielded women from danger, but by the mid-'80s it was threatening to bore us to tears.

Then pleasure made a comeback. Many lesbians identified the adventurous eroticism of gay men as providing inspiration for lesbian sexual exploration. In the past few years, lesbian desire found a voice—and she sounds as hot and bothered as we all hoped she would.

Lesbian sex manuals and magazines, sex shops and strip shows, sex parties, and porn films are all finding their audience. But each of these by-women, for-women erotic productions reflects the tension between sexual pleasure and peril in women's lives. In the introduction to the first lesbian SM anthology, *Coming to Power* (Alyson Publications), the editors informed readers that a debate had taken place within the group about "whether we could add disclaimers to the fiction pieces, a statement akin to 'Remember, this is only fantasy.'" Yet it is inconceivable that any collection of porn intended for a male public—gay or straight—would need such a comment.

Women's awareness of sexual danger often translates into explicit concern with safety and responsibility in sex play, whether that safety is established through prenegotiated SM or unspoken deep intimacy. Lesbian reliance on intimacy has paid off in the creation of a richly interconnected sexual community.

In fact, the lesbian relationship is an increasingly attractive model for some gay men. San Francisco AIDS activist and historian Jenny Terry explains: "Gay men facing AIDS and ARC (Aids-Related Complex) are struggling with how best to create webs of support and care, and how to organize sexual relationships with a real possibility of negotiation around safety. Among gay men, the lesbian relationship is widely seen as a stable emotional unit based on a kind of connection that has nothing to do with anonymity but rather with deep-rooted awareness and familiarity." These qualities are clearly crucial when it becomes important to know something about the people with whom one is having sex.

Ironically, at the very moment when gay men are questioning the value and wisdom of sexual experimentation, some lesbians wonder whether the new openness to greater sexual adventure may mean more high-risk behavior. Even in the AIDS era, most lesbians remain convinced of a certain "immunity" to standard sexual risks. This may be a legacy of our traditionally low rates of sexually transmitted diseases and our foolproof "birth control method." Add to this the fact that only two documented cases of AIDS resulted from lesbian sexual transmission of HIV, and the result is a frighteningly slow response to the risk of infection. Lesbians do not usually practice safe sex until they feel there is a direct need, yet our

his best defense. Vigorous education in the gay community has stabilized the spread of AIDS there.

The media have been sounding the alarm about heterosexual transmission for some time—and indeed it is rising. Still, by far the most likely heterosexual carriers are poor intravenous drug users and their partners. Therefore, the most sensible AIDS-prevention technique is to give kids real reasons and resources to stay away from serious drugs and away from sexual relations with people who use them. Excluding drug users, only 4 percent of people with AIDS are heterosexual. We are all fearful enough about sex; there's no point exaggerating the danger.

Nobody should make assumptions about what kids know about sex. Research shows that while they're highly aware of sex generally, they're often pretty ignorant about the details. Good sex education is safe sex education too. Helping kids to be aware of their bodies—of health and contraception, mastur-

---

new openness to greater sexual experimentation may mean more high risk behavior.

If AIDS continues to spread in our community—and there is little reason to believe that lesbians will be exempt—several reactions are possible. For some it will only confirm the message that women have so long received: Sex is danger. We shouldn't have been pursuing our pleasure after all; if only we had listened to our mothers and our sisters and worked to rid the world of non-monogamy, casual sex, and pornography, we never would have gotten into this mess. Another response, which is already finding an audience within the lesbian community, is to see AIDS as an invader hiding inside that Trojan horse, the bisexual woman. Writer Pat Califia points out that this is a set-up for bisexual bashing: "There is more phobia about bi-women bringing diseases into 'our' community than there ever was before. Name calling is happening instead of safe sex. The idea is that if you are the 'right kind' of lesbian you need not practice safe sex, and if you are not the right kind, then maybe other women should not have sex with you."

A third response is possible. We can learn to hold passion and danger in our heads at the same time, denying neither. Here lesbians and gay men face a similar challenge. That the danger shall temporarily obscure desire for some of us and desire overshadow danger for others is understandable. The challenge is to once again negotiate our desire under fire.

—Wendy Chapkis
On Our Backs

Excerpted with permission from On Our Backs: Entertainment for the Adventurous Lesbian *(Spring 1988). Subscriptions: $19/yr. (4 issues) from 526 Castro St., San Francisco, CA 94114. Back issues: $5 from same address.*

Where can we look for pro-sex messages in the AIDS era?

bation, sensual touching, and fantasy as well as intercourse—and of their feelings about sexuality can only make them better able to practice safe and egalitarian sex in what could be history's most honest chapter of sexual relations.

Sexual behavior, moreover, should never be governed by a separate category of morality. If we want our kids to balance their own desires with responsibility and consideration for others, then we should practice and teach our kids these values in sex, too. Teaching that abstinence is "right" is not only puritanical and ineffective in limiting sexual activity, but it fuels prejudice against people whose sexual expression may be more flagrant, and it implies that disease is a punishment for sin.

AIDS presents one of the biggest challenges in history to our survival as a loving community. Both safety and compassion require us to stop seeing those people who we've been taught to revile as the Other. When we are ruled by fear and alienation, it is easy for extreme attitudes and repressive policies to start sounding reasonable. We must reach deep to find our human similarities and also respect our sexual differences.

The anti-sex hysteria of the 1980s also presents a great challenge to us as lovers. Fear and malaise are counter-aphrodisiac (the number one complaint sex therapists hear is lack of desire). We need not exacerbate these problems with self-righteousness. Married people, who these days seem to have no sensual outlet besides stroking their newborn's cheek and watching the VCR, go around gloating about their maturity and security. Single people are home watching their VCR, too—and looking over their shoulders nervously. With movies like *Fatal Attraction*, it's no wonder. Once envied, singles are now blamed; once considered free, they're now portrayed as trapped.

Where can we look for pro-sex messages in the AIDS era? I found one in the most threatened quarter, the gay community, in the educational comic books distributed by the Gay Men's Health Crisis. These books depict numerous types of gay men gorgeously built and hung every one, having phone sex, masturbating, or role-playing, all with minimum risk and maximum heat. Explicitly, humorously sexual, indeed happily pornographic, these pamphlets are pragmatic: They meet their constituency where it lives and do not try to preach a different way of living. But they imply more—that it's unnecessary to foment aversion to sex through moralizing or hyperbolizing. Death is aversion enough. It's driven many back into the closet and made celibates of countless more.

Instead, the lascivious comic-book hunks are saying: Affirm sex. While death is all around us, let us nurture pleasure—for pleasure is life. Even now, especially now, just say yes.

THE POLITICS OF CHILD SEXUAL ABUSE:

Notes from American History

Linda Gordon

In the early 1970s, when a radical feminist conscious-ness pulled incest out of the closet, we thought we were engaged in an unprecedented discovery. In fact, charity volunteers and social workers a century earlier dealt with incest cases daily, understanding them to be a standard, expected part of the caseload of a child-protective agency such as a Society for the Prevention of Cruelty to Children. How are we to explain this historical amnesia? Like the suppression of so much women's history and feminist analysis, this hiatus was not created simply by the decline in feminism between 1920 and 1970, but by an active reinterpretation of child sexual abuse. I shudder when I think about what this meant: not only because of the incest victims rendered invisible and mute, but also because of its threat to us today, the threat that great achievements in conscious-ness-raising can be rolled back by powerful ideological tanks. My motives in writing a history of family vio-lence were thus far from disinterested.[1]

Charity and social workers in the late nineteenth-century United States were familiar with child sexual abuse and knew that its most common form of abuse was intrafamilial—that is, incest. Ten percent of the family-violence case records of Boston child-saving agencies which I sampled, starting in 1880, contained incest (Gordon and O'Keefe, 1986; Gordon, 1984). Moreover, in their upper-class way these child savers had a feminist analysis of the problem: they blamed male brutality and lack of sexual control. They could safely offer such explanations because they believed the problem to occur exclusively among the Catholic immigrant poor, whom they perceived as of 'inferior

stock,' crowded 'like animals' into urban ghettoes. Thus, ironically, the very upper-class base of child-rescue work at the time promoted the identification of problems unmentionable by standards of Victorian propriety.

Despite these class limitations, the sympathy for child victims entailed by this sensibility was one of the major achievements of the nineteenth-century feminist movement. The attack on male sexual and familial violence was often disguised in temperance rhetoric. American women's historians have recently conducted a reinterpretation of temperance, acknowledging its anti-Catholic, anti-working class content, but also iden-tifying its meanings for women contesting the evils that alcohol created for them and their families: vio-lence, disease, impoverishment, male irresponsibility. Moreover, the feminist anti-violence campaign had significant successes. In the course of the century wife-beating was transformed from an acceptable practice into one which, despite its continued widespread inci-dence, was illegal and reprehensible, a seamy behav-iour which men increasingly denied and tried to hide (Pleck, 1979). Indeed, the whole movement against child abuse which began in the 1870s was a product of a feminist sensibility in several ways: first, in opposing corporal punishment and preference for gentler meth-ods of child training; second, in challenging the sanc-tity of the Victorian home and authority of the paterfamilias. Most manuals of child raising by the last quarter of the nineteenth century recommended phys-ical punishment only as a last resort, and women's legal victories in child custody created a preference for maternal rights to children for a century.

Consider a few examples of incest cases from the late nineteenth century:[2]

> In 1900 a thirteen year old girl has been placed out with a family in which the wife is absent. The SPCC worker reports that the 'child's bed not slept in but [the father's bed is] much tumbled. The girl cries and dreads the night.' (Case #1820A)

> An incest victim reports, sometime in the 1890s, that her father 'told her that it was all right for him to do such things and say such things to her, for all fathers did so with their daughters. Tried to force her to go to a hotel in Boston with him once. Also advised her to go with fellows to get money. Said that if she got in trouble he would help her out. . . .' (Case #2058A)

There were hundreds of these stories telling us not only that incest occurred, but that child-saving agencies were aware of it and taking action against it. The publicity and fund-raising efforts of the Massachusetts Society for the Prevention of Cruelty to Children focussed on intrafamily 'carnal abuse' directly, unembarrassed to include it as part of the need for SPCC intervention.

In the early twentieth century the child-savers' view of child sexual assault changed significantly, and incest was de-emphasized. By the 1920s, although child-protective agencies continued to meet many incest cases, a three-part interpretive transformation had occurred: the *locus* of the problem was moved from home to streets, the *culprit* transformed from father or other authoritative male family member to perverted stranger, the *victim* transformed from innocent betrayed to sex delinquent. In other words, the fact that child sex abuse is overwhelmingly a family problem as obscured; instead it was pictured as rape by strangers on the streets. (Anna Clark has shown how a similar reinterpretation of adult rape took place (Clark, 1987).) This is not to say that there was no extrafamilial sex abuse; there was, but, compared to incest, it was greatly exaggerated in both public and professional discourse.

Several factors contributed to this reinterpretation. The professionalization of social work tended to weaken the influence of feminists and social reformers among child protectors, even as, ironically, more women entered child welfare casework as salaried workers. After the women's suffrage victory in 1920 the organized feminist movement fragmented and weakened. During World War I venereal disease became a major problem for the armed forces (it was for this reason that condoms became widely available at this time, first issued by the Navy to sailors); servicemen were presented as victims of disease-ridden prostitutes. After the war, fears of Bolshevism, sexual freedom, and feminism combined to create a 'pro-family' backlash.

The implications of this reinterpretation of child sexual abuse were pernicious for women and girls. The existence of sexual abuse became evidence requiring the constriction and domestication of girls, and their mothers were blamed for inadequate supervision if the girls were molested or even played on the streets. What was once categorized as carnal abuse, the perpetrators virtually all male, was often now categorized as moral neglect—meaning that the mother was the culprit and the behaviour of the victim was implicated. Some of the 'sex abuse' was relatively noncoercive teenage sexuality. Female juvenile sex delinquency was constructed as a major social problem in early twentieth-century America, and it was a vague, victimless crime. Girls who smoked and drank, dressed or spoke immodestly, or simply loitered on the streets were convicted of sex delinquency in substantial numbers and sent to reformatories (Schlossman and Wallach, 1978). During World War I near armed-forces bases it was the servicemen who were the innocents, their girl partners the sources of pollution. Even girls who had been raped were no longer victims but temptresses. I do not mean to deny that some girls behaved in socially dangerous and self-destructive ways, nor that they sought out sexual adventure but, as many students of sex delinquents and other runaways today have observed, high proportions, quite possibly a majority of these girls, were first victims of sexual assault, typically familial. They were, so to speak, squeezed out onto the streets in search of safety and/or self-esteem from homes that were even more destructive than the street boys or men who exploited them.

Above all, this reinterpretation of child sexual abuse removed scrutiny from family and home, restoring the curtain of impunity that surrounded those sacred institutions. This was the period of the discovery of the 'dirty old man', the 'sex fiend', and the 'pervert', the stereotypical culprit in child sex abuse cases in the 1930s, 1940s and 1950s. As before, I do not wish to deny that such figures existed. Child protection agencies uncovered child prostitution, pornography rings and sex criminals who molested literally scores of children. The victims were not always brutalized; the children of the very poor—not only in the Depression but in earlier decades too—could be bribed into acquiescence and silence with a nickel, an orange, a pail of coal. However, even these nonfamilial molesters were rarely 'strangers'. They were often neighbours, accepted members of communities, often small businessmen or janitors who had access to private space.

There were two peak periods of hysteria about sex crimes: 1937–40 and 1949–55. The panic had official government sponsorship, led by none less that J. Edgar Hoover, head of the FBI. In 1937 he called for a 'War on the Sex Criminal'. Hoover's rantings about 'degenerates' threatening 'American childhood and womanhood' assimilated these sexual anxieties to nationalism, racism and anti-Communism. It bears notice that, in contrast to earlier periods of public agitation against sex crimes, as in campaigns to raise the age of consent in the Progressive era, women's organizations played no role in this campaign (Freedman, 1987).

Meanwhile social workers became less likely to investigate girls' typically euphemistic accusations of their fathers.

In 1935 a mother turned her daughter in for sex delinquency. Investigation reveals that the daughter, fleeing from an abusive father, who also beat his wife severely, had spent most of her time for 4-5 years with her maternal uncle and aunt. She accused her maternal uncle of molesting her steadily. However, the MSPCC physical exam indicated that she was a virgin,[3] so no action was taken. (#3555A)

A battered woman, terrified of her husband, is told by their daughter, who has become a 'sex delinquent,' behaving 'vulgarly,' that her father has criminally assaulted her. The mother says 'she would speak to him.' At court the police chief says he is doubtful about taking up the case as the girl's word is the only evidence the Government could produce; he would not question the father 'as it would be asking [him] to incriminate himself.' The daughter was committed to an institution. (#2057A)

In 1920 a mother is so fearful that her new husband will abuse her daughter (from a previous marriage) that every time she goes out she hires a babysitter to chaperone them. Yet when the daughter, now eleven, says she has been raped by a 'stranger' whom she refuses to name, the social workers not only fail to question whether she might be shielding her stepfather, but decide that her accusation is not credible and brand her a delinquent—a liar, immoral, and uncontrollable. She is boarded out as a domestic. (#3085A)

In 1930 a 14-year-old girl alleges sexual abuse by her widowed father and begs to be taken out of his home. No action is taken until the father brings her to court on stubborn-child charges and she, as well as her younger sister whom she has been trying to protect are sentenced, separately, to institutions. (#3585)

In addition to references like these, in which the agencies did not investigate or prosecute, there were many others in which agency workers simply did not pick up the broad hints that girls threw out, hoping to draw attention to their plight. Social workers ignored statements like, 'I asked my mother for a lock on my door'. These girls were not usually bribed or intimated into silence. Some of the recent discussion of incest emphasizes victims' fearful silence, but this evidence is based on the work of therapists, counselling incest victims years later, who have often by then reconstructed their stories on the basis of their guilt; my evidence, contemporaneous with the abuse, showed that these children were usually very active in trying to get help, more so, for example, than victims of nonsexual child abuse (Gordon, 1986).

Not only did social workers de-emphasize incest, but academic experts dismissed it as an extremely rare, one-in-a-million occurrence (Weinberg, 1955). Psycho-

analytic and anthropological interpretations, associated respectively with Freud and Lévi-Strauss, attributed to incest taboos a vital role in the development of civilization; this logic brought with it the assumption that these taboos were effective and that incest was, in fact, rare; but in terms of impact on treatment of actual cases, Freudian thought did not so much *cause* social workers to deny children's complaints and hints about mistreating as it offered categories with which to explain away these complaints. As Boston psychiatrist Eleanor Pavenstedt commented in 1954:

Most of us have trained ourselves to skepticism toward the claims of young girls who maintain they have been seduced by their fathers . . . We must ask ourselves whether our tendency to disbelief is not in part at least based on denial. The incest barrier is perhaps the strongest support of our cultural family structure, and we may well shrink from the thought of its being threatened. (Pavenstedt, 1954)

So did the dominant sociology of the family, which inverted Lévi-Strauss's functionalism to prove that the incest taboo was operative because it had to be. For example, 'No known human society could tolerate much incest without ruinous disruption' (Gebhard, Gagnon, Pomeroy and Christenson, 1965: 208; Davis, 19490; Bell and Vogel, 1963). The few nonfeminist historians to study incest replicated that error by studying public beliefs about incest, not behaviour (Wohl, 1979; Strong, 1973).

The rediscovery of incest in the 1970s was, then, merely a reinterpretation, and it did not come quickly. Nonsexual child abuse was resurrected as a social problem in the 1960s in a movement led by physicians but stimulated by the influence of the New Left, with its sympathy for youth and critique of authority and the family. Without pressure from feminists, incest first reappeared as gender-neutral. Indeed, the very classification of all forms of intrafamily sexual activity as incest obscures the meanings of these behaviours. For example, sibling sexual activity, or sex between other relatives of approximately the same age, is extremely common, difficult to identify and not necessarily abusive. Mother-child incest is extremely rare and, in my findings, more often than father-child incest, associated with adult mental illness; by contrast incestuous fathers have extremely 'normal' profiles (Gordon and O'Keefe, 1984; Herman, 1981). Yet many child abuse experts throughout the 1970s ignored these gender differences (Kempe, 1980; Money, 1980). Others found ingenious ways of explaining away actuality with speculation about possibility. Thus social worker Kate Rist argued that 'society has created a stronger prohibition against mother-son incest' because 'it is most likely to occur. This has led to the intriguing situation in which father-daughter incest appears to have a lower natural probability of occurrence, is therefore less strongly prohibited, and in practice occurs more often' (Rist, 1979; 682).

Historians do not usually like to speak of the 'lessons of history', as if she were some objective, finally definitive schoolteacher. But in many years of work at the craft, I have never come across a story that so directly yields a moral. The moral is that the presence or absence of a strong feminist movement makes the difference between better and worse solutions to the social problem of child sexual abuse; more, that the very same evidence of sexual abuse will be differently defined in the presence or absence of that movement. Without a feminist analysis, evidence of child sexual abuse means that danger lies in sex perverts, in public spaces, in unsupervised girls, in sexually assertive girls. There are few ironies more bitter than the fact that rape of children—that most heinous of crimes— has also been the crime most drenched in victim-blaming. As with adult rape, child sexual abuse without feminist interpretation supplies evidence and arguments for constricting and disempowering children.

Such a reinterpretation arose again in the United States in the mid-1980s, a reinterpretation aided, of course, by the real and increasing incidence of deranged killers attacking strangers. In the school year 1984/85 my then second-grade daughter was taught *three* separate programmes in her classroom about how to react to sexual abuse attempts, all of them emphasizing strangers, and all of them gender-neutral. The most publicized sexual abuse cases have concerned daycare centres, and often female teachers, although daycare centres remain, on the whole, among the safest environments for children. The statistics about child sexual abuse remain what they were a century ago: the most dangerous place for children is the home, the most likely assailant their father. Similarly a panic about missing children not only exaggerated their numbers a thousandfold, but completely misstated the source of such 'kidnappings': neglecting to mention that noncustodial parents are overwhelmingly the main kidnappers; and that teenage runaways, often from abusive homes, are overwhelmingly the majority of the missing children.

What then is the best policy? My argument should not be taken as an implicit call for de-emphasizing the problem. On the contrary. The children's educational programmes and pamphlets have strengths, particularly in so far as they offer assertiveness training for children: if it feels uncomfortable, trust your judgement and say no; scream loud and run fast; tell someone. Of course it is difficult and inadvisable to sow distrust of fathers, particularly because the more intimate fathers are with children, the more responsibility they have for children, the less likely they will be to abuse them sexually. However, education for children should contain a feminist and an anti-authoritarian analysis: should discuss the relative powerless-

ness of women and girls, and praise assertiveness and collective resistance in girls; should demystify the family and even discuss that ultimately tabooed subject, economic power in the family. Education for boys must be equally brave and delicate. Boys are children too, and often victimized sexually, but they are also future men, and school age is not too early to ask them to consider what's wrong with male sexual aggression, to teach them to criticize the multiple and powerful cultural messages that endorse male sexual aggression.

Probably the most important single contribution to the prevention of incest would be the strengthening of mothers. By increasing their ability to support themselves and their social and psychological self-esteem, allowing them to choose independence if that is necessary to protect themselves and their daughters, men's sexual exploitation could be checked. In the historical incest cases I sampled, one of the most consistent common denominators was the extreme helplessness of mothers—often the victims of wife-beating themselves, they were often ill or otherwise isolated, they were the poorest, the least self-confident and the least often employed of mothers in these case records. This is not victim-blaming; their weaknesses were not their fault, but part of the systematic way in which male supremacy gives rise to incest. It was a gain that wife-beating and incest have become more criminalized, but we cannot expect women to prosecute aggressively if their prospects for single motherhood are so bleak.

Moreover, women's very subordination often contributes to making them child abusers and neglecters. Although women do not usually abuse children sexually, in these case records they were responsible for approximately half the nonsexual child abuse (the same proportion they occupy in many contemporary studies). Unfortunately, feminists have avoided women's own violence towards children and analysed family violence in terms of stereotypical male brutality and female gentleness. Women's violence should not be regarded as a problem that will somehow weaken our feminist claims; on the contrary, these claims should not rest on assumptions of women's superiority—those of us who behave worst may be those who need empowerment most. Women's mistreatment of children also needs an analysis of the damages caused by the sexual division of labour and the pattern of women's exclusive responsibility for child raising. In the US, too, the rather middle-class radical feminist groups never made issues of social services a political priority, although such services are fundamental to women's ability to resist violence, to protect their children, and to parent better themselves.

This is not to say that a good feminist line will solve the problems of child sexual abuse, especially not where the abuse has already occurred. Like everyone else, feminists who deal with policy or individual cases must wobble through many contradictions. For example: the victimization is real, but the tendency to exaggerate its incidence and to produce social and moral panics needs to be resisted. The problem emerges from the powerlessness, the effective invisibility and muteness of women and children, especially girls, but the adult anxiety has led to children's false accusations, and children's sufferings will not be corrected by eroding the due process rights and civil liberties of those accused. Child sexual abuse needs a political interpretation, in terms of male power. However, the prosecution of culprits—however necessary—and the breaking up of families that may result do not always benefit the child victims. Especially if they are incestuous, sex abuse cases have something of the tragic about them, because once they arise, tremendous human damage has already occurred, and a politically correct analysis will not ease the pain. Still, that analysis, situating the problem in the context of male supremacy in and outside the family, is the only long-term hope for prevention.

NOTES

Linda Gordon is Professor of History at the University of Wisconsin/Madison. She is the author of *Woman's Body, Woman's Right* and the forthcoming book on family violence noted below.

1. My book, *Heroes of Their Own Lives: The History and Politics of Family Violence*, is forthcoming from Viking/Penguin US in early 1988. References to my sources and more information on my research methodology can be found there.

2. These and other excerpts are from case records of Boston, Massachusetts, child-protection agencies (see Gordon, 1988).

3. The standard response to a sex abuse allegation was to look at the condition of the hymen (Gordon, 1988).

REFERENCES

BELL, Norman and VOGEL, Ezra (1963) editors *A Modern Introduction to the Family* New York: Free Press.

BREINES, Wini and GORDON, Linda (1983) 'The New Scholarship on Family Violence' *Signs* 8, pp. 490–531.

CLARK, Anna (1987) *Women's Silence, Men's Violence: Sexual Assault in England 1770–1845* London: Pandora Press.

DAVIS, Kingsley (1949) *Human Society* New York: Macmillan.

DUBOIS, Ellen and GORDON, Linda (1983) 'Seeking Ecstasy on the Battlefield: Danger and Pleasure in Nineteenth-century Feminist Sexual Thought' *Feminist Studies* 9, pp. 7–25; also *Feminist Review* no. 11 (1981).

FREEDMAN, Estelle B. (1987) "Uncontrolled Desires: The Response to the Sexual Psychopath, 1920–1960" *Journal of American History* Vol. 74, no. 1, pp. 83–106.

GEBHARD, Paul, GAGNON, J., POMEROY, Wardell and CHRISTENSON, C. (1965) *Sex Offenders* New York: Harper & Row.

GORDON, Linda and O'KEEFE, Paul (1984) 'Incest as a Form of Family Violence: Evidence from Historical Case Records' *Journal of Marriage and the Family* Vol. 46, no. 1, pp. 27–34.

GORDON, Linda (1986) 'Incest and Resistance: Patterns of Father-Daughter Incest, 1880–1930' *Social Problems* Vol. 33, no. 4 pp. 253–67.

GORDON, Linda (1988) *Heroes of Their Own Lives: The Politics and History of Family Violence* New York: Viking/Penguin.

HERMAN, Judith (1981) *Father-Daughter Incest* Cambridge: Harvard University Press.

KAUFMAN, Irving, PECK, Alice L. and TAGIURI, Consuelo K. (1954) 'The Family Constellation and Overt Incestuous Relations Between Father and Daughter' *American Journal of Orthopsychiatry* Vol. 24, pp. 266–79.

KEMPE, C. Henry (1980) 'Incest and Other Forms of Sexual Abuse' in KEMPE (1980).

KEMPE, C. Henry and HELFER, Ray (1980) *The Battered Child* Chicago: University of Chicago Press.

MONEY, John, (1980) Introduction to the incest section in WILLIAMS and MONEY (1980).

PAVENSTEDT, Eleanor (19564) Addendum to KAUFMAN, PECK and TAGIURI (1954).

PLECK, Elizabeth (1979) 'Wife Beating in Nineteenth-century America' *Victimology* Vol. 4, no. 1 pp. 60–74.

RIST, Kate (1979) 'Incest: Theoretical and Clinical Views' *American Journal of Orthopsychiatry* Vol. 49, no. 4, pp. 630–91.

RUSH, Florence (1980) *The Best Kept Secret: Sexual Abuse of Children* Englewood Cliffs, NJ: Prentice-Hall.

SCHLOSSMAN, Steven and WALLACH, Stephanie (1978) 'The Crime of Precocious Sexuality: Female Juvenile Delinquency in the Progressive Era' *Harvard Educational Review* 48, pp. 65–94.

STRONG, Bryan (1973) 'Toward a History of the Experiential Family: Sex and Incest in the Nineteenth-century Family' *Journal of Marriage and the Family*, Vol. 35, no. 3 pp. 457–66.

WEINBERG, S. (1955) *Incest Behavior* New York: Citadel Press.

WILLIAMS, Gertrude J. and MONEY, John (1980) editors *Traumatic Abuse and Neglect of Children at Home* Baltimore: Johns Hopkins.

WOHL, Anthony S. (1979) 'Sex and the Single Room: Incest Among the Victorian Working Classes' in *The Victorian Family: Structure and Stress* ed. Wohl. New York: St. Martin's Press.

Sex in China

Unable for many years to learn the answers to their questions about sex, the Chinese people can now find the information they have long been forbidden to seek.

**Fang Fu Ruan, MD,
and Vern L. Bullough, PhD, RN**

Fang Fu Ruan was a professor of medicine at Beijing University, and is currently Adjunct Professor of Nursing, State University of New York at Buffalo. Vern L. Bullough is Dean of Natural and Social Sciences, State University of New York College at Buffalo, and SUNY Distinguished Professor.

For more than 30 years, the Chinese Republic permitted virtually no information concerning sex to reach the Chinese people, either via publications or any other source, such as classroom instruction. Certain regulations concerning reproductive behavior were strictly enforced. For example, abortions were mandatory for unauthorized pregnancies.

In 1980, health and other publications were once again allowed to publish sexuality-related materials, and the senior author (Ruan) spent five years (1980–1985) writing a health column for several popular national publications in China.

Readers of medical columns in lay newspapers were encouraged for the first time in decades to submit questions about sexuality, and receive answers published in these media. Such information had always been scarce and virtually unobtainable, since the Chinese emphasis on propriety made it almost impossible to discuss sex even in private.

Traditionally, Chinese parents have not explained the facts of life to their children until just before they marry. Since marriage between 1949 and 1980 was not officially sanctioned until young people reached their mid-20s, sexual ignorance was widespread. Many Chinese girls had no idea what was happening to them when they began to menstruate. Inevitably, when people first learned that they could ask (and receive answers to) questions about sex, numerous readers submitted questions to the media. Not surprisingly, many of these questions were rather naïve.

Newpaper and magazine health columns also provided new and valuable sources of research information, which had been forbidden in earlier years. For example, it was now possible to contact a number of homosexuals and transsexuals, and gather important data about them. It also became possible to perform transsexual gender-change surgery in at least one case.

The naïveté of many questions obviously reflected the long period in which there had been absolutely no sex education in China. For example, several women wrote to ask whether they could become pregnant as a result of merely being touched by a man. More than one couple inquired how the wife could become pregnant since "nothing had happened" despite several years of marriage. Correspondence with some of these couples revealed that a number of them had never engaged in sexual intercourse and did not even know what it was! Acutely aware of the need for sex information, the Chinese government officials were at last persuaded to call a national conference on sex education in 1985. In the course of the conference, sex education classes were recommended for all Chinese youth, and the government finally set up such a program in 1988.

The following are typical questions answered in Chinese newspapers' health columns from 1980 to 1985. (Additional information has been added in some instances to aid American readers in understanding the context in which some of the questions were asked and answered.)

Sexual frequency

Question: I read in the booklet *Knowledge of Sex* that the normal frequency for intercourse is once every week or every other week. I have sex with my wife every night and I worry that I am not normal. Am I wrong to have intercourse so often? Should we limit our frequency?

Comment: This booklet, issued after the ravages of the Cultural Revolution had ended, marked the Chinese government's first effort to respond to its citizens' demands for information about sex. The booklet's authors, however, mindful of the forced confessions of wrongdoing by those few professionals who had written about sexual activity before the Cultural Revolution, took a very cautious approach in discussing sexuality. Dr. Ruan's columns marked a new level of frankness.

Answer: China has a long tradition of opinions concerning how often individuals should engage in sexual intercourse. The famous Tang dynasty physician Sun Si-mao (AD 581–682) stated that 20-year-old men should engage in sex at least once every four days; 30-year-old men, once every eight days; 40-year-old men, once every 16 days; and 50-year-old men, once every 21 days. Today we know that this is neither right nor wrong, but depends on the individual. Every person has different sexual needs and the frequency of intercourse therefore needs to be decided by the sexual partners. Thus, if you and your wife enjoy having sex every night, that's fine. There is nothing wrong with this. Your own feelings and wishes about sex are important, but at the same time, you also need to consider those of your wife. Each of you should try to satisfy the other.

Masturbation

Question: I have been told that one drop of semen equals 20 drops of blood, and that the loss of semen, especially through masturbation, will cause neurosis, insomnia, impotence, impaired ejaculation, and other severe disorders. Is this true?

Comment: In China there is much misinformation about masturbation. Several male correspondents were so worried about their practice of masturbation that they had attempted to cut off their penis. Some parents wrote in to say that their sons had committed suicide due to their inability to stop masturbating. Thus, it was imperative to answer this type of question by allaying fear as well as providing factual information.

Answer: No. Semen can be stored by the body only for about a month and is then either absorbed by the body or used up. The loss of semen is therefore not harmful. Masturbation is a normal physiological phenomenon. According to the studies of such internationally known sex researchers as Alfred Kinsey and William Masters (as well as others), masturbation can actually be helpful in certain circumstances. Unfortunately, many people experience totally unwarranted fears and guilt feelings because of false, misleading, and unscientific beliefs and teachings; such fears and guilt feelings often cause needless suffering.

Female sexual arousal

Question: How can I tell when my wife is sexually aroused, and how can I satisfy her?

Answer: This is an old question, but it is just as important today as it was years ago. In one of the classic handbooks on sex, *Yu Fang Pi Chueh (Secret Instructions Concerning the Jade Chamber)*, which predates the modern era, the Yellow Emperor asked: "How can I become aware of the joyfulness [arousal] of the woman?" The answer was given by the character called the Plain Girl, who said: "There are five signs, five desires, and ten movements. By looking at these changes you will become aware of what is happening to the woman's body." She identified these signs: flushing of her face, hardening of her breasts, a growing dryness of her throat, a moist vagina, and finally a transmission of fluid through the vagina. She said that intercourse should begin during the second phase; after the fifth phase, you should slowly withdraw from her.

The Plain Girl also mentioned other signals that indicate a woman's sexual feelings: If she bates her breath, it means that she wants to have sex with you. If her nose and mouth are dilated, she wants to begin sexual activity, and if she embraces you tightly, you will know that she is excited and aroused. If perspiration flows, it means that she is approaching orgasm, and lastly, if her body straightens out and her eyes close, it means that she has been satisfied.

According to a well-known scholar of ancient Chinese sex customs, the five signs described in classical Chinese sexual writings are comparable to those discussed by Kinsey.[1,2] It is clear that ancient Chinese sexologists were observant and that Chinese culture attached great importance to orgasm. Therefore, pay attention to your partner's responses, gain her full cooperation, and you and your partner will discover what works best for you as you both try to attain orgasm.

Sex change

Question: I read that some women want to change their sex to become a man, and vice versa. Is this true? Is it normal? Do we have such people in our country?

Answer: Yes, there are such people and some live in China. This phenomenon, called "transsexualism" in the West, became widespread there during the 1950s and 1960s. The number of transsexuals in China is estimated to be very small, perhaps one in every 40,000 to 400,000 individuals. "Normal" is not a good word to use in discussing these people, for we need to understand and accept them.

Homosexuality

Question: I was surprised to learn that there are men who love other men sexually, and that this is also true of certain women. A newspaper said that this phenomenon is called "homosexuality" in the West, and I believe it just emphasizes the corrupt, rotten, decayed, and degenerate life-style encouraged by capitalism. But more recently, I heard that there are also homosexuals in China. Is this true? Is homosexuality a disease?

Answer: Homosexuality is not a phenomenon that can be labeled as "Western" or "capitalist." Neither is it a disease. People who are attracted to the same sex are found in every country, every culture, every historical period, and every social class. Since China currently forbids any overt display of homosexuality, these people have to live a closeted life—and therefore are not generally recognized.

China, like every other country in the world, has always had homosexuals. Ji Yun, the eminent scholar of the Ch'ing dynasty (AD 1644–1911), stated in his famous *Yuwei Caotang Biji (Notes of the Yuwei Heritage)* that the position of "catamite," a young boy who serves as the sex partner for an adult man, existed at the court of Huang-ti (Yellow Emperor)—the reputed first Emperor of China—more than 4,600 years ago. The surviving literature of the Spring-Autumn period (770–745 BC), and the Warring States period (475–221 BC) of the Chou and Han dynasties (206 BC–AD 220) indicates that homosexuality was accepted by the royal courts. The official dynastic histories show that in the Western Han dynasty alone, all 10 male emperors either had homosexual lovers or at least tolerated and accepted homosexuality. In view of this documented historical information, no one in China can claim that homosexuality was imported from a Western capitalist country.

Teenage sex and pregnancy

Question: I have heard that many teenagers now have sex and that a lot of teenage girls become pregnant. Is this true? Should we teach a teenage son or daughter how to use contraceptives?

Answer: Yes, it is true that many teenagers have sex, and teenage pregnancy is very common. We know this from several kinds of data: In 1985, for example, in a major hospital in Shantong province, 38% of the women who had abortions were teenagers. Healthcare professionals believe that this figure will soon rise to 60%. A survey in this same city showed that 80% of the women have had sexual intercourse before they marry, usually without using any contraceptives.

A rural area in Zhejiang province reported that 66% of the women had had intercourse before they married. The number of abortions performed on girls in Shanghai, the largest city in China, rose from 39,000 in 1982 to 65,000 in 1984. This is the reality that we must face. Traditionally many groups in China opposed any sex education or instruction in the use of contraceptives. They believed that "words relating to sex should never be mentioned." It is time to change this attitude.

The problem of teenage pregnancy needs attention since most of these girls are too young to be responsible mothers, and their male partners are too young to be responsible fathers. Both need time to grow and mature physically and psychologically, and they need more education. Although we can advise them not to engage in sex before they reach adulthood, they tend to ignore what we say. Since they have the right to decide how they will use their bodies, we must teach them about contraceptives and encourage them to use these methods. This will benefit the teenagers and their families, as well as the nation.

Female anorgasmia

Question: I have heard that many women fail to have orgasm. Could you tell me how many? Do Western women have more orgasms than Chinese women? How can a woman achieve an orgasm?

Comment: Many Chinese women do not know what an orgasm is. An American journalist who recently visited Beijing wrote that he had asked a Chinese woman whether she had ever experienced an orgasm, a question never yet asked by a Chinese sex researcher.[3] Upon hearing this question, the woman frowned, puzzled by the question. The journalist then used a more technical expression (common in Hong Kong) to describe what he meant—*gao-chao* (literally, "high tide"). She did not know what this meant either, but once the journalist explained it, she said she had never had any such sensation. When asked about intercourse, the woman explained that it usually lasted three or four minutes, and then her husband would withdraw.

A survey concerning orgasm, taken of a small sample of Chinese women, was conducted by the newly formed group of sex educators and published in 1987. This survey revealed that some 35% of the respondents either had never had an orgasm or had one only occasionally.

Answer: Chinese women can enjoy orgasm as readily as Western women. But first they need to know what it is. The male sex partner must pay greater attention to arousing the woman by engaging in longer foreplay, and by letting her reach orgasm first. Finally, both should enjoy the experience, and stop being concerned about orgasm.

Conclusion

Many changes have taken place in recent years. For example, in 1988 the Chinese government authorized a second pregnancy for families whose first child is a girl. Contraception, in general, is practiced by means of a modified version of the Lippes loop, voluntary sterilizations, or abortion. These methods, however, may be available only to married women in many instances.

In reviewing the questions submitted to the media, it is worth noting that most of the questions came from male readers. Chinese women rarely inquire about sexual matters, unless they relate to pregnancy or menstruation—the only types of sexually related questions Chinese women believe are appropriate to ask.

It is obvious that despite the many questions submitted, much remains to be done in the near future before Chinese men and women have the sexual knowledge necessary to understand and cope with questions regarding sexual functioning. As sex education becomes widely available for young people in China, it will increase their understanding of sexuality and sexual problems. It will also help to provide solutions via sexual counseling and sex therapy.

References

1. Van Gulik RH: *Sexual Life in Ancient China*. Leiden, Holland, EJ Brill, 1961.
2. Kinsey AC: *Sexual Behavior in the Human Female*. Philadelphia, WB Saunders, 1953.
3. Butterfield F; *China: Alive in the Bitter Sea*. New York, New York Times Books, 1982.

AIDS NEWS *Number of cases in U.S.: Over 97,000*

HIGHLIGHTS: FIFTH INTERNATIONAL AIDS CONFERENCE: Montreal, June 4-9

Patricia Kloser, MD

Patricia Kloser is Clinical Coordinator, AIDS Services, University Hospital, Newark, NJ, and Attending Physician, Department of Infectious Diseases, University of Medicine and Dentistry of New Jersey, Newark.

More than 12,000 scientists, physicians, health workers, and people with AIDS (PWA) convened in Montreal to share their ideas and data regarding HIV. This very intense conference drew participants from all over the globe, with a major focus on the management of AIDS as a chronic illness rather than as an infectious disease that can be readily cured. AIDS patients in developed countries today are living longer as clinicians have become more experienced in treating AIDS-related opportunistic infections and the HIV-infected patient.

All of the news, however, was not upbeat. New cases continue to increase, both in the United States and worldwide; the current total number of cases in the United States (97,000) is projected to double by the year 1991. The possibility of a longer than heretofore recognized HIV incubation period during which time serum antibody cannot be detected is particularly worrisome. While HIV antibody is detectable within 6-10 weeks after infection in most cases, this time period can exceed two years in some individuals.

The following highlights represent the developments of greatest interest to the primary care physician, who may diagnose and treat HIV-infected patients in office practice.

EPIDEMIOLOGY

Prevalence
● The World Health Organization (WHO) reports more than 150,000 cases of AIDS from 145 countries, with an estimated 5–10 million HIV-infected people worldwide.

● In the US, more than 97,000 AIDS cases have been reported as of June 1989, with 14,137 new AIDS cases occurring in 1989 alone.

Profile of AIDS in the US
The following figures represent the current distribution of AIDS:

● Adults: Men, 91% (61% in homosexual men); women, 9%.

● Of these cases, 46% are in the 30–39 year age group and 88% are in the 20–49 year group.

● Racial composition: White, 57%; Black, 27%; Hispanic, 15%; other/unknown, 1%.

● Children: As of May 31, 1989, 1,632 cases have been reported in children; 79% of these children have a parent at risk for AIDS.

HIV seroprevalence in the US
● Early randomized studies show 0.6% seropositivity in a general population, outpatient primary care setting.

● Up to 30% of randomly selected males 25–44 years old in two inner city urban hospitals were seropositive.

● In 1987 in New York City, 53% of intravenous drug users (IVDU) tested positive for HIV. Seropositivity was found to be related positively to injection frequency, length of time of drug use, cocaine use, certain ethnic backgrounds, and certain geographic locations.

Trends
● AIDS is now one of the 10 leading causes of death among 1–4 year olds and 15–24 year olds in the US. (Source: Centers for Disease Control [CDC].)

● Among women with AIDS nationwide, 25.6% contracted their disease via sexual contact in 1988, up from 14.8% in 1983.

● The perinatal HIV transmission rate (seropositive mothers to their offspring) is at least 33%.

● At least one in every 1,000 women of childbearing age in the US is HIV seropositive.

● Every state in the US has reported AIDS cases.

● In a recent CDC study, 0.2% of university students tested HIV positive.

● The largest number of AIDS cases currently are in urban areas of New York, California, Florida, New Jersey, and Texas.

● HIV infection rates have been stable among military recruits.

● The incidence of AIDS is increasing among younger

and older adults, women and children, and in minority groups.
- The incidence of infection is decreasing among homosexual men.
- The growth in condom sales is up from a 0.6% increase between 1982 and 1983 to a 20.3% increase between 1986 and 1987.

New developments in patterns of infection
- Pattern I. North America, Europe, Australia, New Zealand, South/Central America, Southeast Asia: Homosexual/bisexual men, IV drug-abusers, heterosexual spread
- Pattern II. Africa, Caribbean areas: Heterosexual spread, blood products
- Pattern III. Asia, Middle East: Low numbers, but increasing in high-risk groups (male/female prostitutes)

TRANSMISSION

Heterosexual: The incidence of cases attributed to heterosexual transmission is rising. These cases remain confined to those whose sexual partners belong to a known high-risk group. The highest rate of HIV seropositivity due to presumed heterosexual transmission is in drug treatment centers (35%) and sexually transmitted disease (STD) clinics (0.4%–5.6%).

Homosexual: Anorectal trauma appears to be associated more frequently than symptomatic genital ulceration with HIV transmission, according to one study. Another study indicates that simultaneous nitrite inhalation and receptive anal intercourse increase the likelihood of HIV transmission.[1]

Hemophiliac: HIV progression with opportunistic infection and decreased T4 levels is more rapid in older adults (age greater than 34).[2]

IVDU: Coinfection with HTLV-1 is associated with risk for progression to AIDS among HIV-positive users. The number of cases directly or indirectly associated with IVDU represents the area of greatest growth now and in the future. Behavior modification in this group is difficult, due to social, political, legal, and economic problems that are not easily solved. Drug rehabilitation on demand, needle exchange, and early education are being attempted in some areas.[3]

VIROLOGY

Each year scientists present new information about retroviruses and about HIV in particular. Much knowledge has been acquired in a short time with the help of our "high-tech" society.

HIV-1: This virulent retrovirus remains the most common cause of AIDS in the US. The virus is heterogeneous (consists of several different strands) in each individual and is even heterogeneous in individual infected cells. It can vary during disease progression in the patient. Selection of more virulent strains may be responsible for disease progression in the individual.

HIV-2: This virus remains the infective agent in Central/West African AIDS, with sporadic cases occurring throughout the world. It is less virulent than HIV-1.

HTLV-1: This virus is endemic in the Caribbean and occurs more frequently in the older age groups. Coinfection with this virus and with HIV-1 is associated with disease progression.

AIDS-RELATED DISEASES

Pneumocystis carinii pneumonia (PCP): This is the most common opportunistic infection that occurs with AIDS, and is associated with the most morbidity and mortality in the AIDS patient. Encouraging treatment results were reported at this conference concerning PCP prevention and treatment, and the increasing rate and period of survival of patients with PCP.

- Prophylaxis: Preventive treatment is recommended for all patients who have had one episode of PCP or whose T4 count is less than 200/mm³. Oral trimethoprim/sulfamethoxazole (TMP/SMX) may be used. Recently the Food and Drug Administration (FDA) approved aerosolized pentamidine for prophylaxis. The suggested dose: 300 mg by the Respigard II nebulizer every four weeks. Studies continue on the use of dapsone, 50 mg/day.[4]

- Treatment: Intravenous treatment with either pentamidine or TMP/SMX is the "gold standard," and most patients respond well to two to three weeks of therapy. Concurrent treatment with steroids has been found useful in some studies. Aerosolized pentamidine has been studied as a treatment modality for mild to moderate PCP, with final results pending.

- Salvage treatment: When PCP is refractory or usual treatments cannot be tolerated, other drugs are available for compassionate or experimental use. Trimetrexate with leucovorin rescue has been used successfully in some cases. Eflornithine shows promise and is being studied. The oral anti-infectives clindamycin and primaquine have also shown early positive results and are being investigated.

Intestinal pathogens: In addition to other diarrhea-causing pathogens, microsporidia and HIV itself have been described as intestinal pathogens. Cryptosporidium is often refractory to treatment, but spiramycin may be of help in up to 40% of patients. Investigational treatment with hyperimmune colostrum may be beneficial. *Isospora belli* may respond to TMP/SMX, sulfadoxine plus pyrimethamine, or metronidazole hydrochloride. In the most difficult cases, parenteral hyperalimentation may be required.

Cytomegalovirus (CMV) infection: Retinitis secondary to CMV infection often responds to treatment with ganciclovir (now approved by the FDA for general use). The drug must be given intravenously for life. Due to bone marrow toxicity, patients may not tolerate this drug long-term. Another drug, trisodium phosphonoformate, or foscarnet, has also shown promise in the treatment of CMV.

Cryptococcus infection: Amphotericin B with or without fluorocytosine (5FC) has been the mainstay in acute and maintenance therapy for cryptococcal infection. Another drug, fluconazole, given orally, has recently shown excellent results in the treatment of acute and chronic infection. This medication is expected to reduce morbidity associated with intravenous drug therapy. Currently this drug is available for the treatment of patients who cannot tolerate amphotericin B. Suppressive therapy for cryptococcal meningitis with ketoconazole, 400 mg/day, has shown encouraging early results.

Anemia: Many patients with AIDS and HIV infection are anemic, either because of their disease or because of side effects associated with toxic reactions to drugs used to treat their illness. Recently, the FDA approved erythropoietin, which stimulates bone marrow production of red blood cells, for use in dialysis patients. The drug has now been approved by the FDA for use in AIDS patients. Similarly, colony-stimulating factor (CSF), which stimulates granulocyte production, but which has not yet been approved by the FDA, may be of benefit for the leukopenia frequently present in these patients. Both agents may be given subcutaneously, are under study at this time, and may become generally available in the near future.

Kaposi's sarcoma (KS): This malignancy in its aggressive form is most common in the homosexual man with HIV disease. Treatment with full-dose zidovudine (AZT) and interferon has been successful, given subcutaneously at induction doses followed by maintenance doses. The patient, or a family member, can be taught to administer the medication at home. Intralesional vinblastine given for oral KS lesions has also been of therapeutic benefit. In advanced cases, more aggressive chemotherapy with multiple agents has yielded positive salvage results.

ANTIVIRALS

AZT: AZT has shown and continues to show benefit as a suppressive treatment for HIV infection. The usual dosage of 200 mg every four hours is tolerated by many patients, but bone marrow toxicity is common. The greatest drug benefit occurs during the first 6–18 months of treatment. Good treatment results continue at a somewhat lower percentage for up to 30 months—the length of time in which it has been studied to date. Newer studies show that AZT may not be entirely effective after prolonged use, since the development of some AZT-resistant HIV strains has been noted. For the present, however, AZT remains the mainstay of treatment for HIV infection as a single agent or in combination with other agents such as acyclovir, ganciclovir, 2'3'dideoxycytidine (DDC) or 2'3'dideoxyinosine (DDI).

INVESTIGATIONAL ANTIVIRALS

DDC: This drug is of the same family as AZT. Possible toxicity: neuropathy. Effectiveness may be enhanced by alternating treatment cycles with AZT therapy.

DDI: This drug has effective antiviral properties, can be given orally, appears to have low toxicity, and thus shows therapeutic promise.

CD4: Given intravenously, CD4 is well tolerated, but still under investigation. Intramuscular and subcutaneous dosage and administration are currently under study.

Colchicine: Generally used in the treatment of gout, this drug has been shown to have antiviral activity *in vitro*. Further studies are under way.

VACCINES

The study of vaccines has yielded exciting news. Jonas Salk, MD, described the results of his vaccine research at the Salk Institute (La Jolla, CA), and the clinical trials to be carried out in HIV-seropositive asymptomatic patients in 1989–1990. The vaccine under investigation appears to be of low toxicity, with promise of becoming an immune enhancer in this population, thus prolonging the asymptomatic state. While a vaccine to prevent HIV infection is considered to be years away, these preliminary studies are seen as a first step toward achieving that goal early in the next century. The French physician Daniel Zagury has continued to produce HIV antibodies in his laboratory at Université Pierre et Marie Curie, Paris; the volunteers who have been injected with his vaccine, gp 160, have shown few toxic effects. The next step in testing this vaccine will be to administer it to selected populations at risk, in order to determine its protective effect.

EDUCATION

General education remains the key to the prevention of HIV disease. All-out campaigns on safe sexual practices, safe IVDU, and safe blood products are being mandated worldwide. AIDS-prevention education now starts in many parts of the world with *pre*-schoolers. It has become obvious that preventive education is a continuous process into adulthood. Never before has it been so important yet so difficult to modify life-style, and reduce high-risk behavior. Preventive education is difficult to implement because it must cross religious, political, economic, language and cultural barriers to be effective. Numerous presentations and posters made a convincing case for the critical importance of worldwide AIDS education. Without it, the survival of entire populations may be at stake.

References

1. Van Raden M, et al: The role of ulcerative genital diseases in promoting acquisition of HIV-1 by homosexual men. Abstract ThAO 17. Multicenter AIDS Cohort.
2. Goedert J, et al: The effect of age on HIV progression in hemophiliacs. Abstract ThAO 26. NCI for the Multicenter Study of AIDS in Hemophiliacs.
3. Weiss S, et al: HTLV I/II co-infection is significantly associated with risk for progression to AIDS among HIV+ IVDU. Abstract ThAO 23. New Jersey, UMDNJ.
4. Guidelines for prophylaxis against PCP in AIDS. *MMWR* 38 (S-5); June 16, 1989.

THE CHEMISTRY OF LOVE

That special feeling is not all in your head. It's all through your body and blood too

John Poppy

John Poppy writes Esquire's monthly Active Health column.

When someone would tell me, "Happier is healthier," I'd say, "Yes, that makes sense," but I couldn't make myself believe it. Don't you notice, they would say, people falling in love don't catch colds; we all staved off the flu until after zero hour on the big-bucks presentation; doctors keep writing best sellers about patients with a "will to live" who outlast the hopeless ones. Yes, yes. Such tales do seem to contain a dose of common sense.

You take a moment to savor the sun's warmth on your face. Your baby holds out her arms to be picked up and the trust in her smile brings a sting of tears to your eyes. If good feelings like these do indeed turn out to be an investment in good health, why walk in the shade with your blues on parade?

But even if the happier-is-healthier lore has always made good sense, it never could hold a sharp-enough edge to carve out clear understandings about health. What happened is an anecdote; only when someone figures out how it happened does it cross over to the realm of dependable, repeatable practice. When you're dealing with something as unbelievable as the workings of the human body, you want all the microscope slides, statistics, and evidence you can collect. You want the scientific method.

Science, in spite of its history of stubbornness about jumping from old paradigms to new ones, has lately been

Even just the thought of making love signals your body to begin releasing neuropeptides, as potent as any drug you can find.

accumulating some truly provocative evidence. Just ten years ago, Norman Cousins' book *Anatomy of an Illness* exposed millions of readers to carefully researched explanations for Cousins' certainty that his *attitude* had a lot to do with his recovery from a painful and supposedly irreversible disintegration of his connective tissue. Here was an observer with credentials so fine that his story had appeared first in 1976 in the *New England Journal of Medicine*. His point got grossly simplified as readers repeated it, and a notion took hold that Cousins had laughed his way back to health. That, he has pointed out many times, is absurd. As he has written since, he used mirth as a metaphor "for the full range of the positive emotions, including hope, love, faith, a strong will to live, determination, and purpose...[and] a capacity for festivity." And he worked with an imaginative doctor, sampling varied medications, doing everything

he could to "mobilize all the natural resources of body and mind."

Cousins' book appeared near the beginning of a period in which a trickle of serious research on those "natural resources" had swelled to a flood. The research has created the field of psychoneuroimmunology, or PNI to anyone who has to say it more than once. PNI is casting light on some mechanisms and pathways by which good feelings actually start up chemical reactions in the body that may boost the immune system—particularly when those good feelings are directed toward other people.

PSYCHONEUROIMMUNOLOGY— the study of how emotions can affect the immune system and how the immune system, in a closing of the loop, can affect the emotions—is not a new word for psychosomatic medicine. The word *psychosomatic* appeared a hundred years or so ago to describe the mind's effect on bodily ailments. Ironically, it kept alive the dualism it was meant to dissolve: Mind. Body. "Our language does not even recognize that the two entities are inseparable," says Dr. Robert Ader of the University of Rochester, the psychologist who pretty much founded PNI fifteen years ago with one study that has become a classic. "But it is really not possible to talk about the mind apart from the body."

Ader speaks with the conviction of one who practically tripped over an unexpected truth. In 1974 he and immunologist Nicholas Cohen were doing a standard taste-aversion study with rats. They gave the rats a saccharine solution to drink, then injected them with cyclophosphamide, a nausea-inducing drug that, incidentally, also depresses immune functions. The rats learned—usually with just one experience—to associate sweet water with throwing up. From then on, they avoided sweet water even though it contained no trace of the nauseating drug. Weeks later, Ader noticed something else: rats were falling ill and dying. Tests confirmed what he suspected—these rats had learned to suppress their own immune systems. That had been thought impossible. Immunologists had envisioned the body's defense department working on its own, independent of the brain. (Never mind that Pavlov's lab conditioned guinea pigs to produce specific antibodies in 1924; that was Russia, not to be trusted.)

"We have simply thrown a monkey wrench" into the old beliefs, Ader said last year. "The immune system is…influenced by both the nervous and endocrine systems. Presumably it is via these same channels that behavior can influence the immune system."

Far from everyone in the biomedical community thinks that has been proved. Ader himself asks, "Will the same things occur in life as in the test tube? Possibly, but we just don't know." Still, "We cannot disavow certain phenomena, like spontaneous recovery from illness, just because we cannot explain them."

For years experiments such as Ader and Cohen's—in which you make the rat sick—have been establishing that under stress, the body can constrict blood vessels, raise blood lipids, and release hormones that degrade some disease-fighting cells in the immune system. (Stress, by the way, is not an outside event such as another driver cutting you off; it is your *response* to the event.) Now other studies are blueprinting the mechanisms that produce the opposite effect.

Long-range surveys—among them a nine-year study of 7,000 people in Alameda County, California, and a longer study of 2,700 people in Tecumseh, Michigan—agree that married people with friends have more than twice the life expectancy (during the survey) of single ones, and are

healthier overall. That isn't surprising. If you're sharing a happy life with somebody, you're not so tempted to take drugs or overeat or drink hard; you probably pay some attention to your looks, which means getting some exercise; it adds up. What is surprising is the single thing that *most* affected longevity: social contact. The more social contact, the lower the death rate, no matter what else people did. The Tecumseh study noted that men who did volunteer work at least once a week outlived men who did none, two and a half to one. Women showed less difference, perhaps because most women spend a lot of time looking after other people anyway. These studies imply that doing something with other people—especially *for* them, in volunteer work, support groups, and community building—is the most powerful of all stimuli to longevity and health.

SAY YOU'RE JUST ABOUT TO pick up your salad fork when your wife puts her hand over yours and says, "Twice this morning I thought about us making love, and each time I felt a rush of warmth all through me. Just *thinking* about sex made me happy."

You smile at each other. And there are scientists who say you have more reason to than you might have believed a few years ago. Your wife's physical sensations were no mere figure of speech. She did, in fact, describe concisely one powerful theory for the connection between social contact—especially bonding experiences—and good health.

The chemistry of love. It was discovered in the early 1970s that the human body produces its own supplies of the chemicals known as neuropeptides from cells in the brain, in other organs and, of all places, in the immune system. Your wife's thought of you, just the thought, signaled nerve endings throughout her body to release neuropeptides. Swiftly, carried in her blood like leaves on a stream, they suffused her. Her remark prompted similar reactions in you.

Neuropeptides are as potent as any drug you can take into your body from outside—one, dynorphin, is a pain reliever nearly two hundred times stronger than morphine. Their major job is to convey information. They make things happen by homing in on "receptor sites" on the surfaces of cells. The richest clusters of receptors have been found deep in the center of the brain, in the areas that control mood and mo-

tivation—the so-called limbic system that includes the hypothalamus (the "brain of the brain" that regulates appetite, rest, temperature, heart rate, sexual desire, and more) and the pituitary gland (the master hormone maker). These receptors are identical to others in distant organs (among them the gonads, kidneys, spleen, and gut), and, of all places again, in the immune system. The implication of all this? Chemicals that fit the juncture points for emotions are probably carrying messages back and forth between brain and immune system.

A clue to the potency of peptide molecules is their purity. They are nothing but strings of amino acids. (The twenty amino acids make all the proteins and peptides in the body. If you think of them as differently colored beads, you can imagine varying their quantities and sequences to make different chemicals.) *Neuropeptides* are short strings, created in nerve cells straight off DNA, the double helix that carries the genetic code.

At least sixty neuropeptides have been identified so far. Some are opiates. That your body makes its own forms of opium and its derivatives (morphine, codeine, and heroin) could explain phenomena such as "runner's high," the subject of a million anecdotes and no test-tube proofs. The endorphins (*endogenous morphines*), now as familiar to athletes as Gatorade, are neuropeptides. Others of the sixty are hormones such as insulin (until recently believed to come only from the pancreas) that regulate body functions; still others are growth factors that help create cells.

Whatever else neuropeptides do, all sixty-plus of them "can be considered mood-altering substances," in the opinion of Candace Pert, a bold researcher in the field. Pert and Solomon Snyder first located the receptors for opium in 1973 at Johns Hopkins. She expanded that work as chief of brain biochemistry in a branch of the National Institute of Mental Health. Now scientific director of Peptide Design, a new company that looks for peptide-based disease cures, she still works as an NIMH guest scientist.

The more Pert thinks about the identical receptor sites in the brain, organs, and immune system, the more convinced she becomes that they will lead to "understanding how mind and body are interconnected, and how emotions can be manifested throughout the body." The more we learn, she has written, "the harder it is to think in traditional terms of a mind and a body. It makes more and more sense to speak of a single integrated entity, a 'body-mind.'" Granting that some scientists find the idea outrageous, Pert sees the receptors for neuropeptides as "keys to the biochemistry of emotion."

Some of those emotions are obvious, she said at the end of a long day at Peptide Design. "You might not have tried heroin, but you can imagine the narcotic effects of the opiate peptides. Other peptides that have potent effects throughout the body and the immune system also have receptors in the mood-mediating parts of the brain. We just don't know yet what feelings those peptides might induce.

"You can go both ways, theoretically, from one realm to the other. In one direction, from changes in the body through emotions to the mind. In the other direction, from pure 'mind'—thought—through emotions into bodily changes."

The neuropeptides flooding through your wife and you moved toward their receptors. Some began making things happen even before they docked—particularly in your immune system. Take their effect, for instance, on the mobile white cells called monocytes, which are pivotal in controlling disease. When a monocyte floating along in the blood recognizes an invader, it eats it, and then prompts B-cells, T-cells, and others to get busy with other work. A monocyte also carries enzymes that produce and destroy collagen, the protein that builds tissue and heals wounds. And it has one other important quality—on its surface, a monocyte has receptors for neuropeptidees. When it "scents" a peptide nearby, it crawls toward it. The result of the extra movement, and the eventual contact, may be an increase in a monocyte's overall activity; research has not yet shown precisely what happens. But nature does nothing uselessly. By putting receptors for chemicals associated with emotion on vital cells in the immune system, nature seems to have constructed a bridge between brain and monocytes, between emotion and immunity.

Not only do cells in the immune system have receptors for neuropeptides, they also *make* the same peptides that the brain produces. Since the brain is rich in peptide receptors, it could receive messages about bacteria and viruses from those immune cells. The immune system might be a listener and a talker too.

THE DRUG TRAP

When you're living a good life, your body is exquisitely balanced, producing the right amount of specific chemical substances at the right time to arouse you, relax you, reduce pain, produce feelings of pleasure, or fortify the immune system. Drugs can do some of the same things, but only temporarily—and only by laying a nasty trap.

The opiates, for example. Those you produce inside, the endorphins, soothe you and please you. So do opiates you get from outside, such as the morphine in heroin. The difference is that external opiates are not always available to you, whereas internal ones are—until you mess with the system. Under normal conditions, your body produces a steady supply of endorphins that are stored in nerve cells, against the times when they're needed to balance the chemicals of arousal that make you jumpy and tense—adrenaline and cortisol, for instance. The minute you stick an opiate in from outside, you signal your body to slack off the production of opiates inside. Meanwhile, it keeps on producing flight-or-fight chemicals. The result: just to keep things in balance, you depend on ever-increasing amounts of a drug from outside.

Simply put, when you take in a drug from outside, your brain attempts to *adapt* to it. A drug molecule either mimics the effects of a molecule that the body makes itself or blocks its effects. It does so by occupying a "receptor" site on the surface of a brain cell, much as a key fits into a lock. The receptor is a complicated molecule itself that can be an on-off valve. Slightly different molecules may compete for the same receptor. One may turn things on (an *agonist*) and the other may turn them off (an *antagonist*). When the one that fits most tightly bumps the other one off, its effect is the one you feel.

Caffeine, nicotine, and other external stimulants play the flip side of the opiates. Caffeine is suspected of speeding up the release of adrenaline. When adrenaline kicks in, the brain normally buffers it with other substances, particularly one called adenosine, that promote tranquility and relaxation. Caffeine has a second effect, though: it is a potent antagonist to adenosine. A short-term result of too much coffee can be a jag of anxiety, even panic. A long-run result seems to be that the adrenal glands get lazy, the adenosine is still waiting in the wings, and you need repeated jolts of caffeine (or nicotine, or last-minute deadlines, or whatever upper you use) to feel normal.

Similarly, Valium, which is not an opiate, seems to do its work mainly as an antagonist, by blocking a naturally occurring peptide, diazepam-binding inhibitor (DBI), which makes you alert and nervous. Snatch the block out of receptors that have been clogged with it for a long time, and the resulting rush of DBI can make you crazy.

Whatever happens, the brain tries to keep things stable. It works for homeostasis. A drug coming in from outside can trick it into signaling a cut in production of your body's own form of that drug; or a boost of its antagonist; or both. Either way, the brain is doing its best to tamp down the effects of the drug and restore stability. Everything in the brain is interlinked, so one reaction affects others, cascading across entire systems in a profusion of yin-yang effects, with peaks on one side and valleys on the other. When you push your brain and body past their ability to match peaks with valleys, you run the risk of addiction, and possibly death. As with any trap, you're better off not putting your foot in it.

"WE FEEL the pursuit of happiness is a reasonable part of the fight for recovery from cancer," Harold Benjamin said in his office at the Wellness Community in Santa Monica, California. Benjamin retired from his law practice in 1982 to open a place where cancer patients and their families can come, free of charge, to augment their conventional medical treatments with "psychosocial support"—camaraderie, group therapy, and information. Since then more than eight thousand people have found it so useful that ten new Wellness Communities are opening in other cities this year.

What they do, essentially, is trigger the interactions between emotions and health that PNI has been documenting. For instance, numerous experiments have shown that laughter reduces the levels of certain hormones that ordinarily rise with stress and also apparently increases the activity of natural killer cells that attack tumors and other cells infected by viruses.

"We never, never tell people that if they come here their cancer will go away," Benjamin said. "It would be absurd to say that changing your point of view cures cancer. There are too many times when biology overwhelms psychology. We do say that people who participate in their fight for recovery along with their physicians—instead of acting as hopeless, helpless, passive victims of the illness—will improve the quality of their lives and just may enhance the possibility of their recovery." He provides details in *From Victim to Victor*, ostensibly a handbook on what the Wellness Community has learned about cancer, but in its lucidity really a book about life.

"*May* enhance the possibility," Benjamin emphasized. "If I had cancer, and decided with my doctor to take radiation, I would take it because I thought it could kill the cancer cells. I would also try everything *else* I could to enhance the power of my immune system to kill more cancer cells. That includes enhancing the quality of my life. People participate so actively in jokefests and visualization and social networking here because they want to get better, not because they want to be happier. And they're happier."

Harold Benjamin is not referring to petty happiness, to trivialities that are self-centered, acquisitive, based on the quick fix of drugs or entertainment. Those variations, along with any chemical changes they might initiate, are short-lived; there is no reason at all to believe that the one who dies with the most toys wins. Rather, it is now clear that the possibilities for satisfaction and health over a lifetime emerge from "activity in accordance with excellence," as Aristotle defined happiness.

The practical fact is that feeling good, even sensual, is healthier than feeling grim, lonely, and depressed. Every detail of what makes it healthier may be figured out someday, but don't bet on it. We are too complex. For now, the clues argue for following common sense rather than waiting for every scientist to be satisfied.

It is part of common sense, by the way, to refrain from falling over the edge into promises that nobody can keep: that if you love enough, or summon up enough optimism, you can armor yourself against all misfortune. Love may boost healing and health, but love does not conquer all, not even, at times, the common cold. The coordination of the body's processes, the artfulness and resilience, are dazzling; yet in the end they will fail. Everyone dies. Along the way, though, loving the textures and colors of the world, your sweetheart's lips, your child's faith in you, all the gifts that fill the day, can contribute to making the best of the life we have been given.

What Keeps Women "in Their Place"?

" . . . Sexual equality will not be achieved until we face up to the fact that inequality is a product of our own behavior and attitudes."

Anthony Layng

Dr. Layng is professor of anthropology, Elmira (N.Y.) College.

During the decade of the 1970s's, women in numerous nations called for the elimination of sexual discrimination. In the U.S., this latest feminist resurgence ambitiously attempted to end all inequalities between the sexes—including those involving employment, political participation, property rights, recreation, language, and education—and some reforms were achieved. An increasing number of women began to act like they were socially equal to men; there has been much talk about teaching girls to be more assertive; and there is now considerable confusion about what constitutes appropriate sex roles. Yet, judging by the fact that the Equal Rights Amendment did not pass and that it presently shows little promise of being resuscitated in the near future, many seem to have concluded that most American women are, by and large, content to remain where they are in relation to men. Further, since women in other industrialized nations have remained essentially "in their place," it appears that there are other formidable obstacles to overcome if we are to bring about such fundamental social change.

Why do sexual inequalities persist in the face of concerted feminist challenges? Is there any realistic basis for us to hope that sexual discrimination ever will be eliminated? What must be done to bring about full emancipation of women? What is it that keeps women "in their place"?

To understand fully how women have been kept "in their place," we first must learn how they came to be there. This requires consideration of the course of human evolution. Prior to 4,000,000 years ago, there was probably little social differentiation based on gender, because the two sexes were not economically interdependent; one could survive quite well without assistance from the other. It is likely that economic interdependence developed only after the evolving human brain reached a size that necessitated earlier birth, before the cranium of an infant was too large to pass through the birth canal. Giving birth earlier meant that the babies were less mature and would be more dependent on their mothers for a longer period of time. Prolonged helplessness of infants eventually created a need for mothers to depend on others for food and protection.

At the same time, more evolved brains enabled us to invent and use tools that resulted in our becoming effective hunters, in addition to being scavengers. Females with helpless infants still could gather and scavenge a variety of foods, but they were likely to be relatively handicapped hunters and so came to depend on males to provide them with a more reliable source of meat.

Increasing brain size and improved hunting skills also meant that some of our ancestors could begin to occupy northern regions where successful hunting was necessary for survival, since those foods that could be gathered were insufficient during some seasons. In such an environment, females with infants would not live long without food provided by others. Under these circumstances, a sexual division of labor made very good sense.

Although biological factors created the especially long dependency of human infants, the solution to this problem may have been entirely cultural. There is little evidence to suggest that any instinct developed at this time which led females to restrict their economic activities to gathering roots and fruits and men to go off in search of game, but doing so was sound strategy. Such specialization—encouraging females to learn and concentrate on gathering, and teaching only males to be hunters—was an efficient and realistic adaptation requiring only a change in our ancestors' learned behavior and attitudes.

So, a sexual division of labor emerged, but what about sexual inequality? The subordination of females was not brought about by this economic change alone, for, although economic specialization by sex made women dependent on men, it also made men dependent on women. Where human populations subsist entirely by what can be hunted or gathered, most of the food consumed is provided by the gatherers—women. Meat acquired by hunters may be given a higher social value than nuts and berries and the like; but, if the technology employed in hunting is very primitive, meat is difficult to acquire and frequently absent from the menu. Thus, when men began to concentrate on hunting, an interdependence between the sexes emerged, each relying on the other to provide food that made survival possible.

BELIEFS AND CUSTOMS

The development of a sexual division of labor may have preceded and even facilitated social inequality, but it did not create male dominance. Although male dominance would be very difficult to achieve in the absence of a sexual division of labor, it takes firm beliefs and customs as well to retain a higher status for men. The following examples illustrate how societies in various parts of the world have directed the socialization of their children to assure that women will be kept "in their place."

• Mythology which justifies maintaining female subordination. Mythology and folklore are used in tribal societies to explain and justify the social *status quo*. The story of Adam and Eve illustrates how sexist myths can be, but some are even less subtle than Genesis in rationalizing male preeminence. Frequently found tales of Amazons or an era when our ancestors lived in matriarchal communities may be functionally equivalent to the Adam and Eve account; although they serve as inspiring models for some women, they may be far more instrumental in reminding men why they must be ever-vigilant in protecting their favored status. So, such tales become an important part of the conservative social learning of children.

• Seclusion based on the concept of pollution. In many horticultural societies, women must retire to a special hut during menstruation, since it is believed that their condition magically would jeopardize the well-being of the community. Their economic inactivity during these and other periods of seclusion serves to indicate symbolically that their economic contributions are of secondary importance. This subconsciously may suggest to children in the community that the labor of men is too important to be so restricted by taboos.

• Segregation of male domains. Many tribal societies have a men's house in the center of each village in which nearly all important political and ritual plans are made. Women are not allowed to enter this house, under the threat of severe punitive sanctions such as gang rape. Since this form of segregation effectively precludes the participation of women in the political arena, they are not likely to develop any political aspirations while growing up.

• Exclusion from sacred public rituals. Tribal societies customarily devote much energy to elaborate religious events, believing that the health of the community depends on these. With very few exceptions, men direct these rituals and play all the key roles; commonly, women merely are observers or participate only in a support capacity. A primary function of these public rituals is to reinforce social values. Since they even attract the full attention of young children, tribal members learn early that men are far more important than women, for they are the ones charged with magically protecting the people.

• Exclusion from military combat. As in the case of religious ritual in tribal societies, war is considered necessary to insure the survival of the community and almost always is conducted exclusively by men. Success as a warrior brings conspicuous prestige and admiration from women and children alike. Here again, the socialization process, instilling norms and attitudes of correct conduct, leads easily and inevitably to the conclusion that everyone's welfare depends on the performance of the men, and that the women should be suitably grateful.

• Exclusion from high-status economic roles. Women in most tribal societies are important producers and consumers, but their economic role is restricted largely to domestic concerns, producing food and goods for kinsmen. When it comes to regulating the exchange of goods between kin groups or with outsiders, men usually dominate such activities. This division of economic roles is fully consistent with the assumption that men are more important socially and more skillful politically. Given such an assumption, the economic differences between the behavior of men and women are likely to seem both proper and inevitable.

• Veneration of female virginity. If the religious, political, and economic activities of women are of secondary importance, then what, besides producing children, is their real value? One might be tempted to speculate that, because children in primitive societies are taught to venerate female virginity, this indicates that the status of women is not so lowly as might otherwise be assumed. However, it seems far more likely that this concern with virginity is an extension of the double standard and a reflection of the belief that the major value of women is their sexuality and fertility, their unexalted role as wife and mother.

• Preference for male children. When parents usually prefer that their next child will be a boy, this attitude may be considered as both a consequence of and contributor to the higher status of men. Before young children are mature enough to appreciate that one sex socially outranks the other, they can understand that their parents hope to have a boy next time. Impending childbirth in a home is given much attention and takes on real importance; this often may be the earliest opportunity for children to learn that males are more valued than females.

• Sexist humor and ridicule are used as important socialization methods in all societies and lend themselves quite effectively to maintaining a sexual hierarchy. Girls who behave like boys, and boys who behave like girls, almost inevitably inspire ridicule. Sexist jokes, particularly when they are considered to be good-natured, are especially effective in this regard. Women who take offense or fail to find such jokes amusing are accused of having no sense of humor, thus largely neutralizing their defense against this social control mechanism.

• Sexual stereotyping. Stereotypes of any sort are likely to be of little use in teaching social attitudes to children unless they are accepted by the children as true images of nature. To believe that women and men behave differently because it is the way they were created helps to prevent misgivings from arising about the social inequality of men and women. To the extent that such status differences are believed to be imposed by human nature, the cultural supports of such inequality are not likely to be recognized and, therefore, will not be questioned.

DO WOMEN ACCEPT SUBJUGATION?

A society which effectively keeps women "in their place" need not employ all of the above techniques to do so; just a few will suffice, so long as there is general agreement throughout the population that the *status quo* of sexual inequality is both appropriate and natural. It is just as necessary that women accept this view as it is for men. Although some reformist writers argue that the subjugation of women was instigated by a male chauvinist plot forced upon unwilling victims, it seems amply evident that these social control mechanisms could not work effectively without the willing cooperation of women. They, too, must believe that they were designed by their creator to be subordinate; religious, political, and economic leadership are less suitable for them; and they have their own domains and should not be so immodest as to attempt to interfere where they do not belong. They, too, must consider military exploits as unsuitable for themselves.

Is this asking too much? Do not women value their virginity and that of their daughters as much as men do? Do they not condemn promiscuous women and at the same time tolerate promiscuous men? Is it not common for

women to hope to have male children, in preference to daughters? Most women accept sexual stereotypes as an accurate reflection of nature to some degree, and they continue to encourage sexist humor by their laughter.

It seems clear that the "lowly" status of women was not brought about by a conspiracy, nor is it perpetuated only by men. There is no reason to view the above social controls as sinister or perverse where women willingly, even enthusiastically, teach their sons to be "real" men and their daughters to admire such men without wanting to be like them. In other words, in tribal societies, it is not male suppression which makes women subordinate.

It is only when we assume a missionary mentality, viewing such societies in light of our own society's values, that we think these women long for emancipation. Such an ethnocentric view fails to recognize that inequality, where it is accepted by all concerned as inevitable and proper, can be advantageous to lower-status individuals as well as to those who outrank them. Dominance hierarchies, like pecking orders, establish and maintain social order, a condition which tribal societies understandably prefer to disorder and uncertainty. Women in traditional societies do not contribute to their own subordination because they do not know any better or because they are forced to comply with the wishes of the men; they do so because they are socialized appropriately in an orderly society which is culturally well-adapted to its environment.

In tribal societies, sexual inequality is relatively high and protest against such inequality is relatively low. However, an increasing number of women in other societies are protesting sexual discrimination and their subordinate position. Most of this dissent comes from stratified and heterogeneous populations, where gossip, ridicule, and taboos are relatively ineffectual social control techniques. Social order in these more complex societies tends to be enforced by laws and specialized agencies, rather than depending upon voluntary compliance. Even in such complex societies, most may be wholly

supportive of the social *status quo*, in spite of their own lowly status. Nevertheless, most of the discontent about sexual inequality comes from these populations.

In spite of such feminist discontent, sexual hierarchies still survive in even highly modernized societies like our own. American women have gained important rights in recent years, but many Americans continue to find Biblical justification for sexual discrimination. Many still think that our nation's economy appropriately remains under the domination of men, and, although the number of exclusively male domains (athletic teams, lodges, clubs, etc.) have been reduced greatly in recent years, a large number still find general endorsement and remain very much intact. Sexual stereotypes continue to enjoy robust health, the double standard is far from moribund, and sexist humor and ridicule seem to have recovered from their recent bout with militant feminism in the 1970's.

Today, in spite of a recent Gallup poll indicating that more than half the women in the U.S. consider themselves to be feminists, the most ambitious goals of the feminist movement have not been realized. However, it has grown increasingly difficult to convince American women that it is proper for them to be socially inferior to men, or that they should behave submissively. It seems that those customs and beliefs which deny opportunity to women in America are going to continue to be questioned by some who are very persuasive. Since a sexual division of labor has become largely anachronistic for our technologically advanced society, we may anticipate that efforts to preserve exclusive privileges for either sex will encounter increasing resistance.

Although tribal societies need to depend on a system of ascriptive statuses to maintain an orderly social structure, we do not. Tribal populations are not at risk in assigning economic roles strictly by sex, because not basing such assignments on individual aptitude and inclination is of little importance where the economy requires only a narrow range of tasks. In modern industrial society, however, where much highly skilled specialization is essential, selecting candidates for such positions from a limited talent pool, from only half of the adult population, places such a society at an unnecessary disadvantage, one which shows up very clearly if that society must compete with other nations which do not handicap themselves in this fashion. Also, traditional American values which exalt equality, opportunity, and achievement (matters of relatively little concern in tribal societies) are bound to give us increasing difficulty if we continue to deny equality to women and so restrict their ability to achieve the success that they desire and that our economy requires.

Since men have been politically dominant in all human societies, it is not surprising that many scholars have concluded that it is our nature, not our nurture, that has necessitated this inequality. Still, if sexual inequality is inevitable, given our nature, why must tribal populations resort to so many cultural methods to keep women subordinate and submissive?

Knowing how women have been kept "in their place" so long is essential if attempts to combat sexual inequality are to have some success. Just as the most effective medical cure is based on accurate causal diagnosis of an illness, so must social reform efforts take into account the nature of that which we would alter. If we recognize the various ways that our society uses cultural means to perpetuate differential socialization for boys and girls, we are prepared better to redesign that process to foster equality between the sexes. Similarly, if we are aware of the customary practices which encourage women to be submissive, we are more able to challenge and change such customs effectively. To fully understand how and to what extent women are kept "in their place" in the U.S., it is important that we understand how various societies effectively accomplish stable inequality.

Before all of this can enable us to eradicate male dominance, it may be that we first must learn why our society continues to deny equality of opportunity to women, for it is unlikely that we do so only as a result of cultural inertia. It may be that inequality is socially functional in ways that we do not understand fully.

Nevertheless, if women are to achieve total equality, if such a fundamental change can be brought about, it will require far more than passing the Equal Rights Amendment or changing discriminatory laws piecemeal. Since longstanding customs which encourage inequality thoroughly are ingrained in our culture, sexual equality will not be achieved until we face up to the fact that inequality is a product of our own behavior and attitudes. Only then might we discard this vestige of our tribal heritage.

THE AMERICAN MAN IN TRANSITION

STUBBORNLY

▲

FOLLOWING

▲

WOMEN'S

▲

EXAMPLE,

▲

MEN

ARE

▲

CHANGING.

▲

THEY

▲

HAVE

▲

NO CHOICE.

PROJECT EDITOR MICHAEL SEGELL

Men are doing a lot of soul-searching these days. The old role models—taciturn John Wayne, macho Stallone, sensitive Alda, workaholic Iacocca—simply have no relevance now. Inspired by women, who have radically re-defined their roles in America, men are casting about for an identity that is comfortably, and truly, masculine. They're in transition, and they're finding it a wrenching, lonely business.

One thing is certain. American men must do something to change—and women have to help them, or risk losing them. On average, men die seven years younger than women. Bio-logy isn't the full explanation—the gap used to be smaller. By one estimate, only two of those years can be clearly attributed to hard-wired differences in male and female biology. The tradi-tional male sex role, characterized by a roll-with-the-punches stoicism and iso-lation, fraught with stress, anxiety and ambivalence, is hazardous to men's health. The body, that exacting task-master and teacher, is telling men to find a new way to be. It's a matter of life and death.

The American man's emotional life is crying out for change, too. Just as feminism encouraged women to enrich their lives by looking outward, the gains women have achieved have indi-rectly suggested to men the benefits of looking inward. Not only is the old male model physically destructive, it's emotionally stultifying—and unaccept-able to many women. The sorry condi-tion of men's interpersonal skills is reflected in a few telling data: At no time in history have there been so many divorced men, so many single fathers—and this at a time when men claim to cherish family and home life more than any other facet of their lives. That they are so inept at it is tearing them apart.

Their current failure to integrate their lives, though, may be tempor-ary—a transition before they reach their ultimate transformation. A new *American Health*/Gallup survey has turned up a remarkable finding: Men and women are in very close agreement on the characteristics that make up an ideal man (see "Perfection Incarnate"). Does this signal an end to the battle of the sexes? Maybe, suggest some of the

authors on the following pages. Many men, by changing themselves, are at least moving toward a rapprochement. Like the early feminists, these men her-ald a shift, however gradual, in the American male psyche. Some—opti-mistically, perhaps—are calling the trend a men's movement.

Our survey documented not only evidence of that shift, but the ambiva-lence, reticence and discomfort ac-companying it. Both men and women agree, for instance, that it's most im-portant for an "ideal man" to be a good husband and father, have a sense of humor and be intelligent. That ideal traveled well even with single people, particularly men, who also rated quali-ties associated with being a family man near the top of the list.

The rise of this new ideal may signal the demise of the old: Both married and single men and women feel that conventionally "male" attributes like physical strength, aggressiveness, toughness and earning power are no longer as important as they once were.

Our poll did, however, highlight

WHAT MEN—AND WOMEN—TOLD US

When It Comes to Defining the Ideal Man, Men and Women Largely

Agree; the Characteristics They Choose, and the Percentage

Choosing Each, Are Shown in "Perfection Incarnate." But When They're

Talking With Friends of the Same Sex, Men and Women

Differ Tremendously, as "Shop Talk and Jock Talk" Makes Clear.

PERFECTION INCARNATE

Qualities of an "Ideal Man"

Being a good husband and father	68%
Intelligence	48%
Sense of humor	46%
Emotional sensitivity	31%
Ambition	30%
Rationality, not being overly emotional	17%
Earning power	17%
Being a good lover	11%
Aggressiveness	9%
Physical strength	7%
Physical attractiveness	5%
Toughness	4%
Sports ability	4%

(Total is more than 100% because respondents could give more than one answer.)

SHOP TALK AND JOCK TALK

Men talk with best friends about:

Work issues	43%
Sports	42%
Goals for the future	28%
Their children	26%
Personal problems and self-doubts	23%
Politics	21%
Books, movies, cultural activities	14%
Romantic relationships	13%
Religion	2%

(Total is more than 100% because respondents could give more than one answer.)

Women talk with best friends about:

Their children	47%
Personal problems and self-doubts	41%
Work issues	27%
Books, movies, cultural activities	23%
Goals for the future	22%
Romantic relationships	15%
Politics	10%
Sports	8%
Religion	2%

(Total is more than 100% because respondents could give more than one answer.)

some differences of opinion among various segments of the population. 45% of college graduates, for instance, think it's good for a man to be emotionally sensitive, compared with only 23% of non-college-graduates. The finding suggests that even though men know they have to abandon their old distant, authoritarian style, they're not quite ready to adopt a demeanor that could label them as wimps.

Men are lonely, too, our poll found. We asked men what they talk about when they get together with their closest friends (see "Shop Talk and Jock Talk"). In contrast to women, who talk mostly about their children and personal problems, men talk about work and sports. Men *say* their families are the most important things in their lives, yet seem unable to talk about them with their best friends. In that sense, men

truly may be isolated from sharing what they really care about.

Men may also be more isolated from their families—or more specifically, their wives—than they would like. Our poll found, for instance, that 29% of men think their best male friend understands them better than their wife or girlfriend. (High as that figure may seem, it falls short of its counterpart among women: 39% of women say their best friend understands them better than their husband or boyfriend.)

The isolation our poll found may be rooted in men's earliest, most primary male relationship. Most sons—daughters, too—feel closer to their mothers than to their fathers. On average, both men and women rate their relationship with their father a 7.5, on a 10-point scale, while mom rates almost a full point higher. The American man may cherish his family, but his children are more attached to his mate.

Perhaps that's one reason why more than half the fathers we polled (51%) would quit their jobs and stay home with their children, if money were not a problem. Clearly, men feel torn between being able to provide their families with more of themselves and being, simply, good providers. The pressures of a two-career family are especially disturbing—70% of married men would prefer that their wives not work, despite the many proven benefits to health and self-esteem that a job provides.

The American male, in short, is in flux. He's trying to shake the old rigid macho values, but he'd still like to be the sole breadwinner and keep his wife in the kitchen. Some college-educated trendsetters think men should feel more emotion, but the rest of the population—particularly men, and to a lesser degree, women—is terrified by the idea. Men still can't share their feelings with other men, preferring to rehash ball games or dissect the nuances of office politics with their best friends rather than reach for what really matters. The "lonely guy" is real.

But some men are breaking down the old models and reconstructing the male role. Men are seeking each other's counsel, healing wounded relationships with their fathers, and exploring, with the help of poetry, myths and fairy tales, what it means to be masculine. Finally, men's groups are meeting with women's groups—a summit of sorts of the sexes—in an effort to raise everyone's consciousness and understanding.

It's an effort to go beyond feminism, beyond "masculinism," toward humanism—a noble direction, whatever your gender.

Sexual Biology and Health

- The Body and Its Responses (Articles 9-12)
- Sexual Hygiene (Articles 13-19)

A change in attitudes toward sexuality is instrumental in opening avenues for more humanistic sexual relations. Indeed, freeing the mind for awareness and acceptance of bodily sensations is an important step toward maximizing sexual expression. But this is only half the story. Of parallel importance is developing a clear understanding and appreciation of the working of the human body. This section directs attention toward these goals.

Most males and females have a great number of misconceptions and a general lack of knowledge concerning the bodily responses of the opposite sex. This less than optimal situation is further worsened by the fact that many individuals have less than a working knowledge of their own bodily responses and functioning during sexual activity. In an effort to develop an understanding of and an appreciation for a healthy sexual awareness, females and males alike desperately need quality physiological information. Several articles in this section focus on the physical sexual response of females and males, laying to rest many of the fallacies that individuals have come to believe. Other articles explain some of the recent discoveries concerning the sexual functioning of males and females.

The physiological dimension of sexuality also includes sexual hygiene. Sexually transmitted diseases (STDs) are often inappropriately labeled "social diseases." This stigmatization may be a reflection of the general negative aura that surrounds sexuality in American culture. Such diseases might be a lesser social problem if people could deal with them as medical problems and seek immediate treatment for themselves and their sexual contacts.

As you read through the articles in this section, you may realize that matters of sexual biology and health are not merely physiological but—as with sexuality in general—are frequently psychological, social, and cultural in origin. The awareness, appreciation, and health of our bodies extends far beyond organic determinants.

The first two articles in the first subsection focus on the importance of touch as the language of intimacy and the most powerful of the communication channels. The last article focuses on the interplay between biology and emotions that can result in optimum sexual functioning and intimacy, or contribute to the "most common (sexual) complaint of the decade"—problems of sexual desire. The last article in the section asks an intriguing question, "Is Orgasm Essential?" as it traces the evolution and purpose of this often sought-after sexual event.

The *Sexual Hygiene* subsection covers a range of topics related to male and female sexual health: sexually transmitted diseases (STDs), urinary tract infections (UTIs), prostate and testicular conditions, and infertility. Each discussion provides information about these diseases or conditions and how they affect individuals and their sexual functioning. The articles also summarize the latest research into treatments and cures as well as predict probable future advances. The sixth article in the subsection, "Demystifying Menopause," provides a clear and informative guide to assist both men and women in better understanding the normal processes of menstruation and menopause. These articles can assist all readers in understanding their own and others' sexual functioning with less embarrassment so they will be better able to address and remedy problem situations if and when they occur.

Looking Ahead: Challenge Questions

Have we as a society put too little or too much emphasis on orgasm? In what ways has our preoccupation with orgasm been problematic?

Why is touch an important issue? How do sensuality and sexuality differ? How can the use of touch be integrated into sex therapy?

In what ways are UTIs and STDs similar? What emotional factors can hinder women and their partners from dealing with them?

In the past, how well prepared were most women for menarche, their first menstruation, or for menopause and the climacteric, the slowing down of their menstrual cycle after menstruation? Do you feel women are more prepared today than in the past? Why or why not? What are the general societal feelings about menstruation?

If we as a society were more comfortable with sexual functioning, would infertility be less traumatic for those affected and their families?

What might be some solutions for coping with the ever-increasing problem of STDs? Besides finding better medical treatments, what needs to be done at the psychosocial and cultural levels?

What attitudes or values contribute to men's uncomfortableness in knowing and/or talking about their bodies? How would your brother, father, or other male close to you react to your giving him "The Healthy Male" article?

CLOSE ENCOUNTERS

Silent but powerful, a touch can comfort, greet, persuade, inflame.
Small wonder societies keep our contacts under tight control.

STEPHEN THAYER

Stephen Thayer, Ph.D., is a professor of psychology at City College and the Graduate Center of the City University of New York.

IN MAY 1985, Brigitte Gerney was trapped beneath a 35-ton collapsed construction crane in New York City for six hours. Throughout her ordeal, she held the hand of rescue officer Paul Ragonese, who stayed by her side as heavy machinery moved the tons of twisted steel from her crushed legs. A stranger's touch gave her hope and the will to live.

Other means of communication can take place at a distance, but touch is the language of physical intimacy. And because it is, touch is the most powerful of all the communication channels—and the most carefully guarded and regulated.

From a mother's cradling embrace to a friend's comforting hug, or a lover's caress, touch has the special power to send messages of union and communion. Among strangers, that power is ordinarily held in check. Whether offering a handshake or a guiding arm, the toucher is careful to stay within the culture's narrowly prescribed limits lest the touch be misinterpreted. Touching between people with more personal relationships is also governed by silent cultural rules and restraints.

The rules of touch may be unspoken, but they're visible to anyone who takes the trouble to watch. Psychologist Richard Heslin at Purdue University, for instance, has proposed five categories of touch based on people's roles and relationships. Each category includes a special range of touches, best described by the quality of touch, the body areas touched and whether the touch is reciprocated.

FUNCTIONAL-PROFESSIONAL touches are performed while the toucher fulfills a special role, such as that of doctor, barber or tailor. For people in these occupations, touch must be devoid of personal messages.

SOCIAL-POLITE touches are formal, limited to greeting and separating and to expressing appreciation among business associates and among strangers and acquaintances. The typical handshake reflects cordiality more than intimacy.

FRIENDSHIP-WARMTH touches occur in the context of personal concern and caring, such as the relationships between extended-family members, friendly neighbors and close work mates. This category straddles the line between warmth and deep affection, a line where friendly touches move over into love touches.

LOVE-INTIMACY touches occur between close family members and friends in relationships where there is affection and caring.

SEXUAL-AROUSAL touches occur in erotic-sexual contexts.

These categories are not hard and fast, since in various cultures and subcultures the rules differ about who can touch whom, in what contexts and what forms the touch may take. In the Northern European "noncontact cultures," overall touch rates are usually quite low. People from these cultures can seem very cold, especially to people from "contact cultures" such as those in the Mediterranean area, where there are much higher rates of touching, even between strangers.

In the United States, a particularly low-touch culture, we rarely see people touch one another in public. Other than in sports and children's play, the most we see of it is when people hold hands in the street, fondle babies or say hello and goodbye. Even on television shows, with the odd exceptions of hitting and kissing, there is little touching.

The cultural differences in contact can be quite dramatic, as researcher Sidney Jourard found in the 1960s when he studied touch between pairs of people in coffee shops around the world. There was more touch in certain cities (180 times an hour between couples in San Juan, Puerto Rico, and 110 times an hour in Paris, France) than in others (2 times an hour between couples in Gainesville, Florida, and 0 times an hour in London, England).

Those cultural contact patterns are embedded early, through child-rearing practices. Psychologist Janice Gibson and her colleagues at the University of Pittsburgh took to the playgrounds and beaches of Greece, the Soviet Union and the United States and compared the frequency and nature of touch between caregivers and children 2 to 5 years old. When it came to retrieving or punishing the children, touching rates were similar in all three countries. But on touches for soothing, holding and play, American children had significantly less contact than those from the other cultures. (Is that why we need bumper stickers to remind us: "Have you hugged your child today?")

Greek and Soviet kids
are held, soothed and touched playfully
much more than American kids.

Men greet people
with fewer lip kisses, embraces and
kinds of touch than women do.

Generalizations about different national or ethnic groups can be tricky, however. For example, despite widespread beliefs that Latin Americans are highly contact-oriented, when researcher Robert Shuter at Marquette University compared public contact between couples in Costa Rica, Colombia and Panama, he found that the Costa Ricans both touched and held their partners noticeably more than the couples did in the other two countries.

Within most cultures the rules and meanings of touch are different for men and women, as one recent study in the United States illustrates. Imagine yourself in a hospital bed, about to have major surgery. The nurse comes in to tell you what your operation and after-care will be like. She touches you briefly twice, once on the hand for a few seconds after she introduces herself and again on the arm for a full minute during the instruction period. As she leaves she shakes your hand.

Does this kind of brief reassuring touch add anything to her talk? Does it have any kind of impact on your nervousness or how you respond to the operation? Your reaction is likely to depend upon your gender.

Psychologist Sheryle Whitcher, while working as a graduate student with psychologist Jeffrey Fisher of the University of Connecticut, arranged for a group of surgery patients to be touched in the way described above during their preoperative information session, while other patients got only the information. Women had strikingly positive reactions to being touched; it lowered their blood pressure and anxiety both before surgery and for more than an hour afterwards. But men found the experience upsetting; both their blood pressure and their anxiety rose and stayed elevated in response to being touched.

Why did touch produce such strikingly different responses? Part of the answer may lie in the fact that men in the United States often find it harder to acknowledge dependency and fear than women do; thus, for men, a well-intentioned touch may be a threatening reminder of their vulnerability.

These gender differences are fostered by early experiences, particularly in handling and caretaking. Differences in parents' use of touch with their infant children help to shape and model "male" and "female" touch patterns: Fathers use touch more for play, while mothers use it more for soothing and grooming. The children's gender also affects the kinds of touches they receive. In the United States, for example, girls receive more affectionate touches (kissing, cuddling, holding) than boys do.

By puberty, tactile experiences with parents and peers have already programmed differences in boys' and girls' touching behavior and their use of personal space (see "Body Mapping," this article). Some results of this training are evident when men and women greet people. In one study, psychologists Paul Greenbaum and Howard Rosenfeld of the University of Kansas watched how travelers at the Kansas City International Airport touched people who greeted them. Women greeted women and men more physically, with mutual lip kisses, embraces and more kinds of touch and holding for longer periods of time. In contrast, when men greeted men, most just shook hands and left it at that.

How do you feel about touching and being touched? Are you relaxed and comfortable, or does such contact make you feel awkward and tense? Your comfort with touch may be linked to your personality. Psychologist Knud Larsen and student Jeff LeRoux at Oregon State University looked at how people's personality traits are related to their attitudes toward touching between people of the same sex. The researchers measured touch attitudes through questions such as, "I enjoy persons of my sex who are comfortable with touching," "I sometimes enjoy hugging friends of the same sex" and "Physical expression of affection between persons of the same sex is healthy." Even though men were generally less comfortable about same-sex touching than women were, the more authoritarian and rigid people of both sexes were the least comfortable.

A related study by researchers John Deethardt and Debbie Hines at Texas Tech University in Lubbock, Texas, examined personality and attitudes toward being touched by opposite-sex friends and lovers and by same-sex friends. Touch attitudes were tapped with such questions as, "When I am with my girl/-boyfriend I really like to touch that person to show affection," "When I tell a same-sex intimate friend that I have just gotten a divorce, I want that person to touch me" and "I enjoy an opposite-sex acquaintance touching me when we greet each other." Regardless of gender, people who were comfortable with touching were also more talkative, cheerful, socially dominant and nonconforming; those discomforted by touch tended to be more emotionally unstable and socially withdrawn.

A recent survey of nearly 4,000 undergraduates by researchers Janis Andersen, Peter Andersen and Myron Lustig of San Diego State University revealed that, regardless of gender, people who were less comfortable about touching were also more apprehensive about communicating and had lower self-esteem. Several other studies have shown that people who are more comfortable with touch are less afraid and suspicious of other people's motives and intentions and have less anxiety and tension in their everyday lives. Not surprisingly, another study showed they are also likely to be more satisfied with their bodies and physical appearance.

These different personality factors play themselves out most revealingly in the intimacy of love relationships. Couples stay together and break apart for many reasons, including the way each partner expresses and reacts to affection and intimacy. For some, feelings and words are enough; for others, touch and physical intimacy are more critical.

In the film *Annie Hall*, Woody Allen and Diane Keaton are shown split-screen as each talks to an analyst about their sexual relationship. When the analyst asks how often they have sex, he answers, "Hardly ever, maybe three times a week," while she describes it as "constantly, three times a week."

How important is physical intimacy in close relationships? What role does touch play in marital satisfaction? Psychologists Betsy Tolstedt and Joseph Stokes of the University of Illinois at Chicago tried to find out by interviewing and observing couples. They used three measures of intimacy: emotional intimacy (feelings of closeness, support, tolerance); verbal intimacy (disclosure of emotions, feelings, opinions); and physical intimacy (satisfaction with "companionate" and sexual touch). The

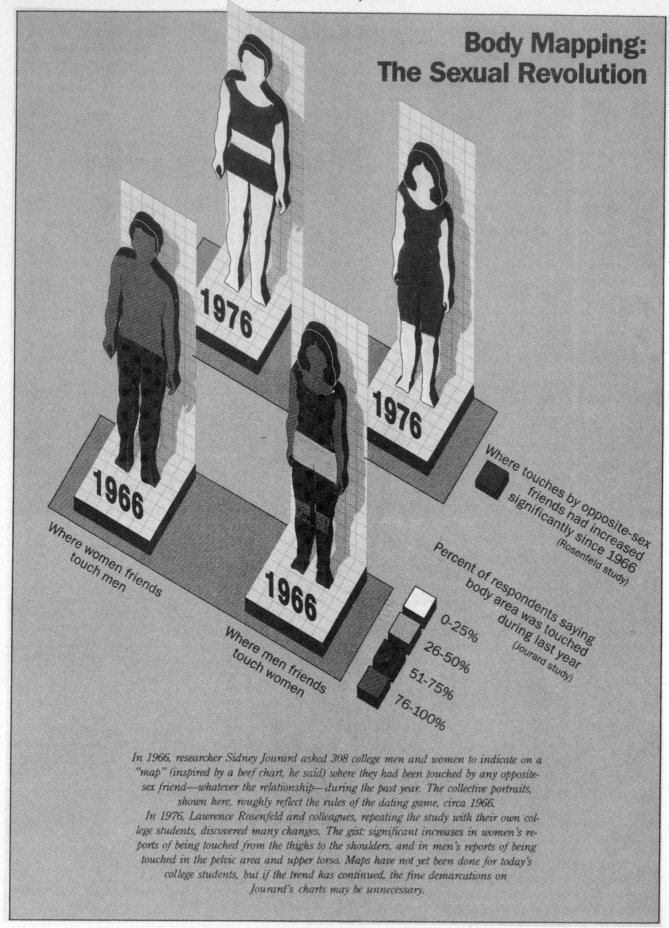

Body Mapping: The Sexual Revolution

1976

1976

1966

1966

Where women friends touch men

Where men friends touch women

Where touches by opposite-sex friends had increased significantly since 1966 (Rosenfeld study)

Percent of respondents saying body area was touched during last year (Jourard study)

0-25%

26-50%

51-75%

76-100%

In 1966, researcher Sidney Jourard asked 308 college men and women to indicate on a "map" (inspired by a beef chart, he said) where they had been touched by any opposite-sex friend—whatever the relationship—during the past year. The collective portraits, shown here, roughly reflect the rules of the dating game, circa 1966.

In 1976, Lawrence Rosenfeld and colleagues, repeating the study with their own college students, discovered many changes. The gist: significant increases in women's reports of being touched from the thighs to the shoulders, and in men's reports of being touched in the pelvic area and upper torso. Maps have not yet been done for today's college students, but if the trend has continued, the fine demarcations on Jourard's charts may be unnecessary.

researchers also measured marital satisfaction and happiness, along with conflicts and actual separations and legal actions.

They found that each form of intimacy made its own contribution to marital satisfaction, but—perhaps surprisingly to some—physical intimacy mattered the least of the three. Conflict and divorce potential were most connected to dissatisfaction with emotional and verbal intimacy.

Touch intimacy may not usually have the power to make or break marriages, but it can sway strangers and even people close to you, often without their knowledge. The expressions "to put the touch on someone" and "that person is an easy touch" refer to the persuasive power of touch. Indeed, research shows that it is harder to say no to someone who makes a request when it is accompanied by a touch.

Politicians know this well. Ignoring security concerns, political candidates plunge into the crowd to kiss babies and "press the flesh." Even a quick handshake leaves a lasting impression—a personal touch—that can pay off later at election time.

A momentary and seemingly incidental touch can establish a positive, temporary bond between strangers, making them more helpful, compliant, generous and positive. In one experiment in a library, a slight hand brush in the course of returning library cards to patrons was enough to influence patrons' positive attitudes toward the library and its staff. In another study, conducted in restaurants, a fleeting touch paid off in hard cash. Waitresses who touched their customers on the hand or shoulder as they returned change received a larger percentage of the bill as their tip. Even though they risked crossing role boundaries by touching customers in such familiar ways, their ingratiating service demeanor offset any threat.

In certain situations, touch can be discomforting because it signals power. Psychologist Nancy Henley of the University of California, Los Angeles, after observing the touch behavior of people as they went about their daily lives, has suggested that higher-status individuals enjoy more touch liberties with their lower-status associates. To Henley, who has noted how touch signals one's place in the status-dominance hierarchy, there is even a sexist "politics of touch." She has found that women generally rank lower than men in the touch hierarchy, very much like the secretary-boss, student-teacher and worker-foreman relationships. In all of these, it is considered unseemly for lower-status individuals to put their hands on superiors. Rank does have its touching privileges.

The rules of the status hierarchy are so powerful that people can infer status differences from watching other people's touch behavior. In one experiment by psychologists Brenda Major and Richard Heslin of Purdue University, observers could see only the silhouettes of pairs of people facing each other, with one touching the other on the shoulder. They judged the toucher to be more assertive and of a higher status than the person touched. Had the touch been reciprocal, status differences would have disappeared.

Psychologist Alvin G. Goldstein and student Judy Jeffords at the University of Missouri have sharpened our understanding of touch and status through their field study of touch among legislators during a Missouri state legislative session. Observers positioned themselves in the gallery and systematically recorded who initiated touch during the many floor conversations. Based on a status formula that included committee leadership and membership, they discovered that among these male peers, the lower-status men were the ones most likely to initiate touch.

When roles are clearly different, so that one individual has

TOUCHY ISSUES

TOUCH IS A GESTURE of warmth and concern, but it can also be seen as intrusive, demeaning or seductive. Because of these ambiguous meanings, touch can sometimes be problematic for therapists, who must be careful to monitor their touch behavior with clients. Because difficult legal and ethical issues surround possible misinterpretation of touch, many therapists avoid physical contact of any sort with their clients, except for a formal handshake at the first and last sessions. But in a number of body-oriented psychotherapies, such as Wilhelm Reich's character analysis and Alexander Lowen's bioenergetic therapy, touch is used deliberately as part of the treatment process; it is meant to stir emotions and memories through the body and not just the mind.

Imagine meeting your therapist for the first time. You are greeted in the waiting room and guided into the consultation room. You have the therapist's full attention as you speak about what brings you to therapy. Twice during the session the therapist briefly touches you on the arm. Before you leave, you make an appointment to meet again.

How are you likely to evaluate your first session? Do you think the therapist's touch might affect your reactions to therapy or to the therapist? Could it affect the process of therapy?

Sessions like the one just described have been studied by psychologist Mark A. Hubble of Harding Hospital in Worthington, Ohio, and colleagues, using therapists specially trained to touch their clients in consistent ways during their first counseling session. Results show that, compared with clients who were not touched, those who were touched judged the therapist as more expert. In an earlier, similar study by researcher Joyce Pattison, trained judges rated clients who had been touched as deeper in their self-exploration.

Although there are clearly some risks, perhaps more therapists should consider "getting in touch" with their clients by adding such small tactile gestures to their therapeutic repertoire.

control or power over the other, such as a boss and a secretary, then touch usually reflects major dominance or status differences in the relationship. But when roles are more diffuse and overlapping, so that people are almost equal in power—as the legislators were—then lower-status people may try to establish more intimate connections with their more powerful and higher-status colleagues by making physical contact with them.

Touching has a subtle and often ambivalent role in most settings. But there is one special circumstance in which touch is permitted and universally positive: In sports, teammates encourage, applaud and console each other generously through touch. In Western cultures, for men especially, hugs and slaps on the behind are permitted among athletes, even though they are very rarely seen between heterosexual men outside the sports arena. The intense enthusiasm legitimizes tactile expressions of emotion that would otherwise be seen as homosexually threatening.

Graduate student Charles Anderton and psychologist Robert Heckel of the University of South Carolina studied touch in the competitive context of all-male or all-female championship swim meets by recording each instance of touch after success and failure. Regardless of sex, winners were touched similarly, on aver-

At swim meets, winners were touched six times more than losers were.

age six times more than losers, with most of the touches to the hand and some to the back or shoulders; only a small percent were to the head or buttocks.

This swimming study only looked at touch between same-sex teammates, since swim meets have separate races for men and women. Would touch patterns be the same for mixed-gender teams, or would men and women be inhibited about initiating and receiving touches, as they are in settings outside of sports? Psychologists David Smith, Frank Willis and Joseph Gier at the University of Missouri studied touching behavior of men and women in bowling alleys in Kansas City, Missouri, during mixed-league competition. They found almost no differences between men and women in initiating or receiving touches.

Without the social vocabulary of touch, life would be cold, mechanical, distant, rational, verbal. We are created in the intimate union of two bodies and stay connected to the body of one until the cord is cut. Even after birth, we need touch for survival. Healthy human infants deprived of touch and handling for long periods develop a kind of infant depression that leads to withdrawal and apathy and, in extreme cases, wasting away to death.

As people develop, touch assumes symbolic meaning as the primary system for expressing and experiencing affection, inclusion and control. Deprived of those gestures and their meanings, the world might be more egalitarian, but it would also be far more frightening, hostile and chilly. And who would understand why a stranger's touch meant life to Brigitte Gerney?

THE POWER OF TOUCH

A lover's touch can heal a bruised ego and calm a raging fever. It can also be the most tender, sensual experience of your life, if you take a moment to learn the language of touch.

Sherry Suib Cohen

ALL GOOD SEXUAL TOUCH IS sensual. A sensual touch is one that gratifies the senses—all the senses. It is voluptuous. It is slow, searching, and attentive to reactions. It gives and receives. It is enjoyed as much by the giver as by the receiver. Although sensual touch is related to sexual touch, it doesn't necessarily lead to sex. Sensual touch is glorious in itself. Wise lovers know that sex does not necessarily mean intercourse but rather sharing the exquisite delight of exploring one another's bodies. A sensitive toucher can evoke wonders. With sensual fingers, a partner's touch can instantly cool head and eyes that are burning with fever. With sensual touch, he or she can instantly gentle your damaged psyche and send it to a calming sleep. And then, when the time is ripe, he or she knows how to transform the sensual touch into the sexual.

Fingers and hands that have practiced the craftsmanship of sensuality can touch your libido, make it surge with desire and burn brighter than you ever imagined possible. The same language of sensual touch that nourishes the infant comes into adult fruition during erotic play.

William H. Masters, M.D., and Virginia E. Johnson, Ph.D., and the many sex therapists who use their methods, allow no intercourse at all in the first few weeks of sex therapy. Couples practice touch—gentle, appreciative, sensual touch—of one another's feet, arms, legs, face, hands . . . and bodies. They carefully learn the art of touch as a process in itself. Intercourse is *not* a goal, they teach. If it happens because both lovers are in the mood, fine. If not, sensual touching is golden anyway.

Intercourse as a goal seems to be a big hang-up in our culture. Most sex therapists warn against it as a sure way to decrease sensual enjoyment. In *Touching for Pleasure: A Guide to Sensual Enhancement,* Susan Dean, Ph.D., a specialist in human sexuality, and Adele P. Kennedy, a sex therapist, advise: "When you are goal-oriented you are no longer in the present. You interrupt your responses when you try to anticipate the next step. Stay focused on the moment, so that you receive all that is being offered. Touch is, in and of itself, the pleasure. Any by-product is coincidental to the experience, although it is to be enjoyed and appreciated. The motivation is to sensitize your body to its intrinsic capacity for pleasure."

Alexandra Penney, author of several popular books on sex, agrees. Great sex, she says, is between two people and not two bodies. It goes far beyond mechanics; there are all kinds of great sex besides intercourse.

We are sexual creatures from the moment of birth. We are sexual because we are sensual, and, once having experienced the pleasure of body electricity, we can anticipate it and even simulate it in our brain. Ever feel a rush of flutters in your groin while reading a sexy passage? You *remember*. Touch is so powerful that it lingers in our bodies even when it's not actually there. That's why audiences flock to superbly written sexual scenes in movies or in print.

The skin, the medium for touch, is such a wondrous conductor of sensual signals that it changes either visibly or in ways that can be felt when it is touched, when it anticipates being touched, or even when it remembers being touched. How many of us have felt an actual warming of the skin, a literal heating-up at the very thought of a single touch from a special person?

But there are many receptors of sexual touch, besides the skin. There's the brain, for example. It interprets touch and tells you whether you should let a caress be enjoyable or despicable. If your brain tells you that the man in front of you is your dream of an ideal sex object, you will enjoy the feel of him. On the other hand, if your brain tells you that he turns you off, the *feel* of him may still be enjoyable, though you *think* it shouldn't be.

Of course, you don't always have to love someone to respond to sexual touch. As Mae West put it, "Honey, sex with love is the greatest thing in life, but sex without love—that's not so bad either." So sensitive are the erogenous zones that if you look forward to being aroused, if you concentrate on responding to sexual touch, if you *think* you'll be turned on, the odds are you will be. After all, people are the sexiest primates on earth; while females in other species are limited in sexual receptivity to times of ovulation, the human female loves making love any time—*if* she's in the mood.

From *New Woman*, April 1987, pp. 40-42. Adapted from THE MAGIC OF TOUCH by Sherry Suib Cohen. Copyright © 1987 by Sherry Suib Cohen. Reprinted by permission of Harper & Row Publishers, Inc.

Learning how to touch is very important in relationships throughout life. The art of touching is a process in and of itself, and is essential in establishing communication between partners. The long-established relationship this couple enjoys has been fortified by understanding and comfort through touch.

Still, as the sex therapists point out, it does help a lot when caring is present. Tenderness, respect, and practice have a way of intensifying physical pleasure. Knowledgeable sexual touch gives us heightened sexual pleasure that a one-night stand never can, as Kennedy realized in a recent encounter with her lover: "[He] had arrived at my house one night to take me out to dinner and a film. We sat down in the living room to discuss which restaurant to go to. As we were talking, he was running his fingers gently over my knuckles, and I was looking through a magazine for dining suggestions. Before I knew it, I was aroused.

"We were both surprised, as there was nothing outwardly conducive to it. Although our conversation or nuances had in no way been sexual, we were connect-ed; and since I had allowed that connection to flow freely, my body responded long before sexual thoughts ever reached my consciousness. It was at that point that I knew that the possibilities of stimulation and response were infinite."

HOW DO MEN AND WOMEN differ in their relationship to touch? Generally, young girls are more likely to be touched than boys are—although that is slowly changing as people become aware of how such actions perpetuate the notion of woman as nurturer. In the meantime, while extra touching may make women warm and affectionate, it also makes them tend to take what they get and not to be assertive in the getting. Many women learn to let themselves accept sexual touching rather than initiate it. They are believed to be more passive sexually, and thus they train themselves to be so. They worry that men will find them pushy, unfeminine, or grabby if they are sexually aggressive in touching. Boys, on the other hand, learn to be the touching aggressors. When they are men, they often have little patience for lying back and receiving touches in foreplay. Lie back and just enjoy? Is that really manly?

Although this attitude seems old-fashioned, it still persists in spite of many studies and books to the contrary. Our generation is supposed to be one of sexual sophistication, yet insidious double standards continue.

Touch is then relegated to a sexual

provocation instead of being a mutual and enduring pleasure in its own right. If one doesn't love to experiment with touch as a conveyance of affection and friendliness, one may never reach the zenith of sexual achievement. Sensual touches must precede sexual intents for both men and women.

A man may place his hand on his partner's breast two seconds after they tumble into bed. Or perhaps he heads straight for her genital area before she has time to catch her breath. He expects that once he touches these sensitive zones her sexual motor will automatically shift into high gear.

But, of course, it doesn't. She feels annoyed, outraged, or, at best, unaroused. Her motor remains in idle position, or perhaps it stalls, chokes, and turns off.

He feels confused or nervous. Is there something wrong with him if his touch doesn't spark a conflagration? He may feel irritated; what a cold potato his partner is! It's not his fault, surely.

And therein, note Masters and Johnson, lies a basic dead-end approach for many relationships. He thinks she's frigid, either because she didn't let him touch her in the crucial place or because, when he did, she wasn't thrilled. She decides he's a boor and a lousy lover. They learn to settle for mediocre. They consider touch merely as a means to an end. They buy sex manuals that teach them how to manipulate body parts—the science of stimulation of disembodied parts. How much better to have a philosophy that celebrates caring, that celebrates sensual touch as an extension of everyday life. Sensual touching should not be chained to the bedroom.

The bottom line is this: we—both men and women—miss sensual touch. We confuse it with sexual intercourse, and so we deny its casual use. And then, ironically, we separate it from sexual touch, which depends on sensuality for its goodness.

Masters and Johnson point out that too many people interpret every sensually loving touch as an invitation to copulate. Bodies hunger for holding as a sensation quite apart from genital penetration.

Marc H. Hollender, M.D., a psychiatrist with the Department of Psychiatry at Vanderbilt University School of Medicine in Tennessee, has said that the need to be held is so compelling for some women that they have intercourse when they may not really want it in exchange for being held.

"The need for touch is a kind of ache," says one woman.

"I'd rather have my husband hold me than have a Cadillac convertible," says another.

"The reason I like to wear big, fuzzy sweaters and be bundled up and held in warm blankets is that it makes me feel like I'm being held," says yet another.

When you know yourself, you'll know when your body and soul need to be touched. What feels like sadness can simply be your disguised need to be held; what feels like hunger or fatigue can be your disguised wish for lovemaking. Your response to touch can help you build a personal and a sensual sense of wellbeing. Touch is glorious. And perfecting it can be a life's work.

Chemistry of Sexual Desire Yields Its Elusive Secrets

Therapists shift focus from mechanics of sex to biology and emotions of desire.

Daniel Goleman

The sex hormone testosterone is a genuine aphrodisiac, with higher levels stimulating sexual desire in men and perhaps in women as well, recent research has shown. But the level of testosterone coursing through a person's body has little direct impact on sexual performance, according to the studies, which have discovered a sharp distinction between the chemistry of desire and that of the sexual act itself.

The findings on testosterone's role in erotic life are part of a series of recent discoveries emerging from laboratories as sexual desire, an urge at once elusive and compelling, yields its secrets to the cold eye of science.

While for several decades scientists have made detailed studies of the psychology and anatomy of sexual arousal itself, it is only within the last few years that desire, the harbinger of arousal, has become a focus for research. The new studies, which aim to aid therapy of individuals and couples who suffer a lack of erotic impulses, are focusing on both the biological and the emotional chemistry of desire.

"Sexual desire is an extraordinarily complicated part of life and there is an enormous range of difference," said Harold Lief, an emeritus professor of psychiatry at the University of Pennsylvania who is a pioneer in identifying and treating problems with desire.

"College students who are asked to press a wrist counter every time they have a sexual thought, fantasy or feeling may count over 300 a day, while other people report that they rarely, if ever, have a sexual desire," Dr. Lief added.

The research is focusing on two kinds of problems. One involves individuals who, as perhaps because of hormonal imbalances or psychological problems, generally feel no sexual urge. The second emphasis is on the psychological and emotional interactions of couples that can destroy desire in people who, in other situations, might have strong sexual urges.

The impetus for the new studies has been the growing realization by sex therapists that many patients who had been treated for difficulties with the mechanics of sexual performance, such as impotence or a failure to reach orgasm, actually suffered from an underlying lack of sexual desire.

"Desire and arousal are two entirely different processes, each under the influence of different factors," said Gayle Beck, a psychologist at the University of Houston.

Most Common Complaint

Today problems with sexual desire rank as the most common complaint treated by sex therapists, even though it is only in the last decade that the problem was given an official diagnosis. A recent survey of 289 sex therapists found that the most common complaint of partners—in 31 percent of couples seeking sex therapy—was a discrepancy between partners in their desire for sex. The second most common complaint, reported by 28 percent of patients, was individuals troubled by either too little or too much sexual desire.

Much of the new research focuses on the biochemistry of desire, particularly the role of hormones, especially testosterone. Testosterone is often called the male sex hormone because it is more prevalent in men, although it fluctuates in the individual with time, and plays a key role in development of masculine traits. But it is also found in lesser quantities in women, in whom its levels fluctuate over the course of the menstrual cycle. Recent studies show that one of its main effects is on desire, and that, contrary to earlier assumptions, it has virtually no role in the sexual act itself.

In a study of men who suffered from extremely low levels of desire as the result of underactive gonads, doses of testosterone increased the men's frequency of sexual fantasies and restored their sexual desire. But the testosterone had no effect on the mechanics of sexual arousal, such as their genital arousal while watching erotic videotapes or fantasying.

This study and others with similar results have led scientists to conclude that testosterone regulates sexual desire. The new study, done by Julian Davidson, a physiologist, and colleagues at Stanford University, was reported in "Patterns of Sexual Arousal," published this year by Guilford Press.

"It's now very clear that testosterone is the biological substrate of desire, at least in men," Dr. Davidson said.

There is less agreement on the relationship between testosterone and desire in women. Studies by Dr. Lief and others have found that in many women sexual desire peaks in the middle phase of the menstrual period, when testosterone levels are at their highest. But other researchers have failed to duplicate the findings.

While there is uncertainty about the role of ordinary levels of testosterone in regulating desire in women, higher doses of testosterone than are normally found in the body are now used to treat the loss of desire in some women who are post-menopausal or who have had their ovaries removed, according to Dr. Lief.

Biochemistry aside, every couple who have ever been at odds know that emotional life shapes their sexual life for better or worse. New studies are pinpointing more precisely which emotions have what effects.

The most common cause of low desire, clinicians say, is marital conflict. New laboratory research shows that, like depression, anger is particularly devastating to erotic desire. Anxiety, on the other hand, can sometimes fan desire, but interferes with the sexual act itself.

In men, desire is more vulnerable to anger, while sexual arousal is more sensitive to anxiety, Dr. Beck has found in research reported at a recent meeting of the American Psychological Association. In the study, male college students used a lever to report their level of sexual desire and a gauge measured their genital arousal while they listened to tapes depicting sexual encounters.

When the tapes portrayed an angry dialogue during the sexual encounter, the students reported a sharp drop in their own levels of desire. But there was little effect on their genital arousal. Tapes designed to elicit anxi-

ety, on the other hand, resulted in the student's having a drop in physical arousal, but none in sexual desire.

The findings suggest that conflict between a couple is more damaging to their desire for sex than would be moderate levels of stress or anxiety, according to Dr. Beck.

"Someone who is preoccupied by worries would be likely to feel sexual desire, but might have trouble getting or staying aroused," she said. "Lovemaking is vulnerable to intrusive, worrisome thoughts because it is largely a skill, while desire is more vulnerable to anger because it operates much like an emotion. While an argument will dampen partners' desire for sex, they could still follow through if they were to become aroused."

Survey of 93 Couples

The judgment of what level of desire is "too low" or "too high" is, of course, a relative one. But to get a sense of what the usual range of desire is for married couples, Joseph LoPiccolo, a psychologist at the University of Missouri, and Jerry Friedman, a sex therapist in Stony Brook, L.I., surveyed 93 couples who, on average, were 34 years old and had been married for 9 years. The survey is reported in "Sexual Desire Disorders," published this month by Guilford Press.

The men generally expressed a greater desire for sex than did their wives. More than 12 percent of the men said they preferred intercourse more than once a day, while about 3 percent of women expressed the same preference. On the other hand, about 4 percent of men and 10 percent of women said they desired sex just once a week. The most common preference was for sex three or four times a week. Fifty percent of women and 42 percent of men expressed this preference.

But desire outpaced reality. Just 2 percent of men and 1 percent of women said they actually made love more than once a day, while 12 percent both of men and of women said the rate of lovemaking in their marriage was once every two weeks or just once a month. And 3 percent of men, but no women, said they made love less than once a month.

The discrepancies between the men

and women in the rates of lovemaking they reported in the survey reflects the very different perceptions of their sex life that couples bring to sex therapy.

"When a couple seeks treatment for a problem with sexual desire, I often hear, 'He's oversexed,' or, 'she doesn't love me anymore,' but I quickly learned to speak only in terms of a discrepancy in desire." Dr. Beck said. "To see one partner or the other as too highly sexed or as having too little desire is unhelpful."

There is a bias in treating couples with a discrepancy in desire, one that too easily blames the partner with the lower level of desire for the problem, said Bernard Apfelbaum, a psychologist at the Berkeley Sex Therapy Group. He points, for instance, to the onus attached to the term frigidity, a word no longer used by sex therapists. When there is a marked discrepancy between partners in their levels of desire, many sex therapists try to help the couple negotiate a compromise rather than focusing treatment exclusively on the partner with the lower levels of desire.

While there is a drop in testosterone levels in men after the 40's, aging tends to bring only a gradual lessening of desire. A sudden drop in desire more often reflects other problems, such as continual marital conflict, according to sex therapists.

"Often the problem is boredom—habituation to one's partner," said Dr. Lief. A study by Dr. Lief of postmenopausal women that compared one group married an average of 25 years with another married just 2 years found that the newlyweds had a much higher level of sexual desire than those who remained in the lengthy marriage. But the level of desire in the newlywed post-menopausal women was not as high as that of young couples.

After marital conflict, depression is the second most common cause of low desire, according to Dr. Lief. What is more surprising, though, is that many of the medications often prescribed for depression can themselves inhibit desire. Not all anti-depressants lower desire, and those that do affect only certain people. The problem is most likely in those drugs that affect dopamine, a brain chemical that interacts with testosterone. Lowered sexual desire can be a side effect of many other drugs, including some prescribed to control anxiety, for psychosis and for hypertension.

Scientists say that a promising research frontier for sex therapists is the interaction between emotions and chemistry, especially levels of testosterone and other sex-related hormones. But so far too little evidence is available to draw firm conclusions.

Sex therapy for too little desire almost always focuses on the quality of the couple's relationship. Apart from out-and-out conflict, difficulties such as the fear of emotional closeness in one partner, or a difference between partners in how much emotional intimacy they feel is comfortable can also cause problems with desire. Often what seems to be a loss of desire is a disguised form of anger, part of a power struggle between the couple, Dr. Lief said.

Paradoxically, some partners first experience a sudden drop in desire when they get married or in some other way move toward a major commitment. In such cases, the partners typically have idealized each other, creating a romantic universe in which neither has any flaws, said David Scharff, a psychoanalyst at George Washington University medical school. But at the point of deeper commitment, the partners may begin to see each other more realistically, discovering traits in each other that do not fit their idealization.

People at this point may also want more than ever to reveal their true selves to the partner because they want to be accepted completely. This may cause the partner to feel he or she is with a different person than imagined.

Loss of Sexual Interest

In some people, the loss of sexual interest occurs while dating, as they become more deeply involved emotionally with their partner. This problem, which Freudians have called the "Madonna/whore complex" when applied to men's views of women, arises in members of either sex when their overly moralistic conscience make them unable to love and have sex with the same person.

The tactics of therapy generally take the obvious route of tackling the problem, such as depression, that is blocking desire. "If a couple is having marital problems, for instance, in therapy we deal with the disharmony, while encouraging the expression of all the affection and tenderness the couple feel for each other," said Dr. Lief. "The rest happens naturally."

Is Orgasm Essential?

Melvin Konner

MELVIN KONNER, *Samuel Candler Dobbs professor of anthropology at Emory University, in Atlanta, is the author of* BECOMING A DOCTOR: A JOURNEY OF INITIATION IN MEDICAL SCHOOL, *which will appear in paperback in July.*

The French call it *le petit mort* (the little death), a convention shared by Shakespeare and other Elizabethans. Its etymological ancestors include the Greek words *orgasmos* (to grow ripe, swell, be lustful) and *orge* (impulse, anger) and the Sanskrit *urj* (nourishment, power, strength). It is surely one of the most fundamental of human satisfactions—a pleasure for which we are at times willing to pay, to take risks, to commit ourselves to lifetimes of unwanted responsibility, even to kill.

Different cultures have taken different views of orgasm and have come up with countless strategies for achieving, avoiding, enhancing, or delaying it. Among the Mundugumor, of New Guinea, Margaret Mead found that lovemaking is conducted "like the first round of a prizefight," with biting and scratching being important parts of foreplay. In Samoa, by contrast, couples work up to the big event slowly and gently: the man is expected to prepare the woman's mind with songs and poetry and her body with playful, skillful hands. Within the tradition of Tantric Buddhism, men have typically been contemptuous of orgasm and have used various stratagems to maintain, for hours on end, the blissful vertiginous state that immediately precedes it. In modern Western societies, some psychoanalysts have decreed that only a disturbed woman would pursue multiple orgasms, whereas others have defined sexual satisfaction as a vital aspect of physical and psychic health.

Indeed, orgasm may be a universal experience, or at least capacity, not only of humans but of primates generally. Male monkeys often let out a whoop at the moment of ejaculation, as if in honor of some explosion of good feeling. For the females, with no event that compares with ejaculation, the inferences have always been more conjectural, but numerous studies have suggested that they too experience a climax. Doris Zumpe and Richard P. Michael, both of Emory University, have found that the female rhesus monkey typically reaches back toward her partner, arms flailing spasmodically, at the moment he ejaculates. Given the unlikelihood that these animals share a stylized expression of concern for their erupting companions, the inference of a whole-body reflex seems reasonable.

For all the attention it has received, though, orgasm has remained something of a mystery. The riddles of how it works and why it exists have never been fully resolved, despite the best efforts of physicians, psychologists, and evolutionists. The renowned sex researchers William H. Masters and Virginia E. Johnson shattered a number of myths about the phenomenon with their massive 1966 study, *Human Sexual Response.* Yet their work left crucial questions unanswered—questions that continue to spawn confusion and controversy. Is orgasm primarily a physical phenomenon, or is it psychological at root? Where within the female sexual organs is it centered: in the clitoris, or in the walls of the vagina? Are the apparent differences between male and female orgasm basic to our biology, or are they mere epiphenomena of culture? And, most interesting: Why did such a sensation evolve in the first place?

One of the first modern, clinical descriptions of orgasm was ventured in 1855, by the French physician Felix Riboud, who, in one dramatic paragraph, identified most of the main elements of the phenomenon as it is now recognized:

The pulse quickens, the eyes become dilated and unfocused. . . . With some the breath comes in gasps, others become breathless. . . . The nervous system, congested, is unable to provide the limbs with coherent messages: the powers of movement and feeling are thrown into disorder: the limbs, in the throes of convulsions and sometimes cramps, are either out of control or stretched and stiffened like bars of iron: with jaws clenched and teeth grinding together, some are so carried away by erotic frenzy that they forget the partner of their sexual ecstasy and bite the shoulder that is rashly exposed to them till they draw blood. This epileptic frenzy and delirium are usually rather brief, but they suffice to drain the body's strength, particularly when the man's over-excited state culminates in a more or less abundant emission of sperm.

That orgasm might also have a psychological dimension was first formally recognized by Sigmund Freud, whose psychoanalytic theory—in a radical departure from the conventional wisdom of the late nineteenth century—initially located the problems of neurotics in the blockage of sexual fulfillment. Through analysis of his patients' jokes, dreams, and psychological symptoms, he attempted to show that the fear of normal sexual feeling caused neurosis, and that only recognizing such fear could bring psychic health. In his case study of Frau Emmy von N., a forty-year-old woman he treated in 1889, Freud attributed severe phobias in part to "the fact that the patient had been living for years in a state of sexual abstinence," adding that "such circumstances are among the most frequent causes of a tendency to anxiety."

Yet, because he misunderstood a crucial aspect of female physiology, Freud ended up describing orgasm in a way that ultimately would prove harmful both to women and to the study of sex. Being something of an evolutionist, he suspected that so impressive an event must exist to assist in reproduction—and must therefore be tied to intercourse. The male peak of pleasure, coinciding almost exactly with ejaculation, seemed nicely attuned to the demands of insemination. Freud reasoned, by analogy, that the vagina should produce a corresponding feminine ecstasy when closed around the organ that so relentlessly seeks a berth in it. To account for the sexual sensitivity of the clitoris (which is entirely external to the vagina), Freud theorized that female orgasm comes in two varieties—one a mere adolescent thrill, the other a product of maturity. He explained the difference in 1920, in *A General Introduction to Psychoanalysis*:

Of little girls we know that they feel themselves heavily handicapped by the absence of a large visible penis and envy the boy's possession of it; from this source primarily springs the wish to be a man which is resumed again later in the neurosis, owing to some mal-adjustment to a female development. The clitoris in the girl, moreover, is in every way equivalent during childhood to the penis; it is a region of especial excitability in which auto-erotic satisfaction is achieved. The transition to womanhood very much depends upon the early and complete relegation of this sensitivity from the clitoris over to the vaginal orifice. In those women who are sexually anesthetic, as it is called, the clitoris has stubbornly retained this sensitivity.

It was not until 1953, when the American sex researcher Alfred C. Kinsey published his ground-breaking *Sexual Behavior in the Human Female*, that scientists began to see just how wrong Freud had

been about this. In Kinsey's study, more than twenty-seven hundred women, interviewed throughout the United States, said they did not typically attain orgasm through vaginal stimulation alone. When questioned about techniques of masturbation, eighty-four percent reported that they achieved "the little death" through massage of the clitoris and the labia. And when, in another part of the Kinsey study, gynecologists examined the genitals of more than five hundred women, ninety-eight percent were found to be sensitive to light touch on the clitoris but only fourteen percent to equivalent touch on the vaginal walls. In the light of these findings, Kinsey declared the supposed transfer of sensitivity from clitoris to vagina a "biologic impossibility." He expressed sympathy for the countless normal women who had been led to expect such a transfer and had imagined themselves dysfunctional when they failed to achieve it. "There is," he wrote, "no evidence that the vagina is ever the sole source of arousal or even the primary source of erotic arousal in any female."

But it was Masters and Johnson who—after studying how hundreds of people actually had sex—really pulled the rug out from under Freud's armchair. In a series of studies conducted between 1954 and 1965 at the Reproductive Biology Research Foundation, in Saint Louis, they went beyond the interview to make the study of sex an empirical science. Equipped with electrodes to measure heart rate and breathing, sensors to gauge the strength of muscle contractions, even cameras to film the inside of the vagina, they set about to observe the act itself. The nearly seven hundred participants were observed not only in intercourse but also in masturbation, including, for women, directed vaginal masturbation with a plastic penis that doubled as a camera. Some of the subjects were old, some were pregnant, some homosexual. But most were just conventional folks in the prime of their lives, doing what came naturally.

Like Kinsey before them, Masters and Johnson did a lot of debunking—and Freud was not their only target. Physicians who thought sex during pregnancy would harm the developing fetus were proved wrong, as were psychologists who thought pregnant women did not desire it. Pundits who believed that aging takes away both impulse and ability were hard-pressed to explain reports of eager septuagenarians with lubricating jelly. And there were startling findings about the routine details of sexual physiology, many of which had never been properly studied. In what would come to be known as the EPOR model, Masters and Johnson

defined four stages of normal sexual response—excitement, plateau, orgasm, and resolution—which involved almost every part of the body.

The excitement phase was described as one of gradual buildup—of increasing muscle tension, vaginal lubrication, and engorgement of blood vessels in the penis, the clitoris, and the nipples. Plateau was a sustained period of excitement, during which heart rate and respiration increase and the skin flushes. Orgasm, the discharge of the built-up tension, was marked by muscle contractions throughout the body (particularly in the genital area), disgorgement of the collected blood, ejaculation in the male, and intense pleasure in both sexes. Resolution was a period of diminishing tension, in which the body returns rapidly through the plateau and excitement levels to an unstimulated state.

Masters and Johnson reported a number of striking similarities in the sexual functioning of men and women, including parallel sensitivities in the penis and the clitoris, flushing of the chest during the plateau phase, and identical rhythmic contractions of the anal sphincter during orgasm. But they uncovered at least one critical difference: in men the resolution phase was accompanied by a complete loss of sexual responsiveness, lasting anywhere from a few minutes (in teenagers) to a day or more (in older fellows), whereas women appeared capable of "returning to another orgasmic experience from any point in the resolution phase." Indeed, women seemed at times to experience one orgasm after another, in uninterrupted succession. This finding, anticipated in Kinsey's interviews, made women seem veritable sexual athletes compared with men. It overturned the Victorian notion of poorer female responsiveness and helped pave the way for a new sort of sexual liberation.

Like Kinsey, Masters and Johnson found no evidence that sexual sensitivity is transferred from the clitoris to the vagina as a woman matures. In fact, they challenged the very existence of vaginal orgasm, suggesting that any female climax achieved through intercourse alone must result from indirect stimulation of the clitoris by the moving labia. (This possibility led the polemicist Shere Hite, in her 1976 book, *The Hite Report*, to characterize vaginal penetration as the "Rube Goldberg" route to sexual satisfaction.)

Most of Masters and Johnson's findings have held up remarkably well, and the clitoris is now recognized as the primary center of female sexual pleasure. Yet some sexologists remain firmly convinced that there *is* such a thing as vaginal orgasm. In fact, one research team, that of

Alice K. Ladas, Beverly Whipple, and John D. Perry, reported in 1982 that they had traced the vaginal orgasm to a particular location—a spot on the innermost third of the front vaginal wall. In a popular book, they dubbed this region the G spot, in honor of Ernest Grafenberg, a physician who had described it in 1950. Other studies have since suggested that some women do experience purely vaginal orgasms, distinct from the clitoral type. And surveys have found that, although women prefer clitoral to vaginal stimulation if asked to choose, most prefer a climax that blends the two. None of this suggests that a woman's capacity for vaginal orgasm has anything to do with maturity or psychological health—or that vaginal orgasm is anywhere near as common as clitoral orgasm. But Freud may have been right in the belief that it exists.

Freud may also have been right to think of orgasm as a partly psychological phenomenon. One curious aspect of the Masters and Johnson outlook was the notion that sexual pleasure—whether male or female—is merely muscular and cutaneous. They didn't come right out and say that, yet they managed to write hundreds of pages on the subject with nary a mention of its mental or emotional aspects. The racing heart, the flushed skin, and the gasps were real, they seemed to suggest, yet the profound emotion that sometimes accompanies those physiological events was as insubstantial as a shadow.

This aspect of Masters and Johnson's work seemed a throwback to the model of emotion advanced by the psychologists William James and Carl Lange around the turn of the century, a model that defined such experiences as joy and sorrow, affection and anger not as primary sensations but as secondary mental reactions to physiological events. Even as Masters and Johnson's work was in progress, however, their physiological bias was being undermined.

One of the first researchers to show definitively that sexual feeling originates above as well as below the chin was the neurologist Robert G. Heath, of Tulane University, who found that certain areas of the brain, when directly stimulated, produce the sensation of sexual pleasure. Heath's study, published in 1972 in *The Journal of Nervous and Mental Disease*, centered on two subjects (a mentally disturbed man of twenty-four and an epileptic woman of thirty-four) who, for therapeutic reasons, had already had electrodes implanted in their limbic systems, the part of the brain that mediates pleasurable emotion.

Not only did neural stimulation induce sexual pleasure, but sexual activity seemed to cause a great deal of neural activity. Heath found that when either patient was sexually stimulated, electrical waves generated within the septal region, which links the limbic system to the hypothalamus, resembled waves whose appearance in other parts of the brain suggests the onset of a seizure. But these subjects were not experiencing seizures—except to the extent that orgasm constitutes one. (Here, Felix Riboud's early characterization of orgasm as an "epileptic frenzy" seems prescient.) Moreover, the electrical changes in the septal area were discernible before the orgasm even began, suggesting that they are not just secondary responses to orgasmic muscle contractions but may play a part in inducing them.

Inspired by such findings, the physiologist Julian Davidson, of Stanford, proposed in 1980 a "bipolar hypothesis" of orgasm, intended to integrate all the known physiological and psychological data. Davidson first undertook to demonstrate that orgasm has many of the features of an altered state of consciousness—that it requires an ability to let go of inhibitions and involves changed perceptions of time, space, and motion. He cited studies showing that both men and women, when asked to write subjective descriptions of orgasm, used such phrases as "loss of contact with reality. All senses acute. Sight becomes patterns of color, but often very difficult to explain because words were made to fit in the real world."

Having established that orgasm occurs in the mind as well as the loins, Davidson posited a hypothetical "organ of orgasm" to mediate between the two. He speculated that this organ—presumably a portion of the nervous system that includes the limbic system and the septal area studied by Heath—interacts with the cerebral cortex to create an altered state of consciousness during sex. Because the cortex processes sensory data, Davidson reasoned that it must bombard the organ of orgasm with "cognitive input," in the form of sight, sound, and fantasy. Meanwhile, according to his model, the organ would continue to generate—and respond to—pelvic muscle contractions. in a dynamic, two-way interchange.

Davidson's model remains largely untested, but it has much to recommend it as a heuristic device. For one thing, it rescues sexual feeling from muscular marginality and puts it back in the center of our experience (and our nervous systems), where most of us sense it belongs. For another, it enables us to talk about the psychological and physical mechanics of orgasm without giving either precedence over the other. For all its virtues as a description of the phenomenon, however, Davidson's model leaves untouched

the central question of why we are subject to orgasm in the first place. Is orgasm an adaptation—a tendency that took hold by bestowing reproductive advantages on creatures who exhibited it, and that has been tailored by natural selection to the contingencies of survival—or does it exist by sheer happenstance?

It seems clear that, in males, orgasm directly rewards behavior associated with ejaculation, with insemination, and thus with reproduction. Various hypotheses have been proposed to account for female orgasm: theorists have speculated that uterine contractions may promote the motility of sperm and thus assist in fertilization (weakly supported); that recovery from orgasm may serve to keep women at rest in a horizontal position while the sperm find their way (a reasonable inference); and that the sensation itself rewards sexual activity (which is undeniable). What makes the largely nonvaginal female orgasm problematic is that, as Alfred Kinsey noted in 1953, "the techniques of masturbation and of petting" induce it more readily than "the techniques of coitus itself." This fact has led some evolutionists, such as Stephen Jay Gould, of Harvard, to argue that female orgasm is not an adaptation at all but a by-product of human development.

Males and females are, of course, variations on a single form; we are indistinguishable at conception but acquire separate characteristics during later stages of development, as hormones act to suppress or exaggerate particular anatomical features. The result is that each sex ends up sporting homologues of the other's distinctive organs. That being the case, it makes no sense, in Gould's estimation, to puzzle over the presence of, say, male nipples; they exist not because they enhance fitness but because they are part of the anatomical tool kit that enables females to develop breasts. Gould applies the same reasoning to female orgasm: it exists not because it fosters reproduction but because the clitoris is the homologue of the penis—"the same organ, endowed with the same anatomical organization and capacity of response."

Gould may be right about male nipples, but the idea that clitoral orgasm is an adaptation, and not just the by-product of one, doesn't seem all that farfetched. For one thing, as Masters and Johnson demonstrated, male and female orgasms are *not* identical phenomena. If, as Gould contends, the clitoris has exactly the same "capacity of response" as the penis, why is female orgasm more gradual, more sustained, and more repeatable than male orgasm? One plausible answer is that male and female sensitivities have been shaped by different selective pressures.

2. SEXUAL BIOLOGY AND HEALTH: The Body and Its Responses

For the males in many species, reproduction can be as simple as inseminating a female. For females, on the other hand, reproduction inevitably entails gestation, labor, and nursing. So it stands to reason that males would be rewarded, in an evolutionary sense, for rough-and-ready copulation—the sort encouraged by prompt, final orgasms—whereas females would do best by choosing carefully among suitors and trying to sustain a bond with one. Female orgasm, with its slower onset and its greater capacity for repetition, would seem far more likely to result from such sustained encounters than from quick, perfunctory ones.

But why, if female orgasm evolved as an aid to reproduction, is it centered largely *outside* the vagina? This is indeed a puzzling fact, but it doesn't automatically negate the adaptationist view. Certainly, a sensation can encourage an activity without being a direct product of it. Our sense of taste, so basic to nutrition, is not confined to the orifice that receives food; gustatory pleasure originates to a significant degree in the nose. No one would argue, on that basis, that taste does not serve to encourage and regulate eating. By the same token, female orgasm may originate outside the vagina and still serve as an inducement to copulation.

Moreover, as we have seen, the vagina has never been definitively desexed.

Whether the G spot really exists I'm not qualified to say, but suppose that there *is* a sensitive region located on the innermost third of the front vaginal wall. What sort of behavior would this encourage? As devotees of the G spot have long been aware, sexual intercourse in the en face, or "missionary," position affords only minimal stimulation to that area, whereas "bestial" intercourse—in the front-to-back position characteristic of nonhuman mammals—maximizes it. (That position, incidentally, also facilitates clitoral touching.) The argument seems to be ripening toward climax: if there is such a thing as vaginal orgasm, it is perfectly tailored to the activity by which our primate ancestors engendered us.

Contagious Fortune

*A less than cheery report
about the sex disease in your future*

David Berreby

NOT SO VERY LONG AGO VENEREAL disease seemed like a minor footnote in the charter of sexual freedom. Syphilis and gonorrhea had an antique ring, redolent of Army training films and old novels. Then came the eighties, when every couple of years seemed to bring a new sexual terror. Quite apart from the specter of AIDS, there were herpes and chlamydia, genital warts and hepatitis. Even as rates of syphilis and gonorrhea declined, doctors were talking about sex diseases with words they'd seldom used before: Poorly understood. Cancer-causing. Incurable.

If it felt like a plague upon humanity, that's understandable. Sexual diseases have always been regarded more as a punishment for vice than the result of infection. And while the sexual revolution was supposed to have liberated us from such puritanical attitudes, the question still remains: what is causing all this sickness? Is it just changing sexual mores, or some ominous new biochemical environment?

The answer is, nobody knows. Neither viruses nor bacteria appear on the scene with road maps and family trees, so it is difficult to say how they've come to infect humans, how they've evolved, or whether, in fact, some still exist. (The World Health Organization declared the world free of smallpox, for example, not because the virus disappeared but because worldwide vaccination made so many humans immune.) In any case, it's sometimes hard to identify a disease mentioned in antiquarian texts. It was thought that syphilis came back from the New World with Columbus (the earliest drawings of syphilitic patients date to about 1497). But some experts now believe that syphilis is one of the repulsive

"plagues" referred to in the biblical book of Leviticus. In fact, a lot of doctors would probably agree with New York gynecologist Sally Faith Dorfman. She thinks that many of the world's approximately 20 sexually transmitted diseases have been around "since the Garden of Eden."

Of course, AIDS is the big exception to the rule that what's new is old in sex diseases. By examining blood samples that have been stored over the years for research, scientists have been able to establish that AIDS is that great rarity, a truly new sex disease in humans. Blood samples from 20 years ago show no trace of exposure, except for certain villages in central Africa, where a few people showed antibodies to HIV, the AIDS-causing virus, back in the 1960s, says Jonathan Zenilman, an epidemiologist at the Centers for Disease Control in Atlanta. That's what has prompted the current theory that AIDS arose in Africa—perhaps as a random mutation of a similar virus found in monkeys, which people in the region capture and eat. It's been speculated that when monkeys are trapped, they scratch. The virus may have been jumping back and forth, therefore, between monkeys and people, and with the right number of mutations it became HIV as we know it today.

HIV belongs to a category of viruses—the retroviruses—that were long thought to afflict only animals. (The "retro" refers to the way the virus works in reverse, copying its genetic code from RNA to DNA.) But it's certainly possible, as some researchers think, that retroviruses have been in human populations for a long time, and either we are better able to detect them now or they are spreading more widely, or both.

What might cause a rare virus to "break out"? Some researchers look to

From *Ms.*, May 1989, pp. 30, 32. Copyright © 1989, Ms. Magazine. Reprinted by permission.

human habits, practices that could transform a rare and hard-to-catch disease into an epidemic. For example, the human immune system, as it has evolved over thousands of years, has never had to defend against disease-causing organisms injected directly into the bloodstream. Dr. David Golde, a professor at the University of California at Los Angeles medical school, speculates that this may be the reason a rare virus seen only in one part of the world could suddenly spread quickly in a population.

If there is to be a new, as yet unknown, sex disease of the nineties it may well come from the family of retroviruses. Already, studies have found a relatively high incidence among intravenous drug users in New York, California, and New Orleans of what Dr. Golde calls a "very worrisome" retrovirus known as human T-cell leukemia virus II (HTLV-II). Once considered so rare only six people in the world were known to be infected, its effects are unknown. But it is believed to be transmitted by sexual intercourse, at least from men to women, and it is closely related to HTLV-I, a virus that causes a rapidly fatal form of leukemia and a neurological syndrome that robs sufferers of muscle control below the waist. HTLV-I was first isolated in 1980, a year after it was linked to leukemia, according to Joseph Rosenblatt, a colleague of Golde's at UCLA.

It frequently takes 10 to 20 years after exposure to HTLV-I for its effects to be known, so it may well be a decade or two before we see the toll of HTLV-II. It is known that from 4 to 20 percent of drug abusers tested in New Orleans and New York were exposed. And in a study reported in the New York *Times* of blood donors in San Francisco, HTLV-II was found to be three times more common than antibodies to HIV.

If HTLV-II is sexually transmissible, as it now appears (though not as easily transmitted as AIDS), there seems little doubt that we've got a new sexual worry coming due around the turn of the century. As for other new sexual diseases, who can say? Viruses and bacteria do mutate and evolve, but it's human change that has had the most impact on venereal disease in the last 30 years.

Take gonorrhea and syphilis. Both were on the way out until crack hit in the mid-1980s. Syphilis, which is associated with having many anonymous sex partners, dropped "like a rock" among gay men, according to Dr. Zenilman, as sex habits changed in response to AIDS. But the rate of infection began to climb among heterosexuals—from a total of 67,000 cases in 1985 to 90,000 in 1988. Crack addicts tend to have a large number of anonymous sex partners—partly

because crack reduces sexual inhibitions, and partly because it leads women into prostitution to pay for their addiction.

Most worrisome about this situation, which Zenilman says has the potential for epidemiological disaster, is antibiotic-resistant gonorrhea. Each year, of the estimated 2 million new cases of gonorrhea, there are about 100,000 that will not respond to penicillin or ampicillin. In those cases, the Centers for Disease Control recommends ceftriaxone, a drug five times more expensive than penicillin. This is not a problem if physicians in private practice are doing the dispensing, but it is cause for alarm when the first line of defense is the municipal health clinic.

Many of the "new" sex diseases that made us so uptight in the eighties were not new at all. What was new was science's ability to detect them. Chlamydia, for example, is a small viruslike bacterium that 20 years ago was associated only with eye disease. When cases of genital infection skyrocketed in the sexually active sixties and seventies, doctors were unfamiliar with the disease. It didn't help that some major symptoms of chlamydia—discharge, painful urination—are the same as gonorrhea, and that many people with chlamydia also had the latter. In fact, chlamydia infections are twice as prevalent as gonorrhea, but for years they remained untreated.

The consequences have not been trivial. If not caught early, chlamydia is likely to cause pelvic inflammatory disease, which can scar the Fallopian tubes and may lead to sterility. "Most tubal infertility is caused by it," says Dr. Zenilman of the CDC. One University of California study concluded that in 1984, some 50,000 American women were being rendered infertile by chlamydia infections each year. And since infants can be infected at birth, chlamydia has been linked to a number of syndromes in newborns.

Unfortunately, chlamydia is not likely to go away anytime soon, mostly because there is not an instant cure—treatment takes a week—and many public health clinics either remain ignorant of it or won't treat it. As one doctor writing in the *Journal of the American Medical Association* explained, "They can't afford it." Thus with 3 to 4 million people catching it annually, chlamydia is likely to be a major sex disease of the nineties, not because it has just arisen, but because medical knowledge and awareness are on the rise.

The same could be said for herpes, about which you might think everything has already been said. But medical science is just now finding out that one to 3 percent of herpes carriers have no symptoms at all, and therefore the disease is being unwittingly spread—especially to babies, who can catch the virus during a vaginal delivery.

Genital warts, which were recorded as far back as ancient Greece, have only recently been linked to cervical cancer. Caused by the human papilloma virus, the warts are sometimes invisible and hard to remove, and sometimes a person with no symptoms at all can be infected. Since it is a particularly difficult condition to treat, doctors have attacked genital warts with lasers, liquid nitrogen, and interferon. No doubt we will hear more about them, too, as the number of infec-

tions spreads, and treatment improves.

But new drugs and treatments are expensive, and every time a new therapy becomes available, the health of the poor suffers in contrast to the middle class. At least in the areas of AIDS, syphilis, and gonorrhea, sex diseases in the nineties will be a more severe problem for the poor than for rest of the population. Not that anyone can really breathe a sigh of relief. For, despite anticipated progress on AIDS and its symptoms, sex in the next decade will be just as fraught with anxiety as it was in this one.

STDs—Sexually Transmitted Diseases

Roger Baxter, M.D.

Dr. Baxter is a fellow in infectious diseases at Mt. Zion Hospital in San Francisco.

Like so many things in life, sexual activity is a two-edged sword. The excitement, joy, and emotional warmth of sex, if not tempered with the knowledge of potential harm, can bring down the curse of a disease. This article describes some of the more common sexually transmitted diseases, how to recognize them, and how they can be prevented.

SYPHILIS

Syphilis was first described in Spain in the early 1500s. Many medical historians believe it was brought there by Columbus and his fellow travelers from the New World. Soldiers spread the disease rapidly throughout Europe while fighting foreign wars.

Today, contrary to popular opinion, we are seeing an upsurge in the number of cases of syphilis in the United States; in fact, 1987 had the highest rate of infection since 1950. The greatest increase in cases and the highest incidence (rate per 100,000) was in black and Hispanic populations.

Syphilis can manifest in a great number of ways; in fact, it has been called the "great imitator" because its symptoms can mimic all kinds of other diseases. It comes in three forms: primary, secondary, and tertiary, depending on how long it has been around before being recognized and treated (we will ignore the problem of congenital transmission in this discussion).

Syphilis is acquired by direct contact with an open sore containing **Tre-ponema pallidum**, the organism that causes the disease. About 3 or 4 weeks later, a primary lesion, called a chancre, will develop at the site of entry (most commonly the cervix or the penis). This is usually a single, firm, painless ulcer, and it may pass unnoticed. It is often associated with large, painless lymph nodes in the groin. Diagnosis at this stage is made by microscopic examination of material taken from the center of the ulcer. Untreated, the **sore** will heal in a few weeks. The **organism**, however, remains intact, and sometime later (usually a few more weeks) reappears as "secondary" syphilis, generally a skin rash accompanied by fever, sore throat, headache, and swollen lymph nodes, and sometimes hair loss. These are so nonspecific that the diagnosis is often missed, even if medical advice is sought. At this stage, the diagnosis is made by blood tests that check the person's antibody response to the infecting organism. Once again, if left untreated, the symptoms will resolve, and the organism will become "latent." The person will feel totally normal, although he or she will continue to be infected. It is only years later that the signs of tertiary syphilis may develop. Although approximately two thirds of untreated people will never have any problem with the disease, the remainder will develop late complications, some with cardiovascular problems and others with neurosyphilis. This manifestation of syphilis is now rare, but when it is present, it can be devastating, with problems ranging from gait and motor disturbances to paralysis and, in some instances, insanity. In general, the disease is not transmissible during the later stages.

Penicillin, discovered by Alexander Fleming in 1929, was found to be effective against syphilis in the early 1940s and remains the treatment of choice today. A person in an early stage of the disease may have a strong reaction to the drug that may result in high fever and intensification of the rash. The rash is due to the killing of the organisms and should not be confused with an allergic reaction.

GONORRHEA AND CHLAMYDIA

Recognized since antiquity, gonorrhea was named by Galen in 150 B.C., from the Greek meaning "flow of seed." At that time it was thought to be only a malady afflicting men, and the penile discharge was thought to be semen. Actually, the discharge is pus, caused by inflammation of the urethra by the organism **Neisseria gonorrhoea**. Today we know that women can indeed be infected, usually with an ascending infection beginning in the cervix. This may present nonspecific symptoms such as lower abdominal pain, vaginal discharge, or vaginal bleeding. If unrecognized at this stage, the infection can spread to the rest of the woman's reproductive organs, leading to pelvic inflammatory disease (PID) and even to infertility. In men the course is usually benign, with untreated disease resolving in a few weeks. The major risk in men is that of spreading infection to others, although complications, such as urethral strictures, blood infection, and arthritis, can occur.

Chlamydia trachomatis is an unusual organism: it is very similar to bacteria, but due to deficiencies in its cell wall, it cannot live outside of cells. Thus, it cannot be grown in regular cultures and cannot be recognized by the usual staining of tissues. It is diagnosed with special culture techniques or stains for detecting the organism by using antibodies to it. It affects the same organs as does gonorrhea and thus causes similar diseases.

When cultures turn out negative in a patient whose urethra is infected, the disease is called "nongonococcal urethritis" (NGU). It is thought that nearly 50% of NGU is caused by chlamydia. Another important fact is that both chlamydia and gonorrhea frequently coexist: this association is so close that physicians are trained to treat both infections if one is found. This is why a doctor may prescribe one medication to be taken once immediately together with one to be taken over one week's time.

Chlamydia can also infect the epididymis in men, manifesting as a painful swelling of the upper part of the scrotum. In women, the organism can cause, as with gonorrhea, an ascending infection of the reproductive tract and may result in infertility. **Lymphogranuloma venereum** (LGV) is also caused by the chlamydia organism. It is unusual in North America but not uncommon in Africa, Asia, and South America. This disease first produces small genital sores that may easily be missed and then enlargement of lymph nodes in the groin.

The most effective therapy against chlamydial infections is tetracycline.

HERPES SIMPLEX

One of the "plagues" of the 1980s, herpes instills great fear in many sexually active adults. Of course, nearly everyone has had a "cold sore" or a "fever blister" at some time or another; did you know that these are also caused

by herpes? In fact, there are two types of the virus, Type I, with a predilection for the mouth and lips, and Type II, which prefers to strike below the belt. By age 6 most of us are infected with Type I. Only the unlucky half of the infected group will go on to develop recurrent sores on the lips, provoked by exposure to sunlight and stress. The others may never know they've been infected and can only find out by being tested for antibodies to the virus. Once you have been infected, the virus is yours for life; it lies dormant inside of one of your sensory nerves. Later, probably in relation to normal ebbs and flows of immunity, the virus becomes activated, travels down the nerve to the lip, and causes the little blisters known so well to many. This means that if you develop lip sores for the first time, no matter what age, it is probably **not** that your kissing partner has just infected you with an evil virus, but that for unknown reasons the virus you **already** harbor has become reactivated.

Type II herpes virus is similar to Type I, except that it prefers to infect body parts "below the belt"–the penis or vulva, and the anus. It is a relatively common disease, but it provokes severe anxiety because of the sensitive areas involved.

Happily, there is hope for those who have herpes. Acyclovir, a relatively new antiviral, is effective both in decreasing symptoms and in shortening the duration of an attack. It also can be taken to prevent the recurrence of attacks. However, nothing can actually "cure" the disease. Hence the joke: "What's the difference between love and herpes?" Answer: "Only herpes is forever."

AIDS

Last, and most seriously, we'll talk about AIDS, acquired immunodeficiency syndrome. AIDS is caused by a virus and is transmitted sexually via semen and cervical secretions. It can also be transmitted via blood, that is, through transfusions or the sharing of needles among illicit drug users. Basically, it infects a certain type of blood cell that is instrumental in your body's

immune system. Over a period of years the cells are destroyed, and with them go your defenses against many of the viruses, bacteria, fungi, and parasites that surround, but normally do not infect, people with an intact immune system. People with this disease fall prey to infection after infection and eventually die. The viral infection can be slowed with a medication, AZT, but so far there is no cure. Although research is ongoing, it is doubtful that a vaccine will be forthcoming within the next few years. Hence, our only way of stopping the epidemic we are now witnessing is by prevention, especially by educating people who are at risk for acquiring the infection.

The bottom line for preventing AIDS is to **avoid contact with bodily secretions that might harbor the virus**. This means, first and foremost, avoiding sexual contact with anyone who admits to risk factors for the disease. Male homosexuality and/or bisexuality is one such risk factor. Although AIDS is not an exclusively homosexual disease, there is a very high prevalence of the virus in the homosexual population due to sexual activity patterns that existed in the early part of this decade and have since been curtailed.

Intravenous (IV) drug abusers are another group to avoid: by sharing needles, a growing percentage have been infected with the virus. Education has **not** much affected this group.

People infected with the virus don't necessarily look sick; you certainly can't tell by looking whether a person is infected or not. Often the only way to tell is by a test for the antibody to the virus. So if you're not positive about your partner's past, avoid contact with body fluids either by avoiding sexual activities or by using a condom. Condoms have been shown to prevent passage of the virus. They will also prevent the spread of the other sexually transmitted diseases discussed earlier.

MISCELLANEOUS

There are a number of other sexually transmitted diseases, but I won't go into great detail about them here.

Trichomonas is a mobile parasite that causes inflammation of the vagina, producing a thin, watery discharge and vaginal itching. Both symptomatic women and their partners should be treated with the appropriate antibiotic for this disease. Epstein-Barr virus causes mononucleosis, the "kissing disease," a febrile (fever-producing) disease of young adults. It can also cause sore throat, swollen lymph nodes in the neck, and even enlargement of the spleen, a vascular organ located up under the ribs on the left side. The disease can last a month or more. Although there is no effective treatment for this ailment, a blood test should be done to establish the diagnosis. This way, at least you can be reassured that there is not some other serious underlying infection.

Scabies and body lice might also be considered "sexually transmitted," as they are passed by any close contact. Itchy (especially at night!) bumps on the hands, abdomen, and genitals are characteristic of scabies. They are definitely diagnosed only by microscopic examination of scrapings of the lesions. Lice and their eggs, on the other hand, can often be seen with the naked eye. These are blood-sucking parasites of three separate species, each with a love of one area of the body: crab, or pubic lice, head lice, and body lice (not so choosy). Luckily, both scabies and lice can be treated with medicated lotions or creams. All clothes and bed linen must also be washed at the time of treatment.

The list of sexually transmitted diseases is even longer than this, but this has probably been enough to throw fear into the most stalwart Casanova. Although most of these illnesses can be easily cured, it's important to remember that some of these infections cannot be, and that AIDS is lethal once contracted.

UTI'S EVERYTHING YOU NEED TO KNOW ABOUT URINARY TRACT WOES

STEPHEN A. HOFFMANN, M.D.

Stephen A. Hoffmann, M.D., *is an infectious disease specialist and emergency room physician at Massachusetts General Hospital.*

Sex is great—it's the morning *after* that Joan M. dreads. She usually awakens feeling as though her bladder's about to burst. But when she does urinate, there's burning and pain, and she feels she can't quite empty her bladder. Next comes a nagging ache in her lower abdomen— and chills.

Sound familiar? Joan's problem is a urinary tract infection (UTI). Up to one in five women get them. (Men usually don't get serious UTI's until old age, when prostate problems set them off.) Until now, not much has been known about how and why women get recurrent UTI's. But new research has brought a better understanding. And now there's no reason for anyone to resign herself to countless bouts. There are preventive steps you can take, new while-you-wait tests and one-dose treatment options; someday, there may even be a vaccine.

Why certain women seem so prone to UTI's has long puzzled physicians. Sure, kidney stones and bladder troubles make anyone more susceptible, but why should otherwise healthy people be so vulnerable to infection? After all, it's normal for bacteria to be found on the skin around the urethral opening (see diagram). Even the intestinal bug *Escherichia coli* frequently crops up. Usually, though, the body's natural defenses keep them at bay. So why are some people so plagued?

In the past, most theories were the stuff of folklore. Neither taking bubble baths, douching, using tampons, nor wiping oneself in the "wrong" direction after a bowel movement has been shown to give UTI bugs a boost.

Research now suggests that some women may be genetically more vulnerable to UTI's, says Dr. Anthony Schaeffer, a professor of urology at Northwestern University Medical School. His team has found that most women with recurrent UTI's have a biological defect in the cells lining the urinary tract: Those cells had sticky surface proteins (called glycoproteins) that attract *E. coli* and allow them to cling and colonize. (The abnormality doesn't cause disease; it just makes it easier for germs to latch on and infection to occur.)

Other researchers looking for a possible way to tell who has the sticky-cell defect have found that women in blood groups B or AB are at higher risk for UTI's. What's more, 85% of women who get recurrent UTI's have P_1 negative blood (P_1 is a specific protein on red cells). That may be an important finding, considering only 21% of Americans are P_1 negative. If further research shows those blood groups truly are markers, scientists could create a new screening test for UTI susceptibility.

It's also possible UTI-prone women simply may have inherited weaker immune systems—and weaker defenses against UTI germs. Given a vulnerable genetic make-up and the right bug, the body's immune system can be overwhelmed.

Women who keep getting UTI's also have less acidic urine, studies show. Dr. Larrian Gillespie, a urologist at the University of California, Irvine, explains that bacteria use urea, a component in acidic urine, to help them thrive. When bacteria multiply, she says, they split urea molecules—leaving the urine less acidic.

She says that's why drinking cranberry juice—which acidifies the urine—is the worst advice you could follow. "It makes about as much sense as putting out a fire with gasoline." Other investigators agree cranberry therapy is a myth. One team reports in the journal *Microbios* that, according to a test tube study, cranberry juice has a certain component that may render bacteria less able to stick to cells on the urinary tract. However, even they say any possible benefits are only temporary. Further studies are in the works.

THE SEX HEX

Sex—especially vaginal intercourse—is now shown to be a major trigger for urinary tract infections. In one study, a team led by Dr. Brian L. Strom at the University of Pennsylvania surveyed the sexual practices of 168 students who were being treated for UTI's and 734 who'd sought care for other kinds of problems at the school's clinic. Result: 95% of the UTI group said they'd had sex in the previous 48 hours, compared with only 26% of the control group. The more times they'd had intercourse, the greater the UTI risk.

Problems arise during sex if penile thrusts abrade the woman's urethra, making it more susceptible to infection, suggests Strom. Thrusting may also push existing bacteria into the

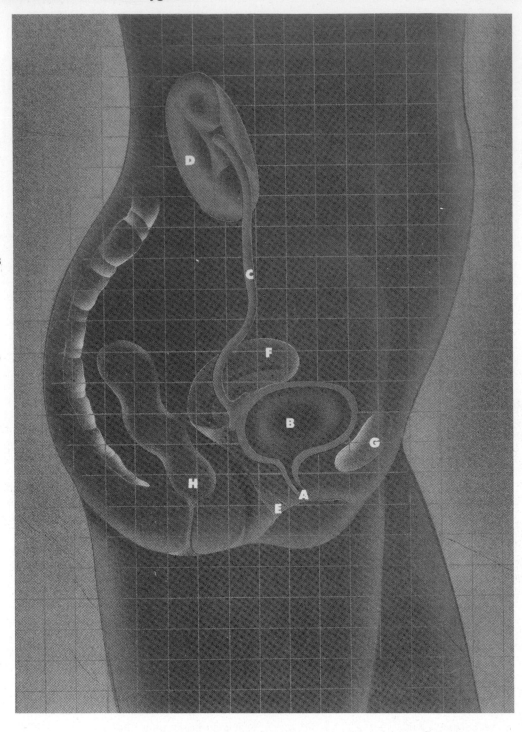

When bacteria infect the urethra (A), it's called urethritis (symptom: burning urination); in the bladder (B), it's cystitis (frequent urination); via the ureters (C), to the kidneys (D), it's pyelonephritis (fever, back pain, nausea). Also shown: vagina (E), uterus (F), pubic bone(G), rectum(H).

bladder. No particular sexual position is inherently dangerous, says Gillespie. It's the angle of the penis against the vagina that leads to UTI's. She suggests UTI-susceptible women try positions in which the man enters at a lower angle so that the clitoris is compressed and the top wall of the vagina is massaged. She says a rocking motion—rather than up-and-down thrusts—spares the woman's urethra unnecessary stress.

Another intriguing finding from Strom's study: Use of a diaphragm increases the chances of infection, though oral contraceptives don't. (The Pill, however, can make some women more susceptible to yeast and vaginal infections, say other researchers.) The diaphragm connection still puzzles many doctors, but Gillespie thinks she has an answer. Her examination of 150 sexually active women with UTI's found that 74% used diaphragms that,

in her estimation, were too large. Gillespie explains that such diaphragms push too hard against the neck of the bladder at the point where urine empties out. During urination, then, the bladder is forced closed before it voids all the urine. Because urine stays around longer in the bladder, bacteria have more time to multiply.

To prove it, Gillespie had the diaphragm-users refitted with smaller devices. (Others switched to another

URINATING SOON AFTER SEX CAN PROTECT AGAINST GETTING A UTI, SAY RESEARCHERS.

contraceptive method.) All were advised to remember to urinate after sex. A year later, 96% of these 81 women were free of infection.

Of course, sometimes *he* is the source of UTI woes. Men, too, can get urinary tract infections—but with very mild symptoms that slip by unnoticed. (For instance, men may simply notice increased urgency to urinate, rather than burning sensations.) So if a woman keeps coming down with UTI's, especially the same type, it may be a good idea for her partner to be checked.

BUG BAEDEKER

Because germs can set up shop throughout the urinary tract (from the urethra all the way up to the kidneys), there are many different types of UTI's. When bacteria infect the urethra, the resulting UTI is called urethritis (tipoff: burning during urination). When the bacteria ascend to the bladder, the infection is called cystitis—from the Greek word *kystis*, for bladder. (No. 1 symptom: frequent urge to void, with or without burning sensations.) If the organisms scale the ureters from the bladder to the kidneys, the result is full-blown pyelonephritis (from the Greek *pyelos*, for pelvis). This is the most dangerous of all UTI's because the infection can damage kidneys, then spread to the circulatory system. (Fever, back pain, nausea and vomiting are its symptoms, though during the early stages signs may be subtle or absent.)

Even though UTI's are common, they can still be confused with many other conditions. Urethritis symptoms are much like those of a vaginal yeast infection or even atrophic vaginitis—the nagging vaginal-wall burning that often occurs after menopause. The bottom line is that any problems with bladder, back or vagina deserve a visit to the doctor. Many times a urinary tract infection is the culprit.

BUG BUSTING

You no longer need to wait hours or days for a doctor to study your urine sample under a microscope or do a culture to tell if you've got a urinary tract infection. Now there's the "rapid urine screening test," which can pick up trace amounts of bacteria in a urine sample within minutes. It can't, however, pick up chlamydia, the sexually transmitted bug that can also cause UTI's. (Chlamydia is just sufficiently

BUG DRUGS

Some of the most common UTI bacteria are now resistant to ampicillin and amoxicillin—two antibiotics long considered the drugs of choice for UTI's. And resistance to another old favorite, Bactrim, is also on the rise. Fortunately, potent new medications have become available within the last year. Here's a guide to the latest UTI-busting drugs (ask your doctor about side effects):

■ Two-Punch Rx: Augmentin combines amoxicillin with another chemical agent called a beta-lactamase inhibitor. This combination punch promises to enhance amoxicillin's effectiveness.

■ Killer Cousin: Keflex (cephalexin) can be more effective than its chemical relative, ampicillin.

■ Small-Dose Suppressors: Macrodantin (nitrofurantoin), when taken regularly in small doses, can actually inhibit new infections. It's also good against a simple UTI, but not a kidney infection.

■ The Young Guns: Ciprofloxacin and norfloxacin are among the newest drugs against UTI germs. Doctors say they're good choices for women with recurring UTI's, especially when the bacteria may have developed resistance to the more common antibiotics. (Ciprofloxacin is not recommended for anyone under 17, pregnant women or nursing mothers; norfloxacin is not for children or pregnant women.)

different to evade routine urine tests, too.) A chlamydia check requires specialized cultures. It's worth the extra effort: If untreated, chlamydia can spread to the ovaries and Fallopian tubes and lead to infertility.

If you test positive for a UTI, the doctor may also wish to make sure the bacteria have not mounted an assault on the kidneys. In fact, up to a third of women with seemingly nothing more than cystitis actually have the beginnings of a kidney infection. All the doctor needs is a urine sample. A clever new assay, the antibody-coated bacteria test, can distinguish between a kidney infection and a UTI.

One of the biggest boons to UTI sufferers is the discovery that when it comes to therapy, a single, large dose of antibiotic often turns out to be just as good as a series of smaller doses given for seven, 10 or even 14 days. One dose is not only cheaper and more convenient, but easier on the stomach. The two pills most often prescribed this way are Bactrim and ampicillin (see "Bug Drugs"). However, the one-shot cure shouldn't be used by pregnant women or people with kidney problems.

Treating *recurrent* infections requires a different tactic. Some studies have shown that repeat infections can be reduced considerably by taking certain antibiotics in *low* doses, either daily or several times a week. More and more physicians are prescribing "suppression" therapy for frequent infections. A relatively new antibiotic, Macrodantin, is especially useful when taken this way. The downside is that side effects may be more common; and surviving bacteria will probably develop resistance to the drug, making the next UTI that much more difficult to treat.

For most women, it would be preferable to take a preventive pill only once in a while, as needed. Now studies show this is possible. Women whose UTI's seem linked to sexual activity may prevent infection by taking an antibiotic after making love. If this is your pattern, it may be worth asking a doctor about this kind of treatment, called antibiotic prophylaxis.

Finally, researchers are working on a vaccine to prevent UTI's. To develop it, they need to find a way to deactivate the UTI germs' virulence factors, the sticky proteins on the bacteria themselves. Researchers hope it will be possible to immunize people with a combination of virulence factors garnered from the most common UTI bacteria and so prevent them from sticking.

Much more work is needed, however. Scientists are learning that some strains are so clever they can change their virulence factors. No one knows just how effective a vaccine will be, either: immunizing people against bacteria that cause UTI's is a tall order.

Meanwhile, here's news you can use today to avoid a UTI tomorrow:
■ Women who use a diaphragm should get the fit checked regularly, especially after giving birth.
■ Drinking lots of water may be helpful—especially before sex—to flush the urinary tract.
■ Urinate soon after intercourse.
■ If you're prone to frequent UTI's, ask your doctor about the value of suppressive antibiotics. If UTI's seem to follow sex, ask about prophylactic medication.
■ If you have a relapse after treatment or have recurrent infections, ask your partner to get a checkup, too. Sharing is nice in a relationship, but not when it comes to infections.

The healthy male: What's going on in there?

What could happen, what happens, and why . . . the facts about his vital parts.

More men than ever are paying attention to their *outsides* with great looking clothes and regular gym workouts. But, even today, most men don't pay enough attention to their *insides*. Women are ignorant of men's systems, too. Here are the facts.

Prostate problems

The prostate gland is located below the bladder and above the rectum. It produces semen, the thick fluid that carries sperm from the *testicles*. Most men develop at least one prostate problem by age 60. The prostate is not a single gland, but rather a collection of 30 to 50 small, gland-cell clusters.

The prostate is almond-sized in young boys. During puberty, the male sex hormone *testosterone* stimulates it to mature to the size of a large walnut, and it begins to produce seminal fluid. (See diagram.)

Here are the most common conditions that affect the prostate:

Prostatitis (inflammation or infection of the prostate)
● *Symptoms*: May include fever; pain in the penis, lower abdomen, lower back, or perineum (the area between the scrotum and the anus); pain or burning on urination and/or ejaculation; an urgent need to urinate frequently; scant urine production; trouble starting to urinate; or frequent night urination.
● *Diagnosis:* Prostatitis may be caused by the *gonorrhea* or *E. coli* bacteria, by the *trichomonas* parasite, or by *chlamydia* or *mycoplasma*, organisms that can't be neatly fitted into any specific category.

All these organisms can be detected by a culture in the doctor's office. The type of culture medium, and the method of obtaining a sample, varies depending on the organism.

● *Treatment*: There is an appropriate antibiotic for each of the organisms causing prostatitis.

Sometimes, "no offending organism can be found," says Dr. Richard Lena, chief of the urology section at the Hospital of Saint Raphael. In that case, he says, treatment may include antibiotics and/or a wide range of nonmedical approaches, such as hot baths and elimination of alcohol (especially red wine), strong teas, spicy foods, and coffee (both caffeinated and decaffeinated) — any of which may irritate the prostate.

Prostatitis-like symptoms may also be caused by *urinary sphincter hypertonicity* (USH), stress-related tension in the muscle that controls urination. Dr. Lena says muscle relaxants are used for this condition, in addition to the above-mentioned lifestyle changes. "Sexual activity can also help relax the muscle," he adds.

Acute or chronic? There are two kinds of prostatitis, acute and chronic. The former causes sudden fever and genital, abdominal, and/or low-back pain. Acute prostatitis usually clears up in about a week of treatment with the correct antibiotic.

Chronic prostatitis causes less severe symptoms but lasts longer. Dr. Lena says it may occur because the organisms are "hidden" in areas of the prostate hard to reach by antibiotics, or because the organisms have become antibiotic-resistant. Chronic prostatitis may require more lab work, longer-term antibiotics, stress management, and the dietary modifications described above.

Prostatitis caused by a microorganism is usually an uncomplicated illness, but if an infected prostate clamps down on the urethra and prevents the bladder from emptying completely, the result may be *cystitis* (bladder infection). Symptoms of cystitis and prostatitis can be quite similar — pain and/or burning on urination, and urinary urgency and hesitancy with scant production.

Like prostatitis, cystitis is not a major medical problem. But if it is left untreated it may progress to a kidney infection, which is considerably more serious and often requires a period of hospitalization.

● *Prevention*: According to Dr. Lena, a high fluid intake may help prevent prostatitis. Good hygiene habits also are important. But, he cautions, these measures are far from foolproof and can't guarantee that a man will never suffer from prostatitis.

A last word of caution. Dr. Lena advises, "If you have something that looks like prostatitis, but it doesn't respond properly to appropriate treatment, you'll want to make sure the symptoms aren't caused by some other disease, such as cancer."

Benign prostatic hypertrophy (BPH) Unlike other glands, which shrink with age, the prostate continues to grow — in some men, up to the size of a grapefruit.

By around age 50, prostate overgrowth (*hypertrophy*) causes noticeable problems in about 20 percent of men. By age 70, that figure rises to more than 50 percent.

"We're not sure why the prostate continues to grow, but we believe it's due to the changed hormonal balance that occurs with age," Dr. Lena says. He stresses that *the growth is not cancer, nor does it predispose a man to cancer*.
● *Symptoms*: The enlarging prostate may pinch the urethra and cause urinary urgency, hesitancy, and, particularly, the need to get up at night.
● *Diagnosis*: BPH can be diagnosed by a digital rectal examination (DRE). To perform a DRE, the physician inserts a gloved finger into the rectum and feels the prostate.

From *St. Raphael's Better Health,* November/December 1988, pp. 6-12. Portions of this article originally appeared in *Medical Self-Care Magazine,* Pt. Reyes, CA 94956, and were written by Michael Castleman.

• *Treatment*: Eventually, a man may grow tired of the inconvenience of BPH and opt for surgical correction, typically a transurethral resection of the prostate (TUR).

With the man under spinal or general anesthesia, the urologist inserts a tiny instrument (*resectoscope*) into the urethra. When electrically heated, the wire loop at the end of the instrument burns away prostatic overgrowth and widens the urethral path.

TURs are considered routine; nonetheless, they're major surgery. Recovery usually involves three to five days of hospitalization and a week of rest.

Although surgical complications are uncommon, several are possible: infection, bleeding that requires transfusion, urinary sphincter damage that causes incontinence, and erection impairment.

But "TUR-related erection problems are psychological in origin," Dr. Lena says. "There's no physiological reason for either nerves or blood supply to be disturbed by the procedure when it's correctly performed."

In most cases, however, TURs result in "dry orgasm." Scarring from the electrocautery usually closes the *ejaculatory ducts*, and so blocks the flow of seminal fluid. After a TUR, orgasm feels as pleasurable as ever, but the man does not ejaculate. If seminal fluid still flows at all, it is released backward into the bladder.

Backward ejaculation, called retroejaculation, may sound strange, but it's of no medical concern. Semen mixes with the urine and passes during urination. No ejaculation means no vehicle for sperm to leave the penis. The testicles continue to produce sperm, but they are reabsorbed by the body, so TURs signal the end of male fertility.

A few years ago, a new technique was touted as an alternative to TURs. The nonsurgical technique uses an inflatable balloon to widen the urethra and make urination easier.

"It sounded good in the press, but it isn't a curative measure," says Dr. Lena. He explains that this "forced balloon dilation" doesn't correct the underlying condition—an enlarged prostate—and so provides only temporary improvement, at best.

Prostate cancer Prostate cancer is extremely common in older men. On autopsy, cancerous cells are found in 10 percent of men in their 50s, one in every three in their 60s, and in three of every four over 80.

Fortunately, most prostate tumors are slow-growing, never spread beyond the gland itself, do not cause symptoms, and pose no threat to life.

Still, fast-spreading prostate cancer is the number three cause of cancer death in men (after lung and skin cancer). Most common in men over 40, it accounts for 20 percent of men's cancers and 10 percent of male cancer deaths. The American Cancer Society estimates 99,000 new diagnoses and 28,000 deaths in 1988.

• *Symptoms*: Early prostate cancer symptoms include: blood in the urine, urinary urgency and hesitancy but scant urine production, and pain.

• *Diagnosis*: Exams are recommended annually for men over 40, whether or not there are any symptoms. Prostate cancer can be detected by a digital rectal examination (DRE). If any hard lumps are detected, a biopsy is performed. Any biopsy that shows cancer also reveals whether it's the slow- or fast-growing kind.

Ultrasound is sometimes advocated for diagnosis, but, insists Dr. Lena, "The DRE is still the diagnostic gold

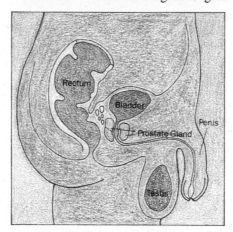

standard." He adds that ultrasound can be useful in guiding biopsies or confirming suspicious exam findings.

• *Treatment*: For slow-growing cancers, treatment decisions depend on the patient's age. Dr. Lena says. "If the man is 70 years or older, it's reasonable to expect the tumor won't give him significant trouble in the next 10 years." In this case, he says, the urologist will keep track of the cancer through regular checkups.

But the situation is different for younger patients, Dr. Lena says. "Any kind of tumor in a younger man — say, one of 50 or so — should be treated aggressively."

Treatment options for fast-growing

prostate cancer include removal of the prostate, radiation therapy, and/or hormone therapy.

Dr. Lena says the decision about which method or methods to use to treat prostate cancer depends on the findings of various additional tests such as CAT scans, bone scans, and blood tests. "The choices we make depend on whether and where the cancer has spread," he says.

Often, the treatment plan includes removal of the entire prostate gland. Until recently, that meant impotence for 90 percent of the men who had the operation. This occurred because the nerves that control erection run along the prostate gland, and were severed when it was removed.

But a technique recently developed by Dr. Patrick Walsh of the Johns Hopkins University preserves many men's ability to have an erection. Dr. Lena cautions, though, "We never spare the nerves if it means compromising our ability to remove all the cancerous cells." All in all, he says, about 50 percent of men who undergo prostate removal can expect to retain potency.

Impotence also can be caused by radiation therapy. Other possible side effects include diarrhea, bowel problems, obstruction of the urethra, and blood in the urine.

Hormone therapy has side effects, too. Because the spread of prostate cancer depends on the male sex hormone *testosterone*, hormone treatment usually works either by removing the testicles— the source of testosterone—or counteracting testosterone with a form of the female sex hormone, *estrogen*. A newer form of hormone therapy blocks the action of a hormone that stimulates testosterone release.

Regardless of the method used, the results of hormone therapy include erection loss, decreased body hair, and breast development. (Breast effects can be prevented with radiation.)

Testicular cancer

The *testicles* are the primary male sex organs. They produce the sperm cells that fertilize the female egg during reproduction. The two oval-shaped testes are suspended below the penis in a pouch of skin called the *scrotum*.

Testicular cancer accounts for only about one percent of all male cancers, but, unlike most other cancers, it is generally found in young men between the ages of 15 and 39. It is less common in middle aged and older men.

Two groups of men have a greater risk of developing testicular cancer — those whose testes have not descended into the scrotum and those whose testes descended after age 6. Cancer of the testes is 10 to 40 times more likely in these men.

Only one testicle is affected in the large majority of testicular cancer cases.

● *Symptoms*: The most common symptom is the appearance of a small, hard lump about the size of a pea on the front or the side of the testicle. The lump is usually painless in the early stages of the disease. Other symptoms may include enlargement of a testicle, a heavy feeling in a testicle, a sudden accumulation of fluid, or blood in the scrotum. If the disease has spread, there may be swelling or tenderness in other parts of the body, such as the groin, breast, or neck. *These symptoms can also be caused by infections or other conditions that are not cancer. Only a doctor can determine if cancer is present.*

● *Diagnosis*: Most testicular cancers are first discovered by men themselves (see box, "Testicular self-exam," page 64). Any swelling, pain, or hard lump in the testicle should be brought to the attention of a doctor. If cancer is suspected, further tests such as tissue biopsies, X rays, and blood tests can determine if it is present and if it has spread.

● *Treatment*: Just a decade or two ago, the outlook for patients with testicular cancer was grim: Fewer than 10 percent lived 5 years after diagnosis. But today, Dr. Lena says, new treatments have led to an overall cure rate of 90 percent.

Treatment always includes surgical removal of the affected testicle or testicles. When, as is common, only one testicle is affected, the surgery does not affect fertility.

Radiation therapy and/or chemotherapy may also be used. "A new, very effective 'triple-threat' chemotherapy regimen has helped us combat this disease," Dr. Lena says.

Erection problems

For many men, "impotence" is among the most threatening words in the English language. It implies not only loss of erection, but also the end of everything traditionally considered masculine: assertiveness, leadership, and self-respect.

Erection problems often wreak havoc on relationships. In their anger and con-

---

MedTerms

Biopsy: The removal and microscopic examination of a sample of tissue.

Benign prostatic hypertrophy: A noncancerous condition in which the prostate swells and pushes against the urethra and bladder.

Bladder: The hollow organ that stores urine.

Chemotherapy: Treatment with anticancer drugs.

Ejaculation: Ejection of sperm and seminal fluid.

Impotence: Inability to have an erection.

Incontinence: Inability to hold urine in the bladder.

Prostatectomy: The surgical removal of the prostate gland.

Radiation therapy: Treatment with high-energy radiation from x-rays or other sources of radiation.

Scrotum: The external bag or pouch containing the testicles.

Testicles: The two egg-shaped glands in which sperm are formed.

Testosterone: A male sex hormone.

Transurethral resection (TUR): The use of a special instrument inserted through the penis to remove prostatic overgrowth.

Ultrasound: A diagnostic procedure that bounces high-frequency sound waves off tissues and changes the echoes into pictures.

Ureter: The tube that carries urine from each kidney to the bladder.

Urethra: The tube that carries urine from the bladder, and semen from the prostate, to the outside of the body.

Urologist: A doctor who specializes in diseases of the urinary organs in females and the urinary and sex organs in males.

---

fusion at what many men experience as betrayal by their bodies, some feel guilty that they cannot "perform." Others blame the problem on their lovers. Many get depressed and withdraw from physical affection altogether. Women involved with nonerective men also typically feel confused, anxious, depressed, and guilty.

Happily, with a little sexual re-education or counseling, the vast majority of erection problems can be resolved with self-care within a few months. For

---

those whose problems do not respond, surgery for penile implants can restore the ability to have an erection.

Medical history first Therapy for erection problems begins with a complete medical history performed by a physician. "We used to think that 90 percent of erection problems were psychological, but now we know that about 50 percent have a physical component," says Wardell Pomeroy, Ph.D., coauthor of the Kinsey Report (1948) that launched scientific sex research, and now dean of the Institute for the Advanced Study of Human Sexuality in San Francisco.

Saint Raphael's Dr. Lena explains that many illnesses can cause erection problems: diabetes, depression, alcoholism, multiple sclerosis, and atherosclerosis, a narrowing of the arteries that supply blood to the penis.

Dr. Lena says a complete accounting of all drugs is also an important part of the medical history, since a large number of widely used drugs can cause erection impairment. These include: alcohol; beta-blocker drugs for heart conditions and high blood pressure; and some drugs used to treat anxiety, depression, ulcers, glaucoma, and irritable bowel syndrome.

If a drug is suspected of impairing sexuality, Dr. Lena suggests, ask your doctor if another type might be substituted, or if a lower dose might be safely prescribed.

Assess sensuality If medical problems are ruled out, a detailed sexual history is in order: When and how did the problem begin? What was happening in your life and your relationship? Do you ever wake up with morning erections? How did you learn about sex? How do you make love?

The answers to these questions provide crucial clues to the problem, Dr. Lena says. Sudden onset with substantial impairment suggests a medical or drug-related problem. Ability to become erect, but not with a lover, suggests a stress, relationship, or lovemaking problem.

Part of a sexual history involves a discussion of the man's (or couple's) feelings about how lovemaking is "supposed" to proceed.

Many men learn about sex at the curbside or in the locker room, and adopt a nonsensual lovestyle almost entirely focused on the genitals and intercourse. But at its most fulfilling, lovemaking is a combination of the sexual and the sensual, and many men's erection problems clear up when they learn how to take a more leisurely approach.

Stress If an erection problem is not the result of illness, drug use, or lack of sensual lovemaking, the next approach is to examine the role of stress in the man's life.

Stress — everything from a leaky faucet to major marital problems — deflates erections by triggering the body's fight-or-flight mechanism.

Stress redirects the blood supply away from the central body — and the penis — out toward the limbs, so the person can defend against attack or flee from danger.

The fight-or-flight reflex has clear evolutionary advantages, but the chronic stresses of modern society have made this adaptation somewhat counterproductive. A man under pressure at work, or with legal, financial, or family problems, may live much of his life in the fight-or-flight mode, and may develop stress-related medical problems or erection problems, especially if he uses alcohol to cope.

Aging Although men in their 40s and 50s may have no trouble raising an erection, it may take them a little longer to do so than when they were twenty years younger. This change is perfectly normal, says Dr. Lena.

Unfortunately, most men who develop age-related erection problems don't fully understand how the aging process affects their sexuality. Quite often, once the man understands these changes, his concerns clear up.

Testicular self-examination

This exam should be performed once a month after a warm bath or shower. The heat will cause the scrotal skin to relax, making it easier to find anything unusual. The procedure is simple and takes only a few minutes.

● Stand naked in front of a mirror. Look for any swelling on the skin of the scrotum.

● Examine each testicle gently with both hands. The index and middle fingers should be placed underneath the testicle while the thumbs are placed on the top. Roll the testicle gently between the thumbs and fingers. One testicle may be larger than the other. This is normal.

● Find the epididymis (a cord-like structure on the top and back of the testicle that stores and transports the sperm). Do not confuse the epididymis with an abnormal lump.

● Feel for a small lump — about the size of a pea — on the front or the side of the testicle. These lumps are usually painless.

● If you do find a lump, contact your doctor right away. The lump may not be due to cancer, but only your doctor can tell.

The surgical solution If erections remain a problem due to illness, or due to a nonorganic problem lasting more than a year, surgery can restore a man's ability to have erections, Dr. Lena says.

He explains that surgeons can insert two basic types of penile implants — a hydraulic system and a hinged, semirigid rod.

The hydraulic system allows for a natural-looking penis either flaccid or erect. It involves two plastic cylinders inserted into the penis, a fluid reservoir implanted in the abdomen, and an inflation bulb implanted in a pocket beside the left testicle.

When the man desires an erection, he squeezes the bulb, which forces fluid from the reservoir into the rod system to produce erection. Afterward, a valve deflates the erection and the fluid returns to the reservoir.

"Because it's more complicated, this method carries with it a greater risk for mechanical problems," says Dr. Lena. "On that basis, it's simpler and more efficacious to use a semirigid rod."

He explains that the semirigid rod is a flexible plastic rod wrapped around a metal wire. Two of these rods are inserted in compartments in the penis. The man bends the rods up for erection, and down the rest of the time. The penis remains permanently semierect, but this is not noticeable in normal clothing, Dr. Lena says.

Even without erection, men are able to experience orgasm and ejaculation, Dr. Lena points out. But penile implants allow nonerective men to resume full sexual activity with their partners, and can restore their reproductive capacity.

INFERTILITY AND THE SEXUAL HEALTH OF THE FAMILY

Linda Hammer Burns, M.A.
Clinical Associate Psychologist
Department of Obstetrics and Gynecology
University of Minnesota
Minneapolis, MN 55455

Abstract

Infertility, which affects an estimated 20% of couples of childbearing age, has been investigated from a number of different perspectives. A great deal of attention has been paid to the sexual health and functioning of infertile couples, but the long-term ramifications of infertility on the sexual health of other family members has received little attention. For families with a history of infertility, sex often has an altered meaning, value, and reality. This may be the result of sexual dysfunction, nonsexual reproduction, or painful identity issues that alter self-concepts. Such experiences cannot help but have an impact on children raised in these families, especially if parents with a history of infertility are not helped to realize the import of their sexuality and sexual functioning on the healthy development of their children.

Infertility as a life crisis has received increasing professional and public recognition in recent years. With increased awareness has come a greater understanding of the complexity of infertility and its psychosocial impact on each individual and on the couple, their marriage, life goals, and family relationships. Whether the cause or the result, sexual dysfunction is a common and often destructive partner of long-term infertility. As a result, the majority of infertile couples will find they must, at some point, readjust their relationship, life view, values, and beliefs, especially in regard to their sexuality.

It is the premise of this paper that the sexual dysfunctions and sexual value dilemmas encountered by an infertile couple have a profound and lasting effect on the sexual health and environment of the couple's family, present and future. Furthermore, the manner in which the infertile couple manage their sexual dysfunctions and value dilemmas influences how they will negotiate other transitions in their family's development, especially those involving the sexuality and gender identity issues of any child(ren) they may parent.

This premise builds on the conceptual framework of Maddock (1983) and Scharff (1976), who assert that sex is a fundamental aspect of family life affecting all members within the family system. Scharff explains, "Sexuality is a central source of communication and growth in the development of relationships between an individual and his parents, spouse, and child. It is the vehicle for and manifestation of crucial interpersonal links" (p. 17). Sexual dysfunctions, common and even prevalent as one cause of infertility, have the potential of creating a problematic sexual atmosphere for children (adopted or born), especially in regard to issues of sexuality and sexual value dilemmas.

Infertility and Sexual Dysfunction

Although there has been an increasing awareness of the impact of infertility on sexual functioning, little attention has been given to the long-term impact of infertility on the sexual health of the family. Infertility is defined as the inability to conceive/carry a pregnancy to live birth after 1 year of regular sexual intercourse without contraceptives. It is estimated that 15–20% of couples of childbearing age are infertile.

Whether the cause or the effect, sexual dysfunction is a very real side-effect of infertility and the medical treatments for it. Sexual dysfunction is defined as any interuption in the individual's and couple's enjoyment or performance of sexual activity. Elstein (1975) described the causes of sexual dysfunction in infertile couples as: (1) psychosexual problems masquerading as cases of infertility (2) incidental findings of psychosexual disturbances in cases of infertility and (3) infertility causing psychosexual problems.

2. SEXUAL BIOLOGY AND HEALTH: Sexual Hygiene

Although there are documented instances of sexual dysfunction causing infertility (eg., unconsummated marriage, excessive masturbation) Kaufman (1969) found that "...emotional tension is not the CAUSE of infertility in most cases, but rather the RESULT of frustration of this basic human need." One common myth is that relaxation will cure infertility. Although this is a prevalent belief, it has not been substantiated by scientific research. In her poem "Trying to Conceive, #4," Marion Cohen (1983) confronts the relaxation myth and describes what couples are willing to do in order to have a baby.

Anything, I'll do anything—
    Temperature charts, Tes Tape, litmus paper,
    Vitamin A, Vitamin E, zinc, manganese
    Abstinence to maximize sperm count,
    Lying on my back with a pillow under my behind
    and my legs up like a beetle.
    Anything, I'll do anything—
    But please—please—don't ask me just to relax.

Inability to conceive or bear children because of physical pathology (known or unknown) often creates feelings of inadequacy, defectiveness, helplessness, and valuelessness (Kraft et al., 1980). Such feelings often result in or contribute to damaged or diminished sexual functioning. For some couples, sex may simply become perfunctory, a means to an end devoid of feelings of intimacy, sharing, or romance.

Erectile dysfunction (impotence) is the most common male sexual dysfunction. Berger (1980) found impotence following diagnosis of azoospermia to be common. Some other factors contributing to impotence are endocrine problems, performance anxiety, and medications to treat infertility. Other male sexual dysfunctions include ejaculatory incompetence, incomplete erection, and oligospermia (Leader et al., 1984; Walker, 1978; Rutherford et al., 1979).

Performance anxiety is experienced by some as "reactive impotence" (Levie, 1962). This includes "sex on demand" or the inability to perform sexually during ovulation. Many men describe their part in the sexual relationship as "stud service" and feel threatened and resentful of this role. Both men and women find that "sex on demand," often associated with months or years of reproductive frustration, makes spontaneous and playful sex difficult to maintain (Mahlstedt, 1985; Rosenfeld & Mitchell, 1979; Walker, 1978).

Anorgasmia, vaginismus, dyspareunia, and lack of sexual desire are the most common forms of sexual dysfunction found in women (Elstein, 1975). Debrovner and Shubin-Stein (1976) found that women with infertility problems were more often the initiators of sex and although they experienced increased sexual activity, they reported decreased sexual desire. Low sex drive or lack of interest in sexual intercourse may be the result of depression, doubts about sexual adequacy or identity, schematized sexual activity.

Sexual identity issues are frequently experienced by both partners, whether or not they have been diagnosed as the partner responsible for the couple's infertility (Bell, 1981). Both men and women frequently seek out other partners for extramarital affairs in an attempt to prove their sexuality; to reassure themselves of their desirability, femininity, or masculinity; to shore up their self-esteem; or to create a child that the partner cannot provide (Mai, 1971; Reddick, 1982; Kraft et al., 1980).

Not infrequently the quiet destruction of a couple's sexual relationship is avoided or ignored by the partners themselves or by their caregivers. Medical caregivers often fail to address sexual issues because of their own discomfort or ignorance. The couple's sexual relationship may be impaired by a belief that sexual problems are an inevitable concomitant of infertility or that sacrifice of sexual satisfaction will ensure the desired child. Some may view the lack of sexual satisfaction as a punishment that must be endured for past sexual indulgences. For many couples the gradual deterioration of their sexual relationship is the result of believing that pregnancy or parenthood will alleviate or ameliorate any sexual problems that may occur during infertility treatments.

The alteration of the infertile couple's sexual relationship often takes place over time in an atmosphere of anxious anticipation of the pregnancy they desire. In his play "Ashes," David Rudkin (1974) describes the ever-hopeful yet routine and lackluster sexuality of an infertile couple.

Colin: You've not been aroused by me at all—All my foreplay reefed on your single expectation of winkling out one clotted pore.
Anne: (Pause.) Getting heavy, love.
Colin: (Put out.) Sorry.
Anne: (Pause. Quieter.) Mop up now.
Colin: Ay. Load delivered, back to yard, cold half of bed. (Sounds of them shifting. Long pause.)
Anne: Perhaps we did it this time. (pp. 9–10)

Of course, sexual problems do not disappear with the arrival of children or with the termination of medical treatments. The long-term effects of sexual dysfunction can potentially affect all family members. More important, and more problematic, may be the belief that sexual functioning can be shut on and off on demand. This cavalier attitude toward sexual health, frequently shared by medical caregivers, is often at the bottom of the sexual problems experienced by many infertile couples.

Infertility and Sexual Value Dilemmas

The reality of reproduction today is that people can and do have babies without sexual intercourse. Reproductive technologies such as artificial insemination by husband or donor, in vitro fertilization, gene therapy, embryo transfer, donor uterus, donor ova, frozen embryos, and surrogate motherhood all provide couples with the opportunity to create and bear children in ways that were impossible in the past (Zimmerman, 1982). On the horizon are even more possibilities, such as in vitro gestation and cloning.

Today, more than in the past, infertile couples face several moral, ethical, and legal dilemmas basic to sexuality and reproduction. These include the desex-ualization of reproduction, challenges to traditional religious beliefs, alteration of traditional concepts of kinship, the child's right to self-identify, and social policy issues. The desexualizing of reproduction has resulted in what Toffler (1970, pp. 240–241) describes as a shattering of "all orthodox ideas about the family and its responsibilities . . . To continue to think of the family, therefore, in purely conventional terms is to defy all reason."

Changing concepts of the family is one of the out-comes of reproductive technology. The children of one family may have a genetic, conceptive, or birth history that differs from that of their parents and siblings. This is true of adopted children or children conceived by reproductive technologies (e.g., artificial insemi-nation by husband or donor, in vitro fertilization, or embryo transfer).

Historically, perhaps when there was less familial variety, issues of paternity and kinship had the poten-tial to tear families apart, creating conflicts and rifts, as exemplified in Strindberg's play, "The Father" (1958).

Captain: Didn't being a father sometimes make you feel ridiculous? I know nothing more absurd than . . . hearing a father talk about 'my children'. He ought to say 'my wife's children'! Weren't you ever afflicted with doubts . . . ?

Doctor: No, as a matter of fact, I never was. And anyhow, Captain, wasn't it Goethe who said, 'A man must take his children on trust'? (p. 51)

When bloodlines or geneology are blurred, histori-cal beliefs and policies about kinship and entitlement are brought under examination. Is parenting a social, biological, or legal status? Boszormenyi-Nagy and Spark (1973) describe the invisible loyalties that have tradi-tionally linked family members and may, in under-ground fashion, continue to affect families. Colon (1978) acknowledged the dilemma faced by both parent and child, stating: ". . . the child's experience of biologi-cal-familial continuity and connection is a basic and fundamental ingredient of his sense of self, his sense of personal significance and his sense of identity" (p. 289). Furthermore, "persons who experience un-resolved emotional cut-offs from significant others are persons at high(er) risk emotionally and psychologi-cally than those who have resolved such cut offs" (p. 290).

Paradoxically men and women today give away or sell their reproductive "materials" (eggs and sperm) with little regard to the invisible loyalties they may have to the child(ren) born as a result of their "dona-tion." Although donation of ova is relatively recent, the donation of sperm without claiming parental rights or responsibilities has been a practice in the United States for over a century (Corea, 1985). In his poem, "To my Children, Unknown, Produced by Artificial Insemination," James Kirkup (1983) illustrates some of the mixed feelings of such a donation.

. . . All I know is,
As a "donor"
I received acknowledgement of

"the success of the experiment"
All boys.
Mission completed . . .

Could I care much less
About the offspring of my loins, sprigs
Of a poet's side-job? I feel your absence
only as I might feel amputated limbs . . . pp. 344–7

Traditionally most religions have held the purpose of marriage to be procreation and childrearing; for some religions this is also the sole purpose of sex. Religious tenants may restrict the infertile couple's access to reproductive technology, forcing them to choose between use of technology, childlessness, or finding another spouse. It may even mean choosing between the child (who affirms the purpose of mar-riage) or being observant of religious teachings. When sexual intercourse is confined to reproduction, cou-ples may need to reconcile the meaning of sexual activity with religious teachings.

Social policy and legal issues regarding sexuality and reproductive technologies are part of an ongoing debate. Owing to lack of well-defined policy and legal definitions, infertile couples exist in an atmosphere in which policy is determined in a piecemeal fashion by medicine, available technologies, insurance compa-nies, and the availability of adoptable children. As the process of policy ad libitum continues, the meaning and value of sexuality, marriage, and parenting con-tinue to evolve. It is apparent that the entire nature of our society has been and will be changed.

For the infertile couple, an important part of the complex developmental process is reworking their value system to incorporate the new realities of their life. It means an honest appraisal and acceptance of their altered circumstances and an integration of those altered realities into their philosophy of life and their value system. The current reality of reproduction requires infertile couples to restructure their beliefs and values about sexuality and reproduction in order to create definitions of manhood, womanhood, and parent-hood that affirm sexuality and validate sexual inter-course as valuable in and of themselves, regardless of their role in reproduction.

Sexuality and Parenting After Infertility

Recognition of these value dilemmas and their impact on sexual meanings in the family is an important first step in the transition to parenthood that most infertile couples eventually will take. From satisfactory perfor-mance of the basic human act of sexual intercourse to a discussion of values and meanings within the family to the growth and development of healthy children and families may seem a gigantic leap. In actuality, it is not. The concept of parental sexual activity and parental values influencing family and child devel-opment is not new. What is new is looking at infertility as a detour in the development of the family, a detour that influences the subsequent growth and health of the family and children. Furthermore, looking at the impact of infertility on family development provides an excellent example of the many levels on which the family operates.

2. SEXUAL BIOLOGY AND HEALTH: Sexual Hygiene

Sex and sexuality have a different meaning for the family with a history of infertility. Instead of meaning intimacy, closeness, sharing, and caring, sex is often a memory of what the couple tried to make and could not. This is exemplified in a story about stillbirth and childlessness, "First Born," by Maeve Brennan (1975).

> There seemed to be no end to the damage—even the house looked bleak and the furniture poor and cheap. . . . He was beginning to fear that Delia had turned against him. He had visions of awful scenes and strains in the future, a miserable life. He wished they could go back to the beginning and start all over again, but the place where they had stood together, where they had been happy, was all trampled over and so spoiled that it seemed impossible ever to make it smooth again. And how could they even begin to make it smooth with this memory, which they should have shared, standing like an enemy between them and making enemies out of them. He would not let himself think of the baby . . . He wanted Delia as she used to be. He wanted the girl who would never have struck at him, or spoken roughly to him. He was beginning to see there were things about her that he had never guessed at and that he did not want to know about. (p. 178)

When the members of the family are not biologically linked or do not share common histories, there are often questions about identity. The child's desire to have information about his genetic history may create identity issues in other family members: parents, siblings, grandparents (Snowden & Mitchell, 1983). There is also the question of the child's right to know his or her genetic heritage versus the birthparent or donor's right to privacy which may challenge parental beliefs about secrecy and honesty. Blum (1983) states, "The boundaries between who is the real parent and who is the real child, between reality and fantasy, may be blurred where reality has been validated or anchored in fantasies and where familial secrecy surrounds adoption" (p. 145).

Understandably, these issues often surface during stages of individuation and differentiation as the son or daughter gains sexual maturity and a separate and mature sense of self. The child's blossoming sexuality may be a bitter reminder of what the parent could not do or it may become a covert opportunity to vicariously live out reproductive fantasies. With the child's attempts at individuation, anxiety may increase as the parent recognizes his or her need to establish a new sense of self or to deal with conflicts in the marriage that were kept underground. Conflict may also surface as a result of the parent's feeling that the child is still "indebted" to him or her as a result of sacrifices made to have the child.

Parents may attempt to sabotage the child's passage into adulthood by denying information about sexual functioning and birth control, by failing to transmit healthy meanings about sexuality (e.g., sex is not shameful), or by discussing sex purely in a clinical or closed fashion. Triseloitis (1973) found that in families in which secrecy and evasiveness about adoption were common, other issues were also avoided: ". . . parents' difficulty over talking to [their children] about their adoption [was connected] with the parents' atti-

tude towards their childlessness, their marital life, to illegitimacy, and sex in general" (p. 46). Children, sensing their parents' discomfort with the topic, may interpret the discomfort as a message that sex is wrong or at least someting the parent does not feel happy about when reminded of it. Parents unable to share their history or unable to build new and positive memories upon the old ones leave a difficult legacy about sex to their much wanted children.

The interaction patterns and the history of the family may result in different patterns of adjustment to parenthood. A continuum of possible outcomes is: child-centered/overprotective parenting; secure/conscientious parenting; and neglecting/abusive parenting. All outcomes are possible for all families, but families with a history of infertility may be more at risk for certain parenting patterns.

Some parents with a history of infertility have reworked their own identity to see themselves primarily as parents. Barragan (1976) concluded that developmental defects in the family, such as infertility, resulted in a child-focused family pattern that hinders the growth of the family. The result is a closed and rigid system with inflexible boundaries and proscribed rules of behavior for both parents and children. By focusing on the long-awaited child, past conflicts and uncomfortable memories can be avoided.

Levy (1966) found that a mother's reproductive history, when troubled, affected her parenting, making her ". . . more apprehensive and protective" than other mothers. The result is parental overprotection or infantilization of their children.

Calef (1972) concluded that infertility and child abuse were manifestations of hostility on the part of parents toward their children. This hostility may be due to the idealization of parenthood or the anticipated and desired child, the limited rewards of parenting in comparison to the large investment of the infertile couple, or any number of other factors.

It is important to note that the legacy of infertility may have either a positive or negative impact on the family's subsequent adjustment to parenthood. The sexual health of the couple, all too often overlooked, is a fundamental factor in the establishment of a healthy foundation for all family members and for healthy parenting.

Conclusion

All too often the sexual disturbances of infertile couples, whatever the magnitude, are avoided or overlooked by the couple or their caregivers. These disturbances may, and often do, affect the couple's sexual attitudes, sexual functioning, and subsequent parenting, as well as the psychosexual development of their children.

It is essential, therefore, for caregivers to respect the **couple's sexual health and to be alert to potential problems. When necessary they should provide early education, intervention, and treatment or appropriate referrals and resources for the couple. Couples and their caregivers must be ever mindful and protective of the long-term sexual health of the couple and not** become focused solely on current medical treatment. Caregivers can help couples to accommodate infertility treatments in their sexual relationship by showing their own willingness to discuss sex with the couple and by not colluding with the notion that parenthood is a panacea that will cure all difficulties: past, present, and future.

It is important for the professional not to overlook the healthy sexual functioning of all members of the family with a history of infertility. The sexual health and pleasure of the couple and individual partners need not be relinquished for the desired child. Nor should the sexual health and development of the child be impaired by a legacy of sacrificed sexual functioning or distorted sexual values and meanings. It is, therefore, incumbent upon both couples and professionals to acknowledge and address the long-term impact infertility may have on a couple's subsequent parenting and family development while valuing the couple's sexual health during the short-term treatment of infertility.

Acknowledgements

Special thanks to professor James Maddock, Ph.D., and Professor Emeritus Gerhard Nueback, Ph.D., both of the Department of Family Social Science, University of Minnesota, St. Paul. I extend special thanks also to Debra Pysno.

References

Barragan, M. (1976). The child-centered marriage. In P.J. Guerin (Ed.), *Family Therapy: Theory and Practice*, New York: Gardner Press, Inc.

Bell, J.S. (1981). Psychological problems among patients attending an infertility clinic. *Journal of Psychosomatic Research, 25*, 1–3.

Berger, D.M. (1980). Impotence following the discovery of azoospermia. *Fertility & Sterility, 34* (2), 154–156.

Blum, H.P. (1983). Adoptive parents: generative conflict and generational continuity. *Journal of the Psychoanalytic Study of the Child, 38*, 141–163.

Boszormenyi-Nagy, I. & Spark, G.M. (1973). *Invisible Loyalties*. New York: Bruner/Mazel.

Brennan, M. (1975). The eldest child. In S. Cahill (Ed.) *Women and Fiction*. New York: New American Library.

Calef, V. (1972). Infertility of parents to children: Some notes on infertility, child abuse, and abortion. *International Journal of Psychoanalytic Psychotherapy, 10* (1), 76–96.

Cohen, M. (1983). Trying-to-conceive poem #4. In M.D. Cohen (Ed.), *An Ambitious Sort of Grief*. Mesquite: Ide House.

Colon, F. (1978). Family ties and child placement. *Family Process, 17*, 289–312.

Corea, G. (1985). *The Mother Machine*. New York: Harper & Row.

Debrovner, C.H. & Shubin-Stein, R. (1976). Sexual problems associated with infertility. *Medical Aspects of Human Sexuality, 10*, (1), 161–162.

Elstein, M. (1975). Effect of infertility on psychosexual function. *British Medical Journal, 3*, 296–299.

Kaufman, S.A. (1969). Impact of infertility on the marital and sexual relationship. *Fertility & Sterility, 20*, (3), 380–383.

Kirkup, J. (1983). To my children unknown, produced by artificial insemination. In R. Graziana (Ed.), *The Naked Astronaut: Poems on Birth and Birthdays*. London: Faber & Faber.

Kraft, A.D., Palombo, J., Mitchell, D., Dean, C., Meyers, S. & Schmidt, A.W. (1980). The psychological dimensions of infertility. *American Journal of Orthopsychiatry, 50* (4), 618–628.

Leader, A., Taylor, P.J., & Daniluk, J. (1984). Infertility: Clinical and psychological aspects. *Psychiatric Annals, 14* (6), 461–467.

Levie, L.H. (1962). The indications for homologous artificial insemination. *International Journal of Fertility, 7* (1), 37–42.

Levy, D.M. (1966), *Maternal Overprotection*. New York: W.W. Norton & Co.

Maddock, J. (1983). Sex in the family system. In J.W. Maddock, G. Neubeck, & M.B. Sussman (Eds.), *Human Sexuality and the Family*. New York: Haworth Press.

Mahlstedt, P.P. (1985). The psychological component of infertility. *Fertility & Sterility, 43* (3), 335–346.

Mai, F.M. (1971). Interesting sexual cases: Psychogenic infertility. *Medical Aspects of Human Sexuality, 5* (7), 26–32.

Reddick, D.H. (1982). Sexual dysfunction: cause and result of infertility. *The Female Patient, 7*, 45–48.

Rosenfeld, D.L. & Mitchell, E. (1979). Treating the emotional aspects of infertility: counseling services in an infertility clinic. *American Journal of Obstetrics and Gynecology, 135* (2), 177–180.

Rudkin, D. (1974). *Ashes*. New York: Samuel French, Inc.

Rutherford, R.N., Klemer, R.H., Banks, A.L. & Coburn, W.A. (1979). Psychogenic infertility—from the male viewpoint. *Pacific Medicine and Surgery, 22* (1), 255–267.

Scharff, D.E. (1976). Sex is a family affair: Sources of discord and harmony. *Journal of Sex and Marital Therapy, 2* (1), 17–31.

Snowden, R. & Mitchell, G.D. (1983). *The Artificial Family: A Consideration of Artificial Insemination by Donor*. London: Counterpoint Books.

Strindberg, A. (1958). The Father from *Three Plays by August Strindberg*. London: Penguin Books.

Toffler, A. (1970). *Future Shock*. New York: Random House.

Triseliotis, J. (1973). *In Search of Origins: The Experiences of Adopted People*. Boston: Beacon Press.

Walker, H.E. (1978). Psychiatric aspects of infertility. *Urologic Clinics of North America, 5* (3), 481–8.

Zimmerman, S.L. (1982). Alternatives in human reproduction for involuntary childless couples. *Family Relations, 31*, 233–241.

Demystifying Menopause

Judith Willis

Judith Willis is editor of the FDA Drug Bulletin, *a periodical for health professionals.*

Generations past called it "change of life." Today we're more apt to call it what it is: menopause. Yet our understanding of this change in a woman's childbearing status may still be clouded by myth and mystification.

Natural menopause is the end of menstruation and childbearing capability that occurs in most women somewhere around age 50. Today women can expect to live about a third of their lives after menopause.

Technically, the term "menopause" refers to the actual cessation of menstrual periods. When a woman has not had a period for a year, then the date of her last menstrual period is retrospectively considered the date of her menopause. However, the term "menopause" has come to be used in a general sense in place of the more proper terms, "climacteric" or "peri-menopause," which encompass the years immediately preceding and following the last menstrual period.

To cut through some of the myth and mystery surrounding the hormonal changes that accompany menopause, it is necessary first to understand what happens in the cycle of a normally menstruating woman.

The menstrual cycle, averaging 28 days, is divided into two phases. The first is called the follicular, or pre-ovulatory, phase and lasts 10 to 17 days. The second is the luteal, or post-ovulatory, phase lasting 13 to 15 days (see illustration).

CHANGING CYCLE

Usually sometime in a woman's early to mid 40s — two to eight years before actual menopause — her menstrual cycle begins changing. Notably, levels of hormones such as estrogen, produced by the ovaries, decrease; ovulation (release of eggs from the ovaries) stops or becomes more infrequent; and the pattern of the menstrual cycle changes.

Initially this may mean heavier and/or more frequent periods. Later, periods may be scantier and less frequent. Lack of ovula-tion may cause some light bleeding or spotting between periods. However, not all women follow this pattern exactly. Some may experience simply a wide variability in the time and quantity of flow, and a few may have little or no change in menstrual cycle. For some women, the unpredictability of menstrual pattern changes is unsettling because social activities can no longer be planned around a specific cycle, and there is no period due date to help determine pregnancy status. And indeed, because most women continue to ovulate at least in some cycles, pregnancy is possible until a woman has actually passed menopause. In fact, in some cultures where women bear many children, it is not uncommon for a woman to give birth to her last child and never menstruate again.

In the vast majority of cases, menstrual irregularities in the years before menopause are simply manifestations of the normal transition in the woman's hormonal status. Sometimes, if these irregularities cause too many problems or if a woman's doctor suspects that the uterine lining is not being shed completely during menstruation as happens during a normal period, the doctor may suggest treatment with a synthetic progesterone, called a progestin, to make the cycle more regular. In cases of extremely heavy bleeding, the doctor may recommend surgery

The age at which a woman has her last period is not known to be related to race, body size, or her age when she began to menstruate. The average age for menopause in American women is 50 to 52. But it is not abnormal for it to occur several years earlier or later. Some studies show that women who have had many children reach menopause earlier. And smokers may experience menopause an average of one to two years earlier than nonsmokers.

Even after menopause, women's bodies continue to produce estrogen, but far less of the hormone is made in the ovaries. Most postmenopausal estrogen is produced in a process in which the adrenal gland makes precursors of estrogen, which are then converted by stored fat to estrogen. However, far less estrogen is produced in this manner than is produced in the ovaries before menopause.

Reprinted from *FDA Consumer,* Vol. 22, No. 6, July/August 1988, pp. 24-27.

HOT FLASHES

*T*he most common symptom of menopause, the hot flush or flash, may begin before a woman has stopped menstruating and may continue for a couple of years after menopause. Although it is known that the hot flash (or "vasomotor flush," as doctors sometimes call it) is related to decreased estrogen levels, exactly how this occurs is not completely understood.

Many women describe the hot flash as an intense feeling of heat. Some say it actually feels like the temperature in the room has risen. Most commonly the sensation starts in the face, neck or chest and may extend to other parts of the body. It is usually accompanied by perspiration and may last a few seconds to several minutes. Increased heart rate and finger temperature have been documented during hot flashes.

About half of the women who have hot flashes visibly blush or have a patchy reddish flush of the face, neck and chest. For some women, the feeling of heat is followed by a feeling of being chilled. The hot flash may be particularly disturbing when it occurs during sleep. This problem, often involving profuse sweating, can awaken the women and is credited for much of the insomnia sometimes associated with menopause.

Up to 75 percent to 85 percent of women have hot flashes, but less than half of all women experiencing a natural menopause have symptoms severe enough to warrant medication. Obese women tend to have a lower incidence of hot flashes, possibly because they have higher levels of estrogen, converted from stored fat.

Many women find they can cope with hot flashes by dressing in layers that can be removed, wearing natural fabrics, drinking cold rather than hot beverages, keeping rooms cooler, and sleeping with fewer blankets.

ESTROGEN REPLACEMENT

*F*or women who cannot get sufficient relief without drugs, hormone replacement therapy may be prescribed. The length of time that a woman is advised to continue taking hormones may vary from several months to several years, depending on her symptoms.

Often abbreviated ERT, estrogen replacement therapy may relieve at least two other postmenopausal problems related to lower estrogen levels: urogenital atrophy and osteoporosis. The first of these involves both the vagina and bladder. The vagina becomes foreshortened, thins, and lubricates less efficiently. Itching, burning and dryness may result. Intercourse may become painful and vaginal infections more frequent. A similar tissue thinning occurs in the bladder, sometimes resulting in urinary discomfort, which may include the sudden and/or frequent need to urinate.

Osteoporosis involves loss of bone mass. It occurs in the elderly of both sexes, but is particularly common in fair-skinned, short, thin women. Smoking is an additional risk factor. It is estimated that 25 of every 100 white women over 60 suffer spinal fractures as a result of osteoporosis.

Although osteoporosis is by no means a universal outcome of menopause, some estimates say that 60 percent of untreated white women will develop some symptoms. In addition to ERT, weight-bearing exercise and sufficient calcium intake — particularly if begun years *before* menopause — may help prevent the bone loss associated with this condition.

Other symptoms experienced by some menopausal women that are probably related to lower estrogen levels include joint pains and sensations of tingling, prickling or creeping of the skin.

Estrogen therapy can be taken in several different dosage forms: vaginal creams, oral tablets, transdermal patches (by which the drug is slowly absorbed through the skin), and intramuscular injection. The first three are the most common dosage forms. The vaginal cream is usually given to relieve local problems of the vagina and bladder.

Although many women report a lessening of symptoms such as headaches and depression when they take estrogen, studies have not consistently shown these to be related to hormone changes. Some believe that these symptoms may be more a byproduct of other factors, such as life changes that a woman may be going through around the age of 50, preconceived and possibly erroneous ideas of what menopause may be like, and a woman's response to society's undervaluation of aging women.

In any case, because of the rare but serious adverse effects associated with estrogen use, ERT would not be considered medically appropriate for other symptoms of lowered estrogen in the absence of hot flashes, urogenital atrophy, or the potential for osteoporosis.

ADDING PROGESTIN

*T*he most serious adverse effect of non-contraceptive estrogen use is a higher risk of endometrial cancer (cancer of the inner lining of the uterus). For a number of years after this relationship was established in the mid-70s, ERT fell into some disfavor.

In the last few years, the use of ERT has again been on the rise, with doctors increasingly prescribing a progestin in the last 10 to 13 days of each estrogen cycle to prevent endometrial hyperplasia (abnormal increase in endometrial cells), a presumed precursor of cancer. It should be noted that FDA has not yet added this use to progestin labeling and is presently evaluating data about both progestins' possible protective effects against endometrial cancer and the possible but unknown cardiovascular risk, which may include an adverse effect on cholesterol.

Postmenopausal women who are on estrogen/progestin therapy may experience some menstrual-like bleeding (although it is usually far lighter than a normal menstrual period). For this reason, some women do not like to take progestins.

The weight of evidence from scientific studies is that there is not a higher incidence of breast cancer in women who take estrogen. However, women who have had breast cancer should not take ERT (except in cases where it is part of cancer treatment), because some tumors are dependent on estrogen for their growth. Others for whom estrogen is contraindicated are those who have a known or suspected estrogen-dependent tumor, may be pregnant, have undiagnosed abnormal genital bleeding, active thrombophlebitis (blood clots) or clotting disorders, or have previously had these when given estrogen.

Since there are some women with a variety of conditions for whom ERT may not be the best choice, the benefits and risks of ERT should be weighed carefully by each woman and her physician.

Less serious side effects of ERT include enlarged and tender breasts, nausea, skin discoloration, water retention, weight gain, headache, and heartburn.

A possibly beneficial side effect of estrogen is that it may raise the levels of the desirable kind of cholesterol known as high-

Hormone Activity During Menstrual Cycle

This drawing describes hormone activity during the menstrual cycle. The hypothalamus (the part of the brain that regulates many basic body functions) and the pituitary (a gland adjacent to the brain that secretes hormones regulating growth and the activity of other glands) are involved in the beginnings of the follicular phase.

The hypothalamus produces gonadotropin-releasing hormone (GRH), which stimulates the pituitary to release two gonadotropins– follicle-stimulating hormone (FSH) and luteinizing hormone (LH). FSH stimulates the development of follicles (sacs that hold the eggs) in the ovary. These follicles produce estrogen.

One follicle becomes dominant, increasing its estrogen production to aid in the maturation of the egg. In response to the estrogen, the endometrium (lining of the uterus or womb) thickens. The estrogen also goes to the pituitary resulting in a midcycle surge of LH. Ovulation–the release of the egg from the follicle–follows. The LH also transforms the ruptured follicle into the corpus luteum (tissue mass necessary to maintain pregnancy).

As the luteal phase begins, the corpus luteum produces both estrogen and progesterone. The progesterone makes the lining of the womb more receptive to the implanting egg. Progesterone also prevents the pituitary from releasing any more gonadotropins and halts further follicular growth. If conception does not occur, the corpus luteum disintegrates and the thickened lining of the womb is shed in menstruation.

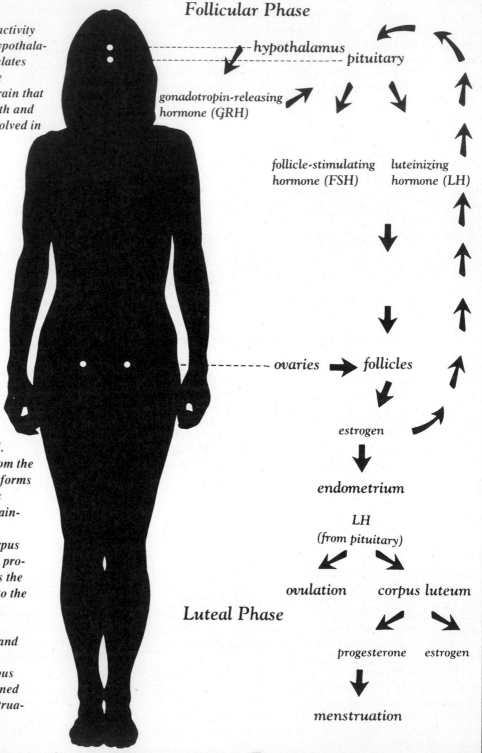

Follicular Phase

hypothalamus — pituitary

gonadotropin-releasing hormone (GRH)

follicle-stimulating hormone (FSH)   luteinizing hormone (LH)

ovaries → follicles

estrogen

endometrium

LH (from pituitary)

ovulation   corpus luteum

Luteal Phase

progesterone   estrogen

menstruation

Terms Your Doctor May Use When Discussing Menopause

Arthralgia – pain in a joint; experienced by some women during climacteric.

Breakthrough bleeding – any visible blood when not expected.

Climacteric – the years leading up to and following the last menstrual period. Also called "peri-menopause."

DUB – dysfunctional uterine bleeding; excessive and/or unpredictable bleeding from the womb, not due to any abnormality, that frequently occurs in the few years before menopause.

Dyspareunia – difficult or painful sexual intercourse.

Endometrium – lining of the uterus (womb).

FSH – follicle-stimulating hormone; stimulates development of sacs that hold the eggs.

GnRH – gonadotropin-releasing hormone; stimulates the release of FSH and LH.

Hysterectomy – surgical removal of the uterus (womb).

LH – luteinizing hormone; stimulates the release of the egg from the sac.

Leiomyoma – also called a fibroid; a non-cancerous growth in the womb that occurs in 20 percent to 25 percent of women before menopause and causes no symptoms in most women.

Menorrhagia – heavy menstrual bleeding and excessively long periods.

Myomectomy – surgical removal of fibroids from the uterus.

Oligomenorrhea – infrequent menstruation with diminished flow.

Oophorectomy – surgical removal of the ovaries, sometimes called castration.

Paresthesia – sensation of tingling, prickling or creeping of the skin; experienced by some women during climacteric.

Withdrawal bleeding – "planned" bleeding while on a medication that occurs during the hormone-free period of a cycle or after progestin has been added to a continuous estrogen cycle.

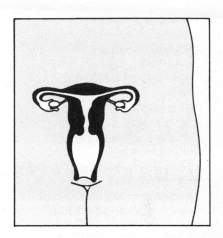

density lipoproteins (HDLs). (See "Knowing Your LDLs from Your HDLs" in the November 1987 *FDA Consumer.*) Scientists think that postmenopausal women who take estrogens may have added protection against heart disease. However, when progestins are added, this effect may be canceled out.

The form of progestin most often prescribed for use with ERT, medroxyprogesterone (brand names Provera, Amen, Curretab and others), seems to only slightly lower HDL levels. ERT, both with and without added progestins, lowers total cholesterol. In contrast to oral contraceptives, which use a higher dose of hormones, ERT appears not to influence blood pressure in any significant way.

Some women who cannot take estrogens can receive a certain degree of relief from hot flashes by taking a progestin alone. But this hormone does not reverse urogenital atrophy, may increase inappropriate hair loss or gain, and may lead to abnormal bleeding.

If it is not advisable for a woman to take an estrogen or a progestin, a doctor may prescribe Bellergal-S, a combination of phenobarbital, ergotamine and belladonna alkaloids, which FDA

has approved for relieving hot flashes. While not specifically approved for hot flashes, clonidine (Catapres and others), a heart drug, is sometimes prescribed for this purpose, and studies show that it gives some relief.

Doctors may also prescribe other drugs for relief of symptoms such as insomnia, headache and depression. FDA has noted that at least one product is being marketed over-the-counter for the relief of "tension, irritability, and stress headache during menopause." The agency is investigating the claims of this product, which contains acetaminophen (the active ingredient in Datril, Tylenol, Panadol and others) and an antihistamine (an ingredient approved for OTC use in allergy, cold, and sleep-aid preparations).

As the proportion of women nearing menopause increases with the advancing age of "baby boomers," it is likely that more attention will be paid to the interests of menopausal women. This focus may provide impetus for a more complete scientific unraveling of the mysteries surrounding this stage of life, so that women may deal with it on a factual basis and be free to live the latter third of their lives in the fullest manner possible.

Sharp Rise in Rare Sex-Related Diseases

Warren E. Leary

Special to The New York Times

WASHINGTON, July 13—In a development all but obscured by the surge in such major sexually transmitted diseases as syphilis and chlamydia, cases of some little known but worrisome venereal diseases have also increased.

The increases have surprised specialists, who had expected a decline because of concern about AIDS. Among the better-known venereal diseases, the number of syphilis cases is creeping up after five years of decline and gonorrhea strains that resist antibiotics represent a growing proportion of the 800,000 cases of that disease reported annually.

Less publicized has been the rise of formerly rare diseases, and health officials are expressing concern. Chancroid, for example, a bacterial disease that causes genital ulcers and enlarged lymph nodes, has increased tenfold in a decade, from a few hundred cases annually to more than 5,000 last year.

Other diseases, such as granuloma inguinale and lymphogranuloma venerium, have increased from a few reported cases annually to hundreds. And, as with all venereal diseases, the reported cases are thought to represent only a fraction of the true incidence.

DIFFICULT TO DIAGNOSE

Health officials believe the true numbers for the diseases are still relatively small, compared with a million cases of genital warts or a quarter-million cases of herpes each year. But the rarity of these conditions makes them harder to diagnose and treat, the officials said.

Dr. Shalom Z. Hirschman, director of the Mount Sinai center for the treatment of sexually transmitted diseases in New York City, said recognizing even common sex-related diseases was difficult for doctors who are not specialists because there are so many diseases and the early signs can be so subtle.

Among the less-known diseases are these:

•Chancroid, a bacterial disease that causes genital ulcers and enlarged lymph nodes in the groin. It can be treated with antibiotic injections and pills, but this can be complicated because of a tendency for the bacterium to develop antibiotic resistance.

•Granuloma inguinale, a bacterial condition that causes ulcers in the genital and rectal areas and that responds well to antibiotic treatment.

•Lymphogranuloma venerium, a disease caused by a strain of chlamydia organism that can cause rectal infections, inflammation, fever and enlarged lymph nodes in the groin. The condition responds to tetracycline.

13 MILLION CASES A YEAR

Any increase in the more than 50 diseases and syndromes classified as a sexually transmitted disease, or STD, is of concern because these conditions, even excluding AIDS, already account for more than 13 million cases and 7,000 deaths annually, according to the United States Public Health Service.

"The rare diseases coming back are symptoms of all STD's regaining a foothold on the population, and of the huge resurgence of STD's in general," said Wendy J. Wertheimer, director of public and government affairs for the American Social Health Association, a private group based in Palo Alto, Calif., that has battled sexual diseases for decades.

The Federal Government will spend $65 million this year on programs and studies against sexually transmitted diseases, and perhaps $40 million more on research, Ms. Wertheimer said. She called this an inadequate response to diseases that cost society $4 billion a year.

The current spread of diseases associated with unprotected sexual acts and promiscuity is especially alarming to health officials because of the associated heightened risk of the spread of AIDS.

Not only does such sexual behavior increase the chances that a person will be exposed to the AIDS virus, but research also suggests that some of these diseases, particularly those that cause blistering and ulcers, may increase the chance that the AIDS virus can find a pathway into the body during sex with an infected partner.

SEX-FOR-DRUGS PROSTITUTION

Dr. Ward Cates, director of the division of sexually transmitted diseases at the Centers for Disease Control in Atlanta, said health officials believe the rising incidence of these diseases is associated with increased sex-for-drugs prostitution and the diversion of local venereal disease control efforts to combat the threat of acquired immune deficiency syndrome.

When AIDS emerged as a major problem, several experts said, many local health departments turned to existing sex disease specialists and facilities to combat it, often providing no new people or money. Responding to the rise in conventional sex-related diseases, some departments are now putting more resources back into that battle, they added.

"It's tough to see something like syphilis increasing after years of decline, particularly in light of the drop seen in the gay male community connected with precautions against AIDS," Dr. Cates said. "But the rates among heterosexuals are rising slowly to cancel out these gains."

New Worries on Sexually Transmitted Disease

Some major forms of venereal disease, such as syphilis and chlamydia have increased dramatically in the United States in recent years. But other sexually transmitted diseases, once extremely rare, are also on the rise. Among them are chancroid, granuloma inguinale and lymphogranuloma venerium. The estimates of annual new infections are from the Federal Centers for Disease Control.

Disease	Symptoms	Treatment
Chlamydia More than 4 million new infections	Urinary tract, rectal or vaginal infections; can cause pelvic inflammatory disease in women, leading to infertility. Can be asymptomatic.	Long-term tetracycline regimen
Gonorrhea 1.8 million	Irritation, discharge, painful urination. Can promote pelvic inflammatory disease in women.	Penicillin or other antibiotics
Cytomegalovirus More than 1 million	Usually none. People with impaired immune systems may develop gastrointestinal problems or blindness; newborns may suffer retardation or death.	None approved in U.S.
Genital warts 1 million	Warts, sometimes painful, on genital organs or rectum. Virus that causes them has been linked to cancer.	Surgical, chemical or cryogenic removal
Genital herpes Up to 500,000	Often asymptomatic. Can cause genital blisters and malaise. In newborns, can cause blindness, hearing problems and death.	Acyclovir, in capsule or ointment form, can suppress symptoms.
Hepatitis B 200,000	Can be asymptomatic. Virus can cause short-term liver inflammation or chronic diseases including cirrhosis and liver cancer.	None. Vaccine can prevent infection.
Syphilis 85,000	Can produce sores but is frequently asymptomatic. Can damage heart, nervous system, brain and other organs. Can cause stillbirth or birth defects.	Highly responsive to antibiotics
Chancroid Up to 10,000	Genital ulcers; enlarged lymph nodes, often painful, in the groin.	Antibiotics
Lymphogranuloma venerium More than 1,000	Genital or rectal infection, enlarged lymph nodes in the groin, pain, fever and inflammation.	Tetracycline
Granuloma inguinale Up to 100	Genital or rectal ulcers. More common in South and Southwest.	Antibiotics

The resurgence of sex-related diseases appears to have started in late 1985, Dr. Cates said. The number of reported syphilis cases nationally has increased 30 percent from 1985 to more than 86,000 in 1987, and is still increasing.

While almost 60 percent of all syphilis

Their rarity makes them harder to diagnose and treat.

cases and 80 percent of the increase were reported from South Florida, California and New York City, 25 of the 49 other reporting areas also had increases, the disease centers reported.

RISK OF AIDS INCREASED

The greatest relative increases in syphilis and other such diseases has occurred among young women and heterosexual men, particularly inner-city black and Hispanic populations.

But experts say the increase in venereal diseases has occurred to some degree in all groups of sexually active men and women.

While there are no vaccines to prevent sexually transmitted diseases other than hepatitis B, most can be cured with no ill effects if detected and treated early.

More than five million new cases of chlamydia occur each year in the United States, according to the disease control centers. But this infection, which can lead to scarring, inflammation and infertility in women, goes largely unnoticed and untreated because it is often asymptomatic, specialists say.

Although there are therapies for most bacterial sex diseases, some can be difficult to treat, particularly in later stages when they may have caused organ damage. Gonorrhea and chancroid bacteria are examples of such organisms that present the added problem of developing resistance to antibiotics, said Dr. John LaMontagne, director of

the microbiology and infectious diseases program at the National Institute of Allergy and Infectious Diseases in Bethesda, Md.

While most bacterial diseases can be treated with a few days or a week of therapy, usually involving an injection

The increase is linked to sex-for-drugs prostitution.

and oral antibiotics, he said some are harder to get at because they hide, sometimes inside ordinary cells.

Among viral diseases, acyclovir is an effective drug for treating herpes lesions, but there is no cure for the millions of adults believed infected.

No treatment exists for human papilloma virus, which causes venereal warts and may be a factor in causing cervical, penile and rectal cancer. Early research indicates interferon, a natural immune system protein, may be effective against some genital warts and tests continue, Dr. LaMontagne said.

Reproduction

- **Pregnancy and Childbirth (Articles 20-23)**
- **Birth Control (Articles 24-30)**

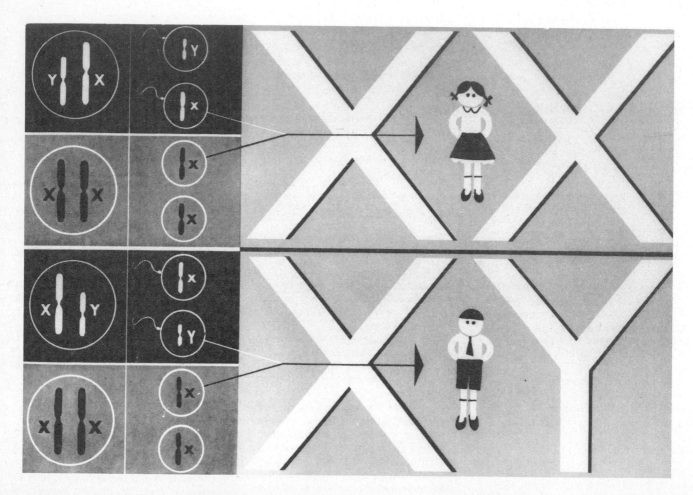

While human reproduction is as old as humanity, there are many aspects of it that are changing in today's society. Not only have new technologies of conception and childbirth affected the *how* of reproduction, but personal, social, and cultural forces have also affected the *who*, the *when*, and the *when not*. Abortion remains a fiercely debated topic, and legislative efforts for and against it abound. The teenage pregnancy rate in the United States is one of the highest in the Western world. The costs of teenage childbearing can be high for the parents, the child, and for society. Yet those who appear most able to bear the rising costs of parenthood—-upwardly mobile, dual-career couples—are choosing in ever-greater numbers to remain childfree. These contemporary trends in procreation constitute interesting and thought-provoking subject matter, and the future will undoubtedly produce more changes—technological, attitudinal, and socio-cultural—in traditional patterns of childbearing.

This section also addresses the issue of birth control. In light of the change in attitude toward sex for pleasure, birth control has become a matter of prime importance. Even in our age of sexual enlightenment, some individuals, possibly in the height of passion, fail to correlate "having sex" with pregnancy. Before sex can become safe as well as enjoyable, people must receive thorough and accurate information regarding conception and contraception, birth and birth control. In addition, it is even more crucial that individuals make a mental and emotional commitment to the use and application of the available information, facts, and methods. Only this can make every child a planned and wanted one.

Despite the relative simplicity of the above assertion, abortion, and even birth control, remain emotionally charged issues in American society. While opinion surveys indicate that most of the public supports family planning and abortion at least in some circumstances, individuals who seek abortions often face stigmatization. A recent Supreme Court decision has opened the door for new restrictions on abortion, while various religiopolitical groups posit and challenge basic definitions of human life, as well as the rights and responsibilities of women and men associated with sex, procreation, and abortion.

Many of the questions raised in this section about the new technologies of reproduction and its control are likely to remain among the most hotly debated issues for the remainder of this century. The very foundations of our pluralistic society may be challenged. We will have to await the outcome.

The first article in the *Pregnancy and Childbirth* subsection urges us to reframe America's problematic teenage pregnancy crisis as a sociocultural rather than a race problem. The second article explores the apparent unfairness associated with men's lack of legal rights regarding decisions about abortion or childbearing. Its conclusion may startle readers who had preconceived ideas about how a male writer would view his rights and responsibilities. The final two articles look at two very different childbearing-related topics: sex during pregnancy, and couples who voluntarily remain childfree. They strive,

however, to accomplish a similar end: permission-giving and normalization of these choices and behaviors.

The first article in the subsection on *Birth Control* focuses on the crisis in developing contraceptives and the misunderstandings surrounding birth control. The next selection deals with contraception for teens. The following article focuses on vasectomy, one of the most effective and least expensive methods of contraception available today. The last two articles in this subsection examine the future of contraception. "Pill Politics" focuses on the controversies surrounding RU 486, a product about which considerable moral questions have been raised. "A Failed Revolution" ponders the sorry state of contraception today: the promises of safe, reliable, accessible contraception still have not become reality. Whether due to failed contraception, non-use of contraception, or other factors, the need for abortion remains. The legal status of abortion is considered in the final two articles in this subsection, "Voting in Curbs and Confusion" and "Abortion: Right or Wrong?"

Looking Ahead: Challenge Questions

Is there hope for reducing teenage pregnancy and childbearing in this country? Why or why not?

Can you offer a better solution to the dilemmas raised in "His Sexuality, Her Reproductive Rights"? How do you feel about Newman's position?

What problems do you foresee for couples who cease sexual expression during late pregnancy due to misinformation and/or fear?

Why is choosing not to have children such an issue? Are attitudes changing? Explain.

What prevents more men and couples from utilizing vasectomy as a birth control method?

Is RU 486 a viable form of birth control? Will it ever be accepted in the United States?

What will facilitate a successful contraceptive revolution, making safe, reliable, inexpensive methods available to all?

What consequences do you foresee if the abortion restrictions predicted in this section become law?

■ TEEN-AGE PREGNANCY

The Case for National Action

FAYE WATTLETON

Faye Wattleton is president of Planned Parenthood Federation of America.

In 1983 a 25-year-old woman with a 9-year-old daughter gave the following testimony before Congress:

> In the tenth grade, my girlfriends and I were all sexually active, but none of us used birth control. I had hopes of a career and I wanted to go to college. One day my mother said, "Towanda, you're pregnant." I asked her how she knew. She said, "I can just tell."
>
> My mother wouldn't even consider abortion. I had nothing to say about a decision that would alter my entire life. A few weeks after the baby was born, my mother said, "You'll have to get a job." The only job I could get was in a bar.
>
> I spent two years dealing with the nightmare of welfare. Finally I went to the father of my child and asked him to take care of her while I went back to school. He agreed.
>
> I am now making some progress. I went to business school and I now have a job working in an office in Washington. But my life has been very difficult. . . . I had ambitions as a child, but my hopes and dreams were almost killed by the burden of trying to raise a child while I was still a child myself.

This young woman's story is relived around us every day. The United States has the dubious distinction of leading the industrialized world in its rates of teen-age pregnancy, teen-age childbirth and teen-age abortion. According to a study of thirty-seven developed nations published by the Alan Guttmacher Institute in 1985, the teen pregnancy rate in the United States is more than double the rate in England, nearly triple the rate in Sweden and seven times the rate in the Netherlands. Throughout the 1970s, this rate rose in the United States, while it declined in such places as England, Wales and Sweden. Each year, more than 1 million American teen-agers become pregnant; about half of these young women give birth.

Teen pregnancy is both cause and consequence of a host of social ills. The teen-agers likeliest to become pregnant are those who can least afford an unwanted child: those who are poor, those who live with one parent, those who have poor grades in school and those whose parents did not finish high school. As the National Research Council points out, teen mothers face "reduced employment opportunities, unstable marriages (if they occur at all), low incomes, and heightened health and developmental risks to the children. . . . Sustained poverty, frustration, and hopelessness are all too often the long-term outcomes." Compounding the tragedy is the fact that children of teen-age mothers are more likely to become teen parents themselves. The burden is felt by the entire society: The national costs of health and social service programs for families started by teen-agers amount to more than $19 billion a year.

Media accounts have tended to represent teen-age pregnancy as primarily a problem of the black community, and implicitly—or explicitly, as in the case of the 1986 CBS Special Report on the "vanishing" black family by Bill Moyers—they have attempted to blame the problem on the so-called degeneracy of the black family. Such distortions of fact are particularly dangerous because they coincide all too neatly with the insensitivity to blacks and the blame-the-victim ideology that the Reagan Administration so disastrously fostered.

High rates of teen pregnancy actually are as all-American as apple pie. Even when the figures for "nonwhite" teens were subtracted from the calculations, the rate of teen pregnancy in the United States in 1981 (83 per 1,000) far exceeded the teen pregnancy rates in all other major industrialized nations. In England and Wales, our closest competitors, the rate for teens of all races was just 45 per 1,000.

The fact of the matter is that teen-age pregnancy rates in the United States have a great deal more to do with class than they do with race. The majority of poor people in this country are white, and so are the majority of pregnant teen-agers. In a report published in 1986, the Guttmacher Institute examined interstate differences in teen pregnancy rates.

It found that the percentage of teens who are black is relatively unimportant as a determinant of overall state variations in teen-age reproduction. It is states with higher percentages of poor people and of people living in urban areas—whatever their race—that have significantly higher teen pregnancy and birth rates.

Teen pregnancy is as grave a problem within many black communities as are poverty and social alienation. One-third of all blacks, and one-half of all black children, live in poverty. And today the pregnancy rate among teens of color is double that of white teens. One of every four black children is born to a teen-age mother; 90 percent of these children are born to unwed mothers. Such patterns can only intensify the problems already facing the black community. Disproportionately poor, blacks are disproportionately affected by the social and economic consequences of teen-age pregnancy.

We need only look to other Western nations to recognize both the cause and the solutions to our teen pregnancy problem. American teens are no more sexually active than their counterparts in Europe; and teen-agers abroad resort to abortion far less often than do those in the United States. There is a major cause for our higher rates of teen pregnancy and childbirth: the fundamental discomfort of Americans with sexuality. Unlike other Western societies, we have not yet accepted human sexuality as a normal part of life. The result is that our children, and many adults as well, are confused, frightened and bombarded by conflicting sexual messages.

Most parents recognize their role as the first and most important sexuality educators their children will have, providing information and sharing family values from the time their children are born. Nevertheless, many parents are unable to talk with their children about such sensitive issues as sex and human relationships. Schools do not fill the gap. Only seventeen states and the District of Columbia mandate comprehensive sex education. As a result, many teen-agers are abysmally ignorant about their reproductive functions.

The mass media, particularly television, only exacerbate the problem. Many teen-agers spend more time in front of the television than they do in the classroom, and their sexual behavior in part reflects what they have learned from this thoroughly unreliable teacher. Nowhere is it more apparent than on television that America suffers from sexual schizophrenia: We exploit sex, and at the same time we try to repress it. Programs and advertisements bombard viewers with explicit sexual acts and innuendo. One study indicates that in a single year, television airs 20,000 sexual messages. Yet rarely is there any reference to contraception or to the consequences of sexual activity.

A substantial number of teens believe that what they see on television is a faithful representation of life. Many believe that television gives a realistic picture of pregnancy and the consequences of sex. And large numbers of teens say they do not use contraceptives because they are "swept away" by passion—surely a reflection of the romanticized view of sex that pervades the mass media.

Network executives, though they apparently have few qualms about exploiting the sexual sell twenty-four hours a day, have the hypocrisy to claim that good taste forbids them to carry ads for contraceptives. Some of the networks recently decided to accept condom ads, though not during prime time, and those ads promote condoms only as protection against AIDS, not against pregnancy. It should not surprise us, then, that America's youths are sexually illiterate, or that 67 percent of sexually active teens either never use contraceptives or use them only occasionally.

We have not failed to resolve this problem for lack of majority agreement on how to do it. A 1988 Harris public opinion survey done for Planned Parenthood found a strong consensus about both the severity of the teen pregnancy problem and about how to solve it:

§ Ninety-five percent of Americans think that teen-age pregnancy is a serious problem in this country, up 11 percent from 1985.
§ Seventy-eight percent of parents believe that relaxed discussions between parents and children about sex will reduce unintended teen-age pregnancy.
§ Eighty-nine percent endorse school sex education.
§ Eighty percent support school referrals of sexually active teens to outside family-planning clinics.
§ Seventy-three percent favor making contraceptives available in school clinics.

School-linked clinics that offer birth control as part of general health care are growing in number in many areas of the country. Community support and involvement are crucial to their development, to insure that the programs are consistent with community values and needs.

Clearly the vast majority of Americans, regardless of racial, religious or political differences, strongly supports the very measures that have proven so effective in reducing teen pregnancy rates in other Western nations. Unfortunately, an extremist minority in this country has an entirely different outlook on sexuality—a minority that has a level of influence out of all proportion to its size. Eager to cultivate the anti-family planning, antiabortion fringe, the Reagan-Bush Administration and its cohorts in Congress sought to whittle down Federal funds for domestic and international family planning, limit sex education in the schools, eliminate confidentiality for birth control and abortion services and block the development of school-linked clinics. These vocal opponents object to everything that has proven successful elsewhere in the industrialized world. Their one and only solution to the problem of teen-age pregnancy is, "Just say no!" But just saying no prevents teen-age pregnancy the way "Have a nice day" cures chronic depression.

There is nothing inherent in American life that condemns us permanently to having the highest teen pregnancy rate in the Western world—nothing that Sweden, England, France, the Netherlands and Canada have been able to do that we cannot.

Parents must talk with their children about all aspects of sexuality—openly, consistently and often—beginning in early childhood. Every school district in the country should provide comprehensive sex education, from kindergarten

3. REPRODUCTION: Pregnancy and Childbirth

through twelfth grade. Community groups need to support the development of school-linked health clinics. The media must present realistic, balanced information about relationships and the consequences of sex. Television, in particular, must end the restrictions on contraceptives advertising. Government—at the local, state and Federal levels—must live up to its obligation to eliminate any financial barriers to family-planning education and services and to foster a community environment in which our children can flourish and aspire to a productive and fulfilling life.

But we must also recognize that the teen pregnancy problem cannot be solved through sexuality education and family-planning services alone. If our efforts are to succeed, society must provide all our young people with a decent general education, tangible job opportunities, successful role models and real hope for the future.

It is only by placing such a comprehensive national agenda at the top of the priority list that our society can protect the creative and productive potential of its youth.

His Sexuality, Her Reproductive Rights

Richard Newman

Richard Newman is a poet working as an adjunct writing teacher at the New York Institute of Technology, Old Westbury, Long Island, NY.

Your lover on the phone is very excited. "Congratulations!" she says. "You're going to be a father! I just got back from the doctor and she tells me I'm pregnant. Isn't that great?" Your heart sinks. You want to scream, "What do you mean, 'Isn't that great?' " You want to tell her to have an abortion.

Or she calls and her voice is slow over the phone, and she has a hard time getting the words out. Finally, she tells you, "I'm pregnant." "Why so glum?" you ask elatedly. "That's wonderful!" She replies, "I want an abortion."

Or she calls and tells you she's already had an abortion. She says she feels guilty for not telling you first but she was afraid. You hang up screaming "Murderer!" into the phone.

Or she tells you she's pregnant and doesn't know what to do. Neither do you. This is the first time the subject has come up.

ABORTION: WHOSE RIGHTS?

These scenarios, each perfectly understandable in its own context, raise questions about the rights of both men and women in relation to the fetuses we create together. Can a man claim a fetus as half his? Can he say that if his lover aborts it against his will, she violated his bodily and reproductive rights? Or can he claim that if he does not want to have a child, she has no right to carry the pregnancy to term? On the other hand, can the woman claim that, since *she* carries the fetus and his body is no longer involved, the man's claims are irrelevant?

An important difference separates these two sets of claims. The man's claim assumes power over the body of the woman. Although his active participation in the reproductive process is

finished, he believes that his feelings about having children are enough to keep the woman from doing what she wants with her body. The woman's claim, however, involves no such power over the man. She merely states that since the sex act is over, he has no bodily and/or reproductive rights to exercise. She refuses to acknowledge his claim to power over her, and instead asserts her right to her own autonomy.

Women's liberation concerns precisely this right of women to their own independence without regard for patriarchal ideas of who, what or how women should be. Women's liberation, in other words, concerns woman-centeredness, or "gynocentry." In the situations described above, the woman's claim concerning her right to abortion is based on a woman-centered sexuality in which her relationship to her own body is more important than her relationship to the man. The man's claims grow out of an hierarchical sexuality in which the woman's body—because of her relationship to him—becomes an object over which he has control. Her body becomes a part of him the way anything we acquire becomes in some way a part of ourselves.

If we men want to redefine the nature of our reproductive and sexual relationships with women, we must look, not to the women, but to other men. From men comes the possibility of a male-centered, male-defined heterosexuality in which our relationships to ourselves and each other become primary. Developing these relationships should command our attention with some urgency because any hopes we have of real and complete male liberation depend on our ability to live our lives without recourse to the possession/oppression of a subservient other—the role into which we coerce the women of our culture.

The politics of abortion seem to me a good place to start defining this male-centered sexuality. This is because the issues concerning women's reproductive choice and men's role in the reproductive process ultimately involve

understanding the boundaries between male and female sexualities.

RELINQUISHING MALE PRIVILEGES

We can begin with what is probably a radical assumption in our culture, an assumption that we shouldn't have to mention at all: that women are fully adult human beings, fully capable of making responsible life decisions. They do this not only within the context of the female community but also, along with fully adult and fully capable men, within the context of the human species. Second, we can recognize a simple biological fact: men do not get pregnant. Because the physical processes of pregnancy, abortion and childbirth are experienced only by women, it is only common sense that the final decision to experience either childbirth or abortion should rest with no one but a pregnant woman. (Just imagine how unreasonable it would be if women decided when and whether men should undergo vasectomy operations.) I accept this right of women to reproductive choice as a fact inaccessible to argument; it simply is, and demands nothing more of me and other men than our full awareness and acknowledgement of this right. To the extent that we lack this awareness, or that we fail in our acknowledgement, we can not enter fully into egalitarian relationships with women.

The politics of abortion is a good place to start defining a male-centered sexuality.

Probably most men would agree with a woman's "right to choose," but I wonder how many of us understand fully the implications of what we are agreeing to.

The politics of reproduction in our culture are such that women have functioned primarily as baby machines without their having much, if any, control over when or whether this function should be performed. Even today, despite the relative availability of birth control, many women—for religious, economic, social or family reasons—have children they can't afford, don't want or shouldn't have all because "that's what women do." The patriarchal institution of monogamous marriage has "privileged" the reproductive aspect of female sexuality by essentially enslaving women to the "duty" of having a family. We have created the notion that a woman without a husband and children lives, by definition, an unfulfilled life. In effect, women acquire fulfillment in a patriarchal culture by prostituting themselves, offering their bodies as sexual and reproductive machines serving the needs of men.

Such a hierarchical relationship between ourselves and women has deep implications for how men perceive our sexuality and our role in reproduction. By presuming to insist that women's sexual biology exists to serve male needs, we have, in essence, confined our reproductive role to one of control. We also have made it virtually impossible, for both men and women, to separate erotic sex from reproductive sex.

In an essay entitled "Erotica and Pornography," Gloria Steinem observed that human beings are the only animals who engage in erotic sex, in sex as "a way of bonding differentness, discovering sameness, and communicating emotion" (1). She also makes the point that the yoking together of erotic sexuality and reproduction, and the insistence that the breaking of this yoke is somehow obscene and pornographic, constitutes a major strategy by which men use religious and political institutions to intimidate women into resisting women's liberation. If a woman, having conceived, can decide without recourse to any authority but herself whether or not to carry her pregnancy to term, she is a woman free to determine the who, what, when, where, why and how of her own sexuality. Her sexuality, then, becomes a part of her whole identity, and she can, at her will, explore whatever other parts of herself she chooses. Her life becomes woman-centered and the patriarchal power of the male collapses.

When the courts of this country granted women the right to abortion, women gained a sexual freedom previously lacking in their lives. However, in our male-dominated society, what the King can grant the King can also take away. Presuming to grant women a right which is intrinsically theirs merely reinforces the same old attitudes about female sexuality. Even though male-

permitted abortion-on-demand allows women, married or not, a necessary option to unwanted pregnancy, it also gives men one more possible reason to insist that women make themselves sexually available to us. Further, if we don't like how they use this "privilege" we have "granted" them, we can take it away. For example, anti-abortionists use this strategy when they point to the rise in the number of teen-age abortions as a reason to make abortion against the law. The fact that the right to abortion can be challenged in court and its availability restricted by law indicates how little of our actual privilege men have relinquished.

Women's right to reproductive choice—if we men understand it fully—not only allows women freedom of sexual expression, both reproductive and erotic, it also leaves men with a minor biological role in the reproductive process. Full reproductive choice for women means they regain the control we previously enjoyed. If a woman, simply by having an abortion, can thwart a man's desire to have children, he loses a great deal of what men traditionally invest in having children to begin with.

Currently, male control of conception and childbirth functions to reinforce heterosexual notions of virility, self-worth and masculinity. Part of the traditional significance for men in the birth of a child is not only that we perpetuate ourselves, but that we *cause* it to happen. Take, for instance, the notion of "fathering" a son to carry on the family name, tradition or business. Also, it was common to blame the lack of a male child in the family on the wife's inability to produce one—as if her interference botched what the husband could, almost by himself, do all along. If women possess complete control over their reproductive biology—which unrestricted abortion on demand provides them—we men may perpetuate ourselves through the birth of a male or female child, but that self-perpetration takes place only by *permission* of the mother.

MALE-CENTERED HETEROSEXUALITY

Merely acknowledging the reality of the male role in reproduction and thereby relinquishing our perceived right to control the process, however, accomplishes little more than an inversion of the present situation. The injustice of men controlling the biology of reproduction will find no remedy in the injustice of women's control over our emotional investment in having children.

I think we men need to redefine our relationship to reproduction, both symbolically and physically. We need to find

a way of being sexual and reproductive that neither exploits others nor puts our sexual and reproductive fulfillment at the mercy of someone else's freedom of choice. We need to put ourselves—not the women (or other men) with whom we make love—at the center of our sexuality. Then we can begin to learn truly who we are as loving and vulnerable human beings.

To the degree that the primary power relationship in patriarchal society is between men and women, gay men, by virtue of their sexual choices, do not participate in one aspect of that relationship: they do not require/ask for the specifically sexual surrender of women. I do *not* mean that gay men, because they are gay, are not sexist. I do not mean that by definition relationships among gay men will not duplicate the sexual hierarchy of the dominant culture. Nor do I mean that the gay male community, simply by existing, subverts the connections between sexism and heterosexism. I *do* mean that relationships between gay men take place in a community which is defined by men in terms of men. Heterosexual men can begin to develop from this aspect of the gay male community a political/physical male-centered sexuality for ourselves that is analogous to the women-centered sexuality I discussed above. Because a male-centered sexuality asserts the primacy of our relationships with ourselves and other men, it will subvert the hierarchy of a heterosexuality organized around our possession and control of women.

Male heterosexual responsibility should begin with the realization that once we fertilize the egg— unless we have agreed beforehand with our partner on the consequences—what happens thereafter is beyond our control.

Probably the most common and easily identifiable aspect of sexist culture is the physical/sexual objectification of women by men. Such objectification is, however, an aspect of any sexual relationship. It is reasonable that bed partners like each other's bodies as bodies. A sexually defined power hierarchy reveals itself when the objectification becomes chronic and represents the entire relationship, or even just the entire sexual aspect of the relationship.

Of course, sexual objectification of men by men does not in and of itself avoid or subvert sexual hierarchies. A homosexual couple may fall quite conventionally into easily recognizable male ("dominant") and female ("submissive") roles. However, if it is the "idea" of the female which determines the hierarchical structure of the relationship, it is possible for each man to recognize himself, if only on a physical level, in the other. Since a chronic hierarchy can only be maintained by the denial of the basic sameness between the two lovers, such recognition will work to subvert the hierarchy.

Recognizing aspects of oneself in another human being and accepting that basic sameness as positive requires a certain amount of self-acceptance, of self-love. A male-centered sexuality will depend upon our claiming the primacy of our relationships with ourselves and other men. I can only love the man in other men if I love the man in me *as a man*. If this self-love becomes the basis for my life decisions, then my art, my science, politics, religion—everything I do, including my sexual activity, becomes an expression of my love for myself. My homo/autoeroticism gives my life its power, and I do not need to depend on someone else's surrender, male or female, to tell me who and what I am. A community in which the primary motivating principle of human action is self-love would honor non-hierarchical social arrangements. The integrity of its communal structure would depend on a constant awareness of, and fidelity to, the basic sameness of each of its members.

HETEROSEXUAL RESPONSIBILITY REDEFINED

Currently, male heterosexual responsibility usually consists of something like "don't get her pregnant unless you're ready to accept the consequences" (i.e., marry her, pay for the abortion). But women either get pregnant or they don't, *and we need to know what we're about if we take the chance that they might*. The basic assumptions are still the same. Since women exist as objects to fulfill male sexual and reproductive needs, traditional male heterosexual responsibility requires that, if we choose to use them, we maintain them properly.

Real male heterosexual responsibility requires that we be aware of and responsible for the consequences *for ourselves* of our own sexual activity, not the use to which we put women-as-objects. How many of us, for instance, can honestly say that before we became sexually involved with a woman we found out whether we agreed on what would happen if she got pregnant—*and then, based on that discussion, decided the extent to which we were willing to become physically involved with her.* I suggest this discussion as the very point at which male heterosexual responsibility starts.

That the physical facts of abortion and childbirth take place within an exclusively female community does not prevent men from having feelings and opinions about those facts. Nor should it prevent us from taking responsibility for what we think and feel. For instance, if a man who believes abortion is murder finds himself involved with a woman who explicitly says she will have an abortion should she become pregnant, that man has a responsibility to himself to avoid *completely* the possibility of her becoming pregnant.

Since he cannot question her right to an abortion, the moral dilemma if she gets pregnant is his, not hers. If she has an abortion because of his sexual involvement with her, he—according to his own ethic—implicates himself in a murder. Since he cannot hold the woman accountable for any beliefs but her own, the responsibility to say "no" is his. The same reasoning would apply to a man who does not want to have a child and a woman who does not believe in abortion.

Male heterosexual responsibility should begin with the realization that once we fertilize the egg—unless we have agreed beforehand with our partner on the consequences—what happens thereafter is beyond our control. We need to start with what we can control: the extent and nature of our heterosexual relationships.

For heterosexual men, the idea that we can and must control only our own participation in our sexual relationships has many implications. It implies a new way of thinking about ourselves that is in direct opposition to the general stereotype of men as people whose sexual responsibility hangs from our penises by a thread which breaks when we get hard.

It means we can tell a woman, "no, I don't want to fuck," out of fidelity to our own beliefs about abortion or our desire not to have children—not simply to avoid the fertilization of an egg.

It means that our choice of sexual partners and the character of our sexual relationships will be determined by our sexual biology (not a comfortable situation for anyone). One possible result is that men will discover a renewed interest in developing—for ourselves as well as our partners—truly safe and effective contraceptives, thereby rendering obsolete the question of abortion.

It means we can assert and explore the fullness of our own erotic selves by insisting that oral, anal and manual sex—or even non-genital intimacy such as massage—are not mere substitutes for or preludes to sexual intercourse. Rather, they are perfectly valid erotic acts in and of themselves.

Finally, it means that men will learn how true erotic fulfillment comes from within ourselves, as a result of understanding who we are, and not from controlling who does what to whom and how often.

REFERENCES

1. G. Steinem, "Erotica and Pornography," in *Outrageous Acts and Everyday Rebellions*. (Holt, Rinehart, & Winston, 1983).

SUGGESTED READING

R. Biale, *Women and Jewish Law*. (Shocken Books, 1984).

M. Daly, *Beyond God The Father*. (Beacon Press, 1973).

D. M. Feldman, *Marital Relations, Birth Control and Abortion in Jewish Law*. (Shocken Books, 1968).

E. Jackson & S. Persky (eds.), *Flaunting It!* (Pink Triangle Press, 1982).

K. Jay and A. Young (eds.), *Out of the Closets: Voices of Gay Liberation*.

E. Koltun, *The Jewish Woman*. (Schoken Books, 1976).

A. Rich, *On Lies, Secrets, and Silence*. (W. W. Norton & Company, 1979).

Yes, You Can

Taboos against sex during pregnancy are old-fashioned. Instead it can be a time of greater pleasure.

Elisabeth Bing

Elisabeth Bing, ACCE, was a cofounder of ASPO/Lamaze and is the author of numerous books on pregnancy and childbirth including Six Practical Lessons for an Easier Childbirth *(Bantam Books, 1977), a classic on psychoprophylaxis in childbirth, and* Making Love During Pregnancy *(Bantam Books, 1977) with Libby Colman.*

"The final three months I have experienced a heightening of sexual enjoyment. Whereas before, I could rate sexual experiences on perhaps a one (routine) to five (very passionate) scale of intensity (depending on my mood beforehand, my degree of fatigue, and the like), I would say that since the sixth month our sexual relations have maintained a higher plateau of intensity, regardless of mood or fatigue. Almost every time, I experience multiple (two or three) orgasms, which is not the norm for me. This is another reason, I'm certain, why we decided not to give up sex during the ninth month: Whatever feels good can't be bad.

"As for orgasms, I've had no fear of their hurting the fetus. I figure they are basically contractions and, if anything, they strengthen my muscles and are beneficial, not detrimental. If at the end of the ninth month, they encourage the baby to come, they don't make any difference one way or another.

"Paul and I certainly feel closer to each other now than ever . . . ."

The above quote is from a contemporary mother-to-be. And it's not unusual or improper. But attitudes toward sexuality and pregnancy have not always been so positive.

In the late 19th century, books were written on the nature of women. This nature, according to received wisdom, undermined a woman's good character, which as a result had to be continuously reinforced. Sexual activity in particular was thought to have pervasive physical and moral ill effects on women.

Authors of that period thought that sexual activity was fraught with unpleasant consequences for women and that it had particularly pernicious effects on their physical and emotional well-being during times of physical change, especially pregnancy. Writing in 1902 in the *Ladies' Guide to Health and Disease,* a man named Kellogg advised women to suspend sexual indulgence during pregnancy to benefit both themselves and their children. He claimed support from ancient medical writers, who called attention to the fact that practicing continence during gestation greatly mitigated the pains of childbirth.

If women rejected this line of reasoning, Kellogg had another to which they surely felt vulnerable. He thought that the "injurious influences upon the child of the gratification of the passions during the period when its character was being formed were undoubtedly much greater than is generally supposed. The punishment for the gratification of the passions during pregnancy was pain in labor for the mother and a warping of character for the child."

While the effects of sexual activity were considered harmful in the main, reproduction was seen as beneficial and free of moral detriment to the mother. The only authentic passion allowed women, according to Kellogg, was motherhood. "Motherly instinct," he wrote, "is without doubt the ruling passion in the heart of the true woman. The sexual nature of woman finds expression in this channel when her life is

 From *Childbirth '88*, Vol. V, No. 2, 1988, pp. 36-38, 40.

a normal one, rather than in the grosser forms of sexual activity."

Our thinking has certainly changed a great deal in the last 100 years. Alfred Kinsey and then William Masters and Virginia Johnson studied and demystified human sexual behavior, and in 1966 Masters and Johnson assessed sexuality in a small group of pregnant women. Since then many studies have been done on sexuality during pregnancy, and one of the most interesting is by Dr. Niles Newton of the University of Chicago. In the "Interrelationship Between Sexual Responses, Birth and Breastfeeding," she compared unmanipulated and undrugged childbirth with sexual excitement. She found 11 characteristics common to both. They are:

1. Changes in breathing
2. A tendency to make vocal noises
3. Facial expressions reminiscent of an athlete under great strain
4. Rhythmic contractions of the upper segment of the uterus
5. Loosening of the mucous plug from the cervix
6. Periodic abdominal contractions
7. Use of a position in which the woman is on her back with her legs wide apart and bent
8. A tendency to become uninhibited
9. Unusual muscular strength
10. A tendency to be unaware of the world and a sudden return to alert awareness after climax or birth
11. A feeling of joy and well-being following climax or birth

The implication is, of course, that neither childbirth nor sexual activity is physiologically or morally harmful. In the last ten years, attitudes toward childbirth and sexuality have continued to improve. All of us involved with expectant couples have become aware of our responsibility as their counselors to help them maintain a satisfying intimate relationship with each other during pregnancy.

Pregnant women often find it extremely hard to retain their good self-image, particularly in the last trimester. They may look at themselves in a mirror and say sadly, "How can anything as big as this still be desirable?" Our culture tells us that the ideal shape

Fears of hurting the fetus during intercourse or orgasm are groundless.

of a woman includes small but distinct breasts, a flat belly, and long, slender legs. How difficult it is for a mother-to-be to see herself larger than she remembers ever having been.

It is important to bear in mind that the shape of ideal woman has changed over the centuries. Fifteen thousand years ago, the voluptuous Venus of Willendorf was viewed as the essence of beauty. The sculpture we have of her portrays a very big woman with enormous breasts. On the other hand, the Venus de Milo represents the ideal image of the ancient Greeks. As all such ideals are relative, it is particularly important that women today not be obsessed by a media version of what they should look like. Indeed, many men find that their wife's new shape excites them and makes them feel protective and loving. Most husbands find the pregnant woman's added roundness and her larger breasts very attractive.

Here is how one woman describes what happened to her and her partner during this period:

"When I became pregnant, I worried that my husband would not like my body and that it would not feel good to him as I grew larger. The reverse happened. Every night he would study me, and as the baby began to move we would watch the 'show' for as much as half an hour every night. My belly was another part of me that he loved, and my early fears were in vain . . . ."

In spite of reassurance, both partners frequently fear they will hurt the fetus during intercourse. It's unfortunate that in our culture we tend to think of coitus as the only way of mak-

ing love. Holding hands, touching, eye contact, even walking together arm in arm are ways of loving.

Many women are afraid to have an orgasm in the last trimester, believing it to reduce the baby's oxygen supply. Orgasm can produce quite noticeable uterine contractions and temporarily slow down the fetal heartbeat, but there is no evidence that these events are harmful to the baby.

As to preterm labor brought on by intercourse, no one has proved that intercourse in the last three months causes early labor. Researchers have been unable to find any differences in birthweight, length of pregnancy, or health of the fetus related to intercourse in the last trimester.

A Time for Understanding

Here is a list of sexual anxieties and joys of women and men during the third trimester of pregnancy.

For women

Joys:
Discovery of new positions for intercourse
New ways of pleasuring
Larger breasts
Freedom from worry about becoming pregnant
Greater sensitivity in genital organs
Sharing changes in body with their partner

Anxieties:
Loss of interest in sex
Physical awkwardness
Harming the fetus
Precipitating preterm labor
Rupturing membranes
Physicians' taboos

For men

Joys:
Being turned on by the increase in size of partner's breasts
Love of the extra weight and roundness of belly
New ways of pleasuring
Challenge of finding new positions

Anxieties: (similar to women's)

Another question couples ask is whether prostaglandin, which is found in the man's ejaculate, can cause early labor. It is true that prostaglandin is occasionally used to induce labor, but its quantity in the semen is too minute to initiate labor.

Frequently, pregnant women have an unusually strong desire for sex, especially during the last three months. Many report that they first experienced orgasm at that time. The explanation is that the added blood supply to the pelvic area (indeed to all the body during pregnancy) can make the genitals especially sensitive and enhance the desire for satisfaction compared to the nonpregnant state. The extra blood supply is also why many women discover the resolution period after orgasm lasts considerably longer than usual. Some women may find that masturbation eases some of these strong desires, while for others frequent masturbation does not seem to relieve the tension. Some women may feel reluctant to masturbate because of the age-old belief that masturbation causes madness or is generally undesirable or because masturbation is considered a poor substitute for sexual gratification. Consequently, pregnancy is a good time for couples to learn cuddling, pleasuring, talking to each other, and finding new and comfortable positions for coitus that accommodate the woman's changing shape.

I would like to end with a quote from Libby Colman's and my book *Making Love During Pregnancy* (Bantam Books, 1977):

"Pregnancy is an opportunity for a man and a woman to draw closer together, to learn about each other in new and different ways. They may have to work hard to stay in touch with each other and with the changes that take place, but their understanding of their sexuality and their acceptance of their bodies will help their love and lovemaking and carry them beyond caring for each other to embrace the family unit."

Saying No to Motherhood

You like babies. You're the last person who can carry on the family genes. You think it's selfish to not have children. Still, something deep down inside you votes against it. Deciding against having children is a relatively recent option for women. With this advice, you can examine your options practically and emotionally and learn how to live with your choice.

VICKI LINDNER

Vicki Lindner is a freelance and fiction writer and the coauthor of Unbalanced Accounts: Why Women Are Still Afraid of Money.

I don't remember when I first realized I didn't have an instinctive drive to give birth to a baby. When I was a child, I played with dolls, but I saw myself not as their mother but as their creative prime mover. If someone had asked me if I expected to marry and have children, I would have said *yes*, because that was what all girls raised in the fifties did when they grew up. I saw no adult women in my New Jersey suburb who were doing otherwise.

When I was 28, I became pregnant while living and working in Japan. In Japan at that time, birth control pills, which I'd run out of while traveling through Asia, were illegal, and the easiest to obtain form of contraception was a cheap abortion. The father and I were in love. Months later, when our transcultural romance came to its confusing close, he looked at me with bewildered eyes and asked, "Why didn't you want to have the baby?" I'd had the nausea, lethargy, and inexplicable terror in my gut extracted like an aching tooth; I'd never thought of *it* as a child.

As I edged into my 30s, and friends began to marry and have children, no biological clock ticked inside me. Either I hadn't grown up yet or I hadn't grown up to be like other women. About the time the proverbial clock should have been sounding a shrill alarm—age 36— my younger brother married a woman who didn't opt for motherhood either. So certain was she that she wouldn't change her mind that my sister-in-law had her tubes tied before she was 30. The responsibility to carry on the Lindner genes fell to me, and I didn't want it. I *wanted* to want it; I wanted to be a normal female, part of a world of close, fertile families, joyfully reproducing themselves. Instead I was a writer, living alone, creating not living beings but characters in books and short stories. On my good days, I thought of myself as a Brave New Woman in a Brave New World, paving the way for others who wished to be different. On my bad days, I felt like a neuter alien from a science-fiction novel.

I'm not sure I ever chose not to have children. That is, I never sat down, counted up the minutes left on my biological clock, and said, "Do I or don't I?" Instead, I feel that my childlessness evolved from a series of life choices, which resulted in a lifestyle and personal temperament that are incompatible with motherhood. I'm not married. I live in a tiny, rent-controlled apartment in Manhattan, and I support my fiction by working as a freelance writer; my income is modest and often unpredictable. I need silence to work (actually, it would be more honest to say I love silence). I'm one of the rare people who like being alone, and I love travel and freedom, too. I want to learn instead of teach, and I am as hungry for new experience as any child; in that sense, I want to remain one. What would I be doing if I had a child? Who would I be? I might be somebody different, somebody more satisfied, or less satisfied, but I would not be the person I define as myself.

Sometimes I like to get off the hook by believing that childlessness chose me. My

From *New Woman*, April 1987, pp. 57-58, 60, 64. Copyright © 1987 by Vicki Lindner. Reprinted by permission.

mother's pregnancies, one of which I witnessed, were nightmares of nausea and anemia. Her mother, my maternal grandmother, died at 44 of a heart attack in the ninth month of a troubled pregnancy. My mother told me the story—of how she

technology have made it possible for women not to have children, society still persuades and pressures us to believe that motherhood is a duty, a virtue, and a delight—our natural calling. Few women dared to consider childlessness, or sup-

quate, a woman who loves her career, or who needs to earn money, might reject the time-consuming responsibilities of raising children. She may look at an exhausted "supermom" friend, struggling to work and raise a child, and say, "I don't want to take this on myself." In short, women who have decided to say *no* to motherhood do not believe kids are compatible with self-fulfillment or necessary to happiness.

The woman who chooses childlessness chooses alone and may feel defensive, ambivalent, and confused, as friends and relatives pressure her to make a pro-baby decision.

had watched her mother die gasping on the floor and had run barefoot through the snow to phone the drunken rural doctor—when I was very young. Yet, it wasn't until I was 35 and searching for convincing reasons to explain my childlessness that I became aware of how these long-known facts (with buried significance) had made me fear pregnancy. For me, the maternal condition conjured specters of sickness and death.

As I write my reasons for choosing childlessness, I imagine my readers, who have bravely overcome their own reluctance and fears to produce lovable namesakes, saying, "What nonsense!" I imagine their faces, bemused, even angry, as they mutter, "Selfish! Neurotic! Doesn't want to grow up! Doesn't know what she's missing. Will die alone and lonely, buried in the sheaves of dried-up manuscript!" The truth is that I don't know whether it is the voice of my readers I hear or a voice inside myself, not yet reconciled to my unusual decision—the part of me that feels guilty! The part of me that believes I had no right to make such a choice.

Recently, I held a baby at a dinner party. I was in awe. This miraculous infant of my species, so helpless, so pliable, seemed made to fit into my body's curves, to merge with them. Too young to know the difference between her mother and other women, she reached for my breast. I handed her back quickly, saying, "I don't want to get my hormones in an uproar!" The guests all laughed, but it wasn't really a joke. Having made my choice, I am afraid that what the world has told me might be true and that a force springing from my female biology, over which I have no control, might still rise up and punish me with regrets.

Why It's So Difficult to Choose Childlessness

■ Not only does the childless choice flout centuries of tradition and social expectations, but also it is a relatively new option. (Birth control was not legally available until the 1930's, and abortion was legalized nationwide only in 1973.) Even though the law and medical

port this option, until the 1970's, when concern about the world's burgeoning population gave some a legitimate excuse to speak out. Author Betty Rollin was one. She wrote a controversial article for *Look* magazine titled, "Motherhood: Who Needs It?" Readers were outraged. "In 1970," Rollin says, "to support childlessness was equivalent to supporting communism. I wasn't antimotherhood, but I suggested that life could be good without having children. My article got more hate mail than any article *Look* had published, except for one about Hitler. People called me a monster!"

Rollin believes that it is easier to make the childless decision now than it was then. "Though pressures to have children are still very great, and there is a lot of guilt attached to not being a mother, it is not totally freakish to choose childlessness in the eighties," she says. Rollin, whose recent book, *Last Wish,* describes her terminally ill mother's suicide, believes strongly in choice—"in diversity, differences, and tolerance. Motherhood is a perfectly good choice, and nonmotherhood is a good choice too. There's no reason why we can't have both."

Why Women Choose Childlessness

■ According to Jean Veevers, a Canadian sociologist who has studied childless couples, most couples who choose childlessness believe they are opting for a pleasant lifestyle over an unpleasant one. They see child raising versus a freewheeling lifestyle as an either/or choice. *Either* they can have the freedom and money to seek experience, travel, and change or quit jobs, *or* they can commit themselves to supporting a stable family. Some, who enjoy deep intimacy with their mates, fear a child's presence would sabotage it. Others think they would sacrifice important career goals for children. As Susan Brownmiller writes in *Femininity,* "Motherhood and ambition have been seen as opposing forces for thousands of years." Since studies show that most fathers shoulder little of the burden of child care, and daycare facilities are expensive and inade-

According to experts, however, the childless choice is often made unconsciously, before we are old enough to form adult lifestyles and beliefs. Some choose childlessness because early childhood experiences or perceptions have made them see parenthood as unrewarding or threatening. Some view pregnancy and birth as repulsive, frightening, or, as I do, dangerous. "They do not see their bodies as being sturdy and resilient," says Lois Kennedy, a New York City psychotherapist. "They do not believe they will survive physical changes."

Others reject parenting because they feel their parents were less happy or prosperous because they had large families and devoted their lives to their offspring. Modern women may feel that their own mothers would have enjoyed richer lives if their interests and talents hadn't been submerged by domestic duties. According to Kennedy, mothers who do not see their own womanhood in a positive light, or who resent their maternal roles, communicate a negative sense of what it meant to be a woman to their daughters. These daughters often identify with their fathers and reject traditional female activities—including having children.

On the positive side, the childless may have known "Auntie Mames," who lived intriguing lives without children. They grew up more able to see themselves as nonmothers than did women without inspirational role models.

Making the Decision

■ The social push to have children is strong, and there are no support groups to help the childless. (The one that existed, the National Alliance for Optional Parenthood, is now defunct.) As a result, the woman who chooses childlessness chooses alone and may feel defensive, ambivalent, and confused, as friends and relatives pressure her to make a pro-baby decision. Instead of regarding her choice as positive or inevitable, she is tempted to blame it on others or on herself. Some defend their own lifestyles by downgrading mothers. "Isn't it better to be doing what I'm doing," they ask, "than scraping Gerber's off the walls?" Others blame children themselves for their lack of desire to have them: kids are noisy, irritating, and expensive. Who would want one? Some say their mates would be terrible fathers. Most of the childless women I interviewed say their own negative qualities—impatience or bad tempers—would make them unfit mothers. Others ask, who would want to raise a child in such an unpredictable and dangerous world? Sometimes the childless offer *all* of the above reasons.

Given the difficulties, how does a woman manage the traumatic decision-making process? Let's look at some women who made the childless choice.

Practical and Emotional Research

Merry Bruns, a commercial model and graduate student in anthropology, presented me with the reading list and pile of books that helped her choose childlessness. "I think people should talk more openly and honestly about this issue," she says. "Most of my friends are either dying to have children or are ambivalent. I feel like I belong to a secret club."

Merry grew up "not thinking about having children." When she was 20, the "big decision" seemed "twenty-five years away. When I turned thirty, my friends started having babies left and right," she says. "At my wedding, people asked not *if* we were going to have them, but *when* we were. 'I have to think about this,' I said to myself, and I researched my decision like I would a term paper." After reading extensively, Merry wrote down the reasons why she wanted a child in blue and why she didn't in black; the black column was much longer. Tops on the black list was, "I like to have complete freedom and control of my life."

Though Merry sees her decision as practical, she researched it emotionally, too. Because she is wholesome and blond, with bright blue eyes, she is often cast as a mother, holding an infant, on modeling assignments. "I would say to myself, 'On a scale of one to five, how do you feel about this baby?' " When her nephew was born, she enjoyed a special relationship with the little boy: "I'd look at Alec and ask, 'Does loving him make me want to have children?' and I'd honestly have to answer *no*. But I tried to stay in touch with new feelings."

A pregnancy, followed by an abortion, which proved physically and emotionally painful, made Merry face up to her choice. Though her husband, who has two adult children by a first wife, didn't want more and was willing to have a vasectomy, Merry opted for a tubal ligation. "I thought it was my responsibility," she says. "I wanted to know *I* wasn't going to get pregnant."

Her father accepted her decision, saying proudly, "You're really your own woman!" But what about her mother? Merry's vivacious smile fades. "I gave

How to Say No

● Write down all the reasons why you don't want children. Don't prejudge them as selfish or superficial. Then write down the reasons why you do. Make sure the *pros* belong to you, not someone else.

● Discuss your feelings about not wanting children with other women who don't want them either or who have serious doubts. From them you will get the support and validation you need. If you can, find an older woman who opted for childlessness and discuss the issue with her. It will help if you learn she has no regrets.

● Hit the bookstore or library (most of the books on the subject are out of print) for information and support. Recommended reading: *Childless by Choice,* by Jean Veevers (Butterworth & Co., 1980); *Pronatalism: The Myth of Mom and Apple Pie* (a collection of essays), edited by Ellen Peck and Judith Senderowitz (Thomas Y. Crowell, 1974); *The Parent Test: How to Measure and Develop Your Talent for Parenthood*, by Ellen Peck and William Granzig (G. P. Putnam's Sons, 1978); *Making up Your Mind about Motherhood,* by Silvia Feldman, Ed.D. (Bantam, 1985); and *Childless by Choice* by Marian Faux (Doubleday, 1984).

● When casual acquaintances or people you sense are unsympathetic to your choice ask why you haven't had children, don't feel obliged to answer this very personal question. Usually they are asking not because they really want to know, but because they disagree. Say firmly but politely, "I can't," and indicate the subject is closed. It will only make you feel insecure to argue this issue.

● Don't let insecurities about your choice lead you to make unsympathetic remarks about children or parenting to parents—including your own. They will respect your choice more if you indicate that you respect theirs.

● When relatives pressure you to provide grandchildren, ask them if and how they are willing to help. Ask for specifics. This tactic may backfire, as some parents want heirs enough to offer child care and financial aid, but often it will discourage further harassment.

● If you don't want children, make sure your boyfriend understands and accepts that before you make a serious commitment.

● Remember, it's 1987—you have a right to say *no* to motherhood. It's not illegal or immoral to remain childless when the world population is increasing by 78 million a year. Think of your decision as positive and appropriate for you. Don't take it to heart when others suggest you are abnormal or selfish. "Society teaches women that they should put the needs of others first; and when they don't, they're selfish," says feminist psychotherapist Annette Lieberman.   —*V.L.*

her my list of reasons and told her to consult them whenever she's inclined to protest. She'll get over it, but right now she thinks I'm selfish."

Fighting Urges

Some women choose childlessness in spite of yearnings to have children. Betty Tompkins, 41, an artist who has let her clock tick with no regrets, ignored "biological urges" because they conflicted with her desire to paint. "When these urges visited, they were very strong," she says, "and I didn't want them. I'd look glowingly at some crying child in the supermarket. I'd have to wait until those feelings went away, because they never had anything to do with what was happening in my life."

Betty, like Merry, viewed her choice as a practical one that had to be weighed against other plans and obligations that, for her, came first. Like most women who choose nonmotherhood, she leads a busy, satisfying, creative life with specific

goals. "It would have been naive to think I could be a full-time exhibiting painter, earn money somehow, and be a full-time mother, too," she points out. "I would have needed another day in every day to do what I'm doing and have a baby."

Though this modern woman chose a twentieth-century option, she respected her body's messages. "I've always been careful with birth control," she says, "because if I got pregnant, I'm not convinced I'd have the courage to have an abortion."

"Postponing" the Choice

Sociologist Veevers found that many women who don't want children postpone the decision indefinitely. They evade pressures by pretending to others—and sometimes to themselves—that they may one day become pregnant. One 36-year-old woman played this complex game. "Let's say my decision is *no* until I change my mind," she says. "I think I will never make a decision *not* to have a child, until biology catches up with me."

According to this woman, her "ambivalence" helps her to avoid uncomfortable moments with friends who are thrilled with new babies and to enjoy a "richer fantasy life. Because I've never made an official decision, I can say, 'Oh, what a cute little baby! What a wonderful thing it is to have your own child,' and imagine doing it myself. But all it takes is for a new mother to say, 'You should have one too,' and the fantasy dissolves. I don't want to do what everybody else is doing, what my mother did! I'm too delicate. I would feel crowded by a baby. Actually, I've made a conscious decision to move in other directions." This woman, who is a photographer, fears she would lose "creativity to maternity."

Some women eventually realize that continued ambivalence implies a negative decision. A California woman says her husband helped her make her childless choice. "He thought having a child might be a romantic idea," she says. "I was curious. What would it be like to have a child with this man? How would it turn out? On my thirty-ninth birthday I said to him, 'I still can't decide. I'm still thinking about it.' And he said, 'Then the answer is *no*.' "

Coping with Fears and Pressures

The greatest fear for women who are childless by choice is that they'll regret their decision in later years. One childless woman's therapist reduced her anxiety by asking if regretful feelings had ever made her want to jump off buildings in the past. "At that point I realized regret was not a lethal emotion," she says. "Fear of regret was not a positive reason to have a child."

Most women who don't want children marry men who don't want them either. But some fear that their mates will change their minds. "I'm afraid that ten years from now he'll divorce me and have a child with a younger woman," says one woman. "Whenever we see a baby, I test the waters. I ask, 'Isn't he adorable? Don't you want to have a baby too?' He always reassures me by saying firmly, 'No, I don't.' "

Those who pressure the childless to have children prey on such fears. These pressures prevent many women from making the childless decision or from feeling comfortable about it. Most of the women I interviewed confessed to feelings of guilt or shame. Many said they felt selfish or had been told they were. Though some labeled negative emotions as "society's trips," others found it hard to distinguish between their own feelings and the feelings of those who were disappointed or angry. "Almost everybody else in the world rejects your choice," says Kennedy. "That's pretty hard to come up against and say, 'I know I'm right.' "

Why do others feel they have an obligation to convince the childless to change their minds? According to Kennedy, those who resort to pressure tactics may have an ax to grind. "Parents see the childless decision as a rejection of their lifestyles and major life accomplishment," she says. "People who love you, and who are happy with their own babies, want you to discover this happiness too. They have trouble acknowledging differences and think you can't possibly know what you're missing." Kennedy believes that no one in our culture can raise children without ambivalence and stress. "It's a very hard job," she says. "Parents get little help from society. Those who experience difficulty raising children need to be validated. They feel that you may hold them in contempt, having made a choice that is more rebellious or creative. They will ask you to explain, but no answer you give will satisfy them, because they are really looking for validation."

The Crisis in Contraception

ELIZABETH B. CONNELL

ELIZABETH B. CONNELL, M.D., is professor of gynecology and obstetrics at Emory University School of Medicine in Atlanta. She has served on the FDA's Obstetrics and Gynecology Advisory Committee and the executive board of Planned Parenthood, and as an advisor to the U.S. Agency for International Development.

THE United States has led the world in contraceptive research and development for many years. Americans have provided most of the basic scientific data, expertise, and manufacturing capability for contraceptive technologies now in use around the world. However, the United States is losing its leadership role in this area—with potentially disastrous consequences for women and men in this country and elsewhere.

The increasingly litigious climate in this country is one major reason for our technological slippage in this field. The growing number of lawsuits against companies that manufacture contraceptives has prompted many to withdraw products such as intrauterine devices (IUDs) from the marketplace. As a result, there are fewer contraceptive options available to Americans than there were a decade ago.

Fear of litigation has also discouraged companies from introducing safer and more convenient contraceptives to the domestic market, although they continue to test and sell new products abroad. It is particularly ironic that a number of excellent products developed by Americans, such as Depo-Provera (an injectible contraceptive) and the copper-bearing IUDs, are now available virtually everywhere in the world *except* the United States.

This situation has been aggravated by widespread public misunderstanding about the risks and benefits of certain birth-control methods. This is particularly true of the pill, whose risks have been grossly exaggerated in proportion to its benefits.

A steady decline in federal funding for contraceptive R&D in recent years has further exacerbated the situation. In 1985, for instance, the National Institutes of Health (NIH) allocated only $7.5 million for contraceptive research, down from $38 million spent by the U.S. government in 1974. The Reagan administration has sliced contraceptive funding for both research and services because of political pressure from religious groups and right-wing organizations.

For all of these reasons, the United States is facing a crisis in the development and use of contraceptives. While everyone is affected, two groups are suffering the most. The first is our teenage population. The United States now holds the dubious distinction of having the highest rate of teenage pregnancies anywhere in the developed world. Our rate is seven times higher than that of the Netherlands, and more than twice as high as that of Canada, Denmark, England, Finland, New Zealand, and Sweden, even though our teenagers are not more sexually active. More than 1 million U.S. teenagers become pregnant each year, with almost half of the pregnancies ending in abortion. If current trends continue, 40 percent of today's 14-year-old girls will be pregnant at least once before age 20.

*P*olitical pressures
and litigation are driving contraceptives
off the market and stifling research
and development in this area.

3. REPRODUCTION: Birth Control

The vast majority of teenagers don't give their babies up for adoption, and they face all the medical and socioeconomic problems that occur when children have children. The Center for Population Options in New York estimates that the cost to the public of teenage childbearing was $16.65 billion in 1986. This figure does not include the costs of housing, day care, special education, and numerous other needs, all of which are steadily increasing as more and more teenagers keep their babies.

While inadequate sex education programs and the lack of easily available contraceptive services play a role in this epidemic, many pregnant teenagers say they failed to use birth control because either they didn't know there were safe and effective methods or they didn't know how to obtain them. Educating teenagers about contraceptives becomes even more of an urgent priority with the looming threat of AIDS and other sexually transmitted diseases.

A different problem exists at the other end of the age spectrum. Women who are beyond the age when the pill is deemed appropriate—35 to 40—still face 10 to 15 years of potential fertility. Yet the options available to these women are narrowing. As a result, many of them (or their husbands) will undoubtedly resort to possibly irreversible sterilization procedures for which they are not psychologically ready. Furthermore, while a vasectomy has some risks of minor side effects, a tubal ligation—a surgical procedure often done under general anesthesia—carries a small but real risk of significant complications.

The current crisis is also creating problems for other countries. Since many developing nations do not have a regulatory agency such as the Food and Drug Administration (FDA), they have traditionally looked to the United States for guidance in evaluating new drugs and devices. So when birth-control methods are discontinued here for economic reasons, or are not approved by the FDA for political reasons, other countries often get the impression that they are unsafe or ineffective. Thus, the decline in contraceptive development and use in the United States is resulting in fewer contraceptive options for those countries. To make matters worse, the current administration has refused to fund any international family-planning organizations that offer abortion counseling or referrals along with other forms of birth control. This could have particularly serious repercussions for nations with uncontrolled population growth.

Sneezing to Prevent Pregnancy

Ever since our ancestors concluded that there was a causal relationship between sexual intercourse and the birth of a baby, both men and women have searched for ways to control their fertility. Some of these techniques seem ludicrous in light of today's knowledge, while others were scientifically quite perceptive. Some were extremely dangerous and even lethal.

Every country had its own superstitions. In Rome around the sixth century B.C., women wore the testicles of a cat in a tube around their waist. Women in other regions believed that sneezing and jumping after intercourse would prevent conception, and still others claimed success from burning moxa-balls (small packets of medicinal herbs) on the abdomen. Barrier devices that prevented sperm from entering the cervical canal were made of numerous plant and animal materials such as cabbages, pomegranates, leaves, animals' ear wax, and elephant dung. The ingestion of heavy metals for contraception killed many women during the Middle Ages, and many women died as a result of mutilating sterilization procedures.

Condoms, in one form or another, have been employed ever since prehistoric times, but the use of modern condoms began with the industrialization of rubber. A modern version of the diaphragm was developed in the late nineteenth century, and spermicides, made from chemicals toxic to sperm, were introduced for contraceptive use around the 1930s and 1940s.

Before the development of the pill and IUDs, barrier contraceptives were the only reliable methods of birth control. But they have to be used with every act of intercourse, and many users find them inconvenient and aesthetically unattractive. Furthermore, these devices are not completely effective in preventing pregnancy—condoms occasionally tear and diaphragms fitted or used improperly do not always prevent sperm from getting into the cervical canal. For these reasons, barrier methods were rapidly replaced by oral contraceptives and IUDs when they became available.

The FDA approved the first oral contraceptive in 1960. The pill contains two female hormones: estrogen, which blocks ovulation, and progestin, which promotes cyclic bleeding. The pill seemed safe and effective during initial clinical tests. However, data accumulated during the mid- and late 1960s, when the pill became more widely used, indicated that there were risks for certain individuals. For instance, use of the early oral contraceptives resulted in a seven fold increase—to 3 in 100,000—in women's annual death rate from thromboembolism, a blood-clotting disease. Pill use also caused a fourfold increase in users' risk of stroke, and a threefold increase in their risk of heart attacks.

However, the risks of heart attacks and strokes appeared only in 35-year-old women who smoked and 40-year-old women who did not: there have been no reported deaths from the pill owing to these cardiovascular diseases in women under the age of

25. Long-term risks apply only to women who have additional risk factors such as age and smoking. Thus, for women without these risk factors, it is far safer to take the pill than to carry a pregnancy to term.

Making a Safer Pill

After these initial risks came to light, researchers modified the pill, lowering the dosage first of estrogen and then of progestin. The amount of estrogen, for instance, declined from more than 100 micrograms to 30 micrograms. As a result, the incidence of serious side effects is considerably lower in the pills sold today. And as the newer, low-dosage pills become more widely used, we can look forward to even fewer long-term cardiovascular side effects. Yet the almost 100 percent effectiveness rate of the early oral contraceptives, when taken properly, has been maintained.

Despite this track record, the use of oral contraceptives has declined. This is largely because the pill's early risks received a disproportionate share of public attention. The first major assault against the pill took place during U.S. Senate hearings held by Sen. Gaylord Nelson's Subcommittee on Monopoly of the Select Committee on Small Business in 1970. In the opening days of these hearings, witnesses antagonistic toward oral contraceptives such as Hugh Davis, inventor of the Dalkon Shield, testified about their risks. This early testimony received extensive media coverage. Only later in the hearings did witnesses such as myself and Alan Guttmacher, president of Planned Parenthood, present a more balanced view of the pill's risks and benefits. But by then the damage had been done.

The legacy of these hearings and later reports about adverse side effects was vividly documented in a 1985 Gallup poll commissioned by the American College of Obstetricians and Gynecologists. The pill showed that the public's fears far exceed the real dangers of oral contraceptives. For example, about 75 percent of the men and women interviewed thought that the pill posed a serious threat to health. Of these, one-third believed that women taking these agents are at risk of developing cancer.

This viewpoint is particularly disturbing because, according to recent studies, the opposite is true. The pill not only does not cause malignancies but actually protects against cancer of the endometrium, the tissue lining the uterine cavity, and the ovary, the latter disease being almost always fatal. Howard Ory, of the Centers for Disease Control (CDC), has estimated that 1,700 hospitalizations for ovarian cancer and 2,000 for endometrial cancer are prevented each year by the use of oral contraceptives. In addition, 23,490 admissions for benign breast disease are averted annually, according to CDC estimates. Studies have shown that the pill continues to offer this protection for at least 10 to 15 years after women stop taking it.

Clinical studies have revealed other health benefits from the use of oral contraceptives. It is now well established that these potent hormonal agents protect against a number of medical conditions including ectopic pregnancy, a potentially fatal condition in which the fetus develops outside the womb in one of the woman's two fallopian tubes. The pill also protects against numerous conditions, including ovarian cysts, fibroid tumors of the uterus, pelvic inflammatory disease, excessive menstrual bleeding, and weakening of the bones (osteoporosis). Yet under intense pressure from some consumer groups, the FDA has not allowed information about these significant health benefits to be included in the packaging for oral contraceptives.

Similarly, the vaginal contraceptive sponge was attacked by two activist consumer groups shortly after its approval by the FDA in 1983. The Associated Pharmacologists and Toxicologists in Washington, D.C., and the Empire State Consumer Association in Rochester, N.Y., claimed that the sponge contained three carcinogens, that its use carried a high risk of toxic shock syndrome, and that it had been inadequately evaluated by the FDA.

These charges culminated in hearings before the House Subcommittee on Intergovernmental Relations and Human Resources in July 1983. All the allegations were essentially refuted by the manufacturer of the sponge, VLI Corp., based on its research data. The NIH, which provided funding for the sponge's development, found no reason for concern. The FDA did not withdraw its approval nor recommend any alterations in the product's labeling. The media, however, focused primarily on the alleged risks of the device and the public once again became alarmed.

In my opinion, the concern about contraceptives—

The pill's early risks received a disproportionate share of public attention.

and indeed all new medications—can be traced to a general belief that all drugs and devices should be totally safe and effective. Given the great scientific advances made in recent years, many people believe there should be no risks associated with medical care. This, unfortunately, will never be true, since it is impossible to develop any agent powerful enough to produce a desired biologic effect that will not have an adverse effect on a few susceptible people. Therefore, every treatment has and will always have its own risk-benefit ratio for any given individual.

The Disappearance of the IUD

The first intrauterine device was invented in the early 1920s. Several centuries before, camel drivers somehow learned that placing pebbles in the uteri of their female camels would keep them from getting pregnant while crossing the Sahara. Foreign bodies inserted into the uterine cavities of women were later shown to induce biochemical changes that were either toxic to sperm or did not allow the implantation of a fertilized ovum.

Like the pill, the early IUDs seemed to be highly effective and safe. However, studies with larger numbers of users soon revealed adverse effects, particularly in the case of the Dalkon Shield. This plastic device was found to be very dangerous because its tail, composed of hundreds of small filaments encased in a sheath, acted as a wick, allowing bacteria from the vagina to ascend into the uterus. Hundreds of cases of pelvic infections resulted from the use of the Dalkon Shield, causing sterility and a number of deaths among women using this IUD.

At least 12,000 lawsuits and more than 325,000 claims were filed against A.H. Robins, the manufacturer of the Dalkon Shield, forcing it to withdraw the IUD and later file for bankruptcy. In this particular case, there seems to be clear evidence of corporate irresponsibility. According to internal memos released during litigation, Robins officials had known of the dangerous wicking tendency of its IUD before they marketed the device.

All the other marketed IUDs had monofilament (single filament) tails, which do not have as much potential for infection. There are two major types of IUDs: the earlier, non-medicated devices made of plastic such as Saf-T-Coil and Lippes Loop, and the more recent medicated devices made out of plastic

to which copper (Copper-7 and Tatum-T) or a progesterone (Progestasert) have been added to increase their effectiveness. The medicated devices are smaller and better tolerated, producing fewer cases of cramping and bleeding than their predecessors. Furthermore, two studies published in the *New England Journal of Medicine* in 1985 showed little or no increased risk of tubal infertility from the use of copper IUDs in monogamous couples. The Saf-T-Coil and Lippes Loop have since been removed from the market for economic reasons.

However, fears aroused by the Dalkon Shield fiasco have prompted a number of lawsuits against the widely used Copper-7. The suits claim a variety of injuries, primarily related to pelvic infections. Most of these suits have been decided in favor of the manufacturer, G.D. Searle.

Despite these favorable judgments, Searle decided in January 1986 that it was no longer economically feasible to continue producing the Copper-7 and the Tatum-T. While sales of the Copper-7 amounted to $11 million in 1985, the successful defense of just four of the Copper-7 lawsuits cost the company $1.5 million. With more than 300 lawsuits pending, Searle found product-liability insurance for both products to be virtually unobtainable.

One decision in a 1986 lawsuit against Searle may discourage some future IUD litigation. U.S. District Court Judge Joseph H. Young in Baltimore declared that the evidence submitted on behalf of 17 Copper-7 users who had sued Searle was nothing but a "series of alternative unsubstantiated theories." He concluded that the "plaintiffs had failed to present sufficient evidence of causation" and rendered a verdict in favor of Searle.

Unfortunately, that court decision will probably not change the decision of Searle and other pharmaceutical companies to stay out of the IUD market. As a result, the newest IUD—the Copper T Cu 380A—may never be brought to the U.S. market. Yet this IUD is the best of the copper devices (it has the highest rate of effectiveness) and has already been approved by the FDA.

At present, at least 2.3 million American women use an IUD. When those devices need to be replaced, most of these women will have to find some other form of contraception. Jacqueline Forrest of the Alan Guttmacher Institute, a New York-based research organization, has statistically estimated that

*I*UDs are no longer available
in the U.S. because companies
cannot obtain liability coverage.

160,000 unintended pregnancies will occur from the discontinuation of IUD production in the United States, resulting in 72,000 live births and 88,000 abortions.

The Controversy over Depo-Provera

Another unfortunate victim of the current medical-legal climate is Depo-Provera (depo-medroxy progesterone acetate), a long-acting injectable progestin that acts by blocking ovulation. The injection is given by a health-care provider once every three months. This route of administration not only allows for long-term effectiveness but is particularly desirable in many areas of the world where medications are perceived to be of value only when given by injection. Depo-Provera has been shown to be extremely safe and virtually 100 percent effective. This agent has been used by more than 11 million women in over 80 countries for more than 20 years with no reported deaths. Yet it has never been approved in the United States because of political reasons.

The FDA's scientific advisory committees, the World Health Organization, and numerous other national and international groups have reviewed the data on Depo-Provera and recommended its use as a contraceptive agent. However, the drug has been the target of various consumer and feminist groups such as the National Women's Health Network, *Mother Jones* magazine, and the Institute for Food and Development Policy.

These opponents have cited animal data on malignancy that are probably irrelevant to women. For instance, beagles given high doses of Depo-Provera developed breast tumors. However, the beagle has a high spontaneous rate of breast lesions, and British scientists have recently stated that it is not an appropriate animal for testing hormonal agents. Two of fifteen rhesus monkeys receiving 50 times the contraceptive dose developed endometrial cancer, but in a tissue not found in the human female. Moreover, this tumor has also been reported to occur in untreated animals. While critics maintain that Depo-Provera can cause birth defects, there is no evidence that this has occurred. Furthermore, this agent is so effective as a birth-control method that the risk of exposing a fetus to the drug is extremely low.

Opponents have also claimed that Depo-Provera causes permanent sterility, but studies have shown normal pregnancy rates approximately one year after stopping the medication. Most women do experience irregular menstrual cycles, and sometimes a complete absence of menses, while using this contraceptive. But this has not been shown to have adverse effects on their health or future fertility.

Despite the agent's long-term record of safety, an FDA Public Board of Inquiry recommended in 1985 that Depo-Provera not be approved without more research to establish its long-term safety. The Upjohn Co. is currently preparing a new application to the FDA based on recent international studies that document Depo-Provera's safety and efficacy.

Other contraceptive agents currently under attack are spermicides, which work by chemically disrupting the membrane covering the head of the sperm. These are manufactured as jellies, creams, and foams and are used either alone or with a diaphragm, condom, or in the vaginal sponge. In 1985, in a non-jury trial in Atlanta, a judge awarded $5.1 million to a woman who claimed that her child's congenital defects resulted from the use of Ortho Gynol, a spermicide made by the Ortho Pharmaceutical Corp. In his decision, the judge cited a study published in 1981 that purportedly showed a link between congenital anomalies and spermicides. However, this study has many methodological flaws and lacks statistical validity. Moreover, the judge made this award even though most of the evidence presented at the trial showed that there is no proven association between the use of spermicides and fetal damage.

Spermicides are low-profit items, and one or two more suits of this magnitude might be enough to convince U.S. companies to discontinue production. Thus, we face the potential loss of these valuable contraceptive agents as well.

In the meantime, there is little chance that new contraceptives will become available in the near future. It is very difficult and sometimes impossible to obtain funds to pursue promising leads for new contraceptive technologies. Two factors are to blame. First, as I mentioned, federal funding of basic research—in both government and university labs—has steadily declined over the last six years. Second, the development of a new product is very expensive (it costs approximately $50 million) and very time consuming (it takes about 15 years to bring an idea to market). Unless companies expect a product to produce a reasonably good financial return, they are unwilling to make a major investment.

Even if U.S. companies decide to develop and test new contraceptives, they may not be able to obtain liability insurance for them. And there is always the fear of litigation, which can occur regardless of the product's safety record in clinical tests.

For these reasons, the number of pharmaceutical companies working in the field of contraception has dropped precipitously over the last decade. The Ortho Pharmaceutical Corp. is the only major U.S. company now committing significant amounts of money to developing contraceptives.

A classic example of this dilemma is a biodegradable contraceptive capsule known as Capronor, developed with NIH funding. This agent is implanted under the skin of the arm and releases a progestin, which also blocks ovulation, for a year. The product has been ready for clinical testing for more than two years, but no company has been able to obtain product-liability insurance in order to supply clinical researchers with the implant.

The same situation will probably apply to IUDs. A new tailless magnetic IUD has been developed by researchers at Emory University and the Georgia Institute of Technology. The magnet is used to detect and remove the IUD, so the tail—which can allow bacteria to pass into the uterine cavity—is no longer necessary. This new device is also almost ready for clinical trials. Yet it is unlikely that this or any other promising new IUD will undergo clinical trials in the United States, at least in the foreseeable future.

The current political climate is also inhibiting the availability of completely new technologies. This is particularly true in the case of RU 486, a steroid compound developed by the Roussel-Uclaf Co. of France and soon to be marketed there. RU 486 acts by suppressing the corpus luteum—a structure that develops in the ovary following ovulation and produces progesterone, a hormone essential to the development of a fertilized ovum.

Taken as an oral tablet, this agent interrupts the normal menstrual cycle and can prevent the implantation of a fertilized ovum. It can also be used to terminate pregnancy. Early data from clinical trials in other countries suggest that terminations induced by this agent carry lower complication rates than those linked with the few abortions performed late in the first trimester and in the second trimester.

However, RU 486 is highly controversial because it places control of pregnancy in the hands of women themselves. It thus circumvents any legislative authority and renders the whole abortion debate moot. Needless to say, antiabortion groups are vehemently opposed to introducing this agent in the United States. Given the current administration's anti-abortion stance, it is highly unlikely that such an agent will be studied and approved in the near future.

Another contraceptive that may not make it to the American marketplace is the Cavity Rim cervical cap, used with a spermicide. Studies conducted with approximately 2,000 American women showed pregnancy rates with this device comparable to other barrier methods. And there are no adverse health effects. Some women prefer the cap to the diaphragm because it is smaller and therefore less apt to affect the vaginal walls. And unlike the diaphragm, it does not put pressure on the urethra and bladder, which can cause urinary tract infections.

However, the FDA classified the cap as experimental in 1981. Therefore, anyone who wished to manufacture this device must accumulate all the data from the various centers where the cap was tested and submit the information to the FDA. This is a time-consuming and expensive exercise. Since the cap—like other barrier methods—would probably not be a major income producer, and insurers would assign manufacturers the same liability as that for the sponge and other vaginal contraceptives, it is unlikely that any U.S. company will pursue FDA approval.

Other contraceptives such as an implant encased in biocompatible plastic, a steroid-containing vaginal ring, and an antipregnancy vaccine have been investigated for more than a decade. But for the same reasons, these products are not likely to reach the American marketplace.

A Male Contraceptive?

Activist women's groups have often charged that there are no male contraceptives available today because most of the researchers are men who only want to work on methods for use by women. In reality, much time and money has been spent trying to develop safe and effective birth control for men.

It is much more difficult to control male fertility. A woman produces only one egg per month and is fertile for only about 12 hours. A man, however, produces as many as 30 million sperm per day and is almost constantly fertile. Preventing the development of a single egg is less difficult than reducing the sperm count to zero for long periods of time.

The World Health Organization has predicted that it will be more than 20 years before a male contraceptive becomes available for general use. Even if one is marketed, it would not eliminate the need for good female methods. Many women may not want to entrust their sexual partners with the sole responsibility for preventing pregnancy.

As the contraceptive crisis worsens, American women are being forced to leave the country to ob-

*The current administration
has cut funding for contraceptive research and services
largely because of pressure from religious
and right-wing groups.*

tain contraceptives. This is already happening with the IUD. The Copper T Cu 380A is now available in Canada, the United Kingdom, and continental Europe, and American women are traveling to these countries to obtain the device. While this solution may not pose an inordinate problem for middle- or high-income women, it does for poorer women. This de facto discrimination cannot fail to have serious social and economic repercussions.

The current crisis is also hurting family-planning activities worldwide. When devices such as the copper IUD are discontinued in the United States for purely economic reasons, other countries believe that they are not safe or effective. Similarly, because of the consistent failure of the FDA to approve Depo-Provera, grave doubts about its safety have begun to affect its use in various parts of the world.

To make matters worse, the U.S. government has drastically reduced funding for international family planning in recent years. In December 1984, the Reagan Administration abruptly terminated 17 years of support for the International Planned Parenthood Federation (IPPF) because it would not renounce its members' rights to carry on abortion-related activities with their own funds. The following year the U.S. Agency for International Development (AID) cut $10 million from support for the United Nations fund for population activities because of its program with China. AID claimed that China coerced women into obtaining abortions, sterilizations, and IUD insertions so the country could attain its population goals. Since the United States has been a primary source of support for such programs for many years, these cuts are hurting many countries' efforts to curb population growth. It is impossible to talk with international colleagues without becoming acutely aware of the immense negative impact we are having on contraceptive programs abroad.

Improving Public Understanding

The track record of the present administration suggests that very little will be done in the next two years to alleviate the contraceptive dilemma. One hopes that the next administration will better understand the need to support the development and use of safe and effective contraceptives. With that in mind, several potential solutions can be explored.

First, efforts must be undertaken by government agencies and the health-care profession to improve the public's understanding of the risks and benefits of available contraceptives. For instance, public ed-

ucation programs, using every type of media to reach the widest audience, should be launched to inform consumers that today's oral contraceptives are extremely safe and effective. Such programs should also spread the news that copper IUDs are safe and effective for monogamous individuals, who have a lower potential for contracting infections, and that no data exist linking spermicides to fetal defects.

People must also be informed that the condom offers our best defense against the spread of AIDS and other sexually transmitted diseases. U.S. Surgeon General C. Everett Koop has taken an admirable stance in advocating extensive public education programs about AIDS and the use of condoms.

The media should also attempt to cover contraceptives in a more balanced and responsible way. Television is perhaps most in need of improvement. Television executives who broadcast programs and ads that sell sex to teenagers should recognize how hypocritical they are in refusing to run public-service announcements about contraception.

Second, ways must be found to curb the increasing number of lawsuits that claim an association between a product and some sort of damage even though there is no scientific evidence for such a link. The public must be made aware that insurance companies do not have unlimited funds in their "deep pockets," and the public ultimately pays the price for unwarranted judgments.

Some so-called experts testify against drugs and devices without any scientific evidence to back up their claims. Many of these "hired guns" would not be allowed to testify if the courts imposed stricter criteria on expert witnesses' training and experience.

One approach to the product-liability quagmire would be to indemnify manufacturers of high-risk medical therapies against certain types of risk. This has already been suggested for manufacturers of vaccines and might also work for developers of contraceptives. Both vaccines and contraceptives carry an unavoidable risk to a very small percentage of users. Some policymakers have suggested a national fund to compensate the few individuals who sustain damage from these otherwise safe and effective drugs.

Finally, federal agencies such as the NIH and the Department of Health and Human Services should increase funding for contraceptive research and services. There is no reason why the United States should lose its leadership status in this area. And there is certainly no reason why women in this country must bear unwanted children because they do not have satisfactory options for birth control.

Kids and Contraceptives

The alarming rate of teenage pregnancy and the inexorable spread of AIDS has raised troubling moral questions and given new urgency to the debate over how best to protect our children

In Boston, where 13 percent of all births in 1983 were to girls 19 and under, the controversy over a plan to distribute birth-control devices in the city's schools is intense. The same kind of furor has accompanied the opening of many clinics that dispense contraceptives or provide family-planning counseling in at least 76 schools around the country. "We have no choice," says School Committee member Abbie Browne, the mother of two teenagers, who favors the plan. But fellow committee member Joe Casper, a father of five, is adamantly opposed to giving condoms to teenagers. "What are we going to do next?" he says. "Put them on for them, too?"

On national television, the 17-year-old hero of "Valerie" lusts after his sultry blond girlfriend. They get into bed together. But there's a little hitch: she doesn't have "protection." The boy decides to postpone their lovemaking until he can buy some condoms. Later, when his mother finds the package of contraceptives, they have a heart-to-heart talk. "Just make sure whatever you do, it's the right time in your life," she advises her son.

Every week more than 130 girls—some of them as young as 12—receive birth-control pills at one of the three clinics for teenagers run by the Chicago Board of Health. Peer pressure to have sex is unrelenting in the South Side ghetto, says director Cheryl Walker. "If a girl gets to be 15 or 16 years old and she hasn't had a baby yet, [her friends think] there must be something wrong with her," Walker says. So Walker takes the angry words of the critics in stride. "We holler when 12-year-olds come in here for contraceptives," she says. "But we holler louder when they come in here pregnant."

Contraceptives in the schools. Teenagers using condoms on television. Twelve-year-olds receiving birth-control pills—at the taxpayers' expense. A decade ago it would have been unthinkable. But the alarmingly high rate of teenage pregnancy and the fear of AIDS and other sexually transmitted diseases have opened up the debate over what to do about the precocious sexual activity of young people; what was once a matter of morality has become a matter of public health. Politicians, educators, doctors and parents have the best interests of their children at heart. And everyone, it seems, wishes that their kids would just say no to sex until they understand the possible consequences. But that's as far as the agreement goes: Abstinence? More sex education? Free access to contraceptives? What is best for the kids—and for all of us?

The statistical portrait of sex and the American teenager will stagger many parents. Each year for the past decade, more than a million teenage girls have become pregnant. Even though the teenage-pregnancy rate has remained fairly steady for the last few years, it is still very high—indeed, it is the highest in the Western world. The number of illegitimate births has soared. In 1984, 56 percent of teen births were out of wedlock, compared with only 15 percent in 1960. About 500,000 teenagers actually become mothers each year; the rest of the pregnancies end in miscarriages or abortions. A shocking one-third of all abortions performed annually in this country are done on teenage girls.

The outlook for the babies, and for the young mothers, is grim. They are most likely to come from low-income households, and chances are that other members of the family—their mothers or their older sisters—have been teenage mothers. If they drop out of school to have their babies, as most girls do, they probably will never finish their education and they will come to depend on public assistance to survive. A third of all teenage mothers have a second child before they turn 20. Because teenage mothers usually do not have access to any prenatal care, they do not know about nutrition; their babies are likely to have low birthweights, which in turn increases the risk of health and developmental problems. The huge number of teenage mothers is one reason why the United States has a high infant-mortality rate: 10.8 infant deaths for every 1,000 live births. According to a report released last week by the Children's Defense Fund, the United States ranked with Belgium, East Germany and West Germany for the highest infant-mortality rate among 20 industrialized countries.

High risk: A potentially more serious threat—AIDS—has forged unlikely alliances in the battle over teenage sex. Public-health experts worry openly that sexually active teenagers will be the next AIDS "high risk" group. In October Surgeon General C. Everett Koop—known for his conservative views on abortion and birth control—came out in favor of early and explicit sex education in schools; he also advocated the use of condoms as protection against AIDS. In December a distinguished panel of researchers from the National Research Council issued a report that advocated making contraceptives available to teenagers.

It is now much more acceptable to talk publicly about contraception. In the last few weeks, condom ads have begun appearing on some television stations and in major newspapers and magazines, including NEWSWEEK. The new openness is mandated by serious public-health concerns. "When it comes to pregnancy and decisions about abortion or whether to bear a child at a young age, then the stakes are high," says Leroy Walters of the Kennedy Center for Biomedical Ethics. "The stakes are even higher with an infection that could be lethal within five to 10 years."

In this atmosphere, it has also become acceptable to talk about chastity—long out of fashion. "Abstinence is our first choice," says Patricia Davis-Scott, who runs a teen health clinic that dispenses contraceptives at DuSable High School in Chicago. The National Research Council panel also endorsed programs that stress delaying sexual activity, although the panel noted in its report that "there is little available evidence to document their effectiveness." Other groups, such as the Washington-based Center for Population Options, which helps schools set up clinics, have made extensive efforts to get kids to postpone sex. The center publishes a booklet called "Make a Life for Yourself" that lists 10 reasons to wait. Among them are: "You don't want to"; "You're not ready"; "You want to wait until you're in love or married"; and "You're not using birth control." Says the center's Debra Haffner, coauthor of the booklet: "We believe in abstinence. There's no question that kids should delay having sex because most adolescents are not ready to have sex." That message seems to be getting across to at least a few stu-

dents. "We tell the kids the best kind of safe sex is abstinence," says Amy Weitz of Planned Parenthood in San Francisco, "and we're seeing more of it." Tina, a 16-year-old from Oakland, Calif., says that fear of AIDS and other diseases has made some of her friends chaste. "We call it the 'Straight Age'," she says.

But most health-care professionals aren't counting on teenagers to stay away from sex. "After food and sleep, you are dealing with the third most powerful drive we have," says Dr. Sheldon Landesman, an AIDS researcher in New York. "And sex is the most powerful nonsurvival drive." There are other forces pushing teenagers into each other's arms as well. A recent Harris poll of U.S. teenagers indicated that more than half have had intercourse by the time they are 17—primarily because they felt pressure from their peers. "My friends say, if you haven't done it, you're not in with the 'in' group," says Nekell McGrith, a 16-year-old sophomore at Harry S. Truman High School in the Bronx.

Jeans ad: Still, only a third of the teenagers who were sexually active said they used contraceptives all the time. Nearly as many (27 percent) said that they never use them. The rest said they used birth control "sometimes" or "most of the time." It's not because birth control is unavailable. Any kid who's not too embarrassed can pick up a package of condoms in the local drugstore. Sometimes kids avoid contraceptives because of ill-founded concerns about their safety. There are other prevalent myths about birth control. Last year the Detroit Free Press asked high-school students to write letters about what was wrong with their schools. Pregnancy was a major topic and many of the responses included popular misconceptions about sex. At Clintondale High School in Mt. Clemens, Mich., for example, some girls thought that you couldn't get pregnant if you wore high heels during intercourse. Other misguided ideas about sex: You can't get pregnant the first time. Douching afterwards will prevent pregnancy. You can't get pregnant standing up. You can't get pregnant if you don't kiss. Many health-care professionals say the level of ignorance among teenagers is astounding—and yet most of these children have had some kind of sex-education class in school. The sexual innuendoes in everything from blue-jean ads to MTV are "overwhelming," says June Osborn, dean of the University of Michigan's school of public health. "Pregnant kids know all about sexuality but they do not know what makes them pregnant."

First clinic: What's the best way for them to learn? Most experts say sex education should start at home, although they concede that few parents feel comfortable talking about sex. Classrooms are another important source of information, but a lot

depends on the quality of the instruction. No study has ever borne out a prevalent notion among adults: that sex education has any effect on students' rate of sexual activity. However, classes combined with school-based clinics offering contraceptives or information about birth control have been proven effective in delaying sex and lowering pregnancy rates. After the first school clinic to offer birth control was started at Mechanic Arts High School in St. Paul in 1973, birthrates were cut nearly in half. "In the schools, you have a beautiful system for follow-up because the nurse in a school has access to kids in a hallway to say, 'How's it going?' " says Gail Fearnley, a nurse-practitioner at school clinics in Muskegon, Mich.

It may turn out that the best hope for getting control of the problem is the most controversial approach. The very idea of school birth-control clinics raises troubling moral questions for many people. When the Portland, Ore., school district opened its first on-campus health clinic a year ago at Roosevelt High School, there were angry pickets. Clinic coordinator Mary Hennrich faced taunts of "devil worshiper" and "whoremonger" on her way to work. "They're well-meaning, concerned people with tunnel vision," says Hennrich of the protesters. "They think all kids are from ideal families in the suburbs and that all parents can talk openly with the kids about sex. It's not at all like that out there." The clinic at the all-black DuSable High School in one of Chicago's poorest neighborhoods

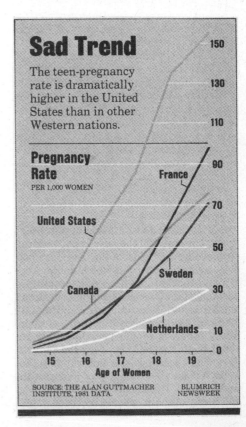

Sad Trend

The teen-pregnancy rate is dramatically higher in the United States than in other Western nations.

Pregnancy Rate
PER 1,000 WOMEN

France

United States

Sweden

Canada

Netherlands

| | | | | | |
|150|130|110|90|70|50|30|10|0|

15 16 17 18 19
Age of Women

SOURCE: THE ALAN GUTTMACHER INSTITUTE, 1981 DATA.

BLUMRICH
NEWSWEEK

is under attack in the courts; 13 black ministers from churches in the area have filed suit to close down the facility, alleging that it is a "calculated and pernicious effort to destroy the very fabric of family life among black parents and their children"—a charge denied by clinic director Patricia Davis-Scott. She says students can participate in the family-planning program only if a parent or legal guardian gives permission. "We are a school which is intimately involved with children and their families," she says. "We're not trying to circumvent parental authority."

Black leaders: Sometimes the opposition spreads beyond the schools themselves. In Boston a task force convened last fall by Schools Superintendent Laval Wilson recommended that clinics be established in two middle schools and two high schools. A powerful lobby lined up against the clinics. Included were Mayor Ray Flynn, members of the school board, local conservatives, prominent black leaders and religious leaders. The Roman Catholic Church set up its own task force and compiled a thorough report arguing that clinics are not only morally wrong but ultimately ineffective. In a letter he sent last fall to Wilson, Cardinal Bernard Law, archbishop of Boston, argued that the clinics would "place the Boston public schools in the position of implicitly condoning or encouraging sexual activity among students." Wilson is expected to decide whether or not to open the clinics in the next two weeks.

Whatever Wilson's decision, school-based clinics will probably continue to grow in popularity—and not just because they give out contraceptives. Many are located in low-income areas, where a substantial portion of the students have no health insurance. Often, the clinics provide the only medical care the kids will get. At Chicago's DuSable clinic, director Davis-Scott says that family planning is only one of 10 health programs—including regular physical examinations and prenatal care. In fact, she says, 80 percent of the students who use the clinic do not participate in the contraceptive program. The demand for clinics like the one in Chicago appears to be great. Wanda Wesson of the Support Center for School-based Clinics in Houston, which has been advising schools on how to open clinics since 1985, says that the center gets about 100 requests for help a month from schools wanting to begin new projects.

But school-based programs are not the only resource available to teens. There are about 5,000 community family-planning clinics around the country that distribute contraceptives to teenagers—often on a confidential basis. At The Hub in the South Bronx, teenagers participate in an after-school program that includes aerobics, karate and computer lessons as well as group discussions about sex and the need for contraceptives. The neighborhood, one of the poorest urban areas in the nation, has a serious teen-pregnancy problem. In 1980, the last year for which such data is available, 179 out of every 1,000 teenage girls in the South Bronx got pregnant—compared to 112 out of 1,000 for all of New York City. (The national rate in 1983 was 108 per 1,000.)

Peer pressure: "They have a lot of family problems—unemployment, alcoholism, suicide," says The Hub's director, Mary Morales. "Our focus is to give these people options other than early child rearing. We want them to know there is more out there than just having kids. If they have self-esteem, they can learn to say no. And children have to be given credit if they withstand peer pressure." With the high rate of drug use in the area, AIDS is also a very real danger for teenagers. Intravenous drug users are one of the major risk groups for the disease and are also thought to be among the main carriers of AIDS to the heterosexual population. "Maybe the best way to get the message across about contraceptives is to say use condoms—if you get AIDS, you're dead," says Morales.

At least some of the youths who use the center seem to have gotten the message. One day last week, five teenagers took part in a group discussion about attitudes toward sex and birth control. All agreed on the need for contraception, but most seemed to think the girl should take care of it. Clive McKay, an 18-year-old high-school senior, talked about "spontaneity" and how hard it is to stop and put on a condom. Dorothy Guttierrez, 19, responded angrily: "Now you have to carry a condom for him! You can stop to go to the bathroom if you have to. Why can't you protect yourself at the same time? Why should it be just the responsibility of the girl?"

Getting boys involved has been difficult in recent years. A generation ago, if a teenage girl became pregnant, she married the father. Now, says Stanford law Prof. Robert Mnookin, a member of the National

Teenagers, Birth Control and AIDS

Americans 13 and older are split over whether schools that dispense birth control encourage sex. But they overwhelmingly believe that parents unable to prevent their child from having sex should help the teenager get birth control.

How worried are you that AIDS will spread widely among the nation's teenagers?

48%	Very worried
24%	A little worried
15%	Not very worried
9%	Not worried at all

If a school dispenses birth-control devices, do you think that will make teenagers more likely to engage in sexual activities or not?

45%	More likely
47%	Not more likely

At what age do you think young people should be first able to get birth-control devices?

3%	8-11
31%	12-15
54%	16-18

Has the fear of AIDS affected the social life and dating habits of teenagers greatly, to some extent or not at all?

13%	Greatly
43%	To some extent
29%	Not at all

Which do you think is the best way to limit AIDS and unwanted pregnancies? By emphasizing:

51%	Sex education
43%	Advocating abstinence

What method of birth control do you think is most appropriate for teenagers?

	13- to 17-year-olds	Total
The Pill	69%	42%
Diaphragm	1%	4%
Condom	26%	34%
Foam	1%	1%
The sponge	2%	2%
Abstinence	0%	8%

If parents are unable to prevent their teenage child from having sexual relations, is it better for them to help the teenager get birth control or not?

76%	Help
16%	Not help

Should teenagers be able to get birth-control devices at the following places, only with their parents' permission or not at all?

	Should be available	Should not be	Only with parents' OK
Family doctor	52%	5%	42%
Clinic	50%	9%	39%
School	24%	41%	32%
Local drugstore	34%	34%	31%

For this NEWSWEEK Poll, The Gallup Organization conducted telephone interviews with a representative sample of 606 Americans over the age of 13 on Feb. 5 and 6. The margin of error is plus or minus 5 percentage points. Some "Don't know" and "Other" answers omitted. The NEWSWEEK Poll © 1987 by NEWSWEEK, Inc.

Research Council panel, "it's more common for her to abort or be a single parent, and for the boy to become difficult to find or wash his hands of responsibility." Mnookin says the attitude of most young boys is: "You take the Pill, you take the risk. If you don't want to have a baby, you have an abortion." Mnookin recommends the enforcement of child-support laws to make it clear to young men one "mistake" can mean 18 years of paying bills.

But other experts say that work with boys has to begin on an even more basic level. Louise Flick, an associate professor at the St. Louis University School of Nursing, has reviewed studies conducted over 15 years on teenagers' attitudes toward sexuality. Boys tend to be less well informed about sex and contraception than girls and have more trouble discussing sex—although they may cover up their discomfort with "macho" talk. The boys' role is crucial in contraception. "Girls say they don't want to use contraceptives because their partners don't want them to," says Morales of The Hub. "The boys say condoms don't feel good, destroy the sensation, are artificial. The condoms made today are so thin, you can't feel them."

Some groups are making special efforts to reach boys. It's not easy. Charles Ballard, who runs the Teen Fathers Program in Cleveland, says that one day he asked a group of 15 boys how many were fathers. Only two raised their hands. When he asked how many had babies, 14 hands went up. "They just don't think like fathers," Ballard says. "They don't connect pregnancy with marriage or husbanding or fatherhood." At least 65 percent of his clients never really knew their own fathers. "No man has ever touched their lives except a policeman," he says, "and he was approaching them with a gun or billyclub in his hand."

Although many boys seem to be able to ignore the responsibilities of parenthood, AIDS has made them think about condoms. Fear of dying isn't the only reason; teenagers often have a hard time believing in their own mortality. "They're terrified of getting AIDS and being labeled homosexual," says Medora Brown, who runs the sex-education program at Como High School in St. Paul, Minn. "That's the issue—they are more afraid of having people call them gay than they are of dying."

Comic strip: Family-planning groups and condom manufacturers are taking advantage of this increased receptivity to contraceptives. A series of Planned Parenthood ads featuring comic strips of young people urges readers to "protect your love with condoms." Condoms are coming out of the wallet; not only are manufacturers placing ads in mainstream publications and TV stations like KRON in San Francisco, they are trying to appeal to younger audiences, experimenting with packaging and hipper slogans. Rev. Carl Titchener of suburban Buffalo dispensed condoms during a sermon on AIDS last Sunday.

Condoms have begun to appear on regular television programs as well—a move that health-care experts say is particularly important since teenagers get many of their ideas about sex from television and movies. In the Harris poll, substantial numbers of teenagers said that they thought television presented an accurate portrayal of sexually transmitted diseases, pregnancy and birth control. Younger teenagers were more likely to believe in television than older teens. "TV has become the major form of sex education," says Dr. Victor Strasburger, head of the American Academy of Pediatrics task force on children and television. The problem is, sex on television isn't very realistic.

Koop and Bennett Agree to Disagree

Secretary of Education William Bennett and Surgeon General C. Everett Koop, two of America's most visible and voluble conservatives, have clashed in recent weeks over the issue of sex education for teenagers. Two weeks ago, in an attempt to head off a looming feud, the two issued a joint statement. They managed to agree on this much: "Education has a fundamental role to play in teaching our young people how to avoid that threat [of AIDS]." On the important questions that lie just beyond, however— what kind of role education should play and how far it should go—they seem to have agreed to disagree. Curiously, it is not the education secretary but the surgeon general who has taken a broader view of what students should learn about AIDS in school.

Last week, at the convention of the National Religious Broadcasters, Koop was out once again stumping for the use of condoms to prevent the spread of AIDS. He repeated the joint statement's position that "the safest approach to sexuality for adults is to choose either abstinence or faithful monogamy." But in the absence of such a choice, he went on, "an individual must be warned to use the protection of a condom." The Koop-Bennett statement had made no mention of condoms, which the surgeon general in November had called the best protection short of abstinence. "Strong, honest and family-centered" sex education (which Koop prefers to call "health and human development") should begin in kindergarten, he told the religious broadcasters, and explain the dangers of sexually transmitted diseases—specifically AIDS—in junior high school.

Moral context: Bennett is moving more cautiously. He says schools should stress abstinence and should teach about sex only as a part of marriage. "In matters like this," he says, "I trust the judgment of the local community instead of the sexperts." Even where sex education is taught, he adds, contraception, abortion and condom-protection should not automatically be made part of the curriculum, nor should contraceptives be dispensed in school. (Koop has not taken a position on contraceptive distribution.) To do so "encourages those children who do not have sexual intimacy on their minds to have it on their minds," he said in a speech last year. Sen. Paul Simon, Democrat of Illinois, who plans in this Congress to reintroduce his bill calling for federal funding of school clinics that might offer family-planning services, suggests that "It's been too long since [Bennett] was a teenager." But Bennett argues that sex education should be taught "in a moral context" and that to dispense contraceptives in schools "is to throw up one's hands and say, 'We give up'."

Koop and others argue, in effect, that sex is a fact of life. Last week, speaking to the religious broadcasters, the surgeon general cited a Michigan State University study that found that large numbers of 9th- and 10th-grade girls watch one to two hours of soap operas every day; the programs show or discuss sex between unmarried partners an average of 1.5 times an hour. "You as Christians will continue to be tested by tremendous questions that arise from the turmoil of current events," he said and urged them to face squarely the sensitive intertwining of sexuality and public health. For non-Christians too, these are frightening issues. And short of a cure, education may be the only answer.

BILL BAROL *with* MARY HAGER *and* PAT WINGERT *in Washington*

3. REPRODUCTION: Birth Control

Lovers usually hop into bed quite spontaneously—with little thought of the consequences. Teenagers raised on these scenes of impulsive romance think they're watching the only course of true love. Last October Planned Parenthood launched an ad campaign with slogans like "When J.R. took Mandy for a roll in the hay, which one had the condom?" and "They did it 20,000 times on television last year. How come nobody got pregnant?" Says Faye Wattleton, president of the Planned Parenthood Federation of America: "Just as sex is integrated into most programming, prevention should be also. It should go hand in hand."

Some television executives are beginning to make changes, partly in response to pressure from groups like Planned Parenthood. "We were avoiding the issues," concedes Al Rabin, executive director of the soap opera "Days of Our Lives." "We had teens losing their virginity. When we wanted her to get pregnant, she'd get pregnant, but we never mentioned contraception." Rabin developed a new story line where a young girl wants to make love with her boyfriend and discusses it with her grandmother, her brother, a doctor and a married girlfriend—all of whom urge her to use birth control. The program even showed her boyfriend buying a condom.

There are changes on prime time as well. The producers of the NBC show "Valerie" say it wasn't easy to convince the network's censors to let them use the word "condom" on a sitcom. "If you can talk about it on the 6 o'clock news," says coexecutive producer Thomas Miller, "why can't you talk about it on 8 o'clock sitcoms?" Miller finally won, but when the show ran Sunday, it was preceded by an advisory from the network that parents watch the show with their children. It won't be the last time condoms appear on television. In April, ABC is going to air a movie called "Daddy" that shows a teenage boy passing a condom to a friend. " 'Daddy' is not a two-hour movie dealing with an unwanted pregnancy that never produces a baby," says Ted Harbert, ABC's vice president for motion pictures. "In our movie, [a teenage girl] has the baby in the first hour and you spend the next hour watching her deal with the consequences." The 22-year-old star, Dermot Mulroney, says he didn't have to do a lot of research on the subject to prepare for his role. "I went to high school in Virginia where, my senior year, there were 52 pregnancies," Mulroney says. "An unplanned pregnancy is as devastating as a death in the family. It changes your life forever."

Low income: As well-intended as all these efforts are, they may be treating only the symptoms, not the disease. Teenagers who begin sex early and don't use contraceptives are likely to come from low-income homes or single-parent families. "They're little kids with grown-up problems," says Kim Cox, a health educator at Balboa High School in San Francisco. They are moved to sex, many of them, not by compassion or love or any of the other urges that make sense to adults, but by a need for intimacy that has gone unfulfilled by their families. "Sex," says Cox, "is an easy way to get it."

Teenagers make important decisions about their lives on their own—without much help from parents. It's not just that adults are uncomfortable discussing sex with their kids, although many probably are. The teenagers don't think they can talk to their parents. In the Harris poll, 64 percent of teenagers said they had never discussed birth control with their parents.

Parents are also reluctant to assert their authority in a positive way. Dr. Catherine Deangelis, a professor of pediatrics and adolescent medicine at Johns Hopkins University in Baltimore who runs an inner-city health clinic for teenagers, says she often sees 13- and 14-year-olds come into her clinic with their mothers—both dressed in jeans. "My first question is how does she know you're her mother? I mean, psychologically, that you are her mother, not her friend?" Deangelis tries to teach parents that they must set limits for their children and teach them right from wrong.

As the problems of teenage pregnancy and the fear of AIDS grow worse, the dilemma will deepen as well: where to draw the line between the rights and responsibilities of parents and society's need to protect itself. Our children—and their children—will be waiting for the answer.

BARBARA KANTROWITZ *with* MARY HAGER *and* PAT WINGERT *in Washington,* GINNY CARROLL *in Detroit,* GEORGE RAINE *in San Francisco,* MONROE ANDERSON *in Chicago,* DEBORAH WITHERSPOON *in New York,* JANET HUCK *in Los Angeles and* SHAWN DOHERTY *in Boston*

Vasectomy Update: Effects on Health and Sexuality

Jonathan P. Jarow, MD

Jonathan P. Jarow is Assistant Professor, Section of Urology, Bowman Gray School of Medicine, Winston-Salem, NC.

Safe and inexpensive, vasectomy is the most commonly selected form of male contraception. Reversal success runs a high 90%, but fertility cannot be guaranteed.

Vasectomy is one of the most frequently chosen forms of contraception in the United States today.[1] Approximately 300,000 vasectomies were performed each year during the past four years—in almost all cases to produce sterility. Some of the procedures are done in conjunction with prostate surgery or to prevent recurrent epididymitis. At one time, vasectomy was performed on aging men in hopes of raising their testosterone levels via Leydig cell hyperplasia.[2] Today, endocrinological, histological, and immunological changes associated with vasectomy are known to occur, but their specific effects are still being investigated.

Sterilization: male vs female

Surgical sterilization leads all other forms of contraception for couples aged 30–44 and for those who no longer desire children. Of the 7 million individuals who underwent surgical sterilization between 1975 and 1980, 58% were women and 42% were men.[3] The risks and benefits of male vs female sterilization may be summarized as follows:

● Vasectomy can be performed on an outpatient basis under local anesthesia; female sterilization, a more complicated procedure, requires general anesthesia.

● Vasectomy has a much lower morbidity and mortality rate than female surgical sterilization.

● Sterilization efficacy rates are similar for both procedures: 0.28 failures per 100 vasectomy cases; 0.33 failures per 100 tubal ligations.[4]

● Shortterm costs of female sterilization are three to four times higher than those associated with vasectomy.

Vasectomy is generally performed by a urologist. In a study of 357 consecutive bilateral vasectomies, the most frequent complication reported was epididymitis (1.5%).[5] Less than 1% of the patients developed minor complications such as hematoma or cellulitis. In a global study of sterilization-associated deaths, only one death was attributed to vasectomy compared to 54 deaths following tubal ligations.[6] Despite these findings, tubal ligation is still the more commonly performed procedure.

Physical, social, and psychological factors undoubtedly play a major role in the choice of procedure. For example, a significant number of tubal ligations are performed in association with cesarean section or vaginal delivery. There are also many men who fear the possible side effects of vasectomy. Most often, vasectomy is chosen by couples who are acquainted with other men who have undergone the procedure, or by those in which the husband is strongly motivated to terminate childbearing, or has used other contraceptive methods in the past. It is important to inform patients undergoing vasectomy that most men become sterile within six weeks of the surgery, but 10% will experience delayed azoospermia (past 180 days).[3] Persistent fertility can occur in as many as 1%–2% of cases.

Endocrine effects

Recent data indicate that there are no significant hormonal changes following vasectomy, nor have gross changes in the volume of vasectomized testes been documented. In one study, in which prevasectomy hormone levels were compared to those obtained six to 24 months postvasectomy, a statistically significant rise in plasma testosterone and luteinizing hormone (LH) was found.[7] Follicle-stimulating hormone, although unchanged at six months, became elevated at two years. Since none of these elevated levels exceeded normal ranges, however, their clinical significance is currently unclear. Yet another study, which followed patients who had undergone bilateral vasectomy for five years, showed a slight elevation in plasma LH but no change in plasma testosterone levels.[8]

Sperm granulomas

Following vasectomy, the testis continues to produce sperm. The sperm is apparently phagocytized within the vas deferens and epididymis, which is a normal, prevasectomy activity. If sufficient pres-

sure builds within the epididymis and vas deferens, however, spontaneous rupture will occur at the ligated end of the vas or more proximally. The resultant immune response leads to inflammation and the formation of sperm granulomas. These granulomas, which vary in size, are composed of sperm debris surrounded by histiocytes and neutrophils. Researchers discovered granulomas in up to 41% of vasectomized men undergoing vasectomy reversal, and vasitis nodosa in 66% of the men.[9] In other studies based on physical examination alone, however, the incidence was as low as 0%. Most sperm granulomas are

---

> ## "Approximately 10% of vasectomy patients request a reversal of the procedure at some later time."

---

asymptomatic, but some can be quite tender or painful. Recommended treatment varies from conservative measures such as sitz baths and nonsteroidal anti-inflammatory drugs to surgical excision.

Vasectomy and immunology

The most widely used tests to determine the presence of anti-sperm antibodies in serum and semen include the gelatin agglutination test (GAT or Kibrick test), the tray agglutination test (TAT or Friberg test), and the sperm immobilization test (SIT or Isojima test). Anti-sperm antibodies have been demonstrated in as many as 70% of patients one year postvasectomy. By contrast, the inci-

dence of agglutinating antibodies in control populations is 2% and that of immobilizing antibodies, 0%. The antibodies are of the IgG and IgM class; titers range from 2–1,024.

Researchers reported in 1978 that the combination of vasectomy and a high lipid diet caused atherosclerosis in Macaca monkeys.[10] They attributed this effect to the deposition of circulating immune complexes composed of anti-sperm antibodies and antigen. Since the atherogenic effect was only significant in the group with a high serum cholesterol level, however, it may only be clinically significant in a population predisposed to atherosclerosis. Moreover, such observations in lower primates have not been observed in humans. In a large cohort study, no increased health risk for vasectomized men was found.[11] Excluding epididymitis-orchitis, the disease incidence for vasectomy patients was similar to or lower than that seen in paired controls. An investigation into the longterm effects of vasectomy (mean, 15 years) also showed no evidence of any increased risk for heart attack.[12]

Testis changes following vasectomy

Studies in animals have revealed a wide variety of testicular changes after vasectomy; however, some of these changes, such as the autoimmune process observed in the guinea pig, are species-related. Other changes appear to be related to the duration of obstruction, the surgical technique employed, or the volume of testicular output.[13] In humans, disordered spermatogenesis, thickening of the tunica propria of the tubular wall, ultrastructural changes in the spermatids, and testicular interstitial fibrosis have all been observed.

Using light and electron microscopic examination in a recent controlled study, interstitial fibrosis was demonstrated in 23% of postvasectomy patients and spermatogenic arrest in 6%.[14] Morphometric analysis revealed a doubling of the seminiferous tubule wall thickness and a 50% increase in tubule diameter. The number of Sertoli cells and spermatids in the testes was found to be significantly reduced in vasectomized men compared to the control population. No significant changes were observed in the Leydig cell population. None of these histological changes, however, suggests that vasectomy poses any significant health hazard.

The mechanism of these testicular changes is unclear. They may be due to an autoimmune phenomena; however, examinations of postvasectomy human testis biopsies for antibodies or immune complexes have been negative. One possible, but unproven mechanism might be a purely mechanical phenomena. The testis, as in other obstructed organs, demonstrates tubule dilatation and wall thickening due to collagen deposition. This may result from a transient increase in the seminiferous tubule pressure.

Vasectomy reversal

Approximately 10% of vasectomy patients request a reversal of the procedure at some later time. Typically, the patient has under-gone vasectomy after having had several children with his first wife, but then remarries a younger woman with whom he wants to start a second family. The surgical success rate (sperm present in the ejaculate) is about 90%; the fertility rate for these couples, however, ranges only from 40%–70%, which is significantly lower than the 85% reported for "normal" couples. This decrease in fertility may be due to the development of sperm antibodies, damage to the deferential nerve, epididymal extravasation, or testicular changes.

Vasectomy reversal may be

"Vasectomy has a much lower morbidity and mortality rate than female surgical sterilization."

---

performed with or without a surgical microscope, although the best results are probably achieved with its use. A vasovasotomy is usually effective, however, if there is a more proximal obstruction, a vasoepididymostomy may be required. Examination of the intravasal fluid for sperm at the time of the operation will determine the patency of the more proximal ductules and guide the surgeon in choosing the correct procedure. Positive prognostic factors for vasectomy reversal include a relatively short interval between vasectomy and reversal (best results occur if done less than 10 years following vasectomy), a finding of sperm granulomas at the vasectomy site, and the presence of intravasal sperm at the time of operation.

Summary

Vasectomy is the most frequently used method of male contraception, and is safe, simple, and inexpensive. Patients are considered sterile when the ejaculate is sperm-free. Vasectomy reversal is possible, but fertility cannot be guaranteed. Vasectomy does not appear to significantly affect the endocrine or exocrine functioning of the testis. The procedure does carry significant immunological consequences, but their effects in humans have not been fully determined. Since clinically evident deleterious effects have not been demonstrated to date, vasectomy is currently recommended as a highly satisfactory contraceptive choice for appropriately selected patients.

References

1. Philliber SG, Philliber WW: Social and psychological perspectives on voluntary sterilization: A review. *Stud Fam Plan* 16:1, 1985.
2. Steinach E: Biological methods against the process of old age. *Med J Rec* 125:77, 1927.
3. Shain RN, Miller WB, Holden AEC: Factors associated with married women's selection of tubal sterilization and vasectomy. *Fertil Steril* 43:234, 1985.
4. Smith GL, Taylor GP, Smith KF: Comparative risks and costs of male and female sterilization. *Am J Publ Health* 75:370, 1985.
5. Tailly G, Vereecken RL, Verduyn H: A review of 357 bilateral vasectomies for male sterilization. *Fertil Steril* 41:424, 1984.

Pill Politics

A new drug makes abortion more personal, private, and convenient. So why do you have to fly to France to get it?

LAURA FRASER

San Francisco journalist Laura Fraser often writes about women's health care issues.

Sometime this year women in five countries can begin taking a pill that could change the nature of abortion as we know it. The pill, an antiprogesterone steroid called RU 486, can end a pregnancy up to three weeks after a missed menstrual period. There are still a few questions about RU 486, but extensive research so far has shown it to be safe enough to be a potential breakthrough for millions of women with unwanted pregnancies. It has been approved for use in France, China, Sweden, the Netherlands, and Britain. But because of political pressure from the right, and the cost of developing and insuring new contraceptives, women in the United States will not have access to RU 486 anytime in the near future—unless they buy it on the black market.

RU 486 HAS BEEN CALLED AN "abortion pill"; critics on the right prefer the term "death pill." But the drug, developed by scientists at the French pharmaceutical company Roussel-Uclaf, works so soon after fertilization that it might more accurately be called the

RU 486 means no waiting, no walking past picket lines, no feet up in stirrups for surgery. When used properly, says one supporter, the drug is "a revolution. I can't wait until we get our hands on it."

"period pill." Taken orally and under a doctor's supervision, RU 486 blocks the hormone progesterone from reaching uterine cell receptors; without progesterone, the uterine lining breaks down, the fertilized egg is dispelled, and menstruation occurs. For a woman whose period is late, using RU 486 means no waiting, no walking past picket lines at abortion clinics, and no feet up in stirrups for surgery. It also means

she will never have to know whether she had actually been pregnant.

Those are attractive features for a potentially enormous market. The failure to use existing contraceptives, most of which are either inconvenient or cause irritating side effects, has combined with method failures to give the United States one of the highest percentages of accidental pregnancies in the industrialized world. More than half of the 6 million pregnancies that occur in the United States each year are mistakes, and half of those pregnancies, or 1.6 million, end in abortion.

When coupled with a small dose of another drug called prostaglandin, taken two days later, RU 486 is over 90 percent effective (see "A Passing Grade"). Researchers don't know why it doesn't work the rest of the time, or why it occasionally produces side effects—heavy bleeding, nausea, fatigue, and, rarely, hemorrhaging. Since RU 486 stays in the body for only about 48 hours, the side effects are usually short-lived. But more research, and perhaps more tinkering, will need to be done before RU 486 can pass FDA requirements for marketing in this country.

So far, preliminary findings on the drug look promising enough to elicit the tentative support of two groups that otherwise have been bitterly divided on

Beyond RU 486

RU 486 ISN'T THE ONLY NEW BIRTH control method in the works. Researchers are developing implants that continuously release low doses of hormones for up to five years, 24-hour vaginal spermicidal pills, reversible vasectomy devices, hormone-blocking nasal sprays, vaginal rings, and once-a-month injections, to name a few.

But, as with RU 486, getting these new contraceptives approved and marketed may be difficult. At present, women and men have the same number of contraceptive options they had when the Pill was introduced 28 years ago.

The future may lie with smaller firms. The IUD, for example, is available in the United States from only two small companies: the Alza Corporation, which markets Progestasert, a device that releases local contraceptive hormones, and GynoPharma, which is marketing the new Copper T 380A. Both companies are small enough that they don't have enormous assets to lose in a liability case, and both have done extensive research and consumer education to be sure that women understand the method to know whether it is right for them. The best way to insure against liability, after all, is to develop a safe product.   —L.F.

the topic of new birth control methods: the family planning establishment—relatively large organizations like the Planned Parenthood Federation of America, the World Health Organization, and the Population Council—and grass roots feminist health activists from the smaller Committee to Defend Reproductive Rights, the Boston Women's Health Book Collective, and the National Women's Health Network. But the support the drug needs most is financial, and that has not been forthcoming: not one U.S. pharmaceutical company has been willing to invest in the research that could lead to the marketing of the drug. And because RU 486 can be used as an abortifacient, a drug that facilitates abortion, the Public Health Act prohibits the use of government money to study or develop it for that purpose.

The slow pace of RU 486's development and marketing in the United States frustrates the drug's supporters. "RU 486 is a revolution," says Debbie Rogow, who works with reproductive health programs in developing countries. When used under proper medical supervision, she says, RU 486 "will change everything. I can't wait until we get our hands on this stuff."

Rogow is particularly interested in the drug's political side effects. "The Right has concentrated its fear of women's sexuality and equality on abortion," she says. "RU 486 is really going to fuck with the anti-abortion movement's strategy. When this thing hits the market, the movement will have been technologically bypassed."

• • • • • •

LEADERS OF THE ANTI-ABORTION MOVEment might be ruffled by Rogow's choice of words, but they would find it hard to disagree with her analysis. They are, in fact, keenly aware that RU 486 could sabotage their best efforts, especially in public relations. "It's more difficult to make the case that this is a developing baby if you don't have pictures of the fetus," explains Richard Glasow, the education director for the

National Right to Life Committee, the largest anti-abortion group in the country. "If you can show people fingers and toes, it's dynamite." Photographs of the menstrual blood that results from the use of RU 486 could hardly have the same effect. If RU 486 were to become available, "the abortion debate wouldn't go away," Glasow says, "but we'd lose some of our best arguments."

Dr. John Willke of the National Right to Life Committee warns that he and his allies will make every attempt to stigmatize the use of RU 486 as much as they have surgical abortion. Willke calls RU 486 "chemical warfare on the unborn," arguing that life starts at fertilization—even though between 40 and 60 percent of all fertilized eggs are never implanted and are sloughed off naturally in menstrual blood. National Right to Life, Willke vows, will boycott any company that attempts to develop or market RU 486.

Abortion opponents have tried the boycott tactic before. They stopped using over-the-counter Upjohn products from 1983 to 1985 because the company was marketing prostaglandins, which cause severe uterine contractions that induce abortion. Prostaglandins

A Passing Grade

SINCE 1982, RU 486 HAS BEEN USED IN clinical trials by over 4,000 women in 20 countries, which is a larger sampling than the FDA would require in the United States. All of the research has shown the drug to be effective only in terminating pregnancy in its earliest stages—up to six or seven weeks after the onset of the last menstrual period. After eight weeks, the drug is virtually ineffective.

Several studies have reported that RU 486, when used by itself, works successfully about 85 percent of the time. One French study, published 18 months ago in the New England Journal of Medicine, reported the results of research on 100 healthy women, with regular menstrual periods, who were given a dose (between 400 and 800 milligrams) of RU 486 within ten days of their missed periods. Within four days, 85 of the women ended their pregnancies. The other 15 bled, but had incomplete abortions, which required follow-up surgery. All of the women bled, similar

to a heavy menstrual period, for between 5 and 17 days, and 26 of the women reported cramping more painful than normal menstrual cramps. A little less than a fourth reported slight nausea and fatigue. During the month that followed the procedure, no additional complications were reported.

Studies using RU 486 in conjunction with prostaglandins have shown improved results. A 1984 study in Sweden revealed a 94 percent effectiveness rate when a small dose of prostaglandin was given intravenously with RU 486. (Prostaglandins also can be given as a suppository or injection.) That study and a British study report that when used together the two drugs bring on an abortion with less blood loss and milder side effects.

The FDA, which would have to approve RU 486 before it could be marketed in the United States, "might accept" the results of some of the studies already carried out in other countries, says FDA spokeswoman Susan Cruzan. But, she adds, the agency "would probably require tests in the United States."   —L.F.

have been approved by the FDA for use only after the first trimester of pregnancy; since more than 90 percent of abortions are performed earlier, prostaglandins were never as large or profitable a market as RU 486 could be.

Right-to-lifers claimed victory in 1985 when Upjohn stopped developing one of its prostaglandins and announced it was getting out of the birth control research business altogether. Company officials, however, insisted Upjohn had been driven out of fertility research by the costs of long product development time and liability insurance. The decision "was not influenced by National Right to Life," says Upjohn spokeswoman Jessyl Bradford.

Upjohn isn't the only company to decide that birth control development is risky business. The brute expense of shepherding a contraceptive through research, clinical trials, and FDA approval is estimated at $30 million to $70 million—a figure that doesn't include the cost of setting aside massive amounts of cash to insure against liability claims—and the process could take as long as 17 years. Twelve other pharmaceutical companies that researched contraceptives in the 1970s have dropped out, leaving only Ortho Pharmaceutical active in the field.

Most research and development is now carried out either by government laboratories or by nonprofit research agencies that get much of their funding from the government. Sixty percent of all contraceptive development funding in the United States now comes from the federal government, up from 25 percent in 1970. Not surprisingly, right-wing political influence is playing a greater role in research priorities.

The Population Council, a nonprofit research organization, has used private foundation money to support low-level RU 486 research at the University of Southern California, in the only experiments in the country that have studied RU 486's use as an abortifacient. (Among its other uses, the drug appears to be effective in treating Cushing's Syndrome, a hormonal disorder usually treated by removing the adrenal glands, as well as certain types of breast cancer and endometriosis. Research also has indicated that RU 486 can be used as a cervical softener, potentially eliminating the need for many cesarean births.) Dr. C. Wayne Bardin, the council's director of biomedical research, says he has received irate letters and phone calls from right-to-lifers, including one from Jesse Helms's office, mistakenly accusing the council of using government funds to publish a book on RU 486. But more often the politicking is less direct. "There are other ways a researcher can be pressured besides just having money cut off for a particular product," he says. "You can have money blocked for some other research you want to do." Abortion foes in Congress and the administration also closely monitor the work of the Population Council, says Bardin, "looking for things that can be used against us."

If it weren't for political pressure, and if money weren't a barrier, Bardin says, "RU 486 would really be a number one priority." The drug's greatest potential, he says, may be in stopping the "enormous carnage" of women around the world from botched abortions—perhaps 200,000 deaths a year, with countless more women left maimed and infertile. He sighs. "But right now all the politicians hear about are people who are opposed to RU 486."

If the process of getting FDA approval and conducting market research for RU 486 began tomorrow, it would still be between five and ten years before the drug was legally available here. And that process is not likely to begin without the vocal support of women who see the drug as a way to get more personal, and political, control over their fertility. Marie Bass, whose political consulting firm has studied the prospects of making RU 486 legally available in the United States, has called for "a countercampaign to the rhetoric and misinformation" of the right-to-life community. A public clamor for RU 486, Bass believes, could outweigh a pharmaceutical company's concerns over a right-wing boycott. The potential for such clamor exists, since RU 486 has the support of most prochoice organizations. But the support is unorganized, at least in part because family planning groups have long been at odds with women's health activists, often accusing feminists of being so zealous in making sure contraceptives are safe that no new products ever make it to the market.

Many researchers and manufacturers, too, blame the stall in contraceptive development more on women's health activists than on the anti-abortion movement. The current liability insurance crisis, they say, discouraged them from staying in the contraceptive business. Expensive litigation like the $2.48 billion Dalkon Shield settlement, which women's groups played a large part in organizing and publicizing, was the final straw. Despite the fact that 2.2 million women were using IUDs that were much safer than the Dalkon Shield—which, unlike other IUDs, was never approved by the FDA—most of the devices were pulled off the market in the wake of the Dalkon Shield lawsuit. Jacqueline Forrest of the Alan Guttmacher Institute, a nonprofit reproductive health research agency, estimates that the withdrawal of the IUD from the American market caused 123,000 unintended pregnancies by former users. Even Norma Swenson of the Boston Women's Health Book Collective, who emphasizes that the Dalkon Shield settlement represents a hard-fought victory for the women's health movement, admits that it had the ironic by-product of "chilling manufacturers."

Swenson's colleague at the Health Book Collective, Judy Norsigian, places the blame for the liability insurance mess elsewhere. "Fear of excessive litigation," she says, "has nothing to do with feminists. It has to do with lawyers." In any event, liability insurance for the manufacture and sale of contraceptives is now, in most cases, impossible to get. That leaves the contraceptive field to very small companies with few assets to attach (see "Beyond RU, 486"), or to large corporations that have some products with huge profit margins, allowing them to bank against the possible costs of litigation. Birth control pills, for example, cost pennies to make and are usually sold for about $14 a cycle. Could RU 486 be as profitable? There's no telling, but Marie Bass believes that "when some drug company sees the possibility of millions of dollars, you can believe it will go through the hoops and get RU 486 on the market."

Feminist groups may have contributed unwittingly to the crisis in contraceptive liability insurance, although the problem is just a small part of a broader liability insurance crisis throughout the U.S. economy. But it is thanks to the vigilance of women's health groups, and to feminists within the family-planning establishment, that pharmaceutical companies, research groups, and the FDA now pay closer attention to women's health. Stringent FDA regulations, extensive labeling, and informed-consent requirements mean that the experiments in the early '60s with dangerous high-dose oral contraceptives are not going to be repeated—nor will another Dalkon Shield likely find its way to the market.

When and if RU 486 becomes legal in the United States, it will probably not be available initially by simple prescription; rather, it will be part of a medical procedure, including counseling and health screening. The procedure will be, in Marie Bass's words, "not as expensive as a surgical abortion," which usually costs at least $200, "but not a whole lot cheaper." The drug's supporters hope that once it becomes more popular, the price will fall. But until RU 486 becomes legal here, the only way American women will be able to get it is through the black market—which, predicts Planned Parenthood president Faye Wattleton, will happen as the drug gains widespread acceptance in other countries. At the Boston Women's Health Book Collective, Norma Swenson argues that RU 486 would save so many women around the world from death by botched abortion that it would be worth it for women's groups to organize its underground use. "Using RU 486 in countries where abortion is illegal," she says, "would be a type of civil disobedience."

Unsupervised use of RU 486 pills, however, could be dangerous. Dr. Louise Tyrer, Planned Parenthood's vice president for medical affairs, ticks off the risks: "Women would use them later in pregnancy than they should; women would use them and not terminate and continue a pregnancy; they would use them and hemorrhage, or have some retained tissue and get an infection and not be aware that they needed to get ahold of the doctor until they were in pretty bad shape." But in countries where women use sticks and coat hangers, or pound on their stomachs until they abort, it may be a question of weighing the risks.

If the medically supervised use of RU 486 proves the drug to be safe and reliable, as virtually everyone monitoring the research believes will be the case, it could greatly ease the lives of American women. Even in the best of circumstances, an abortion is physically painful. And for many women, the real pain is emotional; the decision not to have a child can be a powerful and sad one. Once that decision is made, it is best carried out quickly. Being pregnant and anticipating an abortion is traumatic, especially in a society where, largely because of the efforts of the anti-abortion movement, it is difficult not to internalize the public shame inflicted on a very personal choice.

With the safe and legal use of RU 486, ending an unwanted pregnancy could become even more explicitly a personal matter. But that won't happen without a public outcry for more research and the eventual marketing of RU 486, A coalition of family planning and women's health groups brought us abortion rights in the 1970s; perhaps they can help ensure that a safer, easier way to end pregnancy is available to women in the 1990s.

A Failed Revolution

We expected the perfect contraceptive by now but our choices are more limited than ever before. ELLEN SWEET's investigation found that bottom-line pressure and liability risks have caused most major drug companies to give up the search.

THREE YEARS AGO, A Harris poll found that three fourths of Americans believed that a major breakthrough in birth-control technology was right around the corner—less than five years away. It was an advance eagerly awaited by American women, 60 percent of whom were dissatisfied with all available contraceptives. But today we have no more choices than we had 20 years ago, and technology has yet to deliver a safe, effective contraceptive.

"In the United States, we are losing contraceptive methods faster than we are gaining them," says Richard Lincoln, senior vice president of the Alan Guttmacher Institute, a nonprofit agency doing research and analysis on reproductive health. He and other family-planning experts worry that the birth-control "revolution," heralded by the development of synthetic reproductive hormones in the late fifties, has failed and left us in a crisis that the pharmaceutical industry, paralyzed by liability suits and bottom-line pressure, seems unable to resolve.

The expectation of no-hassle, highly effective birth control dates from the marketing of the Pill in 1960, followed a few years later by the IUD. Now we have an improved, lower dosage, safer Pill; and the sponge has been added to the older forms of birth control—the diaphragm, condom, spermicides, rhythm method, and sterilization. But

we have lost most IUDs. Although dozens of ideas are in the pipeline, only three companies, one of them in the U.S., are actively researching new methods, says Lincoln, as compared to 13 in the early 1970s.

Among the 35 million women in the United States who need birth control at any given time, 12 million women are sterilized or have partners who have had vasectomies, 10 million use the Pill, 4.5 million depend on condoms, 3 million use the diaphragm, 2.5 million were using the IUD (before 1985 when most companies stopped manufacturing it for use in this country), and 1.5 million use the sponge. (See chart, next page.) But the inadequacy of these methods may be judged by the numbers of women who get pregnant unintentionally each year. In 1982, 3.3 million women—6 percent of all women aged 15 to 44—had unintended pregnancies and 1.6 million women had abortions. Half of these pregnancies, or 1.5 million, are the result of not using any contraceptives at all.

1988 Models

The two types of birth-control pill available today are both lower-dose refinements on the original formulation. The "minipill" contains only progestin and—since it leads to irregular spotting—is only prescribed for women who should not take estrogen. The most popular pill combines progestin and estrogen,

the estrogen to suppress ovulation and the progestin to increase the thickness of cervical mucus, preventing passage of sperm, and to decrease the thickness of the uterine lining, preventing implantation of a fertilized egg. The newest versions of this combined pill, marketed since 1983, release the progestin in different amounts at different stages, or phases, of the menstrual cycle. According to Ortho Pharmaceutical, its triphasic pill, Ortho-Novum 7/7/7, is now the most frequently prescribed oral contraceptive in the U.S. The advantage of such pills, says John McGuire, Ortho's vice president of preclinical research and development, is that they allow for lower doses than ever before. To some observers the refinement had as much to do with the company's expiring patent as with safety. (See box, page 112.)

Sixty-six percent of women have used the Pill at one time or another. The cost of a 13-month prescription filled at a drugstore ranges widely—from $115 to $260—but it is considerably cheaper at clinics. During the past year, as patents expired, generic versions have been introduced at prices 30 to 50 percent lower.

Only one IUD is being sold in the U.S. at present—major companies stopped marketing the device following the Dalkon Shield tragedy—and it has been available for the past 12 years. Progestasert, manufactured by the Alza

Corporation, releases a "natural" hormone gradually over the course of a year. Because it must be reinserted annually, it never was as popular as other IUDs. Sometime this spring, a rival, the Copper T 380A manufactured by GynoPharma, which may be left in place for four years, will be available (see box on page 113).

Such copper-bearing IUDs are not new, but no one knows exactly how they, or hormone-releasing IUDs, prevent pregnancy. Most reproductive researchers now believe that the plastic T-shaped device makes fluids in the uterus hostile to sperm, or prevents development of the embryo in cases where conception occurs.

The Progestasert IUD costs about $200, including an office visit for tests and insertion. GynoPharma has not set a price yet. But both companies must factor in the cost of liability.

Sometime this spring, a large rubber thimble with a latex dome and a flexible rim, about half the size of the diaphragm, will almost certainly be approved for sale in this country. Versions of the cervical cap were sold here earlier in the century but it never became popular as it did in Europe. The one about to be approved by the FDA, manufactured by Lamberts Ltd. of London, fits snugly around the cervix, creating a strong suction. It acts as a physical barrier to sperm, a protection that is enhanced when sper-

Reprinted from *Ms.*, March 1988, pp. 75-79. Reprinted by permission.

micide is added.

Unlike the diaphragm, the Prentif cap can be left in place for up to three days, and no additional spermicide need be added. According to Susan Jordan, chair of the National Women's Health Network Committee on Barrier Methods, there are plans once the device is approved to create distribution points from which clinics or practitioners could order the cap. "It won't be available right away from every doctor's office," Jordan warns. "Most doctors will need some training to learn what constitutes a good fit." But Planned Parenthood will help affiliate clinics make the cap available. Its cost is estimated at $140 including fitting, lab tests, and a year's supply of spermicide.

The Today (TM) sponge resulted from a renewed interest in low-risk barrier method contraception. Available since 1984, it has been compared to a marshmallow with a dimple in the middle and a loop on one side. In response to early complaints that it disintegrated and was difficult to insert and remove, the design has been modified. The manufacturer, VLI, recently acquired by American Home Products, Inc., says 70 million sponges have been sold so far. It considers the average user a young, unmarried woman who prefers such features as disposability, the fact that it comes pretreated with a spermicide (nonoxynal 9), and that it can be bought over the counter.

The Funding Problem

Given American women's dissatisfaction with existing methods, why haven't companies increased contraceptive development? "In part, it's because of liability, and in part, return on investments," says Peter F. Drake, biotechnical analyst for Kidder, Peabody and Company, a Wall Street investment firm. Drake singles out the suits brought against the A.H. Robins Company by women who contracted life-threatening and sometimes fatal infections or became infertile from use of the Dalkon Shield, and Judge Robert R. Merhige Jr.'s ruling last December of a $2.48 billion settlement in their favor.

"The other companies think, if the Dalkon Shield could force a major company into filing for bankruptcy, then any contraceptive can cause problems—whether it's inserted or ingested," Drake says.

Drake predicts similar problems for spermicides, following a $4.2 million judgment against Ortho Pharmaceutical for a child born with a birth defect who was conceived during use of one of its products.

"A company spends 10 to 15 percent of its total sales on research and development," says Drake. "It takes, on average, twelve years and $100 million to bring a drug from discovery to market. Why would the company bother with contraceptives when the FDA gives priority to drugs that fight disease?"

The FDA's rigorous requirements for approval of drugs intended for healthy people protect women from some of the worst potential health problems. Before the dangers of the Dalkon Shield became apparent, the FDA regulated medications such as the Pill, but there were no rules governing contraceptive devices. Women's health groups considered the introduction of such requirements a victory, yet now a relatively simple product, the cervical cap, had to undergo extensive animal testing before it was allowed to enter clinical trials here.

While citing the specter of liability and shareholder pressure, Drake did not see pressure from the right-to-life movement as an important factor in the drug companies' retreat. "The issues are much more long-term," he says. Right-to-life groups have taken credit for the Upjohn Company's decision to close down its reproductive research labs in 1985. And the groups have protested once-a-month pills like RU-486, which is about to be submitted for registration in France but may not ever be introduced for approval in this country.

Federal support for research—which accounts for more than half of all money spent—is hampered by short-term commitments based on political and budgetary swings. Moreover, government agencies cannot fund research into abortion-related methods. In addition, there has been a brain drain of good, young talent into other areas of research, especially molecular biology, says Dr. Florence Haseltine, director of the Center for Population Research, where the number of fellowships has been cut in half. There has been a decline in research as well at the universities, where the earliest discoveries are often made.

New Methods

Despite the reluctance of most major companies to invest in contraceptive research, work is continuing at universities and public agencies, as well as smaller private companies. In some cases, however, promising projects were shelved at the point when they could go to clinical trial because of the liability roadblock. In others, innovative solutions have been found (see box, page 113).

In January 1986, the Alan Guttmacher Institute listed more than 30 major methods being sponsored by the eight large nonprofit public organizations responsible for most new contraceptive leads; many collaborate with universities and industry. But, according to Dr. C. Wayne Bardin, vice president of the Population Council and director for biomedical research, "there is not enough money around to complete development of all but a very few by the year 2000."

Here are some of the projects that are most intriguing. VAGINAL PILL: A tablet that, when placed in the vagi-

---

Birth Control

What contraceptives do women choose?
(source: The Alan Guttmacher Institute, from the National Survey of Family Growth, 1982) *

Method	15-19	20-24	AGE 25-29	30-34	35-44
Sterilization					
male	.1%	2.0%	3.6%	9.7%	12.0%
female	0.0	2.2	8.6	18.0	25.6
Pill	15.5	30.7	22.8	11.0	2.1
IUD	.3	2.3	6.8	6.1	4.2
Diaphragm	1.4	5.7	8.2	5.4	2.4
Condom	5.0	5.9	7.1	8.2	6.9
Foam/suppository	.3	1.9	2.1	2.6	2.6
Periodic abstinence	.5	1.9	2.9	2.6	2.6
Other	1.0	2.8	3.0	.9	1.3
Nonusers at risk	9.3	8.2	7.1	5.8	6.0
Not sexually active for previous three months	55.1	15.3	3.3	2.0	1.9
Others not at risk (sterilized for noncontraceptive reasons or pregnant)	11.5	21.1	24.7	27.4	32.2

* The latest available data, which does not reflect the recent unavailability of the IUD or the introduction of the sponge.

A User's Guide—How Safe and Effective Is Your Choice?

HOW SAFE AND EFFECTIVE ARE current methods? The answer is different for each woman depending on age and lifestyle. We might dream about a cheap, easy-to-use, risk-free contraceptive that prevents pregnancy 100 percent of the time. But we will always have to weigh risks against advantages.

Overall, women average about three contraceptive methods during their childbearing years. (See chart, preceding page.) Here is a brief look at the pros and cons of the major methods. Effectiveness rates are based on a survey by James Trussel, Ph.D., and Kathryn Kost of Princeton University.

●PILL. The Pill has a 3 percent failure rate (three pregnancies per 100 women in the first year of use), making it the most effective reversible form of birth control. The Pill is safest for women under 35 who do not smoke. Studies show a clear association between smoking and increased risk of cardiovascular complications such as blood clots and strokes. Results of the CASH (Cancer and Steroid Hormone) Study, a federal project involving 10,000 women aged 20 to 54, are reassuring about the lack of a connection between Pill use and breast cancer even for women using it as long as 15 years. But since such cancers are slow to develop, continued surveillance is necessary. On the plus side, studies show a protective effect of the Pill against ovarian and endometrial cancer. It also decreases the incidence of severe pelvic inflammatory disease (PID). On the other hand, some evidence suggests increased risk of chlamydia infections with Pill use, which can trigger PID and lead to infertility. Chlamydia, the most widespread sexually transmitted disease, is prevalent among young women. Until more is known, women on the Pill who are at risk for infection should be screened for both chlamydia and PID routinely.

●IUD. IUDs have a failure rate of 6 percent. But Gyno-Pharma, the company marketing the new Copper T 380A IUD, claims a failure rate "conservatively" of 1 percent—better than the Pill. This product was under study for more than 10 years by its developer, the Population Council, and tested on more than 3,500 women before the FDA approved it. One improvement in design is a single filament polyethelene string, which is less likely to attract bacteria than the multifilament tail that experts in the Dalkon Shield trial cited as a probable source of PID and other infections. But it is still advised only for women over 25, who do not want to have children and who are in a stable relationship.

●CAP. The FDA-mandated study found the Prentif cap to be almost as effective as the diaphragm, with an 18 percent failure rate. But other health care practitioners, allowed to dispense the cap on an experimental basis, rate it even higher, with a failure rate of 4 to 10 percent. Since the Prentif cap comes in only four sizes, as opposed to eight for the diaphragm, it will not fit every woman. Others may find it harder to insert and remove than the diaphragm.

●DIAPHRAGM. The diaphragm has a failure rate of 18 percent, but rates high in safety. Like the cap, its drawbacks are aesthetic rather than life-threatening: to be fully effective, spermicide must be added for repeated intercourse, and it must be left in place up to eight hours after intercourse.

●SPONGE. Studies show an effectiveness rate comparable to the diaphragm and cap. Some women report that it can flake or disintegrate or flip in the vagina, making it hard to remove, and the company has modifed the design; others complain that it slips during intercourse. A few cases of Toxic Shock Syndrome have been associated with its use, but the Centers for Disease Control estimate that the risk is very low (24 in a million), about half the risk for tampon use.

●CONDOM. No reliable studies have been done on condom effectiveness. Like all barrier methods, condoms protect the cervix from the development of precancerous conditions, and offer the best protection against sexually transmitted diseases such as gonorrhea and chlamydia. They are the only contraceptive that offers some protection against AIDS.

—E.S.

---

na, would slowly release spermicide for up to 24 hours—eliminating reapplication after each act of intercourse. The product was put on hold at the clinical trial stage, three years ago, when the contractor lost its liability insurance.

FILSHIE CLIP. A surgical method of sterilization that destroys the least possible amount of Fallopian tube, holding out a better chance for later restoring the tubes.

VAGINAL RING. Softer and smaller than the rim of a diaphragm, the ring fits around the cervix and can be worn continuously except during menstruation. It releases progestin and estrogen locally to avoid side effects.

NORPLANT(TM). A system of six silicone-rubber rods the size of matchsticks that are implanted in the upper arm in fanlike fashion and continuously release progestin into the bloodstream for up to five years before having to be replaced. The device, manufactured by a Finnish company, has already been approved in 10 countries and will be submitted to the FDA this year.

INJECTABLES. A shot of progestin that would last three or six months, and, further down the line, a progestin-bearing pellet, the size of a grain of rice, that would last a year and then dissolve.

DISPOSABLE DIAPHRAGM. A diaphragm incorporating a pre-measured dose of spermicide that could be discarded after one use. The contractor has held up clinical trials for lack of liability insurance.

CONTRACAP. Contracap's cervical cap resembles a large contact lens with a one-way valve in the center that would allow menstrual discharges to flow out but prevent sperm from swimming in. Some women may welcome the fact that it requires no spermicide and can be left in for up to a year. Trials in the U.S. and England had unacceptably high pregnancy rates, but the Illinois company says new trials of a modified design begun in China a year ago are more promising.

OVABLOC (TM). Silicone plugs that block the Fallopian tubes and offer a nonsurgical alternative to sterilization. This product is already available in Holland.

"NO-SCALPEL" VASECTOMY. An "almost bloodless" method of vasectomy that involves using special instruments to make a tiny puncture in the scrotum has been developed in China. And researchers at the University of Western Ontario have recently discovered that a single injection of a natural ingredient, glycerol, directly into animal testicles completely stops sperm formation without decreasing libido.

LHRH. Different researchers are trying to find a modification of the brain hormone that controls the pituitary, triggering both sperm production in men and ovulation in women. No formulations so far have completely wiped out sperm, or eliminated the problem of menstrual irregularities in women. After failing to produce a nasal spray that delivers the hormone, scientists are more hopeful about injectable microcapsules that would slowly release the hormone over a period of months.

INHIBIN. One of many nonsteroidal gonadal factors, as these water-soluble proteins are called, inhibin is able in animal studies to suppress sperm production without interfering with testosterone production. If it works similarly with humans—researchers expect trials to be completed by the late 1990s—it would mean a reversible form of birth control for men that did not interfere with their libido. Inhibin is also able to suppress ovulation in women without the potential side effects common to steroids, such as blood clotting, weight gain, and hypertension, but researchers at an international conference in January decided to make the development of a male method their top priority, says Dr. Gary Hodgen, director of the Contraceptive Research and Development Program, which sponsored the conference.

Another protein, which blocks the action of a hormone in the testes themselves without interfering with male sex drive, was isolated recently by Leo Ricchert, Ph.D., and a team of researchers at the Albany Medical College in New York State.

BEYOND THE YEAR 2000: Look for small patches of progestin that attach like adhesive strips to the skin, similar to the estrogen patches recently marketed that help prevent premature menopause; a device for reversible vasectomy; and more male methods, including a "natural" product, gossypol, which is a derivative of cottonseed oil, discovered in China.

The *Ms.* Perspective

How do we evaluate this brave new world of reproductive technology being developed largely by men for women? How can women influence the contraception of tomorrow?

First of all, we must help those who design birth-control products to consider the "users' perspective," as Judith Bruce defines it in a recent article in *Technology in Society* (Vol. 9, No. 3). As Bruce puts it, "Users are consumers, and no product—espe-

---

Small, Innovative Companies Are Willing To Take the Risks

AS THE LARGE COMPANIES have cut back on contraceptive development, citing low profits or the specter of lawsuits, smaller ones have stepped in to fill the gap. Eager to get a share of the $1.5 billion birth-control business, they may be more willing to take risks than the larger pharmaceuticals. Some have a pet product they have nurtured through arduous preclinical and clinical testing.

A good example is what happened with the IUD. Two years ago, Searle and Ortho stopped making their IUDs, claiming low demand and reduced profits. That left the field wide open to Alza, a small Palo Alto, California, company specializing in drug delivery systems, including the new estrogen patches for menopausal symptoms. Alza developed its IUD, Progestasert, 12 years ago, but the disappearance of its more successful competitors gave it renewed incentive to claim a larger piece of the market.

In what Alza president Jane Shaw, Ph.D., calls a "fairly unique undertaking," the company created a package information sheet that spells out risks in detailed, clear language intended to be read together and discussed, point by point, by doctor and patient. They then refined the pamphlet after consulting with doctors, women's health activists, and other user groups.

"While it doesn't absolve the physician of responsibility, it does guarantee a better informed user, and that reduces the probability of suits," explains Judy Norsigian of the Boston Women's Health Book Collective.

The model prompted GynoPharma, a company formed in 1984 to develop ideas and market gynecological products already in development, to try the same approach with its patient information pamphlet for the copper-bearing IUD it plans to bring out this spring. Developed by the Population Council and already in use in Canada and 29 other countries, this device lay on the Population Council's shelf in the U.S. for several years before GynoPharma took it on. The company, based in Somerville, New Jersey, hopes that at least half of the 700,000 women now wearing the Copper 7 IUD who are scheduled to have it removed this year will switch over to their brand. Roderick Mackenzie, a former president of Ortho Pharmaceutical who started the company, believes that he understands why the larger pharmaceuticals fear to tread where his own smaller company is going: "Picture yourself as chairman of a multibillion dollar corporation in which, by comparison, a relatively small division is the source of adverse publicity impacting the entire corporation," he says. GynoPharma has already licensed a new vaginal spermicide and a vaginal ring that it hopes to bring to market in the next two or three years.

Gynex, started by former executives of Searle, another leading pharmaceutical, is developing a tablet based on a by-product of beans that delivers natural sex hormones that are effective in much lower doses than current formulations of the Pill. Clinical trials began in the United Kingdom last year. According to vice president Stephen Simes, the Deerfield, Illinois, company is subsidizing its long-term research by developing generic products, including the first FDA-approved oral contraceptive.

Wisconsin Pharmacal, a small company outside Milwaukee, is developing a disposable female condom that would be the first barrier contraceptive designed specifically to help women protect themselves against AIDS and other sexually transmitted diseases. The polyurethane device consists of two rings and a large male condom: the woman inserts the inner ring to fit around the cervix, which pulls in the sheath; the outer ring stays outside on the labia. Mary Ann Leeper, Ph.D., vice president of Phoenix Health Care Inc., which has invested in the product, says that it is beginning clinical tests in the U.S.

Meanwhile, the only major U.S. drug company doing active contraceptive research, Ortho Pharmaceutical, is concentrating on the development of new progestins that would not change the lipid (fat) levels in women—a major cause of cardiovascular problems sometimes associated with use of the Pill. John McGuire, vice president of preclinical research and development, says that the new drug is available in Europe; and it has been submitted to the FDA for approval. McGuire also says that his in-house research staff has more than doubled over the past 10 years. Other products under investigation include a spermicide that would last up to 24 hours (clinical trials will begin within 18 months), and, further down the road, injectable progestins to last up to six months. On the distant horizon: immunological approaches that generate antibodies to fertility in men and women.

—E.S.

---

cially one to be employed by healthy people—will be accepted if its intrinsic properties (the hardware) or its service delivery mechanisms (the software) are inimical to the user's personal, physical, and cultural needs."

Women's contraceptive choices, Bruce goes on to say, are more than "tastes": they are part of a survival strategy for control of our bodies. Ideally, a virtual "cafeteria" of choices would be available, as Norma Swenson of the Bos-

ton Women's Health Book Collective imagines it. Men and women would share equally in deciding who takes the risks or bears the inconvenience of a given method. But in reality, however much women want more male involvement and responsibility, most prefer to have direct control over their reproductive lives. For example, the condom is not acceptable to many women because it depends on male cooperation. The IUD, albeit riskier, gives more control, but makes us dependent on someone else for its insertion and removal. In fact, the more high tech the method, the more dependent women are on that outside provider of service.

A responsive technology would take such concerns into account by giving women the greatest number of independent options. For example, Norplant, the new implant system about to be submitted for approval to the FDA, is intended to provide a continuous supply of a low level of progestin for up to five years. But partly as the result of consultation with women's health groups, its developers decided *not* to make it biodegradable. This was to allow for easier removal if a woman decided to stop using it before the five years were up.

The new technology will also have to respond to the changes in women's lifestyles. For example, as more women delay childbearing into their thirties and even forties, and as more women have their first sexual experiences in their teens, they will need contraception for a longer period of time before their first child is born. This makes certain methods, such as the IUD, less appropriate because of the risk of infertility.

Similarly, the increase in sexually transmitted diseases and the recent spread of AIDS to the heterosexual population is forcing women and men to learn new forms of social behavior. Condoms offer the most protection of any existing methods against AIDS. The short-term solution requires men to share in making sure they are protecting their partners from infection. This could have a positive effect on men's responsibility for birth control by forcing men and women to speak more frankly together about sexuality. But the longer-term challenge for birth-control technology is to find new, low-risk methods that protect against both pregnancy and disease.

Voting in Curbs and Confusion

How five likely state restrictions might work

For many years now the fight over abortion has played out in the black-and-white slogans of political placards: Yes or No, Pro-Choice or Pro-Life. With the Supreme Court's ruling in *Webster v. Reproductive Health Services*, the battlefield shifts to the fine print of state regulatory codes. Legislature by legislature, law by law, clause by clause, partisans on both sides of the issue will struggle for control of the future of abortion in this country. As a result of last week's historic ruling, states have substantial opportunity to restrict women's access to abortions for the first time in 16 years. Wrote Chief Justice William Rehnquist in his plurality opinion: "There is no doubt that our holding today will allow some governmental regulation of abortion that would have been prohibited" in the past. In effect, the majority invited the states to pose further challenges to *Roe v. Wade* in a series of test cases. The states are eager to R.S.V.P. "The battleground is going to be in the state legislature as we seek to plumb the outer limits of constitutionality under the new standard," said Kenneth Connor, president of Florida Right to Life.

The combatants' first task will be figuring what those new standards are. To supplant *Roe's* trimester scheme, Sandra Day O'Connor proposed a vague, new principle: regulations are acceptable if they do not place an "undue burden" on women. Many constitutional experts interpret this to mean that states may adopt almost any restriction, short of banning the procedure outright.

Anti-abortion legislators are planning to put that presumption to the test by introducing restrictive new bills as soon as possible. Five states already have statutes on the books declaring their intention to ban abortions at the first opportunity. After the court's decision the Louisiana Legislature

passed a resolution calling on district attorneys to enforce state laws similar to the ones upheld in *Webster*. Florida Gov. Bob Martinez announced a special session of the legislature to consider enacting new abortion measures. At the same time pro-choice advocates proved they were ready to wage war on the microregulatory front. Several legislatures are considering laws spelling out their commitment to choice. New York Gov. Mario Cuomo vowed to fight attempts to ban abortions from public hospitals.

With the *Webster* decision, anti-abortionists won the right to regulate in two key areas: public funding and viability testing. The court has agreed to review three other cases that could create further roadblocks to abortion; they would affect parental consent for teens and licensing standards for abortion clinics. If the past is any guide, the strictures will have their greatest effect upon the poor, the young and the uneducated, who may lack the financial or emotional resources to navigate the new abortion obstacle path.

Of the myriad regulations states are now likely to consider, the following five could have enormous impact:

Viability Testing: A Brave New World

Webster's most stunning—and most confusing—contribution to the constitutional canon was its ruling on fetal-viability testing. The medical and scientific community maintains that the earliest point of fetal viability has remained at 24 weeks for some years and is not going to change, barring evolutionary shifts in human development or leaps in medical tech-

nology. Nevertheless, the court majority upheld the Missouri statute requiring physicians to test for fetal viability at 20 weeks, apparently to allow for a four-week margin of error in dating gestational age. O'Connor seemed to limit her support to "medically prudent" procedures, and the majority granted doctors some discretion in deciding whether to perform tests on all 20-week patients. Still, *Webster* creates a brave new world of government-controlled intervention into patient-physician relations, leaving many doctors uneasy about their new legal obligations.

The tests at issue were sophisticated ultrasonography, which could add an estimated $125 to $250 to the cost of an abortion, and amniocentesis, which could increase the cost by about $450. Ultrasound is a relatively quick, painless and safe procedure. Amniocentesis, by contrast, is an invasive test in which a doctor inserts a hollow needle into a woman's abdomen to extract amniotic fluid from the uterus; it has about a 1 percent miscarriage risk and can cause hemorrhaging or infection. In attempts to determine fetal viability, medical technicians would analyze the fluid for the presence of surfactant; its absence would indicate that the fetus's lungs were too immature to permit survival outside the womb. In a series of amicus briefs in this case, many doctors argued that amnio does not provide useful information about lung maturity until about the 28th week, making it a risky and pointless exercise. The requirement could delay abortions by two or more critical weeks; if a 19- or 20-week abortion were postponed by three weeks, its cost could triple in that time to approximately $2,000. "They're making us add extra roadblocks, extra costs and extra interventions to prove that the baby isn't mature, which we already know," says Howard Schwartz, an obstetrician-gynecologist in Kansas City.

In practice, only a tiny percentage of all abortions takes place after 20 weeks (chart). Few doctors are willing to do the operations after that point except in such instances as severe fetal abnormality or a health risk to the mother. But according to pro-choice supporters, right-to-life lobbyists have convinced some politicians that late-term abortions are commonplace enough to warrant restrictive legislation. "[Anti-abortion activists] have been very clever in creating this myth that women have abortions right up to the time of delivery for frivolous reasons," says Colleen Connell, reproductive-rights director of the American Civil Liberties Union in Illinois.

At present, only Missouri mandates viability testing, but other states are expected to follow with related measures. In Illinois, for example, a bill now in conference would require a physician who believes there is a possibility of survival outside the womb to perform an abortion in a hospital with life-support equipment. Louisiana, which forbids aborting a fetus capable of life outside the womb, has a law on the books requiring ultrasound before all abortions. Though the state is currently prohibited from enforcing the sonogram provision, Louisiana would probably get a go-ahead from the current court. Given the rarity of late-term abortions, viability testing may ultimately have little practical application. But its symbolic force will certainly be felt if conservative legislatures follow Missouri's lead in upcoming sessions.

Tough Limits on Public Funding

Starting in the late 1970s, Congress and many states cut Medicaid funding for most abortions, leaving poor women to scrape together enough money to terminate unwanted pregnancies. At present, only a few states provide public funds for abortion on demand. Now, with *Webster*, the court has further limited the access of poor people by upholding the right of states to ban abortions in public facilities. In the past few years, Missouri and other states have passed laws stipulating that public hospitals can be used for abortions only when necessary to save the life of the mother. Similarly, Missouri now forbids doctors from using public funds when performing or assisting in an abortion, unless maternal life is at stake.

At first glance, such restrictions would not seem to affect women who can more easily afford abortions. But many may find themselves locked out of private facilities as well. "The public/private distinction in American hospital care is nearly moot," the National Abortion Federation report-

The Who, When and Where of Abortion

Each year three out of every 100 American women age 15 to 44 choose to end unwanted pregnancies—1.5 million abortions in all. Only .01 percent of abortions occur after 24 weeks, and most of those are for urgent therapeutic reasons.

Age:	ESTIMATED RATE PER 1,000 WOMEN IN CATEGORY
15-17 years	32.2
18-19 years	62.4
20-24 years	54.6
25-29 years	33.0
30-34 years	17.9
35-39 years	9.8
40 and over	3.4

Race:	
White	23.0
Nonwhite	52.6

Family Income:	
Under $11,000	62.2
$11,000-$24,999	32.5
$25,000 and over	16.5

FIGURES ABOVE BASED ON 1987 DATA

Length of Pregnancy:*	1983	1973
8 weeks and under	50.3%	38.2%
9-10 weeks	26.9%	29.8%
11-12 weeks	13.3%	17.5%
13-15 weeks	5.3%	6.0%
16-20 weeks	3.4%	7.2%
21 weeks and over	0.8%	1.4%

*TIME SINCE LAST MENSTRUAL PERIOD

Locations:*	
Hospitals	13%
Abortion clinics	60%
Other clinics	23%
M.D.'s offices	4%

*1985 FIGURES

SOURCE FOR ALL: THE ALAN GUTTMACHER INSTITUTE

ed last week. "A thread of public funding and involvement touches most areas." For example, Reproductive Health Services, the St. Louis facility that unsuccessfully challenged the Missouri law, was a private clinic with tangential ties to the state. With such a broad definition of "public," many private facilities may find it difficult to escape the long reach of the law.

As a result of the court's ruling, the availability of abortions is likely to decline as the cost mounts. The regulation is likely to have greatest impact in states with strong right-to-life movements. In Missouri, for example, doctors in public facilities performed only 90 of the state's 17,382 abortions reported last year. The reasons: many physicians switched to private practice or relocated to another state because they anticipated restrictive legislation and also didn't want to endure the harassment of anti-abortion protesters.

Many women will be forced to seek out-of-state abortions—incurring travel expenses and losing time and income in the process. More than 1,000 Missouri residents crossed the border in search of abortions last year. Staffers at Reproductive Health Services say out-of-town patients often sleep in their cars in the clinic parking lot because they can't afford local accommodations. The indigent and the young, who tend to rely on public hospitals, will be hardest hit by the stiff laws. Florida state Rep. Lois Frankel raises the alarming prospect that women with AIDS won't be

able to afford to terminate their pregnancies. Pro-choice advocates argue that banning abortions at public facilities is tantamount to eliminating legal abortion for many poor or young women. "It's like saying you have the right to vote, but you can't get to the polling place," says Nancy Gertner, an attorney with the Massachusetts chapter of the ACLU.

With the court's blessing, several states may follow Missouri's example in a related area: banning the use of public funds to "encourage or counsel" a woman to have an abortion. Because Missouri Attorney General William Webster contended that the law applied only to state fiscal officers, the court did not rule on the constitutionality of prohibiting publicly paid doctors and hospital workers from counseling patients. Nevertheless, such laws can have a dampening effect on the free exchange of information. Health-care workers on Missouri's payroll say they were told not to discuss abortion with women seeking help. Abortion-rights supporters say that poor women will again bear the brunt of such regulations. "If state facilities are even prohibited from giving them information, these women are not going to be able to know where to go," says Matty Bloom, executive director of Planned Parenthood of Miami. "It will set up a two-tiered system where women with means can fly to exercise their freedom of choice, whereas those without means are forced into childbearing."

What the Future Could Hold

If new laws are passed restricting abortion in your state, are the following likely to happen or not? (Percent saying likely)

60% A lot fewer abortions will be performed.

72% More women will die because of illegal abortions.

69% Poor women will not be able to get safe abortions.

64% There will be greater use of birth control.

75% More unwed teenage girls will become mothers.

63% There will be more mistreated children.

cause they've waited too long to admit their pregnancies, they might face later and more costly abortions; for example, a termination that cost $225 at 12 weeks might cost $450 a month later.

While anti-abortion forces move ahead on parental-consent laws, pro-choice advocates are readying their own challenges. Later this month a California appellate court will consider a suit in which the ACLU contends that, under the state constitution, minors have the same privacy rights as adults. Both sides will be watching closely for guidance from the Supreme Court next term.

New Standards for Abortion Clinics

At the moment the overwhelming majority of abortions take place in clinics. Next year that could change—with stunning repercussions for the practice of abortion in this country. The Supreme Court has agreed to hear *Turnock v. Ragsdale,* a case involving an Illinois law that requires private abortion clinics to meet standards similar to those mandated for operating rooms in full-care hospitals. In 1983 the court knocked down a law limiting abortions outside a hospital setting, on the ground that the regulation would increase the cost of an abortion for no medical reason. O'Connor dissented from the majority opinion.

If the court rules in favor of Illinois in *Turnock,* the number of abortion clinics in the state—and ultimately around the country—could drop dramatically. Those remaining might have to raise fees substantially to cover the costs of complying with the law. Average abortions could cost closer to $750, rather than the current $213. Again, the young and the poor would be affected most adversely. "One of the wonderful things about clinics is that we've been able to keep prices low," says Carol Wall, executive director of Planned Parenthood of Southeastern Pennsylvania. "Actually, $240 is a lot of money for some poor women, but a lot of people do scrape it together even if they have to go to 10 different people. I don't know about $500." But the restriction wouldn't affect just the poor. "Ninety percent of all abortions take place in exactly the kind of clinics that don't comply with the regulations we're talking about," says Colleen Connell of the Illinois ACLU.

Pro-choicers say there is no medical evidence to support the need for upgraded facilities. First- and early-second trimester abortions are generally performed under a local anesthetic, with no incision; many doctors regard such abortions as one of the safest surgical procedures. But right-to-life

A Parental Role in a Teen's Decision

Of the more than 1 million teenagers who get pregnant each year, 42 percent decide not to have the babies. Girls between 15 and 17 account for 11 percent of all abortions. The fate of these minors will hang in the balance next fall, when the Supreme Court hears two cases involving parental-consent requirements.

In the past the court has upheld such laws, as long as teens had access to a "judicial bypass" giving minors the opportunity to convince a judge it is not in their best interest to inform parents about abortions. In *Ohio v. Akron Center for Reproductive Health,* the justices will consider a case involving notification of one parent, as well as the state's attempt to eliminate its bypass provision from the books. The court has also agreed to hear arguments arising from a 1981 Minnesota statute forcing a girl to inform *both* parents—even a divorced parent without custody or an incestuous father who is also the father of the fetus. This court leaves little doubt of where it stands on notification and consent rulings. "Four members of the court don't think much of adult women," says Thomas Webber, executive director of Planned Parenthood of Minnesota. "They probably aren't going to think much more of young women." The only questions are whether the court will permit states to impose a two-parent provision and whether it will continue to insist on bypass procedures.

At present 13 states have parental-notification laws and 12 require the consent of at least one parent; many of them, however, are under court injunctions not to enforce the statutes. Massachusetts is considering a bill—albeit one unlikely to pass—that would allow parents to testify at their daughters' judicial bypass hear-

ings. Surprisingly, even some pro-choicers support parental notification on pro-family grounds. "It's an interesting coalition that includes people interested in parenthood," says Wisconsin state Rep. Robert Welch, a right-to-life legislator. "Whether they believe in abortion or not, they think parents should know."

Activists on both sides of the abortion issue cite the Minnesota law to buttress their positions on parental notification. Soon after the law took effect, the birthrate in Minneapolis climbed 38.4 percent for 15- to 17-year-olds, while the birthrate for 18- to 19-year-olds, who were not covered by the regulation, rose just 0.3 percent. Right-to-lifers consider the statute a triumph of deterrence. "The state has an interest in protecting minors from their own immature and many times improvident decisions," says Ann-Louise Lohr, staff counsel at Americans United for Life. Pro-choice activists view the law as a disaster. The requirement was designed to bolster family life, but critics contend it in fact caused dissension in many families. In a state where 42 percent of minors do not live with both parents, the two-parent stipulation was not easy to comply with; in some cases the state had to track down fathers who had abandoned their wives and children years before.

Many minors want a parent with them during an abortion. Opponents of consent requirements say that it is precisely the kids who come alone who need court protection. "Most teens do talk to their parents. But when they can't, they can't," says Pat Kibler, Virginia public-affairs coordinator for Planned Parenthood. "The ones least well equipped to become teen mothers, the ones who don't have support from family, they'll be the ones having babies." Among teenagers hoping to wish away their pregnancies, the parental-consent requirements can only delay the inevitable. Be-

117

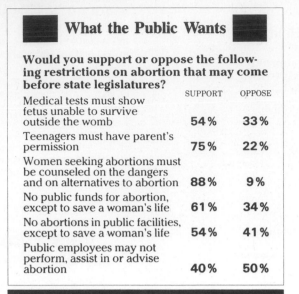

What the Public Wants

Would you support or oppose the following restrictions on abortion that may come before state legislatures?

	SUPPORT	OPPOSE
Medical tests must show fetus unable to survive outside the womb	54%	33%
Teenagers must have parent's permission	75%	22%
Women seeking abortions must be counseled on the dangers and on alternatives to abortion	88%	9%
No public funds for abortion, except to save a woman's life	61%	34%
No abortions in public facilities, except to save a woman's life	54%	41%
Public employees may not perform, assist in or advise abortion	40%	50%

advocates say they are only trying to protect women. "The ACLU is objecting to regulations which promote safe and sanitary conditions for women seeking abortion," says Laurie Anne Ramsey, director of education of Americans United for Life in Chicago. "It is so ironic that the ACLU has moved back-alley abortions onto Michigan Avenue."

The Illinois law entered the books in the mid-1970s as a barely disguised attempt to reduce the availability of abortions. The then state representative Henry Hyde, now a prominent right-to-life congressman, said at the time that the state should "at least regulate the abortion mills so they will not proliferate." Abortion-rights advocates worry that the court's rulings, taken together, could make it all but impossible for poor women or teenagers to get abortions. For example, a state could prohibit public hospitals from performing abortions and, at the same time, impose onerous restrictions on private clinics. The effect of that would be to say, "You still have a right to an abortion, but we've taken away all the providers," says Thomas Webber of Planned Parenthood. Activists on both sides believe *Turnock* may be the case that finally forces the court to address *Roe* head-on. *Roe* said that since women have a constitutional right to abortion, states cannot restrict their ability to obtain one. If the court now allows Illinois to impose strict licensing standards on clinics without demonstrating a medical need for them, it will cut at the constitutional core of *Roe*.

'Informed Consent': Graphic Literature

Opponents of abortion believe that the more a woman knows about abortion, the less likely she is to have one. The right-to-life movement has long sought to enact "informed consent" laws, which would force a would-be patient to receive information about fetal development and abortions before going ahead with the procedure. The regulations could include anything from counseling on the supposed risks of abortion to viewing pictures of developing fetuses. To supporters of choice, however, "informed consent" is nothing more than a code for explicit, often off-putting and sometimes distorted information imposed on a woman at a vulnerable moment.

Anti-abortion activists are putting informed consent high on their legislative agenda: they plan to introduce laws soon in several states, including Pennsylvania. That state furnished the 1986 lawsuit *Thornburgh v. American College of Obstetricians and Gynecologists,* in which the Supreme Court invalidated informed consent because of the statute's "anti-abortion character." But today the ball is in a different court: O'Connor, Rehnquist and Byron White, all dissenters in *Thornburgh,* would now be likely to uphold such regulations.

Under the proposed informed-consent statutes, states may ask doctors to show patients detailed pictures of the fetus in utero, or photographs of aborted fetuses. Right-to-lifers want women to be told not only about adoption, but about counseling, support groups and financial assistance for pregnant woman. Related measures might impose a 24- to 72-hour waiting period on a woman seeking an abortion.

Right-to-lifers admit that they intend for the laws to reduce the number of doctors willing to perform abortions. Some physicians might not want to bother with the new protocol; others might object on moral and medical grounds to forcing graphic literature on their patients. But the primary target, of course, is the woman herself. Anti-abortionists believe informed-consent laws would intimidate those who were wavering. Though most people would agree that a woman should not undertake abortion lightly, it may not be the state's place to try to talk her out of it.

Restrictions like informed consent are just a beginning. In the aftermath of last week's ruling, right-to-life groups are moving quickly to develop new test cases that might once and for all topple *Roe.* Some states will introduce bills requiring the presence of a second doctor during late-term abortions, ostensibly to represent the interests of the fetus. Other restrictions may test the outer limits of the Constitution—and perhaps common sense. Burke Balch, state legislative coordinator for the National Right to Life Committee, says his organization is considering "innovative" proposals to ban abortions in cases where a couple failed to use contraception. Short of putting an assistant D.A. under the bed, it is unclear how states would enforce this rule.

"It's clear that geography now equals destiny," says John Glaza, executive director of Idaho's Planned Parenthood. The post-*Webster* world will look more and more like the one that existed pre-*Roe.* Where a woman lives, how much she earns and what she knows will determine whether she can obtain a safe, legal abortion. In his concurring opinion, Antonin Scalia deemed abortion a "political issue" more than a legal one. So from now on, state legislators will grapple with ethical, medical and legal complexities that even the Supreme Court could not resolve. Their conclusions will have a profound effect on one of the most important—and intimate—decisions of a woman's life.

ELOISE SALHOLZ *with* ANN MCDANIEL *in Washington,* PATRICIA KING *in Chicago,* ERIK CALONIUS *and* DAVID L. GONZALEZ *in Miami*, NADINE JOSEPH *in San Francisco and bureau reports*

ABORTION:

Right or Wrong?

Edd Doerr

Mr. Doerr, Religion Editor of USA Today, *is executive director, Americans for Religious Liberty, Silver Spring, Md.*

IS abortion a constitutionally protected women's right? Or is it the killing of innocent unborn persons, and therefore a wrong to be prohibited by law?

Since the women's rights movement began getting state legislatures to liberalize abortion laws about 20 years ago—and especially since the Supreme Court's 1973 *Roe v. Wade* ruling, which held that a constitutional right to privacy covers a woman's right to choose to terminate a problem pregnancy—bitter battles over abortion have become a permanent feature of the American scene. Congress and state legislatures have fought over proposals to outlaw or sharply curtail abortion, bills to require spousal or parental consent, and Federal and state Medicaid funding for abortions for poor women. Demonstrators have sought to close down clinics and/or discourage their clients. Extremists have burned and bombed clinics. Politicians are torn between vocal voters and groups which are either pro-choice or "pro-life." The issue sharply has divided the religious community, both between and within denominations, and the controversy seems unlikely to abate for many years.

In recent years, almost 1,600,000 abortions have been performed annually in the U.S. About 69% of the women having abortions are white and 31% nonwhite, while 19% are married. In 1983, 61% had had no prior abortions, while 21% had had one. Slightly over 27% of abortions were performed for women 19 and under,

"At the heart of the public policy controversy over abortion is the question of when a fetus becomes a person."

56% for women in their 20's, and 16% for women in their 30's.

Almost half of all abortions take place before eight weeks of gestation, 77% before 10 weeks, 90.5% before 12 weeks, and 99.2% before 20 weeks. Only about 100 abortions (less than 0.01%) take place after 24 weeks.

Most abortions, 87%, are performed in non-hospital facilities, while 91% of rural and 50% of urban counties have no abortion facilities at all. Many women have difficulty finding a clinic or other facility, especially after the 12th week of gestation.

The average charge for non-hospital abortions at 10 weeks in 1986 was $238. Since 1977, virtually no Federal Medicaid funds have been available for abortions for poor women, though, in 1985, 14 states and the District of Columbia covered the costs of 187,500 abortions for poor women

Although the fact is not well-known or appreciated, abortion before "quickening" (the point at which a woman first notices fetal movement, at 16-18 weeks of pregnancy) was legal, widely accepted, and

apparently far from uncommon throughout the U.S. until state legislatures began banning it, except when necessary to save a woman's life, around the time of the Civil War. As the Supreme Court has noted, states enacted laws in the mid- to late-19th century for three basic reasons: "a Victorian social concern to discourage illicit sexual conduct"; a concern for the health of women, as abortion was dangerous and did not become safer than bearing children until after antibiotics were in common use toward the middle of the 20th century; and the states' newfound "interest—some phrase it in terms of duty—in protecting prenatal life." Historians also have shown that "turf wars" over who was to provide medical care often were involved. Physicians, rather than clergymen, provided the impetus for the restrictive laws. By 1970, however, public and professional opinion had become increasingly supportive of the liberalization of state abortion laws.

The watershed event in the rapid development of abortion rights, of course, was the Supreme Court's ruling in 1973 in *Roe v. Wade*, a case brought by a Texas woman who had been denied approval for a hospital abortion. After showing that a line of decisions going back to 1891 "recognized that a right of personal privacy, or a guarantee of certain areas or zones of privacy, does exist under the Constitution," with roots of that right found variously in the First, Fourth, Fifth, Ninth, and Fourteenth Amendments, and "in the penumbras of the Bill of Rights," the Court held in *Roe* that the "right of privacy . . . is broad enough to encompass a woman's decision whether or not to terminate her pregnancy."

"The detriment that the State would impose upon the pregnant woman by denying this choice is apparent," the Court added. "Specific and direct harm medically diagnosable even in early pregnancy may be involved. Maternity, or additional offspring, may force upon the woman a distressful life and future. Psychological harm may be imminent. Mental and physical health may be taxed by child care. There is also the distress, for all concerned, associated with the unwanted child and there is the problem of bringing a child into a family already unable, psychologically or otherwise, to care for it. In other cases, as in this one, the additional difficulties and continuing stigma of unwed motherhood may be involved. All these are factors the woman and her responsible physician necessarily will consider in consultation."

However, while concluding that the constitutional "right of personal privacy includes the abortion decision," the Court held that the "right is not unqualified and must be considered against important state interests in regulation," such as the interest of assuring that abortions are performed only by qualified medical personnel and, late in pregnancy, a certain interest in potential human life.

The State of Texas argued in *Roe* that a fetus is a "person" within the language and meaning of the Fourteenth Amendment. The Court disagreed, holding that the term "person" in the Constitution nearly always "has application only postnatally." The Court added that "We need not resolve the difficult question of when life begins. When those trained in the respective disciplines of medicine, philosophy, and theology are unable to arrive at any consensus, the judiciary, at this point in the development of man's knowledge, is not in a position to speculate as to the answer." "In short," the Court concluded, "the unborn have never been recognized in the law as persons in the whole sense."

Roe v. Wade thus became the Magna Carta of the abortion and women's rights movements. Obviously, however, the story does not end there. A powerful movement, led at first by the bishops of the Roman Catholic Church and joined later by televangelists such as Jerry Falwell and Pat Robertson, began the campaign to overturn *Roe*, or at least to throw as many roadblocks as possible in the way of women seeking to terminate problem pregnancies. The growing pro-choice forces proved sufficiently strong to block passage of constitutional amendments designed either to outlaw abortion or to authorize states to do so. Nonetheless, anti-choice or "pro-life" forces have been powerful enough to stop most Federal and state Medicaid funding of abortions for poor women, to deny publicly provided abortions to armed forces and Peace Corps personnel and dependents, and even to try to cut off Federal funding of domestic and international family planning agencies whose activities actually reduce demand for abortions. Social pressures have been responsible for the decisions of many public hospitals not to offer abortion services.

Public opinion and abortion

Since 1973, debate over abortion rights has raged incessantly. Catholic bishops, fundamentalist leaders and TV evangelists, and conservative politicians have campaigned vigorously against abortion rights. Other religious bodies and leaders, women's and civil liberties groups, and many moderate-to-liberal politicians have defended freedom of conscience on abortion, though at a much lower decibel level and certainly with a great deal less resources.

Where does public opinion stand? The most recent major test of opinion occurred in November, 1986, when statewide referenda on constitutional amendments were held in Massachusetts, Rhode Island, Arkansas, and Oregon. Massachusetts voters, by 58% to 42%, defeated a proposed amendment to the state constitution which would have allowed the legislature to limit or prohibit abortion, eliminate Medicaid funding for abortions for poor women, and prohibit private insurance coverage for abortions. In neighboring Rhode Island, a similar amendment was voted down 65% to 35%. Since Massachusetts and Rhode Island are 50% and 67% Catholic, respectively, and as the Catholic bishops strongly supported the amendments, the votes in the two states clearly showed very strong support for the pro-choice position.

On the same day, Oregon voters rejected by 54% to 46% an amendment aimed not at prohibiting abortion, but only at cutting off state funding for medically necessary abortions and those for victims of rape and incest. In largely fundamentalist Arkansas, voters unexpectedly defeated, by a paper-thin margin, an amendment which would have sought to outlaw abortion by having the state declare constitutionally that personhood begins at conception.

The most extensive recent polls were released in January, 1988, by Hickman-Maslin Research, a Washington-based political polling group, clearly showing that most Americans favor keeping abortion as a legal option for women who so choose by a 56% to 37% margin. Support for choice was highest in the Northeast (69%), lowest in the South (45%). Support increased with educational level and was higher in urban than rural areas. Democratic (59%) and independent (58%) support was higher than Republican (52%); liberal support higher (79%) than conservative. The pro-choice position was supported by Catholics 52% to 40%, by Baptists 50% to 42%, by other Protestants 56% to 36%, and by "Jewish/other/none" respondents 69% to 26%. White fundamentalists opposed choice 55% to 34%, while southern white fundamentalists opposed it 62% to 29%.

Looking at the question from a different angle, 39% believed that abortion should be available to any woman who wants one, 49% said abortion only should be allowed "under certain circumstances," while only 10% said it should not be allowed. From a still different angle, a constitutional amendment to make abortion illegal was opposed 63% to 31% (Catholics, 60% to 35%; Baptists, 55% to 37%; other Protestants, 64% to 30%; "Jewish/other/none," 73% to 19%; white fundamentalists favored an amendment 50% to 45%).

The entire spectrum of Americans were in strong agreement (78% to 20%) with the statement "Abortion is a private issue between a woman, her family and her doctor; the government should not be involved." By a 74% to 23% margin, respondents agreed that, "Since nobody knows for certain when life begins, people should follow their own moral convictions and religious teachings on the abortion issue." By 60% to 38%, the poll respondents disagreed with the statement "Abortion is such an important moral issue that the government has to play a role." The differences between men and women respondents on these questions were negligible.

The bottom line is that, no matter how questions about abortion rights are worded or whether the question is put in an opinion poll or a statewide political referendum, most Americans favor keeping abortion as a legal option for women with problem pregnancies.

Terms for debate

At the heart of the public policy controversy over abortion is the question of when a fetus becomes a person. A fetus is certainly a living organism from conception on. Genetically, it is human, and it is biologically individually unique, except in the case of identical twins. However, when is it to be regarded as a "person" with legal rights?

The "pro-life" movement generally holds that a fetus is a person and should be regarded as a *legal* person from conception. As a publication of the National Right to Life Educational Trust Fund puts it, "From this and all other scientific information, we are compelled to recognize that there is no essential difference between the fertilized ovum we all once were, and the embryo, the fetus, the infant, adolescent and adult we all grew or are growing to be.'' This view (criticized often as reductionist), essentially a religious view, has been espoused chiefly by the Catholic bishops, some Orthodox Jewish leaders, and a large number of fundamentalist Protestant clergy, such as Jerry Falwell, Pat Robertson, Jim Bakker, and the late Francis Schaeffer.

Fundamentalists cite biblical texts to support their view of early fetal personhood, but most biblical scholars would agree with Baptist theologian Paul D. Simmons that there is no clear prohibition against abortion in the Bible, though abortion certainly was common when the Jewish and Christian scriptures were being written.

The pro-choice case is much more complicated. Opinion varies as to when a fetus becomes a person and as to when and under what circumstances choosing the abortion option may be moral. However, there is a consensus that the decision to continue or to terminate a problem pregnancy legally should be left to the individual woman. The pro-choice position is espoused by a wide spectrum of religious bodies, such as the 31 groups which make up the Religious Coalition for Abortion Rights.

Pro-choice positions have been taken by the American Baptist Churches, American Ethical Union, American Friends Service Committee, American Humanist Association, American Jewish Congress, American Lutheran Church, American Protestant Hospital Association, B'nai B'rith Women, Catholics for a Free Choice, Central Conference of American Rabbis, Disciples of Christ, Church of the Brethren, Episcopal Church, Lutheran Church in America, National Council of Jewish Women, Reformed Church in America, Reorganized Church of Jesus Christ of Latter Day Saints, Union of American Hebrew Congregations, Unitarian Universalist Association, United Church of Christ, United Methodist Church, United Presbyterian Church, United Synagogue of America, and Young Women's Christian Association of the U.S.A. All of these organizations speak up for the sanctity of human life and insist that respect for persons requires that women enjoy the right to freedom of conscience. They also would tend to agree that the freedom of conscience position taken by the Supreme Court in *Roe v. Wade* is consistent with the U.S. constitutional tradition of separation of church and state, and that government action to prohibit choice would be tantamount to government imposition of a religious creed.

What does science have to say about when personhood begins? "Personhood," of course, is not a scientific term, but, rather, one used in law, philosophy, and theology. Nonetheless, science can provide information as to when certain structures or functions are present in a fetus.

"Pro-life" writers point to such landmarks in fetal development as when the heart starts pumping, when reflexes begin, when certain muscle activities begin, etc., but can personhood be reduced to mere biology? Such a view surely undervalues what it means to be fully human.

Anthropologists have shown that cultures vary widely as to when they attribute personhood, with some of them not assigning it until months after birth. Catholic theologian Marjorie Maguire, who is strongly pro-choice, usefully points out that, in our culture, pregnant women subjectively attribute personhood to a fetus at different stages of development, often in relation to whether the pregnancy is wanted or unwanted.

Since the functioning of born persons as human—with the capacity to be aware, sense, reason, and make moral judgments—is related to the development of the neocortex and central nervous system, the science of neurobiology can tell us a great deal about when a fetus acquires the neural equipment necessary for personhood. Prospective neocortical cells begin to move into position only after seven weeks of gestation. The first neocortical synapses are not formed until 19 to 22 weeks. After reviewing the latest findings of neurobiology, biologist Michael J. Flower concludes that "it is probably not until after 28 weeks of gestation that the fetal human attains a level of neocortex-mediated complexity sufficient to enable those sentient capacities the presence of which might lead us to predicate personhood of a sort we attribute to full-term newborns." Neurobiology, then, does not support the notion that abortions, 99.99% of which take place before 24 weeks, involve the termination of human persons.

An article of this length can not possibly cover this complex subject as thoroughly as one would like, but the bottom line of even a much more extended analysis would be that there is no good reason why our country should retreat from the constitutional protection it finally has extended to women to determine for themselves if and when they will produce children. Indeed, that protection can and should be made more complete and secure.

Interpersonal Relationships

- **Establishing Sexual Relationships (Articles 31-33)**
- **Responsible Quality Relationships (Articles 34-37)**

Most people are familiar with the term "sexual relationship." It denotes an important dimension of sexuality: interpersonal sexuality, or sexual interactions occurring between two (and sometimes more) individuals. This unit focuses attention on these types of relationships.

No woman is an island. No man is an island. Interpersonal contact forms the basis for self-esteem and meaningful living; conversely, isolation results in loneliness and depression for most human beings. People seek and cultivate friendships for the warmth, affection, supportive-

ness, and sense of trust and loyalty that such relationships can provide.

Long-term friendships may develop into intimate relationships. The qualifying word in the previous sentence is "may." Today many people, single as well as married, yearn for close or intimate interpersonal relationships but fail to find them. Fear of rejection causes some to avoid interpersonal relationships, others to present a "false front" or illusory self that they think is more acceptable or socially desirable. This sets the stage for a "game of intimacy" that is counterfeit to genuine intimacy. For others a major dilemma may exist: the problem of balancing closeness with the preservation of individual identity in a manner that at once satisfies the need for personal and interpersonal growth and integrity. In either case, partners in a relationship should be advised that the development of interpersonal awareness (the mutual recognition and knowledge of others as they really are) rests upon trust and self-disclosure: letting the other person know who you really are and how you truly feel. In American society this has never been easy, and it is especially difficult in the area of sexuality.

The above considerations in regard to interpersonal relationships apply equally well to achieving meaningful and satisfying sexual relationships. Three basic ingredients lay the foundation for quality sexual interaction. These are self-awareness, acceptance of the partner's state of awareness, and a free and open sharing of each partner's awareness through communication of feelings, needs, and desires. Without these, misunderstandings may arise, bringing into the relationship anxiety, frustration, dissatisfaction, and/or resentment, as well as a heightened risk of contracting AIDS or another STD or experiencing an unplanned pregnancy. Indeed, these basic ingredients, taken together, may constitute sexual responsibility. Clearly, no one person is completely responsible for quality sexual relations.

As might already be apparent, there is much more to quality sexual relations than our popular culture recognizes. Such relationships are not established on penis size, beautiful figures, or correct sexual techniques. Rather, it is the quality of the interaction that makes sex a celebration of our sexuality. A person-oriented (as opposed to genitally-oriented) sexual awareness coupled with a leisurely, whole body/mind sensuality and an open attitude toward exploration make for quality sexuality.

The subsection on *Establishing Sexual Relationships* opens with an article examining the reasons why men and women actually experience fewer and less satisfying intimate relationships than they desire. In the next article, the differences in male/female thinking about love, sex, and

relationships are highlighted. The final article, "How Do You Build Intimacy in an Age of Divorce?" explores personal and cultural inhibitions to intimacy and its cornerstone: trust. It offers insightful suggestions for taking the "intelligent leap of faith" into the level of intimacy for which we yearn.

The first article in the *Responsible Quality Relationships* subsection, "Major Mergers," may seem to contradict the advice to trust given in the last one in the preceding section. Yet it offers some important advice about economic matters that couples involved in joint ventures would be wise to consider. The next selection is actually a set of articles grouped under the title "Sexual Pursuit." Each ponders the state of intimate relationships. Changes associated with the women's and men's liberation movements, AIDS, and other sociocultural forces are discussed with a variety of conclusions and perspectives. The final two articles continue in the vein of exploring dilemmas inherent in '80s intimate relationships. "Not Tonight, Dear" discusses the growing problem of ISD (Inhibited Sexual Desire). "I Love You, But Can I Ask a Question?" provides suggestions about how to ask a potential partner those difficult "safe sex" questions.

Looking Ahead: Challenge Questions

What do you see as the greatest barriers to satisfying intimate relationships? Are there some people who are destined to fail at establishing and/or maintaining them? If so, who and why?

What do you think are the reasons for the differences in male/female thinking about love, sex, and relationships?

What makes you most fearful of trusting or intimacy? Why?

What about sexual pursuit in the "old days" do you wish was still here today? What are you glad has changed?

Have you ever lost interest in sex? What are some reasons why others might do so?

Have you or your friends found a comfortable way to ask the questions you want to ask of potential sexual partners? If yes, how? If not, why not?

Barriers in the Initiation of Intimate Heterosexual Relationships and Strategies for Intervention

Susan Sprecher

Kathleen McKinney

SUMMARY. One problem for which men and women commonly seek help from social workers is difficulty in initiating intimate heterosexual relationships. The lack of a meaningful intimate relationship can lead to feelings of loneliness and distress, which can contribute to more severe problems, such as alcoholism, drug abuse, and suicide. The problems of initiating intimate heterosexual relationships are discussed, including the specific barriers of physical unattractiveness, fear of rejection, shyness, and traditional sex-role norms. Research evidence is presented that indicates how people can overcome these barriers and initiate the relationships they desire.

INTRODUCTION

Social workers, counselors, and therapists work with the special problems and needs of many different groups. But, whatever a group's unique issues, one of the fundamental needs of all people is love and intimacy. Thus, it is critically important for those in the helping professions to understand the array of problems men and women can face in initiating intimate heterosexual relationships.

In this chapter, we first summarize research that indicates that many people *desire* more (or better) relationships than they actually have and that this discrepancy can cause them to feel lonely. Second, we discuss why people don't always act on their desires and at least *try* to establish the relationships they would like to have. Special focus will be given to four barriers that can prevent people from initiating relationships: physical unattractiveness, fear of rejection, shyness, and traditional sex roles. Next, we summarize the research that indicates where and how men and women typically meet each other and form relationships. Finally, we offer possible solutions on how men and women can overcome these barriers and how counselors can help them do so.

LONELINESS— DESIRED RELATIONSHIPS EXCEED ACHIEVED RELATIONSHIPS

Loneliness is defined as the distress experienced as a result of perceiving a discrepancy between desired and achieved social rela-

tionships (Perlman & Peplau, 1981). Loneliness can be experienced for two general types of relationships (Weiss, 1973). *Emotional loneliness* exists when one desires but does not have an intense intimate relationship that is characterized by self-disclosure, sharing, love and, possibly, physical intimacy. *Social loneliness* is experienced as a result of a lack of a social network of friends and acquaintances.

The state of loneliness, regardless of its source, is not pleasant. People who are lonely also experience sadness, depression, boredom, self-pity, helplessness, alienation, and insecurity (Rubenstein & Shaver, 1982). These are the feelings that can lead to other problems, such as drug and alcohol abuse, clinical depression, and even suicide.

If people *achieved* social relations (in both quantity and quality) to the same degree that they *desired* them, they would not experience loneliness. Unfortunately, loneliness is a very common experience for many Americans. For example, in one national survey 26% of Americans reported feeling "very lonely or remote from other people" when asked to report on feelings experienced during the previous few weeks (Bradburn, 1969).

The desire of men and women for intimate heterosexual relationships has been the subject of research that we have conducted with our colleagues (Marwell, McKinney, Sprecher, DeLamater & Smith, 1982). In our study, students at the University of Wisconsin were asked how many opposite-sex classmates they would be interested in "spending an hour (with) for the purpose of deciding whether this is someone you would like to date." More than 80% of the men and 66% of the women indicated that there were one or more persons in the classroom with whom they would like to spend time. To another question about interest for persons *outside* the class, 90% of the men and 80% of the women reported that there was at least one such person they would like to meet. Men indicated an average of 19 women, and women an average of seven men. Evidence also indicates that, when people experience loneliness,

The authors would like to express appreciation to the following people for providing comments on the chapter: Lynn Atkinson, John DeLamater, Charles Fisher, Terri Orbuch, and Stevens Smith. Gratitude also goes to Gerald Marwell for helping to develop the authors' interest in this topic.

Address reprint requests to Dr. Susan Sprecher, Illinois State University, Department of Sociology, Anthropology & Social Work, Normal, IL 61761.

From *Journal of Social Work & Human Sexuality*, Vol. 5, No. 2, Spring/Summer 1987, pp. 97-110. Copyright © 1987 by The Haworth Press, Inc. Reprinted by permission.

what they report desiring is an intimate relationship (Cutrona, 1982).

If men and women desire intimate relationships and are attracted to specific others, why don't they simply pick up the phone and ask one of them out for a date? In the next section, we will discuss why some people have a difficult time approaching the opposite sex.

BARRIERS THAT PREVENT DESIRED HETEROSEXUAL RELATIONSHIPS

The fact that some people have not developed the intimate heterosexual relationships they desire suggests that barriers operate to prevent them from doing so. In our research (Marwell et al., 1982), we were interested in exploring which barriers are particularly important. We developed a list of 21 possible barriers based on face validity and on the open-ended responses of students in a pretest. The items represent two general types of barriers. Some are internal to the individual. These would include, for example, shyness and fear of rejection. Other barriers are external, and may either arise because of circumstantial factors or because of characteristics of the desired potential date (e.g., he/she seems difficult to approach).

The respondents in the final study were asked to think about one specific opposite-sex person whom they would like to get to know better and to rate each barrier (on a seven-point scale) according to how important it was in preventing them from getting to know this person. Items that were rated as important barriers (mean of 4.0 or greater) by *both* men and women were: "I have been too shy to approach him/her," "I do not think he/she would be interested in me," "I don't want to make a fool of myself" (internal barriers), "I have not had the right opportunity," "I have never been alone with him/her," and "I think he/she is in a relationship with someone else" (external barriers).

In the next four sections, we will focus more specifically on common barriers to the initiation of heterosexual relationship. These barriers are: being (or perceiving oneself as) physically unattractive, fear of rejection, shyness, and traditional sex roles.

Physical Unattractiveness

When people are asked what characteristics are important in a dating or marriage partner, they do not rate physical attractiveness as very important (Hudson & Henze, 1969; Hudson & Hoyt, 1981; Tesser & Brodie, 1971). People's *actions*, however, indicate that physical attractiveness is exceedingly important, particularly when they meet others who are potential dating partners. Walster, Aronson, Abrahams, and Rottman (1966) found that for freshman college students randomly matched for a dance, the major determinant of how much the date was liked was how attractive he/she was. This was more important than the date's intelligence, personality, and social skills. Numerous other studies also demonstrate that people prefer to date attractive others (e.g., Brislin & Lewis, 1968; Tesser & Brodie, 1971).

The research cited above suggests that physically unattractive people are less likely to be approached by the opposite sex for a date. There is also evidence to indicate that people's physical attractiveness influences whether they do the approaching. Interestingly, the research indicates that being unattractive is a barrier to initiating relationships for men, while being attractive can be a barrier for women.

Reis, Wheeler, Spiegel, Kernis, Nezlek and Perri (1982) studied how physical attractiveness affected college students' social participation. The men and women in this study completed several social competence measures and kept a daily record of every interaction that lasted 10 minutes or longer for a period of 7 to 18 days. From the daily diaries the students maintained, the researchers discovered that attractive men reported initiating more of their social interactions with the opposite sex than did the unattractive men. Furthermore, the attractive men had more social interaction with the opposite sex; that is, they interacted with more women and for longer periods of time. Attractive women, on the other hand, were less likely to initiate contacts with the opposite sex than were their less attractive peers. Furthermore, more attractive women did not have significantly more interactions with the opposite sex than did unattractive women.

Fear of Rejection

While most people find rejection to be somewhat unpleasant, because it can lower self-esteem and lead to embarrassment in front of others, certain people are particularly anxious about having their advances rejected. Evidence indicates that those who are shy, unattractive, or have low self-esteem are more likely to experience fear of rejection (Kiesler & Baral, 1970; Krebs & Adinolfi, 1975; Reis et al., 1982).

However, even nonshy, attractive, and high self-esteem individuals can experience fear of rejection under certain circumstances. A necessary condition for experiencing fear of rejection is that the goal (a date) is desired and the acceptance is uncertain. If we knew that the other would accept our offer (for example, if we had heard from friends that he/she had expressed interest in us) then we would probably experience no or little fear of rejection.

Many times, however, the likelihood of acceptance is not known. This uncertainty can prevent individuals from initiating relationships even though both parties may actually be interested. For example, two of the barriers rated in the Marwell et al. (1982) study as important reasons why men and women had not approached someone to whom they were attracted were "I do not think he/she would be interested in me" and "I do not want to make a fool of myself." Furthermore, several laboratory studies indicate that choices for a dating partner are affected, in part, by the probability of acceptance. People are not likely to choose as potential dates those who they think are unlikely to accept their offer (Huston, 1973; Shanteau & Nagy, 1979).

Shyness

Another barrier to the initiation of new heterosexual relationships is shyness. Both shyness and fear of rejection can be considered aspects of a general feeling of inadequacy regarding intimate relationships. Shyness has been defined as "the general tendency to be inhibited and awkward in social situations and to experience unpleasant affect in the presence of others" (Cheek & Busch, 1981; p. 573).

As pointed out by Snyder, Smith, Angelli and Ingram (1985), there are several common features of shyness or social anxiety. Shyness arises in social situations and has an affective component that often involves feelings of apprehension and nervousness, a cognitive component including evaluation concern, and behavioral aspects such as inadequate social responses. All of these characteristics make it difficult for the shy person to initiate desired heterosexual relationships.

Shyness can inhibit the formation of relationships in several different ways. First, the shy person may have difficulty feeling safe and secure enough to trust another, which in turn inhibits self-disclosure, a necessary condition for establishing and maintaining intimate relationships (Zimbardo, 1977). Second, because shy individuals are typically overly concerned with their evaluation and acceptance by others, and with the potential costs of new relationships, such as ridicule and embarrassment, they may use a series of buffers or barriers to control their contact with others (Schlenker & Leary, 1982, Snyder et al., 1985; Zimbardo, 1977). They may avoid new people and new situations, and refrain from eye contact. Such buffers serve to decrease social interaction directly as well as indirectly, because these behaviors can be viewed negatively by others who may then decrease their own efforts to initiate contact with shy persons.

Sex Roles

A fourth barrier to the initiation of new heterosexual relationships is traditional sex-role norms. Sex roles refer to the attitudes, behaviors, and personality characteristics that a particular culture considers appropriate for a male or female. Parents, peers, church, school and the media all serve as agents of socialization across the lifecycle. According to traditional sex roles men are expected to be aggressive, competitive, in control, sexual, dominant, athletic, strong, and independent, whereas women are supposed to be the opposite—submissive, passive, nonsexual, nonathletic, warm, nurturant, and dependent.

If men and women adhere strictly to traditional sex roles and courtship behaviors, they may encounter obstacles in getting relationships started. This may be a particular problem for women, who feel that it is inappropriate to ask a man out directly or who lack the sense of personal power to do so. In support of this, the Marwell et al. (1982) study found that women rated the item "I have been waiting for him/her to approach me" as an important barrier preventing them from initiating heterosexual relationships, and more important than did men. Traditional sex roles can also be a barrier to men in establishing relationships. Men may not initiate relationships because they may presume that the burden (and risk) of initiating the relationship will be totally theirs and that they will be expected to bear the entire financial cost of dating. In the Marwell et al. (1982) study, for example, men rated "I do not know her name and/or phone number" and "I cannot afford the money" more highly than did women as important barriers to the initiation of relationships.

What happens if women break away from traditional sex roles and ask men out for a date? The evidence indicates that, despite some advances toward equality (e.g., Allgeier, 1981; Clark & Hatfield, 1981), the outcome may not be completely positive. Jason, Reichler and Rucker (1981) found that "most important" relationships lasted, on the average, nine months less when the woman asked the man out on the first date than when the man initiated the first date. Men may be embarrassed, feel their prerogative is being usurped, or view the female in negative terms when a woman asks them out or tries to make the first contact. (However, for evidence that women may actually make the first subtle move in certain settings, see Perper & Fox, 1980.) Finally, studies show that men and women (especially those who are traditional themselves) view more negatively and like less those who express sex-inappropriate or cross-gender behavior (Korabik, 1982; Richardson, Bernstein & Hendrick, 1980).

HOW PEOPLE MEET OTHERS

Although people have barriers to overcome in the process of initiating heterosexual relationships, many relationships do manage to develop. Perhaps the most valuable information counselors can give men and women who have failed to establish intimate heterosexual relationships is *where* and *how* successful others have met their dating partners. In fact, the lack of opportunity and the unavailability of partners may be the most critical barriers to overcome. In this section, we summarize research that indicates the processes by which many heterosexual relationships get started.

In our investigation of how college students meet their dates (Marwell et al., 1982), we interviewed a random sample of 136 college sophomores about the process by which they met "the last person since coming to the university with when you have had some experience in which the two of you were definitely a 'couple.'" More than one-third of the males and 43% of the females were introduced to their partner by a third party. The third party was most often a friend, but some introductions were also made by siblings, employers, and professors.

The importance of introductions from friends was also demonstrated by Knox and Wilson (1981) in a study of 334 college students. They found that 33% of the students reported having come to know their dating partner through a friend. This way of meeting a dating partner was mentioned more frequently than any of the other possible responses, which included "at a party," "at work" and "in class."

Meeting a dating partner through friends is not limited to college students. In fact, this way of meeting a partner may become more important as age increases. Jason et al. (1982) administered a questionnaire on how relationships begin to single women in a variety of singles' settings. (The average age of these women, who represented a variety of backgrounds, was 27.4.) They found that introductions from friends was one of the primary ways the women met a dating partner, and it was particularly important for the older respondents (ages 28-37).

While most of the aforementioned studies were conducted with small samples, one large-scale study was conducted of single adults in America (Simenauer & Carroll, 1982). Three thousand men and women between the ages of 20 and 55 from 36 states participated in the study. One of the many questions asked in this study was, "Where do you meet most of the men/women you date?" The most common response from both men and women was "through friends." Thirty-three percent of the men and 36% of the women responded in this way.

Why are introductions so important? As Marwell et al. (1982) pointed out, an introduction from a third party helps to legitimize the relationship. The authors note:

> The friend has the right to interact with each of the two partners and he/she essentially vouches for the fact that the other person is "all right." The friend also makes it improbable that the other person will behave in a rudely rejecting manner, and may also imply with the introduction that the two partners are both "available" and appropriate for one another (pp. 5-6).

In other words, introductions may help individuals overcome (or at least, deal with) some of the barriers previously discussed. For example, shy people may rely on introductions from friends to help break the ice. Those who fear rejection may need the friend's verification that it will be unlikely that they will be immediately rejected. Women who adhere to strict sex roles may use introductions as a subtle way to initiate a relationship.

Research has also demonstrated that a variety of settings is important. For example, parties were the most important setting for meeting dating partners in the Knox and Wilson (1981) study. The single women surveyed by Jason et al. (1981) reported that school, work, bars, and parties were important locations for meeting others. In Simenauer and Carroll's study, social gatherings, bars (discos, nightclubs etc.), singles functions, and work were popular settings for meeting others. And the college sophomores in Marwell et al. (1982) most frequently met their partners at parties in dorms, apartments, and fraternities, or in classes.

The particular setting in which men and women meet does seem likely to affect the process by which they move from the unacquainted to the acquainted, and then on to the "couple" stage, but systematic research has not been conducted to examine whether or how meeting setting affects the development of a relationship. Some settings are created solely for men and women to meet each other (e.g., dances, fraternity/sorority mixers, singles bars, and special singles functions). This type of setting may be defined as a relationship-building one because attendance is usually a way of communicating interest in developing relationships.

In other types of settings, people interact for nonsocial reasons. For example, in work settings, classes, and in certain task-oriented groups, people are present to accomplish tasks. Their interaction with others is not necessarily of a coupling nature. Some decision has to be made to convert the relationship into a dating one, and usually this conversion does not take place immediately after meeting. Thus, one of the differences between the two settings is that in the second setting, the individuals have more information about each other before they begin a dating relationship. While this may make the initiation process easier in some ways, it can also make it more difficult. Once a relationship has been defined in a certain way (as coworkers or casual acquaintances), it may be difficult to redefine it in another way.

OVERCOMING MORE DIFFICULT BARRIERS

The information on where and how couples meet may help guide the lonely to the right settings. However, there are also more specific strategies that counselors can suggest to individuals in order to overcome the four barriers previously discussed.

One can deal with the barrier of *unattractiveness* both directly and indirectly. Directly, men and women can actually alter and improve their appearance by manipulating hairstyle, make-up, clothes and jewelry, and through exercise and weight control. However, it may not be worth sacrificing everything to improve one's attractiveness, because research shows that being of average attractiveness provides almost the same interpersonal benefits as being very attractive (for more discussion of this point and a summary of relevant research, see Hatfield & Sprecher, 1986). Indirectly, individuals can increase their feeling of attractiveness by associating with others of equal or lesser attractiveness levels (rather than greater attractiveness) so that comparisons provide positive feedback, by realistically seeking potential partners of equal attractiveness and, finally, by playing up other positive aspects of the self, such as intelligence, personality, humor, and abilities. This last strategy can be best utilized in settings where these characteristics may be more important than appearance (e.g., work, school).

If one accepts social skills deficits as one influence on *fear of rejection* and *shyness* (Bellack & Hersen, 1979; Curran, 1977), then one strategy for dealing with these barriers involves teaching people effective social skills such as negotiation, verbal and nonverbal communication, and etiquette (for example, through therapeutic interventions utilizing role-playing). Furthermore, because shyness and fear of rejection are related to how one feels about oneself, exercises to improve appearance and boost self esteem are useful.

Overconcern with evaluation by others is another factor related to fear of rejection and shyness, and counseling and exercises can be used to help people keep such concern at an appropriate level. Individuals have to be taught to focus more on the other than on the self, because self-focus hinders social performance (Schlenker & Leary, 1982).

Sometimes counselors will encounter clients who present themselves as more shy than they really are. Men and women may present themselves as shy if it can-be used as a valid excuse for poor performance. This is what is called a "self-handicapping strategy." Snyder et al. (1985) found that shy men (but not shy women) were likely to report symptoms of shyness if it could be used as a valid excuse for failure. People who present themselves as shy, perhaps because they need an excuse for lack of success in dating, need to work on new self-presentations.

Because all of the above strategies for helping those who are shy or who fear rejection will not make such people socially adept over-

night, it may be useful for them, in the interim, to gain some interpersonal confidence by asking friends to provide introductions.

Given the strength, length, and success of the socialization process in teaching *traditional sex roles* in our culture, this barrier to the initiation of heterosexual relationships is particularly difficult to overcome. At the least, individuals need to be aware of how their traditional sex roles limit their ability to form new heterosexual relationships. This can help them better understand some of their failures to make new contacts. Second, people can learn to practice cross-gender role behaviors by talking to, observing, and modeling the role behaviors of opposite-sex friends and siblings or of more androgynous same-sex friends and siblings. Finally, individuals might reduce the traditional sex-role barrier by seeking partners who have an androgynous sex-role orientation or who are able to accept androgynous behavior in others. This should reduce the chance of role expectations being violated and the negative outcomes that such violations produce. In fact, evidence indicates that such pairings have more positive interactions. For example, Ickes and Barnes (1977, 1978) found that male-female pairs of strangers, in which at least one member was androgynous, had significantly more positive interactions (more smiling, gesturing, eye contact, and liking) than pairs consisting of a traditional male and traditional female.

SUMMARY AND CONCLUSIONS

Unfortunately, it is likely that there are many relationships that were "meant to be" but never happened because one or both parties didn't have the courage or the opportunity to make the first move. In this chapter, we described some of the barriers that can prevent the initiation of heterosexual relationships and some ways of overcoming these barriers. Although it is important for the social worker/counselor to know how to help a distressed, lonely client overcome general feelings of inadequacy concerning the initiation of relationships, it is also important that focus be given to the opportunities the client has to meet the opposite sex. Becoming a socially confident and assertive person will not matter if there are no opportunities to meet potential partners. It is important that the individual who desires intimate heterosexual relationships have the opportunity to be around the opposite sex in appropriate settings and also to develop a social network of friends who can provide introductions. In fact, the social worker can be instrumental in creating the conditions ideal for igniting intimacy by introducing singles to each other, by holding group sessions, and by finding other legitimate settings for uncoupled men and women to interact.

REFERENCES

Allgeier, E. P. (1981). The influence of androgynous identification of heterosexual relations. *Sex Roles, 7,* 321-330.
Bellack, A. S. & Hersen, M. (1979). *Research and practice in social skills training.* New York: Plenum.
Bradburn, N. (1969). *The structure of psychological well-being.* Chicago: Aldine.
Brislin, R. W. & Lewis, S. A. (1968). Dating and physical attractiveness: A replication. *Psychological Reports, 22,* 976.
Check, J. M. & Busch, C. M. (1981). The influence of shyness on loneliness in a new situation. *Personality and Social Psychology Bulletin, 7,* 572-577.
Clark, R. D., III & Hatfield, E. (1981). Gender differences in receptivity to sexual offers. Unpublished manuscript, 1981.
Curran, J. P. (1977). Skills training as an approach to the treatment of heterosexual social anxiety. *Psychological Bulletin, 84,* 140-157.
Cutrona, C. E. (1982). Transition to college: Loneliness and the process of social adjustment. In L. A. Peplau & D. Perlman (Eds.), *Loneliness.* New York: John Wiley and Sons.
Hatfield, E. & Sprecher, S. (1986). *Mirror, mirror: The importance of looks in everyday life.* New York: State University of New York Press.
Hudson, J. W. & Henze, L. F. (1969). Campus values in the mate selection: A replication. *Journal of Marriage and the Family, 31,* 772-775.
Hudson, J. W. & Hoyt, L. L. (1981). Personal characteristics important in mate preference among college students. *Social Behavior and Personality, 9,* 93-96.
Huston, T. L. (1973). Ambiguity of acceptance, social desirability, and dating choice. *Journal of Experimental Social Psychology, 9,* 32-42.

4. INTERPERSONAL RELATIONSHIPS: Establishing Sexual Relationships

Ickes, W. & Barnes, R. D. (1977). The role of sex and self-monitoring in unstructured dyadic interactions. *Journal of Personality and Social Psychology, 35*, 315-330.

Ickes, W. & Barnes, R. D. (19778). Boys and girls together—and alienated: On enacting stereotyped sex roles in mixed-sex dyads. *Journal of Personality and Social Psychology, 36*, 669-683.

Jason, L. A., Reichler, A. & Rucker, W. (1981). Characteristics of significant dating relationships: Male versus female initiators, idealized versus actual settings. *The Journal of Psychology, 109*, 185-190.

Kiesler, S. B. & Baral, R. P. (1970). The search for a romantic partner: The effects of self-esteem and physical attractiveness on romantic behavior. In K. J. Gergen and D. Maslow (Eds.), *Personality and Social Behavior*. Reading, MA: Addison-Wesley, pp. 155-165.

Knox, D. & Wilson, K. (1981). Dating behaviors of university students. *Family Relations, 30*, 255-258.

Korabik, K. (1982). Sex-role orientation and impressions: A comparison of differing genders and sex-roles. *Personality and Social Psychology Bulletin, 8*, 25-30.

Krebs, D. & Adinolfi, A. A. (1975). Physical attractiveness, social relations, and personality style. *Journal of Personality and Social Psychology, 31*, 245-253.

Marwell, G., McKinney, K., Sprecher, S., DeLamater, J. & Smith, S. (1982). Legitimizing factors in the initiation of heterosexual relationships. Paper presented at the First International Conference on Personal Relationships, Madison, WI.

Perlman, D. & Peplau, L. A. (1981). Toward a social psychology of loneliness. In S. Duck & R. Gilmour (Eds.), *Personal relationships: 3: Personal relationships in disorder*. New York: Academic Press.

Perper, T. & Fox, V. S. (1980). Special focus: Flirtation behavior in public settings. Paper presented at the Meeting of the Eastern Region of the Society for the Scientific Study of Sex, Philadelphia.

Reis, H. T., Wheeler, L., Spiegel, N., Kernis, M. H., Nezlek, J. & Perri, M. (1982). Physical attractiveness in social interaction: II. Why does appearance affect social experience? *Journal of Personality and Social Psychology, 43*, 979-996.

Richardson, D., Bernstein, S. & Hendrick, C. (1980). Deviations from conventional sex-role behavior: Effect of perceivers' sex-role attitudes on attraction. *Basic and Applied Social Psychology, 1*, 351-355.

Rubenstein, C. M. & Shaver, P. (1982). The experience of loneliness. in L. A. Peplau & D. Perlman (Eds.), *Loneliness*. New York: John Wiley and Sons.

Schlenker, B. R. & Leary, M. R. (1982). Social anxiety and social presentation: A conceptualization and model. *Psychological Bulletin, 92*, 641-669.

Shanteau, J. & Nagy, G. F. (1979). Probability of acceptance in dating choice. *Journal of Personality and Social Psychology, 37*, 522-533.

Simenauer, J. & Carroll, D. (1982). *Singles: The new Americans*. New York: Simon and Schuster.

Snyder, G. R., Smith, T. W., Angelli, R. W. & Ingram, K. E. (1985). On the self-serving function of social anxiety: Shyness as a self-handicapping strategy. *Journal of Personality and Social Psychology, 48*, 970-980.

Tesser, A. & Brodie, M. (1971). A note on the evaluation of a computer date. *Psychonomic Science, 23*, 300.

Walster, E., Aronson, V., Abrahams, D. & Rottman, L. (1966). The importance of physical attractiveness in dating behavior. *Journal of Personality and Social Psychology, 4*, 508-516.

Weiss, R. S. (1973). *Loneliness*. Cambridge, MA: MIT Press.

Zimbardo, P. G. (1977). *Shyness*. Reading, MA: Addison-Wesley.

Study Defines Major Sources of Conflict Between Sexes

Differences are found in what disturbs men and women.

Daniel Goleman

In the war between the sexes, virtually all combatants consider themselves experts on the causes of conflict. But now a systematic research project has defined, more precisely than ever before, the points of conflict that arise between men and women in a wide range of relationships.

The new studies are showing that the things that anger men about women, and women about men, are just about the same whether the couple are only dating, are newlyweds or are unhappily married.

The research is the most sophisticated yet conducted, and some findings are surprising. Although a vast body of literature cites heated arguments over money, child-rearing or relatives as frequent factors in disintegrating marriages, those conflicts seldom emerged in the new studies.

Instead, the research often found more subtle differences, like women's feelings of being neglected and men's irritations over women being too self-absorbed. There were also more pointed complaints about men's condescension and women's moodiness.

Upset by Unfaithfulness and Abuse

Some forms of behavior bothered both sexes about equally. Both men and women were deeply upset by unfaithfulness and physical or verbal abuse. But the most interesting findings were several marked differences between men and women in the behaviors that most disturbed them.

Sex, not surprisingly, was a major problem, but men and women had diametrically opposed views of what the problem was. Men complained strongly that women too often turned down their sexual overtures.

In contrast, the most consistent complaint among women was that men were too aggressive sexually. This conflict may be rooted deep in the impact of human evolution on reproductive strategies, according to one theory, or it may simply reflect current power struggles or psychological needs, various experts say.

Help in Counseling Couples

Understanding the sources of trouble between the sexes, psychologists say, could do much to help couples soften the impact of persistent problems in their relationships, and help therapists in counseling couples having difficulties.

"Little empirical work has been done on precisely what men and women do that leads to conflict," said David M. Buss, a psychologist at the University of Michigan who conducted the studies. The results were published in May in the *Journal of Personality and Social Psychology*.

Dr. Buss conducted four different studies with nearly 600 men and women. In the first, he simply asked men and women in dating relationships about the things their partners did that made them upset, hurt or angry.

The survey yielded 147 distinct sources of conflict, ranging from being disheveled or insulting to flirting with others or forcing sex on a partner.

In the second study, Dr. Buss asked men and women who were dating or who were newlyweds how often they had been irked by their partner's doing any of those things. From these results, Dr. Buss determined that the complaints fell into 15 specific groups. He then had another group of men and women rate just how bothersome those traits were.

Men said they were most troubled by women who were unfaithful, abusive, self-centered, condescending, sexually withholding, neglectful or moody.

Many men were bothered, for example, if their partner was self-absorbed with her appearance, spending too much money on clothes, and being overly concerned with how her face and hair looked.

Women complained most about men who were sexually aggressive, unfaithful, abusive, condescending, emotionally constricted, and those who insulted the woman's appearance, neglected them, or openly admired other women.

Many women were also bothered by inconsiderate men. For instance, they complained about a man who teases his partner about how long it takes to get dressed, or who does not help clean up the home or who leaves the toilet seat up.

'Basic Differences in Outlook'

Other research has produced supporting findings. "We've seen similar points of conflicts in marital fights," said John Gottman, a psychologist at the University of Washington whose research involves observations of married couples while they fight.

"Many of these complaints seem to be due to basic differences in outlook between the sexes," Dr. Gottman added, citing men's complaints that women are too moody, or that women dwelled too much on the feelings.

"That is the flip side of one of women's biggest complaints about men, that they're too emotionally constricted, too quick to offer an action solution to an emotional problem," he said.

"Generally for women, the natural way to deal with emotions is to explore them, to stay with them," he continued. "Men, though, are stoic in discussing

The War of the Sexes: 2 Views of the Battlefield

Based on a new study of close to 600 men and women, many areas of conflict for couples are the same for both sexes. But here are the main areas where men and women diverge sharply over how upsetting certain behaviors are:

What Bothers a Woman About a Man

SEXUAL DEMANDS: Making her feel sexually used; trying to force sex or demanding it.

CONDESCENSION: Ignoring her opinions because she is a woman; treating her as inferior or stupid; making her feel inferior.

EMOTIONAL CONSTRICTION AND EXCESS: Hiding his emotions to act tough; drinking or smoking too much.

NEGLECT: Unreliability; not spending enough time with her or calling when promised; ignoring her feelings or failing to say he loves her.

THOUGHTLESSNESS: Being unmannerly, belching, for instance, or leaving the toilet seat up; not helping clean up the home; teasing her about how long it takes to get dressed.

What Bothers a Man About a Woman

SEXUAL REJECTION: Refusing to have sex; being unresponsive to sexual advances; being a sexual tease.

MOODINESS: Acting "bitchy" or otherwise being out of sorts.

SELF-ABSORPTION: Fussing over her appearance, worrying about her face and hair; spending too much on clothes.

Source: David A. Buss, Ph.D.,
University of Michigan

their emotions; they don't talk about their feelings as readily as women. So conflict over handling emotions is almost inevitable, especially in marriages that are going bad."

For couples in the first year of marriage, Dr. Buss found the sexual issues to be far less of a problem than for most other couples. Instead, women tended to complain that their new husbands were inconsiderate and disheveled.

"You'd expect that sex would be the least troubling issue for a couple during the honeymoon year," Dr. Buss said. "Even so, newlywed men were still bothered somewhat about their wives' sexual withholding, but the wives didn't complain much about their husbands being sexually aggressive."

Nevertheless, the overall finding that men tend to see women as being sexually withholding, while women see men as too demanding, also fits with other findings. Researchers at the University of New York at Stony Brook found in a survey of close to 100 married couples that the husbands on average wanted to have sex more often than did the wives.

Problems Compounded

In the last of Dr. Buss's series of tests, married men and women were asked about their main sources of marital and sexual dissatisfaction. A new set of complaints emerged, along with the previous ones cited by dating couples and newlyweds. The more dissatisfied with the relationship, the longer the list of complaints.

For example, the more troubled the couple, the more likely the husband was angered by his wife being too possessive, neglecting him and openly admiring other men.

The dissatisfied wives, by contrast, added to their list of complaints that their husbands were possessive, moody and were openly attracted to other women.

Sex was especially problematic for unhappy married men and women.

"The sexual complaints are standard in unhappy marriages," Dr. Gottman said. "But it tends to crop up even in otherwise happy marriages. Generally, women have more prerequisites for sex than men do. They have more expectations about what makes love-making O.K. They want emotional closeness, warmth, conversation, a sense of empathy."

He added: "Sex has a different meaning for women than for men. Women see sex as following from emotional intimacy, while men see sex itself as a road to intimacy. So it follows that men should complain more that women are withholding, or women say men are too aggressive."

Investment in Reproduction

Dr. Buss sees his results as affirming the importance of evolution in shaping human behavior. "The evolutionary model that I use holds that conflicts occur when one sex does something that interferes with the other's strategy for reproduction," he said.

His view is based on the theory put forth by Robert Trivers, a social scientist at the University of California at Santa Cruz, who proposed that women are more discriminating than men about their sexual partners because biologically women have to invest more time and energy in reproduction than do men.

Men on the other hand stand to gain in terms of reproductive success for having sexual relations with as many women as possible, the theory holds.

"To some degree the sexes are inevitably at odds, given the differences in their strategies," Dr. Buss said.

Even so, Dr. Buss does not see evolution as explaining all his findings. "The sources of conflict between men and women are much more diverse than I predicted," he said.

Some of that diversity may be caused by sex roles. "Men and women are socialized differently as children," said Nancy Cantor, a social psychologist at the University of Michigan. "Men, for example, are not expected to be as open with their emotions as women, while women are expected to be less aggressive than men. So you'd expect a list very much like he found."

Dr. Gottman offered another explanation, saying: "The categories sound like much of what we see in couples' fights. But they miss what underlies all that: whether people feel loved and respected. Those are the two most important dimensions in marital happiness."

How do you build
INTIMACY
in an age of divorce?

CARYL S. AVERY

Caryl S. Avery is a New York-based free-lance writer specializing in health and psychology.

Given one wish in life, most people would wish to be loved — to be able to reveal themselves entirely to another human being and be embraced, caressed, by that acceptance. People who have successfully built an intimate relationship know its power and comfort. But they also know that taking the emotional risks that allow intimacy to happen isn't easy. Preconditioned on the sharing of feelings, intimacy requires consummate trust. And today trust is in short supply.

Few adults under 40 can remember a world without cynicism. Faith is no longer fashionable, and a quarter-century of wars and double-dealing in high places has eroded our confidence in institutions we once revered. The personal realm seems similarly shaky. With one of two new marriages ending in divorce and countless others existing in name only, trusting someone to be honest and committed over the long haul is increasingly difficult.

This isn't to say that the concept of marriage or commitment has fallen into disfavor — in fact, among certain age groups the marriage rate is up, and a new National Opinion Research Council survey finds that for Americans monogamy is still the ideal.

But ideals aside, the "till death do us part" of the marriage vow rings increasingly ironic. "Nobody goes to a wedding today without somewhere in the back of their mind wondering how long the marriage is going to last," says psychologist Judith S. Wallerstein who, with writer Sandra Blakeslee, authored the wave-making book *Second Chances: Men, Women and Children a Decade After Divorce.* Clearly, an anticipation of dissolution is not the best foundation on which to build a relationship that will be rich and meaningful. And it's the ultimate saboteur of trust, since it's the sense of continuity and permanence provided by commitment that creates an atmosphere in which trust can flourish.

Although trust in a partner means different things to different people — dependability, loyalty, honesty, fidelity — its essence is emotional safety. Trust enables you to put your deepest feelings and fears in the palm of your partner's hand, knowing they will be handled with care. While feelings of love or sexual excitement may wax and wane over time, ideally, trust is a constant. When you have it, you have it all. The challenge for most of us is not to let the spectre of deception in love interfere with finding the intimate connection we want and need.

When the world — or your own past — plants seeds of doubt, how is it possible to overlook them? Clearly, people's capacity for trust in intimate relationships varies widely, depending many factors — early upbringing, the quality of their parents' relationship, their own experiences with love. Because nobody emerges unscathed from that early infantile period when "basic trust" — the sense that the world is fundamentally a kindly place — is formed, none of us is 100% trusting, or trustworthy.

Yet the more trusting we are, the more likely we are to be trusted by others — a finding that has come out of the research of Julian Rotter, a professor of psychology at the University of Connecticut. This theory of reciprocity can be used to help build trust, Rotter believes: Take the risk of trusting, and you may be trusted in return. Initially, this requires the sophisticated skill of sensing just how far to risk your trust, what John and Kris Amodeo, authors of *Being Intimate,* call making an "intelligent leap of faith." True trust is felt, not willed, they say. It must be developed over time, by sharing your innermost thoughts and feelings gradually, and seeing how they're received.

"John made it clear from the beginning that he'd accept my feelings no matter what they were," says Kass Patterson, 28, a legal secretary who married John, 31, almost a year ago after a three-year courtship. "Since my teenage years, I'd never trusted a man; I was betrayed so often. But John proved over and over that he was true to his word. And he allowed me to be me."

Two years into the relationship, John lost his job in the oil and gas industry and remained unemployed for about a year; he didn't want just another job but a career that would make him happy. Kass, however, was ready to get married and began wondering, aloud, if John was the man for her: Was he a stable person, would he be a good provider? John's reaction: "I tried to reassure her that I was doing this for both of us. I said, 'If you can wait, thank you; if you can't, do what you must.'"

Despite the doubts, deep down Kass knew that John was a go-getter and would get back on track. So she waited. Looking back she says, "Making it through that hard time, I know I can make it through anything; I have even greater confidence in John. But I know I hurt him back then and regret having done it."

Says John, now a successful restaurateur, "It was hard when she was questioning my values, but she shouldn't regret it — she was looking for the man of her dreams."

To be able to be oneself and not have to disown one's values to please another — that's what intimate love is all about. John and Kass achieved it because they knew themselves, accepted each other and were willing to take a risk. By validating Kass's need to look for her dream man, John gave her space to find it in him.

the intelligent leap of faith it takes to get on to

the more serious business of loving another person requires that we first increase our awareness of the forces — both social and personal — that would undermine it. The divorce rate isn't the only sign flashing "danger." There are novels and films about fatal attractions and dangerous liaisons, television shows that make infidelity look positively routine, tabloids that report every relationship rift and rupture. Trash sells, trust doesn't. But trash makes trust seem increasingly improbable.

To adopt that mindset is to court trouble. Your inclination may be to trust less — but then you'll pay the price of being trusted less. Or you might be inclined to put less into the relationship, while researchers find that the more you invest, the more commitment increases.

external messages like

these can sabotage our sense of trust. And in addition, we have to grapple with internal impulses. There's the tendency to idealize others and compare their "perfect" relationship to our own. The "investment model," as defined by psychologist Caryl E. Rusbult of the University of North Carolina, asserts that we feel satisfied with what we have to the extent that it exceeds our expectations or our handy comparisons. But what can possibly compare with perfection?

Another powerful element, the flip side of idealization, is the habit of sitting in judgment of other people's relationships in a way that confirms the elusiveness of caring, intimate partnerships. What looks "bad" to us — she

takes separate vacations, he has a number of women friends — may work fine for them. Our intolerance of others' creative solutions, says one expert, leads us to draw inappropriate, negative conclusions about the quality of their love — and about the possibilities of love in general.

The tendency to lump all your past failed relationships together also can undermine present and future bondings. You can't realistically attribute a failed marriage to a breach of trust when there never was trust — or the potential for it — to begin with. The issue in this case is bad choice of partner, not bad faith. Still, it can *feel* like betrayal, so it's important to examine the causes of poor choices — and how to avoid them.

Judith Wallerstein found the question of choices particularly striking in the daughters of divorce she observed over 10 years as part of her landmark study. She believes that many of these women select wrong because they're afraid to select right. "They're so scared of abandonment or betrayal that they pick men they're sure of not losing or don't care about losing," she says. Even those who initially adjust well to parental divorce often experience a delayed reaction. "These women are afraid to risk, and you can't trust or love without risking."

To break out of their pattern, Wallerstein says, women who can't trust need to realize their anxiety has less to do with the present than with the past. "Sometimes therapy is necessary, but often these women can work through their fears themselves. Talking with others who have the same problem can be helpful, as can a good love affair where one feels heard and understood and respected."

sons of divorce fare no bet-

ter. According to Wallerstein, many of them bury the feelings that flow from their parents' divorce and become constricted emotionally. As a result, they tend to lead lonely, insular lives, dating seldom if at all, and are extremely vulnerable to rejection from women.

But children of divorce aren't the only ones who select poorly or are unusually vulnerable to hurt. Many women in particular don't see themselves as choosers and consequently are so happy to be chosen they jump too quickly, notes Rosalind Barnett, a psychologist in Weston, Massachusetts. If the relationship ends, they feel betrayed, as if they had lost their best friend. But in reality, they'd never tested the friendship to begin with.

Wendy and Steve Herstein have four children, run a business and have been married for more than 25 years. Yet until recently, each often had one foot out the door, literally or figuratively.

"Whenever we had a fight, I'd storm out of the house and Wendy would yell, 'Don't come back, I want a divorce,'" says Steve. "That made me so angry I'd shout, 'If that's what you want, that's what you'll get.'"

Since it wasn't what either of them *really* wanted, they'd eventually decide they couldn't get divorced because their lives were too intertwined — the kids, the business, etc. "But the real reason," says Wendy, "was that there was a personal commitment."

That commitment eventually led them into therapy,

where Wendy discovered that her calls for divorce were caused by fear of abandonment. "Since my parents divorced when I was four, the thought of Steve leaving me was something I couldn't handle," she says. "His storming out felt like desertion, so I'd end it. Now I've stopped threatening him with divorce just because he walks out the door; I see a fight as a disagreement that's going to end, instead of a marriage that's going to end."

the cornerstone of commitment

is exactly this attitude: the feeling on the part of both partners that the marriage will last — not because of the kids or the finances but because the relationship itself is valued and cherished. Steve and Wendy were able to harness the power of their commitment to find a solution for other problems within the marriage. And in any relationship, trust is inspired when both partners communicate that the relationship is a priority, something they want to invest in for their own benefit and their partner's.

Scott M. Stanley and Howard Markman, psychologists and co-directors of the Center for Marital and Family Studies at the University of Denver, call this kind of commitment *personal dedication* and believe that it's the key determinant of relationship stability. The other determinant they identify, *constraint commitment,* includes all the forces, internal and external — religious and moral beliefs, social pressures, children, joint possessions — that motivate a person to stay in a relationship even if not dedicated to it. Interestingly, constraints are not perceived as negative by couples so long as their dedication remains high. "In fact, happy couples barely notice them and, when they do, tend to think of them positively, as signs that they're truly connected," says Stanley.

How a couple demonstrates their dedication is, of course, a personal matter, and often nonverbal: It can be a willingness to do things for each other, spending time together, making personal sacrifices on the other's behalf, being consistent. Self-disclosure is a part of it too, because sharing what's inside — even if what's inside isn't pretty — is the supreme act of faith in another.

Love flourishes in a mutual universe of shared secrets, deep understanding, complete acceptance.

◆━━━◆

building trust

also requires sharing the feelings of everyday life. Many couples find this uncomfortable, especially when the feelings are negative — whether or not they have anything to do with the relationship. But for intimacy to develop, partners must be able to express their emotions and have them heard.

If, for example, your spouse tells you she got criticized at the office and is feeling really down, "a trust-enhancing response would be, 'Sounds like you're upset. Why don't we talk about it?' " says Markman. "A trust-busting response: 'I had a tough day, too.' " The first approach validates her feelings; the second discounts them. To continue in the validation mode, he adds, "stay with discussing the problem, don't try to solve it. More than a solution, most people just want an ear."

Of course, it's one thing to listen to your partner complain about her boss, another to sit there calmly while she criticizes you. But that's exactly what pastoral psychotherapist Harville Hendrix prescribes in his book *Getting the Love You Want: A Guide for Couples.*

Hendrix, who is an ordained minister, has developed a rage-containment exercise to help couples express their anger constructively. In it, the angry or "expressive" partner briefly communicates his or her frustration, but without attacking or blaming the other. Then the "receiving" partner paraphrases the frustration, affirming the expressive partner's right to be angry but not necessarily agreeing with the reason. After this, the angry person can convert the frustration into a behavior-change request.

Scott Stanley suggests a different way of dealing with anger. By identifying the immediate underlying hurt and expressing *it* instead of rage, you can use anger to increase trust and intimacy.

For example: A woman is angry because she feels her husband doesn't spend enough time with her. She can either attack ("You don't care about anyone but yourself") or express the frustration and disappointment underneath ("I know your job is important, but spending so little time with you makes me sad").

"Most people attack because it's safer," says Stanley. "Sharing your real feelings is riskier: On the one hand, it's your only hope of getting the caring acknowledgement you want; on the other, you leave yourself open to rejection." But even that will at least tell you where you stand with your partner.

a final, vital step

toward overcoming the doubts that block intimacy is to examine the validity of your own expectations about a relationship. When expectations are unconscious, uncommunicated, unrealistic — unreasonable — we can feel we've been betrayed when we haven't been. And that perpetuates our feelings of distrust.

"Betrayal implies that someone has made a promise and broken it," says psychologist Norman Epstein of the University of Maryland in College Park. "But often we feel betrayed when no deal was ever made. We may have wanted or *expected* something from another person, but he or she never agreed to give it." For instance, a woman may marry expecting her husband to do 50% of the housework, even though she never discussed this with him.

When he fails to "follow through," her trust plummets.

In another scenario, a man accuses his wife of disloyalty when she fails to take his side in an argument with a friend. "Not only was *she* unaware of his concept of loyalty prior to this event," says Epstein, "I doubt he'd ever given the matter a thought."

Then there are the Unreasonables: Believing that if your spouse truly loves you, she should be able to read your mind; that partners in "good" relationships rarely disagree; that "being in love" feels a certain way and shouldn't change over time.

When feelings of betrayal, even subtle ones, seep in, look at your own expectations as well as your partner's shortcomings. One way, Stanley suggests, is to write down *everything* you expect from your current relationship. Include both intangibles (independence, emotional support) and tangibles (kids, a house in the country, frequent vacations). With these expectations in mind, try keeping a journal of every time your partner — or anyone else for that matter — disappoints you. Instead of stewing about those disappointments, *face* them. Ask yourself why you felt betrayed: "What did I expect that I didn't get?" And "Is it OK to expect it?"

You may find that some of your expectations don't stand up to such scrutiny, that you can let go of them. The ones that still seem reasonable to you are worth fighting for in the name of intimacy.

When Judith Wallerstein told Margaret Mead how upset she was over her early findings on children of divorce, Mead reportedly said, "There is no society in the world where people have stayed married without enormous community pressure to do so." Now that the pressure's off, you can take it as an omen — or a challenge. John Patterson, whose parents and sister are divorced, has made his choice about his marriage to Kass: "When most people say 'I do,' they regard it as 'I did.' They take it for granted that love will be easy. I intend to work at it."

Major Mergers

Whenever partnerships, romantic or otherwise, are in the offing,
decide what's __mine__ and what's __ours__ beforehand

Grace W. Weinstein

Joint accounts demonstrate commitment and strengthen a relationship.

Joint accounts preclude privacy and undermine independence.

OPPOSITE POINTS OF VIEW? YES. YET both statements are true. Because joint ownership has both advantages and disadvantages, deciding how to own and manage money and property demands careful consideration. Some assets probably should be owned jointly while others should not. If you're trying to decide how to handle income and assets in a new or ongoing relationship, here's what you need to know.

Legally speaking, all joint ownership is not alike. The form called "tenants in common" suits singles buying property together (see box), but is generally not appropriate for marriage partners because either can sell her or his share at any time and because the survivor does not automatically inherit the property. If you're married, "joint tenancy" or "tenancy by the entirety," depending on where you live and what kind of property you're talking about, protects you during life and also provides this vital "right of survivorship" after death.

Practically speaking, you'll want to own some assets jointly and some individually. You'll also want to differentiate between property you have before and that you acquire after marrying.

State laws differ but usually recognize that you continue to own whatever assets you bring into marriage. You can sell the property or borrow against it, as you please—so long as you keep it in your name alone. Put your husband's name on the title, however, and you're giving up a measure of control. No matter how fervent your love, think twice before you do so. We all know that true love, these days, doesn't necessarily last forever.

Assets you acquire together during marriage are a different story. In the nine "community property " states (Arizona, California, Idaho, Louisiana, Nevada, New Mexico, Texas, Washington, and Wisconsin), such property is automatically considered joint property, owned by both of you in equal measure. In the other 41 states, you have to make a decision (although property acquired while you live in a community-property state remains community property even if you later move to another state, notes Elizabeth S. Lewin, author of *Financial Fitness for Newlyweds*).

Try this course of action. Even if you want to mingle most current income, keep property that you brought to the marriage in your own name. Keep property that you inherit or that is a gift to you personally (from your parents, for example) in your own name. Then, should worst come to worst, you won't be in the position of a friend of mine. She had to scrape together the money to buy the half of her home that "belonged" to her ex-husband—even though the funds to purchase that home had come solely from her parents. Had "Joan" segregated that money so that she could prove its source in court, she would have had a stronger claim on the jointly owned home.

You *should* own the family home jointly,

partly because a home is such a powerful symbol of commitment and partly because neither of you would want the other to be able to sell the old homestead out from under. But owning other property jointly reduces each partner's control over the property in a way that makes effective money management difficult.

With stocks and bonds, for example, it will take both signatures to sell. If one of you is out of town, ill, or just plain stubborn, it can make it impossible for the other to take appropriate action. Instead, why not take turns investing, putting equivalent assets in each name? Many couples find this approach has an added benefit of reducing friction over how much risk to assume and what kind of investment to choose.

With joint bank accounts, by contrast, either partner is free to withdraw all the funds at any time. But each partner also knows exactly what the other is spending. And, with one checkbook and two check-writers, each can scramble accounts by forgetting to make checkbook entries. I recommend three checking accounts per couple (marrieds or live-togethers)—a joint household account for convenience, plus individual accounts to give each partner financial independence.

One of the reasons for keeping separate accounts is, of course, "just in case . . . " Who owns which property isn't supposed to matter under the equitable distribution divorce laws of most states, but it does in fact make a difference to the judges who make the decisions.

If you've been through a divorce, you know this all too well. If you're entering a second marriage, you'll probably be extra careful about keeping some assets separate. Here's an additional tip from financial planner Rianne Leaf, a district manager with IDS Financial Services in Minneapolis: if you sell your house to move in with your new husband, and use the money from the sale to buy an insurance policy on his life, make sure that you are not only the beneficiary of the policy but also its owner. That way, because a life insurance policy can be borrowed against or cashed in, you keep control of your own money.

First marriage, second, or third, it's important to reach an understanding about how you will own property and how you will manage your money. You may want to consider a legally drawn prenuptial agreement, particularly if one or both of you has been married before and has children. Such agreements, once considered a threat to the institution of marriage, are now accepted by courts almost everywhere.

Perhaps you don't own enough to make a formal prenuptial agreement necessary. Even then, suggests Marjorie A. O'Connell, a Washington, D.C., attorney, you should make yourself put "what ifs" on paper. What if either of you decides to go to graduate school? To stop work? What if one of you inherits a sizable sum? Receives down payment money for a house from parents?

Contract or not, discuss (preferably in advance) whose paycheck will be used for what and whose name goes on which property. Sort out your expectations about what will happen in various money situations and you'll be less susceptible to conflict later on.

Terms of Cohabitancy

WHETHER FOR REASONS OF LOVE OR economy, more and more singles are buying houses together. If you're thinking of doing so, protect yourself by drawing up a written agreement designed to resolve any potential problem before it occurs. Martin Shenkman, a New York City real estate attorney who is the author of *The Total Real Estate Tax Planner*, suggests that your agreement include the following:
• Who owns what percentage of the house and how much each will contribute toward the down payment and monthly upkeep.
• What happens if one of you runs into financial reverses and can't meet monthly obligations; Shenkman builds a loan provision into the agreements he writes to cover this contingency.
• Who else can live in the house.
• Under what circumstances either of you can make financial commitments for the other; you don't want to come home from a trip and find that your house-mate has committed $10,000 to replacement windows, but you do want him or her to be able to make emergency repairs.
• What happens if one of you moves away, becomes disabled, or dies. If death severs the partnership (and young people, unfortunately, sometimes die), your agreement should provide the terms on which the estate will sell the half-interest to the other partner within a specified period of time. You might also want to take out an inexpensive term life insurance policy on each other, enough to buy out the other's interest. **—G.W.W.**

SEXUAL PURSUIT

LOVESTRUCK

Reigniting an Old Romance

Gilbert Deering Moore

WHO WOULD HAVE THOUGHT THAT LOVE COULD ENDURE, even after all this time? Even after the fighting and the fury, the betrayals on both sides, the bitterness over the babies, the rancor running wild over the money and property? Even after the depth of the rift and the terrible ugliness when everybody's dirty laundry was out in the open?

Who would have thought that you could bury love six feet under, then dig it up 10 years later, and it would still have the breath of life? Who would have dreamed that the feeling could stay so strong, so sweet like it is, so tender, even after all this time?

The woman was through with me—too through. Through with my womanizing, dope-smoking, my reckless way of living. And I was through with her—her basic bitchiness and her head-strong ways. But it turns out we're not through at all. We're just beginning.

Ten years ago we were all washed up. One harsh day in November I came home from work to find the woman packing, preparing to leave me. The children were already shipped off to stay with Grandma. The time for our third and final breakup was ripe.

People split up long before one of the parties moves out. They still "live together"—they're still under the same roof. But they sleep in separate beds, eat at separate tables. They come and they go, but they don't speak.

The handwriting was on the wall for as long as a year before. I tried very hard to prevent the breakup, but there was an inevitability about it.

Part of the problem was that I was into heavy dope-smoking, and the effects of it used to frighten her. I thought marijuana was this marvelous painkiller and bountiful source of creativity.

This was illusion: the wonderful weed took my pain and multiplied it by four, shackled my muse, drove me to the brink of paranoid madness.

But the heart of the trouble was my womanizing. All the time we were together, I was steady playing the cheating game, steady chasing after luscious females. I used to meet them on the street, on planes and trains, in bars and workplaces. And having met them, I was forever making secret arrangements to see them in the underground. None of my exploits remained much of a secret, however, because I tended to leave incriminating evidence lying about. I was careless and, perhaps, callous.

SEX TIPS

BE SMART!
Do it with someone you like.
—Molly Ivins

SEX TIPS

ARTS & CRAFTS
Using a Magic Marker, paint tiny happy faces on your partner's condom. Watch them wink and expand as he does.
—Comedian Susan Vass

Things came to a head that fall as she changed jobs. The new environment gave her fresh perspective on her life and new confidence in herself. It also put her in the company of adoring men and made her less and less tolerant of my shaky ways. Suddenly the tables were turned. Whereas she had always been the one who was jealous and insecure, worried about some "outside agitator," now it was my turn to stew.

The day of disaster finally came. The woman was leaving me. She didn't want any further discussion about it. I pleaded with her to stay and work things out. She was adamant. The woman walked out the door and she didn't look back.

So now I had to deal with the pain: the pain of jealousy and rejection and self-reproach; the pain of vain regret and irretriev-

From *Ms.*, May 1989, pp. 45-52, 54-56. Copyright © 1989, Ms. Magazine. Reprinted by permission.

able loss. Furthermore, I had to deal with it by myself, for there were no lovely ladies left to hold my hand, and no men I cared to face, given my pathetic condition.

When a woman is in pain, she can call up her sister, her girlfriend, her mother. She can tell the whole sad story, chapter and verse—how the bastard brutalized her, left her high and dry. When a woman suffers a broken heart, she can cry with dignity.

A man with a broken heart is in big trouble. There's no place to go with his humiliation and his tears. His he-man friends will laugh at him. A man has no business crying in the first place—certainly not because some witch left him. This is what my daddy might have said, had I been silly enough to unburden myself at his feet.

So I find myself alone, with a big knife sticking out of my heart. I go into a little room and close the door. I smoke my dope; I guzzle my Sneaky Pete wine. I rush to kill the pain. But the pain is powerful and nothing I do can kill it. 'Cause the knife is in me and the blade is thick. The wound is deep and the bleeding is bad. I'm stuck. I can't pull it out and I can't leave it there. So I lie and I bleed and I die . . .

I call her treacherous, I call her whore. Snatch up her pretty clothes and burn 'em. Grab her picture off the wall and burn that too. I shatter her fine crystal and her lovely looking glass. I wish deep-seated evil on the witch. I pray that she should rot in hell . . .

I get down on the floor and I wallow and I crawl and I cry like a baby. The woman is gone. And the babies are gone with her. And there is not one effing thing I can do about it . . .

The days pass. The nights come and I dream long ugly dreams. She is naked, stretched out in the bed—queen-size. Got them long legs way up in the air. And on top of her is this dude I know. The two of them are into it. The two of them are gruntin' and groanin' and sweatin' like racehorses . . .

I am made to sit there and watch. My eyes are fixed in their sockets. My skin crawls. And the two of them? They laugh, they feast, they love, and they mock me . . .

I always wanted to catch her—catch her with the stuff on her nose like she used to catch me. And the time came when I commenced to follow her 'round. And I opened her mail. And I listened in on her phone calls. And I sniffed her dirty drawers, looking for clues, hoping to trap her, but it never worked. The only time I caught her was in a dream, a long dream I had over and over. Except the times were such that my faculties were all askew. Who could tell where the border was between the world of dreams and the realm of the real?

I went underground, withdrawing from polite society to live like a monk. I left the opulent corporate world I used to work in, went where the work was hard and the pay was peanuts. Isolated, I relived my whole life in my head. Sensitized now to pain, I began to realize the terrible suffering I caused my wife and the other women I got involved with.

SEX TIPS

PICK & PLAY!

1. Safe: Buy sex toys.
   Invite your lover.
   Use them together.
   Talk about the experience.
2. Safer: Buy sex toys.
   Invite your lover.
   Use them individually.
   Talk about the experience.
3. Safest: Buy sex toys.
   Don't invite your lover.
   Use them on yourself.
   Talk about it on the phone
   to your therapist.
   —Comedian Janice Perry,
   a.k.a. Gal

> *I thought every relationship would necessarily get old. It ain't necessarily so. I look at the woman sometimes and desire sweeps through me like fire through a forest.*

It was the end of an era, the death of one way of living and the birth of another. When I was younger, I played it fast and loose. I was the playboy. He struts about, flaunts his manliness, "conquers" woman after woman. He is *much* man. Yet inside beats the heart of a self-centered child whose only purpose is to gratify himself. When it comes to the gratification of his primary needs, he is ruthless and cruel and unfeeling.

He wears the mask of the great lover, but behind his disguise is a greedy little boy whose capacity for love is seriously impaired. Eager to take love, he has precious little to give. He rushes headlong to be intimate, yet real intimacy is the last thing he wants.

He wants to be known as a great lover, but by this he means not someone who feels deeply but someone who fucks well. His preoccupation is not love in the heart but technique in the head. Still, he understands the importance of love to women, and in his exploitation schemes he is always willing to feign a love he does not feel. The name "playboy" is well chosen, for the primary instinct of this Don Juan is to play. His principal plaything is the woman—her and that priceless toy between her legs.

Once upon a time I felt compelled to play the role of a Don Juan. One woman could not satisfy me, no matter how lovely her looks, how subtle her wit. No matter how fantastic she was in bed. One woman cannot satisfy the Don, nor two or three or four. He requires a *chain* of women passing through his life in endless procession. Possessed of a strange inner force (some call it demonic), the Don Juans of this world wage a lifelong war against women, endlessly moving to conquer them and bend them to their iron wills.

Don Juans come in all sizes, shapes, colors, and creeds. They hail from the four corners of the earth, though each continent produces a breed peculiar to its climate. We in the United States have, of course, our species of machismo, and produce a many-splendored breed composed of white boys as well as black, Latin boys (to whom we must give special credit for the Don Juan legend), and Jewish ones too. Among the Don Juans are rich boys who own boats and planes and emeralds, and poor boys who scarcely have pots to pee in. What they all have in common, what makes them brothers under the skin, is their burning ambition to become great playboys of the Western world.

My daddy was a "ladies' man." So was my big brother Charlie. So were a string of first cousins I once lived with. So was a certain rake of a roommate I had in college. Most of these "role models" of mine had wives and children to support. But off to the side, they had their extra ladies: women they slept with, made babies with, and frequently established semisecret homes with.

I remember, when I was a timid teenager in Jamaica, watching my big brother in action fencing with the ladies. I myself was so terribly frightened of the female—these lovely, remote creatures who held awesome powers of rejection over the male of the species. They could break your heart so easily. One wrong turn of the head, one baleful bat of an eyelash and they could crush you with their tender might. My brother Charlie, on the other hand, was completely unfazed by women. He always knew what to say to them and when to say it.

I used to stand there on this big veranda we had overlooking a great, busy street, and my brother used to stand there watching the women go by. When he saw the right cutie-pies, he would call out to them. Lo and behold, they would stop and Charlie would go downstairs and run his game on them, feeding them a line of his lyrical bullshit. In short order Charlie would score again.

Then I studied under Jake, this big stud I used to live with when I was going to college. Many people wondered what we could possibly have in common. I was a serious straitlaced egghead, and Jake was an ex-con, a dude of the streets. Jake used to enjoy whipping me at chess—"the intellectuals' game"—and he enjoyed teaching me how to be the great cocksman he was.

Starting with the landlady's daughter, there was a long string of women he used to cavort with, and every evening when I came home from class I would find him in the sack with someone different. Jake passed on to me the secret of his success with women. Be tough, he used to say. Let them pour their hearts out. Let them do the falling in love. You maintain your cool. When they cry, when they become hysterical, just turn your back and walk away. Never blow your cool.

Once upon a time I embraced the philosophy of hedonism that sensual pleasure is the principal good in life. And so, like the bobcat stalks the reindeer, I made it my business to track the luscious female wherever I could find her. The fact that I was in love with one particular woman, married to her and making babies, in no way restrained me.

On the surface, I'd been having a grand time sleeping in all those beautiful beds, but when you peeped behind the mask you saw a face contorted in pain. Except that, being a man conditioned to keep out of touch with feeling, I'd been a stranger to my pain and to my innermost self.

Belatedly I was learning that the endless pursuit of pleasure does not in the end bring pleasure. A man pursues the pleasures of love; he escapes the pain of love, but only for a little while. So there was more to a man than met the eye. Quite apart from his brain and his broad shoulders and his big bamboo, a man had a heart every bit as fragile as the female's—quite often, more so. A man could be stern like steel one minute and the next soft as apple jelly.

After two years of agonizing reappraisal, I made up my mind to start fresh somewhere else. I went to Chicago to visit an old

SEX TIPS

LET'S PRETEND!
You be Snow White and have your partner pretend to be each of the seven dwarfs in succession (many men have Grumpy and Sleepy down anyway).
—Comedian Janice Perry, a.k.a. Gal

friend and abruptly decided to cut the Apple loose. I lived in the Windy City with another woman for four years. The relationship was, in a word, beautiful. And yet there was some elusive something missing from it. All I knew was that I did not feel that all-consuming passion I thought would be necessary if I were ever to chance marriage again. I tried, while we were together, to be different, to be faithful in a way I never was

before. Still, after four years, we parted, continuing to be friends, if not lovers.

Meanwhile, my wife in New York was no longer my wife. She had met and married someone else. But, after four years, the marriage crumbled; she frankly admitted that the whole thing was a mistake. We were regularly in touch—writing letters, making long-distance telephone calls and the occasional visit to "pick up the kids, drop them off." Terribly civilized about the whole thing, all the rancor from the past apparently gone. We were pals now, you might say, the kind of pals who laugh and talk and reminisce about a shared past. As recently as September last, this is the way we were.

Now comes fall 1988 and our daughter Vanessa—suddenly terribly grown up—is packed and ready to go off to college. I fly in from Chicago and the four of us (Mommy and Daddy, son Justin, plus Vanessa) drive up to Connecticut where Vanessa will begin school. It's like old times having the family together and happy again, if only for this special occasion.

Conversation is congenial but still careful between the former lovers. We talk about the children—how phenomenal it is that they aren't babies anymore. We talk about the intervening relationships we've had. We swap stories and ply each other with details: what it was like living with somebody else. Nobody thinks the unthinkable. Nobody broaches the subject of how we feel about each other now. Nobody says one word about getting back together again. Who would have the nerve to propose so preposterous a thing!?

Mind you, the thought popped into my mind more than a few times on this visit, but I was not prepared to speak it. There were several moments of private crisis when I looked at the woman and secretly turned to mush—another subject I did not care to broach.

Vanessa now safely ensconced in school, I drive Mommy and Justin back to New York, get on a plane, and fly back to Chicago. And, ostensibly, the Moore family is gone back to being the way it was—split down the middle. Except that now, instead of talking once every three months or so, the woman and I are talking every day, sometimes two, three times a day. And instead of careful, abstract conversation, the talk grows ever more tender, ever more pointed. And, before you know it, the woman dares to speak of love, and the man dares to confirm it.

We begin to make plans. We must get back together again, remarry. The coming Christmas seems the perfect time. Then Christmas appears too far away. How about Thanksgiving? I quit my job in Chicago, rent a truck, pack it with all my earthly possessions, and I race cross-country, back to the Apple.

These are contradictory times we live in. On the one hand, we see love touted everywhere—plastered on billboards and made banal on TV screens. Many scoff at it, say cynical things about it, say there is no such thing. On the other hand, many are afraid to feel it, and some are leery of others feeling it for them.

Who wants to be strung out and vulnerable, have happiness depend on what someone else says and does or fails to say and do? Many of us have the memory of a double cross branded on our souls. Many of us, badly burned, are none too eager to go back for more. And so we have those who are perpetually making love, perpetually performing the act of love, yet always backing away from love.

But it turns out that love is real—every bit as exhilarating as poets promise. The woman and I have a love at once old, tested in the fire, and at the same time new, brand-new, resurrected from the dead. We are like you new lovers who can't see enough of each other and hang on each other's every word. Who hold hands and play footsie under tabletops, sit in restaurants after the food is finished, gazing into each other's eyes. Every touch tingles, every kiss lifts you off the ground. The sun goes down and you race to the sack and do it all night long, and in the daytime too. The closeness is too sweet to be believed, the excitement too heady to reckon about.

But our love is old and seasoned, too, with that certain ease not to be scoffed at. After all, we've known each other 20 years, so there are a host of pretenses we don't have to make, parlor games we don't have to play. The newly met carry the burden of being perpetually charming. We skip all that.

4. INTERPERSONAL RELATIONSHIPS: Responsible Quality Relationships

In our culture we prize new things—the latest model car, the most recently developed computer—and disparage everything old. Our technology breeds in us a perpetual discontent. We can never enjoy the latest gadget for we are too busy anticipating that it will shortly be made obsolete. We reach for a new relationship with the same limited expectations that we have when picking up a new ballpoint pen.

When I was younger, I thought every relationship would necessarily become old and tired. It ain't necessarily so. The passion is still there, even after all this time. I look at the woman sometimes and quiver like a schoolboy. Desire sweeps through me like fire through a forest. And, then, there are moments when passion subsides and a certain tenderness comes to the fore. I walk down the street holding the woman's hand and it thrills me. I feel complete, lacking for nothing.

This is a far cry from the old days when I was always terribly uptight while walking the street holding a woman's hand. Sometimes it was because the woman was white and I was perpetually on guard lest some angry, jealous white man leap to the attack. But no matter what color she was, I didn't want to hold her hand. I wanted to be perpetually available to the chance female who might pass us by.

In modern parlance, the word "lover" has been stripped to its barest essentials to mean hardly more than an occasional lay. It's so easy to be cynical about love and dismiss it as a ruse to rake in the gullible. Sooner or later we wake up with a bleeding heart over some unworthy somebody, and that somebody takes our bleeding heart and tosses it in the air like a Frisbee.

But if you're lucky, as I am, your love is a fortress. It protects you from the hellishness of the street and the marketplace where tenderness is for fools, brutality passes for strength, where dogs devour dogs with relish.

I do believe that nobody gets away with anything, except for a little while: not even the slickest of the slick playboys, not even the coolest of the cool dudes. As I grow older, I learn to place higher and higher premiums on friendship—the older the friendship, the higher the premium.

If you're lucky, as I am, your lover is your closest friend, maybe even your oldest. She's seen me at my lowest ebb and my times of triumph. Between us there is an invisible contract establishing the terms of our mutual affection and respect. Unlike the business contract—which takes no chances, spells out every detail, and covers all contingencies in a spirit of mutual mistrust—the love contract is eternally nonspecific. The love deal leaves everything to chance, and is willing to take incredible risks.

There is a richness in old love that no new hot flash can match. The past we share—all of it, the pain and suffering as well as the joy—is a vast treasure trove the two of us draw on. She has her scrapbook of ugly memories as I have mine. Each of us is subject to doubts and suspicions, to flashes of mistrust. But a powerful current surges through us—an overwhelming need to touch and be touched, a powerful need to love and see that love returned. A need to transcend the awful solitude of this tomb called the body. A need to reveal ourselves, to unveil the deep secrets at last. ♦

ZIPLASH
A Sexual Libertine Recants

Erica Jong

IN THE EIGHTEENTH CENTURY, CLEVER AND LITERATE WAGS used to amuse themselves by writing mock epitaphs. Since I'm a dropout from a Ph.D. program in eighteenth-century English Lit. at Columbia, it has often occurred to me to pen my own tombstone as a paraphrase of Keats. His reads, "*Here lies one whose name was writ in water.*" Mine would say, "*Here lies one who first said Zipless Fuck.*"

The phrase haunts me still. It clings to my name in various dictionaries of quotations (where, after publishing 14 books, this is my only contribution to the culture). And it may be all that the general reader remembers about "that sexy dame," to paraphrase a popular magazine, "who flew to fame." If, as Andy Warhol maintained, we will all get to be famous for 15 minutes, it's for damn sure we don't get to choose the reason for our notoriety. "Why can't you just be rich and anonymous?" my 10-year-old daughter Molly often asks me. Why indeed. Sometimes I dream of selling my name to a Japanese conglomerate and disappearing into a nom de plume.

In the early seventies, when I was writing *Fear of Flying*, puritanical censorship still held sway in sexual mores. It seemed quite radical to see a delicious-looking stranger on a train, have lustful fantasies about him, and consummate the fantasies there and then. This act of "ziplessness" was always much better in the imagination than in the flesh. In the imagination, the fantasy lover looked like Gerard Philipe and talked like Richard Burton. In reality, he was more likely to look like Martin Short and to speak like Pee Wee Herman. The zipless fuck—even in *Fear of Flying*—was always better as a dream. Even Isadora Wing, at the end of the book, rejects the reality in order to keep the fantasy green. But apparently, some people didn't read that far. Books often get famous for the wrong reasons, and often they are most talked about by those who have read them least.

I never *advocated* the zipless fuck. I merely *chronicled* it. And now, 16 years later, I am asked to defend it. I refuse. Our society has had a decade and a half of experimentation with random sexual freedom. We have discovered that it is neither so very sexy nor so very free. My generation is disillusioned with sex as a social panacea. We look longingly at the marriages of our parents and grandparents and wonder how on earth they managed to stay best friends for so long—or even worst friends for so long! But at least they had someone to read the newspaper with. Alone in our single-parent families, still searching for the one great love, we begin to smell a rat. We begin to realize that life consists of little moments of compromise, of joy, of embracing the primal flux. Sex is too volatile and overwhelming a force to use indiscriminately. When we use it indiscriminately, it is dulled and tarnished. When we use it indiscriminately, it takes its revenge by using us indiscriminately. There is finally no substitute for love, for spiritual sharing, for commitment, for cherishing each other. Perhaps fantasy is meant to remain fantasy. Isadora Wing's zipless fuck was always better as fantasy than when she tried to act it out. A careful rereading of the novel shows that free love was never so very free at all. ♦

NICE GIRLS DO

Or Want To

Katie Monagle

THE "NEW MORALITY" IS GIVING ME A BAD CASE OF DÉJÀ VU, even though I'm only 23. This time the danger of AIDS is the rationale for sticking to "old-fashioned" values that create a sexual double standard and legitimate only heterosexual relationships with people of one's same race and class. However, I got these same messages during my childhood and teen years—only then there wasn't a convenient disease to mask the sexual politics. Then, the reasons for holding people, especially women, in check were based on ideas of class and respectability, religion, racism, and homophobia.

When I began my official journey into sexuality with my first real kiss at 14, I had few inhibitions other than keeping my hymen intact until I was at least in love, if not married. I was attending an all-girl, nun-run Catholic high school. When I got to see boys, what registered was the tingly possibility of a fooling-around kind of fun, and the more pragmatic goal of being socially acceptable: there was obviously something wrong about a girl without a beau.

Kissing and making out were the most fun I'd ever had. I lost my library card, forsook *The Love Boat* and *Fantasy Island*, and concentrated on the telephone and my social life. I knew my precoital sexual activity needed to be kept from my parents. They had always told me, and I knew they were sincere, that sex inside marriage is beautiful. Until I was 14, I believed them.

Later, I reinterpreted their message to fit my life: sex inside *love* is beautiful. I figured that until love knocked at my heart, anything but the actual deed could be done. To me, as to many teenagers, my parents weren't the most reliable judges of right and wrong—my peers were, and I still remember when I got the message from them that I was doing something wrong.

SEX TIPS

DON'T FORGET! Sex is a really precious form of communication that is magical, and that we don't get in other kinds of connections with people. Perhaps this is why, even in the Age of AIDS, we are driven to communicate sexually. A particular spiritual place in ourselves is touched, a self that we don't wear out on the street, that we don't necessarily talk about, that in fact doesn't have words.
—JoAnn Loulan, author and marriage and family counselor

The day after a newly acquired "best" friend and I had double-dated, she teased me—amid a group of her old and my new friends—about how she and her date had laughed at the way my date and I shook the car with our enthusiastic "making out." Those few minutes of my life in the sunny courtyard of an old New Orleans convent and girls' school linger sharply in my memory nine years later. Instead of titters and mutual girlish confidences, my new friends looked uncomfortable, and eyed me appraisingly. I felt gross, as though—despite my "virginity"—I belonged to the ranks of the sleazy, easy girls.

Now these narrow-minded values I've spent almost half my life trying to escape are the cornerstone of "the biggest social movement since the sixties" (this information is courtesy of *Good Housekeeping*'s New Traditionalist ad campaign). Young people are more conservative now than a generation ago, we're told. Casual sex is out. Heterosexuality and monogamy are in, lauded as the only ways to have Safe Sex and Beautiful Relationships.

I feel threatened by the New Morality. It's not just sex that's under attack—it's my ability to be me, whoever I am, without being subjected to painful censure in my personal or professional life. I'm seeing not just more conventional relationships among my peers, but also a license to censure other people's decisions about how to run their sex and their lives. Although my friends in the urban Northeast are politically liberal, socially permissive, and not particularly monogamy-minded, I'm afraid I won't be very comfortable outside our circle.

Whether due to the old morality or the new, the pressure is on to be monogamous—single or married. Jane,* a 23-year-old New York woman pursuing a promising career in finance, believes, "People would think I was crazy if I just slept with someone—even if they weren't thinking in terms of AIDS." Liz, 24, an old friend who lives with her boyfriend in Queens, New York, senses condescension and pity for women who are not married or almost-married—especially from women who sowed their oats during freer days and now have naturally evolved into monogamy. "The glamour of being single is gone," Liz says.

And it's not only our sex lives that Liz sees endangered by the New Morality. "I think AIDS will just make people more prejudiced than they already are—make them think it was wrong and foolish to have been liberal in any way. There are all these people out there who aren't prejudiced against blacks or homosexuals in the stereotypical sense—don't use nasty labels—but who feel that AIDS is a 'minority problem.' People are being prejudiced in a covert way."

Mark, who is 25, a Wall Street attorney, and gay, says that in the gay community the emphasis is not on how much sex one has, but on taking precautions and communicating honestly about one's sexual and drug use history. Still, "People think I should cut down on the number of my sex partners rather than making sure I'm totally safe. Deep down, everyone wants to find one person to fall in love with, but in the meantime they would have casual sex. Now 'in the meantime' is gone."

But the double standard that always went along with monogamy—setting limits on women and gays but leaving promiscuous heterosexual men uncensored—is still with us. Brian, a 24-year-old San Franciscan still prowling on the singles scene, has been the lover of almost 40 women in his short lifetime. Yet he sheepishly

* *Names have been changed.*

admits to living by the double standard: "If I have sex with someone, afterward I shouldn't have to feel like, 'Wow, I don't like this person anymore' because she's had sex with me. But sometimes I do feel that, if it's a one-night stand."

Of women who carry condoms in their purses, Brian says, "I think maybe these girls sleep around a lot and that's why they're carrying these condoms." He explains that "all guys are sluts," but "when I say 'male slut' I kind of think positively. A male slut is a guy who is good with the girls, a guy who can pick up women." About female "sluts," though, Brian thinks "negatively. That's terrible, but it's true."

Yet Brian—he who doesn't like women who carry condoms— will now, because of AIDS, "always wear a condom. I used to claim I couldn't get a hard-on if I wore a rubber," he confesses. "That was my big philosophy. When I was having sex, it was like, 'Grunt, I hope you have, grunt, grunt, something. No? Okay, we'll chance it.' Now I'll use a condom. It's important. I don't want to die for it."

I used to have problems asking men to wear condoms. They'd say no, or whine and prophesy that it just "wouldn't work." I'd get embarrassed by the fact that I could produce a condom when they couldn't—it made me look so eager. Finally I got tired of the conflict with the men and myself, and blew off even suggesting prophylactic protection for a while. Hell, we lily-white and middle class aren't really in danger anyway. Right?

For that, I suffered. I suffered a minor medical problem. I suffered a blow to my personal pride: never have my feminist politics been more pertinent to my real life, and I failed myself. And my partner.

Well, I don't have a problem anymore. I want sex, I want my life, and I want to live my life with a sense of pride in myself— which means doing what I know is responsible and right, even if it makes me uncomfortable sometimes. Besides, I didn't like the fact that a little bit of sexism intimidated me enough to suppress my principles and endanger people's lives.

However, I do think AIDS is being used as an excuse for moving back into the old 1950s-style morality. I am aware of AIDS and, despite the old adage "Never say never," I will never have sex without protection before my partner and I have carefully examined each other's doctor's certificates. But I'm also determined not to allow all this hysteria and conservative social coercion to box me into believing I can't have sex again till I've picked my white-bread mate for life. Monogamy, bigotry, and homophobia won't save me from the hazards of modern life.

There have been a lot of places in my life where I didn't feel free to be me—it wasn't cool, respectable, or attractive. I wasn't happy in those places because I couldn't be part of a community. Sometimes I'm not brave enough to be different in a seemingly united world. So I don't want caution to turn into rights-reducing fanaticism that makes all sorts of people into outsiders. We still have some degrees of freedom, medically and socially, about what we do in bed, with whom, and why. I want that freedom for myself, and I endorse it for others. And I still wanna have fun. ♦

FEARLESS FLYING

Singles on the Prowl

Maggie Rafferty

BEFORE AIDS, THERE WAS HERPES. BEFORE REAL FEAR THERE was doubt. Early in the 1980s we began to take a second look at our lifestyles. Casual sex had long been divorced from making love, but we didn't feel any loss until the cold sores began. This was something we could relate to— paying prices. The question was still open on how high prices would go before demand peaked. The curve turned down when AIDS hit the streets.

At least you'd think that would be the case, wouldn't you? Well, actually, there's been little real change in our sexual consumerism. The three-dates-before-sex rule has become all of five dates. We're still sleeping with people we haven't met yet. Instead of closing our eyes and crossing our fingers that he isn't married, we hope he isn't contagious.

The one-night stand is down but not out. It's hot and crowded at New York City's Cafe Iguana. The bar is packed. The place is a subway station and, according to the bartender, the decision is always being made whether to take the express or the local with the attractive patron in the next seat.

"Lena" and "Sylvia" haven't planned on taking anyone home tonight, but they haven't planned against it, either. Sylvia is 26 and recently started as a registered representative for a Wall Street brokerage house. She claims a standard of ethics and a healthy respect for greed. "I've seen others in my field grab for too much too soon and too blindly. If my life was a portfolio, it would be diverse, with a broad foundation in medium- to long-term growth stocks." She starts laughing at her own joke: "A quick buck is like a quick fuck—exciting, energetic, but leaves you craving pizza at 3 A.M."

Lena has been Sylvia's roommate since they graduated from New York University. A paralegal for a midsize law firm with her sights set on going solo, Lena says, "I'm not going to live my life scared or stupid. I'll take the studied risk. The guys here have money—the drinks aren't cheap and neither are the clothes," she continues. "I mean, they're our own kind. A slut I'm not, but I've slept with a guy on the first date and I probably will again. I trust my instincts; they're going to protect me a lot better than plastic."

With a flick of her polished fingers and a smirk on her polished mouth, Lena dismisses the chances of getting AIDS from heterosex as slim or none: "Too many people being paranoid with too little evidence."

Sylvia isn't into arrogance. "I've picked up two guys in the last year—to sleep with. Honestly, I don't have a lot of experience with instant intimacy. A few months ago, I met someone here. We had a few drinks, traded some mutual experiences, and started feeling warm and cozy with one another. I let the movie studio in my head take over. We rented a room at the Pierre, bathed and drank champagne, and went to bed. The right moment to discuss safety just didn't happen. I remember thinking that I should be concerned," she adds, "but I guess I was hoping he would bring it up. The danger and surprise of it were what attracted me, though, turned me on. Sometimes I get very bored with preparing, plotting, graphing, and organizing. I didn't catch anything, not even a cold."

After Sylvia leaves with a trader from a competing firm, Lena and I share a cab uptown. She tells me I'm much too paranoid about all the AIDS stuff. In New York City, she declares, we're

> *Now, instead of closing*
> *our eyes and crossing*
> *our fingers that he*
> *isn't married, we hope*
> *he isn't contagious.*
> *The one-night stand*
> *is down but not out.*

more likely to be mugged or hit by a car.

Counselors at the New York City Department of Health regularly hear disbelief from persons who discover they are HIV-positive although they aren't in any of the well-publicized "at-risk" groups. They didn't make the distinction between at-risk *people* and at-risk *behavior*.

We women are still shy. Not wanting to ask indelicate questions or stop an embrace to tear open little wrappers, we will, nonetheless, get naked. Judy Macks, former Director of Training for the AIDS Health Project in San Francisco, has said that many women—because of low self-image and poor communication skills—are reluctant to discuss sex with their partners.

Among women who use the personals ads and dating services, there seems to be an idea that a man's status protects against his being mean, boring, or contagious. The usual personal ads or singles services clients are between 25 and 40, have white-collar professional jobs, and look for others like themselves. The main question women have is if they'll be matched with someone from similar social and economic backgrounds.

Helena Amram, owner of the international meeting service Helena, finds that few clients make the medical standing of potential dates a major issue. Amram's service is one of a few whose screening procedures include requesting a doctor's letter stating that the client is free of communicable diseases; but such letters aren't foolproof, given the possible six-month lag between exposure to the virus and the time antibodies show up in testing. The Together dating service—more typical of the genre than Helena—doesn't require proof that a client is free of STDs. That doesn't seem to worry the clientele.

"Cathy," 34, highly recommends personals ads for meeting men. She's had a number of very fun, likable dates and two short but worthwhile relationships. Talented, well read, articulate, Cathy is working on a law degree after 10 years as a reading specialist.

This tall, striking blond usually seems to be in charge, but her comments about condoms belie that impression. "Sometimes I ask the guy to use protection, sometimes not," she says. "It depends on the situation, how comfortable I feel around him. Also, some won't wear them; they feel insulted. After you go out with someone a few times you can judge what they're about."

In fact, Cathy rarely uses condoms, although she's bought quite a few. "Every so often I feel paranoid, usually after reading some article." Explaining that she was "much wilder after college and really up to a year or so ago," she asserts, "if I had AIDS, I'd know by now. I'm careful, but not deeply worried. We'll probably find a cure in a few years. A condom isn't 100

percent secure either. Nothing is, except celibacy, and I'm not ready or willing for that."

A reluctance to broach the use of condoms was mentioned by a number of women. This is ironic since, says a friend highly placed in the condom industry, women are the targets of today's condom advertising because they are more susceptible to it than men. Women have historically taken responsibility for birth control.

Some women seem to feel that dating the boy-next-door or the boy-next-desk is sufficient protection against STDs. "Barbara," a midwesterner transplanted to urban New England, has a solid job with a solid insurance firm, and a house with a porch. A self-described liberal, she feeds a fair and open mind through an exceptionally broad reading list—prompting the thought that she'd have equally solid knowledge and reasoning about so timely a topic as AIDS.

Wrong, wrong, wrong. To Barbara, AIDS is a gay/junkie disease and she's freezing her own blood, just in case. She usually dates men she meets in the neighborhood. "I know something about them before they get to my door," Barbara reasons, "their ex-wives, good and bad habits, hobbies. It's like getting a résumé prior to the interview."

Barbara doesn't sleep with every date, and never on the first date. She doesn't buy condoms at all, but will use them if her partner suggests. "I still get embarrassed buying tampons," she says. "Anyway, I don't go out with drug users, and obviously not with gays, so unless he's hemophiliac, I'm safe." Though apparently not afraid of STDs, Barbara focuses on the contaminated blood supply: "I've arranged to put aside my own blood in case I ever need a transfusion. Doesn't hurt to prepare, I guess."

Women are thinking about the "now," not the "then," when they assume that you get to know something about a man because you work with him 40 plus hours a week. Where was he last year, last job?

Elaine works so many hours that she rarely meets people in other than work-related situations. She's relaxed, has a sharp sense of humor and looks that shout high tea and scones at London's Savoy. As a financial planner for a commercial real estate firm, working an 80-hour week is common for her.

"You learn a lot about a person in a 10-hour planning session," Elaine maintains. "If you don't, you're not very bright, are you? The fact is, I don't believe it'll happen to me, or any of my friends. The closest I've come to using a condom is asking the man, 'Are you safe?' and giggling into his chest.

"Now that I have the money and am starting to get the time for a spontaneous weekend or a wild night out," Elaine continues, "I'm told to put the brakes on and approach the man with a list of questions, as if I were his prospective employer. You could be married 50 years and still not know everything about him for sure."

A 1987 survey among singles, ages 18 to 34, living in New York, measured reactions to a safe sex ad campaign. Over 80

SEX TIPS

FANTASIZE!
Accept your mate for who he is, then pretend he's someone else.
—Comedian Rita Rudner

percent of those surveyed thought sexually active people should carry condoms and *women* should get their partners to wear them. The flip side is that over 60 percent of the sexually active respondents reported not using condoms at all or only some of the time.

AIDS is a feminist issue—we are at risk. Sleeping only with those who fit a nonrisk profile is putting our health in the hands of strangers. Mary Fleming, former director of the Illinois State AIDS Hotline, feels that we underestimate the practices of the white middle class. IV heroin and cocaine use are factors in that

group. Elizabeth Whelan, executive director of the American Council on Science and Health, infers that younger middle-class women aren't seriously concerned about AIDS and other STDs. An even more frightening indication of future AIDS/STD demographics is a 1986 study done in Massachusetts. Seventy percent of the 16- to 19-year-olds surveyed were found to be sexually active, but only 15 percent said they had changed to safe sex practices.

So, as yet, the AIDS plague seems not to have made much difference in our dating behavior. That's too bad—because it should. ◆

MODERN ROMANCE

A Lesson in Appetite Control

Mary Gaitskill

AT SOME POINT BETWEEN THE AGES OF 13 AND 14 I WAS BESET with romance fever. What I mean by that (and what I'll mean for my purposes here) is that excruciating hybrid of hormones and emotions that can, at any time, roar up out of the personal murk in a swollen rose-colored blur and wrap itself around anyone, however inappropriate. It can feel like love but it's different; while love has to do with who and what is being loved, romance can totally ignore such details. Romance has more to do with the person who is doing the feeling; it is the projection of some deeply subjective longing.

Being 14 and in a fever, my romanticism was ready to attach itself to even more than the usually absurd objects—my overweight cross-eyed math teacher, the pouty bleached-blond bad girl sitting in front of me, the dumpy dandruff-encrusted, pasty-faced psychiatrist my parents sent me to. Mainly, though, it pulsated around a large muscular oily boy two grades ahead of me, with whom I had had a few sweaty dates.

My feelings about him were certainly sexual, but, partly because I didn't really know what sex was, these feelings were monstrously dilated and distorted by my equally strong feelings of romance. When I fantasized having sex with him, I didn't picture anything happening below the waist: it was searing eye contact and intense jaw-setting action; there was a thunderstorm raging outside and flowers filling my dimly lit canopied boudoir. Never mind that we could barely hold a conversation; delirious with imaginings I more or less engineered the event, which finally took place on the floor of the garage, and it took several weeks for me to recover from the shocking clash between my fantasy and the actual painful, grunting, odorous occurrence.

Many people have had an experience like this, with various gradations in the gap between the real and the romantic. Some people react by repudiating their romantic feelings as lies and illusions—in fact, *The Concise Oxford Dictionary* defines "romance" as "an exaggeration," "a picturesque falsehood," or, as a verb, to "exaggerate or distort the truth, esp. fantastically." Even those adults who describe themselves as romantics tend to append words like "hopeless" to their description as though they know they're being foolish, but that it's a nice kind of foolishness proving how idealistic they are.

At 14, I wasn't about to decide that romance was a crock. My stubborn will to romance simply burrowed underground where it continued to live, finding nurturance in the crevices and claw holds of what was, I'm afraid, a series of seedy and preposterous adolescent experiences. In other words, since I was unable to find romance in the forms I'd been taught by popular culture to expect it—Valentines, flowers, declarations of pure love,

gooey theme music that came out of nowhere—I saw it in unconventional places, in those unexpected moments of tenderness and communication that can occur between people in the most superficially unromantic circumstances.

I had, for various complex reasons, learned very little about intimacy and love, about the tension between desire and personal territory, about the space between my needs and the needs of others. All this confusion was exacerbated by the way in which romance was presented to adolescent girls at that time and probably still is: as an inexplicable idealized feeling that you could have for someone you just glimpsed across the room, based mainly on their appearance, a feeling that would end in love and marriage, a feeling that was totally disconnected from and incompatible with anything else in daily life, even sex. It is this disconnection that seems to me the oddest feature of our idea of romance.

Just a few years ago, I had a romantic experience that was very different from my first. I developed an intense crush on a man I worked with, an adorable big-eyed honey who could actually carry on a conversation. The same level of fantasy was in operation as the first time around—except that this time there were no flowers, no thunderstorms, the lights were on full blast and there was major action below, above, and all around the waist. There was only one thing preventing me from luring him into the metaphorical garage; he had a live-in girlfriend.

This situation, which sounds hideously painful, became a sort of epiphany for me. Somehow, in a startling outburst of maturity, I was able to place my romantic feelings in the context of my other feelings for him. I don't mean I suppressed my romantic feelings, or tried to control them—quite the contrary. I allowed them to exist and respected their realness without throwing all of my emotional weight on them. In this way I was able to enjoy my feeling of tenderness for him while allowing space for a gentle, calm, sensitive connection between the truth of who he was and the limits of our relationship.

What I learned from this experience came in mighty handy when, further down the road, I found myself involved with a handsome sexbomb playboy who was a lot of fun but who was clearly not Mr. Right. Although I knew I wasn't in love with him and never would be, I found myself assailed in the night by enormous fanged fantasies of ultimate romantic communion, fantasies in which we performed the most incredible sex acts to the thundering sound track of our equally incredible emotions. None of this had anything to do with what was actually happening between us, but the more I tried to deny my romantic outburst the closer I got to the edge of an obsessional abyss.

Then, on some barely conscious level, I shifted gears. I stopped trying to control and contain my feelings. Instead I simply allowed myself to feel them—to respect their reality in the context of my other feelings for the guy, which ranged from friendship to attraction to disinterest. Throughout the affair, I was able to enjoy my hot romantic feelings for him, and to see him for who he was— which, if you must know, was a charming meatball.

This of course goes against our conventional concept of romance, which is defined as incomprehensible and overwhelming; women, especially, are taught to regard it as a ferocious onset, a feeling that will render them helpless, swooning, and incapable. Whatever turns you on. But remember: to feel helpless and out of control isn't the same thing as being helpless and out of control. Romance is as real as lust, friendship, and love, but it is only part of a shifting spectrum of possible responses. There's nothing wrong with wanting to make out in a flower-filled room while a thunderstorm rages. There's also nothing wrong with wanting to rip off someone's clothes and roll around on the garage floor with them. It's when these feelings don't acknowledge each other that you court disappointment.

By fetishizing romance in the ways that we do, disconnecting it from other feelings and then placing such enormous weight on it, we make it hard for it to flower. For it is only when romance allows for and works with emotional intimacy as well as the power of gut-level sexual passion that all at once, there is loud theme music playing, the flaming sun is setting, you are bursting out of your bodice—or whatever your fantasy is. ◆

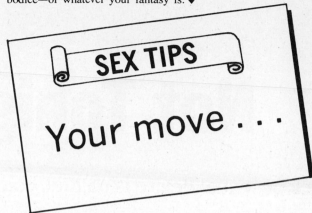

Not Tonight, Dear

Lack of sexual desire is painful, complicated and surprisingly common

As far as their friends can tell, 31-year-old Anne, a bank executive, and her husband, Bob,* a corporate financial officer in his late 30s, lead a busy, happy married life. Only Anne and Bob know the truth: that it has been, mostly, busy. Once they set off to work from their large house in a wealthy Chicago suburb, they seldom see each other again until around 10 p.m., after Anne has put in a couple of hours at a health club. Even then there is a notable absence of intimacy. In their eight years together, Anne and Bob have enjoyed only one year of what she calls "quasi-normal" sex. For the rest, she acknowledges, it has been largely "a marriage of avoidance"—all the sadder because they care for each other deeply. On the rare occasions when they do try sex, the attempt expires without passion. As a result, says Anne, who has been a patient at the Sexual Dysfunction Clinic of Loyola University, "we don't even have much desire to even try."

Meanwhile, Anne grapples with a feeling of lonely failure. "I'm a normal person," she says. "I do well in business. Is this part of my life that weird and freaky, or are other people in the same boat?"

In fact, Anne's problem is far from freaky. Psychiatrists and psychologists say they are seeing a growing proportion of patients with such complaints—people whose main response to the sexual revolution has been some equivalent of "Not tonight, dear." Clinically, their problem is known as Inhibited Sexual Desire (ISD), a condition marked by the inability to muster any interest in the great obsession. "The person with low sexual desire will not feel 'horny' . . . He will not be moved to seek out sexual activity, nor will he fantasize about sex," wrote psychiatrist Helen Singer Kaplan in a 1979 book that first called wide attention to the problem.

Dirty secret: Over the past decade ISD has emerged as the most common of all sexual complaints. By varying estimates, anywhere from 20 to 50 percent of the general population may experience it at some time, to some degree. One clinician goes so far as to call it "the plague of the '80s," although, like many of his colleagues, he doesn't think it's because the problem is growing, but because more people have grown willing to talk about it. The full dimensions of ISD may never be known. In a culture that exalts sex, the absence of desire remains something of a dirty little secret. Many couples still have difficulty acknowledging the problem, even when they seek help. David Kantor, cofounder of the Family Institute of Cambridge in Massachusetts, says he is "astounded" at the number of couples in therapy who claim

It's the new Yuppie disease. Busy two-career couples make up the largest contingent of turned-off patients

initially to have a good sex life, when in truth it is in drastic decline. "I've had couples come in who hadn't had sex for 15, 19 years," he says.

ISD can also be harder to diagnose and treat than other sexual problems. There is no single cause for the condition. It can result from depression, stress, marital discord or from physical causes such as hormone deficiencies. Often, it stems from a more elusive source—a "fear of intimacy," which some experts say is an endemic feature of relationships in the '80s. Sex is perhaps the ultimate act of intimacy, and people can feel profoundly vulnerable in the letting go of defenses that it entails. In getting "close," they may be afraid of getting hurt. Therapists commonly encounter patients who find it easier to make love

with relative strangers than with a spouse. "Sometimes it seems that people in our culture are more afraid of intimacy than they are of sex," says Kaplan. Freudian-oriented therapists see Oedipal undercurrents in the problem: a husband or wife may subliminally evoke the image of a parent, thus calling into play the incest taboo.

At a simpler level, inhibited desire can be caused by performance anxieties—brought on, to some extent, by the images of sexual athleticism relentlessly purveyed in the movies and on television. Both men and women worry that they are not up to those largely mythical standards. But the onus seems particularly great on men. Many men who seem to be suffering from inhibited desire may really be avoiding sex because they are afraid they won't be able to deliver the goods. Those fears have been exacerbated by the new aggressiveness of women. "Twenty years ago," says Dr. Peter Wish, a Framingham, Mass., psychologist, "husbands dragged their wives in [for sex counseling]. Now it's the opposite. Women are no longer willing to settle, and men are under more pressure to perform."

Sheer fatigue: In gay communities and among heterosexual singles, anxiety about AIDS is noticeably dampening sexual desire. But busy two-career couples make up the largest contingent of ISD patients. Usually they complain of sheer fatigue or the boredom of routine, once-a-week sex. Jennifer Knopf, codirector of Northwestern University's Adult Sexuality Program, is seeing so many such turned-off young professional couples that she calls ISD "the new Yuppie disease." A couple discovers they can't just "put the kids to bed, flip a switch on, become physical, catch up on work and go to sleep," she says. On the other hand, some therapists argue, the traditional stay-at-home housewife may be equally prone to ISD. In truth, it can hit anyone. But on average, therapists agree they are seeing more young people than old, more women than men with the complaint. One review of population studies

*The names of patients in this article have been changed.

done over the past half century estimated that up to 15 percent of men and 35 percent of women suffered from the problem.

Research data on ISD is still skimpy, since it was identified as a clinical entity only in the past decade. In their landmark 1966 book, "Human Sexual Response," William Masters and Virginia Johnson had postulated there were four phases of response in lovemaking: excitement, plateau, orgasm and resolution. But in 1979 Kaplan divided human sexual response into the three stages of orgasm, excitement and desire, which are each subject to separate problems. Some people, for instance, might feel desire for sexual intercourse without being sufficiently aroused to carry it out; others could be aroused to the point of orgasm, without feeling any real desire or pleasure. "Patients describe such experiences as similar to eating a meal when one is not really hungry," wrote Kaplan.

By 1980, DSM III, the diagnostic manual of psychiatry, officially adopted Kaplan's three-phase formulation, listing ISD as a disorder of the desire phase. This year the manual added a related item: "sexual aversion disorder," a phobic reaction so strong that a person with the problem may not be able to bear being touched in a suggestive way. Doctors are finding that a large number of such patients actually suffer from a form of panic. Kaplan estimates that in the population she treats, as many as a third who avoid sex actually have panic disorders.

Therapists point out that not all episodes of inhibited desire are cause for concern. Short-term declines in interest may be normal. Sometimes patients merely need reassurance that their sexual frequency is up to par. Dr. Debora Phillips, an assistant professor of psychiatry at the University of Southern California, Los Angeles, says she never gives her clients a standard for frequency except to reassure them: "If they say, 'We've been married for only 10 years and we only have sex twice a week, isn't that horrible?' then I will say, 'Oh, you're way above the national average'."

'Hidden agenda': There is no true benchmark for frequency. By the second year of marriage, it usually declines to about half the rate of the first year, and the curve continues to drop with age and the duration of the marriage. A Kinsey report on sexual practices found an average frequency of 2.4 times a week. ("He gets the two, I get the point four," went a contemporary joke.) More recent surveys tend to confirm that figure. But there can be wide variations, depending on age and conditions. Acceptable frequency now is generally seen as whatever keeps a couple happy. As Dr. Richard Hanish, a Boston-area psychologist puts it, there is a problem only "if a once-a-month marries a once-a-day." But that difference in desire can be critical. In

an address to the American Bar Association, Phillips called the conflict over frequency "the hidden agenda" of divorce. It is, she says, "one of the highest causes of marital unhappiness."

The converse is also true: marital unhappiness is one of the most frequent causes of inhibited desire. ISD patients, in fact, may have a normal sexual impulse, but according to Kaplan, a "turnoff mechanism" such as anger or anxiety squelches it. In Kaplan's view—and many therapists agree—the mechanism is most apt to be triggered by marital discord. Says Harvard professor of medicine Dr. Daniel Federman: "Often, ISD cases are really relational problems, and not intrinsically sexual."

That is surely the case with Anne and Bob, who are still trying to solve their difficulties. As Anne tells it, Bob is a pent-up, angry man who has difficulty making his needs known. She, on the other hand, is sensitive to slights, and Bob's stinging criticisms make her feel inadequate. After a year of sex once or twice a week, they stopped wanting each other, and she is convinced that their squabbles were the main cause. "It's the little things that build up to [the point] where I'm scared to have sex because nothing's going right," she says.

Sometimes it is more than "little things." In two-career marriages, particularly, there may be an underlying power struggle that spills over into the bedroom. Northwestern's Knopf tells of one such couple who are currently her patients. The two had an unwritten "contract," she says, agreeing that both should work; but it was implicit the man should have the better job. When the wife took a superior job, the husband, threatened and angry, lost his desire for her. Then the wife also lost desire: although she liked her work, she felt guilty about straying from the traditional role. Sometimes, inhibited desire can also be an unconscious stratagem for maintaining the upper hand by withholding sexual gratification.

For all the new openness about sex, there is not much communication between couples in such conflicts, and usually they will benefit from straightforward marriage counseling. "The problem is what is happening with their mouths, not with their groins," says Dr. Domeena Renshaw, head of Loyola University's Sexual Dysfunction Clinic. "The couple is really avoiding the argument, not the sex."

Cuddling sessions: When the roots of ISD run deeper, patients are treated with a combination of talk therapy, to get at the source of the difficulties, and behavioral exercises that help them relearn desire. Bill and Mary came to see Dr. Ron Podell, director of the Center for Sexual Science in Los Angeles, at a point where they hadn't had intercourse for months. The couple had been married seven years, Bill for the

second time—his first wife had left him after three years. As is customary in therapy, Podell first checked to see whether there might be a biological cause, such as a hormone imbalance, but there was none. "They were covertly angry and couldn't express their feelings," he concluded. "They couldn't even cuddle anymore."

It turned out that Mary had a hostile, violent father; she had been physically abused as a child. Bill's father had left home, and his mother was a domineering woman whom he had never seemed able to please. "They each had significant fears of rejection, so that becoming intimate frightened them," notes Podell. They kept pre-

One patient's lack of desire and fear of intimacy came from a deep childhood fear of abandonment

tending everything was fine, but if they saw a movie that had heavy sex in it, it made them acutely uncomfortable because that was lacking in their lives. They did not know how to approach each other. "I needed attention and warmth that I didn't get when I was younger, and he could never give me enough," Mary says. "Bill would mistake my touching or cuddling for a demand for sex. He was always pulling away and I was always reaching out." For his part, says Bill, he was "in a frustrating situation of trying to please my wife and not being able to get an erection. If this were the '50s, we probably would have split up or else just lived out our lives in a nonsexual marriage."

Instead, Mary finally persuaded him to see a urologist, who referred the couple to Podell. Bill, a "John Wayne-ish" former Marine by Mary's description, still resisted. When the therapist questioned him he would snap, "I can't answer, I'm too embarrassed to talk about such things." Gradually, Podell got him to see that his lack of desire came from a fear of getting close—a fear that his wife would abandon him as he had been abandoned in childhood and by his first wife. Meanwhile, Podell gave the pair "homework" to do, in the form of nonsexual touching and cuddling sessions. For months only Mary initiated and Bill would just go along. For the first month they were also fully clothed. Then Podell told them they could strip to their underwear. They were as shy as strangers at first, but gradually learned to hold each other and discuss how they felt. "Sometimes," says Mary, "it was just five minutes of cuddles in the den. I just needed the warmth and to know that this person cares about me."

After a year and two months of treatment, Bill and Mary gained considerable insight into the way they were "sabotaging" their sexual relations. They then had their first sexual intercourse in a year and a half. "We have a much closer marriage," says Mary. "There's definitely more romance . . . I'm very proud of Bill for being as strong as he was to go through all this."

Like many therapists, Podell believes desire disorders are the hardest sexual problems to treat because the causes can be so subtle. "Who the hell ever experiences the fear of intimacy?" he says. "What does that feel like?" It is a concept that patients don't immediately grasp. Usually, he notes, "they will say, 'I don't know what you're talking about. I'm just not turned on.' It's really helping a person confront, week after week, what they're feeling." While they are talking through their problems with the therapist, the homework gets them interacting in a sensual way, without the immediate threat of having to perform. It is a way of "deconditioning" their anxiety. "You make the sessions nondemanding," Podell explains, "and gently increase the amount of stimulation each week."

Minimize anxiety: Many therapists encourage patients to set a romantic mood before approaching sex—have a glass of wine, read a sexy book, fantasize, even masturbate—anything to minimize anxiety, which is antithetical to feelings of desire. In line with behavior-modification techniques, Debora Phillips develops "hierarchies" of anxiety-provoking actions or situations. For example, an "approach" hierarchy could range from being kissed on the lips to intercourse itself, on an anxiety scale of mild to moderate to intense.

Despite refinements in understanding and treatment, researchers still have much to learn about ISD. (This year the American Psychiatric Association changed the name of the disorder to the more technically accurate "hypoactive sexual desire," although it is still generally referred to by its old name.) Treatment remains problematic, success rates vary. Some therapists put the figure as high as 80 percent, with anywhere from six weeks to 18 months of therapy. Kaplan gives a conservative estimate of 50 percent.

What is certain is that for far more people than have yet been counted, sexual passion is not the easy, inexhaustible impulse that the popular culture unstintingly portrays. As one ISD patient wistfully observed not long ago to his psychiatrist, Dr. Tom Stewart of Boston's Beth Israel Hospital: "The sexual revolution has come and gone, and I've yet to fire my first shot."

DAVID GELMAN *with* SHAWN DOHERTY
in Boston, ANDREW MURR *in Chicago,*
LISA DREW *in New York and*
JEANNE GORDON *in Los Angeles*

You're supposed to quiz your date about AIDS—but figuring out how is tough

I love you, but can I ask a question?

■ Their second date ends in her apartment, where she offers him a brandy snifter and dims the lights. He runs his finger down her cheek. "I think I'm falling in love with you," he murmurs. "Oh, I feel it too," she sighs, "but . . . well, there's something I need to ask." She pauses. "Have you ever used drugs intravenously, had a blood transfusion or slept with another guy?"

If you're single, AIDS is the latest bogyman to haunt your social life. By now you've absorbed the axioms: "Practice safe sex." "Know your sexual partner." But platitudes are one thing. Knowing what to say when your date declares his love in your living room is quite another. How do you—delicately—probe someone's sexual history, and can you believe what you're told?

If you're heterosexual and don't hang out with IV drug users, the chance of hooking up with someone infected with the AIDS virus is probably small. On the other hand, "safe sex" has a nice ring to it, but there's really no such thing—only precautions to reduce your risk. No one these days disagrees that the era of ultra-casual sex is over. Judith Sills, a Philadelphia clinical psychologist and author of *A Fine Romance: The Psychology of Successful Courtship*, says that with AIDS in the wings the danger of jumping into bed with a stranger far outweighs the fleeting pleasure such meetings afford. Sills doesn't mince words with clients when they talk about spending the night on a first date. She commands: "You can't do that any more—I don't care what kind of car he was driving."

Time to get acquainted

In place of the one-night stand, welcome the return of lingering courtship. "There was some virtue after all in the old stuff about necking and petting," says Oakland psychologist Bernie Zilbergeld. "It gives you some time to get to know the person and to look for red flags." Next month, Zilbergeld and colleague Lonnie Barbach will release an audiotape, "An Ounce of Prevention: How to Talk With a Partner About Smart Sex" ($8.95 in bookstores, or $10.95 including shipping by calling (800) 341-1950, ext. 88). The tape has advice, among other things, on how to bring up the subject of AIDS and what to do about testing.

In slowing down the race to the bedroom, you can raise the subject of AIDS and gently ask a few questions about your partner's sexual past. But don't put too much stock in the answers. It might help to pretend you're an arms-control negotiator and your partner is working for the Soviets. As with hostile nations, lies even between longtime bedfellows are not unknown. In a University of California–San Francisco survey of people tested anonymously for infection with the AIDS virus, more than 25 percent said they did not intend to inform their sexual partners of a positive result.

There are other reasons to distrust your lover's talents as a historian. Over the years, people simply forget exactly where they were and who they were with. And even the most honest paramour is unlikely to know the intimate secrets of his past loves. In short, though far from perfect, condoms provide more-reliable protection than any question you can ask.

That doesn't mean talking about sexual basics with your partner is a bad idea. Such conversations offer a forum for expressing concern and setting the sexual ground rules. "Most people find that what they are doing is establishing the meaning of their sexual involvement, and they use the talk as an entree to an agreement about condoms," says Sills. If nothing else, the interchange can serve as a barometer of intimacy, the bottom line being, "If you can't talk about it—don't do it."

The best timing for a candid talk obviously is not late at night after a few drinks or during a passionate embrace.

"One has to be very careful not to offend," advises Dr. Ruth Westheimer, perhaps the media's best-known sex adviser. "That is why I advise waiting until the relationship is such that a conversation like this can be engaged in without danger." Take it easy, Westheimer warns: "Don't make it the Spanish Inquisition." And don't pursue the subject over dinner, or you might lose your appetite. Her nomination for an opening line: "Look, we live in crazy times; there is this crazy disease. I hope you understand, honey, that we ought to talk about previous relationships."

Frank discussions, of course, don't ensure happy endings. More than one promising lover has stalked out the door upon close questioning—but you're better off without him. If your date turns out to be in a group that runs a high risk for AIDS, who needs an intimate relationship? AIDS tests are probably not the solution, unless you want to abstain from sexual activity for three months or more—the time it takes for AIDS antibodies to appear after a person is infected. Getting tested does make sense, on the other hand, if you're in a long-term, monogamous relationship and want to be sure both you and your partner are in good health.

Recent surveys hint that Americans are revising their attitudes about dating and sex, but there's no evidence that sexual practices have changed—except that drugstore condom sales jumped 18.7 percent in the first half of 1987, the latest period for which figures are available. Their actual *use* may increase more slowly—many men don't like them, and women are often reluctant to take the lead in sex. All that must change, says Margie Nichols, executive director of New Brunswick's Hyacinth Foundation AIDS Project: "When a man won't use a condom, women are going to have to be willing to say, 'Forget it.' "

by Erica E. Goode

Sexuality Through the Life Cycle

- Youth and Their Sexuality (Articles 38-41)
- Adults and Their Sexuality (Articles 42-45)

Individual sexual development is a lifelong process that begins at birth and terminates at death. Contrary to popular notions of this process, there are no latent periods during which the individual is nonsexual or noncognizant of sexuality. The growing process of a sexual being does, however, reveal qualitative differences through various life stages. This section devotes attention to these stages of the life cycle and their relation to sexuality.

As children gain self-awareness, they naturally explore their own bodies, masturbate, display curiosity for the bodies of the opposite sex, and show interest in the bodies of mature individuals such as their parents. Such exploration and curiosity are important and healthy aspects of human development. Yet it is often difficult for adults (who live in a society that is not comfortable with sexuality in general) to avoid making their children ashamed of being sexual or showing interest in sexuality. When adults impose their ambivalence upon a child's innocuous explorations into sexuality, or behave toward children in sexually inappropriate ways, distortion of an indispensable and formative stage of development occurs. This often leaves profound emotional scars that hinder full acceptance of self and sexuality later in the child's life.

Adolescence, the social status accompanying puberty and the transition to adulthood, proves to be a very stressful period of life for many individuals as they attempt to develop an adult identity and force relationships with others. Because of the physiological capacity of adolescents for reproduction, sexuality tends to be heavily censured by parents and society at this stage of life. Yet individuals and societal attitudes place tremendous emphasis on sexual attractiveness—especially for females, and sexual competency—especially for males. These physical, emotional, and cultural pressures combine to create confusion and anxiety in adolescents and young adults about whether they are okay or normal. Information and assurances from adults can alleviate these stresses and facilitate positive and responsible sexual maturity if there is mutual trust and willingness in both generations.

Sexuality finally becomes socially acceptable in adulthood, at least within marriage. Yet routine, boredom, myths, and/or a lack of communication can exact heavy tolls on the quantity and quality of sexual interaction. Extramarital sexual encounters are often sought despite the fact that such activity is conventionally stigmatized as infidelity. The problem of infidelity is not as easy one to solve. Current scholarly opinion maintains that infidelity and extramarital relations are two separate phenomena.

Sexuality in the later years of life is again socially and culturally stigmatized because of the prevailing misconception that sex is for young married adults. Such an attitude is primarily responsible for the apparent decline in sexual interest and activity as one grows older. Physiological changes in the aging process are not, in and of themselves, detrimental to sexual expression. A life history of experience, health, and growth can make sexual expression in the later years a most rewarding and fulfilling experience.

Youth and Their Sexuality begins with an article about sexual abuse versus sex education. The next article explores perceptions and distortions of body image and sexuality, especially in young women. The author argues in favor of early sex education designed to teach values. The next article focuses on questions commonly asked by college students in Human Sexuality courses, revealing that there is still a lot they want to know about their sexuality. The final article in the section summarizes a study of masturbation, a behavior familiar to nearly all men and women but rarely discussed in either everyday conversation or professional research journals.

Adults and Their Sexuality explores marital and other relationships, sexuality, and aging, in an attempt to distinguish myths from reality. The subsection begins with two articles that assert that sex after 35, and even after 50, can be better than ever. The next article outlines an approach to the care of the elderly that maintains their dignity as sexual people, while the final piece presents the results of a survey of older men and women on love, sex, and aging. All four articles strive to establish the point that although aging affects sexuality and sexual functioning, sexual feelings, needs and relationships among older people are very similar to those of younger people and at least as important to their health and well-being.

Looking Ahead: Challenge Questions

What are some of the problems that youth have in dealing with their sexuality? What do parents and adults need to do differently in order to help adolescents? Do you agree or disagree with the statement that sexual knowledge is the best weapon against irresponsible sexuality? Support your position.

Before you took this course, did you think other college students had questions about sex? Because there exist so many questions, do you think that sex education has failed? Why or why not?

Do you feel that talking about male and female masturbation is necessary? What benefits could come from increased discussion of this taboo topic?

How does advancing age affect romantic relationships? Sexual relationships? Can sex for older people bring new freedom and joy? How does sexuality fit with your image of older people?

SEX IN CHILDHOOD: AVERSION, ABUSE, OR RIGHT?

Dean D. Knudsen, Ph.D.
Department of Sociology and Anthropology
Purdue University
West Lafayette, IN 47907

Abstract

Childhood sexuality has become a new focus of attention with the public awareness of child sexual abuse, but there are many unresolved issues. First, the incest taboo is no longer an adequate control on adult-child sexual activities. Second, definitions of sexual abuse are imprecise and inconsistent across county and state lines, resulting in varied levels of enforcement or legal action. Third, an emphasis focused only on the right to say no denies the choice that is inherent in the concept of "rights." A major conclusion is that sex education designed to teach values about sexuality is essential and must begin very early.

Sexual behavior by children has been a problem for parents, schools, and law enforcement for generations. In recent years, the concern about sexual abuse by adults has refocused the issue of child sexual activities. One approach has been to define all activities involving adult-child sexual contact as sexual abuse, giving law enforcement and child protective services an easy way to deal with such behavior. Many questions remain concerning other issues of sexuality in childhood, however. Some consensus exists about the extreme behaviors that should be defined as abusive, but even such terms as *incest*, *molestation*, and *rape* have several meanings. In addition, there are some persistent issues, including consent versus victimization and the rights of children to engage in sexual activities, that are largely unresolved.

This paper is directed toward the general issue of sex in childhood. Three perspectives will be examined: 1) that the incest taboo and the natural aversion among humans to sex with intimates—especially with adults and family members—provides an adequate and appropriate level of control over sexual abuse; 2) that sexual activities for children—especially with adults—is harmful to children, and thus protection and control of children are essential; and 3) that sexual activities are a right of the child if the child desires them—even with adults. Each of these views will be examined, and research that supports or contradicts the various positions will be noted.

Background

Public concern about childhood sexuality is of relatively recent origin. Prior to the eighteenth century, little attention was paid to such sexual activity, but after religious moralists and medical personnel condemned it, child sexual behavior gradually became defined as sinful or harmful (Fishman, 1982). Masturbation, for example, was seen not only as evil but also as the cause of many illnesses, including epilepsy, hysteria, sterility, and insanity (Neuman, 1975). Parents were encouraged to discipline their children to eliminate such self-abuse and thus prevent sickness and disease. Through the years, various techniques, including fear, brutality, and superstition were employed to eradicate masturbation, though with limited success at best (Schultz, 1980a; Gagnon & Simon, 1973).

Heterosexual behaviors and relationships similarly were controlled on the ground that children lacked the physical maturity and cognitive abilities to deal with such experiences, and the concept of "age of consent" was applied, especially to girls, to preserve their moral innocence. Originally "age of consent" apparently referred to the male's ability to enter into commercial agreements or to bear the armor required

*The author wishes to express appreciation to Barbara Carson and members of the Sorento Seminar for their helpful comments on an earlier draft of this paper.

From *Journal of Sex Education and Therapy*, Vol. 13, No. 1, Spring/Summer 1987, pp. 16-24. Copyright © 1987, JSET. Reprinted by permission.

for battle. Only later, during the thirteenth century, was it applied to females under the age of 12, and by the sixteenth century the age of 10 was established as the legal age of consent for males and females in England and America. However, the economic conditions that spawned childhood prostitution were so severe and prostitution was so widespread that as late as 1880 no charge of sexual assault could be made against a man if a child, regardless of age, gave voluntary consent to sexual intercourse (Schultz, 1980b).

Criminal laws were enacted in the late nineteenth century to eliminate childhood prostitution and other forms of sexual abuse by adults. By increasing the age of consent, the laws were designed to protect children from sexual exploitation and effectively denied children the right to engage in any sexual activities (Schultz, 1980a). Changing conceptions of childhood and the concern for protection and control that characterized the child-saving movement (Platt, 1969) also were incorporated into the juvenile justice system by the beginning of the twentieth century, resulting both in a paternalism and in an ambiguous legal status for children and youth.

Since 1900, laws in most states have offered protection of girls and young women through "statutory rape" codes and relatively high ages of consent, and more recently, by child protective services. Despite changing laws, however, and the new legal definitions of childhood that extend it to ages 16–18 in most states, few efforts are made to protect females over the age of 14 (Russell, 1984). The use of higher ages would technically classify those young women who voluntarily or willingly engaged in sexual intercourse below the age of 16—about one third to one half of all females (Zelnick, Kim and Kanter, 1979; Furstenberg, 1976)—either as victims of criminal behavior with possible prosecution of their partners, or as incorrigible individuals subject to possible incarceration (e.g, Wooden, 1976). As a result, few efforts are made to prosecute consensual sexual activity among teenagers.

Most of the current concern about excluding children from sexual experiences is directed toward younger ages, especially those under 12, whose physical and emotional immaturity is viewed as sufficient reason for their protection. This approach is buttressed by beliefs about the natural asexuality of infants and children, by moral codes, and by a genuine concern about the negative effects of early sexual stimulation. Some recent research offers challenges to these beliefs, however, concerning both the physiological functions of small children and the inevitability of negative consequences from early sexual experiences.

Physiological Capabilities of Children

Many adults believe that most sexual functions are possible only with the onset of puberty, though research now suggests that a wide range of sexual behaviors can occur at very early ages. Martinson (1976) has noted that male infants are capable of penile erections and that vaginal lubrication has been recorded for female babies, functions that indicate a physical capac-

ity for sexual activities and intercourse almost from birth. Other observations among small children have indicated that autoerotic behavior such as masturbation or exhibiting may occur by age 2, and is common among boys and girls by 6–7 years of age. In addition, heterosexual play among preschool children involving exploration, genital manipulation, and coital training, that is, positions and movements associated with coitus, has been reported (Langfeldt, 1981a). Though Freud termed these years "the Latent Period," it is clear that many preadolescent children have sexual capacities—including orgasms and even pregnancy (Borneman, 1983; Janus and Bess, 1976; Kinsey, Pomeroy, & Martin, 1948).

To say that children are physically capable of sexual activities does not imply that they interpret such behavior in the way that most adults view sexuality, however, because children lack both knowledge of and experience with the cognitive and emotional dimensions of sexuality. Researchers have described this ability in various ways—as imagery (Byrne, 1977) and as sexual maturity (Borneman, 1983) or as concept formation (Langfeldt, 1981b)—all of which refer to erotic fantasies that appear at very young ages and develop over time, through social experiences, into adult sexuality. At the physiological level, the entire range of sexual activity including sexual intercourse appears to be possible for most humans at very young ages; it is the social and cognitive aspects of sexuality that distinguish adult and child sexual understandings of sexual behavior.

Sociohistorical Factors in Defining Appropriate Child Sexuality

Numerous historians and researchers have noted that children and childhood have different meanings today than in the past (e.g., Aries, 1962; deMause, 1974; Demos, 1971; Pollock, 1983; Postman, 1982; Suransky, 1982; Synott, 1983). While several historical eras might be constructed on the basis of varied criteria, the changing perspective of childhood sexuality is represented by the development from "property," to "protection," to "personal" paradigms (Lee, 1982). In preindustrial society, children were viewed as property whose sexuality was recognized and accepted as a part of life. With the development of schools and changes in families as a part of the industrial revolution, the protection of childhood innocence was sought through the removal of children from the sexuality of adult life. Protection became an adult responsibility that included both the observing and making of decisions in the "best interests" of children. With the emergence of individual rights—especially the right of a child to veto the parental choice of marriage partners—the shift toward a personal paradigm was begun, in which personal rights for children would replace adult protection. One consequence of this movement is the view that young children should be able, if they wish, to choose to engage in the entire range of sexual activities available to adults (e.g, Holt, 1974).

The current ambiguity in legal definitions of sexual abuse and consent and in parental understanding of child sexuality, in part reflects a failure to address the changed understandings and increased knowledge about sexual abuse, incest, molestation, and sexual activities. In the United States, for example, the term *incest* may be used to describe diverse sexual activities that range from an unwanted touch to sexual intercourse; that occur once or over long periods; that occur between nuclear family members as well as consanguineous, affinal, or step-relatives; and that may be consensual or involve force or threats (Bixler, 1983). The genetic factors that often have been cited as a basis for the incest taboo are more scientifically and clearly understood now than when most legal definitions were written. Similarly, the social factors noted to be associated with incest—such as family role conflict, sibling or spousal jealousy, or extrafamilial alliances—that once were cited as reasons for the incest taboo (e.g, Davis, 1949), no longer appear to affect family patterns in an era of mobility and high divorce. While the concept of sexual abuse has obscured some difficult issues, much ambiguity remains about appropriate sexuality for children. In addition, little consensus exists among legal jurisdictions, intervention agencies, and protective service units about the appropriate means of dealing with either children or adults involved in sexual activities or the effects of those sexual experiences on children (e.g. Finkelhor, Gomes-Schwartz, and Horowitz, 1982).

Definitions of Sexuality

Various positions have been taken regarding childhood sexuality and the protection of children from sexual exploitation. Historically, the incest taboo and the assumed natural aversion to sex among intimates have been the means by which children were protected from sexual abuse by family members. The emergence of child abuse as a social problem redefined child protection less as a family responsibility, and social services were developed to supplement or replace the incest taboo as a form of control over sexuality of and against children. A third view defines sexual activities as a right for children, and the decision to become involved is left to the child. Each of these perspectives will be developed more fully and evaluated by examining the existing research literature.

Childhood Sexuality as Aversion

Aversion to sexual activities with family members, usually associated with the incest taboo, is frequently expressed by incest victims who felt that those experiences were "bad" or "wrong"—even as they occurred. Some researchers see these feelings as a natural consequence of intimate social experiences in all small groups, and especially in private family life (e.g., Bettelheim, 1969). Other researchers, however, view the incest taboo as a defense and a social control mechanism against a natural sexual attraction among primary family members. They see the taboo as necessary to prevent sexual activities that would have important social, biological, and psychological consequences

(DeMott, 1980; Renshaw & Renshaw, 1977). Both views would suggest that a genuine aversion to intrafamily sex exists and is buttressed—if not created—by the incest taboo and its strong moral and legal supports.

It has become evident that incest is not rare, suggesting that aversive feelings about intrafamilial sexual behaviors clearly are no longer powerful enough to prevent adults from engaging children in consensual and forced sexual behaviors. The failure of incest taboo in recent decades has been tied to the social changes that have occurred in Western societies in the past 50 years. The sexual revolution and the increased divorce rate with the complementary increase in stepparents have had important consequences for higher levels of sexual contact (e.g., Finkelhor, 1979b, Russell, 1984). Similarly, the contemporary pattern of small, mobile, vertical family units and the loss of extended family ties may foster incestuous relationships because each individual's need for affection and physical intimacy must be satisfied largely from within the nuclear unit (Henderson, 1972; Parker & Parker, 1986). Other researchers suggest depersonalization and compartmentalized life-styles (Taubman, 1984) as factors in the declining power of the incest taboo.

In general, the aversion argument proposes such social changes as sexual permissiveness, changing sex and gender roles, disrupted and reconstructed families, the emphasis on economic success, and the dependence on the family for non-ego-threatening abuse. Not all males in chaotic social settings persistently seek sexual experiences with children, however, suggesting that other individual factors are involved as well. Efforts to deal with this question focus on the breakdown of inhibitions or prohibitions against sexual behaviors directed toward children by adults. Araji and Finkelhor (1986) have suggested that disinhibition theories offer explanations at both the individual and sociocultural levels. At the individual level, impulse disorder, senility, alcohol problems, psychosis, situational stress, and the failure of incest avoidance mechanisms have been identified. Cultural tolerance, pornography, and patriarchal prerogatives are seen as sociocultural conditions that contribute to disinhibition. It may also be that the incest taboo is not learned by all members of society, leading to different levels of strength or salience of the prohibitions against sex with family members, just as other norms have uneven adherence.

Responses of excitement, participation, or disgust to adult overtures reflect earlier experiences with sex and the degree to which these behaviors were rewarded, ignored, or punished (Howells, 1981). Because of the adult's ability to manipulate the child, there is little evidence of physical force being used—at least initially—in most sexual abuse (Plummer, 1981), though it is common for threats, coercion, or bribes to be used to maintain a relationship. Adults may interpret the initial acceptance of contact by children as interest or desire, whether or not such views are supported by the child's behavior following the contact. Such submission is important, for as Frude notes, "the most powerful factor in reducing inhibitions may be a daughter's apparent acceptance of the behavior"

(1982). Others (e.g., Meiselman, 1978; Finkelhor, 1979b) also have reported on the passivity or willing participation of young women in sexual activity with fathers. Because reactions to sexual activity on the part of the offender as well as the child are learned, the lack of immediate negative responses may be viewed as an apparent willingness of young children to participate, thereby further encouraging the perpetrator. Such processes are probably more descriptive of opportunistic abusers rather than of pedophiles who engage in continued or repeated sexual acts with children and probably are not affected by incest taboos in their behavior (e.g., DSM–III, 1980). The fact that boys learn different responses than girls to touch and body contact at early ages also may be a factor in gender victimization in sexual abuse. By the early years of elementary school, the male response to touch is aggressive physical action, whereas females respond with deference and acceptance (Gunderson, Melas, and Skor, 1981).

It is clear that the incest taboo has not prevented adults from seeking sexual activities with children within their kinship group, and intrafamily intimacy has not resulted in a universal aversion to sexual behavior with kin. Thus, several proposals that would emphasize the legitimacy of child sexual activity have been made. Johnson (1977), for example, has suggested that the traditional approach to the sexuality of the young—trying to eliminate it—has failed and that responsibility and enhancement of sexual expression are preferable. Separating abuse from normal or acceptable sexual activity has obvious merit; however, the ambiguity of intentions has presented an important problem for those responsible for protecting children.

Childhood Sexuality as Abuse

The concern with child protection rests on the perspective that children are primarily victims of adult actions and that exposure of a child to any type of sexual activities before the child reaches an appropriate level of maturation has serious negative consequences and thus should be defined as abuse. This view has been based on one or more of several judgments: 1) that adult-child sex is wrong because physical or maturational differences result in damage or harm to the child, 2) that premature sexualization draws the children into adult life and deprives them of the freedom of childhood, 3) that sex at an early age leaves emotional and psychological damage that often appears in later life, and 4) that children cannot give informed consent to sexual activities with adults because by their nature children lack the power and knowledge to give consent (Finkelhor, 1979a). In essence, children are seen as incapable of, disinterested in, or too immature for appreciating the significance of sexual activities and the consequences of their sexual behavior; thus they must be protected from too early exposure and its effects.

Despite the obvious appeal of such an approach to childhood sexuality, some serious questions remain. The first argument, that adult-child sex is unnatural due to size difference and that it produces physical harm and damage to the child, primarily applies only to that small proportion of the cases that involve attempted or achieved sexual intercourse. Schultz has noted that "no more than 5 to 10 percent of sexual abuse involves physical injury" (1980). Other types of physical effects such as AIDS, gonorrhea, or syphilis, are serious and cannot be ignored. Unfortunately, these problems are not unique to child abuse or child victimization where their control would appear to be more feasible than among adults; in fact, on the basis of current public health concerns, it is apparent that adulthood does not necessarily bring a greater ability to deal with them.

The second issue, premature sexualization, ignores the fact that children have extensive interest in sexual activities, however immature and exploratory they may be. The exposure of children to television and the varieties of sexuality expressed through that medium probably have reduced the adult-child differences in sexual understanding that once existed (e.g., Postman, 1982). Though premature sexualization may be an irrelevant issue to many children who have been exposed to a wide range of sexual activities from infancy, other children may be incapable of understanding the full meaning of sexual behaviors, with some serious consequences for their behavior. Unfortunately, data are inadequate to assess the extent or importance of this problem.

Third, the evidence also is far from convincing in the documentation of psychological damage (Conte, 1985). Early reports about sexual abuse came from clinical observations that emphasized the severe negative impact of child sexual abuse, especially coerced sexual activities. These studies suggested that there is a wide range of short- and long-term reactions of victims: anxiety and fear, guilt and shame, depression, grief, sense of stigma, somatic complaints, and learning and behavioral problems (Browne and Finkelhor, 1986). The significance of such reports must be qualified by the fact that the population under observation is selective, that is, the very persons most likely to experience emotional reactions and thus seek assistance in dealing with them are the subjects for these research reports. The lack of representative samples of control groups in most of these studies precludes generalizations about the extent and severity of trauma of sexual experiences with adults, because no comparable evidence is available from those people not traumatized by such activities. Nevertheless, *some* careful, recent clinical research supports the conclusion that sexual abuse produces trauma for children (e.g., Friedrich, Urquize, & Beilke, 1986; Husain & Chapel, 1982; Rogers & Terry, 1984; Rosenfeld, 1979; Ruch & Chandler, 1982; Scott & Stone, 1986; Sgroi, 1982).

Other clinical studies, as well as much research based on larger, representative samples, are less consistent in documenting the pervasive, negative consequences of sexual abuse, however. Indeed, the evidence about the extent and inevitability of trauma is contradictory at best. Several recent studies indicated that perhaps one third of the children who have engaged in some form of sexual activities with adults do not define the experience as negative (e.g, Bernard, 1981; Brunold, 1964; Constantine, 1981; Curtois, 1979; Emslie & Rosenfeld, 1983; Gagnon, 1965; LaBarbera, Martin & Dozier, 1980; Mayer, 1983:15–16; Ramey, 1979; Trepper & Traicoff, 1983:15; Tsai, Summers, & Edgar, 1979; Yorukoglu & Kemph, 1966). Such findings strongly suggest some modifications of the general conclusions drawn from clinical samples that *all* sexual contacts between children and adults have negative consequences for children. Evidence indicates that factors that appear to contribute to trauma for both sexes are: 1) the use of force, and 2) fathers or stepfathers as perpetrators (Browne & Finkelhor, 1986).

A few studies of boys also suggest early experiences may be related to homosexuality (Sandfort, 1982; Ingram, 1979), though such interpretations lack sufficient data to be convincing (DeJong, Emmett, & Hervada, 1982; Farber, Showers, Johnson, Joseph, & Oshins, 1984). It is too early to draw conclusions about long-term consequences for young children who have been victimized without obvious trauma. Though clinical studies often have documented the negative effects for adults of sexual contacts during childhood, such data also are inevitably selective and it remains to be determined if serious problems will develop for all children who experience early sexualization with adults.

No adequate explanation has been offered for these diverse findings, but the nature and intensity of reactions by parents and professionals to the situation is often mentioned as an important factor in generating trauma among victims (Colonna & Solnit, 1981; Conte & Berliner, 1981; Constantine, 1981; Elwell, 1979; Walters, 1975). Additional support for the idea that adult reactions are important comes from a study of communes (Berger, 1981) that suggested that sexuality expressed freely among and between children and adults had few negative consequences—unless the contact had been forced.

Clearly, the attitudes and actions of parents and children toward all sexual activities are important, not only those responses to events that are classified as sexually abusive. Because the term *sexual abuse* is often applied to a range of activities—sexual intercourse, fondling, oral-genital contact, indecent exposure to a child, involvement of a child in obscene performances, and even suggestive, provocative speech—the age and maturation of the child is an important factor in the reactions by both adult and the child to the incident or activity. Some studies attempt to incorporate maturation as a part of the definition of victimization and limit abuse to behavior between adults and children whose ages are at least 5 years apart (e.g., Finkelhor, 1979b; Mrazek and Kempe, 1981), though the psychiatric definition of pedophilia refers to age differences of 10 years or more between participants (DSM–III, 1980). Other researchers have focused on all unsought sexual experiences and include actions by age peers or perpetrators who are even younger than the victims (e.g., Russell, 1984). Current research,

however, offers no consistent evidence that there is greater trauma either for those of younger ages at the onset of abuse or for those whose sexual experiences were of longer duration (Browne & Finkelhor, 1986).

Finally, there is an unfortunate lack of data that would help clarify the issue of age at which the average child can give informed consent. Classifying all sexual activities involving young children—whether with peers or adults—as abuse rests upon a system of age stratification and age segregation that assumes privacy and isolation of children from the adult world. The idea that 12-year-old children are unable to give consent because they lack the knowledge and capacity to make responsible decisions or to accept the consequences of sexual behavior assumes an ignorance and immaturity about sex and life that probably no longer exists for many, if not most children.

If, as some supporters of early sex education claim, the issue of sex is treated as a natural and normal part of life, children of very young ages exposed to sexuality—either as observers or participants—may see a wide range of sexual behaviors as acceptable. Thus, many activities currently defined as abusive, such as parental nudity, exposure to sexual activities of parents, or even fondling or caressing, all of which are often considered abusive and may account for 90% of all sexual experiences of small children (Plummer, 1981), would not be considered inappropriate by parents or the child who had been exposed to these from infancy. To be sure, this perspective does not address the issue of acceptance or responsibility for the consequences of sexual behavior that is implied by the concept of consent; nevertheless, the reality that most sexual practices between children and adults are neither exploitive nor misunderstood by children is an important qualifier to the perspective that *all* adult-child contact is child sexual abuse.

Ironically, the emergence of child protective services in response to parental abuse of children and the development of programs to treat and prevent sexual abuse coincide with changes in modern societies that threaten to eliminate childhood as a distinctive period of life. A large number of recent publications have noted a blurring of childhood and adult life due to communication media, especially television (Postman, 1982); to early education experiences (Suransky, 1982); and to changing patterns of family life (Schultz, 1977); all of which have eroded the dependency, segregation, and innocence of children. Causal linkages between the observation of sexual behaviors by a child and his or her initiation of personal sexual activity remain inadequately specified. For a child who has been exposed to television and movies during the past 20 years, however, sexual behaviors, pregnancy, childbirth, drug use and abuse, rape, physical and sexual violence, abortion, alcoholism, suicide, and the possibility of a nuclear holocaust—all problems that once were reserved for consideration by those recognized by adults (Meyrowitz, 1984; Rooke & Schnell, 1983), are no longer secrets. As a result, childhood for most children in modern societies probably is not as innocent and carefree as parents assume. Instead, it involves many experiences that accelerate learning—preschools, enriched curricula, and television programs, all of which result not only in social skills, but also in a basic knowledge of sexuality (Allgeier, 1982; Goldman & Goldman, 1982) and a curiosity and interest in it. Unfortunately, the new knowledge gained through mass media ultimately may provide a more violent and exploitative and a less humane and sensitive view of sexuality than that taught by peer groups.

Childhood Sexuality as a Right

The children's rights movement probably reached its zenith in the late 1960s and early 1970s. Despite its relative dormancy for over a decade, however, the idea of sexual rights for children has been and continues to be attacked from various sources, so that any discussion of childhood sexuality is viewed as a campaign by pedophiles to justify their behavior (e.g., Constantine & Martinson, 1981; DeMott, 1980). *Time* magazine, for example, noted: ". . . a disturbing idea is gaining currency within the sex establishment: Very young children should be allowed, and perhaps encouraged, to conduct a full sex life without interference from parents or the law" (1981).

Unfortunately such attacks obscure some important issues. First, this view tends to group and define all sexual activities of children as abuse, even those based on curiosity. In addition, there is an unstated assumption that sexual abusers are "dirty old men" who prey on strangers, a perspective that is contrary to the evidence of most research. Indeed, most studies report that at least three fourths of sexual abuse victims are abused by family members or friends who are loved and trusted. Those children who are victimized by strangers or acquaintances tend to be emotionally deprived, socially isolated, desirous of tenderness and affection, or largely ignored by parents (Finkelhor, 1981). In short, they are very vulnerable to attention and expressions of affection—"easy targets."

There appears to be little middle ground between those who advocate sexual rights for children and those who define all sexual experiences of children before an age of consent as abusive. As noted earlier, much research has documented that child sexual contact with an adult does not always result in negative emotional or social consequences. Some studies have reported that trauma, guilt, shame, and deception occur when force or coercion is used by the offender, or in situations in which the child has little sexual knowledge or defines sex as dirty or shameful, especially in families that are characterized by marital disputes or poor communication (e.g., Constantine, 1981; Colonna & Solnit, 1981; Emslie & Rosenfeld, 1983; Trepper & Traicoff, 1983). Some cases may produce a form of the "self-fulfilling prophecy"; that is, those who believe that a child is too immature for sex or who believes such experiences inevitably produce psychological trauma often create the circumstances and conditions that result in those problems for the child.

Fundamental human rights of children, for those who espouse this view, include sexual rights, or the right to choose to be sexual, that is, to engage in a range of sexual actions if they choose to do so. In the words of Mary Calderone (1977), these rights include the right to know about sexuality, the right to be sexual, the right of access to educational and literary materials, and the right of the unwilling or inappropriate audience to have its privacy or peace of mind protected.

Defenders of the sexual rights of children include those whose ideological position is that childhood sexual contact is beneficial to the child (Summit & Kryso, 1978). Noting that the physiological capacity for sexual activities exists in very young children, they argue that understanding the social significance of sex involves learning and experience that can occur at nearly any age if parents and other adults are able to approach sexuality in a rational and consistent manner. Thus nearly all sexual activities should be seen not as abusive, but in fact, as important experiences in the maturation process that enable children so exposed to recognize and avoid exploitative sexual relationships. Such a view has important implications for child protection services.

Recent materials for sexual abuse prevention have emphasized the rights of children over their bodies but have ignored some implications of such an approach. Illusion Theater in Minneapolis, for example, uses the TOUCH Continuum as a tool to identify "good," "confusing," and "bad" touches, and gives the message to children that ". . . NO ONE, whether stranger, acquaintance or relative, has the right to force or trick them into sexual contact or touch" (Anderson, 1981:2). The King County Rape Relief program in Seattle also emphasized the child's right to say NO to unwanted touch (Fay et al., 1979). Empowering children in this way may well prevent some unwanted sexual contact and exploitation. Nevertheless, the concept of right includes the issue of choice, and thus the emphasis on the *right* to say no implies that a child also has the right to say yes to wanted touches and the pleasures that go with them. For a sizable proportion of children, yes may be their choice if the concept of rights is emphasized. Further, if rights to say yes are recognized, is the right for children to initiate sexual behavior included as well? Such total control over one's body is a power that many parents are unwilling to grant to their teenagers, to say nothing of prepubertal children, in part because of the ambiguity about the final result of sexual activity, for example, sexual intercourse, the fear of premature sexualization of the child, pregnancy and unwanted parenthood, and the stigma of having an unmarried child become a parent.

Issues about children's rights, and the age at which they should be recognized, derive from a lack of consensus about competency, consent, and maturity, and how to define and measure them, as well as from different values about sex. The general confusion about values and appropriate sexual behavior—for children, youth, and adults—also presents ambiguous expectations to children, especially given the fact that most mass media expose people of all ages to the same images of sexuality. Emphasis on sexual rights for young children demands early education to provide knowledge and awareness of the meaning and responsibilities associated with sex. Only then can ignorance be eliminated, thus enabling children to prevent adult exploitation of them. Such a program could be effectively begun by parents before school age and continued throughout childhood.

Summary and Conclusion

Three perspectives regarding childhood sexuality have been presented here. Each reflects a different view of childhood and sexual behavior. In addition, definitions of sexual abuse that include all sexual contact between a child and an adult are not correct because they assume that all children who have sexual experiences are innocent victims of adult manipulation and exploitation that the children would have avoided had they been given the opportunity or been empowered to do so. Such interpretations *may* include a majority of cases, but clearly do not include all types of adult-child sexual activity. Further, conditions of modern life have weakened familial controls over children and have altered family patterns that have protected children from exposure to sexual activities in the past. In short, parents and child protection personnel cannot predict when abusive situations will occur or how to identify a sexual offender (Howells, 1981) and lack the ability to control the circumstances in which sex abuse may occur. Thus children are exposed to sexual activities and to sexual experiences that are assumed to have serious negative consequences but which cannot be totally eliminated, leaving children vulnerable to exploitation if they are not able to protect themselves.

Finally, despite the opposition to granting children rights to express their sexuality because of moral grounds or immaturity, the "best interests" of the child may be served by emphasizing children's rights. Parents and professionals should recognize that knowledge and information are the best ways to prevent exploitation of children. Extending rights to include decisions about sexual behavior demands that children have a more complete knowledge of sexuality and that adults examine their assumptions about the appropriate role of sexuality in childhood. Ultimately the best prevention is the child's ability to sense potential exploitation and to confront it. A society that cannot offer the social control over adults and children that existed a half-century ago provides choice de facto; appropriate choices can only be made with adequate information, suggesting that a program of education is mandatory.

A further implication is that the definition of sexual abuse can and should be revised to focus on *Unwanted* sexual contact between children and between children and adults. In one sense, this is a slight extension of current practice, because sexual contact is rarely reported if it is enjoyed by the child, and often is defined as abusive only after the child grows older or is exposed to information that causes him or her to revise earlier views.

Unfortunately, there is no simple answer to this complex issue. However, the importance of providing information about sex, of teaching values, and of sensitizing children to their possible exploitation cannot be overemphasized. Only then can the genuine problem of sexual abuse be addressed adequately.

References

Allgeier, E.R. (1982). Children's interpretations of sexuality. *Siecus Report, 10* (5/6),8–10.

Anderson, D. (1981). *Touch and sexual abuse: How to talk to your childrem.* Minneapolis, MN: Illusion Theatre, Sexual Abuse Prevention Program.

Araji, S., & Finkelhor, D. (1986). Abusers: A review of the research. In D. Finkelhor (Ed.), *A sourcebook on child sexual abuse.* Beverly Hills, CA: Sage.

Aries, P. (1962). *Centuries of childhood: A social history of family life.* New York: Alfred A. Knopf.

Berger, B.M. (1981). Liberating child sexuality: Communal experiences. In L. Constantine & F. Martinson (Eds.), *Children and sex.* Boston: Little, Brown and Company.

Bernard, F. (1981). Pedophilia: Psychological consequences for the child. In L. Constantine & F. Martinson (Eds.), *Children and sex.* Boston: Little, Brown and Company..

Bettelheim, B. (1969). *Children of the dream.* New York: Macmillan.

Bixler, R.H. (1983). Multiple meanings of incest. *The Journal of Sex Research 19*(2), 197–201.

Borneman, E. (1983). Progress in empirical research on children's sexuality. *Siecus Report, 12*(2), 1–5.

Browne, A., and Finkelhor, D. (1986). Initial and long-term effects: A review of the literature. In D. Finkelhor (Ed.), *A sourcebook on child sexual abuse.* Beverly Hills, CA: Sage.

Brunold, H. (1964). Observation after sexual traumata suffered in childhood. *Excerpta Criminologica, 4,* 5–8.

Byrne, D. (1977). The imagery of sex. In J. Money & H. Musaph (Eds.), *Handbook of sexology.* New York: Elsevier/North-Holland Biomedical Press.

Calderone, M.S. (1977). Sexual rights. *Siecus Report, 5*(1), 23.

Colonna, A.B., & Solnit, A.J. (1981). Infant sexuality. *Siecus Report, 9*(4), 1–2, 6.

Constantine, L.L. (1981). The effects of early sexual experiences: A review and synthesis of research. In L. Constantine & F. Martinson (Eds.), *Children and sex.* Boston: Little, Brown and Company.

Constantine, L., & Martinson, F. (1981). Childhood sexuality: Here there be dragons. In L. Constantine & F. Martinson (Eds.), *Children and sex.* Boston: Little, Brown, 1981.

Conte, J.R. (1985). The effects of sexual abuse on children: A critique and suggestions for future research. *Victimology, 10*(1–4), 110–120.

Conte, J.R. & Berliner, L. (1981). Sexual abuse of children: Implications for practice. *Social Casework, 63,* 601–606.

Curtois, C.A. (1979). The incest experience and its aftermath. *Victimology, 4*(4), 337–347.

Davis, K. (1949). *Human Society.* New York: Macmillan.

DeJong, A.R., Emmett, G.A., & Hervada, A.A. (1982). Epidemiological factors in sexual abuse of boys. *American Journal of Disease of Children, 136*(11), 990–993.

deMause, L. (Ed.). (1974). *The history of childhood.* New York: Psychohistory Press.

Demos, J. (1971). Developmental perspectives on the history of childhood. *The Journal of Interdisciplinary History, 2*(2), 315–327.

DeMott, B. (1980). The pro-incest lobby. *Psychology Today, 13*(10), 11–12, 15–16.

DSM–III (1980). *Diagnostic and Statistical Manual of Mental Disorders* (3rd ed.). Washington, DC: American Psychiatric Association.

Elwell, M.E. (1979). Sexually assaulted children and their families. *Social Casework, 60*(2), 227–235.

Emslie, J., and Rosenfeld, A. (1983). Incest reported by children and adolescents hospitalized for severe psychiatric problems. *American Journal of Psychiatry, 140*(6), 708–711.

Farber, E.D., Showers, J., Johnson, C.F., Joseph, J.A., & Oshins, L. (1984). The sexual abuse of children: A comparison of male and female victims. *Journal of Clinical Child Psychology, 13*(3), 294–297.

Fay, J., Adams, C., Flerchinger, B.J., Loontjens, L., Rittenhouse, P., & Stone, M.E. (1979). *He told me not to tell.* Renton, WA: King Co. Rape Relief.

Finkelhor, D. (1979a). What's wrong with sex between adults and children? Ethics and the problem of sexual abuse. *American Journal of Orthopsychiatry, 49*(4), 691–697.

Finkelhor, D. (1979b). *Sexually victimized children.* New York: Free Press.

Finkelhor, D. (1981) *Four preconditions of sexual abuse: A model.* Paper presented at the National Conference of Family Violence Research, Durham, NH.

Finkelhor, D., Gomes-Schwartz, B., & Horowitz, J. (1982). *Agency management of sexual abuse: Responses and attitudes from a survey of Boston professionals.* Paper presented at the annual meeting of the Massachusetts Psychological Association, Boston.

Fishman, S. (1982). The history of childhood sexuality. *Journal of Contemporary History, 17*(2), 269–283.

Friedrich W.N., Urquize, A.J., & Beilke, R.L. (1986). Behavior problems in sexually abused young children. *Journal of Pediatric Psychology, 11*(1), 47–57.

Frude, H. (1982). The sexual nature of sexual abuse: A review of the literature. *Child Abuse and Neglect, 6,* 211–223.

Furstenberg, F.F., Jr. (1976). *Unplanned parenthood: The social consequences of teenage childbearing.* New York: Free Press.

Gagnon, J. (1965). Female child victims of sex offenses. *Social Problems, 13*(2), 176–192.

Gagnon, J., & Simon, W. (1973). *Sexual Conduct: The Social Sources of Human Sexuality.* Chicago:: Aldine.

Goldman, R., & Goldman, J. (1982). *Children's sexual thinking.* Boston, MA: Routledge and Kegan Paul.

Gunderson, B.H., Melas, P.S., & Skor, J.E. (1981). Sexual behavior of preschool children: Teacher's observations. In L. Constantine & F. Martinson (Eds.), *Children and sex* (pp. 45–61). Boston: Little, Brown and Company.

Henderson, D. (1972). Incest: A synthesis of data. *Canadian Psychiatric Association Journal, 17,* 299–313.

Holt, J. (1974). *Escape from childhood.* New York: Dutton.

Howells, K. (1981). Adult sexual interest in children: Considerations relevant to theories of aetiology. In M. Cook & K. Howells (Eds.), *Adult sexual interest in children.* New York: Academic Press.

Husain, A., & Chapel, J.L. (1982). History of incest in girls admitted to a psychiatric hospital. *American Journal of Psychiatry, 140*(5), 591–593.

Ingram, M. (1979). Participating victims: A study of sexual offenses with boys. *British Journal of Sexual Medicine, 6,* 22–26.

Janus, M. (1983). On early victimization and adolescent male prostitution. *Siecus Report, 13*(1), 8–9.

Janus, S.S., & Bess, B.E. (1976). Latency: Fact or fiction. *The American Journal of Psychoanalysis, 36*(3), 339–346.

Johnson, W.R. (1977). Childhood sexuality: The last of the great taboos? *Siecus Report, 5*(4), 1–2, 15.

Kinsey, A.C., Pomeroy, W.B., & Martin, C.E. (1948). *Sexual behavior in the human male.* Philadelphia: Sanders.

LaBarbera, J.D., Martin, J.D., & Dozier, J.E. (1980). Child psychiatrists' view of father-daughter incest. *Child Abuse and Neglect, 4* 147–151.

Langfeldt, T. (1981a). Processes in sexual development. In L. Constantine & F. Martinson (Eds.), *Children and sex.* Boston: Little, Brown and Company.

Langfeldt, T. (1981b). Sexual development in children. In M. Cook & K. Howells (Eds.), *Adult sexual interest in children.* New York: Academic Press.

Lee, J. (1982). Three paradigms of childhood. *Canadian Review of Sociology and Anthropology,19*(4), 592–608.

Martinson, F.M. (1976). Eroticism in infancy and childhood. *The Journal of Sex Research, 12,* 251–261.

Mayer, A. (1983). *Incest: A treatment manual for therapy with victims, spouses and offenders.* Holmes Beach, FL: Learning Publications.

Meiselman, K. (1978). *Incest: A psychological study of causes and effects with treatment recommendation.* San Francisco: Jossey-Bass.

Meyrowitz, J. (1984). The adultlike child and the childlike adult: Socialization in an electronic age. *Daedalus, 113*(3), 19–48.

Mrazek, B., & Kempe, C.H. (Eds.). (1981). *Sexually abused children and their families.* Oxford: Pergamon Press.

Neuman, R.P. (1975). Masturbation, madness, and the modern concepts of childhood and adolescence. —*Journal of Social History, 8*(1), 1–27.

Parker, H., & Parker, S. (1986). Father-daughter sexual abuse: An emerging perspective. *American Journal of Orthopsychiatry, 56*(4), 531–549.

Platt, A. (1969). *The child savers: The invention of delinquency.* Chicago: University of Chicago Press.

Plummer, K. (1981). Pedophilia: Constructing a sociological baseline. In M. Cook & K. Howells (Eds.), *Adult sexual interest in children.* New York: Academic Press.

Pollock, L.A. (1983). *Forgotten children: Parent-child relations from 1500 to 1900.* Cambridge: Cambridge University Press.

Postman, N. (1982). *The disappearance of childhood.* New York: Delacorte Press.

Ramey, J.W. (1979). Dealing with the last taboo. *Siecus Report, 7*(5), 1–2, 6–7.

Renshaw, D.C. & Renshaw, R.Y. (1977). Incest. *Journal of Sex Education and Therapy, 3*(2), 307.

Rogers, C.M., & Terry, T. (1984). Clinical intervention with boy victims of sexual abuse. In I. Stuart & J. Greer (Eds.), *Victims of sexual aggression: Treatment of children, women and men.* New York: Van Nostrand Reinhold.

Rooke, P.T., & Schnell, R.L. (1983). *Discarding the asylum: From child rescue to the welfare state in English-Canada, (1800–1950).* Lanham, MD: University Press of America.

Rosenfeld, A.H. (1979). Incidence of a history of incest among 18 female psychiatric patients. *American Journal of Psychiatry, 136*(6), 791–795.

Ruch, O., & Chandler, S.M. (1982). The crisis impact of sexual assault on three victim groups: Adult rape victims, child rape victims, and incest victims. *Journal of Social Service Research, 5*(1/2), 83–100.

Russell, D. (1984). *Sexual exploitation: Rape, child sexual abuse, and workplace harassment.* Beverly Hills, CA: Sage.

Sandfort, T. (1982). Pedophile relationships in the Netherlands: Alternative lifestyle for children? *Alternative Lifestyles, 5,* 164–183.

Schmidt, G. (1977). Introduction, Sociohistorical perspectives. In J. Money & H. Museph (Eds.), *Handbook of sex-*

ology (pp. 269–281). New York: Elsevier/North-Holland Biomedical Press.

Schultz, L.G. (1980a). The sexual abuse of children and minors: A short history of legal control efforts. In L. Schultz (Ed.), *The sexual victimology of youth*. Springfield, IL: Charles C. Thomas.

Schultz, L.G. (1980b). The age of sexual consent: Fault, friction, freesom In L. Schultz (Ed.), *The sexual victimology of youth*. Springfield IL: Charles C. Thomas.

Schultz, L.G. (1980c). Diagnosis and treatment—Introduction. In L. Schultz (Ed.), *The sexual victimology of youth*, Springfield, IL: Charles C. Thomas. (1986).

Scott, R.L., & Stone, D.A. (1986). MMPI measures of psychological disturbance in adolescent and adult victims of father-daughter incest. *Journal of Clinical Psychology*, 42(2), 251–259.

Sgroi, M., (Ed.). (1982). *Handbook of clinical intervention in child sexual abuse*. Lexington, MA: D.C. Heath.

Summit, R., & Kryso, J. (1978). Sexual abuse of children: A clinical spectrum. *American Journal of Orthopsychiatry*, 48(2), 237–251.

Suransky, V. (1982). *The erosion of childhood*. Chicago: University of Chicago Press.

Synott, A. (1983). Little angels, little devils: A sociology of children. *Canadian Review of Sociology and Anthropology*, 20(1), 79–95.

Taubman, S. (1984). Incest in context. *Social Work*, 29(1), 35–40.

Time (1981). Cradle-to-grave intimacy. September 7, p. 69.

Trepper, S., & Traicoff, M.E. Treatment of intrafamily sexuality: Issues in therapy and research. *Journal of Sex Education and Therapy*, 9(1), 14–18.

Tsai, M., Summers, S., & Edgar, M. (1979). Childhood molestation: Variables related to differential impacts on pychosexual functioning in adult women. *Journal of Abnormal Psychology*, 88(4), 407–417.

Walters, D.R. (1975). *Physical and sexual abuse of children: Causes and treatment*. Bloomington, IN: Indiana University Press.

Wooden, K. (1976). *Weeping in the playtime of others: America's incarcerated children*. New York: McGraw-Hill.

Yorukoglu, A., & Kemph, J.P. (1966). Children not severely damaged by incest with a parent. *Journal of the American Academy of Child Psychiatry*, 5(1), 111–124.

Zelnick, M., Kim, Y.J., & Kantner, J.F. (1979). Probabilities of intercourse and conception among U.S. teenage women, 1971–1976. *Family Planning Perspectives*, 11(3), 177–183.

Double Vision

PENNY WARD MOSER

Why do we never match up to our mind's ideal?

IN 1959, I WAS THE BEST TEN-year-old baton twirler at the Dundee, Illinois, Fall Festival. I was also the skinniest baton twirler. In my sequined leotard, I resembled nothing more than a sparkly red clothespin. All through my childhood, I looked like one of the orphans in "You can help feed this child" ads. Except for my frizzy Tonette-waved hair, my knees were my most outstanding feature.

For the first eighteen years of my life, I was a human Cuisinart. I simply processed huge quantities of food and grew taller without changing very much at all. I was thirteen, 5'5" and 110 pounds when the horror of my predicament struck. There I was, awash in a sea of angora sweaters, nylon stockings and slow-dance parties, and I found myself without a body. I had arms and legs and all, but other girls were acquiring soft, round body parts that I lacked. Annette Funicello betrayed me when she suddenly sprouted huge breasts that made her name jiggle on her Mouseketeer T-shirt. Full-page ads for high-calorie potions cried out, "Don't let them call you skinny!" We all knew that what men wanted was Marilyn Monroe, Jayne Mansfield or Sandra Dee. I can still remember choking down triple helpings of mashed potatoes, butter and milk, trying to round out my body. I wasn't very successful, but did remain a hell of a baton twirler.

My how times have changed. Today, at 124 pounds, I think I'm too heavy, even though I barely make the low-normal weight range on standard height/weight charts. In the last twenty years, something has influenced me to believe that the ideal body is very, very thin. Indeed, the quest for a perfect, lean body has become a sort of national pastime. In one survey, 81 percent of adults said they were dieting to lose weight. Seven hundred thousand attend weekly Weight Watchers meetings. We trot dutifully to exercise classes and buy millions of copies of diet books, no matter how far-fetched the concept. We jam tapes into our VCRs: tapes from the fit and famous, from weight trainers, even from diet specialists who, at the push of the Play button, pop onto the TV screen and yell for twenty minutes.

There's nothing wrong with sensible dieting to keep obesity at bay. But today, for normal-weight and even slender people, dieting has taken on the aspect of war. The enemy is the stuff that scientists call adipose tissue and that the rest of the population knows as fat. Although there are growing numbers of men in the battalions, most of the foot soldiers are women. (Some studies show men tend to have positive images of themselves, even when they're overweight; women tend to look at themselves with a more negative eye.) In an effort to be thin, women are ignoring signals from their bodies, fighting against their genes and—increasingly—become casualties.

At the University of South Florida, associate professor of psychology Kevin Thompson, Ph.D., thinks he's figured out part of the problem: Our mind's eye makes us bigger than we really are. And the more we worry about our body images, the more we tend to mentally blow ourselves up. He's designed a test to show us how we see ourselves.

This is how I've come to be standing in a darkened little lab room, wearing a spiffy hot-pink leotard and tights. I am going to take Dr. Thompson's body-image test.

A graduate student fiddles with some little wooden dowels that slide on a board atop an overhead projector. When I move the dowels, I can narrow or widen the light beams projected onto the wall ten feet in front of me. To take the test, I stare at the wall and move the beams until I think I have projected my own body size. I am going to estimate the widths of key points on my body—the ones Thompson thinks people worry about the most: my face (across the cheekbones), waist, hips and thighs.

This should be easy. "Let's see," I think. "If I were standing there...." I move the light beams in and out. "Hmmm. My waist is—no, it's bigger. Not that big. Ah, this is right. But hey, my thighs aren't that wide, at least not if I push my knees together real hard. Now my hips...."

When I finish positioning the light beams, the grad student measures me with body calipers. At that moment, I officially fall into the legion of 95 percent of Thompson's "normal" women subjects—I had overestimated my body size. Only by about 4 percent, mind you, but still, my imagination had added about five pounds. Even so, I didn't do badly. Consider this: A study Thompson did showed that not only did 95 percent of women overestimate their body size, they overestimated by an average of 25 percent. Smaller women did the most overestimating. The most extreme overestimations, up to 75 percent, are among young women with eating disorders—anorexia and/or bulimia.

It was such a person who first led Thompson to his field of research. "In 1978, my first patient as a student therapist was a young woman who was 5′8″ and weighed 85 pounds. She pulled at the skin on her arms and said, 'Look! Don't you see how fat I am?' She was a nutrition major. That sort of hit me in the face." So what does this all mean? Thompson recently completed several studies to detail the causes of body-image distortion. He says, "It seems to be largely correlated with a lack of self-esteem. The better people feel about themselves, the less they tend to overestimate their size."

One psychiatrist I talked with suggested the Barbie doll first exposes our young psyches to slim-think. Barbie is impossibly long-legged and slim, with large, high, perky breasts. But nobody is going to grow up to look like Barbie. To prove this, I measured a Barbie doll, then measured myself. I used our hips as the constant, and with a little math found that for me to look like Barbie, my bust would have to grow twelve inches, my waist would have to shrink ten inches and I would have to be 7′2″.

Each person has, after all, about ten

Proof that self-image begins in our heads: Nine out of ten women studied overestimate their own body size

thousand taste buds that are on the side of the enemy. Early man, sitting around tearing apart a ground sloth with his bare hands, trying to stuff it down before a tiger came along and made dinner of it and dessert of him, probably didn't stop to think it would be better sautéed with onions. Man used to live quite nicely on a few handfuls of insects a day. If a woman had a few locusts for breakfast, a few more for lunch, and was looking forward to her husband throwing a few locusts on the grill for dinner, she probably wouldn't get up from her desk at three o'clock and pace around the office having a locust attack.

Why can't men and women just be happy being a little on the round side? Not health-hazard fat, but soft and cuddly? One reason may be that we have made sex into an art form. Something people do for a good time without, for the most part, making babies. A plump body, psychologists say, has historically been associated with maternity. To bear a healthy child, lug it around the field and nurse it—maybe through hard times—would take a woman with some adipose tissue reserve. In many cultures men still like their mates a little heavy to downright fat.

Women still have babies today, but American society thinks of sex as more recreational than procreational. And our lower infant/child mortality rate means a woman doesn't have to have ten kids to see that one lives.

It's theorized, then, that the lean woman symbolizes sex for fun, not sex for motherhood. The problem is that nobody has told her genes about this. A woman's biological systems are still primarily geared up for baby-making.

In the last few weeks before a baby is born, and during about the first year after, its body makes fat cells. Some people make fat cells during puberty; but, for the most part, a cute toddler has most of the fat cells she's going to have. Then—and here's the problem—as a girl grows and develops a lifestyle, so do her fat cells. Although science is only beginning to unravel the mysteries of fat cells, it is clear they vary from person to person, behaving as if they have minds—or, it seems to me, appetites—of their own.

A friend of mine, a retired physician, says we have all simply "entered an age of total narcissism." I'd like to think I'm not a part of that. But I am. The thin cues dance in my mind. They're ballerinas. Now that I'm forty, my body wants to gain weight I don't want it to. My mouth would like to send my hips and thighs more M&M's and french fries. Now if Thompson's body-image test is right, I'm not as big as I think I am, and I still have that five pounds to play around with. But in the back of my mind is the knowledge that I do not come from skinny people. And the rest of my life will be a contest between my genes and my jeans.

What College Students Want to Know About Sex

Everything that they don't know yet, which, according to the authors, amounts to more than you would think possible.

Sandra L. Caron, PhD,
and
Rosemarie M. Bertran, MSW

Sandra L. Caron is a health educator, Cornell University, Ithaca, NY. Rosemarie M. Bertran is a therapist at Fairmount Children's Center, Solvay, NY.

Do you have to have sex to have a baby?" "Is sex habit-forming?" "Is cunnilingus good for your teeth?" "Can you get pregnant from swallowing semen?" These and many other questions are commonly asked by young adults attending college, and they may come with these questions to your office, too.* Contrary to the widely held belief that college students know all about sex, the fact is that despite the widely available sexual literature, and explicit sex on television and in popular films, many students know very little about their sexuality. While some are reasonably knowledgeable and comfortable with their own sexuality, others, far more typically, are not. Worse, they're often embarrassed by what they perceive as their excessive ignorance, and fear ridicule if they openly seek the information they need.

Most typically, students come to college with many misconceptions and a host of questions about human sexuality, which reflect their particular stages of psychosexual development. Thus, if you quickly review the typical college student's levels of development, you'll better understand the source of these young adults' questions, and provide the answers and sexual information they seek.

*The questions quoted in this article are selected from among those raised by students in a human sexuality course at a large eastern university, and are in the students' own words. The course is popular and always over-registered; thus, the majority of students were juniors and seniors. Questions were collected anonymously on 3″ × 5″ cards on the first day of class during 1983–1986, and are generally representative of commonly asked questions.

College students' psychosocial/sexual stages of development

New choices and values. As a result of geographical separation from their parents and living in a new environment that invites and encourages reevaluation of values, most college students are suddenly confronted by many new social and sexual issues. They are thus forced to come to grips very quickly with such questions as "Who am I?" "What is my role in life?" and "What value systems do I want to align with?" If they can't answer these satisfactorily, they become confused, and may experience a psychological crisis. They realize that they are no longer subject to their parents' definition of their role, but this may heighten their bewilderment. Typically, issues of identity are presented in questions about sexual behavior, heterosexuality/homosexuality, and body image.

Common questions and their answers

Q: *Is it true that it is harder for a woman to orgasm than a man?*
A: I'm assuming you are referring to sexual intercourse versus masturbation. Although it may take a woman longer to become aroused, she tends to stay aroused longer than the man. Awareness and consideration of individual differences enhance lovemaking. Most women need stimulation of the clitoris. Intercourse is usually not the most effective way to get it. The vagina is often too far from the clitoris for intercourse alone to provide sufficient stimulation for orgasm.

Q: *Is it normal for a man, on occasion, not to be able to get an erection while being stimulated?*
A: Yes. Physical and emotional factors may interfere. A man who is overtired or overstressed is not at his best in anything. Be understanding and patient.

Q: *I have never had sex with someone of the same sex, but have often admired their bodies. Is this unusual?*
A: No, this is not unusual. All of us can admire both male and female human bodies with pleasure. A trip to an art museum demonstrates that the human body has great beauty. It would be sad if one could see beauty only in one sex.

Q: *Which is better in a penis—length or width?*
A: The vagina is quite adept at accommodating to penis size, and many women actually prefer stimulation around the clitoris and vaginal opening to deep thrusting, which some women find painful. Pleasant stimulation doesn't require a large penis (in width or length).

Q: *I have heard that each time a man ejaculates his sperm count decreases. Can a man become sterile from a ultra-active sex life?*
A: Sperm are continually being produced in the testes. Barring severe injury, you're likely to have a lifelong supply.

Q: *How can I tell if a woman is ready to make love?*
A: Women's bodies usually signal readiness with lubrication, pelvic motion, and greater intensity. Many women feel comfortable telling their partner when they are ready. If you are not sure, gently ask your partner to tell you when she is ready.

Q: *I am a virgin and my boyfriend isn't. He says it's okay that we're not having sex, but my friends say our relationship will never last. Should I be concerned?*
A: Since every person is unique, every relationship is unique. If you and your boyfriend are comfortable with your relationship why worry about what your friends say? If you're not comfortable, I suggest you talk it over with your boyfriend rather than your friends. It's ultimately up to you and him to decide.

Q: *How important are simultaneous orgasms?*
A: Not very. In fact, "separate turns" may be even more pleasurable, especially in a new relationship where you are getting to know each other. Most people find they are unable to fully experience their own sensations while trying to give pleasure to their partner.

Q: *Do men really enjoy giving oral sex, or do they do it just to please their partner?*
A: Some men (and some women) enjoy oral sex and some do not. That's a decision for you and your partner to talk about. Why don't you ask him?

Q: *Is it possible to become aroused and/or have an orgasm while under the influence of alcohol?*
A: Most drugs, including alcohol, numb sexual feelings and depress sexual function unless taken in very small amounts. Alcohol may loosen inhibitions or tensions to make intimacy more approachable, but at the same time may diminish physical awareness and make orgasm unlikely. Many a partygoer has been dismayed to find his performance impaired after an evening of heavy drinking.

Learning about intimacy. One of the tasks of young adulthood is to develop the capability of intimacy, the giving of oneself to another believed worthy of trust. Without intimacy in a relationship, the individual feels a sense of *isolation,* which leads to despair and loneliness. Typical areas of con-

Questions about body image, virginity, thoughts/fantasies, STDs, and body functions

Body image
Can a penis be curved and still be normal?
Why do womens' genitals differ so much from one woman to the next?
Which is better in a penis—length or width? How big is the normal penis?
Do big-breasted women get aroused quicker than others?
One of my breasts is definitely bigger than the other—is this a deformity?
What is a circumcised penis? Is it better?
Why do we have pubic hair?

Virginity
What exactly is a virgin? Can guys be virgins too?
Is being a virgin at my age (21-years-old) psychologically damaging?
Is a female virgin scared of sex or of the size of a big man's penis?
Is being a virgin the same thing as being frigid?
I'm a virgin and my boyfriend isn't. He says it's okay that we're not having sex, but my friends say it will never last. Are they right?

Thoughts/fantasies
Is it strange to think about having sex with my brother?
Is my relationship in trouble if I think of other people when I have sex with my partner?
I've never had sex with someone of the same sex, but have often admired their bodies. Is this unusual?

Sexually transmitted diseases (STDs)
What is a sexually transmitted disease? What is gonorrhea?
Can you tell the type of person who gets sexually transmitted diseases?
How is AIDS contracted?
Would I know if I had a sexually transmitted disease?
Can a sexually transmitted disease kill you?
Can you really get a sexually transmitted disease from a toilet seat?
Can oral sex cause you to get an infection?
Who do you go to see if you think you might have a sexually transmitted infection?
I got a vaginal infection, but I didn't have sex. How is that possible?

Body functions/parts
Why do I have a moist spot on my underwear?
Do guys menstruate?
What's the purpose of menstruation?
Should women douche? How is it done?
Why do vaginas smell differently?
Does the G-spot exist? Where is it?
Does it hurt when a guy has an erection?
I don't get anything out of having my breasts touched—is there something wrong?
Do you really "lose it" if you don't "use it"?
What is the most sensitive part of the penis?
Is it normal for a man, on occasion, not to be able to get an erection while being stimulated?
How and where do you locate a woman's clitoris?

cern therefore focus on relationships, social issues, and the mysterious "opposite sex."

The physician's essential role in sexual counseling
College students' questions directly reflect their success (or lack) in mastering these stages of development. They involve rela-

tionships, masturbation, virginity, homosexuality, intercourse, orgasm and ejaculation, birth control and pregnancy, and sexually transmitted diseases.

A review of questions commonly asked by college students indicates that they fall into two broad categories: those based on the need for specific factual information, and those that reflect the students' intense concern with their physical/sexual normality. While you may well be surprised at the often enormous lack of factual knowledge, you'll need to present a review of basic facts about reproductive physiology and sexuality in such a way that you don't point out the student's ignorance and so threaten his/her self-esteem. For example, you can use such phrases "As you probably already know . . . " and "As you may be aware . . . " as tactful introductions to factual information. If you have any doubts about the extent of the student's knowledge, it's best to err on the side of giving too much rather than too little information.

Fears concerning "normality." The gnawing fear of adolescence, "Am I normal?" often haunts college students as well. In this age group, however, the fear focuses specifically on sexual concerns and intimate relationships. For despite the generally more liberal attitudes about sex, prevailing social customs and sexual taboos continue to prohibit the free exchange of information about sexual topics. Thus, aside from hasty comparisons in the locker room, few young people have the opportunity to compare their bodies to those of others. Such questions as "Am I normal?" most often refer to "Am I the right shape and size?" Still another concern for normality relates to sexual experience, eg, "Am I the last

Questions about masturbation, anal sex, homosexuality, and oral sex

Masturbation

Exactly what is masturbation?

Do girls masturbate?

What is mutual masturbation?

Is masturbation considered abnormal if it continues into adulthood?

Is it bad to still masturbate if you have a girlfriend?

Is it normal to masturbate every day since age 13?

How often do college men masturbate on the average? College women?

Why do some women masturbate with cucumbers?

Do girls who masturbate ejaculate like boys?

Anal sex

What is anal sex?

How safe is anal sex? Is it dangerous?

Can you get diseases from anal sex?

Is it normal to enjoy anal sex with a woman?

How did man get the idea for anal sex?

Homosexuality

Is a guy who masturbates a homosexual?

Can homosexuals identify other homosexuals in a crowd?

When I masturbate I think of my friend. I just picture him and think about him. I don't want to have sex with him, or with any man. Does my masturbation fantasy mean that I'm gay?

How can two people of the same sex be attracted to each other sexually?

Besides oral sex, what do lesbians do in bed?

What causes homosexuality? Is there a cure?

Oral sex

What is oral sex?

Do men really enjoy giving oral sex, or do they do it just to please their partner?

What do people mean when they talk about body fluids being exchanged during oral sex? Are these fluids harmless if ingested?

Is cunnilingus good for your teeth?

What percentage of sexually active women enjoy swallowing during fellatio?

Describe oral sex—is it painful or dangerous?

Is semen good for acne if swallowed?

Is oral sex unhealthy?

virgin in the universe?," "Is it okay not to want sex all the time?," and "I never pass up a sexual opportunity—is this unusual?"

Sexual techniques. Students

Questions concerning pregnancy/birth control

Can you become pregnant before/during/after your period?

Can you get pregnant the first time you have sex with someone?

When is the best (safest) time for a woman to have sex without the worry of pregnancy?

Can you get pregnant from swallowing semen?

Is it possible to get pregnant without actually having sex, and if so, how close can you come?

Do you have to have sex to have a baby?

How long does the penis have to stay in the woman's vagina to let sperm out?

What is a rubber?

What is the safest method of birth control?

How do you use the Pill? How does it work?

How do you put a condom on?

Do you swallow foam? Before or after sex?

What is a diaphragm? What does it look like?

How soon after conception does a woman know if she is pregnant?

Questions about relationships and the other sex

How do you French kiss?

How far can a "good girl" go on a date?

Do guys know where a woman's clitoris is?

Do guys get turned on as much by girls with small breasts as opposed to girls with big ones?

Is it possible to be in love with two people at once?

How do you know when you're in love?

How long does it take to fall in love?

What do guys look for in a girl?

Do guys really have friendships like girls (or do they just talk about cars/sports/etc)?

How can you tell if your partner is responding to your touch without having a running commentary?

Can a guy who you date rape you?

Why can't men ever take "No" for an answer?

When my boyfriend won't take "No" he goes ahead and has sex with me anyway. It upsets me; he says it's OK. Is it?

and over again: "Is it okay if she's on top?," "What's the right way to get a woman ready for intercourse?," and "Is it okay that I enjoy masturbating with a vibrator?" Finally, many young people need to be reassured that their thoughts and fantasies are within normal limits. Generally speaking, all thoughts and fantasies may be regarded as normal, unless they are obsessive.

Confidentiality. This is a crucial issue for college-age students, who are now entitled to the confidential status given to adults. If you have known and treated these students since they were infants, you may find it difficult to see them as the adults they now are.

Guiding the student toward sexual maturity

Young people in general and college students in particular are sensitive about their need for adequate information and their newly achieved status as adults. It will take tact and warmth—essential qualities in the delicate balancing act of recognizing that a young person's questions may reveal a shocking lack of information and providing that information without condescension. Similarly, it is important to use correct terms for body parts and functions. Accurate terminology not only permits more precise communication; it also enables people to talk more freely and with less embarrassment.

In order to make the student feel that you are "approachable," try to convey the attitude that all questions are permitted, and that "There's no such thing as a dumb question." Commend the student for seeking accurate information in a straightforward way.

If you prefer to counsel students only about physical facts, and feel uncomfortable talking

are insatiable in their attempts to learn about sexual techniques, reflecting a prolific interest in reading how-to books and viewing steamy films. Amazingly, the same questions are asked over

Common questions about intercourse

Is it true that during sex people get stuck together like dogs?
Does it hurt to have sex?
How is the penis put into the woman? Where?
Can a guy's penis be too big for a girl?
Are you supposed to only have sex in the dark?
What is the most enjoyable sexual activity?
Do my parents still have sex? I find this hard to believe.
Is too much sex bad for your penis?
Can too much sex endanger your health?
Do certain foods make you horny?
Until what age can you have sex?
Can you have sex after age 100?
Is sex during a girl's period messy? Does the tampon get in the way?
Can you jeopardize your longevity by having too much sex?
Does the average woman think about sex as much as the average guy, or do guys just verbalize thoughts more?
Do girls really need foreplay?
Are certain positions better than others?
How do you know if you are ready to have sex?
Is sex the most important thing to college guys? Why?
Does penis size matter in having sex?
How come I'm always horny or thinking about sex?
During sex, how can I tell if the man is ejaculating if he doesn't tell me?
What's the youngest age one can have sex?
Is it possible to have sex once you become pregnant?
Is it unusual that I don't always need sex?

about relational issues and the psychological dynamics of sex, you may wish to refer the student in need of this information to the college health service or a local family planning agency, such as Planned Parenthood.

Remember: the most predictable fact about college students' questions about sex is that they will have them. If you are familiar with these students' psychosocial/sexual stages of development, are approachable, and anticipate their frequently surprising questions, they will also feel free to ask them, and with your advice, progress more contentedly along the road of healthy sexual development.

Recommended readings

Boston Women's Collective: *Our Bodies, Our Selves.* New York, Simon and Schuster, 1984.

Calderone MS, Johnson EW: *The Family Book About Sexuality.* New York, Simon and Schuster, 1980.

Carrera M: *Sex: The Facts, The Acts, and Your Feelings.* New York, Crown, 1981.

Erikson EH: *Identity: Youth and Crisis.* New York, Norton, 1968.

Zilbergeld B: *Male Sexuality. A Guide to Sexual Fulfillment.* Boston, Little, Brown & Co, 1978.

Questions about orgasm/ejaculation

I've heard that each time a male ejaculates his sperm count decreases. Can a man become sterile from an ultra-active sex life?
Is it true that men must have ejaculations fairly regularly for physical reasons?
If you have too many ejaculations can you run out of sperm quicker? At what age?
Can you ever hit bottom?
Is it possible to become sexually aroused and/or have an orgasm while under the influence of alcohol?

Why do guys reach orgasm after 30 seconds? Is it my fault?
Can orgasm be reached just by holding hands/being with someone you love?
Why do girls hold off having an orgasm longer than guys?

Is there such a thing as multiple orgasm?
I think I've had an orgasm, but I'm not sure. How do I know?
Do men ever really "come in their pants"?
What's the difference between the terms "coming" and "orgasm"?

Is it unhealthy for a male to have several orgasms within a limited amount of time?
How long should a male take to come?
Is it true that once you've reached a certain point or have gone so far, a guy must ejaculate? Does it hurt?
What is the maximum number of times a guy can come in one night?
How important are simultaneous orgasms?

Masturbatory Behavior in College Youth

Joan D. Atwood, Ph.D., C.S.W.
Coordinator, Marriage and Family Counseling
Graduate Programs
Hofstra University
Hempstead, NY 11550

John Gagnon, Ph.D.
Professor of Sociology
State University of New York, Stony Brook
Stony Brook, NY

Abstract

A number of areas of investigation are relevant to the consideration of adolescent and young adult masturbatory practices. First it is necessary to determine the incidences and rates of the activity. Currently there is a genuine lack of data on masturbatory incidences and frequencies and thus a need to do some "social accounting." How common is masturbation among contemporary youth? How frequently do they masturbate? These are the principle questions addressed in this paper. In addition to incidences and rates, we examine trends in masturbatory conduct: do the incidences and frequencies of the activity change over time? The specific time periods that are examined are (1) retrospectively reported high school masturbatory behavior and (2) masturbation during each year in college.

Inquiries into the area of human sexuality that we would now recognize as having some scientific merit began approximately 70–80 years ago. However, while other areas of sociological inquiry accumulated both researchers and publications with great rapidity (for example, the study of social stratification, the family, or juvenile delinquency), research in the field of human sexuality has been comparatively retarded. As a result, the accumulated body of knowledge in this area tends to be relatively sparse and in some cases, for example, masturbation, nearly nonexistent.

In addition, there has been a shift in the character of sex research in two major ways. First, there has been movement from discussions of clinical cases to survey research and laboratory research. As a result, the more recently accumulated body of data tends to be more systematically gathered than that of the past. Second, there have been diferent approaches to these kinds of issues. Traditionally, sexual conduct was largely explained in biological, psychological, or clin-ical terms. Often interest was focused on what might be called deviations from "normal" sexuality, such as prostitution or homosexuality, without a consideration of what normal might be. More recently, there has been a steady increase in interest by sociologists in these areas of research. Even so, for the most part, sociological sex research has also considered primarily issues of sexual deviance. Concomitantly, there has been little sociological work on the coventional socio-sexual development of heterosexuals and sex as a normal component of the life cycle, except for studies of premarital coitus.

Masturbation is among the least studied aspects of sexual activity. Aside from the Kinsey (1948, 1953) data, and a few other smaller surveys, there is almost no systematic information about masturbation. And there is little information available on the role of masturbation in socio-sexual development. Further, no empirical studies have examined the relation of masturbation to the nonsexual components of the life cycle.

When considering adolescent and young adult masturbatory practices, certain areas of investigation are relevant. But first it is necessary to determine the incidences and rates of the activity. Currently, there is genuine lack of data on masturbatory incidences and frequencies and thus a need to do some "social accounting." More importantly, however, it is necessary to look at the developmental aspects of masturbatory behavior (as individuals move from high school through college) in order to examine the impacts of these earlier sexual activities on later sexual and nonsexual aspects of life. To date, an analysis of masturbation in the context of normal socialization has not been performed. The analysis of the data for this study will be the first attempt at examining these relationships.

From *Journal of Sex Education & Therapy,* Vol. 13, No. 2, Fall/Winter 1987, pp. 35-42. Copyright © 1987, American Association of Sex Educators, Counselors, and Therapists. Reprinted by permission.

5. SEXUALITY THROUGH THE LIFE CYCLE: Youth and Their Sexuality

As a result of survey data gathered by Gagnon and Simon (1973) on the role of sexuality in normal adolescent development, there exists a body of data that will allow us to locate masturbation within this larger social psychological context. The data gathered on a sample of male and female college students included data on a wide range of topics relating both to sexual and nonsexual aspects of conduct. Contemporaneous information about these attributes was procured for both the college years and retrospectively from the period either pre-college or specifically in high school. Thus, there are data on masturbation for students in each of the four years of college as well as information at least in retrospect on the same topics prior to their entry to college.

The incidence of masturbation among individuals and how frequently they masturbate depends upon many factors, but perhaps the most important is whether the individual is a man or a woman. Because of Kinsey's (1948, 1953) prior finding of very high differences between men and women in the incidences and rates of masturbation, throughout the present paper data will be analyzed separately for men and women.

Sample

The data for this research come from a national sample of college students secured in 1967 at 12 selected colleges. These institutions are representative of all accredited 4–7 year public and private colleges or universities with enrollments over 1,000 which are co-educational, nonsectarian, and not predominantly black. A sample of 100 students, stratified by gender and year in school, was drawn from each college. Black students were deleted from the final set of cases, leaving 1,177 white students for this analysis. The resulting sample of 1,177 students contains 593 males and 584 females (see Table 1).

The sampling frame was designed by Seymour Sudman of the National Opinion Research Center (NORC) and interviewing was performed by the NORC staff. The interviewers were all female, primarily between 30 and 40 years of age. Face-to-face interviewing methods were employed.

There are several problems involved in the present study. First, the fact that the interviewers were all female creates a possible problem of concealment or enlargement of answers due to embarassment or boasting. This problem, of course, is not unique to the present study and should be considered by all sex researchers. However, the interviewers used in the present study had previous training and experience in the administration of questionnaires. Furthermore, they were inured to the sensitive topic of sexuality by engaging in discussions on this topic with the research staff prior to interviewing. These training procedures enabled the interviewers to establish a warm, comfortable atmosphere, thereby minimizing the possibility of distorted responses.

A second problem with the present study has to do with cohort effects. For example, the current freshmen may not resemble the current seniors when they were freshmen. Third, there may be a migration problem. There may have been selectivity in dropout of members of the senior class during the four years of college—usually due to academic problems. However, in a review of the studies investigating the impact of college upon students, Feldman and Newcomb (1969) reported that conclusions about average freshman-senior changes drawn from longitudinal methods generally agreed with cross-sectional methods. Fourth, since the pre-college data are retrospective in nature, they are possibly subject to some distortion. There are no differences in recall over the 4 years of college, however (that is, freshmen and seniors report the same rates of masturbation during adolescence), which suggests some stability in recall. Thus the present findings are restricted to college students, who are respresentative of the upwardly mobile and educationally stable middle class.

Despite these problems, inherent in any study of a college population, the study of college students does provide some opportunities. First, it is a population in which to examine various aspects of socialization after childhood, and second, these aspects can be studied in a relatively controlled environment.

Results

The gender differences that were apparent in the Kinsey studies were also evident in the present study. Whereas Kinsey reported that approximately 93% of the men and 40% of the women in the college-educated group masturbated by age 25, in the present study, approximately 93% of the men and 48% of the women masturbated by age 25 (see Figure 1). Note that although the present study was conducted almost 20 years after the Kinsey studies, using different sampling techniques, the findings are strikingly consistent.

Age At First Masturbation

Table 2 represents the accumulative incidence of year of onset of masturbation. The specific question that the college students were responding to was:

For males: Masturbation is very common in our society. How old were you the first time you were able to make yourself come to climax by masturbating yourself?

For females: How old were you the first time you were able to make yourself come to climax by touching your

Table 1
Sample Group by Gender and College Year

	Males (% of sample)	Females (% of sample)
Freshmen	151 (25.5)	138 (23.6)
Sophomores	145 (24.5)	151 (25.9)
Juniors	150 (25.3)	147 (25.2)
Seniors	147 (24.7)	148 (25.3)
Total	593 (100)	584 (100)

Figure 1
Accumulative incidence of masturbation for men and women

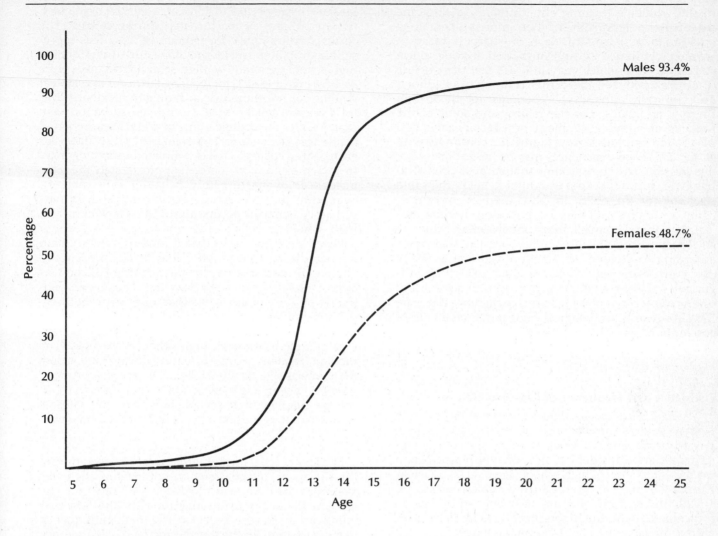

own breasts or sex organs (by masturbating yourself) after you began to menstruate?

The median age for male entrance into masturbatory conduct was 13; the corresponding figure for women is 14. These results for women, however, must be interpreted cautiously. Because of the upper age limit of the present study, we are unable to ascertain whether or not women enter into masturbatory conduct at later ages; also, because of the phrasing of the question, women were unlikely to report any masturbation before menstruation. Kinsey (1953) reported that women tend to learn about masturbation over the entire life cycle, including adulthood and old age. He reported that for women there is a slow but steady increase until the age of 35 in the number of those engaging in masturbation. Incidence of masturbation thereafter remains constant throughout the life cycle. In contrast, the onset of masturbation for men appears to be an adolescent phenomenon, with 80% of the men masturbating by about age 15. From Table 2, however, it is also clear that those women who learn to masturbate do so only slightly after men. (There is only a 1-year difference.)

Table 2
Accumulative Incidence of Year of Onset of Masturbation

Age	Males		Females	
	N	%	N	%
6	1	.18	0	0
7	1	.36	0	0
8	3	.91	1	.35
9	3	1.46	0	.35
10	16	4.38	0	.35
11	24	8.76	6	2.48
12	95	26.10	31	13.47
13	154	54.20	50	31.20
14	122	76.46	65	54.25
15	60	87.41	50	71.98
16	34	93.61	33	83.68
17	14	96.16	17	89.71
18	12	98.35	14	94.67
19	7	99.63	7	97.15
20	1	99.81	5	98.92
21	0	99.81	3	100.00
25	1	100.00	0	100.00
	548		282	

Of those who masturbated, only 11% of women began after age 17, indicating that there is something in the women's learning environments at this time that makes at least some of them more vulnerable to masturbation. Also, this lack of sharp increase in women's entrance into masturbation at adolescence as compared to males' may indicate that there is less of a break between the earlier training of childhood and the early adolescent experience for them than there is for males. For the males, and some of the females, at adolescence, many new factors come into play, so to emphasize developmental continuity with earlier childhood experiences may be misleading. Also, it is possibly wrong to assume that because childhood behavior appears sexual to adults it holds the same meaning for the child. In sum, there is, of course, some continuity with the past, but upon entering adolescence there is much more involvement with the social aspects of sexuality, an involvement that varies according to gender. As Gagnon and Simon (1973) point out, "This period between 14 and 20 (the end is variable) is when young people begin to act out and practice the conventional scripts which organize the physiological, psychological, and social elements of conventional social responses."

Incidence and Frequency of Masturbation

The high school period. Exact comparisons with the Kinsey studies cannot be made for the high school period because in the present study the college students reported incidences and rates of masturbation for the entire span of high school (ages 14–17), whereas Kinsey's data were grouped from adolescence to 15, 16–20, and so forth. Because Kinsey's groupings do not coincide with the high school ages in the present study, direct comparisons cannot be made.

In the present study, 88% of the men and 40% of the women reported that they masturbated during high school. The median frequency of masturbation for men was slightly more than once per week (see Table 3). The corresponding figure for women was less than once per month. The gender differences that were apparent for incidence of masturbation were also evident for rates of masturbation. Not only do more men masturbate during high school, but they also masturbate more frequently.

The college period. The gender differences that were apparent for the high school period were also evident for the college period. Approximately 80% of the men reported that they masturbated during college. The corresponding figure for women is 32%. This represents a drop in the incidence of masturbation from the high school period. (The high school incidences were 88% for men and 40% for women.) In order to establish whether or not there was a change in incidence over the 4 years of college, incidences of masturbation were examined for the specific 4 time periods. These reported incidences of masturbation remained fairly stable for each year in college. That is, within gender categories, freshmen and seniors reported approximately the same incidences of masturbatory behavior (see Table 4), suggesting that the decrease in those engaging in masturbatory behavior occurs during the transition from high school to college and not over the 4 years of college. Men also masturbated more frequently than women during college (see Table 5). The median frequency of masturbation for men during college was approximately once every 2 weeks. The corresponding figure for women is less than once per month.

Thus, for men, there is a decrease in how many individuals masturbate and how often they masturbate as they move from high school to college. (The median frequency of masturbation during high school for men was slightly more than once per week.) Among women, fewer engaged in masturbatory activity in college than in high school; however, the rates of masturbation remained fairly stable for the 2 time periods.

In order to see if masturbatory rates changed during the 4 years of college, frequency of masturbation was examined for each year in college (see Table 6). The median frequency of masturbation for the first-year men was once every 2 weeks. The median frequency of masturbation for the fourth-year men was also once every 2 weeks, suggesting that the decrease in rates of masturbation occurred during the transition from high school to college. Once the transition into college was made, the rates remained fairly stable. Among women, the median frequency of masturbation remained stable across the 4 years of college—less than once per month. Rates of masturbation, then, among women, remained constant not only as they moved from high school to college, but also during the 4 years of college. Thus although rates of masturbation for the women were lower than that of the men, they were generally more stable.

Table 3
Frequency of Masturbation during High School by Gender

Frequency of masturbation	Males (%)	Females (%)
Daily	5.2	0
Twice per week	26.4	6.9
Once per week	27.6	6.9
Once every 2 weeks	12.7	8.7
Once per month	15.2	20.8
Less than once per month	12.9	56.7
N =	519	231

Table 4
Incidence of Masturbation for Each Year in College by Gender

Year in school	Males (%)	Females (%)
Freshmen	76.8	31.8
Sophomores	72.6	21.8
Juniors	86.6	31.9
Seniors	82.9	41.2
N =	477	185

Change Over Time

At this point in the analysis, it is possible to examine specific patterns of masturbatory behavior. For example, if frequency of masturbation during high school is crosstabulated with frequency of masturbation during college, change over time can be examined in more specific detail. Table 7 for men and Table 8 for women represent the frequency of masturbation during high school by the frequency of masturbation in college. For those men who masturbated both in high school and college, overall rates of masturbation either decreased (43.0%) or stayed the same (30.0%). For women, masturbation rates generally stayed the same (24.8%) or stopped altogether (20.0%; see Table 9).

If the percentages are examined for each year in school, the overall male trend remains constant (see Table 10). Rates of masturbation decrease from high school to college or remain the same. For women, overall rates of masturbation either remained the same or stopped altogether. This was true for the first-through third-year women. The group of women most likely to report that they stopped masturbating in college was the sophomores (41.2%). For senior women, however, rates of masturbation either stayed the same (27.6%) or women began masturbating (25.0%). This lends support to the Kinsey finding that women enter into masturbation throughout adolescence and even later.

The median frequency of masturbation for the men who masturbated only in college was once per month, indicating that this group did not differ from those who masturbated both in high school and college. Men and women, then, who only began masturbation in college masturbate as often as those who have been masturbating all along.

For the group of individuals who only masturbated during high school, the median frequency for men was once per month. The corresponding figure for women was less than once per month. This indicates a difference in rates among men. Those men who eventually stopped masturbating when they entered college masturbated less frequently during high school than the rest of the men who masturbated during this time period. The rates for women remained constant.

The Nonmasturbators

Earlier it was found that approximately 93% of the men and 48% of the women in the present sample masturbated to orgasm at some point in their lives.

Table 5
Frequency of Masturbation during College by Gender

Frequency of masturbation	Males (%)	Females (%)
Daily	3.1	0
Twice per week	18.9	6.5
Once per week	20.7	7.0
Once every 2 weeks	19.7	10.3
Once per month	17.8	21.6
Less than once per month	19.7	54.6
N =	477	185

Table 6
Frequency of Masturbation in College by Year in College and Gender

	Males				Females			
Frequency	Fresh. (%)	Soph. (%)	Jr. (%)	Sr. (%)	Fresh. (%)	Soph. (%)	Jr. (%)	Sr. (%)
Daily	1.72	4.6	2.3	4.1	0	0	0	0
Twice per week	18.9	14.7	20.0	21.3	4.5	12.1	6.4	4.9
Once per week	21.5	23.8	22.3	15.6	9.1	6.1	6.4	6.6
Once every 2 weeks	25.0	18.3	16.9	18.8	15.9	0	12.8	9.8
Once per month	13.8	17.4	20.0	19.7	31.8	24.2	10.6	21.3
Less than once per month	19.0	21.1	18.5	20.5	38.6	57.6	63.8	57.4
N =	116	109	130	122	44	33	47	61

Table 7
Frequency of Masturbation during High School by Frequency of Masturbation during College for Males

Frequency of masturbation of high school	Frequency of masturbation during college						
	Daily (%)	Twice per week (%)	Once per week (%)	Once every 2 weeks (%)	Once per month (%)	Less than once per month (%)	Not in college (%)
Daily	33.3	40.7	14.8	3.7	0	3.7	3.7
Twice per week	2.2	40.1	29.2	19.0	5.8	3.6	0
Once per week	0.7	9.1	26.6	23.8	21.0	9.8	9.1
Once every 2 weeks	0	7.6	6.1	28.8	22.7	25.8	9.1
Once per month	0	0	6.3	8.9	26.6	36.7	21.5
Less than once per month	0	0	6.0	6.0	10.4	35.8	41.8
Not in high school	3.6	21.4	14.3	10.7	14.3	14.3	21.4

Table 8
Frequency of Masturbation during High School by Frequency of Masturbation during College for Females

Frequency of masturbation of high school	Frequency of masturbation during college					
	Twice per week (%)	Once per week (%)	Once every 2 weeks (%)	Once per month (%)	Less than once per month (%)	Not in college (%)
Twice per week	31.3	37.5	0	12.5	12.5	6.3
Once per week	6.3	12.5	12.5	31.3	12.5	25.0
Once every 2 weeks	5.0	5.0	20.0	25.0	35.0	10.0
Once per month	4.2	4.2	14.6	22.9	43.8	10.4
Less than once per month	0.8	0	1.5	9.9	36.6	51.1
Not in high school	3.9	3.9	7.8	7.8	41.2	35.3

Table 9
Distribution of Change in Masturbation by Gender

	Male (%)	Female (%)
Only before high school	1.1	6.4
Only in high school	11.9	20.0
Decreased	43.0	18.4
Stayed the same	30.3	24.8
Increased	10.0	10.6
Only in college	4.0	11.7
N =	547	282

This finding illustrates that for some men, the person who has never masturbated is more unusual than those who have. Among women, masturbation was just as likely to occur as not. It may be true that those men who never masturbated and those women who masturbated as often as the men represent individuals who have unusual characteristics. For example, Greenwald (1971) stated, "I have observed that many people who have severe sexual problems have never masturbated" (p. 54). McCary (1973) stated, "Indeed those who do not practice masturbation or have never done so, are far more likely to be suffering from an emotional or sexual problem than those who have masturbatory experience" (p. 156). Kaplan (1974) stated, "In contrast to men, where the absence of adolescent masturbation raises a suspicion of psychiatric disturbance, women who have never masturbated are not necessarily pathological. Even so, absence of masturbation is a frequent finding in the histories of women who later complain of orgasmic difficulties" (p. 110). Spitz (1962) reported that "those persons who first learned of the practice of masturbation during late adolescence (the 20's) tended to be emotionally disturbed." These ideas will be explored in later papers.

The nonmasturbators were asked why they never masturbated (see Table 11). The reason most often cited for not masturbating was "no urge" (about three fourths of each gender), with a substantial proportion (about 40%) mentioning immorality. These percentages are remarkably similar to those reported by Kinsey (1948, 1953). In his sample, 44% reported no masturbation because it was morally wrong and 81% had not done it because they had no need to do so.

In order to ascertain whether or not the nonmasturbating students had any interest at all in self-stimulation, they were asked the following question:

During high school, how often did you find yourself aroused without coming to climax when thinking about sex, or looking at or touching your own body?

This question was asked for the high school as well as the college period. Nonmasturbatory arousal during high school occured among another 5.2% of the men and 21.8% of the women. The median frequency of arousal during this period was once every 2 weeks for men and less than once per month for women. For men, this represents a lower median frequency than was present among those who masturbated.

During college, 5.1% of the men reported that they were sexually aroused without masturbating. The median frequency of sexual arousal for the nonmasturbating men during this period was once per week. The corresponding figure for women is once per month. Among the men, these figures represent an increase in frequency of sexual arousal from the high school period. Among women, they represent an increase in both reported incidence and frequency of sexual arousal, perhaps indicating increased sexual interest and the possibility that masturbation will occur in the future.

Discussion

The earlier onsets, higher incidences, and higher frequencies of masturbatory activities for men than for women reflect different patterns of sociosexual development for the two genders. These differences stem from different role expectations about sexuality for men and women. Therefore, our understanding of the acquisition and practice of sexuality can be enhanced if we try to relate what persons do sexually within the context of what they are expected to do as men and women.

For example, during adolescence, the sources of information about masturbation are less common for women. Kinsey (1953) reported that the most common way women learned about masturbation (57% as compared to 28% of the men) was through self-discovery.

Table 10
Distribution of Change in Masturbation in College by Year and Gender

	Males				Females			
	Fresh. (%)	Soph. (%)	Jrs. (%)	Srs. (%)	Fresh. (%)	Soph. (%)	Jrs. (%)	Srs. (%)
Before high school	2.2	0.8	0.7	0.7	6.0	10.3	4.2	5.3
Only in high school	11.2	16.7	9.7	10.3	28.4	41.2	29.6	14.5
Decreased	41.8	40.9	45.5	43.4	16.4	17.6	19.7	19.7
Stayed same	31.3	27.3	31.0	31.6	25.4	17.6	28.2	27.6
Increased	10.4	12.9	7.6	8.1	17.9	5.9	11.3	7.9
Only in college	3.0	1.5	5.5	5.9	6.0	7.3	7.0	25.0
N =	134	132	145	136	67	68	71	76

Table 11
**Reported Reasons Why Students Did Not Masturbate
by Gender**

Reported reasons	Males		Females	
	%	(N)	%	(N)
Immoral	40.0	(30)	42.7	(213)
Health	6.7	(30)	5.2	(213)
Appearance	3.3	(30)	2.8	(213)
Shame	8.7	(30)	29.6	(213)
No urge	77.4	(31)	71.7	(212)
Other	13.3	(30)	17.5	(212)

For most men (75%) masturbation is learned from either verbal or printed sources. Learning about masturbation often takes place in a peer-dominated environment, and the peer group functions differently for men and women. Through the peer group, men and women learn to attach different meanings to their sexuality. Men learn to be more genitally oriented; women learn more romantic orientations and therefore tend to be more heterosocial in the sociosexual development. Women are trained to protect their virginity whereas men are given social rewards for being sexual. Men more often discuss specific sexual acts with peers; women are more concerned with discussing boyfriends, love, and marriage and the overall relationship usually takes precedence over simple sexual release. The consequences of this differential socialization is that women learn to be sensual while men learn to be sexual. She learns to be charming and attractive, the object of male desires; however it is he, not she, who is "supposed" to have these desires. Thus she learns to be more relationship-oriented while he learns more sexual orientations. In the all-male groups of early adolescence there is a pattern of learning and developing attitudes that are quite explicitly sexual toward the self and toward females. The homosexual groups of females during early adolescence are commonly learning a less sexual and more affectional version of the world.

A further point is that many women frequently do not know that they should or could have orgasms. Thus the sexually emerging adolescent receives the full brunt of this polarizing societal creation, the double standard.

During later adolescence, interpersonal relations with the opposite sex take precedence over the homosocial groups that were common during adolescence. The movement into later adolescence and the concomittant increase in opportunities for sociosexual activity can be described as a situation in which males—committed to sexuality and less trained in the rhetoric of romantic love—interact with females who are committed to romantic love and relatively untrained in sexuality.

By the time individuals reach college they are aware of well-defined social expectations for adult sexual conduct and most are beginning to act out conventional sociosexual behaviors. For both genders, there is a legitimation of heterosexual activity by peers along with an increase in the amount of sexual activity. For men, masturbation now generally represents an activity of early adolescence or a behavior that occurs when a sexual partner is not available. This redefining of proper age-graded sexuality may serve to depress masturbatory incidences and rates during the college period. It is perhaps possible that for a small percentage of individuals, masturbation decreases or stops altogether because early masturbation could be exploratory in nature and people may not realize the social stigma attached to the activity. When they learn the negative social definitions, they may stop.

Women, on the other hand, often learn about their own sexual responsiveness in a heterosexual situation—through mutual masturbation, petting, or sexual intercourse. For some women, this represents the first encounter with sexuality via their genitals and may serve to encourage curiosity and self-exploration.

For both the men and women in the study, the college period is the time for all these changes. It is also a period when some loss of privacy occurs. Usually, there are at least two students to a room; bathrooms are more or less communal, and it is not very often that students find themselves alone. Masturbation, however, is a solitary activity. Thus, some students may reduce masturbation when they enter college simply because of the lack of opportunity to be alone.

Masturbation is the first sexual activity for many individuals. Its incidences and rates are affected by a complex array of factors—two of which are differential socialization and differential definitions of social and sexual situations.

References

Feldman, K. and Newcomb (1969). *The impact of college on students*.

Gagnon, John H. & Simon, William. (1973) *Sexual conduct: Social sources of human sexuality*. Chicago: Aldine Publishing Co.

Gagnon, John H. (1977). *Interaction of gender roles and sexual conduct*. Revised Version of a Paper Written for the Conference on Sex and its Psychosocial Derivitives. Stanford University, Jan. 28–30.

Greenwald, H. (1971). Sex away from home. *Sexual Behavior, 1* (6) 8–14.

Kaplan, H.S. (1974). *The new sex therapy*. New York: Brunner/Mazel.

Kinsey, A.C., et al. (1948). *Sexual behavior in the human male*. Philadelpia: Saunders.

Kinsey, A.C., et al. (1953). *Sexual behavior in the human female*. Philadelpia: Saunders.

McCary, J.L. & McCary, S. (1973). *Human Sexuality*. Belmont, CA: Wadsworth.

Spitz, Rene A. (1962). Autoeroticism reexamined: The role of early sexual behavior patterns in personality formation. *Psychoanalytic Study of the Child. 17*, 283–315.

● Experts have discovered that, thanks to changes in both our bodies and our attitudes, women can—after the first blush of youth—look forward to ever more satisfying intimate relations.

SEX Better After 35

BY SHERRY SUIB COHEN

My mother-in-law worried incessantly about her daughter's lack of interest in marriage at an early age.

"You'd better meet a man before you lose your bloom," she daily and direly warned. "Bloom" to all who knew my mother-in-law was her euphemism for an irresistibly appealing state of youthful and romantic sexuality. My mother-in-law was no dope about sexuality: she met her man when she was in full bloom at 18, and held his interest for more than 50 years of marriage.

It was clear to my mother-in-law that the "losing of bloom" occurred somewhere in the early twenties, but it wasn't nearly as clear to the rest of the family, who indulged in spirited arguments about when the loss of bloom really occurred. You lost your best bloom at 25, thought a cousin. Bloom definitely lasted till 30, claimed another. It was my husband who settled the matter one day, to our infinite relief.

"You don't even *find* your bloom until you're thirty-five," he pronounced with the air of one who knows. I could only smile a self-satisfied (but modest) smile.

Because he's right. So many women over 35—even considerably over 35—overwhelmingly concur that their sex lives are more richly textured and satisfying than ever before. More in touch with their bodies, less inhibited about expressing desires to partners, infinitely more confident, women beyond midlife find that sex gets better and better! Bloom doesn't flee at all: rather, with proper nurturing, it becomes a fully mature, gorgeously erotic blossom.

A number of factors, both biological and psychological, determine sex drive and experts offer new evidence in both arenas suggesting that sex after 35 can be even more pleasurable than in the early years. While virtually every expert agrees that social and emotional influences bear far greater responsibility than physical influences for intensified sexual interest, the biological players in the passion game are, nonetheless, compelling.

● **Hormones are in our favor**

The higher the level of the sex hormone testosterone in the body, the stronger the sex drive for both men and women, maintains Niels Lauersen, M.D., associate professor of obstetrics and gynecology at the Mount Sinai School of Medicine in New York. Estrogen, the female hormone, naturally suppresses or counteracts the effects of testosterone in young women. But as a woman ages, her estrogen level gradually diminishes while her testosterone level stays constant. The fortunate result: Since there's less estrogen to suppress the testosterone, says Dr. Lauersen, "it's definitely possible that many women will feel sexier and more passionate as the years pass."

● **Only as men and women pass their mid-thirties do their mismatched sex drives operate in tandem**

"Biology has planned that girls are far less sexual than boys . . .," says Barry McCarthy, Ph.D., a professor of psychology at American University in Washington, DC, clinical psychologist at the Washington Psychological Center. "[young men] don't need much from their partners; their primary aim is to score and achieve ejaculation. Women, on the other hand, need more intimacy and touching to connect deeply, but often, in their early sexual experiences, they simply don't get what they crave.

. . . male and female sexual tracks are miles apart."

As men age, however, says Dr. McCarthy, to their astonishment, just thinking about sex often no longer gives them an erection. They need more tactile help from their partners. "To the happy surprise of many women in their late thirties and forties," concludes Dr. McCarthy, "men and women finally begin to merge onto the same sexual track. They need each other's attentive stimulation, caring and tenderness for successful lovemaking. Since the best aphrodisiac is an involved and aroused partner, sex after thirty-five becomes a slower, more foreplay-rich kind of lovemaking."

● **Females also reach orgasm more readily when they're older**

Many women say they have had to grow into deeply orgasmic pleasure by trial-and-error sexual relations over the years. As they get used to *expecting* arousal, it becomes easier to achieve orgasm. Jerry Lanoil, Ph.D., assistant professor at New York Hospital, Cornell Medical Center, Westchester Division, and a psychologist in private practice in Manhattan who leads sex-therapy programs, says, "it's sort of a self-fulfilling prophecy. If you have confidence that pleasure will come, it usually does.

"Some women report a certain bodily relaxation after childbirth that appears to make it easier for them to achieve orgasm," Dr. Lanoil adds. "This new easiness melds with their partners' lessening need to prove themselves 'studs' or sexual athletes. Because an over-forty male is not so obsessed with ejaculation, part of his attention can be transferred from his penis to his partner."

Self-worth Encourages Satisfaction

Of far greater consequence than the biological factors that pave the way for better sex after 35 are the enormous psychological influences. Sex no longer exists as the secretive, frantic gropings of adolescence or the often selfish, conquest-driven sessions of early adulthood. Perhaps most significant, men and women, graduated from the first blush of young-adult sexuality, tend to take more time for lovemaking.

And "time" is the operative word, says Robert N. Butler, M.D., a Pulitzer Prize winner, former director of the National Institute on Aging and Brookdale Professor of Geriatrics and Adult Development at the Mount Sinai Medical Center in New York. The passage of time is what acts as a comprehensive dictionary for those interested in learning the sensual language of love.

"Actually, men and women learn two languages of love at different stages of life," explains Dr. Butler. "The first is biological and instinctive and occurs in the early years of sex. It is a tumultuous language, volatile, urgent, explorative and bent on self-discovery. But, ah—the second language of love . . .

"It is a far more lyric expression," says Dr. Butler, "that is not instinctive and must be learned as people mature. It means clearing up old grudges and irritations so you don't waste your sexual energy in negativity. The secret of learning the second language of love lies in learning how to give, how to listen. It implies sensitivity and playfulness as well as passion; laughing, teasing, sharing secrets as well as fears. It involves a responsibility to maintain romance—even soupy romance. It is gloriously sexual."

And, continues Dr. Butler, sometimes "it need not involve the sex act at all."

Sex without the sex act?

Absolutely, says Laura Shapiro Kramer, 39, and married to the same man for ten years.

"Intercourse alone is not how I think of sex anymore," she says. "I think of sex as the warm embrace before we go out. Or the way, sometimes in bed, we kiss and rub those places on each other that we know ache after a long day. Or feet touching in a restaurant, or holding hands when we walk, or—best of all—the way he gets up from a chair for me when he's been waiting and I arrive. I find that irresistibly sexual.

"Before I was married I had a fairly extensive sexual life," she continues. "Then I married. At first, having kids was frightening to me. I was trying to work too, and it threw my professional life off balance. That really affected our sex life. Also, in my twenties and early thirties I didn't know how I wanted life to be so I never paid attention to the moment in which I lived. We were both pretty fragmented."

But in this past year, Laura says, something changed. "I started to focus in, really pay attention to all my riches. I think I fell in love with my life and that made it easy to find romance with my husband. We grew up this year and be-

gan to pay attention. It's like a muscle we're trying to stretch.

"For the first time," she says, "it's very important to me to be beautiful in his presence. He's learned to say, 'you look fantastic' and I love to hear it. There are no performances, but there is heavy-duty romance. The kisses, the holding, the appreciation of each other: There's nothing like it for the deepest sexual fulfillment."

For Victoria Secunda, "Finally being satisfied with myself as a mother and as a professional writer has had a great deal to do with my increased sexual pleasure." After a failed first marriage, Victoria finds her late forties with her second husband, Shel, a photographer, infinitely more sexually exciting than her earlier years. "I have greater control over my life and feel more secure about who I am. The first time around, I suddenly had to shift from being the world's oldest living virgin to being a sexually informed wife. In reality, I was awkward and unsure of myself in bed, and had a hard time expressing my own wants and needs."

Victoria is tall, beautifully elegant, and she can't help but be aware of her magnetic personal presence. Is she worried about the physical effects of aging on her looks, on her sexuality?

"I'm in much better shape now than I was fifteen or twenty years ago because I don't take my good health for granted as I used to. I eat sensibly, work out and know that when I come in from a three-mile run covered with mud, my husband will still find me sexy."

Her husband has been listening to her say this. "She's *particularly* sexy when she's covered with mud," he says.

Taking the Time for Pleasure

One of the psychological pluses of sex after 35 is the increased aptitude for *patience* that many women develop. Susan Brody is in her mid-forties and has learned the virtues of 'try, try again.' A legal secretary when she was married at 20, she found herself in a marriage where it was clear that she was more interested in sex than her husband was.

"Nothing like that for giving one a secure self-image," she comments. "I remember fantasizing about sex constantly, but the reality was that I was sleep-deprived and often in bed by eight-thirty. My children were small and made enormous demands on me. Privacy was often nonexistent."

After she was divorced at 41, Susan took more control of her life. She left her job, which gave little chance for independent action, and became an entrepreneur in the personnel business. And she met a terrific guy. Was the sex terrific? No. Very far from terrific.

"Twenty, even ten years before, I wouldn't have given him a second chance. But, in my forties, I tried harder to make it work."

"See him, but forego the sex," advised a friend.

"That lasted about 10 minutes," notes Susan. "Crummy advice."

"We were new at this singles game and both of us pretty inexperienced for all of our experience. Still, because we were a little older, we didn't have to start from the beginning, but from somewhere in the middle. He was so nice and so interesting."

They decided to go away for a weekend. Not bad. Then they went away again. Better.

"Within one month of the time when I thought sex with this man was so unsatisfying," says Susan, grinning, "we were wonderful together. Once we grew to like, then love each other, our sexual pleasure intensified a thousandfold. Now, we're married—and expect to be marvelous in bed when we're ninety."

"It's amazing," says Sheila Jackman, Ph.D., director of the Division of Human Sexuality at the Albert Einstein College of Medicine in New York, "how the mid- and post-childrearing ages often bring a sexual rejuvenation to women who were just too busy to bother much before. It's almost as if women, having done a decent job with their families, feel more competent to trust themselves in the sexual arena. They no longer have to look to friends and mates to ask, sometimes silently, 'am I OK?' "

This ability to relax extends to the bedroom. A playful quality in lovemaking often eludes many men and women when they are young and green. They take their sexuality too seriously. Many are trapped in a cinema version of what sex is supposed to be, darkly mysterious, even a lot of work to preserve all that mystery, all that pressing of the right buttons. No one ever told them that you could laugh when you were making love—in fact, that mirth was both provocative and sensual. As one woman in her sixties puts it, it seems ironic that the farther one gets from childhood, the freer one feels to "horse around."

And finally, we come to a ticklish subject: menopause. According to Joseph W. Goldzieher, director of endocrine research and a professor in the department of obstetrics and gynecology at the Baylor College of Medicine in Houston, Texas, "This is a time when women burst free from previous sexual stresses because they are liberated from worry about contraceptives, cramps, missed periods and childrearing."

As one lusty 58-year-old put it, "I consider menopause God's reward for a lifetime of service." Yet another woman referred to her postmenopausal years as a "magical bank account: the more it was drawn upon, the higher the balance of pleasure in the account."

Certainly, there are some physical effects of female aging that are not quite such a reward to enhanced sexuality. In addition to the fabled hot flashes, when ovaries stop manufacturing estrogen, decreased vaginal lubrication and thinning vaginal walls may lead to coital discomfort. Still, estrogen-replacement therapy is available and many specialists, Dr. Goldzieher among them, feel that most women of menopausal age

not only benefit sexually but also substantially cut their risks for developing osteoporosis and heart disease later in life if they opt for such treatment.

Still, uneasiness about aging lingers. I was unable to find a woman who would have it in print that she's gone through the "Big M." There was nothing left to do but come out of the closet myself. My husband and I are both in our fifties, and I have just gone through menopause. Nothing to it, mashed potatoes, has been my experience. Talk about an overrated event.

Our bodies, to look at them closely,

may be a tad lumpy, and we are sometimes surely a trifle creaky. But when we climb into bed, these same bodies, familiar with each other and with making love, can anticipate every cue and respond to it. We have learned to trust each other, not to steal the scene or hog the stage. Every now and then we throw in a new trick to keep the act fresh.

These bodies dive into the act of love with more grace and confidence than ever before. Is there sex, better sex, after 35? You better believe it. And it just keeps getting better.

Good Sex Makes Good Marriages

EDWIN KIESTER, Jr.

EDWIN KIESTER, Jr., is a contributing editor of 50 PLUS who specializes in medical topics. He wrote "Stand Up and Fight," the story of nursing home advocate Pat McGinnis.

LET'S CALL THEM couple A. They had been married for nearly 30 years, and for most of that time their sex lives had been joyously active. She used to joke that she had only to undo the top button of her blouse and her husband became aroused. But lately, when she undressed he scarcely seemed to notice. Sex became disappointingly irregular, then rare. The once wonderful relationship deteriorated into frustration and unhappiness.

Not so with couple B. She, too, had passed 50 and no longer had the figure of a prom queen. His hair was gray, and his face was lined with wrinkles. Yet the two radiated happiness and (she confided to friends) their sex lives had never been better.

Why the difference between the two partnerships?

The answer is simple, according to Dr. Herant Katchadourian, a Stanford educator, lecturer, psychiatrist and author of "50: Midlife in Perspective" (W.H. Freeman). "For all their age and experience," he says, "couple A had not learned some basic facts of life—that as the body changes with age, sexual response changes, too." In other words, they expected to react like newlyweds in the bodies of 50-year-olds, and when they didn't, they became frustrated and unhappy. Couple B, on the other hand, had learned to go with the flow. Recognizing

that time had wrought changes in their bodies as it had in their lives, they adjusted and adapted, in bed as elsewhere, secure and affectionate in their relationship.

The stories of both couples are based on actual case histories, and serve to illustrate how lovemaking is transformed with time. "Sex in the young is fast and furious," notes Dr. Katchadourian. "It is ignited easily and fizzles out like fireworks. Some of us grow old but never outgrow this style. But men and women who grow in sexual sophistication along with the years can find vast new vistas of sexual satisfaction in midlife. With the passage of time, it is possible to expand sex into a different and in some ways a richer experience, which amply compensates for whatever deficits are incurred."

The message is clear: for willing learners who make the effort, sex after 50 can be better than ever.

The bearded Katchadourian, 55, is hardly the only voice preaching the gospel of better sex to the 50-plus generation. "Doctor Ruth" Westheimer, for example, has become a television celebrity with her spirited commentary on the subject. The best-seller list is crowded with books purporting to disclose the secret of lifelong sexual satisfaction with the same partner. Indeed, for a subject once taboo, discussed either in whispers or snickers, older sex has come forcefully out of the closet. And as the 50-plus generation continues to grow in size, we can expect to hear more expert advice on the topic.

Few experts, however, will have the professional and academic cre-

dentials to match Katchadourian's. In 20 years, the Syrian-born, Beirut-raised scientist and scholar has taught an entire generation of Stanford students the ABCs of sex. His straightforward, no-nonsense lectures in human biology, combining elements of anatomy, physiology, psychology and social responsibility, have become the most popular in the university's history: more than 10,000 students have taken his courses.

Katchadourian himself became a "sex expert" almost by accident during the so-called sexual revolution of the 1960s. "We had this situation, as did many colleges, of increased sexual activity, student pregnancies, venereal disease, and we felt students needed to know more in order to cope," he recalls. "I served as assistant professor of psychiatry at the time, and I was appointed to a committee to discuss our responsibilities in the area. We came back and recommended teaching a course in human sexuality. And someone said, 'Well, Katchadourian, why don't *you* teach it?' I protested that I didn't know anything about the subject, had never even taken a course in medical school. One of the deans said, 'I've been at Stanford for 20 years, and not knowing anything about a subject has never stopped anyone from teaching it before.' So I went off to the Kinsey Institute for study, and the next fall we started the course with 70 students. The second year we had 400. The following year, 1,000 showed up, and we had to transfer the lectures to Memorial Auditorium."

Later, Katchadourian added a

From *50 Plus*, July 1988, pp. 26-29. Copyright © 1988 by Retirement Living Publishing Co., Inc.

course in adult development to "prepare students for their lives after college—what to expect physically and psychologically at ages 30, 40, 50 and later." And about the time he himself passed 50, he turned his attention to the concerns of his contemporaries. In lectures to alumni and off-campus groups, he explored the emotional and physical changes of reaching mid-life—with particular emphasis on the role of sexuality.

To attend a Katchadourian lecture is to discover anew that sex is a popular topic, regardless of the age of the audience. At a recent Stanford-sponsored conference in Los Angeles, for instance, several hundred men and women attended to hear him discuss "Sex and Intimacy in Midlife." Some appeared to be as young as 30; others might have been in their 70s. Many attended as couples, and some held hands during the lecture.

Katchadourian carefully points out that many of his listeners are already practicing what he preaches. "It would be easy to overstate the problems and ignorance about middle-aged sex," he says. "The fact is, I see heads nodding in the audience, as if to say, 'What's all the fuss about? We already knew that.'" Sadly, however, a combination of misunderstanding and lack of knowledge threatens the relationships of others.

Take the case of couple A. When her husband no longer looked admiringly at her, the neglected Mrs. A might understandably have felt that she had grown old and unattractive. That could be a partial explanation, but a minor one. The most likely explanation lies with Mr. A, not his wife.

"If a young man sees a half-naked woman, he gets an erection very fast, without touching her or her touching him," notes Katchadourian. "As men become middle-aged, they lose the ability to respond to purely psychological stimulation. A typical couple is not aware of this perfectly normal change. So a woman blames herself for their diminished sex life—she thinks she's lost her sexual attractiveness. Yet if she were to physically stimulate her husband, she would find him as re-

sponsive as ever. If he asked her to, that is. Unfortunately, people don't talk about these things, even people married for 25 or 30 years. They try to solve the problem by sweeping it under the rug."

As a result, Katchadourian says, a self-fulfilling prophecy is set up. A woman feels that because she's past 50, she's no longer attractive, and her husband's presumed disinterest "proves" it. He, in turn, finds that he's no longer aroused by the sight of his wife's body; that "proves" he's getting old. They've been conditioned to believe such changes will happen with age, and so their sexual interest wanes. Yet the sex lives of other couples of equal years, like couple B, simply improve, like fine wine.

How does human sexual response change with the years? And how can couples become more like Mr. and Mrs. B, and less like the unfortunate Mr. and Mrs. A? Here are Dr. Katchadourian's answers.

Physical changes: The changes in sexual response simply mirror those going on elsewhere in the body. "We are all born with a certain reserve of physical function that is more than adequate to last us through life, but declines as we get older," Katchadourian says, "You can't perform at the peak you did 20 years earlier. The same thing happens with respect to sexual function. Nothing drastically changes; the genital organs continue more or less as they are, and orgasm is no less pleasurable than in the past. However, definite changes in sexual response *do* take place.

"Oddly, people often recognize and accept the physical changes but not the sexual ones," adds Katchadourian. "A 50-year-old man can still be athletic, but he no longer expects to break Olympic records. The sexual adjustment is really no different from the overall adjustment that we all have to make to the fact that time has a certain impact on our bodies. The real impact depends on how we react to the changes and whether we help or, in some ways, hinder what the body is trying to do."

Two physiological phenomena are central to sexual arousal, performance and orgasm. Vasoconges-

tion, in which more blood enters an area of the body than comes out, accounts for the male erection and the swelling of genital tissues in the female. Muscular contractions dictate the sexual movements that culminate in orgasm. With age, however, the circulatory flow lessens; the muscles relax. Men have more difficulty attaining and maintaining an erection. Erection may be softer and at less of an upright angle. Orgasm may be less forceful, and slower to achieve. It becomes more difficult for a man to become aroused again after intercourse.

Hormonal changes are involved, too. A woman usually has reduced vaginal lubrication after menopause. The loss does not interfere with sexual desire, but may cause irritation during intercourse. Estrogen supplementation and/or the use of lubricating gels can prevent this problem.

Physical illness can also handicap the 50-plus relationship. Diabetes can cause impotence, arthritis often makes intercourse painful, and even the fear of illness, as in the case of a cardiac patient who worries about overtaxing his heart, can take a toll. Medication for chronic illness also may dampen sexual response, as do alcohol abuse, anxiety and depression.

It should be noted that although physical changes occur in everyone, there is no magic age at which they take place. Nor is the rate of decline the same in every person.

Psychological changes: "Both sexes undergo a sort of mid-course correction," Katchadourian explains. For example, many women become more assertive sexually, possibly because there is no longer a fear of pregnancy. Others might feel that, having finished raising the children, they can now concentrate on their own needs again.

As for men, they often become, in Katchadourian's words, "more mellow." Kinsey Institute research has shown, for example, that men after 50 think less about sex and have fewer sexual fantasies than when they were younger. For some men, after having achieved their anticipated station in life (or given up the struggle), it is no longer necessary to be aggressive. For the first time, they enjoy being led and comforted.

Unless poor sex is only one symptom in the decay of the entire relationship, most of the changes noted above can heighten sexual enjoyment. Take the matter of duration of orgasm. The problem of the younger male is often premature ejaculation—Katchadourian's "fast and furious" fireworks. The older man's greater staying power can bring more pleasure to both partners. "If an older male is able to calm down and pace himself," Katchadourian says, "he can become a fabulous sexual partner." Moreover, because sex occurs less often, each episode can achieve an optimal high. And a closer balance in assertiveness between the sexes takes some of the pressure off the male to perform. "He no longer feels the need to be a virtuoso," notes Katchadourian.

For those couples for whom sex has fallen into a predictable routine, midlife may be the time to change the rules. "When the children are gone and the couple is alone in the home, why must sex be postponed until the eleventh hour at night?" Katchadourian asks. "Why not early mornings? Why not weekend afternoons?" He cautions, however, that the very routine may be comforting to some people. "You have to combine the solace of routine and stability with the excitement of doing things a bit differently. For some people, sex in a different surrounding is stimulating and highly desirable. Others are perfectly happy in their own bedrooms."

Somewhat the same advice applies to innovations in techniques and positions. Katchadourian's own textbook, "Fundamentals of Human Sexuality" (Holt, Rinehart and Winston) describes and illustrates coital positions; Katchadourian also recommends "The Joy of Sex" (Crown) by Alex Comfort. But, he adds, books and manuals aren't the whole answer to an improved sex life: "There is some value in reading about what other people say should be done, but ultimately you have to do it yourself. It's like reading a Michelin guidebook. It tells you that there's a two-star restaurant in Paris and what kind of food is served there, but that's not the same as going there and tasting the food for yourself."

For some couples, the need for innovation can be fulfilled by fantasy. Sexual daydreams do no harm, Katchadourian says, *if* the partner doesn't mind. "If a man wants to fantasize that there's another woman in the room, or the woman to dream of a romantic interlude with another man on a tropical island, well, imagining things or making up stories costs nothing if it doesn't disrupt the relationship. But if the partner perceives the fantasy as a hidden wish—today you talk about it, tomorrow you do it!—that can become threatening and unacceptable."

> *For some people, sex in a different surrounding is stimulating. Others are perfectly happy in their own bedrooms.*

Exercising your imagination is one thing; to keep sexually active, Dr. Katchadourian believes that it is just as important to maintain physical vitality. "Taking care of yourself makes a great deal of difference," he says. "That goes for whether you're overweight, in bad physical condition, or a heavy smoker or drinker. Moreover, keeping sexually active seems to be the most important factor of keeping sexually alive. It's the same old story—use it or lose it, and that's true even for older persons who are alone. After all, there is masturbation. People still feel a little uneasy even talking about that because it sounds like kid stuff. But so far as keeping the body in running order is concerned, there is no difference between intercourse and masturbation. It's a worthwhile activity in and of itself."

In summing up his philosophy, Katchadourian notes that "people who are in a committed relationship basically should do what they should have been doing all along: anticipate as much as possible what change is going to take place, make the necessary adjustments, and don't fight the advance of time—go with it.

"After 50," he adds, "you have more time, more money, more leisure, and the greater opportunity of working on the relationship in all its aspects—the requirements of courtship, health, and of working together. Of course, sex has to be put into context, fit into the overall frame of life. It's more important for some people, less important for others. People can make it the very basis of day-to-day living, others don't bother with it.

"We're beginning to have a different perception of what it means to be 50, 60, 70," Katchadourian concludes. "When you see a 70-year-old man in great physical shape, you're no longer surprised. Who plays tennis these days? Who jogs? Who skis? Who rides bicycles? Being older by no means is incompatible with any of these—nor is it incompatible with an active sexual life."

WHAT DOCTORS AND OTHERS NEED TO KNOW

Six Rules on Human Sexuality and Aging

Richard J. Cross, MD

Dr. Richard J. Cross is a member of the SIECUS Board of Directors. He is a Certified Specialist in Internal Medicine, and Professor Emeritus at the Robert Wood Johnson Medical School, New Jersey.

Most of us find that our definition of old age changes as we mature. To a child, anyone over forty seems ancient. Sixty-five and older is the common governmental definition of a senior citizen, and it is the definition that I will follow here, although the author who is 73 long ago found it not entirely acceptable. There is, of course, no specific turning point, but rather a series of gradual physical and emotional changes, some in response to societal rules about retirement and entitlement to particular benefits.

Demographically, the elderly are a rapidly growing segment of the population. In 1900, there were about three million older Americans; by the year 2000, there will be close to 31 million. Because of high male mortality rates, older women outnumber men 1.5 to 1, and since most are paired off, single women outnumber single men by about 4 to 1. By definition, the elderly were born in, or shortly after, the Victorian era. Most were thoroughly indoctrinated in the restrictive attitudes toward sex that characterized these times.

The Six Rules

In my opinion, the care of the elderly could be significantly improved if doctors and other health workers would remember and apply the following six, simple, basic rules:

1. All older people are sexual.

They are not all sexually active, as is also true of the young, but they all have sexual beliefs, values, memories, and feelings. To deny their sexuality, is to exclude a significant part of their lives. In recent decades, this simple truth has been repeatedly stated by almost every authority who has written about sexuality, but somehow the myth persists that the elderly have lost all competence, desire, and interest in sexuality, and that those who remain sexual, particularly if sexually active, are regarded as abnormal and, by some, even perverted. This myth would seem to have at least three components. First, it is a carryover of the Victorian belief that sex is dangerous and evil, though necessary for reproduction, and that sex for recreational purposes is improper and disgusting. Second, is what Mary S. Calderone, SIECUS co-founder, has called a tendency for society to castrate its dependent members: to deny the sexuality of children, of the disabled, of prisoners, and of the elderly. This, perhaps, reflects a subconscious desire to dehumanize those whom we believe to be less fortunate than ourselves in order to assuage guilt feelings. Third, Freud, and many others, have pointed out that most of us have a hard time thinking of our parents as being sexually active, and we tend to identify all older people with our parents and grandparents. For whatever reason, it is unfortunate that young people so often deny the sexuality of those who are older. It is even more tragic when older people themselves believe the myth and then are tortured by guilt when they experience normal, healthy, sexual feelings. Doctors and other health workers need to identify and alleviate such feelings of guilt.

How many older people are sexually active? In an admittedly somewhat biased sample, Ed M. Brecher reported in *Love, Sex, and Aging*, (Little, Brown and Company, 1984) that the proportion of both males and females who are sexually active declines, decade by decade, ranging from 98% for married men in their 50s to 50% for unmarried women of 70 and over. At each decade, there are also some people who are inactive. It is important to accept abstinence as a valid lifestyle as well—at any age—as long as it is freely chosen.

2. Older people have a particular need for a good, sexual relationship.

To a varying extent, the elderly experience and must adapt to gradual physical and mental changes. They may find themselves no longer easily able to do the enjoyable things they used to do; their future may seem fearful; retirement and an "empty nest" may leave many with reduced incomes and no clear goals in life; friends, and/or one's lifetime partner, may become ill, move away, or die; and the threat of loneliness may be a major concern. Fortunately, most older people are not infirm, frustrated, fearful, poor, bored, and lonely but, nonetheless, some of these elements may be affecting their lives. An excellent antidote for all is the warmth, intimacy, and security of a good, sexual relationship.

3. Sexual physiology changes.

In general, physiological changes are gradual and are easily compensated for, if one knows how. But when they sneak up on an unsuspecting, unknowledgeable individual, they can be disastrous. Health workers need to be familiar with these changes and with how they can help patients to adapt to them.

Older men commonly find that their erections are less frequent, take longer to achieve, are less firm, and are more easily lost. Ejaculation takes longer, is less forceful, and is smaller in amount. The refractory period (the interval between ejaculation and another erection) is often prolonged to many hours or even days. The slowing down of the sexual response cycle can be compensated for simply by taking more time, a step usually gratifying to one's partner, especially if s/he is also elderly. But in our society, many men grow up believing that their manliness, their power, and their competence depend on their ability to "get it up, keep it up, and get it off." For such an individual, slowing of the cycle may induce performance anxiety, complete impotence, and panic. Good counseling about the many advantages of a leisurely approach can make a world of difference for such an individual.

The prolonged refractory period may prevent a man from having sex as often as he formerly did, but only if he requires that the sex act build up to his ejaculation. If he can learn that good, soul-satisfying sex is possible without male ejaculation, then he can do it as often as he wants.

Finally, many men (and sometimes their partners) need to learn that wonderful sex is possible without an erect penis. Tongues, fingers, vibrators, and many other gadgets can make wonderful stimulators and can alleviate performance anxiety.

Some women find the arrival of menopause terribly depressing; others feel liberated. If one has grown up in a society that believes that the major role for women is bearing children, then the loss of that ability makes one feel no longer a real woman.

The most common sexual problems of older women, however, is atrophy and drying of the vagina, which can make intercourse uncomfortable and painful, particularly if her partner is wearing an unlubricated condom. The obvious, simple solution is to use one of the many, water-soluble lubricants that are available at drugstores. Saliva is a fairly good lubricant and it does have four advantages over commercial products: 1) It is readily available wherever one may be; 2) It is free; 3) It is at the right temperature; and 4) Its application is more intimate than something from a tube. An alternative approach attacks the root of the problem. Vaginal atrophy and drying result from decrease in estrogen. They can be reversed by estrogen replacement which also prevents other consequences of menopause like hot flashes and loss of calcium from the skeleton. But estrogen administration does increase the risk of uterine cancer, therefore each woman and her doctor will need to balance out the risks and benefits in her particular situation.

Aging inevitably changes physical appearance and, in our youth-oriented culture, this can have a profound impact on sexuality. It is not easy to reverse the influence of many decades of advertisements for cosmetics and clothes, but doctors can at least try to avoid adding to the problem. Many medical procedures, particularly mastectomy, amputations, chemotherapy, and ostomies, have a profound impact on body image. It is of utmost importance to discuss this impact before surgery and to be fully aware of the patient's need to readjust during the post-operative period. When possible, involvement of the patient's sex partner in these discussions can be very helpful.

4. Social attitudes are often frustrating.

As indicated above, society tends to deny the sexuality of the aged, and in so doing creates complications in their already difficult lives. Laws, regulations, and customs restrict the sexual behavior of older people in many ways. This is particularly true for women, since they have traditionally enjoyed less freedom and because, demographically, there are few potential partners for heterosexual, single women, and many of the few that are available are pursuing women half their age.

Some have suggested that the best way for an older woman to find a sex partner is to become a lesbian. Few, however, have successfully made this transition and for many, homosexuality is completely unacceptable.

When doctors see an older woman, they can, at the least, inquire about the possibility of sexual frustration and, if it is present, be understanding. Some women can be encouraged to try masturbating, and some will find a vibrator a delightful way to achieve orgasm.

Older people are living in a variety of retirement communities and nursing homes. This brings potential sexual partners together, but tends to exaggerate the gender imbalance. In retirement "homes," single women often outnumber single men, eight or ten to one. Furthermore, rules, customs, and lack of privacy severely inhibit the establishment of intimate relationships. Administrators of such homes are often blamed for this. Some are, indeed, unsympathetic, but we must also consider the attitudes of the trustees, the neighbors, and the legislators who oversee the operation, and particularly the attitudes of family members. If two residents establish a sexual liaison, it is often followed by a son or daughter pounding the administrator's desk and angrily shouting, "That's not what I put Mom in here for!" In the immortal words of Pogo, "We have met the enemy, and they are us."

5. Use it or lose it.

Sexual activity is not a commodity that can be stored and saved for a rainy day. Rather, it is a physiologic function that tends to deteriorate if not used, and it is particularly fragile for the elderly. If interrupted, it may be difficult (though not impossible) to get restarted. Doctors should work with the patient and partner on reestablishing the relationship, if that is desired.

6. Older folks do it better.

This may seem like an arrogant statement to some, but a lot depends on what is meant by "better." If the basis is how hard the penis is, how moist the vagina, how many strokes per minute, then the young will win out, but if the measure is the satisfaction achieved, the elderly have several advantages. First, they have usually had considerable experience, not necessarily with many different partners. One can have a lot of valuable experience with a single partner. Second, they often have more time, and a good sexual relationship takes a lot of time. The young are often pressured by studies, jobs, hobbies, etc., and squeeze their sexual activities into a few available minutes. Older folks can be more leisurely and relaxed. Finally, attitudes often improve with aging. The young are frequently insecure, playing games, and acting out traditional roles because they do not know what else to do. Some old folks have mellowed and learned to roll with the punches. They no longer need to prove themselves and can settle down to relating with their partner and meeting his/her needs. Obviously one does not have to be old to gain experience, to set aside time, or to develop sound attitudes. Perhaps the next generation of Americans will discover how to learn these simple things without wasting thirty or forty years of their lives playing silly games. One hopes so.

In summary, older people are sexual, often urgently need sexual contact, and encounter many problems, some medical, most societal. Doctors and other health providers need to be aware of these problems and need to help those who are aging cope with them.

love, sex and aging

A surprising and reassuring report.

EDWARD M. BRECHER

Science writer, social historian and investigative reporter, Edward M. Brecher, the author of Love, Sex and Aging, *also wrote the award-winning* Licit and Illicit Drugs, *a Consumer Union report published in 1972.*

The popular concept for years, nurtured by earlier Victorian attitudes and later television diets—that young is beautiful and old is, well, just respectable—has contributed to the terror of growing older, the fear of losing the capacity to love and to make love.

Surveys conducted by Dr. Alfred Kinsey a quarter of a century ago did little to alleviate these fears, for they did not reach beyond middle age. Questions such as, "At what age do men and women begin to lose interest in sex?" and, "At what age do they begin to lose their capacity for sexual enjoyment?" went unanswered. Six years ago, Edward Brecher of West Cornwall was commissioned by Consumer Union to secure answers to sex-and-aging questions. Sixty-six years old at the time, Brecher had a personal as well as professional interest in the research, and in cooperation with the editors of Consumer Reports Books, he drafted and mailed 10,000 questionnaires to men and women between ages 50 and 93 all across the country. A staggering 42 percent of the surveys was returned—and the answers were as unique and individual as they were revealing. Taken together, they confirmed the heretofore unsaid: Men and women are as sexually active when they can be for as long as they want to be.

Following are highlights of the surprisingly reassuring findings, from *Love, Sex and Aging: A Consumers Union Report* (Little, Brown and Company and Consumer Reports Books, 1984).

COMING OUT OF THE CLOSET

The late humorist Sam Levinson once recalled: "When I first found out how babies were born, I couldn't believe it! To think that my mother and father would do such a thing!... My father, maybe; but my mother—never!"

It is hardly surprising that today's young people, taught to think of their parents as nonsexual even when those parents were in their 20s and 30s, continue to think of their parents (and other older people) in their 50s and beyond as *still* nonsexual.

A 58-year-old husband and father wrote to us: "It has been my experience that children in the 15-to-25-year range are horrified if not disgusted at the thought of their 45-to-60-year-old parents having intercourse." He recalled that he, too, was disgusted, decades ago, when he first realized that *his* parents were having sex—and that his wife had reacted similarly when she first realized this about *her* parents. "Something should be done—and I can't suggest what," he continued, "to convince (young people) that a married couple having intercourse in their 50s, 60s, and later is normal, natural, even beautiful, but definitely not dirty or weird or odd."

Many older people have devoted themselves to keeping the secret of their sexuality not only from their children and other young people, but from one another as well. The result is that they themselves are seriously misled about the nature and extent of sexuality in their own generation. Some of them even wonder whether their continuing sexuality is "abnormal" or "perverted." "I must be an animal to (still) desire sex," wrote a troubled 71-year-old widower.

How can such misconceptions about love and sex after 50 be corrected? Clearly, older people themselves must supply the data, demonstrating that their sexuality is no longer something to hide or be ashamed of.

"Let us silver-haired sirens out of the closet!" implored a 54-year-old divorcée. "We have a lot to 'show and tell' the world."

SEXUAL CHANGES WITH AGE

What proportion of men and women experience a decline in sexual function after the age of 50? For men, the answer is: *all men*. What's more, for most men past 50, this is not a recent phenomenon. Most of them have experienced a progressive decline ever since sexual function peaked in their early 20s, or before. This decline is visible in many ways:

- It takes most older men longer to get an erection.
- When fully erect, the penis is not as stiff as formerly.
- The erection more frequently disappears prior to orgasm.
- It takes more stimulation of the penis to reach orgasm.
- Sex more frequently terminates without orgasm.
- The refractory period (the time it takes to have another erection after orgasm) is longer.

In addition, interest in sex and desire for sex tend to decrease.

Among women, vaginal lubrication during sexual arousal is the precise physiological equivalent of male erection—and, as might be expected, the quantity of lubrication goes down as women age. The details, however, have not been worked out for vaginal lubrication. No one knows, for example, whether it takes older women longer to lubricate, or whether they more fre-

From *Connecticut Magazine*, November 1984, pp. 66-69. Based on the book, LOVE, SEX AND AGING, by Robert M. Brecher and the Editor of Consumer Reports Books. (Little, Brown and Consumer Union, 1984.)

'Let us silver-haired sirens out of the closet! We have a lot to "show and tell" the world.'

quently lose lubrication during sexual arousal, or whether it takes more physical stimulation to achieve lubrication in the later years. Nor has the female "refractory period" following orgasm been studied decade by decade. There is evidence of a modest decline in sexual interest and desire among women as among men in their 60s and 70s.

What is astonishing, however, is not the *decline* in sexual function. Rather, it is the high proportion of women and men who *retain* an interest in and an enjoyment of sex even in their 70's and 80's. The tables provide the details.

TABLE A shows the proportion of men and women in the Consumers Union study who remain sexually active (either with a partner or through masturbation or both) during the decades from age 50 on. Even among those past 70, 65 percent of the women and 79 percent of the men report continuing sexual activity.

TABLE B shows the *frequency* of sexual activity. Even among those past 70, more than half of those sexually active report sex once a week or more often.

TABLE C presents similar data for sexual *enjoyment*. Sixty-one percent of the sexually active women past 70 and 75 percent of the men continue to rate their own enjoyment of sex as "high."

Many of those who filled out the Consumers Union questionnaire, moreover, have refused to sit idly by as age has progressively dampened their physiological responses. Instead, they have sought and found techniques for maintaining and in some cases even enhancing their sexual enjoyment despite functional losses.

SEXUAL FANTASIES

More than half of the sexually active men and women who filled out the Consumers Union questionnaire said that they sometimes, usually, or always engage in fantasy during sex with a partner. Among those who masturbate, moreover, more than 75 percent of both men and women reported that they engage in sexual fantasy during masturbation.

An example is supplied by a 52-year-old husband who wrote: "I need an attractive female to stimulate (arouse) me. Physically, I am as fit as I was thirty years ago, while my wife has deteriorated into a pot-bellied slob. Seeing her in clothes turns me off—let alone seeing her in the nude."

He accordingly conjures up for himself a fantasy woman who is "young...long hair, pleasant voice, obvious and firm breasts (not necessarily large), firm belly and 'Oriental' navel, shapely legs...small feet. This dream creature indicates friendliness so there is no risk of rejection. We engage in tentative touching, leading to caresses, and slowly proceed to the ultimate union....

"A less frequent dream: I am 'captured' by a bikini-clad maiden who proceeds to manipulate my body until I reach an agonizing ecstacy."

A 64-year-old wife wrote similarly: "The sexual side of my marriage was never very good." So she engages in fantasies like this one:

"I see myself (younger than I am) with a man who is strong and sure and tender. I see us dancing, driving, parking on the cliff to watch and hear the sea crashing on the rocks—always aware of each other, always reaching toward the ultimate, wondrous culmination, yet prolonging the anticipation. I feel his hands gently removing my dress, my underclothes, lingering on my body, caressing me as I caress him. I feel his body against mine and desire rises, rises, filling me, filling me, and I want that moment to last forever and ever. And I dream that this time, *this* time, there will be that perfect, earth-shaking realization of sexual love. An overwhelming joy in each other, then quiet and peace and sleep in each other's arms."

An 82-year-old widow described her wish-fulfillment fantasy more briefly: "While masturbating, it's fun to pretend that the relationship is with a loved one who lives far away. Murmuring sweet

---

THE FOUNTAIN OF ETERNAL YOUTH

The slim young man I married
Has slowly gone to pot;
With wrinkled face and graying pate,
Slender he is not!
And when I meet a mirror,
I find a haggard crone;
I can't believe the face I see
Can really be my own!

But when we seek our bed each night,
The wrinkles melt away:
Our flesh is firm, our kisses warm,
Our ardent hearts are gay!
The Fountain of Eternal Youth
Is not so far to find:
Two things you need—a double bed,
A spouse who's true and kind!
                    —74-year-old wife

---

nothings, encouraging him to hold out a bit longer—and imagining I'm holding him close at the climax."

Many of the fantasies reported by these older men and women are "reruns" of actual experiences years earlier. Thus a 69-year-old husband still likes to rerun in fantasy "an experience with a girl when I was 37. She was fantastic in bed—a passionate, manipulating, hot-blooded sylph."

An 85-year-old widow recalled similarly that 15 years ago, when she was 70, "I had a sudden, violent love affair that lasted about three months. It remained my fantasy for over ten years!"

Many of the reruns reported, however, were not of extramarital affairs but of prior sexual encounters with one's own spouse. Thus a 67-year-old husband wrote: "It may sound unusual, but when I have [a fantasy during] sex with my wife, it includes her." A special feature of these reruns, of course, is that in the fantasy, both partners are young and fresh again. A 55-year-old wife explained: "I need to think 'sex' thoughts to get into a mood where I can get aroused and complete the sex act, including orgasm. I think back to when we were first married, were young and more attractive physically."

Men, too, have such "rejuvenation fantasies." One 72-year-old husband, after describing his gradual loss of sexual potency, added that in his fantasies "I'm young again—a straining, eager bull."

In marked contrast to such experienced fantasizers is the 66-year-old wife who wrote: "I can honestly say that I have *never* had sexual fantasies." Another wife, aged 59, asked in bewilderment, "What is a sexual fantasy?"

Many women and men who use pornographic materials appear to fall between these extremes; they can fantasize on their own—but find pornography helpful for fantasy enrichment.

WHY SOME WIVES AND HUSBANDS STAY FAITHFUL

The religious, legal, social, and economic penalties against adultery no doubt help keep some spouses from engaging in extramarital sex. Dearth of acceptable or available partners may be another factor. But the reasons given by our respondents were for the most part much more personal; they seemed to arise directly out of the circumstances of each particular marriage.

"I cannot approve of sex outside marriage," wrote a wife of 54. "That is 'defil-

'I'm young again—a straining, eager bull,' says a 72-year-old husband of his fantasies.

ing' my marriage bed whether it be done by my husband or me."

A second 54-year-old wife echoed these views: "Sex is such an intimate part of our marriage, I could not help but feel the marriage diminished if either of us had sex with someone else."

A 65-year-old wife wrote: "I find my love for my husband has more depth, a stronger feeling and mellowed like rare wine. If either partner of the marriage has to seek outside for sex, then that marriage should be ended."

Other wives reported that they have remained faithful—but expressed some small regrets. A 70-year-old wife wrote: "At times I regret having known only one man sexually; but if I had my life to live over, I would probably do the same."

"I sometimes wish I had had more heterosexual experience," a 56-year-old wife wrote. "I have not done so out of loyalty to my husband but would have liked to."

A 67-year-old wife recalled: "I tried to get my husband's permission for outside sex after he could no longer function. He was shocked—and refused! I have too much respect for him, and we together have other 'fun activities'—so it isn't important. Our being together is important."

Our faithful husbands expressed a similar range of views. One wrote, at age 59, that "trust and fidelity outweigh the satisfaction of conquest and change of partners that seem so attracting." Another, 55, said: "I have a very healthy and active sex life with my wife. After being married for thirty-five years, I feel that my sex life now is better than ever before. In view of this situation, I have never found it necessary to seek activity outside my marriage."

A husband of the same age wrote: "If the husband wishes sex outside of marriage…the wife should have the same prerogative, which I doubt many men would accept. Marriage is more fruitful and fulfilling if there is no outside sex by either spouse."

A faithful 50-year-old husband said he would engage in extramarital sex if the opportunity came along: "[My] wife never was enthusiastic about sex. About five or six years ago, she began to say it was "undignified" or "like animals" or "not suitable at our age" and gradually stopped completely….Because of the above, I would feel justified in having sex with someone else, but never have—mainly because I don't know how to find a partner without fear of discovery, embarrassment, etc."

A 54-year-old husband sadly reported that his wife is not sexually aroused by his efforts. He continued:

"It has occurred to me many times to have an affair but I have never done so. My reasons for contemplating this action are (1) to prove that I am still viable sexually; (2) [to prove] that I could be attractive to another female; (3) [to prove] that my technique was adequate…; (4) to test my theory that some other woman would be more easily aroused by my sexual advances. I also fear this sort of encounter to the extent that I cannot tolerate rejection in any form. On a higher level, I firmly believe in the institution of marriage, family and all that this entails. Furthermore, my wife would not be understanding or compassionate to this sort of frailty."

WHY SOME WIVES AND HUSBANDS SEEK (AND FIND) EXTRAMARITAL SEX

We had expected to compile an anthology of reasons given by our adulterous respondents for engaging in outside sex paralleling the reasons given above for refraining. Such reasons might include a spouse who is no longer physically able to have sex, marital incompatibility, boredom with marriage, a desire for variety, a feeling that life is slipping past, and so on. Some respondents did give such reasons, but for quite a few others, adultery "just happens"

—and for still others, it arises out of a complex set of circumstances that cannot be summarized simply.

Adultery takes two markedly different forms. Many of our adulterous wives and husbands have engaged since 50 in the activity commonly known as *cheating*—sex outside marriage without the knowledge or consent of the spouse. Others have engaged in sex outside their marriage with the knowledge and sometimes with the consent of their spouse. In a few marriages, indeed, adultery is a mutual and cooperative enterprise.

A much higher proportion of husbands than of wives in our study (23 *vs.* 8 percent) reported one or more extramarital affairs since age 50. For many husbands, however, these are likely to be mere brief and casual encounters. One husband of 60, for example, said he is in love with his wife and enjoys sex with her once a week —but in addition, he has had "five or six" encounters with other women since age 50. He explains: "Sex outside marriage is exciting and fun. Makes one feel younger for a while."

A 67-year-old husband wrote: "I have been faithful to my present wife since 50 except for one occasion which more or less fell into my lap. I was anxious to see whether I was still functioning—and very pleased with the results." His partner was also married. "We both decided not to continue [due to] constant fear of being

---

QUALITY OF COMMUNICATIONS

That open, constructive communications become increasingly important during the later years of a marriage was noted by several respondents—including a 55-year-old husband, married for 35 years, who wrote: "When you are young, love is predominantly influenced by sexual activities. In later life, you still relate love to sex—but other things become more important. These things are companionship, doing things together, communicating [with] and relating to your wife."

A 70-year-old wife, married for 43 years, wrote: "[Nowadays] we travel together more, spend more evenings together at home reading, and we feel less need to entertain friends or relatives….When we were young we bought fewer books, read less and discussed what we did read with more heat and less mature judgment, it seems to me….We are more honest

with each other [now] on likes and dislikes…and yet we are more considerate of each other's feelings. We really know each other better."

Communications need not always be verbal, of course—as one husband points out: "Problems of all kinds are seen through together. You have this background, and you communicate with each other by a look, a touch, a feeling."

But for some wives and husbands, nonverbal communication, however tender, is not enough. They need the communication of verbal sharing, and love withers in its absence. Wrote an unhappy wife: "I find myself at a total loss for want of anything to talk about [with my husband]. We can spend the entire evening together —he staring at the boob-tube….I reading or needlepointing—and I can't think of one word to say to him even if you paid me a dollar a word."

> 'I tried to get my husband's permission for outside sex after he could no longer function. He was shocked—and refused.'

found out—and it really wasn't that much fun for a long-time relationship."

When adultery is found out, of course, it sometimes leads to divorce—but not always. Nearly 250 of our wives and husbands remain married despite the fact that one spouse knows of the other's adultery. A smaller number reported that *both* wife and husband have had outside sex with each other's knowledge and consent. Half a dozen of these older couples reported engaging in "swinging": outside sex as a sort of cooperative adventure, in each other's presence or even in the same bed.

This broad spectrum of responses—ranging from wives and husbands for whom lifelong monogamy is the only acceptable lifestyle to those who accept outside sex for both partners—is a dramatic example of a theme that runs throughout our study:

All older people are not alike. No stereotype of "the aging" or "the aged" can do justice to the richly variegated patterns of life as it is actually being lived by many in their later years.

"BETTER TO WEAR OUT THAN RUST OUT"

I have been in love with the same woman for 53 years, and we have never cheated or been untrue to each other. We have complete trust in each other. The only trouble with a relationship like this is, when one of us passes on, it is going to be catastrophic for the one left behind."

So writes an 80-year-old husband of his 75-year-old wife. Asked what he regretted in his life, he reached back 60 years to recall his one and only encounter with a prostitute. "It was the most disgusting sexual experience I ever had." He added, however, that if he hadn't had that experience, "I wouldn't know how disgusting it could be."

Both he and his wife reported that they have no intimate friends and no desire to make new friends; they are too busy and hardly ever lonely. Both said that they are currently in love—with one another, of course.

"Participating in sex interests me only with my wife," the husband stated. They have sex about once a week; the husband says he reaches orgasm "almost always." His wife confirmed this, adding that she reaches orgasm "every time." She continued:

"Love in the later years is an enduring love—not the great passionate love of the teens but a greater love. You enjoy the knowledge that you are loved and wanted, that you are still beautiful to your husband. You have shared happiness, sorrows, death—watching your sons leave for the wars, seeing your friends grow old and feeble, then dying. You hold out your hand and your husband clasps it, then draws you near. Sleeping close together.

Having sex whenever you want...."

The husband summed up:

"My wife and I both believe that keeping active sexually delays the aging process. Neither of us is troubled with false modesty....We keep our interest alive by a great deal of caressing and fondling.... We feel it is much better to wear out than to rust out."

TABLE A
PROPORTION OF MEN AND WOMEN WHO REMAIN SEXUALLY ACTIVE (WITH A PARTNER OR ALONE) AFTER AGE 50

	In their 50s	In their 60s	Age 70 and older
WOMEN	93%	81%	65%
MEN	98%	91%	79%

TABLE B
FREQUENCY OF SEX (WITH A PARTNER OR ALONE) AMONG SEXUALLY ACTIVE MEN AND WOMEN AFTER AGE 50

	In their 50s	In their 60s	Age 70 and older
WOMEN Sex at least once a week	73%	63%	50%
MEN Sex at least once a week	90%	73%	58%

TABLE C
ENJOYMENT OF SEX BY SEXUALLY ACTIVE MEN AND WOMEN AFTER AGE 50

	In their 50s	In their 60s	Age 70 and older
WOMEN High enjoyment of sex	71%	65%	61%
MEN High enjoyment of sex	90%	86%	75%

Old/New Sexual Concerns

- Sexual Orientation (Articles 46-49)
- Sexual Abuse and Violence (Articles 50-53)
- Focus: Condoms vs. AIDS (Articles 54-59)

This final unit deals with several topics that are of interest or concern for different reasons. In one respect, however, these topics have a common denominator: They have all recently emerged in the public's awareness as "social issues." Unfortunately, public awareness of issues is often a fertile ground for misinformation and misconceptions. In recognition of this, it is the overall goal of this section to provide some objective insights into pressing sexual concerns.

The first of the four articles in the *Sexual Orientation* subsection strives to clarify the reader's understanding of how children appear to develop their sexual orientation. "Straight or Gay?" dispels many common parental myths and fears, especially about the development of boys. The next two articles explore homosexuality and homophobia—the fear of homosexuality—in the adolescent period. Dr. Gary Remafedi outlines a model for healthy sexual development of gay and lesbian adolescents. Next, Jay Friedman asserts that homophobia is detrimental to the maturation of all adolescent males, whether they become homosexual or heterosexual. The final article, "Homosexuality: Who and Why?" summarizes current perspectives on causation and characteristics of homosexuals. It concludes that it would be more appropriate to refer to sexual orientation options in the plural—homosexualities and heterosexualities—since research has found as many differences within the groups as between them.

Sexual abuse and violence is another topic of ongoing concern. These acts of violence are especially pernicious when an acquaintance, a relative, or a parent is involved. The trust that may have existed is destroyed and the relationship may be damaged beyond repair. The psychological scars of child sexual abuse and incest may last for years and may not heal without professional help. It is "the hurt that keeps on hurting."

Some of the most devastating and flagrant violations of individual sexual and personal integrity arise from the misuse of sex as a means of humiliation and violence. Rape is an example of this. Public awareness of the threat and incidence of rape must increase in order to dispel long-held myths about this crime. It must be emphasized that rape is not a sex act; it is a crime of violence.

Another kind of sexual abuse or misuse has begun receiving media attention: sexual harassment. Like sexual abuse, incest, and rape, it has existed for some time prior to its gaining media attention. Also like its related abusive behaviors, sexual harassment is surrounded by myths, misinformation, and tendencies to "blame the victim."

The first article in the *Sexual Abuse and Violence* subsection focuses on child sexual abuse and incest. It describes characteristics of victims and offenders, and examines the implications of these traumatic experiences for victims, families, and society. The second article examines sexual harassment in the '80s, and includes information that will surprise and educate everyone. The last two articles explore two types of rape not commonly given significant media attention: "date rape" and male rape. Each author emphasizes the importance of society's view of rape being inclusive of all victims and all situations. Only with increased media attention will these victims receive the support and validation they need to recover.

Again this year, the *Focus* topic is Acquired Immune Deficiency Syndrome (AIDS). AIDS has been a very prominent topic in the professional and popular media for the past few years, and it continues to be the subject of much emotional debate. Although the causes and origins of AIDS and what behaviors are most closely linked with AIDS are somewhat better understood by many men and women at risk, the battle to contain and eventually conquer AIDS is far from over. The first two articles in this section focus on condoms—the number one publicized avenue to safer sex. Each provides important information for the public to increase the effectiveness of this risk reduction strategy. The third article identifies the role of education in the prevention of AIDS. The fourth article outlines a special kind of AIDS education: how schools can ethically safeguard health and manage hysteria when a student with AIDS attends the school. "Flirting With AIDS" sounds like something no sane person would want to do, but according to the next article the majority of heterosexual women who responded to a *Self* magazine survey are doing just that. The closing article in the AIDS subsection overviews the hope for the future. Current research and development of drugs that can treat, cure, or prevent AIDS is summarized.

Looking Ahead: Challenge Questions

Why do so many individuals in American society experience homophobia? In what ways does it harm homosexuals? Nonhomosexuals? What are some of the main problems associated with child sexual abuse for parents, for society, and for the victims? What are some ways to combat this problem? Why is incest generally considered even worse than other types of sexual abuse?

How would you have defined sexual harassment before reading the article in this section? In what ways has your view changed after reading it?

Is date or acquaintance rape a problem for many college women? What are some of its causes, and what relationship changes may prevent it? What are some long-lasting effects of rape?

To what extent do you think of male victims when you think of rape? How has Jim Senter's article changed your perceptions?

How has society reacted to the discovery and spread of AIDS? Has the existence of AIDS changed the way people think about sex and express themselves sexually? Why or why not? Have you seen any changes among college students you know? Why do people "flirt with AIDS" and what, if anything, can be done about this?

Straight or Gay?

Researchers are unraveling the origins of homosexuality.

David and Barbara Bjorklund

David Bjorklund, Ph.D., is professor of psychology, Florida Atlantic University, and author of *Children's Thinking* (Brooks-Cole). **Barbara Bjorklund** is a teaching and research associate in the department of psychology at Florida Atlantic University.

We are both professionals in the field of child development. Ask either of us how gender develops and we will give you a two-hour lecture beginning with chromosomes and ending with socialization processes. Ask about homosexuality and we can give you a dozen different theories and cite research that supports or refutes each one. But let us see our four-year-old Nicholas after playing "beauty shop" with our seven-year-old Heidi, barrettes in his hair and fingernails painted pink, and our reaction will not be different from most parents: We feel uncomfortable, are not quite sure what to say, and at best, we laugh nervously.

Why is this reaction so common, especially for parents of boys? It's probably because, in our culture, boys are given little leeway in their gender-appropriate behavior. Many parents are afraid that cross-sex behavior in young boys may lead to homosexuality, and if their sons do turn out to be gay, think, There's something I did that turned my son gay.

This attitude persists despite the fact that times are changing: It's okay for men to stay at home and take care of the kids while women pursue high-powered careers; we need to show our children that men can cry

> *"...Some evidence indicates that prenatal hormones not only determine one's sex but also greatly influence which sex one will be attracted to...."*

and women can get angry. Still, many parents worry that diminishing the distinction between the sexes may lead to sexual confusion and homosexuality. And despite our beliefs that homosexuality is not morally offensive or perverted, we fear the effects that the prejudice of other people may have on our children should they turn out to be gay.

In recent years, homosexuality has become more and more visible. The tragedy of AIDS has also increased the public's knowledge. Publicly we know of gay movie idols, gay politicians, and gay athletes. Privately we know of colleagues, friends, and family members who are homosexual. It is estimated that between 4 and 10 percent of the population is homosexual. But for parents, this new openness has only generated more questions and fewer answers. Is homosexuality something some boys (and girls) are just born with, like blond hair or birthmarks? Or is it something we cause, by protecting them too much or too little?

There has been no shortage of research into the origins of male homosexuality (in contrast to the little done on lesbianism). Most early theories placed the cause of homosexuality in the environment. In fact, it seems likely that homosexuality has multiple causes, that the origins of homosexuality can be different for

Prenatal Gender Development

Genetic sex differences are determined at birth, when the sperm, carrying either the X or Y chromosome, fertilizes the egg. Sex hormone production and physical sex development take slightly longer. By twelve weeks' gestation, the major sex organs have formed, and sex differentiation is complete.

Conception	XX (girl)	XY (boy)
By 6 weeks		TESTES are formed.
By 8 weeks	OVARIES are formed.	ANDROGEN production begins.
By 12 weeks	Lacking ANDROGEN exposure, female sex organs develop: UTERUS, CLITORIS, VAGINA.	ANDROGEN is absorbed into fetal tissue producing male sex organs: SCROTUM, PENIS.

How "sexual inversions" occur.

In a recent review of the scientific literature, Lee Ellis, Ph.D., of the State University of North Dakota at Minot and M. Ashley Ames of Indiana University at Bloomington cite evidence for four possible causes of prenatal conditions that result in "sexual inversions" in humans. Perhaps the most prevalent cause of the extreme cases (for example, male chromosomes, female genitals) are genetic mutations of the fetus, which involve either failure to produce the usual hormones or inability to utilize the hormones already present. Drugs taken during pregnancy, such as progestins (used to prevent miscarriage in the 1950's), barbiturates, marijuana, and alcohol, have been shown to be associated not only with sexual inversions but also with cross-sex behavior. Prenatal maternal stress, such as that experienced in Germany during World War II, has been shown to be associated with an unusually high proportion of homosexuals born during that period. Finally, and more speculatively, under some circumstances a mother's immune system may affect her developing fetus. Although the evidence for this comes mainly from animal research, Ellis and Ames suggest that hormones during pregnancy, which usually inhibit the mother's immune system from affecting the fetus, sometimes may not be produced. As a result, the mother's "immune system might chemically destroy some of the substances vital for sexual differentiation." **—D.B. and B.B.**

different people. Recent research evidence makes it clear that environmental factors play a much less important role than was previously believed, and that one's sexual preference (whether homosexual or heterosexual) is largely determined by certain biological conditions existing before birth.

Some false assumptions.

The oldest, most prevalent myth about homosexuality is that a dominant mother and a weak father are the main ingredients for a homosexual son. This explanation says the son grows up wanting to be like his strong mother instead of his passive father. But a twelve-year project conducted by psychologists Alan Bell, Martin Weinberg, and Sue Kiefer Hammersmith of the Kinsey Institute for Research in Sex, Gender, and Reproduction found little evidence to support this belief.

The researchers surveyed the lives and backgrounds of over 1300 men and women who represented the black and white races as well as homosexual and heterosexual orientations. Bell and his colleagues asked homosexual and heterosexual men if they had felt similar to their mothers while growing up or had wanted to be like their mothers. Somewhat surprisingly for those who hold the "dominant mother" view, homosexual men were no more apt to express a wish to be like their mothers than heterosexual men. In fact, the Kinsey researchers stated that "the connection between boys' relationships with their mothers and whether they become homosexual or heterosexual is hardly worth mentioning."

How about the weak father part of the theory? Here the evidence was less clear. Homosexual men were less apt to report positive relationships with their fathers than were heterosexual men. Many of the homosexual men in the Kinsey study were labeled by their peers as "sissies" and recalled having feminine interests as boys, and this may have caused many of the fathers to feel uncomfortable with their sons. However, the Kinsey researchers do not believe that the fathers' reactions *caused* their sons' homosexuality.

Other possible family causes were investigated by the Kinsey research team, and it was found that quality of the parents' marriage, parents' wish for a daughter, birth order, being an only child, having all sisters or all brothers, and quality of relationships with siblings were not apparent causes of homosexuality.

The findings of the Kinsey researchers indicate that we generally do not need to worry that something we do will "cause" homosexuality in our sons. And we need not worry that our nontraditional careers, family roles, or personalities lead to homosexuality. Domineering mothers and weak fathers do have homosexual sons but so do weak mothers and domineering fathers and the entire parental spectrum in between.

This belief is echoed in a recent book by Carolyn Welch Griffin, Marian J. Wirth, and Arthur G. Wirth, *Beyond Acceptance* (Prentice-Hall). Based in part on interviews with parents of lesbians and gays, the authors state unequivocally that parents should not feel that their son's or daughter's homosexuality was caused by some failure on their part. Such fears and guilt are unwarranted and unconducive to developing a positive relationship between parents and homosexual offspring. (See "Growing Up Gay."

The parents' influence.

Although the nature of the parent-child relationship seems not to be a major cause of homosexuality, in some cases, suspicions that their child may be "different" can cause parents to react problematically. Richard Green, M.D., professor of psychiatry at UCLA School of Medicine and the author of *The "Sissy Boy Syndrome" and the Development of*

Homosexuality (Yale University Press), followed 44 "feminine" boys from early childhood to adulthood. The behavior that distinguished these boys from the control group of traditionally masculine boys was extreme. They frequently expressed wishes to be girls throughout their childhood. They played with girls almost exclusively, they played girl-type games and not boy-type games, and they often dressed in girls' clothing.

Although the parents of these boys claimed not to have encouraged such activities, there was evidence that indicated otherwise. Some parents, for instance, had pictures in the family albums of their sons dressed in girls' clothing, and many mothers reported reacting positively to such cross-dressing for a few years. When parents encourage a son to pretend he is a daughter, it is a rejection of the integral part of the child, and although it doesn't cause homosexuality, it can cause feelings of inadequacy and low self-esteem.

Like the Kinsey researchers, Green also found a pattern of fathers rejecting their "feminine" sons. Compared with the control group, the fathers of the "feminine" boys were more apt to express displeasure with their sons. The poor father-son relationship, because the boy fails to demonstrate typical male behavior and interests, points to one potential source of trauma that some homosexual men may experience.

Fathers need to be accepting of their sons and their sons' interests. If a son doesn't want to go along to a football game, fathers can take them to concerts or museums. If a son doesn't want to play ball, a father can introduce him to other sports such as canoeing or cycling. There is no argument that fathers are the most important influence on the man their sons are to become. Fathers need to be reminded that being a man involves more than sexual orientation. Fathers need to be close to their sons to model honesty, integrity, generosity, sensitivity, and all the virtues they want for their sons regardless of their sexual orientation.

The seduction myth.

Another popular theory holds that young boys are "seduced" into becoming homosexuals by older males. The Kinsey Institute researchers found no support for this. Homosexual men generally recalled their first homosexual experiences as being with males close to their own age.

In fact, the childhood sexual experiences reported by homosexual and heterosexual men in the Kinsey study were strikingly similar. Both reported early sexual play with both boys and girls. And many homosexual men initially had heterosexual encounters. However, the experience itself is not as important as the feelings that accompany it. Homosexual men found sexual play with women to be less enjoyable and emotionally unfulfilling. Significantly more homosexuals than heterosexuals reported feelings of arousal and awareness of their sexual orientation during late childhood and adolescence—often before any type of sexual experience had occurred.

Homosexuality is not something

boys "catch" from being around homosexual men. We need not be overly cautious about the sexual orientation of our sons' teachers, coaches, and adult friends. Homosexual adults are no more apt to be sexually interested in our children than heterosexual adults. It's unfortunate in this day and age that parents need to keep such a close eye on the adults who supervise their children, but they don't need to be more cautious about homosexual adults than they are about heterosexual adults. Child molestation is a totally different subject, a psychopathic behavior that is not related to sexual orientation.

More important, we need not keep our sons away from favorite relatives who may be gay. And we need not be overly concerned about our sons'

Growing Up Gay

Kids who feel "different" need their parents' love and support.

Although many gays report feeling "different" all through childhood, the realization that one is homosexual typically doesn't hit home until adolescence. The teen years are difficult for most children, but they are particularly difficult for gays. While other teens are learning how to date and establish romantic relationships, many gay teenagers are learning how to hide their feelings. Teens fear to deviate far from the conventions of the crowd. Being homosexual is viewed as being about as different as an adolescent can be, and heterosexual teenagers are usually sufficiently insecure with their own sexuality that they fear accepting a peer whose sexual preference is so different. Adolescence can be a very difficult time indeed for young people who are first discovering their homosexuality.

According to Fort Lauderdale psychologist Hilda Besner, Ph.D., one of the most difficult things homosexual adolescents and young adults must face is telling their parents about their homosexuality. However, Dr. Besner states that the communication difficulties of talking to their parents is often not something new. Children who feel different growing up usually recognize that their feelings are not socially "proper" and often have no one to talk to about this. Who can they share their feelings with? Parents are often quietly aware that something is

different with their children but choose to ignore it or even degrade it ("Why can't you be more like your brother?"). Children feel as if there is something wrong with them, and their parents are often the origins of these feelings. Children feel their parents are the last people they can tell.

Besner emphasizes that parents must be approachable for their children—all of their children. However, Besner also recognizes that not all parents will be easily able to accept their child's homosexual orientation. It is important, she says, for parents to get in touch with their own feelings first, even if those feelings are not positive. Parents must then provide an ear for their children. They don't have to be thrilled with what their children may tell them, but the message they give should be, "I'm available, and although I may not like everything I hear, I want to hear it." Children need to develop a sense of self-worth, a sense that although they may feel different from others, there is nothing *wrong* with them. Parents need to send the message to their children of acceptance and unconditional love. In their book, *Beyond Acceptance*, Griffin, Wirth, and Wirth state that parental support enriched the lives of homosexual children, leading them to greater self-acceptance and the courage to face an often hostile world.

—D.B. and B.B.

early sex play with other boys causing homosexuality. Boys commonly experiment with other boys in preadolescent sex play, but their adult sexual orientation is affected by the feelings they bring *into* the experience, not feelings that result *from* the experience.

The role of biology.

Is homosexuality based on biological factors? First, is it genetic—that is, does it run in families? There is some indirect evidence supporting this position. For example, studies of identical twins indicate that if one twin is homosexual, the other is also apt to be homosexual. Of course, in all but a few rare circumstances, twins share not only the same genes but also the same home environment, making it difficult to ascertain the actual root of the homosexuality.

Other research has indicated that genes have an indirect effect on sexual orientation through hormones. For example, it is well established that prenatal hormones determine the genital structure of the fetus. (See "Prenatal Gender Development.") However, under certain rare conditions, things don't go exactly according to plan. For example, if androgen is not produced by the male fetus's testes, or is not absorbed into the fetal tissue, a female develops, despite the presence of the male XY chromosomes. Similarly, if sufficient quantities of androgen are introduced to a female fetus, male genitals develop, despite the female chromosomes. Such prenatal "sex inversions" have been demonstrated experimentally in mammals including rats and sheep. Similar situations have been found to occur in humans as a result of genetic errors (for example, an inability of a male fetus to absorb androgen) or other environmental factors that result in atypical hormone exposure for the fetus.

The presence of prenatal sex hormones not only affects the development of the genitals but also affects the developing brain. John Money, Ph.D., professor emeritus of psychiatry and behavioral sciences and pediatrics at Johns Hopkins University in Baltimore and one of the most influential researchers in the field of gender development, points out that in certain cases in which female animals were exposed to very high doses of androgen prenatally, not only were their external sexual organs those of males, but so was their *mating* behavior. In other words, the prenatal exposure to sex hormones affects not only the construction of the genitals but also the sexual orientation and behavior of the animal. In a related study, female sheep exposed to doses of androgen prenatally were born with female genitals but, as adults, were sexually attracted to other females. That is, sufficient doses of androgen at critical times in development produced adult homosexual behavior in these female animals. Related findings have been reported in other species, in both males and females.

> **"...Many homosexual men had childhood interests and self-images indistinguishable from those of boys who grew up to be heterosexual...."**

The impact of prenatal hormones on animals' sexual orientation has led researchers to assume that, for humans, prenatal hormone activity sets the stage for later sexual development. There is some evidence, although the matter is controversial, that prenatal hormones not only dictate which genitals a person is born with but also greatly influence which sex one will be attracted to. Money believes this to be true, and he thinks prenatal hormones are partly responsible for certain sex-related behaviors some young children exhibit. For instance, Money considers "feminine" behavior in little boys to be attributable to their prenatal hormonal makeup. An improper hormone exposure before birth, Money theorizes, causes the child to be more attentive to and interested in girls' activities and preferences.

Will "sissy" boys become gay?

If John Money is correct about prenatal hormones, and if homosexual boys being more attracted to opposite-sex behavior, then boys who act "feminine" should be more apt to grow up to be gay than boys who are more "masculine." Of the 44 "feminine" boys Richard Green followed to adulthood, 33 grew up to be homosexual or bisexual (75 percent). Of the control group, none grew up to be homosexual and only one became bisexual (3 percent).

In the Kinsey Institute study, the adult homosexuals differed from the heterosexuals on three measures of childhood gender nonconformity: how much they disliked typical boys' activities, how much they enjoyed typical girls' activities, and how feminine they felt themselves to be while growing up. This is not to say that the feminine behavior *caused* the homosexuality, but of all the factors measured in the study, it was the one that best signaled future adult homosexuality. However, parents should keep in mind that 11 of Green's 44 "feminine" boys grew up to be heterosexual, and approximately 11 percent of the Kinsey Institute's group of adult heterosexuals also reported enjoying typically feminine activities as children. That is, not all boys with feminine interests grow up to be homosexuals.

As should also be apparent, not all homosexual men act effeminately. For example, 18 percent of the homosexual men in the Kinsey Institute study described themselves as "very masculine" as children. Furthermore, more than half of the homosexual men in the Kinsey study did *not* profess a childhood enjoyment of typical girls' activities, and very few described themselves as being "feminine" as they were growing up. Although feeling "very masculine" and having interests in boys' activities were mentioned more frequently in the heterosexual group, many of the homosexual men in the Kinsey study had childhood interests and self-images indistinguishable from those of boys who grew up to be heterosexual.

What these findings mean is that parents need not stop their boys from playing "beauty shop" or cuddling dolls. Feminine activities are not the root of homosexuality. In fact, if Dad takes some of the responsibility for child care, playing with dolls may reflect a son's emulation of his father. And boys who prefer noncontact sports, such as swimming, to football will not necessarily grow up to be gay. Nor does the fact that a boy likes football mean he will grow up to be straight. However, the research indicates that *extreme* nongender conformity may be a good predictor of adult homosexuality.

There is no "cure."

Many parents become alarmed when they discover their adolescent or adult son is gay. Some parents search for a reversal, believing that some form of therapy will change their child's homosexuality.

There is little evidence, however, that any kind of therapy can change one's sexual orientation. In fact, researchers warn that the two types of treatment commonly used to "cure" homosexuality—hormone therapy and behavior modification—are largely misdirected.

According to Money, hormonal influence on erotic orientation takes place before birth. Later hormones in adolescence and adulthood simply "switch on" the erotic circuits in the brain, regardless of whether the hormones are male or female. Giving a homosexual hormone treatment

can make him or her either a more active homosexual or less active homosexual—not a heterosexual.

Behavior modification treatment is based on the notion that homosexuality is simply faulty learning of one's erotic orientation. Therapists who employ this "treatment" attempt to punish erotic responses to homosexual thoughts and visions and to reward erotic responses to heterosexual thoughts and visions. These therapies, however, are far from successful; little evidence exists that homosexuality is due to faulty learning in the first place. Any success reported has been with self-referred bisexuals, and no successes have been reported to last more than two years.

In 1973, the American Psychiatric Association stated that homosexuality was not a mental disorder. In fact, if a gay man decides to undergo treatment, it is usually for problems secondary to his homosexuality, such as anxiety or depression. Although family therapy can be helpful in strengthening relationships between a homosexual and his or her parents, psychotherapy is not a "cure." This is made clear by the Kinsey re-

searchers, who state that therapists should not attempt or expect to change a homosexual's erotic orientation. Rather, they argue, "it would probably make far more sense simply to recognize it as a basic component of a person's core identity and to help the client develop more positive feelings about and respect for his or her sexual proclivities."

Can being a sensitive, approachable, and unconditionally loving parent prevent one's child from being homosexual? Probably not. But being sensitive, approachable, and unconditionally loving *will* foster a strong family relationship, providing a child with feelings of high self-esteem and self-worth. Children who grow up in such families have the greatest chance of becoming well-adjusted, productive members of society, no matter what their erotic orientation. Becoming a parent is not simply claiming a guaranteed prize; it is opening oneself up to the possibilities of life, and having a homosexual child is but one of them. We can't always choose the roles parenthood gives us, but we can choose to do them well.

The Healthy Sexual Development of Gay and Lesbian Adolescents

Gary Remafedi, MD, MPH

Assistant Professor of Pediatrics
Medical Coordinator, Adolescent Health Program
University of Minnesota

Defining healthy sexual development for the gay or lesbian teenager is an exciting, but formidable, task. From the outset, it must be understood that all aspects of sexuality have a social context. Beginning at a very early age, children learn the culture's unique parameters of healthy sexuality; and the lessons are repeated, rehearsed, and reinforced throughout the life cycle. This process of sociosexual learning is so effective that almost everybody (except perhaps youngsters who grow up in the most chaotic home environments) understands the culture's basic sexual norms. Every detail, from gender-appropriate hairstyles to attitudes toward sexual intercourse, is mastered — as is the ability to recognize deviations from the norm in other people.

The specific rules governing sexual development are not invariate among all human societies. There are as many variations on healthy sexual development as there are ethnic, racial, religious, and other subcultures. Unlike other species, whose courtship, mating, and childrearing behaviors are "brain-coded" or otherwise instinctual, humans learn their culturally-specific sexual scripts from adults and peers in the immediate environment. The ultimate measure of healthy human sexual development is the extent to which sexual values and norms are incorporated and corresponding sexual behaviors are appropriately enacted. Thus, "healthy" sexual development can be viewed as a personal evolution of socially adapted sexual feelings and expressions.

Almost all children in Judeo-Christian societies are raised with a heterosexual identity: they learn to experience emotional intimacy and sexual gratification with persons of the opposite gender. The message is taught by parents and by other adults, by peers, by the media,

and is embodied social institutions. The road to healthy heterosexual development is fairly well-marked, leading in the general direction of monogamous heterosexual relationships and (often) parenthood. And, despite problems such as unprotected premarital sexual intercourse and its untoward consequences, the bulk of sexual research suggests that today's adolescents are quite traditional in their sexual values and compliant with sociosexual convention. Most of them successfully internalize the sexual teachings of the culture (for better or worse) and thereby meet previous criteria for healthy development.

If the emergence of an adaptive sexual identity is a sign of health, some developmentalists would argue that a homosexual outcome is problematic. After all, homosexuality can hardly be considered to be "adaptive" in modern American society. Homosexuality is still widely regarded as an illness, as a moral deviation, or as a criminal behavior. Eric Erikson[1] wrote that the central task of personality development during young adulthood is the achievement of intimacy within a *heterosexual* relationship. If this were the case, then general personality development — as well as sexual development — might be compromised in homosexual persons.

Of course, the last two decades of sexual orientation research have not supported this conclusion. Perpetual developmental limbo is not a certain fate for homosexual persons. Studies of emotionally and socially competent homosexual adults illustrate that "normal" development does indeed occur in spite of widespread societal disapproval. This remarkable phenomenon raises an important question: "How do some homosexual people actually flourish in, or in spite of, a heterosexual society?" The answer is the key to understanding healthy sexual development for homosexual children, adolescents, and adults.

Modern American gay and lesbian people live within multiple, sometimes conflicting, subcultures. They spend the bulk of their time within heterosexual society; and they are also members of other ethnic, racial, or religious subgroups. Each group has its own unique sexual standards and beliefs that must be regarded by its members. Homosexual communities also play a critical role in the lives of lesbian and gay persons. These communities offer an arena of competency and a safe haven for the women and men who otherwise are set apart from the majority subculture by sexual orientation. Within lesbian and gay subcultures, the negative effects of social stigma are modulated, social supports are built, important information is exchanged, sexual behaviors are modeled, and friendships and romantic relationships are identified. The positive effects of identification within a supportive and familiar subculture cannot be overstated. For example, the beneficial impact of community affiliations on HIV risk reduction among gay men has been described as one of the most dramatic events in the history of health education.

Recalling the previous definition, I propose that healthy sexual development for homosexually-oriented persons is the evolution of sexual attitudes, feelings, and behaviors which, *overall*, enhance adaptation in the various subcultures to which they belong. At the very least, healthy sexual development demands a positive homosexual core identity and the skills to adapt to other subgroups as well. Both conditions are essential to a healthy sexuality. Assimilation within the majority culture, without positive homosexual identity, can lead to self-hatred or disastrous consequences, as in the case of the lesbian adolescent who becomes pregnant to hide her homosexual feelings. Conversely, inability to "fit" within nongay subcultures can lead to extreme vulnerability. Witness the relentless maltreatment of gay-identified boys in most American schools.

Thus, for gay adolescents and adults, successful sexual development means discovering and internalizing the sexual values and norms of the homosexual community and, at the same time, adjusting to (or at least surviving in) other worlds too. If the concept is difficult for the reader, consider the challenge for a teenager who is newly exploring homosexual feelings!

Under the general rubric of a socially-adaptive sexual identity, healthy sexual development for gay and lesbian persons includes several other specific characteristics, the first being an ability to achieve emotional intimacy with another person of the same gender. Historically, emotional (and physical) intimacy for gay and lesbian people has not been confined to monogamous, long-term relationships. Although such arrangements may be adaptive in the AIDS era, there were other times in the recent past when extended relationships with other men or women were exceedingly dangerous. Healthy homosexual persons have always found unique ways to express intimacy, in the safest possible ways, using a diversity of relationship types.

A second characteristic of healthy homosexual development is the ability to achieve physical sexual gratification with someone of the same gender. This not only requires a functional reproductive physiology but also the ability to experience sex as psychologically pleasurable and rewarding. It also implies freedom from sexual scripts that are injurious to self or others, including those behaviors that might transmit HIV.

Finally, healthy sexual development entails an affirmative self-concept as a homosexual person; and a sense of being a lovable, respectable, and competent woman or man. Healthy sexual development includes learning the skills to resist degrading treatment, to reject sexual violence, and to refuse social limitations based on gender or sexual orientation.

Of course, healthy sexual development for a member of an oppressed sexual minority group is not an easy process. There are no manuals, schools, institutions, or easily visible role models for guidance. In fact, the path is obscured by misinformation, fear, and shame. Sexual development for gay and lesbian people is a function of experiential learning; and mistakes are punishable by fatal sexually transmitted diseases, social ostracism, and other harsh penalties. The development of a healthy sexual identity against such odds is a testimony to the resilience of adolescents and adults who survive the crisis of "coming out." Ultimately, their developmental progress must not be judged against a heterosexual standard, but by their ability to find unique strategies to bridge divergent and conflicting sexual subcultures.

Reference

1. Erikson, E.H. Childhood and society. New York: Horton, 1950.

Acknowledgements: This article was supported in part by Grant #MCJ-000985 from the Department of Health and Human Services, Public Health Service, Bureau of Maternal and Child Health and Resources Development.

The Impact
of Homophobia on
Male Sexual Development

Jay Friedman, BA

Director, Institute on Relationships, Intimacy and Sexuality
Director of Education, Planned Parenthood of
Northern New England

My vision of ideal sexual development for boys… How many times did I break into laughter, in the past few weeks — crumpled pages of impossible dreams piled on the floor — wondering if I was working on a romance novel rather than a journal article. Then it hit me: *homophobia — the disease of suspicion.*

Last week, after a presentation at a school in rural Maine, a group of boys asked me if I was gay. The next day, in the school's gym, the same group of boys decided I was "cool," and not a "fag," because they had watched me play basketball and had decided that I was good. Upon returning to Vermont, I reviewed evaluation forms from a teacher training session that I had given on homosexuality and homophobia. One teacher wrote: "I question whether Jay should be doing these lessons on sexual identity. He does not seem distant enough from the topic."

I believe that homophobia, which I define as more than a fear or hatred of homosexuals and homosexuality but a fear of being perceived as gay, is perhaps the *greatest* pressure boys face while growing up. It sparks male hatred of women and fear of closeness to other people.

Homophobia begins in elementary school when "girl," "sissy," "queer," "virgin," and "fag" are the worst put-downs boys can hear. Many boys, at that time, also begin to enjoy the "skirt game"— dropping their pens on the floor as an excuse to look up a girl's skirt at her "underwear." Meanwhile, music, television, and advertisements teach them that women are objects for men's sexual pleasure. Then homophobia begins to play itself out in locker-room talk where "the guys" boast of "scoring." To be "cool," and to avoid being called "gay," boys forcibly push for intercourse with girls. Recent studies indicate that the average age of first intercourse for inner-city boys is 12. Even masturbation is affected by homophobia and mysogyny. In the hallways, and in sexuality education classes, boys often say, "only fags masturbate" or "why masturbate, you can always find an ugly girl willing to have sex." Homophobia thus encourages boys to label people based on stereotypes; to compete with and distance themselves from other boys; and to objectify, and even rape, girls.

• • •

The image is clear in my mind: a large billboard featuring a jean-clad, shirtless, 16-year-old boy encouraging males to practice masturbating with a condom in place. A vision of the future? No. Surprisingly, I saw these posters in train stations in Sweden two years ago. The image remains vividly in my mind as a symbol of ideal sexual development for boys. The poster — in its entirety — affirmed being male. It affirmed being sexual, with masturbation as an acceptable expression of sexual behavior. And, it affirmed being responsible.

• • •

In my vision of ideal sexual development, all young people will partipate in comprehensive sexuality education in their schools, which will demystify sexuality, including homosexuality, normalize "sex talk," and help boys overcome the need to sexualize everything in their lives. Such education will raise self-esteem and will empower all youth, regardless of their sexual orientation.

Sexual development will begin earlier than adolescence. Dads will serve as role models for their sons — and their sons will cherish fatherhood, will break down traditional barriers, and will show genuine affection for their children. Such men — in their roles as coaches, corporate heads, and parents — will not diminish any injury or defeat by saying, "Shake it off, get out there and compete. We don't want any sissies out there, only winners!"

Boys will respond to "girl" putdowns by saying, "Thank you. There are qualities of being female that I am proud to possess." The new males will counter sexism, heterosexism, and other forms of oppression, realizing that these hurt them by reinforcing rigid gender role sterotypes. Men, as women's rights and gay rights activists, will welcome everyone into their traditional positions of power, as judges, clergy, military and police officers, school administrators, doctors, attorneys, and politicians. Boys will treat all women as sisters. They also will love and respect their partners and will take responsibility for using birth control and for practicing safer sex. In my ideal world, boys will grow up in an environment that encourages them to talk with each other, to share their feelings, and to get nurturance and support from both scxes.

Perhaps, most importantly, society will expect men to be nothing less than what they have the positive potential to be. In this ideal world's romance novels, boys who become men that are sensitive, loving, gentle, and caring, will be appreciated and truly desired.

· · ·

To the teacher who questioned my closeness to this issue, and to other educators questioning their role in regard to homophobia, I offer this challenge. We cannot afford to be anything but close to this issue. Otherwise, our silence only promotes oppression, and it hurts the young men and women whose lives we care about so deeply.

Homosexuality: Who and Why?

Melvin Konner, M.D.

Melvin Konner, an anthropologist and physician, teaches at Emory University.

In the bad old days, when homosexuality was considered a mental illness, a friend of mine was trying to go straight. He was seeing a distinguished psychoanalyst who believed (and still believes) that what some call a life style and still others call a crime is a psychiatrically treatable disorder. Through six years of anguished analysis, my friend changed his sexual orientation and married. His wife was wonderful—they had been friends for years—but he died unexpectedly of a heart attack at the age of 42, six months after the wedding. I am not superstitious, and I don't blame anyone, least of all his wife; he was happy with her. But a nagging question remains: Is it possible that my friend's doctor was trying to change something that should have been left alone?

He had been homosexual for years, and had had at least one stable long-term relationship. But he lived in a society that condemned him on religious and medical grounds. He "freely" chose to change through psychoanalysis. But this was a limited sort of freedom, and though he in fact did change—as some have—he did not live to find out how the change would work.

Those bad old days are over; yet a rising tide of bigotry against gay people has followed the AIDS epidemic. Religious fanatics point to AIDS as proof of God's wrath. Some gay men and women have begun to ponder again the nature of their sexual orientation, and parents wonder: Who becomes gay?

Neither science nor art has yet produced a single answer. Yet perhaps that in itself is an answer: that anything so complicated and various and interesting could have a single origin seems wrongheaded. Socrates and Tennessee Williams, Sappho and Adrienne Rich, to take only four people, representing only two cultures, seem certain to have come to their homosexuality in four such different ways as to make generalizations useless. In the further reaches of the anthropological universe, we find variations that knock most folk theories for a loop.

Consider the Sambia of New Guinea, described by Gilbert Herdt in "Guardians of the Flutes." They belong to a group of cultures in which homosexual practices are actually *required* of boys for several years as rites of passage into adulthood. After adolescence, the young men abandon homosexual practices, marry women, father children and continue as heterosexuals for the rest of their lives.

The lesson is threefold: first, a culture can make such a rule and get every person to conform; second, years of obligatory homosexuality apparently do not commit the average man to a lifetime of homoerotic desires. The third lesson may be drawn from the life of Kalutwo, a Sambia. He grew up stigmatized as the illegitimate son of an older widow and had no contact with his father. He showed unac-ceptably strong homoerotic attachments, and never adjusted to a heterosexual relationship, having four marriages without issue—possibly unconsummated—by his mid-30's. According to Herdt and the psychoanalyst Robert Stoller, Kalutwo would have been homosexual anywhere.

The conclusion is reasonable. In every population, some men—most estimates say 5 to 10 percent—are drawn to homoerotic pursuits, whether they are punished, allowed or required. The percentage of strongly homoerotic women is generally estimated to be smaller, though in bisexuality women are said to outnumber men. But it should be remembered, definitions vary, and biases in such estimates are inevitable.

Some homosexuality was said to be present in all of 76 societies examined in one cross-cultural study, including the Tahitians, the Mohave Indians and a number of Amazonian tribes. In 48 (64 percent), it was condoned; in no society was it the dominant mode. Thus, all the societies had homosexuality, and the majority accepted its inevitability.

Not so our society. The Judeo-Christian tradition condemned homosexuality unequivocally, ending Greco-Roman tolerance. Yet centuries of condemnation, culminating in the Nazi attempt to physically exterminate homosexuals along with Jews and other "undesirables," have failed to make this minority acquiesce. Where do homosexuals come from, and how do they persist in the face of such persecution? In April 1935, with the Nazi's noose tightening around homosexuals, Sigmund Freud wrote to the mother of a gay man, "Homosexuality is assuredly no advantage, but it is nothing to be ashamed of, no vice, no degradation, it cannot be classified as an illness." Yet he went on to attribute it to "a certain arrest of sexual development" and then to deny that successful reorientation through psychoanalysis was possible, at least not "in the majority of cases."

Freud's sensitive formulation is remarkably close to the one we would give today. Although few accept his notion about arrested sexual development, most psychiatrists agree that sexual orientation is difficult to change, and that change is not intrinsically desirable. But a person's sexual orientation may be linked in some poorly understood way with anxiety, depression and other medically defined symptoms that can be treated, regardless of what may happen to sexual orientation.

Extensive research on the psychological development of homosexuals, by Allan Bell and others at the Kinsey Institute, found no support for most theories. The only factor implicating parents was (for both sexes) a poor relationship with the father — something shared by Kalutwo.

Yet some characteristics of the child could be predictive. For both sexes, but especially for males, gender nonconformity in childhood predicted homoerotic adaptation in adulthood. Other studies have drawn the same conclusion. The most dramatic, called "The 'Sissy Boy Syndrome' and

Age-old questions on the subject abound. Even after many studies, there are few, if any, authoritative answers – and prejudice is rife.

the Development of Homosexuality," was published in 1987 by Richard Green, a psychiatrist at the University of California at Los Angeles. His was the first study starting with childhood and following through to adulthood, rather than asking adults about their memories. Boys dissatisfied with being boys — cross-dressing, avidly pursuing traditional girls' games to the exclusion of boys' games, and the like — had a high likelihood of growing up gay. Two-thirds to three-fourths became homosexuals. No homosexuality appeared in a control group.

GREEN'S UNEXPECTEDLY STRONG findings have been variously interpreted as showing that male homosexuality is innate or that early childhood environment is key. Either way, some gay men are *intrinsically* homoerotic. Some studies have pointed to genes. For example, identical twins are more likely to share the same sexual orientation than nonidentical twins. And in a recent study by Richard Pillard and James Weinrich, homosexual men were four times as likely to have a homosexual brother (21 percent) as were heterosexual men. Although these familial patterns could be interpreted as stemming from shared early experiences, it is at least equally likely that they are due to shared genes.

Nevertheless, the rare "sissy boy" syndrome cannot account for the majority of even male homosexuals, and for females the predictive power of "tomboyishness" is less strong. Frequently, homosexual orientation is not accom-panied by these or any other departure from typical gender roles. In the last decade, one study after another — as well as the expressive literature that followed the increased tolerance of the 1970's — has shown that homosexuals differ enormously from one another. As Bell and Martin Weinberg concluded in another book: "We do not do justice to people's sexual orientation when we refer to it by a singular noun. There are 'homosexualities' and there are 'heterosexualities.' " Life styles, personalities, behaviors, hopes and dreams all show tremendous variation among people who share either of those labels. No uniformity, psychological, hormonal or genetic has been found.

Bell and Weinberg write that their "least ambiguous finding . . . is that homosexuality is not necessarily related to pathology." In 1974, the American Psychiatric Association conceded the truth of this observation, essentially made by Freud. In that year — three years after my friend's death — homosexuality was removed from the association's list of diagnostic categories. In the current official diagnostic manual, it is represented by only a vestige: "persistent and marked distress about one's sexual orientation," a subcategory under "Sexual Disorder Not Otherwise Specified." This allows homosexuals who are distressed by their sexual orientation to seek psychiatric help to change it. A good therapist will understand that the distress is not necessarily intrinsic, but may be the product of continued social prejudice. As Freud put it in his 1935 letter to the mother about her homosexual son, if he "is unhappy, neurotic, torn by conflicts, inhibited in his social life, analysis may bring him harmony, peace of mind, full efficiency, whether he remains a homosexual or gets changed."

In fact, if the psychiatrist is fair-minded, the same diagnostic subcategory will admit patients dissatisfied with their heterosexual orientation and wanting to become gay. Adrienne Rich — whose lesbian poems are perhaps the most beautiful recent love poetry — has described a syndrome she calls "compulsory heterosexuality." It refers to the requirement of universal heterosexual adaptation imposed on American women, who she believes are, like all other women, naturally bisexual.

In this realm, diagnoses will not help much. The most common recent answer to the main questions about sexual orientation has been something like "I'm O.K.; you're O.K." But, better, is the reply to that bit of psychobabble provided by Fritz Perls, the founder of Gestalt psychotherapy: "I'm not O.K.; you're not O.K. — and that's O.K." As for religious pieties, they are even less helpful than diagnoses. Fear of AIDS is understandable, but it's really beside the point. If AIDS were God's punishment for gay men, then gay women would presumably be God's chosen people, for they have the lowest rates of AIDS and other sexually transmitted diseases. Perhaps in an atmosphere of tolerance and compassion, we can all do better at finding out — and becoming — who we really are.

Shattered Innocence

CHILDHOOD SEXUAL ABUSE IS YIELDING ITS DARK SECRETS TO THE COLD LIGHT OF RESEARCH.

Alfie Kohn

Alfie Kohn's book, No Contest: The Case Against Competition, *has just been published by Houghton Mifflin.*

No one would claim today that child sexual abuse happens in only one family in a million. Yet that preposterous estimate, based on statistics from 1930, was published in a psychiatric textbook as recently as 1975. Sensational newspaper headlines about day-care center scandals seem to appear almost daily and, together with feminist protests against sexist exploitation, these reports have greatly increased public awareness of what we now know is a widespread problem.

Even so, the most recent scientific findings about child sexual abuse—how often it happens and how it affects victims in the short and long term—have received comparatively little attention. These findings suggest that as many as 40 million people, about one in six Americans, may have been sexually victimized as children. As many as a quarter of these people may be suffering from a variety of psychological problems, ranging from guilt and poor self-esteem to sexual difficulties and a tendency to raise children who are themselves abused.

The startling figure of 40 million is derived from several studies indicating that 25 to 35 percent of all women and 10 to 16 percent of all men in this country experienced some form of

abuse as children, ranging from sexual fondling to intercourse. In August 1985, *The Los Angeles Times* published the results of a national telephone poll of 2,627 randomly selected adults. Overall, 22 percent of respondents (27 percent of the women and 16 percent of the men) confided that they had experienced as children what they now identify as sexual abuse.

Some victims of abuse may be reluctant to tell a stranger on the telephone about something as traumatic and embarrassing as sexual abuse, which suggests that even the *Times* poll may have understated the problem. When sociologist Diana Russell of Mills College sent trained interviewers around San Francisco to interview 930 randomly selected women face-to-face, she found that 357, or 38 percent, reported at least one instance of having been sexually abused in childhood. When the definition of abuse was widened to include sexual advances that never reached the stage of physical contact, more than half of those interviewed said they had had such an experience before the age of 18.

Confirming the *Times* and Russell studies is a carefully designed Gallup Poll of more than 2,000 men and women from 210 Canadian communities. The results, published in 1984, show that 22 percent of the respondents were sexually abused as children. As

with Russell's study, that number increases dramatically, to 39 percent, when noncontact abuse is included.

John Briere, a postdoctoral fellow at Harbor-University of California, Los Angeles Medical Center, has reviewed dozens of studies of child abuse in addition to conducting several of his own. "It is probable," he says, "that at least a quarter to a third of adult women and perhaps half as many men have been sexually victimized as children."

One reason these numbers are so surprising, and the reason estimates of one family in a million could be taken seriously for so long, is that many children who are sexually abused understandably keep this painful experience to themselves. In the *Times* poll, one-third of those who said they had been victimized also reported that they had never before told anyone. Many therapists still do not bother to ask their clients whether abuse has taken place, even when there is good reason to suspect that it has.

Studies demonstrate that most child sexual abuse happens to those between the ages of 9 and 12 (although abuse of 2- and 3-year-olds is by no means unusual), that the abuser is almost always a man and that he is typically known to the child—often a relative. In many cases, the abuse is not limited to a single episode, nor does the abuser usually use force. No race, ethnic group or economic class is immune.

All children do not react identically to sexual abuse. But most therapists would agree that certain kinds of behavior and feelings occur regularly among victims. The immediate effects of sexual abuse include sleeping and eating disturbances, anger, withdrawal and guilt. The children typically appear to be either afraid or anxious.

Two additional signs show up so frequently that experts rely upon them as indicators of possible abuse when they occur together. The first is sexual

abuse, it is far more difficult to draw a definitive connection between such abuse and later psychological problems. "We can't say every child who is abused has this or that consequence, and we are nowhere near producing a validated profile of a child-abuse victim," says Maria Sauzier, a psychiatrist who used to direct the Family Crisis Program for Sexually Abused Children at the New England Medical Center in Boston. In fact, some experts emphasize that many sexual abuse victims emerge relatively unscathed as adults. Indeed, David

der," people whose relationships, emotions and sense of self are all unstable and who often become inappropriately angry or injure themselves. "Not all borderlines have been sexually abused, but many have been," Briere says.

Briere, working with graduate student Marsha Runtz, has also noticed that some female abuse victims "space out" or feel as if they are outside of their own bodies at times. And he has observed that these women sometimes have physical complaints without any apparent medical cause. Briere points out that these two tendencies, known as "dissociation" and "somatization," add up to something very much like hysteria, as Freud used the term.

Other therapists believe the label Post-Traumatic Stress Disorder (PTSD), which has most often been applied to veterans of combat, may also be an appropriate diagnosis for some of those who have been abused. Symptoms of the disorder include flashbacks to the traumatic events, recurrent dreams about them, a feeling of estrangement from others and a general sense of numbness. "It feels to me like the fit is very direct to what we see with [victims of] child sexual abuse," says Christine Courtois, a psychologist from Washington, D.C. "Many victims ... experience the symptoms of acute PTSD." She describes an 18-year-old client, abused by her father for nine years, who carved the words "help me" in her arm. In the course of dealing with what had happened, she would sometimes pass out, an occasional response to extreme trauma.

Even when no such serious psychological problems develop, those who were sexually abused often display a pattern of personal and social problems. Abused individuals in psychotherapy have more difficulties with sexuality and relationships than do others in psychotherapy, for instance. And women who have been victimized often have difficulty becoming sexually aroused. Ironically, others engage in sex compulsively.

Abused women often feel isolated, remain distrustful of men and see themselves as unattractive. "Some [victims] become phobic about intimacy. They can't be touched," says Gail Ericson, a social worker at the Branford Counseling Center in Connecticut. "These women feel rotten about

---

AT LEAST 25 PERCENT OF ALL WOMEN AND 10 PERCENT OF ALL MEN IN THIS COUNTRY EXPERIENCED SOME ABUSE AS CHILDREN, RANGING FROM SEXUAL FONDLING TO INTERCOURSE.

---

preoccupation: excessive or public masturbation and an unusual interest in sexual organs, sex play and nudity. According to William Friedrich, associate professor of psychology at the Mayo Medical School in Rochester, Minnesota, "What seems to happen is the socialization process toward propriety goes awry in these kids."

The second sign consists of a host of physical complaints or problems, such as rashes, vomiting and headaches, all without medical explanation. Once it is discovered that children have been abused, a check of their medical records often reveals years of such mysterious ailments, says psychologist Pamela Langelier, director of the Vermont Family Forensic Institute in South Burlington, Vermont. Langelier emphasizes that children who have been sexually abused should be reassessed every few years because they may develop new problems each time they reach a different developmental stage. "Sometimes it looks like the kids have recovered," she says, "and then at puberty the issues come back again."

While there are clear patterns in the immediate effects of child sexual

Finkelhor, associate director of the Family Violence Research Program at the University of New Hampshire, has warned his colleagues against "exaggerating the degree and inevitability of the long-term negative effects of sexual abuse." For example, Finkelhor and others point out that studies of disturbed, atypical groups, such as prostitutes, runaways and drug addicts, often find that they show higher rates of childhood sexual abuse than in the general population. Yet according to the estimate of Chris Bagley, a professor of social welfare at the University of Calgary, "At least 50 percent of women who were abused do not suffer long-term ill effects."

If 50 percent survive abuse without problems, of course it follows that 50 percent do not. And Bagley, in fact, has conducted a study indicating that a quarter of all women who are sexually abused develop serious psychological problems as a result. Given the epidemic proportions of sexual abuse, that means that millions are suffering.

Briere, for example, has found a significant degree of overlap between abuse victims and those who suffer from "borderline personality disor-

themselves—especially their bodies." As a group, adults who were sexually abused as children consistently have lower self-esteem than others. Other studies have found abuse victims to be more anxious, depressed and guilt-ridden.

Might there be a connection between the high incidence of child sexual abuse among girls and the fact that women tend, in general, to score lower on measures of self-esteem than men? Bagley believes that this disparity may simply reflect the fact that in our society, more women are abused: Seven of ten victims are girls, so any random sampling of men and women will pick up more abused women than men,

those in Russell's survey who had been abused as children reported that they were later victims of rape or attempted rape. Abuse victims "don't know how to take care of themselves," Courtois says. "They're easy targets for somebody, waiting for victimization to happen." This may be due to poor self-image, lack of assertiveness or the feeling that they deserve to be punished.

Women, of course, are not to blame for being victims. "In a society that raises males to behave in a predatory fashion toward females, undermining a young girl's defenses is likely to be exceedingly perilous for her," Russell says, since childhood abuse "could

that the prognosis is particularly bad for those who have been abused by more than one person. Counselor Claire Walsh, director of the Sexual Assault Recovery Service at the University of Florida, has paid special attention to this subgroup. She studied 30 women who were in psychotherapy and who had been abused by their fathers, 18 of whom had also been abused by at least one other person. Walsh found a different psychological profile for those who had been molested by more than one person, which included more anxiety, fear and flashbacks. She also believes that PTSD may show up more often when there is more than one abuser.

Another important variable is the age of the abuser. Russell found that victims are most traumatized if their abuser was between the ages of 26 and 50.

Victims seem to experience more serious problems if force is used during the abuse and if the abuser is a close relative, but evidence for these claims is not conclusive.

Obviously, large gaps remain in the research on the long-term effects of child sexual abuse. This is not very surprising given how new the field is. Most of the studies reported here have been conducted since 1980, and the five scholarly journals devoted to the subject have all been launched within the last two years. Only in 1986 was the groundwork finally laid for an American professional society dealing with sexual child abuse.

There is no question that the field already has produced striking findings. "We now clearly know that sexual abuse is a major risk factor for a lot of later mental-health problems," Finkelhor says. "What we don't yet know is who is most susceptible to these problems, how other experiences interact with abuse or what can be done."

Finkelhor adds that research on child sexual abuse "should teach all social scientists and mental-health practitioners some humility. Despite several generations of clinical expertise and knowledge of childhood development, it was only very recently that we came to see how incredibly widespread this childhood trauma is.

"It may make us realize that there are other things about childhood that we don't have a clear perspective on as well," he says.

*S*INCE GIRLS IN OUR SOCIETY ARE ABUSED MORE COMMONLY THAN BOYS, PERHAPS IT'S UNDERSTANDABLE THAT WOMEN, AS A GROUP, HAVE LOWER SELF-ESTEEM THAN MEN.

perhaps enough of a difference to account for the gender gap in self-esteem.

In one study, Bagley discovered that half of all women with psychological problems had been abused. "The reason for the higher rate [of psychopathology] for women is the higher rate of sexual abuse in women," he says. Other researchers might not support so sweeping a conclusion, but Bagley points to a study of his that showed that nonabused men and women have comparable self-esteem.

One of the most disturbing findings about child abuse is its strong intergenerational pattern: Boys who are abused are far more likely to turn into offenders, molesting the next generation of children; girls are more likely to produce children who are abused. Two of five abused children in a study conducted by Sauzier, psychologist Beverly Gomes-Schwartz and psychiatrist Jonathan Horowitz had mothers who were themselves abused.

In addition, victimization can lead to revictimization. Nearly two-thirds of

have stripped away some of [her] potential ability to protect" herself.

Men who were abused, meanwhile, are likely to be confused about their sexual identity, deeply ashamed, unwilling to report the experience and apt to respond aggressively. Says Jack Rusinoff, a counselor in Minneapolis who works with male victims, "I have one 5-year-old boy who's already on the road to being an abuser." This boy, like many others, has displayed sexual aggression, even at this age. Langelier, who has seen more than 200 victims over the last three years, notes that her young male clients are sometimes caught reaching for others' genitals or "making demands for sexual stimulation."

Is there any indication, given this variation in psychological outcome, why one case of childhood sexual abuse leads to serious adult problems while another does not? So far, only two characteristics of abuse have consistently been linked with major difficulties later on. For one, studies by Bagley, Briere and others have shown

SEXUAL HARASSMENT
'80s-STYLE

More subtle now—and more costly.

Brian S. Moskal

This is a quiz. Read each incident and answer "Yes" or "No" as to whether you think the situation presents a case of sexual harassment.

• Jackie thinks Bob is very well-built. She often stares at his body when she thinks he isn't looking. Although he hasn't told her, Bob has noticed Jackie looking and, frankly, it makes him uncomfortable. Sexual harassment?

• At a Christmas party, Barbara's boss has too much to drink. He tells her how beautiful she is and that she understands him better than his wife. He says he intends to make an obvious token of his appreciation of her and her work. Then he asks to drive her home. Is this sexual harassment?

• Sylvia hates the days when she has to work with Jeremy, a co-worker with whom she once had a stormy and romantic relationship. Jeremy hasn't gotten over Sylvia and persistently asks her to come back to him. Sylvia tells her manager about the situation, and he replies that they should try to work it out, reasoning that it is best for

him to stay out of Sylvia's personal business. Is this sexual harassment? Is the manager liable?

• A new clerical-support person in your area of responsibility tells you that she feels uncomfortable during breaks. She says the men who are in the designated break area tell crude jokes and pass around girlie magazines while she is there. Sexual harassment or not?

• Your manager and one of your colleagues are having an affair. Since the affair started, your colleague has received better and easier work assignments, a bigger raise, and a recent promotion. Until their relationship began, you had been the star of the department. Sexual harassment?

The answer to all five questions is "Yes." All five could result in sexual-harassment charges being brought against individuals and the company.

In the first example, Jackie is creating what's called a hostile working environment for Bob. He could file a sexual-harassment charge without even telling Jackie that her looks are unwelcome.

Barbara's partying boss likely is in deep trouble. This is an example of quid pro quo (something for something) sexual harassment. Sex in exchange for raises or promotions are other forms of actionable sexual-harassment cases.

Jeremy had better get the message from Sylvia that their affair is over. Both he and Sylvia's manager are liable under sexual-harassment laws. If the manager does nothing, Sylvia would not only have a case against both, but also the corporation would be legally liable for perhaps millions of dollars in claims.

The new clerical-support person is being subjected to a hostile environment. Sexually suggestive posters hanging on the walls, even in a private office, can offend someone and make the poster owner liable for his or her actions.

The affair between your manager and your colleague is an example of third-party sexual harassment. Your status has been diminished not because of a change in your work ability but because your colleague has gained an unfair advantage.

This is sexual harassment, '80s-style, more subtle than the boss chasing his secretary around the desk. It's also more pervasive, and more expensive, than many may be aware of.

Here's a shocking statistic: Sexual-harassment complaints by female employees were reported at 90% of the nation's largest corporations last year, according to a survey by *Working Woman* magazine. In addition, more than one-third of the companies were sued by alleged victims, a quarter had been sued repeatedly, and each spent an average of $6.7 million a year in sex-harassment related costs (based on absenteeism, low productivity, and employee turnover).

Two-thirds of the complaints, the survey reports, were made against immediate supervisors and upper management. The overwhelming number of incidents were reported by women complaining about unwanted and unwelcomed attention from men.

The survey suggests that many companies are responding to the problem, partly because they fear the adverse publicity and litigation costs associated with harassment complaints. Two out of ten sexual harassers are eventually fired, and others are given written or oral warnings.

It's an expensive issue. In 1987 a record $3.2 million was paid by one company, K mart Corp., to settle a single case. A court settlement, bad publicity, and damaged recruitment can cost more than a company spends annually for employee health and medical benefits.

Under Title VII of the Civil Rights Act, sexual harassment is a form of sex discrimination, and the usual remedies apply—back pay, reinstatement or front-pay injunctive relief, and attorney's fees.

But just what is sexual harassment? In short, unwelcomed sexual advances, requests for sexual favors, and other verbal (sexual jokes) or physical conduct (pinching, arms wrapped around

HOW MUCH DO I KNOW ABOUT SEXUAL HARASSMENT?

A TEST FOR EMPLOYEES
TRUE OR FALSE?

1. If I just ignore unwanted sexual attention, it will usually stop. [T] [F]

2. If I don't mean to sexually harass another employee, there's no way my behavior can be perceived by him or her as sexually harassing. [T] [F]

3. Some employees don't complain about unwanted sexual attention from another worker because they don't want to get that person in trouble. [T] [F]

4. If I make sexual comments to someone and that person doesn't ask me to stop, then I guess my behavior is welcome. [T] [F]

5. To avoid sexually harassing a woman who comes to work in a traditionally male workplace, the men simply should not haze her. [T] [F]

6. A sexual harasser may be told by a court to pay part of a judgment to the employee he or she harassed. [T] [F]

7. A sexually harassed man does not have the same legal rights as a woman who is sexually harassed. [T] [F]

8. About 90% of all sexual harassment in today's workplace is done by males to females. [T] [F]

9. Sexually suggestive pictures or objects in a workplace don't create a liability unless someone complains. [T] [F]

10. Telling someone to stop his or her unwanted sexual behavior usually doesn't do any good. [T] [F]

Answers: 1) FALSE. 2) FALSE. 3) TRUE. 4) FALSE. 5) FALSE. 6) TRUE. 7) FALSE. 8) TRUE. 9) FALSE. 10) FALSE.

A TEST FOR MANAGEMENT PERSONNEL

1. Men in male-dominated workplaces usually have to change their behavior when a woman begins working there. [T] [F]

2. An employer is not liable for the sexual harassment of one of its employees unless that employee loses specific job benefits or is fired. [T] [F]

3. A court can require a sexual harasser to pay part of the judgment to the employee he or she has sexually harassed. [T] [F]

4. A supervisor can be liable for sexual harassment committed by one of his or her employees against another. [T] [F]

5. An employer can be liable for the sexually harassing behavior of management personnel even if it is unaware of that behavior and has a policy forbidding it. [T] [F]

6. It is appropriate for a supervisor, when initially receiving a sexual-harassment complaint, to determine if the alleged recipient overreacted or misunderstood the alleged harasser. [T] [F]

7. When a supervisor is talking with an employee about an allegation of sexual harassment against him or her, it is best to ease into the allegation instead of being direct. [T] [F]

8. Sexually suggestive visuals or objects in a workplace don't create a liability unless an employee complains about them and management allows them to remain. [T] [F]

9. The lack of sexual-harassment complaints is a good indication that sexual harassment is not occurring. [T] [F]

10. It is appropriate for a supervisor to tell an employee to handle unwelcome sexual behavior if he or she thinks that the employee is misunderstanding the behavior. [T] [F]

11. The *intent* behind employee A's sexual behavior is more important than the *impact* of that behavior on employee B when determining if sexual harassment has occurred. [T] [F]

Answers: 1) FALSE. 2) FALSE. 3) FALSE. 4) TRUE. 5) TRUE. 6) FALSE. 7) FALSE. 8) FALSE. 9) FALSE. 10) FALSE. 11) FALSE.

Source: ©1988 by Anderson-davis.

the shoulders) of a sexual nature when (1) submission to such conduct is made either explicitly or implicitly a term or condition of employment; (2) submission to or rejection of such conduct by an individual is used as a basis for employment decisions affecting that individual or third parties; or (3) such conduct has the purpose, in effect, of unreasonably interfering with an individual's work performance or creating an intimidating, hostile, or offensive working environment.

In the '80s a greater proportion of cases involves co-workers rather than boss-subordinate incidents. In addition, sexual harassment today can be more subtle and even more threatening to women than ever before.

There's the member of upper, upper management and part owner of a 650-person business who was fond of checking out the women's locker room at the company's physical-fitness center in the early afternoon. That's when a certain female employee would often exercise and shower so that she would miss the peak hours of fitness-center use. He would not so innocently knock on the locker room door and quickly push it open in the hope of seeing her in the buff. After the woman complained to a human-resources professional, a lock was placed on the door. The next time Mr. Big tried to get in he was stymied. The woman, without ever confronting one of her ultimate bosses, resolved the situation. And Mr. Big got the message when he found the lock on the door.

"I sometimes think we haven't touched the real issue," says Neil E. Schermitzler, Chicago-based director of human resources, central region, Wang Laboratories Inc. "I sense there continues to be a need for management and employees to really understand what sexual harassment is and get with the 1980s. There is still a lot of confusion over the subject. It's an issue of power and exclusion.

Many women continue to feel unempowered or disenfranchised in the workforce. They feel their livelihoods are in jeopardy. In a day of visible litigation, many sexually harassed people are hesitant to go through company procedures to resolve the issue or through the legal process because they might feel like lepers or it will take too long. The predominant number of sexually harassed women are still afraid of retribution from their immediate manager," adds Mr. Schermitzler.

For the most part, males are still downright ignorant about what constitutes sexual harassment. "It's hard for some men to realize that what they might get away with in a single's bar or other social situations isn't acceptable behavior in the business environment," observes Mr. Schermitzler.

"There isn't a good understanding or comprehension that people's jobs and careers are on the line. I blame it on the lack of education and training at the corporation. It's a hard lesson to learn. Men still think sexual harassment is a joking matter."

Supervisors, management, and the corporation itself can be held legally liable for tacitly approving, condoning, or ignoring cases of sexual harassment. It's surprising that, with so many women in the workforce believing they are subjected to major and minor forms of sexual harassment, more legal cases aren't filed.

"It's so rampant and so devastating that if people don't address the issue, it could mean the downfall of a company," asserts Anthony M. Micolo, vice president, human resources, Dime Savings Bank of New York. "Sexual harassment is very widespread. In a way, it's like rape—it happens much more often than it's ever reported. A lot of people are harassed, yet they don't initiate formal complaints because they feel they will be blamed for instigating it or will become outcasts in the company."

In addition, "sexual-harassment verdicts against companies create bad press and can hurt a company in its future recruitment efforts. It's a negative, and if a company has a negative reputation for sexual harassment, people don't want to work there. Outside of the bottom line, the intangibles are just huge," says Mr. Micolo, who is the author of several books on the human-resources function.

Sexual harassment isn't a joke, even though many harassers see it that way. Nor is it a compliment to women. Even a comment that may sound innocent to many men— "that's a nice dress"—can be a form of sexual harassment.

"Men say they are complimenting women, but women don't take it as a compliment," observes Odessa Komer, United Auto Workers' vice president and director of the Women's Dept. In the case of union workers involved in sexual-harassment cases, the local, the national, and even the international union can be sued.

Who gets harassed? After examining sexual-harassment charges filed with the Illinois Equal Employment Opportunity Commission over a two-year period, David E. Terpstra, a professor of business at the University of Idaho, found that "less serious" rather than "more serious" forms of behavior prompted the filing of charges. "We found that most of the charges were based on unwanted physical contact, offensive language, sexual propositions unlinked to threats or promises, and socialization or date requests."

The age of the filers ranged from 18 to 50; however, the majority were clustered in the 20-to-35 age group. Of the 81 people who filed charges, 95% were women. By education, 41% of the filers had a high-school education, 38% had a college degree. By occupation, 25% were secretarial/clerical, 26% were semiskilled or unskilled, 18% were paraprofessional/technical, 5% were skilled craft, 3% were professional, 12% were in sales, and 11% were administrative/managerial.

The percentage of filers by salary were: less than $10,000—39%; $10,000 to $14,999—25%; $15,000 to $19,999—25%; and $20,000 or more—10%.

How does a company protect itself from cases of sexual harassment? First and foremost, there should be a strict company policy banning any forms of sexual harassment. Second, there ought to be a training and education program that outlines examples, subtle and not so subtle, of sexual harassment.

"Once a company has a corporate policy, men are much more careful. Policies make every employee, supervisor, and member of management aware," says Kathy B. Willingham, personnel director at AnSon Gas Corp., Oklahoma City. "Policies are a first step a company can take to protect itself. The second is to have an outlet for sexually harassed people to use as a complaint route." It can be a human-resources professional, ombudsman, ombudswoman, or a member of management who is sensitive to issues of harassment and isn't the alleged victim's immediate supervisor. It's usually best to have a member of the same sex listen to the complaint.

"It's much better for a company to handle sexual-harassment complaints inside the company rather than going outside for solutions and resolution. If it goes outside, it increases the corporation's liability and you can bet you'll lose money," says Ms. Willingham.

Once companies are made aware of a complaint, they should investigate it on a thorough and prompt basis—"a couple of days, not weeks or months. You must literally investigate 'as soon as possible,'" stresses Ellen J. Wagner Esq., president of Creative Solutions Inc., Red Bank, N. J. Her firm specializes in the legal aspects of the human-resources function.

The corporate policy must state that the company will take action based on its findings. That action must be spelled out and could include a verbal warning, a suspension, a departmental transfer, or dismissal.

"People must be put on notice that this is serious business," states Ms. Wagner.

HIDDEN RAPE
The shocking truth behind the statistics

Darian Dizon

Darian Dizon is a magazine editor who lives in New York City.

The Sunday morning sun was just peeking into the California sky when the rapist dropped Jeri*, a 34-year-old divorced mother of two, back at her house. She doesn't remember the drive home, except for the one thought that played over and over in her mind: "If I can wash him off me, I'll be all right." Once she was inside her home, Jeri checked on her children and thanked God her teen son and young daughter were still asleep. Then she went to her bedroom, quickly threw off her clothes and stepped into the shower. She turned on the water as hot as she could stand and let it run over her body until it turned cold, but neither the water nor her tears could wash away the horrible memory of the previous night.

He was on top of her. He was saying, "You're a big girl now, baby. You've been around. Who do you think you're kidding?" Then he raped her, and she felt as if she were being stabbed with a knife. But the deepest cut of all came from the voice she heard inside her head: "It's your fault: You *went* to his apartment."

His name was Dirk. Today he was Jeri's rapist; last night he had been Jeri's date.

"Rape by a known assailant" has many aliases—date rape, hidden rape, cocktail rape, acquaintance rape, presumptive rape. According to a bulletin issued in 1985 by the Bureau of Justice Statistics, of the 1.5 million rapes and attempted rapes that occurred between

*NAMES HAVE BEEN CHANGED TO PROTECT PRIVACY.

1973 and 1982, 486,000—or 32 percent—were committed by "non-strangers." Of those attacks, only 45 percent were reported to the police. Rape crisis counselors across the country say that such official tallies seriously underestimate the number of rapes by known assailants: These professionals report that up to 80 percent of their hotline calls involve rapes by men the women knew. Why this discrepancy? Like Jeri, the vast majority of date- and acquaintance-rape survivors don't officially report the incident because they fear that their complaint will be dismissed as "unfounded," and because they fear that their attacker will claim consensual sex as a defense. No wonder this crime is called hidden rape. And yet, the attacks continue.

"Women are three times more likely to be raped by an acquaintance than by a stranger," says Diana E. H. Russell, Ph.D., professor of sociology at Mills College in Oakland, California, whose book *Sexual Exploitation* (Sage, 1984), includes an analysis of a study she conducted in 1978 of 930 San Francisco women. Dr. Russell found that 49 percent of the women she interviewed had been raped or almost raped at least once by someone they knew (other than a relative), and of those women who had been attacked by a date, only one percent had reported the attack to the police. Conversely, only 11 percent of the women said they had been raped or almost raped by a stranger, but 30 percent of those attacks had been reported to the police.

COULD IT HAPPEN TO YOU?

Research indicates that date or acquaintance rape is most likely to happen to women between the ages of 16 and 24 (see "What Can You Tell Your Daughters?"). However, it also can and does happen to women of all ages. And that means divorced and widowed women, too.

"Many of my clients are in their thirties and forties and newly single," says Flora Colao, M.S.W., founder and supervisor of the St. Vincent's Hospital Rape Crisis Center in New York City and coauthor, with Tamar Hosansky, of *Your Children Should Know: Personal-Safety Strategies for Parents to Teach Their Children* (Harper & Row, 1987). "They say, 'I spent twenty years with only one man. I didn't know the rules when I started dating again.'"

The crime of date or acquaintance rape is easy for a rapist to deny and hard for a victim to prove, because most incidents don't involve weapons or cause injuries other than vaginal trauma. Even the rapist himself seems like a perfectly respectable man—until the attack.

LeAnne's story is typical. A 28-year-old legal secretary who lives and works in New York City, she met Jim at a coed jazz-dance class she attended two nights a week. "I thought he was pretty nice, although I certainly didn't have my eye on him," says LeAnne. However, she didn't think it would "hurt" to have drinks with him one Friday night after class; nor was she alarmed when he suggested they go to his apartment a few blocks away and listen to music. "Once we got there, though, he just lunged at me," she says. "He kept pinning me down, forcing his knees between my legs. Well, after a while—I just couldn't fight anymore."

In extensive interviews with 600 rape victims, Gail Abarbanel, director of the Rape Treatment Center in Santa Monica, California, found a certain pattern to acquaintance rapes: They usually occur on weekends between 10 P.M. and 2 A.M. Unlike stranger rape, the attack often takes place on the man's "turf" (in his car or home), continues longer (up to four hours), and is achieved by enough violent bullying—verbal and physical, but without the use of a weapon—to make a woman fear for her well-being or her life.

Elizabeth, a 39-year-old waitress who lives in Delaware, was badly battered during her attack. She had gone out to dinner with a man she had recently met. They were joined by this man's best friend, Tony, and his date. All during dinner, Tony flirted with Elizabeth, but she ignored him. When Tony learned that he lived in Elizabeth's neighborhood, he offered to drive her home after dropping off his date. "How about a nightcap?" he suggested. He seemed like a nice enough person. And, after all, he was "a friend of a friend," so she invited him in. After one drink, he began kissing her. Pushing him away, she said, "Stop, or I'll scream." That's when he got rough and began punching her in the face. Elizabeth remembers being "so afraid he was going to kill me that I lay there and prepared to die."

"BUT HE WAS SUCH A NICE GUY"

If there is one trait that the survivors of date rape can be said to have in common, it is this: trust. Why shouldn't a woman trust a blind date set up by a coworker, the man that a brother or friend introduces as his buddy, or a guy who seems nice enough? Yet that trust often proves to be dangerously misplaced. With her defenses down, a woman is extremely vulnerable to date rape, and her reaction time, in sensing that danger and protecting herself, is slow.

In an article published in the November 1974 issue of *The American*

Journal of Psychiatry, Ann Wolbert Burgess, R.N., D.N.Sc., professor of psychiatric nursing at the University of Pennsylvania School of Nursing in Philadelphia, and Lynda Lytle Holmstrom, Ph.D., a sociology professor at Boston College, put forward their findings concerning the common

psychological repercussions of rape, which they identified, for the first time, as *rape trauma syndrome.* The symptoms—sleeping and eating disorders, sexual dysfunction, phobias and flashbacks—may last from several months to several years. "All rape victims have difficulty recovering from

WHAT CAN YOU TELL YOUR DAUGHTERS?

The numbers don't lie: Date and acquaintance rape is a crime most often committed against young women. "The average age of a victim is eighteen," says Mary P. Koss, Ph.D., professor of psychiatry at the University of Arizona Medical School in Tucson and one of the country's leading researchers on date rape. In a study conducted in 1984 and 1985 of 3,187 women on 32 college campuses, she found that 84 percent of women who had been raped knew their offender; 57 percent were dating their attacker.

No wonder experts feel that acquaintance rape should rank as an important subject of family discussion. Says Gayle Stringer, education coordinator of King County Rape Relief, a crisis center in Renton, Washington, "We get as many reports of date and acquaintance rape after a football game or church outing as after a late-night party." In their booklet, *Where Do I Start? A Parents' Guide for Talking to Teens About Acquaintance Rape* (Kendall/Hunt Publishing, 1984), Stringer and Py Bateman, executive director of Alternatives to Fear, a Seattle-based educational organization for the prevention of sexual assault, offer parents the following tips:

•**Discuss sexual rights and responsibilities with your children.** This should be done as soon as they show an interest in the opposite sex. In a study conducted in the late 1970s at the University of California in Los Angeles, about half of the high school boys and girls surveyed said that forced sex was sometimes okay—if, for instance, a boy spent a lot of money on a date or if a girl excited him sexu-

ally. Girls need to be told that boys must be given clear messages, and that girls *can* say no; boys need to be told that respecting a girl's "no" makes them more, not less, manly.
•**Pick a calm, private time to have such discussion.** Before the prom or after a date is not the right time to bring up the subject of date rape. A weekend walk or drive might offer a better opportunity to talk.
•**Respect the fact that your teen is a sexual being.** Telling a young person, "No fooling around!" only denies his or her sexuality. Instead, state your preferences ("I don't think petting is wise"), give your reasons ("The situation may get out of hand") and keep the discussion open-ended ("You may not agree, but I'm always here to talk").
•**Offer your teenager a "hassle-free bailout."** Teens often find themselves in situations—a wild party, drunken friends—that make them vulnerable to date or acquaintance rape. Tell your kids, "If you're in trouble, call me. I'll come get you, no questions asked. We'll have a cooling-off period and then later, we'll talk." Such an agreement doesn't let your child off the hook, but it *can* get that young person out of danger.
•**Find someone else to handle the discussion if your kids won't listen to you.** "Enlist another person's help—a trusted relative, a family friend," says Bateman. "Parents who don't warn their children about date rape are just deluding themselves into thinking that it'll never happen to their kids. And that kind of delusion can lead to disaster."

—D.D.

being raped, but date- or acquaintance-rape victims have an added issue to deal with," says Dr. Burgess, "especially if their offender was known to them. And that issue is how to relearn to trust people."

Wanda, a 32-year-old beautician who lives in Seattle, is struggling through that process now. "It's not just that I don't trust men," she says. "I don't trust anybody." A young widow with two children, Wanda had become friendly with her new neighbors—Sally, a dental hygienist, and her fiancé, Phil, a carpenter. One night, after dinner at Sally and Phil's house, Phil insisted on walking Wanda home. "Hey, I'm a gentleman," he told her. But once Wanda had unlocked her front door he was anything but. He wrenched both her arms back behind her and threw her on the couch. "He raped me twice—once there and once on my bed," says Wanda.

Wanda later learned that Phil went back home and told Sally, "I just f----- your friend." But like many girlfriends and wives of accused rapists, Sally refused to listen to Wanda's side of the story and told people, "I can't believe she did this to me." One police officer who questioned Wanda implied that perhaps Wanda wanted to break up her friends' relationship. Even Wanda's sister asked her, "Why did you let him walk you home?" The tendency to "blame the victim" is even more pronounced in cases of date rape. Says Kathleen Degen, M.D., a psychiatrist in private practice in Branford, Connecticut, and former psychiatric consultant for the Crime Victim Assessment Project-Rape Intervention Program at St. Luke's-Roosevelt Hospital Center in New York City, "The attacker and victim are often part of the same circle of friends. No one believes that this 'nice' guy could do what the victim says he did, so she is not believed." Tragically, friends and family often desert these women just when they most need support.

Betrayal is keenest when a boyfriend or husband refuses to accept a survivor's innocence. "My husband left me because of this," says Natalie, a 33-year-old accountant in Grand Rapids, Michigan, who was raped by a prospective client during an out-of-town trip. "I went to my client's apartment after a dinner meeting because he said he had some papers for me,

and that's when he raped me. I so desperately needed my husband, Joe, to be there for me, but he couldn't handle it. He thought that I must have led the guy on."

WAS IT MY FAULT?

In trying to understand what has happened to them, stunned survivors often become their own harshest critics. They ask themselves the same questions others ask them: Should I have seen the danger? Did I unwittingly lead my attacker on? What did he see in me?

After she was raped and sodomized by her roommate's boyfriend, Lisa, a 26-year-old department store manager who lives in Atlanta, says she called herself "a slut, a whore, every name in the book." It doesn't matter that this man tricked her into coming to his apartment by calling, while her roommate was out of town, and pretending to be suddenly, desperately ill. Lisa—a practicing Catholic—still felt guilty.

Today, 18 months after Phil raped her, Wanda still has backlashes of doubt. "Doubts about myself, for one," she says. Why didn't I see the danger earlier? Maybe I *was* flirting when I thought I was just being friendly."

According to Flora Colao of the St. Vincent's Hospital Rape Crisis Center, one of the hardest challenges to a date-rape survivor is learning to trust herself again. "Many of these women were self-confident before they were raped. Now they question their own judgment. They ask themselves, 'Why couldn't I see it coming?' "

IS THERE ANY WAY TO TELL?

The sad truth is that date-rapists often do seem "nice," but they may have Jekyll-and-Hyde personalities. "These men can be highly sociable and seductive on one hand, yet predatory and opportunistic on the other," says Robert Prentky, Ph.D., clinical psychologist and research director of the Massachusetts Treatment Center in Bridgewater, a maximum security facility for rehabilitating sex offenders. Says Mary P. Koss, Ph.D., professor of psychiatry at the University of Arizona Medical School in Tucson and one of the country's leading re-

searchers on date rape, "Because these men appear and act 'normal,' they get away with it by making a woman believe that she was partly at fault. Women leave these situations not knowing whether they were *really* raped."

While experts agree that there is no easy way for a woman to identify the man who is inclined to rape, they do believe that such men often exhibit certain telltale signs. "Watch out for the guy who has a macho attitude, who thinks men are better than women, who breaks minor traffic laws—such as speeding or running stop signs—and who seems to depend on membership in a group as a source of self-esteem," says Andrea Parrot, Ph.D., assistant professor in the department of human service studies at Cornell University in Ithaca, New York, and author of *Coping with Date Rape and Acquaintance Rape* (Rosen Publishing, 1988).

SEX IS NOT A MAN'S RIGHT

Looking back on her own attack, Jeri now sees that, in many ways, Dirk fit the profile of a date-rapist. "Until Dirk assaulted me," she says, "I just thought he was a very attractive guy who lived in my neighborhood. So I was happy when he invited me to a party. The funny thing was I probably had the best time I'd ever had at a party. He paid so much attention to me. But once we were alone in his apartment, everything changed. It was like being with a different person."

Another trait common to many date-rapists is their belief that forcing sex is perfectly normal behavior. These men believe that sex is a man's right, his "entitlement"; that when a woman says "no," she really means "yes"; and that, above all, a man should always be in control.

To other date-rapists, a date with a woman automatically promises sexual activity. Says Dr. Degen, "These men mistake a woman's interest in going on a date with them for a desire to have sex with them. Some of them will say, 'Sex is fun—how could you not want it?' They don't see the distinction."

Jeri, for example, was shocked when Dirk phoned her after the rape to ask her out again. When she confronted him with what he'd done, he laughed and said, "I thought you didn't take my calls because I was bad in bed."

Many experts believe that a culture such as ours, which sanctions male aggression, reinforces the date- or acquaintance-rapist's belief that he is seducing a woman rather than raping her. Says Dr. Parrot, "The message these men hear is 'do it.' Look at what happened to the characters on the TV soap opera *General Hospital*. Luke raped Laura, then she fell in love with him and married him. In last season's final episode of *Moonlighting,* Maddie came home and found David in her bed. She was furious and told him to leave. But David grabbed her and kissed her. As angry as Maddie was, she melted in David's arms and the show ended as they were making passionate love. Shows like this give men permission to rape."

All too often this support for the attacker carries over into court. Despite the recent widespread passage of shield laws that prevent a rape victim's sexual history from being introduced in court, attorneys are frequently able to convince a judge that such information is necessary to their client's defense. They can also argue that, because of the defendant's prior relationship with the victim, he had rightly assumed that she had agreed to have sex with him.

Says Leigh Bienen, a New Jersey public defender who specializes in rape law, "Perhaps what's needed is a statute establishing that a prior acquaintance or relationship between the defendant and victim shall not presume consent." Such a statute might encourage women to press charges. Jeri, LeAnne and Lisa did not. Says Lisa, "I wanted to put the whole thing behind me as quickly as possible."

Wanda and Elizabeth, on the other hand, did report their rapes. "I didn't want any other woman to have to go through what I did," says Wanda. (The case ultimately went to trial; Phil was found guilty and sentenced to six years in prison.) Elizabeth took action in order to help her "get control of my life." (Tony was found guilty, but he is now free on appeal.)

When women worry about rape, they usually worry about stranger-rape. To protect themselves, many women install dead-bolt locks on their doors at home and check the backseat of their car before climbing behind the wheel.

But as necessary as these precautions are, they do nothing to protect women from rape by an acquaintance. Here are some pointers on how women can best avoid, or escape, this most frightening situation.

•**Set your own limits in social situations.** Communicate those limits clearly—and beware the man who won't respect your wishes. Personal limits can range from "No petting on the first date" to "I never leave with a man I've just met" to "Two drinks—tops." The man who tries to persuade you to bend your rules is a man who may be trouble.

•**Be alert to certain behaviors.** A date-rapist will most often proceed step-by-step, from intrusion (he invades your personal space—easy to do in a crowded place), to desensitization (he puts an arm around your shoulder or smoothes your hair—anything to establish physical contact) and finally to isolation (he suggests that the two of you go somewhere more private).

•**Speak up immediately if you don't like his behavior.** Tongue-tied? Try practicing Dr. Parrot's formula for assertiveness: "When you do X, I feel Y, and I'd like you to stop." Don't worry about sounding rude or hurting his feelings. Rape-crisis counselors have a slogan: "Better rude than raped."

•**Don't give inconsistent messages.** Says Dr. Parrot, "If you say 'no' with your mouth and 'yes' with your body language, a man will ignore what you're saying." For example, if a man unbuttons a woman's blouse and the woman says 'no' unconvincingly, the man will continue. "But if a woman assertively says to the man, 'Take your hands off me!' and then removes his hand, she is showing that she means what she says."

•**Avoid situations where alcohol and drugs are present.** Studies indicate that up to 50 percent of all rapists had been drinking prior to, or at the time of, the attack. And a woman who has been drinking is less able to defend herself.

•**Trust your instincts.** If a man makes you uncomfortable, end the relationship. You owe no explanations to anybody.

IF YOU ARE ATTACKED
But what should you do if you are attacked? Pauline Bart, Ph.D., a professor of sociology in psychiatry at the University of Illinois in Chicago, and coauthor, with Patricia O'Brien, of *Stopping Rape: Successful Survival Strategies* (Pergamon Press, 1985), says that, based on research from her study of 94 rape victims, conducted in the late 1970s, a woman should try to escape as soon as possible, before the attack escalates. But when escape was not possible, Dr. Bart found that a combination of physical resistance and yelling proved to be the most effective methods of stopping a rape attempt. Women in Dr. Bart's study who cried or said "I have my period" or "I'm a virgin" or who tried to reason with the rapist were rarely successful in fending off the attack. Dr. Prentky cautions, however, that using physical resistance, may also increase your chances of being seriously injured, because an angered rapist is more likely to become violent. In general, experts agree that there is no single correct course of action; you must do what *you* think best to *survive*.

Rape-crisis counselors also urge women to report the assault—to a trusted friend or helping professional and to the police—and to seek medical attention as soon as possible. Hospitals may collect samples of fluids, fibers and hairs found on your clothes and your body to submit as evidence in court. "Do not wash or bathe," advises Judith Rowland, an attorney in San Diego and founder of the California Center on Victimology. "If the attack occurred in your home, leave everything where it is. We want to get a positive I.D."

If a clock were to sound its alarm each time a woman is sexually assaulted in this country, it would ring at least once *every six minutes*. It is crucially important that all women recognize their own vulnerability and learn to recognize a potential date-rapist. "The week before it happened to me, I saw a newspaper article about date rape," says Jeri. "But I thought the women in that article let it happen. Now I know differently, but it's too late. I hope it's not too late for others. That's why I'm sharing my story, because maybe it will save even one woman from going through what I went through."

For more information on date and acquaintance rape, write:
Alternatives to Fear, 1605 17th Ave., Seattle, WA 98122.

Male Rape: The Hidden Crime

Jim Senter

Jim Senter tends his wildflower garden in Durham, NC, and keeps busy working on the program for male survivors at the local rape crisis center. He also works for People Allied For Child Advocacy, a national child rights alliance.

Six years ago, I was raped; and like other rape victims, I have had a hard time coping with the physical and emotional results of that experience. As a man, I have found the silence surrounding male rape the hardest thing to understand and accept. I must break this silence now.

On August 12, 1981, I was on a Greyhound headed east from Denver. It was early morning, and we were just pulling into St. Louis. Like travelers often do, I was thinking of home, and the river that threaded its way through my dreams and the place I grew up in. I left the bus station, stretched aching muscles, and crossed the street to stand by the wharves watching the Mississippi flow by. "Hey, where're you from?" a voice exclaimed behind me. I turned and saw a man dressed in a polo shirt and slacks. "New Orleans," I replied absentmindedly. I went back to staring at the water, thinking "I could take a canoe and be home in a week easy."

"Hey, New Orleans," he spoke again, "you wanna shot of whiskey?" The muscle in my back that was torn when I lifted the engine into a friend's car the week before screamed for relief. I agreed. "Why not? I have an hour-and-a-half to wait anyway."

"Come on up here," he said as he strolled onto the empty loading dock next to a line of empty tractor trailers. I followed; and as I approached, his arm went around my shoulders and I smelled the scent of stale wine.

"Do you put out?" he asked. The question was so out of context my only response was "What?" as he shoved me into the trailer. "Do you put out? You know what I mean," he said with a leer. As his hand went to my belt, I was

motionless with disbelief. "What's going on?" I thought.

"Bend over," he said shortly. "This isn't happening. This can't be happening," I thought as I tried to get away and was thrown against the side of the trailer. The pain that went shooting through my shoulder nearly made me faint.

"Don't do that again. Bend over," he said again. "No," I replied, vaguely feeling that I wanted nothing to do with what was going down. "Bend over," he said with a shove, his voice raising to an impatient, demanding tone.

"What is this guy going to do if I don't?" I thought, beginning to be frightened. "Stop, " I said frantically as the pain filled my mind and I began to realize I was trapped. "Stop. You're hurting me. STOPYOU'REHURTING-ME!" "No I'm not. Be quiet." "I'm not here to this guy. I'm not here. . . ."

The Invisible Victim

Collectively, our conscious and unconscious view of women as powerless commodities and men as powerful actors, combined with feminists' understandable focus on helping female rape victims, has worked to keep male rape victims invisible. For example, Webster's New World Dictionary (1975) defines rape as "the crime of having sexual intercourse with a woman or girl forcibly and without her consent, or, *statutory rape*, with a girl below the age of consent; 2) any sexual assault upon a person." The gender-specific nature of the primary definition of rape is echoed in much of the later literature on the subject. "Rape is a crime against women" (Medea and Thompson, 1970) and "large numbers of males are not being raped, beaten up, or murdered by large numbers of females" (Russell, 1979). "Rape is nothing more or less than a conscious process of intimidation by which all men keep all women in a state of fear" (Brownmiller, 1978).

Over the past few years, male rape

survivors, with growing frequency, have found the courage to speak of our lives and pain. We have started contacting rape crisis centers for help. The media, particularly in the New York City and San Francisco areas, have focused attention on isolated incidents of male rape. A small number of cases have even made it into the courts.

Denial and Silence

Despite these developments, few rape crisis centers have felt the need to alter their programs to encourage men seeking help. In some cases, these institutions are actively involved in denying male rape for political purposes. Brownmiller, Medea and Thompson, and Russell are uncritically cited as sources in articles published today, and their material is used in the training of rape crisis center volunteers. Public awareness of male rape lags far behind that of people working in the anti-rape movement. The victim-blaming attitudes of law-enforcement, medical and social service professionals for the most part remain unchallenged even today. These things create an environment that encourages the denial of male rape.

The insistence that rape occurs strictly between men and women is neither supportable nor useful. It distorts the reality and complexity of the problem we face. This view of women as victims and men as victimizers, although appropriate in many cases, does not describe the underlying causes of the situation. Men aren't born rapists, just as women aren't born victims. The causes of rape must be sought in other things besides genetics and simplistic sociology.

Rape is a crime of violence, and violence flourishes in an environment of alienation. The causes of rape are to be found in the countless subtle ways our economic and social institutions separate us from our true selves and from each other. I'm not advocating that we

From *Changing Men*, Spring/Summer 1988, pp. 20-21. Copyright © 1988 by Jim Senter.

forget the atrocities perpetrated on women by men. I *am* advocating that we take an honest look at rape and recognize that, in a culture of violence, we can all be victims. We must face this reality and recognize the dangers which threaten us all, if we are to create a more humane society.

The statement, "Rape is a crime against women," tells me that I was imagining things. It tells me a significant event in my life didn't happen. This denial of my experience, pain and blood angers me. The rage I feel in response to these statements is similar to the response women have when they were told by police and the courts, "You weren't raped. You really wanted that to happen."

This denial is echoed by the refusal of people to talk about the rape of men. For months after I was raped, I tried to cope with a maelstrom of emotions: despair, pain, anger, guilt, self-loathing. In order to gain some perspective on my situation, I reached out to people and tried to explain what happened to me. The response: silence. The statement, "I was raped . . ." ended many conversations. The silence made me think, "What's the matter with me? Why are people ignoring me? Maybe I did do something wrong."

Most people don't want to deal with the reality of rape. I dealt with it because I had to. But my healing was prolonged because there was no one to tell me that sexual dysfunction and feelings of boundless anger, guilt, sadness and worthlessness are natural—almost inevitable—parts of the response to rape. What I went through was infinitely more difficult because of the absence of a shoulder to cry on, or a voice telling me it's alright to feel violated. I don't know if anyone I talked to had ever heard of a man being raped. I don't know if the silence I found was the result of the apparent strangeness of my situation. No one ever told me that, but I like to think so. The alternative—that people just don't care—is one I don't like to consider.

Men Breaking Silence

A long road stretches between St. Louis and the place where I sit writing this. The journey I've taken has been a slow growth of confidence and strength that has enabled me to move from total shock to a more healthy way of dealing with the world. Although I'd like to forget—and sometimes I actively pursue forgetfulness—every aspect of this growth is imprinted in my memory. I am still afraid of men who might be rapists as well as women who may accuse me of being a rapist. I am scared of how I may express the rage I feel just thinking about those situations. I am still afraid, but I have found my voice.

Remembering, I despair. I feel a mixture of physical and emotional pain, the sense of the crossing of boundaries which shouldn't be crossed. Someone has crossed the boundary of my skin and stolen the basis of my identity, my ability to control my body. I remain confused and unable to get a handle on what happened to me. I feel like nothing more than a rag for someone to come in. I go through the paces unaware of my surroundings while I think over and over, "How could I have let this happen?"

I remember one night curled up in bed. I hug my knees and cry out of loneliness; and as I cry, I speak out loud, "It's alright to feel hurt. It's alright to feel powerless," over and over until I fall asleep.

Remembering, I feel singled out, isolated, separated by events from everyone for all time. No one has gone through this. No one can help me. The world stinks. I hate it all. I am outraged at the fact that a person can gain physical dominance over another and take pleasure from creating pain.

Remembering, I feel betrayed by those who voice concern about rape and, for whatever reason, leave me alone and staggered; and I am angry at this betrayal.

Remembering, I numb out. I refuse to think or feel about what happened. I try to put it behind me and get on with my life, but I can't forget. I realize the situation demands action, and with this realization, write my story.

The issue is rape. Rape is a crime, a crime of violence. The crime is the same, and the human responses to this crime are the same, regardless of the sex of the participants. Conversations I have had with other rape victims—both male and female—about our reactions to rape, as well as comparisons I have made between my own experience and the descriptions of the aftermath of rape written by women, have shown this to be true.

Although the basic patterns of response are the same, there may be differences in the way these patterns are expressed, due to differences in sex role socialization. Because men are encouraged to be self-reliant, to view ourselves as powerful and in control, the understandable reluctance to talk about victimization may be accentuated. Also, we often don't get support when we are being emotional. Because of this, we may—more frequently than women—be unemotional in the way we express the initial trauma of rape. These things may be true, and it is reasonable to assume they are true; but we don't known enough about the variation in response of male rape victims to say for sure.

Men today are in the same place women were 15 years ago. Male rape victims do exist. It does happen, the silence, the absence of healing services, and persistent attitudes to the contrary. As it was in the past when women first joined together to break the silence and to share their experience and pain, so now it is time for us men to join together to break the silence that torments our minds and turns our hearts away from the things we love. This silence breeds hatred. And hatred nourishes the pain we suffer.

Men today are in the same place women were fifteen years ago. Male rape victims do exist. Now is the time to break the silence.

References

Brownmiller, Susan. 1978. *Against Our Wills: Men, Women and Rape*. (Bantam Books, New York). p. 5.

Medea, Andra, and Kathleen Thompson. 1974. *Against Rape: A Survival Manual for Women*. (Farrar, Straus and Giroux, New York). p. 11.

Russell, Diana, 1979. "Pornography and Violence: What Does the New Research Say?" in *Take Back the Night: Women and Pornography*, Laura Lederer, ed., (William Morrow and Co., New York). p. 23.

Patient Guide: How to Use a Condom

Prepared by the editors of **Medical Aspects of Human Sexuality** in collaboration with Reed Adams, PhD, Emanuel Fliegelman, DO, and Alan Grieco, PhD.

Reed Adams is Adjunct Professor of Sociology, The Johnson C. Smith University, Charlotte, N.C.

Emanuel Fliegelman is Professor of Obstetrics and Gynecology, Philadelphia College of Osteopathic Medicine, and Director, Human Sexuality Program, Osteopathic Medical Center of Philadelphia.

Alan Grieco is a clinical psychologist in private practice in Winter Park, FL.

Sexual abstinence is the only sure way to prevent pregnancy and sexually transmitted diseases, including AIDS. If you do decide to have sex, correct use of a condom will help you to protect yourself and your partner against these risks. This guide tells you how to use a condom for maximum protection.

How to Buy Condoms

Do buy a supply of latex, reservoir (nipple)-end, lubricated type condoms. They're available in different colors, textures, and sometimes in two different sizes. A good quality condom is the most important feature for safer sex.

Do check expiration date on outer package.

Do check name of lubricant: it should contain nonoxynol-9, which provides a chemical barrier against sexually transmitted diseases.

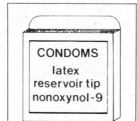

CONDOMS
latex
reservoir tip
nonoxynol-9

Do store in a cool dry place.

Do carry a condom with you at all times.

Don't buy condoms made of any material other than latex. (Only latex prevents passage of harmful germs.)

Don't buy old (outdated) condoms.

Don't store condoms in hot glove compartment of car. Heat can damage the condom.

Don't carry in hip wallet for long periods of time—this shortens shelf life.

Don't be shy about buying condoms—40% are sold to women.

How to Put the Condom On

Do remove rolled condom from package.

Do roll condom down on penis as soon as it is hard, *before* you start to make love (foreplay).

Do leave ¼–½ inch extra space at tip of condom to catch the ejaculate if the condom has no nipple.

Don't unroll condom; instead, carefully roll on all the way toward the base of the penis.

Don't put condom on only when you are ready to enter your partner—it may be too late. Drops of semen may ooze from the uncovered penis before ejaculation, and may infect or impregnate your partner.

Don't twist, bite, or prick condom with a pin—this will damage it and allow fluid to leak out, possibly infecting your partner.

How to Take the Condom Off

Do hold the condom at the rim; remove soon after ejaculation.

Do keep used condom away from partner's genitals and other areas of the body as well.

Don't let penis go soft inside partner—condom may drop off, and protection is lost.

Don't tug to pull condom off—it may tear.

Don't allow semen to spill on your hands or body. Wash hands or body parts if contact occurs. Wrap condom in tissue and dispose of safely.

Don't allow semen to come in contact with a skin break, cut, or open wound.

Special Points to Remember

▶ If you buy unlubricated condoms, you may need to buy a lubricant. Use only water-soluble lubricants such as spermicidal jelly or water.

▶ Don't use oil-based lubricants such as petroleum jelly or vegetable oil with latex condoms, since they can damage the condoms.

▶ Never use a condom more than once.

▶ Correct use of condoms increases comfort, and promotes a sense of security in having safer sex.

How to talk about condoms with a resistant, defensive, or manipulative partner

If the partner says:	*You can say:*	*If the partner says:*	*You can say:*
"I'm on the Pill, you don't need a condom."	"I'd like to use it anyway. We'll both be protected from infections we may not realize we have."	"What kinds of alternatives?"	"Maybe we'll just pet, or postpone sex for a while."
"I *know* I'm clean (disease-free); I haven't had sex with anyone in X months."	"Thanks for telling me. As far as I know, I'm disease-free, too. But I'd still like to use a condom since either of us could have an infection and not know it."	"This is an insult! Do you think I'm some sort of disease-ridden slut (gigolo)?"	"I didn't say or imply that. I care for you, but in my opinion, it's best to use a condom."
"I'm a virgin."	"I'm not. This way we'll both be protected."	"None of my other boyfriends uses a condom. A *real* man isn't afraid."	"Please don't compare me to them. A real man cares about the woman he dates, himself, and about their relationship."
"I can't feel a thing when I wear a condom; it's like wearing a raincoat in the shower."	"Even if you lose some sensation, you'll still have plenty left."	"I love you! Would I give you an infection?"	"Not intentionally. But many people don't know they're infected. That's why this is best for both of us right now."
"I'll lose my erection by the time I stop and put it on."	"I'll help you put it on—that'll help you keep it."	"Just this once."	"Once is all it takes."
"By the time you put it on, I'm out of the mood."	"Maybe so, but we feel strongly enough for each other to stay in the mood."	"I don't have a condom with me."	"I do." or "Then let's satisfy each other without intercourse."
"It destroys the romantic atmosphere."	"It doesn't have to be that way."	"You carry a condom around with you? You were planning to seduce me!"	"I always carry one with me because I care about myself. I have one with me tonight because I care about us both."
"Condoms are unnatural, fake, a total turnoff."	"Please let's try to work this out—an infection isn't so great either. So let's give the condom a try. Or maybe we can look for alternatives."	"I won't have sex with you if you're going to use a condom."	"So let's put it off until we can agree." or "OK, then let's try some other things besides intercourse."

Adapted from the article "Cutting the Risks for STDs" by Alan Grieco, PhD, which appeared in the March 1987 issue of *Medical Aspects of Human Sexuality.*

Can you rely on
CONDOMS?

More people are counting on condoms for protection against AIDS. We tested some 40 varieties for defects and strength.

Close to half of some 3300 readers surveyed for this report told us that they had changed their sexual habits in response to AIDS. "More condoms, more consistently" was one of the major themes. Heeding public-health warnings, Americans have helped boost condom sales more than 60 percent over the past 2½ years. People who had never considered condoms before—women and gay men, especially—are now buying and using them. Women, for example, purchase 40 to 50 percent of condoms today, up from 10 percent a few years ago. Often the women are single, and often it's disease—not birth control—that's on their mind.

Just how good are condoms for preventing sexually transmitted disease? How effective a product are the condom manufacturers sending to market? And how often do condoms break?

Condom manufacturers say they get one or two consumer complaints per million condoms sold—and not all of those involve breakage. When we asked readers, however, about one in four said that a condom had broken in the past year. Nearly one in eight reported at least two incidents of breakage. On the basis of those reports and the number of condoms readers estimated using, we calculated that about one condom in 140 broke. But they break more often in some activities than in others.

Anal intercourse, one of the riskiest activities for contracting AIDS, is also one of the most punishing for a condom. (Anal sex isn't limited to gay or bisexual readers: One in 10 of the heterosexual men surveyed reported having engaged in heterosexual anal intercourse using a condom.) We calculated the breakage rate for anal sex among survey respondents at one condom in 105, compared with one in 165 for vaginal sex.

The disparity could result from such factors as differences in brands or lubricants used. But just as likely, it's due to the nature of anal sex itself. Indeed, many condoms now carry a disclaimer that they're solely for vaginal sex; that other uses can result in breakage.

When condoms are intact, though, how good are they? In principle, latex condoms can be close to 100 percent effective. (Most condoms are made of latex; fewer than 5 percent are fashioned from lamb intestine. See the box on page 220.) Under a scanning electron microscope at 30,000

power, the surface of a latex condom appears somewhat bumpy but shows no pores. When stretched, the latex remains a continuous pore-free membrane. It won't even let water—one of the tiniest of molecules—filter through.

Such an intact barrier shields the wearer's penis from exposure to germs in cervical, vaginal, or rectal secretions or lesions. For the partner, the condom prevents contact with potentially infectious semen and any lesions on the wearer's penis.

A number of laboratory experiments

have explored whether various sexually transmitted germs—some less than one-fiftieth the size of a sperm cell—can get through latex condoms. Condoms filled with a solution containing high concentrations of a sexually transmitted microbe are suspended in a sterile liquid medium. Then the medium is cultured to determine whether any microbes have passed through the latex. Some experiments use an apparatus to simulate intercourse, to check if mechanical stress affects porosity.

Such experiments have confirmed that intact latex condoms won't let even the smallest microbes through. So compelling is the evidence that since 1987 the U.S. Food and Drug Administration has let manufacturers list a roster of diseases that condoms, when used properly, can help prevent: syphilis, gonorrhea, chlamydia, genital herpes, and AIDS.

Outside the lab

Data gathered since World War I also

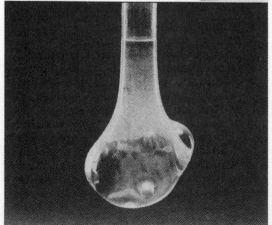

Of six LifeStyles lines, above, three models performed well in our airburst test—Conture, Extra Strength Lubricated, and Stimula Vibra-Ribbed. A fourth, Nuda, failed somewhat more often. But many samples of two brandmates—LifeStyles Extra Strength with Nonoxynol-9 (a spermicide) and LifeStyles Nuda Plus—were grossly defective. When they were filled with water (see photo at left), bulges sometimes appeared, revealing thin spots. The same lines did poorly in airburst testing.

In airburst testing, condoms are inflated until they break, as the maximum pressure and volume they can withstand are monitored. Condoms can burst in various ways. Below, high-speed photography records two possibilities. The burst happens so quickly that it takes a stroboscopic flash, firing at one-millionth of a second, to capture the event.

Photographs by Andrew Davidhazy

confirm the condom's value in disease prevention. The rates of sexually transmitted disease among condom users are typically a fraction of the rates among nonusers. Most times, condoms help cut risks substantially, though not quite to zero.

Scientists also gauge the condom's effectiveness from its performance as a contraceptive. A contraceptive's failure rate is calculated as the percentage of women who have an unwanted pregnancy while using the method over one year's time. For condom users, failure rates have ranged from roughly 5 to 15 percent.

But experts often point out that many contraceptive failures stem from human error, not defective condoms. A couple may not use condoms every time, from start to finish, or may not use them correctly.

Motivation may also play a role. Married women who rely on condoms because they don't want a child under any circumstances have fewer failures than married women who turn to condoms to delay an otherwise wanted pregnancy. Researchers say that strong motivation to use condoms properly could theoretically cut failure rates to 1 or 2 percent.

The FDA's role

When they became popular in the 1930s, many latex condoms—one report estimates as many as three-fourths—were in some way defective. That prompted Congress to ask the FDA to start testing condoms, which the agency has done for 50 years. Until recently, testing had been a low priority. But in the face of AIDS, the FDA has dramatically stepped up its program, putting more than 100 staffers into the effort.

Since April 1987, inspectors have shown up unannounced at condom factories to review records and sample condoms at random, checking for cracks, mold, dry or sticky rubber, and the like. Chiefly, however, the agents run a standard water test—filling condoms with about 10 ounces of water—to spot pinholes. If they find leaks in the equivalent of more than four per 1000 condoms in a production run, that entire lot must be destroyed—often tens of thousands of condoms or more. Imports are inspected, too, at their port of entry.

Over the first 15 months of the program, FDA inspectors checked more than 150,000 samples from lots representing 120 million condoms. The agents had to reject about one lot in 10 of domestic condoms because too many leaked. Imports turned out to be worse—one in five lots were rejected.

Condom quality has been improving, though. Since the new FDA program's inception, defect rates have been cut in half, and far fewer lots are currently being

scrapped. Apparently, the Government presence acts as a strong incentive to improve quality control. And most companies themselves are testing every condom for pinholes electrically.

Gauging condom strength

For this report, we checked some 16,000 condoms in all, either at CU or at a contract laboratory that specializes in testing contraceptive devices. Our samples included 37 varieties of latex condoms from all major U.S. manufacturers and three imports from Japan. Like the FDA, we ran the standard water test on most, examining a total of 250 samples of each.

We turned up one or two leaky samples in 18 different models, products of all major manufacturers. But the overall leakage rate for each model, projected from the failures, fell well within the Government's tolerance of four failures per 1000 condoms.

The leakage test did highlight potential problems with two *LifeStyles* models, however. When we filled them, bulges appeared at thin spots near the tip of some samples (see photo on preceding page). The condoms didn't leak, but the bulges suggested a potential for breakage in use—a potential underscored by a different test on samples from the same lots.

Strength—or resistance to breakage—is related to the ability of the latex to withstand stresses and remain intact. One test of strength involves cutting a band of latex from a condom's shaft and stretching it to the breaking point. That test is part of the voluntary standard domestic producers comply with. But condoms can have problems elsewhere that the test won't pick up. We instead turned to airburst testing, a method used routinely in Canada, Australia, and several European countries.

The airburst test

In airburst testing, condoms are inflated under controlled conditions until they break—often with a loud bang after having reached watermelon size. The volume and pressure of air a condom withstands before bursting are both recorded. We believe those values are likely to be related to a condom's potential to resist breakage in actual use.

Although an airburst test isn't required in the U.S., it is all but certain to be adopted into U.S. standards in the future. In fact, a number of American manufacturers already use such a test, because they export to countries that demand it.

To pass our airburst test, a condom had to withstand a minimum volume of 15 liters of air and a minimum pressure of 0.9 kiloPascal (roughly 0.13 pounds per square inch), two values proposed for an international standard now under discussion. For most models, we tested 100 samples, 20 from each of five lots, in an attempt to examine lot-to-lot consistency. In instances where we didn't obtain five lots, we took the total number of condoms sampled from each brand model into account statistically in projecting a model's overall failure rate in the test.

Some flunked too often

Our results produced three performance groups. We project that only about 1.5 percent (or fewer) of the condoms in the top group of the Ratings would fail the airburst test. We judge that to be a realistic quality level—in line with the proposed international standard.

Generally, condoms toward the top of the first Ratings group took the most volume, pressure, or both. On average, they withstood double the minimum values for pressure and volume. Some took triple the required pressure or triple the volume. But even condoms toward the bottom of the group exceeded the minimum values, typically by at least 40 percent.

For condoms in the middle Ratings group, we project a maximum airburst failure rate of 4 percent, higher than we'd prefer to see.

The two condoms in the worst group—*LifeStyles Extra Strength with Nonoxynol-9* (a spermicide) and *LifeStyles Nuda Plus*—flunked, with more than 10 percent projected failures. In some lots, up to half the tested samples failed. (Note that the *LifeStyles Extra Strength* model without spermicide performed so well that it earned the number two spot in the best group.)

Last October, the manufacturer of *Life-Styles*, Ansell Inc., issued a voluntary recall for defective lots of *LifeStyles Extra Strength with Nonoxynol-9*, including several of the lots we tested. The recall, prompted by health officials in Hawaii, covered about 6 million condoms manufactured more than a year earlier. The problem, according to the manufacturer, arose from a machine intermittently contaminated with oil, a substance that can weaken latex. Very little of the stock remains in stores, the company said.

There was no recall of Ansell's *LifeStyles Nuda Plus* line. Like the *Extra Strength with Nonoxynol-9*, some samples of *Life-Styles Nuda Plus* condoms showed bulges during the water tests, a result of thin spots. But it was impossible to tell from our airburst test whether the thin spots or some other factor was the reason samples

Skin condoms: Unresolved questions

Skin condoms are made from lamb cecum, a pouch forming part of the animal's large intestine. They typically cost several times what latex condoms cost; but as an alternative, "skins" have several things to offer.

They're promoted as more "natural feeling" than latex, and indeed many survey respondents who prefer skins noted the condoms' "greater sensation." Skins are also strong. The brands we checked—*Fourex Natural Skins* and *Trojan Kling-Tite Naturalambs*—withstood more than 10 times the pressure that typical latex condoms took in airburst testing.

For the one or two percent of people allergic to latex, such condoms may be the only choice. (Some allergic reactions stem from the chemicals used on certain latex condoms and may disappear if you try another brand.)

Skin condoms are packed wet, so we had to devise a leakage test different from the standard water test. We inflated the condoms under water and looked for bubbles, as you might check an inner tube for leaks. We found no problems. But that's not to say skin condoms aren't porous at all.

Under a scanning electron microscope, the membranes reveal layers of fibers crisscrossing in various patterns. That latticework endows the skins with strength but also makes for an occasional pore, sometimes up to 1.5 microns wide. That's

smaller than a sperm, a white blood cell, or even some gonorrhea bacteria. But it's more than 10 times the size of the AIDS virus, and more than 25 times the size of the hepatitis-B virus.

The pores aren't tunnels through the skin's wall. They occur in individual layers of the skin's multilayered membrane. So some experts believe that skin condoms can still offer protection against small viruses. To get to the outside, such a virus would have to zigzag through each layer's tortuous fiber structure, somewhat like negotiating a maze. But, given enough time, the virus might be able to do so. Since skin condoms are a natural product, they can also have thin spots, which might contribute to porosity.

Laboratory evidence on whether the AIDS virus can pass through skin condoms is limited to only a few small studies. One study has demonstrated passage; three others

have not. Similar studies show that skin condoms do pass the smaller hepatitis-B virus but usually not the herpes virus, which is slightly larger than the AIDS virus.

The relevance of these results to condoms in actual use isn't known. For example, lab studies typically use virus suspended in blood serum or tissue-culture media, not real semen. Semen has greater surface tension—it forms a glob—so any suspended material may have a harder time migrating outward.

Skin condoms work well as contraceptives. But, apparently because of the skins' possible porosity, the FDA doesn't allow their packages to carry the disease-prevention labeling that latex condoms may carry. It remains an open question whether the skins' relative strength outweighs their potential to pass small microbes. In view of the uncertainty, CU's medical consultants advise latex condoms for disease prevention.

Readers report on condoms

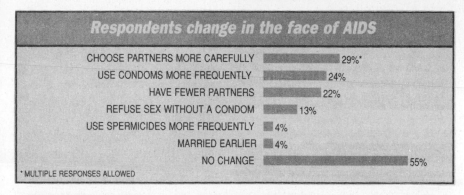

Respondents change in the face of AIDS

CHOOSE PARTNERS MORE CAREFULLY	29%*
USE CONDOMS MORE FREQUENTLY	24%
HAVE FEWER PARTNERS	22%
REFUSE SEX WITHOUT A CONDOM	13%
USE SPERMICIDES MORE FREQUENTLY	4%
MARRIED EARLIER	4%
NO CHANGE	55%

*MULTIPLE RESPONSES ALLOWED

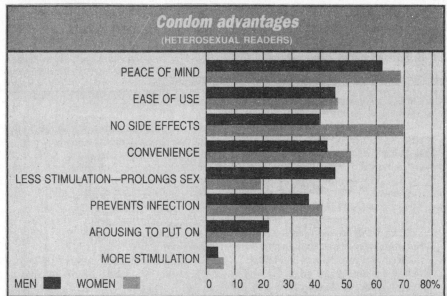

Condom advantages
(HETEROSEXUAL READERS)

PEACE OF MIND
EASE OF USE
NO SIDE EFFECTS
CONVENIENCE
LESS STIMULATION—PROLONGS SEX
PREVENTS INFECTION
AROUSING TO PUT ON
MORE STIMULATION

MEN ■ WOMEN ▪ 0 10 20 30 40 50 60 70 80%

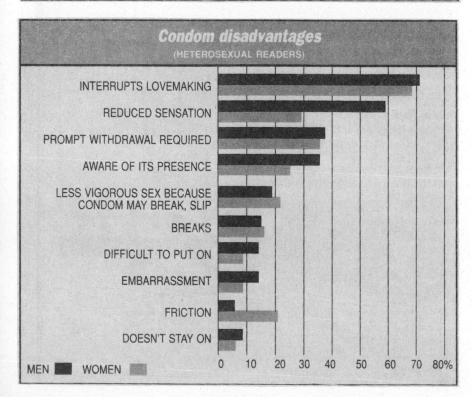

Condom disadvantages
(HETEROSEXUAL READERS)

INTERRUPTS LOVEMAKING
REDUCED SENSATION
PROMPT WITHDRAWAL REQUIRED
AWARE OF ITS PRESENCE
LESS VIGOROUS SEX BECAUSE CONDOM MAY BREAK, SLIP
BREAKS
DIFFICULT TO PUT ON
EMBARRASSMENT
FRICTION
DOESN'T STAY ON

MEN ■ WOMEN ▪ 0 10 20 30 40 50 60 70 80%

In response to a query last year in CONSUMER REPORTS, almost 3300 readers participated in a survey about their use of condoms. They filled in an eight-page questionnaire, which also included questions about their knowledge of AIDS.

As a group, these readers were younger than the average mix of CONSUMER REPORTS subscribers (most were between 25 and 45). And 80 percent were men, compared with some 60 percent for our readership. Because of such differences (and the volunteer aspect of the survey), we can't generalize our findings to all subscribers. But the information we received was still instructive.

Two-thirds of the respondents were currently using condoms for birth control (sometimes along with another method). But disease—AIDS in particular—also had a major impact on condom use. In 1979, when we last reported on condoms, only 8 percent of the respondents checked "avoidance of venereal disease" as a reason for using condoms. Now 26 percent cited diseases such as AIDS and herpes as a reason for using condoms with their regular partner. Of the respondents who had "occasional partners"—about a quarter of the sample did—two out of three mentioned disease prevention.

Ten percent of the respondents reported being gay or bisexual, about the same as what's estimated for the U.S. overall. Most gay readers—85 percent—told us they personally knew someone with AIDS. Among exclusively heterosexual readers, 19 percent personally knew a person with AIDS.

Forty-one percent of heterosexuals living alone said they used condoms as protection against AIDS. Only 7 percent of married readers said they did. Among gay and bisexual respondents, the figure soared to 77 percent. Some readers used condoms for oral sex, too.

Condoms chiefly confer peace of mind, their greatest advantage, readers said. But condoms also interrupt lovemaking, their biggest drawback. About two-thirds of our respondents noted that major advantage and that major disadvantage.

Heterosexual men and women were pretty much alike in reporting the condom's pluses and minuses. Men, however, were twice as likely to complain about reduced sensation. (Yet nearly half the men praised condoms precisely because less stimulation allowed them to prolong sex.) Women were far more likely to favor condoms for the lack of side effects.

of those condoms tested so poorly.

Across most brands, we were surprised at the variability we sometimes observed either between packages or within a single package: A brightly colored condom in a box of plain ones, or vice versa; differences in the shape of the same product; unlubricated condoms mixed in with lubricated ones; or textured condoms showing up among plain ones. Mistakes like that point to an industry-wide sloppiness in some aspects of quality control.

The role of spermicides

Nonoxynol-9, the active ingredient in most over-the-counter spermicides, kills sperm cells through a detergent action that attacks the cell membrane. Nonoxynol-9 also kills various organisms that cause sexually transmitted disease, including AIDS, gonorrhea, syphilis, chlamydia, herpes, and hepatitis B. Even concentrations well under 1 percent have inactivated the AIDS virus in the lab. So nonoxynol-9 spermicides, used with a condom, can provide something of an extra safety net, should the condom break.

Some condoms now come with a spermicide in their lubricant. However, the amount of nonoxynol-9 in condoms is no

Readers judge the brands

Two condoms tested—one *Sheik* and one *Trojan*—come closest to a no-frills model: They're not lubricated, textured, tinted, contoured, or equipped with a reservoir tip. For the rest, though, you can find every conceivable permutation of those features. Store shelves are stocked with dozens of varieties.

According to our survey, the features readers appreciate most are lubrication and the reservoir tip, preferred by about three in four. Substantial minorities—some 35 to 40 percent—liked extra-thin, extra-strong, or spermicidally lubricated condoms. For each of those three features, though, at least 10 percent of the readers said they *wouldn't* use condoms that had them.

Condom strength, important to many readers, was even more favored among women and gay men. Both of those groups also leaned toward spermicide lubrication. Textured (ribbed) condoms, often touted as enhancing a woman's pleasure, got a mixed reaction from women: A little more than one-fourth preferred the texture but nearly an equal number said they wouldn't use such condoms. Gay men tended to avoid skin condoms, presumably because such condoms may offer less protection against viruses (see the box on page 220).

Most readers have used a variety of condoms. We asked for preferences from respondents who had experiences with particular brand models. We've charted the percent of heterosexual respondents who told us they prefer a specific brand versus those who say they would not want to use it again. (Gay respondents appeared to have different opinions but were too few to provide a brand-by-brand listing.) All brands listed were rated by at least 150 respondents—in most cases by more than 300. We also note the advantages and disadvantages readers reported.

Respondents as a group expressed ambivalence about a number of brands, often with a large split in pro and con votes. The most extreme case: *Mentor* condoms, which almost 30 percent liked and almost 40 percent vetoed.

Mentor is unique among all models tested. It features a special applicator "hood" and an inner ring of adhesive to hold the condom on the penis. That helps prevent slipping and leakage. Readers told us: *Mentor* stays on (correct); is difficult to don (right again—instructions are more complex than a regular condom's); and costs too much (right, too—we paid more than $18 a dozen).

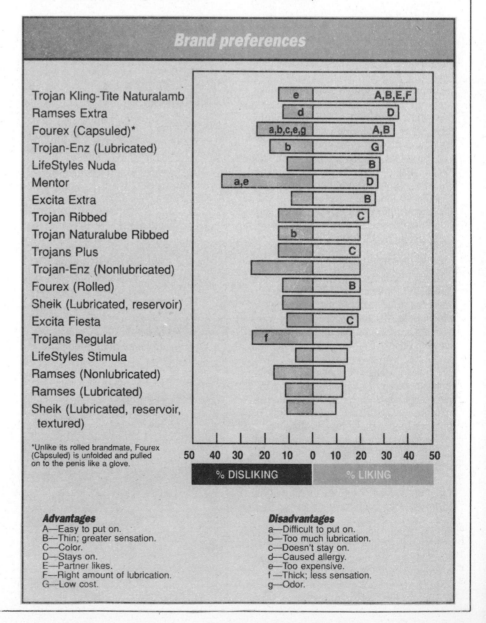

Brand preferences

Brand	Advantages noted	Disadvantages noted
Trojan Kling-Tite Naturalamb	A,B,E,F	e
Ramses Extra	D	d
Fourex (Capsuled)*	A,B	a,b,c,e,g
Trojan-Enz (Lubricated)	G	b
LifeStyles Nuda	B	
Mentor	D	a,e
Excita Extra	B	
Trojan Ribbed	C	
Trojan Naturalube Ribbed		b
Trojans Plus	C	
Trojan-Enz (Nonlubricated)		
Fourex (Rolled)	B	
Sheik (Lubricated, reservoir)		
Excita Fiesta	C	
Trojans Regular		f
LifeStyles Stimula		
Ramses (Nonlubricated)		
Ramses (Lubricated)		
Sheik (Lubricated, reservoir, textured)		

*Unlike its rolled brandmate, Fourex (Capsuled) is unfolded and pulled on to the penis like a glove.

50 40 30 20 10 0 10 20 30 40 50

% DISLIKING   % LIKING

Advantages
A—Easy to put on.
B—Thin; greater sensation.
C—Color.
D—Stays on.
E—Partner likes.
F—Right amount of lubrication.
G—Low cost.

Disadvantages
a—Difficult to put on.
b—Too much lubrication.
c—Doesn't stay on.
d—Caused allergy.
e—Too expensive.
f—Thick; less sensation.
g—Odor.

substitute for a vaginal spermicide, which can be applied more copiously. The nonoxynol-9 in spermicides varies in concentration from about 1 to 12 percent. If a high concentration causes irritation, try a product with a lower one.

Spermicides are formulated so that they can be used with latex diaphragms and thus shouldn't damage latex condoms. As yet, the safety and efficacy of spermicides for preventing disease transmission in anal sex remains unknown.

Precautions with condoms

Air pollution, heat, and light can all spoil latex condoms. So never open one until you're ready to use it, and store condoms in a dark, cool, dry place.

Condom packets should be opened gently to avoid damaging the contents. If the condom shows any signs of deterioration—sticky, discolored, or dried-out latex—discard it.

Some condoms come in translucent or transparent packets, which could hasten aging. We also found some individual packets not quite sealed, which could also hasten aging. And some packets were hard to tear apart. The Ratings give details.

Stored properly, condoms can last up to five years. Most brands tell the manufacturing date. Spermicide condoms give an expiration date for their nonoxynol-9.

If a condom breaks, having a foam spermicide handy to apply quickly may help. It's no guarantee against pregnancy, because sperm cells travel very fast; but it still might help to kill disease organisms. Douching is unreliable, because it might push semen up through the cervix.

Recommendations

Using condoms is part of what public-health authorities now call "safer sex"—practices that can reduce your risk of exposure to AIDS and other sexually transmitted diseases. For that purpose, it makes sense to choose from among condoms that performed well in our airburst test. No in-use research has yet shown conclusively that the better a condom performs in a laboratory test, the more it will resist breakage in actual use. But we think it's only prudent to make that assumption.

The first group of condoms in the Ratings had the fewest failures in our airburst test. The models in that group are listed in order of how much they exceeded the minimum values of pressure and volume. Although we would consider any of them safe by current standards, we suggest you choose from the upper portion of the group if you, like many of our survey respondents, encounter broken condoms as often as once or twice a year.

Our tests did not address other aspects of condom use, perhaps most importantly

that of sensitivity. Still, the variety of condoms in the top Ratings group offer just about any mix of features you and your partner may prefer.

To be effective, condoms must be used consistently, not just some of the time. Surprisingly, among the readers surveyed who have "occasional partners," less than half say they use condoms every time. The notion that it's possible to guess when protection is or isn't needed invites disaster. As one AIDS researcher put it, trying to "take someone's sexual history" is far more fallible than using a condom.

There's a right way to use condoms. Place the rolled condom over the tip of the

erect penis. If the condom has a reservoir tip, squeeze out the air. Otherwise, leave a half-inch space at the end (and squeeze out the air). Unroll the condom down the length of the penis (uncircumcised men should first pull back the foreskin). Right after ejaculation, grasp the condom firmly at the ring and withdraw before losing the erection; that will prevent spillage. Use a new condom for each act of intercourse, and avoid any genital contact before putting the condom on.

A condom lubricated with spermicide may offer some extra protection against disease. But using a separate vaginal spermicide with a condom is more effective.

Safe use of lubricants

Lubricants to use with latex condoms

Most readers who responded to our survey preferred prelubricated condoms (see preceding page). But just over half supplied their own lubrication or supplemented that already on the condom. That can lessen chances of breakage. But it can also *increase* the risk of breakage if you use an oil-based lubricant, as one in eight readers did.

Oil-based lubricants weaken latex considerably. Mineral oil, baby oil, vegetable oil, petroleum jelly, cold cream, and hand lotions containing such oils can all affect latex. We tried some of those lubricants on latex condoms and saw condom performance suffer markedly in airburst testing: At least half of the samples of each condom tested failed. At body temperature, oiled latex will weaken in minutes.

The lubricants safe for condoms are water-based. They include surgical jellies, such as *K-Y Lubricating Jelly* and *Today Personal Lubricant*, both of which we tested. But don't confuse water-based with water-soluble products, which may not be safe for latex. Lotions that wash off easily can still contain damaging oils. Check the label or ask a pharmacist.

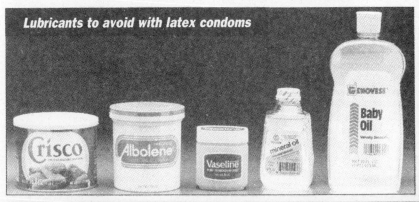

Lubricants to avoid with latex condoms

Guide to the Ratings

Grouped by projected failure rate in airburst testing, adjusted statistically for number of samples tested; within groups, listed in order of decreasing volume and pressure withstood in test. Differences between closely ranked models are not significant.

1 Price. Average price CU shoppers paid in New York City area stores for one dozen condoms.

2 Lubrication. Some models come with "dry" lubrication (D), typically a silicon-based oil. Others are wet-lubricated (W), with a water-based surgical jelly.

3 Spermicide. These models contain the spermicide nonoxynol-9, but concentrations and amounts vary. Most labels say that their spermicide lubricant is no substitute for the use of vaginal spermicide.

4 Texture. Ribbing or stippling around the shaft.

5 Contour. Shapes varied considerably. Some condoms are flared, others tapered, yet others have contouring for more snug fit.

6 Variability. Inconsistencies included: large differences in airburst performance among lots tested (A); color variations among or within packages (C); lubrication variations within packages (L); shape variations among or within packages (S); and texture variations among or within packages (T). Some models come in strips, and in some lots it was hard to separate the individual packets (P). For some models, we didn't test enough lots to check lot-to-lot differences in airburst results (X).

Ratings

Latex condoms

Brand and model	Price 1	Lubrication 2	Spermicide 3	Texture 4	Contour 5	Variability 6	Comments
■ The following models had a projected maximum failure rate of 1.5 percent.							
Gold Circle Coin	$2.75	—	—	—	—	X	A,E,N
LifeStyles Extra Strength Lubricated	5.63	D	—	—	—	—	N
Saxon Wet Lubricated	4.47	W	—	—	—	X	B,G
Ramses Non-Lubricated Reservoir End	5.96	—	—	—	—	S,X	F
Sheik Non-Lubricated Reservoir End	3.43	—	—	—	—	P,X	F
Excita Extra	6.60	D	✔	✔	—	P	A,C
Kimono	7.64	D	—	—	✔	X	A,D,G
Sheik Elite	4.83	D	✔	—	—	—	A,C,M
Koromex with Nonoxynol-9	6.56	D	✔	—	—	—	C,K
Excita Fiesta	6.77	D	—	✔	—	P,X	C,J
Embrace Ultra-Thin	3.36	D	—	—	✔	L	B,C,F
LifeStyles Stimula Vibra-Ribbed	5.08	D	—	✔	—	P	B,C
Ramses Extra with Spermicidal Lubricant	5.80	D	✔	—	—	P	A,C
Lady Trojan	5.25	W	✔	—	—	X	A,F,H
Trojan Plus 2	5.25	W	✔	—	✔	X	A
Protex Secure	4.32	D	—	—	—	C,S	C,F,H
Protex Touch	3.87	D	—	—	—	—	C,H
Protex Arouse	4.00	D	—	✔	✔	C,S,T	C,J
Trojan-Enz	3.56	—	—	—	—	—	—
Lady Protex with Spermicidal Lubricant	4.14	D	✔	—	—	C	C,H
Sheik Fetherlite Snug-Fit	5.42	D	—	—	✔	P,X	C
Trojan Naturalube Ribbed	5.30	W	—	✔	✔	—	H
Protex Contracept Plus with Spermicidal Lubricant	4.61	D	✔	—	—	C	C,H
Lady Protex Ultra-Thin	3.97	D	—	—	—	C,X	C,H
Trojan-Enz Lubricated	4.41	W	—	—	—	—	H
Trojan Ribbed	5.15	D	—	✔	—	—	D,J
Today with Spermicidal Lubricant	6.16	D	✔	—	✔	X	A,G,I
LifeStyles Conture	4.28	D	—	—	✔	—	B,C
Trojans	3.74	—	—	—	—	—	L
Trojans Plus	5.07	D	—	—	✔	—	D,J
Yamabuki No. 2 Lubricated	7.32	D	—	—	✔	X	A,C,J,M
Wrinkle Zero-0 2000	7.32	D	—	✔	✔	—	A,C,J
■ The following models had a projected maximum failure rate of 4 percent.							
Sheik Non-Lubricated Plain End	4.08	—	—	—	—	—	L
Ramses Sensitol Lubricated	5.82	D	—	—	✔	P,S,X	C
Pleaser Ribbed Lubricated [1]	3.46	D	—	✔	✔	—	C,F
Ramses NuFORM	6.26	D	—	—	✔	P	C
Mentor	18.62	D	—	—	—	—	A,O
LifeStyles Nuda	4.69	D	—	—	✔	—	B,C
■ The following models had a projected maximum failure rate of more than 10 percent.							
LifeStyles Extra Strength with Nonoxynol-9	8.07	D	✔	—	—	A	F,I,N
LifeStyles Nuda Plus	5.40	D	✔	—	✔	A	A,C,I

[1] Now called **Saxon Ribbed Lubricated**.

Specifications and Features
Except as noted, all: • Have reservoir tip. • Showed small lot-to-lot variation in strength. • Did not vary among or within packages in color, lubrication, or texture. • Had opaque individual packet. • Were sealed in individual packets, packed in strips, and easy to separate and open. • Had a slight odor. • Have a natural latex color.

Key to Comments
A—Instructions judged better than most.
B—Instructions judged worse than most.
C—Packets translucent; could hasten aging.
D—Packets transparent; could hasten aging.
E—Individual packets not sealed; could hasten aging.
F—Many packets not airtight; could hasten aging.
G—Individual packets hard to open.
H—Has unpleasant odor.
I—Had thin spots.
J—Comes in assorted colors (*Excita Fiesta, Wrinkle Zero-0 2000, Yamabuki No. 2*); comes in pink (*Protex Arouse*); comes in golden yellow (*Trojans Plus, Trojan Ribbed*).
K—Comes with wallet for purse or pocket.
L—Has plain tip.
M—Thinner than most (roughly, 0.05 mm).
N—Thicker than most (roughly, 0.08 mm or more).
O—Has applicator and adhesive to hold condom on penis.

AIDS and the College Student: The Need for Sex Education

Sandra L. Caron, PhD, Rosemarie M. Bertran, MSW and Tom McMullen, Syracuse University

Kay comes home from college for the weekend, and on Saturday night runs into her old high school sweetheart, Bill. They spend the night together in his apartment. The next day, while Bill is at the library studying, Kay rummages guiltily through his things to see if he's found a new girlfriend. She finds a card from a local health agency which says he's tested positive for AIDS antibodies. Scared and confused, she panics. What should she do? Confront him and admit she's been going through his stuff? She thinks, "Why didn't he tell me? We could have used a condom." She decides not to tell him because he wouldn't forgive her for sneaking around. Instead, she returns to college to her boyfriend, Jim, without mentioning her "fling." She continues to have unprotected sex with Jim because she fears that if she now insists he wear a condom, he'll know she's been unfaithful.

College students don't need much sex education, right? These modern kids, exposed by the media to all areas of life, already know all about sex. Their own experience has prepared them to be comfortable, open, and mature in their relationships with others. Unlike prior generations, they are knowledgeable and sophisticated.

Wrong. As one can see from the true scenario above, college students struggle with ignorance, misconceptions, doubts, and fears about themselves and others, just as much and just as painfully as did their predecessors. The difference, fortunately, is that today's young people are growing up in a society that permits more open discussion of sexual topics than in previous generations.

As a society, we are now more knowledgeable about our bodies, psychological processes, the interplay of emotion and body, and social processes than ever before. In addition, we live in an "information age" that provides easy access to accurate information. Indeed, we are more likely to be faced with the problem of choosing which facts, among an overabundance, are significant. Among college-educated adults, few sexual topics are in "taboo closets" anymore; many feel more distressed by exposure to and inept handling of sensitive subjects than by prohibitions.

Clearly, in an age touted to be one of great sexual openness,

we still have many problems to solve. It would be naive to suggest that adequate or even ideal (whatever "ideal" may be) sex education at any, and all, levels will solve the social ills of our complex society. Knowledge, however, can be used to alleviate and avoid much human suffering. And putting knowledge in the hands of young people increases their options *and* their capacity to choose among them. We know of no instance in which people, young or old, are better served by ignorance. Choice permits and enhances the individual's ability to develop as a human being; ignorance prohibits choice and adversely affects the quality of life.

Knowledge About AIDS

Just what do college students know about AIDS? Do they believe they are at risk? Has their awareness of AIDS resulted in changes in sexual and dating behaviors? To find out, we conducted a survey of Syracuse University students during the spring term, 1987. The survey consisted of one-to-one interviews with students in bars on "Marshall Street," near the university. Subjects were male and female, mostly undergraduate students. Interviews were generally conducted during the most popular hours of 9 p.m. and 2 a.m.

The instrument was a one-page interview that consisted of structured, open-ended questions regarding the student's opinion and knowledge about AIDS. Interviewers were members of the Peer Sexuality Program at Syracuse University. More than 350 interviews were completed. Returns have not yet been tabulated completely, but our initial impressions are the following.

1. *Most students exhibit a great lack of knowledge and factual data about AIDS.*

2. *Most students fail to see any relevance between ongoing media stories about the growing incidence of AIDS and their personal behavior.* Students frequently indicated that they believed they were not in "high risk" groups and equated this with little or no risk at all. Often unconcerned about risk, they failed to see that high risk *behaviors* placed them in jeopardy. Frequent comments included: "Well, I'm not a slut, I don't sleep around that much, and I'm not gay."

3. *The level of denial among students is high.* For example, students often commented, "Everyone should be concerned about AIDS." But when the interviewer countered with, "Are you?" the answer was almost invariably, "No." Students often reported their conviction that they had the ability to "know" or intuit which sexual partners were "safe." Commonly, they conveyed the conviction that they were personally immune. Only a small minority indicated anxiety about having been exposed. Students often commented that they believed this to be a greater issue for homosexuals than for heterosexuals.

4. *There is a general unreadiness among students to deal pragmatically with the threat of AIDS in their relationships.* Students talked freely about sex and STDs with interviewers, but expressed unwillingness to discuss these topics with their sexual partners. Many reported that generally they had unprotected sex and indicated that they would not talk with a new sexual partner about AIDS, STDs, or the use of condoms. In general, students equated "safer sex" with "not-fun-sex." Some wondered how to bring up the question of AIDS with a new partner without insulting him/her. The unwillingness of students to deal pragmatically with the threat of AIDS is closely related to, and dependent upon, the level of denial discussed above.

5. *Some students reported that AIDS was changing social attitudes regarding sexual and dating behavior.* There is less approval for the "one night stand." "People think twice before picking someone up." Some women indicated increased interest in men who are virgins, wanting to avoid "the guy who's been around" or "the womanizer." It is interesting to see the shift in women's attitudes away from the traditional interest in experienced men, and towards virgins. Some men also indicated their preference for an inexperienced or less-experienced sexual partner, but this is, of course, a more traditional view.

Recommendations for Education

The recommendations, below, are based on our preliminary findings in this study. Those who are planning, and/or developing, educational programs about AIDS for college students are also advised to consider the two recent articles listed at the end of this article.

Our recommendations are directed toward influencing the behaviors of people who do not believe themselves to be at risk of exposure. Ideally, these program recommendations should be carried out in a warm, supportive environment that invites open discussions. Our experience with education suggests that the best approach is a group of peers—students of the same approximate age and educational level—working together. Such programs should be conducted by educators who are knowledgeable about sexual issues and comfortable with open discussion. The following guidelines have been developed from our study.

1. *Provide factual information about the incidence and transmission of the AIDS virus.*
   Most students in our study demonstrated significant factual deficits. Many believed, for example, that AIDS was transmitted through casual contacts, such as sneez-ing or sharing beer bottles. Presenting solid, clearly stated information will significantly alleviate many fears.

2. *Debunk myths.*
   As stated previously, students widely believe that they are not at risk and/or that they can intuitively recognize which people carry the AIDS virus. Such beliefs permit students to rationalize high-risk behaviors. Education about AIDS should therefore describe high-risk behaviors, explain why engaging in such behaviors jeopardizes the health of the individual, as well as others, and give information on available tests to identify the presence of AIDS antibodies in a person.

3. *Discuss options.*
   Students should be made aware of the potential choices they have to provide varying levels of protection against the AIDS virus. Certainly abstinence should be recognized and discussed as a possible choice. Another option is "safer sex" (which should be clearly distinguished from "safe sex"), which can be achieved through the proper use of condoms with spermicides. Students clearly should understand that this is not 100 percent protection against the transmission of the AIDS virus. Sexually active students, especially, should be made aware of the availability and limits of testing.

4. *Discuss ethical issues.*
   Each individual has a responsibility to himself or herself, as well as to others. Responsible behaviors include taking adequate steps to protect oneself, discussing openly the risk between sexual partners, and not concealing significant information from sexual partners.

5. *Present dramatization of effective coping behaviors.*
   Brief plays, skits, and role-playing all provide opportunities to model responsible sexual behaviors. Actors may be recruited from the drama department, from among peer educators, from the student body at large, or even from the audience. Dramatic presentations should include open discussion of the use of condoms and other protection, frank inquiries about personal risk, and how to deal with casual sexual encounters.

Conclusion

In closing, it is useful to review some basic knowledge: that AIDS is already present in the heterosexual population, as well as among homosexuals; that college students, as a group, tend to be more sexually active than other segments of the adult population; and that college students are a significant proportion of our population, not only in numbers, but also in terms of their future influence. These are our upcoming professionals—the privileged, who will be our future leaders. For their own sake, and for the sake of our society, this group should have the information, knowledge, and wisdom to make sound decisions for themselves and others.

Additional Resources

Hirschorn, M. W. (1987, April 29). AIDS is not seen as a major threat by many heterosexuals on campuses. *The Chronicle of Higher Education.*

The years of living dangerously. (1987, April). *Newsweek—On Campus.*

Helping Schools to Cope With AIDS

A case of AIDS can cause chaos in a school system that has made no plans to deal with such an event. This author outlines helpful procedures you can suggest that will prevent confusion and controversy.

Michael I. Grady, MD

Michael I. Grady is Medical Director, Boston Public School System, Boston, MA.

Physicians have always been deeply involved in school health programs, and for good reason. While most children are able to learn and make progress in school, their achievement potential is largely determined by the state of their physical, mental, and social health. Fortunately, school health programs have made tremendous strides in the early detection, management, and prevention of diseases and other medical conditions in recent years. For example, the mandated immunization for school-age children has greatly decreased the incidence and spread of communicable diseases. Similarly, vision and hearing tests, and such new programs as scoliosis screening have made possible the early identification and treatment of children with problems in these areas.

AIDS, the newest and perhaps the most frightening medical enemy to threaten society today, now challenges the entire school community, as well as the nation at large. Although the first few cases of AIDS were reported only six years ago, well over 47,000 Americans—including over 600 children—have contracted the disease since then. Moreover, this is only the tip of the iceberg, since some 1.5 million people are believed to be infected with the virus in this country alone. According to current projections, 270,000 of these are expected to have the full-blown disease by 1991. Individuals with AIDS have now been reported in each of the 50 states and the District of Columbia. As the Surgeon General, C. Everett Koop, stated recently, "AIDS is no longer possibly headed in your direction, it has probably already arrived."

My experience as medical director of the Boston public schools has shown that three components are essential for any effective school-based program on AIDS: A physician-consultant who is knowledgeable about AIDS; a policy concerning school attendance of HIV-infected students (including those with ARC or AIDS and those without any symptoms); and appropriate educational programs for school health professionals, teachers and school staff, students, parents, and others concerned with the problem of AIDS in the schools.

Urgent need for a physician-consultant

Every school system, regardless of size, requires the services of a physician to advise and assist in making medical decisions that affect the school population, especially on issues as complex as AIDS. Depending on the specific needs and size of the school system, the physician's services may be required full-time or part-time, or he or she may be employed as a consultant. In smaller educational systems, the physician-consultant can advise not only the school committee in charge of health affairs, but also the school health director, if that individual is not a physician.

AIDS policy

All school systems in the United States must establish an attendance policy for students with AIDS, ARC, and those with a positive HIV blood test but no symptoms. This should be done on a statewide basis. Such a policy must be developed in anticipation of the first case of AIDS, in a deliberate and thoughtful manner, together with appropriate school and community representatives. Schools cannot wait until one or more cases of AIDS, ARC, or

HIV-positive students are discovered, because at that time, the pace of events often makes it impossible to start from scratch. A consensus must have been reached and a mechanism of action readied *before* the need arises.

To accomplish this, the Boston

Public Health Fact Sheet

The Massachusetts Department of Public Health works to maintain, protect, and improve the health and well-being of the people of the Commonwealth. AIDS has recently received national attention and raised many issues for people. Following are some of the common questions raised by citizens of the Commonwealth, with answers that are provided by research physicians and experts of the Governor's Task Force on AIDS.

In what bodily fluids has the AIDS virus (HIV) been isolated?

The virus is found primarily in blood and semen. It has also been isolated in smaller amounts in saliva and tears. No studies have detected the virus in sweat, urine, or feces but scientists are investigating these possibilities. Precaution should always be taken in handling any of these substances, but transmission by any means other than sexual contact or direct injection with infected blood has never been demonstrated.

How contagious is AIDS?

Research shows that large amounts of infected fluids such as blood and sexual discharges must enter the body to spread the disease. Fluids that carry the HIV virus in small amounts, such as tears or saliva, are not a means of transmitting the virus casually. These infected fluids would have to enter the body through open wounds. The body's first defense is intact skin, which provides a barrier to any invading organism. Therefore, the AIDS virus cannot be transmitted by a kiss, a water fountain, swimming pools, door knobs, shared pens, or surfaces in restrooms. The virus is transmitted by sexual contact, sharing of needles, and blood to blood contact.

Can the virus live for a long time outside the body?

Unlike bacteria, the virus cannot reproduce outside a living cell. The AIDS virus needs a host to give it life. This host is the T-cell, part of the body's immune response. Once the virus is outside of the body, it becomes fragile and susceptible to changes in the environment such as heat and light. Household bleach (1 part bleach to 10 parts water) kills the virus, as well as hot sudsy water used to clean utensils. In the 13,000 households where AIDS has been diagnosed, no family members have caught the disease by casual contact.

How do children and babies get AIDS?

Four ways: blood transfusions; by the virus crossing into the fetus' blood through the placenta; through exposure to an infected mother's blood during childbirth; and possibly through breast milk.

Is it safe to allow children with AIDS to attend school?

Upon recommendation of the Governor's Task Force on AIDS, the Department of Public Health issued a policy on school attendance for children with AIDS. The policy, consistent with the guidelines issued by the Centers for Disease Control, and endorsed by the Department of Education, is based on sound scientific findings and allows a child with AIDS under the care of a personal physician to attend regular classes, with the following exceptions: open skin sores that are not able to be covered; inappropriate behavior such as biting or frequent incontinence; or if the child is too ill. The child also may be excluded from classes if there is an outbreak of any illness in the school.

Public School System (BPSS) in March 1985 formed a school committee of concerned individuals to set up an AIDS policy. The members included the medical director, school nurses, teachers, administrators, parents, students, custodians, and public health officials. During the following two months, the committee worked to devise an attendance policy, which was approved in June 1985 by Boston's Superintendent of Schools. Essentially, the policy states: All students with AIDS, ARC, or asymptomatic HIV infection are able to attend regular classes unless (1) the student has skin eruptions or weeping lesions that cannot be covered, or (2) the student exhibits inappropriate behavior such as biting. A plan was also set up to provide alternative education via home instruction for any student unable to attend school.

Once the group was established, it held numerous meetings in addition to those devoted to establishing the AIDS policy, to educate its members about AIDS and the ramifications of the disease. They also learned ways of responding to and educating the public about AIDS before any cases of the disease appeared in one of the schools and became public knowledge. With the AIDS policy in place for the Boston school system, we were able to prevent confusion and controversy in September 1985, when the public became aware that a student in one of Boston's public schools had developed AIDS. As a result of the educational program provided for students, parents, and school personnel, the student remained in school throughout the year without disruption in that particular school or in the system at large.

In contrast to our experience, many other school systems throughout the country have ex-

---

> ## Cleanup procedure for contaminated body fluid spills
>
> Blood, vomitus, or any other discharges of any body fluid from any person or child at the school site should be cleaned up as follows:
> 1. Obtain a plastic bag to dispose of all materials used in cleanup.
> 2. Wear disposable gloves.
> 3. If possible, wipe up fluids with disposable materials and discard them into a plastic bag.
> 4. Wash the contaminated area with a solution of one part bleach to ten parts water* (one pint or eight ounces of bleach to 1¼ gallon [10 pints] of water). Wash mop in bleach solution and let dry.
> 5. Clean sinks and toilets with bleach.
> 6. If you use sawdust for major spills, pick it up with cardboard, and discard both into a plastic bag. Treat the area with bleach, as explained in No. 4 above.
> 7. Discard all disposable materials, including gloves, into a plastic bag, then seal and discard it as instructed.
> 8. Wash hands thoroughly with soap and water.
>
> *Or equally effective disinfectant

---

perienced periods of controversy over students with AIDS, and on the question of whether to allow them to attend school. Many of these school systems had no AIDS policies at the time the infected students were discovered, which aggravated the situations.

When a school child develops AIDS

Schools have information regarding students' medical histories through our Health Services. Parents as well as students are assured that this information is kept in strict confidence. If a student has AIDS or ARC, only those with a need to know—the principal, school nurse, teacher(s) of the student, medical director, and superintendent—are informed about the student's diagnosis.

As soon as we learned that a child in one of our schools had developed AIDS, an educational forum was held for all the parents in that child's school. The city and state health officials who had pre-

viously worked with the policy committee attended this forum. We informed the parents of our existing AIDS policy, reassured them, and educated them about AIDS and its transmission. Subsequently, we sent all parents of the 60,000 students who attend the Boston public schools an informational packet that included information about the AIDS policy, a public health fact sheet on AIDS, and a list of telephone numbers for further information. While all parents received this information in English, those of foreign origin were sent another version in their own language.

Continuing AIDS education for school personnel

The committee formed during the spring of 1985 realized that any AIDS policy would be effective only if an educational program was developed at the same time to ensure that participants were updated about the disease.

In order to establish a truly

Hotline questions about AIDS

Are these statements true or false? (See answers below.)

(All are based on *actual questions* Community Health Nurses have answered on the AIDS Hotline at the Department of Health & Hospitals.)

	True	False
1. Mosquitoes can transmit AIDS by biting someone with AIDS and then biting a noninfected person.	___	___
2. You can acquire AIDS by using a toilet seat that has been used by someone with AIDS.	___	___
3. A child with AIDS attending school is in more danger of getting sick than making someone sick.	___	___
4. You can get AIDS by taking a bite of a sandwich or a sip of a drink that someone with AIDS has had.	___	___
5. You can get the AIDS virus by giving blood or getting an immunization.	___	___
6. You can tell by looking at someone if they have AIDS or the AIDS virus.	___	___
7. If you are into I.V. Drugs you are at risk for getting AIDS.	___	___
8. You can get AIDS by close skin contact—shaking hands or hugging.	___	___
9. You need to be careful with bodily fluids from anybody when cleaning up spills.	___	___
10. If you have sex with a lot of people you don't know very well you might be at risk for getting AIDS.	___	___

1. False   2. False   3. True   4. False   5. False   6. False   7. True
8. False   9. True   10. True

useful program, we identified and trained resource persons to act as sources of information and as teachers. Inasmuch as most of the informational needs at that time were medical in nature, personnel from the City of Boston Department of Health and Hospitals trained all 75 Boston school nurses as educators. These training sessions began in the spring of 1985. Since that time, the school

nurses have continued to attend inservice sessions at regular intervals, to review the present program as well as to receive new information on AIDS. School custodians who might become exposed to students' body fluid spills also attended periodic educational training sessions conducted by medical personnel. Recently, we added health/science teachers from the middle- and high schools

to the standing group of resource personnel.

Educational program for students

While the nurses/teachers were being trained, we also developed a program for the students. We determined that this program would have to be factual, informative, and compassionate. Our major concern was to overcome their lack of knowledge, correct widespread misinformation, and teach risk reduction techniques. We planned the first program for the middle and upper grades. These students are old enough to understand the disease and its ramifications, and are most likely to consider becoming, or already are, sexually active. To meet their needs effectively, we developed a 28-minute videotape.* This video is loaned to schools upon request, subject to availability. It fits well into a classroom schedule in that it allows time for an introduction by an instructor, and for followup questions and answers. Although one such teaching session does not cover the entire subject, it is a helpful starting point that leads to further discussion in the students' health/science classes. The videotape has still other advantages. It makes it possible to

● present to all students the same facts concerning a specific medical condition;

● graphically demonstrate the experiences of a young, articulate person who has AIDS, and

● include a number of frequently asked questions (and their answers) in a true-false format.

In the spring of 1986, the school nurses started to present this pro-

---

* This videotape may be obtained by writing to: Boston Public Schools Health Services, 26 Court Street, Boston, MA 02108.

gram to the staff (teachers, teachers' aides, secretaries) of the 123 schools in the Boston school system to educate them about AIDS, as well as to familiarize them with what the students were learning.

Since these student educational programs were established, they have been *recommended* for grades 7–12, and *mandated* for grades 8, 10, and 12. Initial evaluations by the program presenters have been very positive. The Boston school system is now planning to broaden the AIDS education program for these grades by incorporating the newly available state curriculum on AIDS.

At this time, too, the committee on AIDS education is preparing questions and answers appropriate for inclusion in the elementary school health curriculum. Obviously, younger children do not need a formal medical course on AIDS. Nevertheless, these children will be asking questions about AIDS, and their teachers should be able to discuss and answer them. Thus, a subcommittee will shortly develop a curriculum on AIDS for the elementary grades. This will be reviewed by the overall committee of concerned constituents, and subsequently forwarded to the Superintendent of Schools for his approval. The nurses and teachers in the elementary schools will then be trained and the program will become a part of the overall elementary health curriculum.

School employees who develop ARC or AIDS

When a teacher or other school employee is found to be HIV-positive, or develops either ARC or AIDS, the Employee Policy, issued as part of the School Superintendent's "Guidelines and Procedures concerning AIDS" is followed. It states "The Boston School Department recognizes that employees with life-threatening illnesses, including, but not limited to, cancer, heart disease, and AIDS may wish to continue to work. As long as employees are able to meet acceptable performance standards, and medical evidence indicates that their condition is not a threat to themselves or others, employees shall be assured of continued employment. Federal and State laws also mandate, pursuant to the laws protecting disabled individuals, that those individuals not be discriminated against on the basis of their handicaps, and that if it becomes necessary, some reasonable accomodations be made to enable qualified individuals to continue to work."

Confidentiality

On the issue of confidentiality of an employee's medical condition, the "Guidelines" state: "Employers should always remember that an employee's health condition is personal and confidential. Personnel and medical files or information about employees are exempt from public disclosure by M.G.L. C. 4, §7 (26). In addition, information relating to a specifically-named individual, the disclosure of which would constitute an unwarranted invasion of personal privacy, is exempt. Thus, special precautions should be taken to protect such information regarding an employee's health condition in order to prevent instances of disclosure that may invade the personal privacy of employees. Only those managers with a clear need to know should be informed of an employee's health condition."

Conclusion

The success of any school-based curriculum on AIDS must include a broadly representative committee that has credibility, access to appropriate medical consultants, and the capability to prepare and implement educational programs appropriate for school health professionals, students, parents, school staff, and the public. One or more physicians knowledgeable about AIDS should serve on such a committee. If further assistance is needed, public health physicians or agencies must be consulted. It is important to be open and honest about what is known, as well as what is not known about this illness. If this is done, the necessity for an educational program in the schools will become apparent to all those involved, who will then be willing to support its execution.

Until medical researchers come up with a cure for the disease and a vaccine to prevent it, physicians must take a leading role in assisting educators to prevent the spread of AIDS, and help them manage the education of HIV-infected children in their system.

Flirting with AIDS

*500 Women Like You Report in on the Big Gap
Between What We Know and What We Do*

Caryl S. Avery

All women—singles, live-togethers, even marrieds—need to protect a little, or a lot, against AIDS. But few are. Some encouraging, some disturbing results of a startling new Self *survey.*

Advice on how to protect yourself against AIDS abounds, but what are women like you actually doing about it? To find out, *Self* interviewed over 500 heterosexual women (252 were married or living with someone, 264 were single), ages 20 through 45, throughout the country. What we discovered: While some women are backing up attitudes with action, many more have good intentions about taking precautions but less-than-optimal follow-through. Ahead, new insights into where denial may be tripping you up—and new incentive to combat it.

What singles need most:
Healthy skepticism
Considering that the first step in preventing a wide heterosexual AIDS spread is raising people's consciousness to the *possibility* of one, it's encouraging that over eight out of ten single women surveyed (85%) were concerned about contracting the disease. Problem is, a substantial number of them aren't doing anything about it. While 53% say they have changed their behavior either "drastically" or "moderately," a whopping 31% haven't changed their actions at all.

What's more, the ones at potentially greatest risk—the 50 or so dating more than one man—were the least concerned and the least inclined to make major changes. This is especially surprising considering that, as a whole, the singles were rather conservative sexually, averaging only 1.7 sex partners in the past year. Of

those who were playing the field, half slept with under three men in the past year, a third with three to five. From them you might expect more caution regarding AIDS, but not so.

"It appears that many of these women have unrealistic notions about their invulnerability," says Martha Gross, Ph.D., a sex therapist and psychologist in private practice in Washington, D.C. "They are rationalizing risky behavior."

For example: When asked if they delay intercourse with men they are attracted to because of fear of AIDS, 36% of *all* the singles said, "Yes, until I feel I know him well," 15% indicated "Until marriage," 14% "Until we agree to become monogamous," 7% "For a specific number of dates—about 5." Only 8% said "Yes, until we've both been tested for the AIDS virus"—the only truly safe choice in the bunch. And one fifth said they don't put off having intercourse at all.

Now hold on to your hats: Of those *dating more than one man*, over one quarter didn't postpone lovemaking. And 57% said they wait until they know their partner well. Well-intentioned, but naive.

Despite admonitions to "know your partner," experts know from experience with female AIDS patients that that's virtually impossible. Not that you shouldn't *try*, but don't bet your life on it.

For starters, "men do not talk about bisexual experiences," says June Osborn, M.D., dean of the School of Public Health at the University of Michigan. "And that poses a substantial risk for anyone dealing with what she thinks is a perfectly ordinary new date. I don't care how well you get to know each other, the chances of it coming out in conversation are practically zip."

The same is true for a drug experimentation episode, she says. "Take, for example, somebody who visited New York City five years ago, tried shooting up and later learned about AIDS—he's not likely to say, 'Hey, I just want to mention that a few years ago I did this really dumb thing.' Especially if he's trying to 'make it' with you. So you have to have a little healthy skepticism with new sexual partners."

If you don't think any of this could apply to "the kind of men" you date, you're definitely not alone. More than nine out of ten of the singles we surveyed stated that as far as they know, they have not had sex with a bisexual in the past decade. "I think they are greatly underestimating the number of bisexual men," says research biologist Mathilde Krim, Ph.D., founding chair of the American Foundation for AIDS Research (AmFAR).

Although there are no firm data on the number of bisexual men in the United States today, we can get some idea from the 1948 Kinsey statistics. Kinsey had men rank themselves on a scale of 0 to 6, where 0 meant they'd had only heterosexual experiences and 6 meant they'd had only homosexual experiences; the numbers in between represented some combination thereof. The study found that 50% of American men were "Kinsey zeros" (completely heterosexual); 4% were "Kinsey sixes" (completely homosexual); leaving 46% who had had one or more homosexual, as well as heterosexual, experiences.

Not only are people disinclined to talk about bisexuality and drug abuse, they may not even *know* what they've done in the past (for instance, if they were "under the influence"), or remember it (we tend to repress behaviors we're ashamed of or uncomfortable with), or realize that a particular behavior put them (and therefore you) at risk.

"So a person doesn't have to be lying or deceitful for you to be deceived," says Constance Wofsy, M.D., codirector of AIDS activities at San Francisco General Hospital and principal investigator of Project AWARE, a study of women aged 18 to 50 who have had five or more sex partners in the last three years or have been exposed to men in risk groups. "I can confirm that by the luck of the draw there are women—in all walks of life, including white, middle-class, professional women—who have been infected by partners who had provided no clue that there was a risk."

So "precautions" like holding off for a certain number of dates or until the two of you are monogamous or even married (since neither monogamy nor marriage "dis-infects"), while better than nothing, are not sufficient.

This doesn't mean you *shouldn't* hold off or ask about his past—you might get honest answers. What it does mean is if you're truly concerned about safety but you and he don't opt to be tested, your best bet is using latex condoms and a spermicide containing nonoxynol-9. Not 100% safe, but a *lot* safer.

The condom conflict

Although 85% of the single women reported being worried about AIDS, only 38% of them said they usually bring the subject up with new men they're dating—suggesting a big gap between attitudes and actions.

Another example of the words/action split: While the overwhelming majority of singles (88%) thought condoms were either completely (14%) or somewhat (74%) effective in protecting against the AIDS virus, only 37% bought and carried them; 53% relied on men to have them! "This is astounding, considering men's well-known dislike of condoms. Too many women are not taking responsibility for their health," says Dr. Gross. "I think it's not so much embarrassment over buying condoms as it is fear of threatening their relationship."

This seems confirmed by the fact that four out of ten singles said that if a man refused to wear a condom, they would sleep with him anyway—6% unconditionally, 33% if they considered him low-risk. Interestingly, significantly more of the older women seemed willing to rely on their judgment about a partner's risk. "Apparently they feel with age comes wisdom," Dr. Gross says. "In other areas that may be true, but here, with age comes a greater chance of hitting a partner with a 'speckled' sexual history."

You can be aware of the AIDS danger, savvy about carrying condoms and committed to using them—and still give in to unconscious conflicting needs at the last minute. "I hear that all the time," says Anke A. Ehrhardt, Ph.D., director of the HIV Center for Clinical and Behavioral Studies at New York State Psychiatric Institute and Columbia-Presbyterian Medical Center. "The woman had a condom and was *determined* to use it, then gave in when the man resisted because she didn't want to risk the relationship." The only way you can prevent this from happening, she says, is by discussing the issue with your partner in advance.

Abstaining from anal sex: Not the entire answer

But some warnings appear to be getting through loud and clear. Chief among them: that anal intercourse increases the efficiency of transmission of the virus, and therefore the risk.

How many women have at least *tried* anal sex? The figures vary: A 1983 *Playboy* survey with roughly 20,000 female respondents found 61%; a 1984 *Self* survey of 11,000 readers, 51% (up 13% from 1980). The majority of sex experts we recently asked estimate that conservatively 30% of women have tried it, though considerably fewer practice it regularly.

In our present survey, almost a fifth of the singles report having had anal intercourse, but 45% of those say they now avoid it because of fear of AIDS—roughly twice as many as have given up oral sex, which has been cited as potentially risky but never proven to be.

But believing "If I don't have anal sex, I'm safe" is either a rationalization or a misunderstanding of the facts: *You don't have to have anal intercourse to become infected; plain old vaginal intercourse (especially unprotected) will do,* if you're unlucky enough to choose a partner who has the virus.

Marrieds: A false sense of security?

Women who are married or living with a man have a harder time believing they could be at risk. Of the 252 marrieds or live-togethers (coupled for an average of 9.6 years), only one out of eight (12%) was worried about having been exposed to AIDS beforehand.

This sense of security is realistic for the 46% together for more than ten years, as it's believed HIV has been in this country only since 1977. But not so for the rest, if they (and/or their partners) were sexually active prior to this relationship. And, in fact, the women in our study married under ten years (*especially* those married under three) were significantly more concerned than those married over ten years.

Not only were most marrieds not very troubled about the possibility of having picked up the virus from a sex partner prior to marriage, they also weren't much concerned about contracting it from their spouse. Only 8% said they were worried about what their partner might have done before they tied the knot—or since.

This is especially surprising considering 13% said their partner has not been faithful. And that 13% figure is way below the generally estimated 70% infidelity rate for men. In other words, many women may have a false sense of security based on either wishful thinking—that their partner has been faithful—or denial—that even if he hasn't, it wouldn't put them at risk for AIDS.

Not to mention that nearly 20% of the married or live-together women reported having been unfaithful themselves. And that 60% of the infidelities (his or hers) occurred within the last three years—that is, since it's been known that AIDS does not discriminate, that it affects straights as well as gays.

A dangerous double standard

Still, marrieds don't totally have their heads in the sand. Seven out of ten said that if they found out their partner had had an affair, they'd insist he be tested before resuming sex; over half would insist he use condoms.

But while the majority of women would take some action to protect themselves if their husband strayed, a *minority*—four out of ten—would accord their partner the same opportunity by confessing their own infidelity. The rest either flat-out wouldn't tell (27%) or would only if they thought they might have been infected (31%).

"That's worrisome," says Dr. Krim. "It means they recognize the seriousness of infidelity in the present situation, but don't accept responsibility for telling if they are the unfaithful ones."

Prepregnancy testing: A must?

Most women in a position to have children, however, would set aside personal fears—about threatening the future of a relationship or finding out they were infected—if they were planning to get pregnant: Over eight out of ten of the marrieds agreed with the statement that "since infected women can transmit the AIDS virus to their unborn, women contemplating pregnancy should be tested." Nine out of ten felt that anyone who tests positive—that is, has antibodies to the virus, and is thus assumed to be a carrier—should not bear children.

But of those who believe prospective mothers *should* be tested, only three quarters said *they* would be tested. One quarter would just hope for the best. Again, a gap between attitude and action.

"Testing might be unnecessary if a woman and her husband are virgins when they marry," says Dr. Krim. "But the average woman who lives in an urban area and has had a number of boyfriends over the last five years should be tested. She has a responsibility not only to herself, but to her child. Many infected babies die within a year or two and suffer horribly." Besides, she emphasizes, "it's likely that the result will be negative, and then you can stop worrying."

Deal with the risk—don't deny it

Whether individual women are worried for themselves or not, our study sug-

gests a collective AIDS *angst:* Almost two thirds of the women believe there will be a major epidemic in the heterosexual population. One fifth already know (or knew) someone with AIDS or ARC (AIDS-related complex).

But confusion still reigns. While some seven out of ten women give points to the media for accurately reporting the heterosexual risk "based on current knowledge," about the same number don't think much of that knowledge; 74% feel "doctors don't really know all the ways AIDS is transmitted."

In this kind of situation, the *real* risk is denying the risk ("Nobody knows what they're talking about anyway, so what the hell") or exaggerating it ("Even holding hands isn't safe anymore"). Everybody deals with ambiguity and uncertainty differently. The necessity is to deal with it responsibly.

The emerging strategy to contain AIDS

The worst lies ahead, yet there is new hope for extending victims' lives

Heart disease and cancer still kill more people annually. But AIDS continues to command center stage in the world of medicine, not so much for the deadly toll it has exacted to date as for the impact still to come. The army of 11,000 AIDS experts who gathered in Montreal last week for the fifth international conference on the disease agreed that the AIDS time bomb has yet to explode full force.

By conservative estimates, some 5 million people around the world will have active cases of AIDS by the year 2000, 1 million to 1.5 million of them in the U.S. alone. And the World Health Organization (WHO) estimates that an additional 15 to 20 million by then will be infected with human immunodeficiency virus, or HIV, which causes the disease. Even with stepped-up programs for prevention and education, WHO projects that twice as many will become infected in the 1990s as in the 1980s. In the U.S., the share of those infected will increasingly be young, black or Hispanic, and poor.

Yet there is hope amid the grim statistics. Waging an all-out research effort now costing almost $1 billion a year in the U.S., scientists are fast closing in on the mechanisms the virus uses to spin its lethal web. Researchers have identified the virus's key genes and proteins and have capitalized quickly on this knowledge to initiate novel approaches to drugs and vaccines. Half a dozen vaccines are in the early stages of testing, with several already showing promise in animal studies. One approach, being led by polio-vaccine pioneer Jonas Salk, is to develop a vaccine that would both prevent initial infection and help people already infected by forestalling development of full-blown AIDS.

Clever virus. Such rapid progress, unprecedented against a newly discovered viral disease, does not obscure the fact that much remains unknown. "This virus is very clever," says Dr. Luc Montagnier, the French researcher who co-

discovered HIV. "It will be many years before we fully determine how it works." Most troubling still, he says, is how the virus manages to remain dormant for so long. Most people do not develop AIDS until five to 10 years after becoming infected. Doctors still cannot say unequivocally whether everyone infected with the virus will ultimately develop AIDS. They do know, however, that some people's immune systems put up a tougher fight against the virus than do others'.

However, scientists do not have to understand the virus fully to beat back its ravages with new drugs. The experts in Montreal agreed that controlling AIDS and the infections that accompany the disease, if not curing them, is within sight. About 20 anti-HIV drugs, alone or in combination, are currently being tested, and some 7,000 AIDS patients are in formal drug trials. "There is much reason to be optimistic that we can develop a strategy to contain the infection and to keep many AIDS patients alive for years," says Dr. Anthony Fauci, director of AIDS research at the National Institutes of Health. Among the most promising drugs is one that takes advantage of scientists' identification of the key protein on the surface of immune-system cells to which the virus usually binds. Called soluble CD4, the drug keeps the virus from latching onto cell surfaces by sopping up the virus in the bloodstream.

Only one drug, AZT, has been approved so far to treat AIDS directly, and studies presented at the conference show that AZT does extend the lives of most of those who take it. But its greatest benefit seems to come in the first 12 to 15 months. After that, the death rate rises. The virus, moreover, can become resistant to AZT. This makes finding other agents to send against the virus more imperative. Under intense pressure from clinicians and AIDS activists to release experimental AIDS drugs more quickly, the Food and Drug Administration is likely to expedite the approval process when alternatives to AZT come along.

The therapy issue that dominated the Montreal conference, however, was the treatment of infected people who show

no signs of illness. An increasing number of doctors think such treatment is warranted, and thousands of HIV-infected people, mostly homosexual men, are already taking one or more drugs to stave off AIDS. But many at the conference urged caution. "We don't yet know whether the risks of long-term side effects outweigh the benefits here," says Fauci, noting that infected persons may have to take a preventive drug for years. One possible alternative would be treating the disease just as it takes hold. Dr. James Mason, assistant secretary for health, told conferees that the U.S. Public Health Service may soon formally urge all infected persons to be monitored regularly for signs of imminent disease so that drugs could be administered to those in the earliest throes of AIDS. Several key blood tests now allow this because they can detect which infected people have the highest risk of developing AIDS or are in the very early stages of the disease.

Seeking the infected. The who-gets-treated issue will vastly complicate the social, ethical and economic quandaries that already surround AIDS. If drugs can prevent the onset of AIDS, that argues powerfully for aggressively seeking out all infected people. Any mention of forced testing or mandatory reporting of the names of those voluntarily tested for HIV antibodies, however, draws the ire and protest of civil-rights groups and AIDS patients. They say that discrimination against the infected in housing, jobs and health insurance is all too real, and because of the chance they will be revealed, high-risk people still shy away from being tested.

It is not clear who would pay for the costly drugs. Of the 1 to 1.5 million people in the U.S. currently infected with HIV, as many as 250,000 could qualify for immediate treatment, at an annual cost of $5,000 to $15,000 each. With insurance companies and Congress already balking at covering the rising costs of AIDS care, sparks will surely fly if studies now under way do confirm a clear benefit for treating the infected.

by Steven Findlay with Joanne Silberner in Montreal

Glossary

—A—

abnormal: anything considered not normal, i.e., not conforming to the subjective standards a social group has established as the norm

abortifacients: substances that cause termination of pregnancy

acquaintance (date) rape: when a sexual encounter is forced by someone who is known to the victim

acquired immunodeficiency syndrome: fatal disease caused by a virus that is transmitted through the exchange of bodily fluids primarily in sexual activity, and intravenous drug use

activating effect: the direct influence some hormones can have on activating or deactivating sexual behavior

actual use failure rate: a measure of how often a birth control method can be expected to fail when human error and technical failure are considered

adolescence: period of emotional, social, and physical transition from childhood to adulthood

adultery toleration: marriage partners extend the freedom to each other to have sex with others

affectional: relating to feelings or emotions, such as romantic attachments

afterbirth: the tissues expelled after childbirth including the placenta, the remains of the umbilical cord and fetal membranes

agenesis (absence) of the penis (ae-JEN-a-ses): a congenital condition in which the penis is undersized and nonfunctional

AIDS: acquired immunodeficiency syndrome

ambisexual: alternate term for bisexual

amniocentesis: a process whereby medical problems with a fetus can be determined while it is still in the womb; a needle is inserted into the amniotic sac, amniotic fluid is withdrawn, and its cells examined

amnion (AM-nee-on): a thin membrane that forms a closed sac to enclose the embryo; the sac is filled with amniotic fluid that protects and cushions the embryo

anal intercourse: insertion of the penis into the rectum of a partner

androgen: a male hormone, such as testosterone, that affects physical development, sexual desire, and behavior. It is produced by both male and female sex glands and influences each sex in varying degrees

androgyny (an-DROJ-a-nee): combination of traditional feminine and masculine traits in a single individual

anejaculation: lack of ejaculation at the time of orgasm

anorchism (a-NOR-kiz-um): rare birth defect in which both testes are lacking

aphrodisiacs (af-ro-DEE-zee-aks): foods or chemicals purported to foster sexual arousal; they are believed to be more myth than fact

apotemnophilia: a rare condition characterized by the desire to function sexually after having a leg amputated

areola (a-REE-a-la): darkened, circular area of skin surrounding the nipple

artificial embryonation: a process in which the developing embryo is flushed from the uterus of the donor woman 5 days after fertilization and placed in another woman's uterus

artificial insemination: injecting the sperm cells of a male into a woman's vagina, with the intention of conceiving a child

asceticism (a-SET-a-siz-um): usually characterized by celibacy, this philosophy emphasizes spiritual purity through self-denial and self-discipline

asexuality: characterized by a low interest in sex

autoerotic asphyxiation: accidental death from pressure placed around the neck during masturbatory behavior

autofellatio (fe-LAY-she-o): a male providing oral stimulation to his own penis, an act most males do not have the physical agility to perform

—B—

Bartholin's glands (BAR-tha-lenz): small glands located in the opening through the minor lips that produce some secretion during sexual arousal

behavior therapy: used of techniques to learn new patterns of behavior, often employed in sex therapy

berdache (bare-DAHSH): anthropological term for cross-dressing in other cultures

bestiality (beest-ee-AL-i-tee): a human being having sexual contact with an animal

birth canal: term applied to the vagina during the birth process

birthing rooms: special areas in the hospital, decorated and furnished in a nonhospital way, set aside for giving birth; the woman remains here to give birth rather than being taken to a separate delivery room

bisexual: refers to some degree of sexual attraction to or activities with members of both sexes

blastocyst: the morula, after five days of cell division—has developed a fluid-filled cavity in its interior and entered the uterine cavity

bond: the emotional link between parent and child created by cuddling, cooing, physical and eye contact early in the newborn's life

bondage: tying, restraining, or applying pressure to body parts for sexual arousal

brachioproctic activity (brake-ee-o-PRAHK-tik): known in slang as "fisting"; a hand is inserted into the rectum of a partner

brothels: houses of prostitution

bulbourethral glands: also called Cowper's glands

—C—

call boys: highly paid male prostitutes

call girls: more highly paid prostitutes who work by appointment with a more exclusive clientele

cantharides (kan-THAR-a-deez): a chemical extracted from a beetle that, when taken internally, creates irritation of blood vessels in the genital region; it can cause physical harm

case studies: an in-depth look at a particular individual and how he or she might have been helped to solve a sexual or other problem. They may offer new and useful ideas for counselors to use with other patients

catharsis theory: suggests that viewing pornography provides a release for sexual tension, thus preventing antisocial behavior

celibacy (SELL-a-ba-see): choosing not to share sexual activity with others

cervical cap: a device that is shaped like a large thimble and fits over the cervix; not a particularly effective contraceptive because it can dislodge easily during intercourse

cervical intraepithelial neoplasia (CIN) (ep-a-THEE-lee-al nee-a-PLAY-zhee-a): abnormal, precancerous cells sometimes identified in a Pap smear

cervix (SERV-ix): lower "neck" of the uterus that extends into the back part of the vagina

cesarian section: a surgical method of childbirth in which delivery occurs through an incision in the abdominal wall and uterus

chancroid (SHAN-kroyd): a venereal disease caused by the bacterium *Hemophilus ducreyi*: and characterized by sores on the genitals which, if left untreated, could result in pain and rupture of the sores

child molesting: sexual abuse of a child by an adult

chlamydia (kluh-MID-ee-uh): now known to be a common STD, this organism is a major cause of urethritis in males; in females it often presents no symptoms

chorion (KOR-ee-on): the outermost extra-embryonic membrane essential in the formation of the placenta

chorionic villi sampling (CVS): a technique for diagnosing medical problems in the fetus as early as the 8th week of pregnancy; a sample of the chorionic membrane is removed through the cervix and studied

cilia: microscopic hair-like projections that help move the ovum through the fallopian tube

circumcision: in the male, surgical removal of the foreskin from the penis; in the female, surgical procedure that cuts the prepuce, exposing the clitoral shaft

climacteric: mid-life period experienced by both men and women when there is greater emotional stress than usual and sometimes physical symptoms

climax: another term for orgasm

clinical research: the study of the cause, treatment or prevention of a disease or condition by testing large numbers of people

clitoridectomy: surgical removal of the clitoris; practiced routinely in some cultures

clitoris (KLIT-a-rus): sexually sensitive organ found in the female vulva; it becomes engorged with blood during arousal

clone: the genetic duplicate organism produced by the cloning process

cloning: a process involving the transfer of a full complement of chromosomes from a body cell of an organism into an ovum from which the chromosomal material has been removed; if allowed to develop into a new organism, it is an exact genetic duplicate of the one from which the original body cell was taken; the process is not yet used for humans, but has been performed in lower animal species

cohabitation: living together and sharing sex without marrying

coitus (KO-at-us or ko-EET-us): heterosexual, penis-in-vagina intercourse

coitus interruptus (ko-EET-us or KO-ut-us): a method of birth control in which the penis is withdrawn from the vagina prior to ejaculation

comarital sex: also called mate-swapping, a couple swaps sexual partners with another couple

combining of chromosomes: occurs when a sperm unites with an egg, normally joining 23 pairs of chromosomes to establish the genetic "blueprint" for a new individual. The sex chromosomes establish its sex: XX for female and XY for male

coming out: to acknowledge to oneself and to others that one is sexually attracted to others of the same sex

Comstock Laws: enacted in the 1870s, this federal legislation prohibited mailing information about contraception

condom: a sheath worn over the penis during intercourse to collect semen and prevent disease transmission

consensual adultery: permission given to at least one partner within the marital relationship to participate in extramarital sexual activity

controlled experiment: research in which the investigator examines what is happening to one variable while all other variables are kept constant

conventional adultery: extramarital sex without the knowledge of the spouse

coprophilia: sexual arousal connected with feces

core gender-identity/role: a child's early sense and expression of its maleness, femaleness, or ambivalence, prior to puberty

corona: the ridge around the penile glans

corpus luteum: follicle cell cluster that remains after the ovum is released, secreting hormones that help regulate the menstrual cycle

Cowper's glands: two small glands in the male which secrete alkaline fluid into the urethra during sexual arousal

cross-genderists: transgenderists

cryptorchidism (krip-TOR-ka-diz-um): condition in which the testes have not descended into the scrotum prior to birth

cunnilingus (kun-a-LEAN-gus): oral stimulation of the clitoris, vaginal opening, or other parts of the vulva

cystitis (sis-TITE-us): a nonsexually transmitted infection of the urinary bladder

— D —

decriminalization: reducing the legal sanctions for particular acts while maintaining the possibility of legally regulating behavior through testing, licensing, and reporting of financial gain

deoxyribonucleic acid (DNA) (dee-AK-see-rye-bow-new-KLEE-ik): the chemical in each cell that carries the genetic code

deprivation homosexuality: can occur when members of the opposite sex are unavailable

desire phase: Kaplan's term for the psychological interest in sex that precedes a physiological, sexual arousal

deviation: term applied to behavior or orientations that do not conform to a society's accepted norms; it often has negative connotations

diaphragm (DY-a-fram): a latex rubber cup, filled with spermicide, that is fitted to the cervix by a clinician; the woman must learn to insert it properly for full contraceptive effectiveness

diethylstilbestrol (DES) (dye-eth-a-stil-BES-trole): synthetic estrogen compound given to mothers whose pregnancies are at high risk of miscarrying

dilation and curettage (D & C): a method of induced abortion in the second trimester of pregnancy that involves a scraping of the uterine wall

dilation and evacuation (D & E): a method of induced abortion in the second trimester of pregnancy; it combines suction with a scraping of the inner wall of the uterus

discrimination: the process by which an individual extinguishes a response to one stimulus while preserving it for other stimuli

dysfunction: when the body does not function as expected or desired during sex

dysmenorrhea (dis-men-a-REE-a): painful menstruation

— E —

E. coli: bacteria naturally living in the human colon, often causes urinary tract infection

ectopic pregnancy (ek-TOP-ik): the implantation of a blastocyst somewhere other than in the uterus, usually in the fallopian tube

ejaculation: muscular expulsion of semen from the penis

ejaculatory inevitability: the sensation in the male that ejaculation is imminent

ELISA: the primary test used to determine the presence of AIDS in humans

embryo (EM-bree-o): the term applied to the developing cells, when about a week after fertilization, the blastocyst implants itself in the uterine wall

endometrial hyperplasia (hy-per-PLAY-zhee-a): excessive growth of the inner lining of the uterus (endometrium)

endometriosis (en-doe-mee-tree-O-sus): growth of the endometrium out of the uterus into surrounding organs

endometrium: interior lining of the uterus, innermost of three layers

epidemiology (e-pe-dee-mee-A-la-jee): the branch of medical science that deals with the incidence, distribution, and control of disease in a population

epididymis (ep-a-DID-a-mus): tubular structure on each testis in which sperm cells mature

epididymitis (ep-a-did-a-MITE-us): inflammation of the epididymis of the testis

episiotomy (ee-piz-ee-OTT-a-mee): a surgical incision in the vaginal opening made by the clinician or obstetrician if it appears that the baby will tear the opening in the process of being born

epispadias (ep-a-SPADE-ee-as): birth defect in which the urinary bladder empties through an abdominal opening, and the urethera is malformed

erectile dysfunction: difficulty achieving or maintaining penile erection (impotence)

erection: enlargement and stiffening of the penis as blood engorges the columns of spongy tissue, and internal muscles contract

erogenous zone (a-RAJ-a-nus): any area of the body that is sensitive to sexual arousal

erotica: artistic representations of nudity or sexual activity

estrogen (ES-tro-jen): hormone produced abundantly by the ovaries; it plays an important role in the menstrual cycle

estrogen replacement therapy (ERT): controversial treatment of the physical changes of menopause by administering dosages of the hormone estrogen

ethnocentricity: the tendency of the members of one culture to assume that their values and norms of behavior are the "right" ones in comparison to other cultures

excitement: the arousal phase of Masters and Johnson's 4-phase model of the sexual response cycle

exhibitionism: exposing the genitals to others for sexual pleasure

external values: the belief systems available from one's society and culture

extramarital sex: married person having sexual intercourse with someone other than her or his spouse; adultery

— F —

fallopian tubes: structures that are connected to the uterus and lead the ovum from an ovary to the inner cavity of the uterus

fellatio: oral stimulation of the penis

fetal alcohol syndrome (FAS): a condition in a fetus characterized by abnormal growth, neurological damage, and facial distortion caused by the mother's heavy alcohol consumption

fetal surgery: a surgical procedure performed on the fetus while it is still in the uterus

fetishism (FET-a-shizm): sexual arousal triggered by objects or materials not usually considered to be sexual

fetus: the term given to the embryo after two months of development in the womb

fibrous hymen: unnaturally thick, tough tissue composing the hymen

follicles: capsule of cells in which an ovum matures

follicle-stimulating hormone (FSH): pituitary hormone that stimulates the ovaries or testes

foreplay: sexual activities shared in early stages of sexual arousal, with the term implying that they are leading to a more intense, orgasm-oriented form of activity such as intercourse

foreskin: fold of skin covering the penile glans; also called prepuce

fraternal: a twin formed from two separate ova which were fertilized by two separate sperm

frenulum (FREN-yu-lum): thin, tightly-drawn fold of skin on the underside of the penile glans; it is highly sensitive

frottage (fro-TAZH): gaining sexual gratification from anonymously pressing or rubbing against others, usually in crowded settings

frotteur: one who practices frottage

—G—

gamete intra-fallopian transfer (GIFT): direct placement of ovum and concentrated sperm cells into the woman's fallopian tube, increasing the chances of fertilization

gay: slang term referring to homosexual persons and behaviors

gender dysphoria (dis-FOR-ee-a): term to describe gender-identity/role that does not conform to the norm considered appropriate for one's physical sex

gender transposition: gender dysphoria

gender-identity/role (G-I/R): a person's inner experience and outward expression of maleness, femaleness, or some ambivalent position between the two

general sexual dysfunction: difficulty for a woman in achieving sexual arousal

generalization: application of specific learned responses to other, similar situations or experiences

genetic engineering: the modification of the gene structure of cells to change cellular functioning

genital herpes (HER-peez): viral STD characterized by painful sores on the sex organs

genital warts: small lesions on genital skin caused by papilloma virus, this STD increases later risks of certain malignancies

glans: in the male, the sensitive head of the penis; in the female, sensitive head of the clitoris, visible between the upper folds of the minor lips

gonadotropin releasing hormone (GnRH) (go-nad-a-TRO-pen): hormone from the hypothalamus that stimulates the release of FSH and LH by the pituitary

gonorrhea (gon-uh-REE-uh): bacterial STD causing urethral pain and discharge in males; often no symptoms in females

granuloma inguinale (gran-ya-LOW-ma in-gwa-NAL-ee or -NALE): venereal disease characterized by ulcerations and granulations beginning in the groin and spreading to the buttocks and genitals

group marriage: three or more people in a committed relationship who share sex with one another

G spot: a vaginal area that some researchers feel is particularly sensitive to sexual stimulation

—H—

hard-core pornography: pornography that makes use of highly explicit depictions of sexual activity or shows lengthy scenes of genitals

hedonists: believers that pleasure is the highest good

hemophiliac (hee-mo-FIL-ee-ak): someone with the hereditary sex-linked blood defect hemophilia, affecting males primarily and characterized by difficulty in clotting

heterosexual: attractions or activities between members of opposite sexes

HIV: human immunodeficiency virus

homophobia (ho-mo-PHO-bee-a): strongly held negative attitudes and irrational fears relating to homosexuals

homosexual: term applied to romantic and sexual attractions and activities between members of the same sex

homosexualities: a term that reminds us there is not a single pattern of homosexuality, but a wide range of same-sex orientations

hookers: street name for female prostitutes

hormone implants: contraceptive method in which hormone-releasing plastic containers are surgically inserted under the skin

hot flash: a flushed, sweaty feeling in the skin caused by dilated blood vessels, often associated with menopause

human chorionic gonadotropin (HCG): a hormone detectable in the urine of a pregnant woman

human immunodeficiency virus: the virus that initially attacks the human immune system, eventually causing AIDS

hustlers: male street prostitutes

H-Y antigen: a biochemical produced in an embryo when the Y chromosome is present; it causes fetal gonads to develop into testes

hymen: membranous tissue that can cover part of the vaginal opening

hypersexuality: exaggeratedly high level of interest in and drive for sex

hyposexuality: an especially low level of sexual interest and drive

hypospadias (hye-pa-SPADE-ee-as): birth defect caused by incomplete closure of the urethra during fetal development

—I—

identical: a twin formed by a single ovum which was fertilized by a single sperm before the cell divided in two

imperforate hymen: lack of any openings in the hymen

impotence (IM-pa-tens): difficulty achieving or maintaining erection of the penis

in loco parentis: a Latin phrase meaning in the place of the parent

in vitro fertilization (IVF): a process whereby the union of the sperm and egg occurs outside the mother's body

incest (IN-sest): sexual activity between closely related family members

incest taboo: cultural prohibitions against incest, typical of most societies

induced abortion: a termination of pregnancy by artificial means

infertility: the inability to produce offspring

infibulation: surgical procedure, performed in some cultures, that seals the opening of the vagina

informed consent: complete information about the purpose of a study and how they will be asked to perform given to prospective human research subjects

inhibited sexual desire (ISD): loss of interest and pleasure in formerly arousing sexual stimuli

internal values: the individualized beliefs and attitudes that a person develops by sorting through external values and personal needs

interstitial cells: cells between the seminiferous tubules that secrete testosterone and other male hormones

interstitial-cell-stimulating hormone (ICSH): pituitary hormone that stimulates the testes to secrete testosterone; known as luteinizing hormone (LH) in females

intrauterine devices (IUDs): birth control method involving insertion of a small plastic device into the uterus

introitus (in-TROID-us): outer opening of the vagina

invasive cancer of the cervix (ICC): advanced and dangerous malignancy requiring prompt treatment

—K—

Kaposi's sarcoma: a rare form of cancer of the blood vessels, characterized by small, purple skin lesions

kiddie porn: term used to describe the distribution and sale of photographs and films of children or younger teenagers engaging in some form of sexual activity

kleptomania: extreme form of fetishism, in which sexual arousal is generated by stealing

—L—

labor: uterine contractions in a pregnant woman; an indication that the birth process is beginning

lactation: production of milk by the milk glands of the breasts

Lamaze method (la-MAHZ): a birthing process based on relaxation techniques practiced by the expectant mother; her partner coaches her throughout the birth

laminaria (lam-a-NER-ee-a): a dried seaweed sometimes used in dilating the cervical opening prior to vacuum curettage

laparoscopy: simpler procedure for tubal ligation, involving the insertion of a small scope into the abdomen, through which the surgeon can see the fallopian tubes and close them off

laparotomy: operation to perform a tubal ligation, or female sterilization, involving an abdominal incision

latency period: Freudian concept that during middle childhood, sexual energies are dormant; recent research tends to suggest that latency does not exist

lesbian (LEZ-bee-un): refers to female homosexuals

libido (la-BEED-o or LIB-a-do): a term first used by Freud to define human sexual longing, or sex drive

lumpectomy: surgical removal of a breast lump, along with a small amount of surrounding tissue

luteinizing hormone (LH): pituitary hormone that triggers ovulation in the ovaries and stimulates sperm production in the testes

lymphogranuloma venereum (LGV) (lim-foe-gran-yu-LOW-ma-va-NEAR-ee-um): contagious venereal disease caused by several strains of *Chlamydia* and marked by swelling and ulceration of lymph nodes in the groin

—M—

major lips: two outer folds of skin covering the minor lips, clitoris, urethral opening, and vaginal opening

mammography: sensitive X-ray technique used to discover small breast tumors

marital rape: a woman being forced to have sex by her husband

masochist: the individual in a sadomasochistic sexual relationship who takes the submissive role

massage parlors: places where women can be hired to perform sexual acts

mastectomy: surgical removal of all or part of a breast

menage à trois (may-NAZH-ah-TRWAH): troilism

menarche (MEN-are-kee): onset of menstruation at puberty

menopause (MEN-a-poz): time in midlife when menstruation ceases

menstrual cycle: the hormonal interactions that prepare a woman's body for possible pregnancy at roughly monthly intervals

menstruation (men-stru-AY-shun): phase of menstrual cycle in which the inner uterine lining breaks down and sloughs off; the tissue, along with some blood, flows out through the vagina; also called the period

midwives: medical professionals, both women and men, trained to assist with the birthing process

minor lips: two inner folds of skin that join above the clitoris and extend along the sides of the vaginal and urethral openings

miscarriage: a natural termination of pregnancy

modeling theory: suggests that people will copy behavior they view in pornography

molluscum contagiosum (ma-LUS-kum kan-taje-ee-O-sum): a skin disease transmitted by direct bodily contact, not necessarily sexual, that is characterized by eruptions on the skin that appear similar to whiteheads with a hard seed-like core

monogamous: sharing sexual relations with only one person

monorchidism (ma-NOR-ka-dizm): presence of only one testis in the scrotum

mons: cushion of fatty tissue located over the female's pubic bone

moral values: beliefs associated with ethical issues, or rights and wrongs; they are often a part of sexual decision making

morula (MOR-yul-a): a spherical, solid mass of cells formed by 3 days of embryonic cell division

Müllerian ducts (myul-EAR-ee-an): embryonic structures that develop into female sexual and reproductive organs unless inhibited by male hormones

Müllerian inhibiting substance: hormone produced by fetal testes that prevents further development of female structures from the Müllerian ducts

myometrium: middle, muscular layer of the uterine wall

— N —

National Birth Control League: an organization founded in 1914 by Margaret Sanger to promote use of contraceptives

natural childbirth: a birthing process that encourages the mother to take control thus minimizing medical intervention

necrophilia (nek-ro-FILL-ee-a): having sexual activity with a dead body

nongonococcal urethritis (NGU) (non-gon-uh-KOK-ul yur-i-THRYT-us): urethral infection or irritation in the male urethra caused by bacteria or local irritants

normal: a subjective term used to describe sexual behaviors and orientations. Standards of normalcy are determined by social, cultural, and historical standards

normal asexuality: an absence or low level of sexual desire considered normal for a particular person

normalization: integration of mentally retarded persons into the social mainstream as much as possible

nymphomania (nim-fa-MANE-ee-a): compulsive need for sex in women; apparently quite rare

— O —

obscenity: depiction of sexual activity in a repulsive or disgusting manner

onanism (O-na-niz-um): a term sometimes used to describe masturbation, it comes from the biblical story of Onan who practiced coitus interruptus and "spilled his seed on the ground"

oocytes (OH-a-sites): cells that mature to become ova

open-ended marriage: each partner in the primary relationship grants the other freedom to have emotional and sexual relationships with others

opportunistic infection: a disease resulting from lowered resistance of a weakened immune system

organic disorder: physical disorder caused by the organs and organ systems of the human body

organizing effect: manner in which hormones control patterns of early development in the body

orgasm: (OR-gaz-em) pleasurable sensations and series of contractions that release sexual tension, usually accompanied by ejaculation in men

orgasmic release: reversal of the vasocongestion and muscular tension of sexual arousal, triggered by orgasm

orgy (OR-jee): group sex

os: opening in the cervix that leads into the hollow interior of the uterus

osteoporosis (ah-stee-o-po-ROW-sus): disease caused by loss of calcium from the bones in post-menopausal women, leading to brittle bone structure and stooped posture

ova: egg cells produced in the ovary; in reproduction, it is fertilized by a sperm cell; one cell is an ovum

ovaries: pair of female gonads, located in the abdominal cavity, that produce ova and female hormones

ovulation: release of a mature ovum through the wall of an ovary

ovum transfer: use of an egg from another woman for conception, with the fertilized ovum being implanted in the uterus of the woman wanting to become pregnant

oxytocin: pituitary hormone that plays a role in lactation and in uterine contractions

— P —

pansexual: lacking highly specific sexual orientations or preferences; open to a range of sexual activities

PAP smear: medical test that examines a smear of cervical cells, to detect any cellular abnormalities

paraphilia (pair-a-FIL-ee-a): a newer term used to describe sexual orientations and behaviors that vary from the norm; it means "a love beside"

paraplegic: a person paralyzed in the legs, and sometimes pelvic areas, as the result of injury to the spinal cord

partial zone dissection (PZD): a technique used to increase the chances of fertilization by making a microscopic incision in the zona pellucida of an ovum. This creates a passageway through which sperm may enter the egg more easily

pedophilia (peed-a-FIL-ee-a): another term for child sexual abuse

pelvic inflammatory disease (PID): a chronic internal infection associated with certain types of IUDs

penis: male sexual organ that can become erect when stimulated; it leads urine and sperm to the outside of the body

perimetrium: outer covering of the uterus

perinatally: a term used to describe things related to pregnancy, birth, or the period immediately following the birth

perineal areas (pair-a-NEE-al): the sensitive skin between the genitals and the anus

Peyronie's disease (pay-ra-NEEZ): development of fibrous tissue in spongy erectile columns within the penis

phimosis (fy-MOS-us): a condition in which the penile foreskin is too tight to retract easily

pimps: men who have female prostitutes working for them

placenta (pla-SENT-a): the organ that unites the fetus to the mother by bringing their blood vessels closer together; it provides nourishment and removes waste for the developing baby

plateau phase: the stable, leveled-off phase of Masters and Johnson's 4-phase model of the sexual response cycle

polygamy: practice, in some cultures, of being married to more than one spouse

pornography: photographs, films, or literature intended to be sexually arousing through explicit depictions of sexual activity

potentiation: establishment of stimuli early in life that form ranges of response for later in life

pregnancy-induced hypertension: a disorder that can occur in the latter half of pregnancy marked by a swelling in the ankles and other parts of the body, high blood pressure, and protein in the urine; can progress to coma and death if not treated

premature birth: a birth that takes place prior to the 36th week of pregnancy

premature ejaculation: difficulty that some men experience in controlling the ejaculatory reflex, resulting in rapid ejaculation

premenstrual syndrome (PMS): symptoms of physical discomfort, moodiness, and emotional tensions that occur in some women for a few days prior to menstruation

preorgasmic: a term often applied to women who have not yet been able to reach orgasm during sexual response

prepuce (PREE-peus): in the female, tissue of the upper vulva that covers the clitoral shaft

priapism (pry-AE-pizm): continual, undesired, and painful erection of the penis

primary dysfunction: a difficulty with sexual functioning that has always existed for a particular person

progesterone (pro-JES-ter-one): ovarian hormone that causes uterine lining to thicken

progestin injection: use of injected hormone that can prevent pregnancy for several months; not yet approved for use in the United States

prolactin: pituitary hormone that stimulates the process of lactation

prolapse of the uterus: weakening of the supportive ligaments of the uterus, causing it to protrude into the vagina

promiscuity (prah-mis-KIU-i-tee): sharing casual sexual activity with many different partners

prostaglandin: hormone-like chemical whose concentrations increase in a woman's body just prior to menstruation

prostaglandin or saline-induced abortion: used in the 16-24th weeks of pregnancy, prostaglandins, salt solutions, or urea is injected into the amniotic sac, administered intravenously, or inserted into the vagina in suppository form, to induce contractions and fetal delivery

prostate: gland located beneath the urinary bladder in the male; it produces some of the secretions in semen

prostatitis (pras-tuh-TITE-us): inflammation of the prostate gland

pseudonecrophilia: a fantasy about having sex with the dead

psychosexual development: complex interaction of factors that form a person's sexual feelings, orientations, and patterns of behavior

psychosocial development: the cultural and social influences that help shape human sexual identity

puberty: time of life when reproductive capacity develops and secondary sex characteristics appear

pubic lice: small insects that can infect skin in the pubic area, causing a rash and severe itching

pubococcygeus (PC) muscle (pyub-o-kox-a-JEE-us): part of the supporting musculature of the vagina that is involved in orgasmic response and over which a woman can exert some control

pyromania: sexual arousal generated by setting fires

— Q —

quadriplegic: a person paralyzed in the upper body, including the arms, and lower body as the result of spinal cord injury

— R —

random sample: a representative group of the larger population that is the focus of a scientific poll or study

rape trauma syndrome: the predictable sequence of reactions that a victim experiences following a rape

recreational marriage: extramarital sex with a low level of emotional commitment performed for fun and variety

refractory period: time following orgasm during which a man cannot be restimulated to orgasm

reinforcement: in conditioning theory, any influence that helps shape future behavior as a punishment or reward stimulus

resolution phase: the term for the return of a body to its unexcited state following orgasm

retarded ejaculation: a male who has never been able to reach an orgasm

retrograde ejaculation: abnormal passage of semen into the urinary bladder at the time of ejaculation

retrovirus (RE-tro-vi-rus): a class of viruses that reproduces with the aid of the enzyme reverse transcriptase, which allows the virus to integrate its genetic code into that of the host cell, thus establishing permanent infection

Rh incompatibility: condition in which a blood protein of the infant is not the same as the mother's; antibodies formed in the mother can destroy red blood cells in the fetus

Rho GAM: medication administered to a baby soon after delivery to prevent formation of antibodies when the baby is Rh positive and its mother Rh negative

rhythm method: a natural method of birth control that depends on an awareness of the woman's menstrual-fertility cycle

RU-486: a progesterone antagonist used as a postcoital contraceptive

rubber dam: small square sheet of latex used to cover the vulva, vagina, or anus to help prevent transmission of HIV during sexual activity

— S —

sadist: the individual in a sadomasochistic sexual relationship who takes the dominant role

sadomasochism (sade-o-MASS-o-kiz-um): refers to sexual themes or activities involving bondage, pain, domination, or humiliation of one partner by the other

sample: a small representative group of a population that is the focus of a scientific poll or study

satyriasis (sate-a-RYE-a-sus): compulsive need for sex in men; apparently rare

scabies (SKAY-beez): a skin disease caused by a mite that burrows under the skin to lay its eggs causing redness and itching; transmitted by bodily contact that may or may not be sexual

scrotum (SKROTE-um): pouch of skin in which the testes are contained

secondary dysfunction: develops after some period of normal sexual function

selective reduction: use of abortion techniques to reduce the number of fetuses when there are more than three in a pregnancy, thus increasing the chances of survival for the remaining fetuses

self-gratification: giving oneself pleasure, as in masturbation; a term typically used today instead of more negative descriptors

self-pleasuring: self-gratification; masturbation

semen: (SEE-men): mixture of fluids and sperm cells ejaculated through the penis

seminal vesicle (SEM-un-al): gland at the end of each vas deferens that secretes a chemical that helps sperm to become mobile

seminiferous tubules (sem-a-NIF-a-rus): tightly coiled tubules in the testes in which sperm cells are formed

sensate focus: early phase of sex therapy treatment, in which the partners pleasure each other without involving direct stimulation of sex organs

sex therapist: professional trained in the treatment of sexual dysfunctions

sexual addiction: inability to regulate sexual behavior

sexual dysfunctions: difficulties people have in achieving sexual arousal

sexual harassment: unwanted sexual advances or coercion that can occur in the workplace or academic settings

sexual individuality: the unique set of sexual needs, orientations, fantasies, feelings, and activities that develops in each human being

sexual phobias and aversions: exaggerated fears of forms of sexual expression

sexual revolution: the changes in thinking about sexuality and sexual behavior in society that occurred in the 1960s and 1970s

sexual surrogates: paid partners used during sex therapy with clients lacking their own partners; only rarely used today

shaft: in the female, the longer body of the clitoris, containing erectile tissue; in the male, cylindrical base of penis that contains 3 columns of spongy tissue: 2 corpora cavernosa and a corpus spongiosum

shunga: ancient scrolls used in Japan to instruct couples in sexual practices through the use of paintings

situational homosexuality: deprivation homosexuality

Skene's glands: secretory cells located inside the female urethra

smegma: thick, oily substance that may accumulate under the prepuce of the clitoris or penis

social learning theory: suggests that human learning is influenced by observation of and identification with other people

social scripts: a complex set of learned responses to a particular situation that is formed by social influences

sodomy laws: prohibit a variety of sexual behaviors in some states, that have been considered abnormal or antisocial by legislatures. These laws are often enforced discriminatorily against particular groups, such as homosexuals

sonograms: ultrasonic rays used to project a picture of internal structures such as the fetus; often used in conjunction with amniocentesis or fetal surgery

spectatoring: term used by Masters and Johnson to describe self-consciousness and self-observation during sex

sperm: reproductive cells produced in the testes; in fertilization, one sperm unites with an ovum

spermatocytes (sper-MAT-o-sites): cells lining the seminiferous tubules from which sperm cells are produced

spermicidal jelly (cream): sperm-killing chemical in a gel base or cream, used with other contraceptives such as diaphragms

spermicides: chemicals that kill sperm; available as foams, creams, jellies, or implants in sponges or suppositories

sponge: a thick polyurethane disc that holds a spermicide and fits over the cervix to prevent conception

spontaneous abortion: another term for miscarriage

Staphylococcus aureus (staf-a-low-KAK-us): the bacteria that can cause toxic shock syndrome

statutory rape: a legal term used to indicate sexual activity when one partner is under the age of consent; in most states that age is 18

sterilization: rendering a person incapable of conceiving, usually by interrupting passage of the egg or sperm

straight: slang term for heterosexual

streetwalkers: female prostitutes who work on the streets

suppositories: contraceptive devices designed to distribute their spermicide by melting or foaming in the vagina

syndrome (SIN-drome): a group of signs or symptoms that occur together and characterize a given condition

syphilis (SIF-uh-lus): sexually transmitted disease (STD) characterized by four stages, beginning with the appearance of a chancre

systematic desensitization: step-by-step approaches to unlearning tension-producing behaviors and developing new behavior patterns

— T —

testes (TEST-ees): pair of male gonads that produce sperm and male hormones

testicular cancer: malignancy on the testis that may be detected by testicular self examination

testicular failure: lack of sperm and/or hormone production by the testes

testosterone (tes-TAS-ter-one): major male hormone produced by the testes; it helps to produce male secondary sex characteristics

testosterone replacement therapy: administering testosterone injections to increase sexual interest or potency in older men; not considered safe for routine use

theoretical failure rate: a measure of how often a birth control method can be expected to fail, when used without error or technical problems

thrush: a disease caused by a fungus and characterized by white patches in the oral cavity

toxic shock syndrome (TSS): an acute disease characterized by fever and sore throat, and caused by normal bacteria in the vagina which are activated if tampons or some contraceptive devices such as diaphragms or sponges are left in for long periods of time

transgenderists: people who live in clothing and roles considered appropriate for the opposite sex for sustained periods of time

transsexuals: feel as though they should have the body of the opposite sex

transvestism: dressing in clothes appropriate to the opposite sex, usually for sexual gratification

transvestite: an individual who dresses in clothing considered appropriate for the opposite sex, and adopts similar mannerisms, often for sexual pleasure

trichomoniasis (trik-uh-ma-NEE-uh-sis): a vaginal infection caused by the *Trichomonas* organism

troilism (TROY-i-lizm): sexual activity shared by three people

tubal ligation: a surgical separation of the fallopian tubes to induce permanent female sterilization

— U —

umbilical cord: tubelike tissues and blood vessels arising from the embryo's navel connecting it to the placenta

urethra (yu-REE-thrah): tube that passes from the urinary bladder to the outside of the body

urethral opening: opening through which urine passes to the outside of the body

urophilia: sexual arousal connected with urine or urination

uterus (YUTE-a-rus): muscular organ of the female reproductive system; a fertilized egg implants itself within the uterus

— V —

vacuum curettage: (kyur-a-TAZH): a method of induced abortion performed with a suction pump

vagina (vu-JI-na): muscular canal in the female that is responsive to sexual arousal; it receives semen during heterosexual intercourse for reproduction

vaginal atresia (a-TREE-zha): birth defect in which the vagina is absent or closed

vaginal atrophy: shrinking and deterioration of vaginal lining, usually the result of low estrogen levels during aging

vaginal fistulae (FISH-cha-lee *or* -lie): abnormal channels that can develop between the vagina and other internal organs

vaginismus (vaj-uh-NIZ-mus): involuntary spasm of the outer vaginal musculature, making penetration of the vagina difficult or impossible

vaginitis (vaj-uh-NITE-us): general term for inflammation of the vagina

values: system of beliefs with which people view life and make decisions, including their sexual decisions

variable: an aspect of a scientific study that is subject to change

variation: a less pejorative term to describe nonconformity to accepted norms

varicose veins: overexpanded blood vessels; can occur in veins surrounding the vagina

vas deferens: tube that leads sperm upward from each testis to the seminal vesicles

vasectomy (va-SEK-ta-mee *or* vay-ZEK-ta-mee): a surgical division of the vas deferens to induce permanent male sterilization

villi: the fingerlike projections of the chorion that form a major part of the placenta

viral hepatitis: inflammation of the liver caused by a virus

voyeurism (VOI-yur-izm): gaining sexual gratification from seeing others nude or involved in sexual acts

vulva: external sex organs of the female, including the mons, major and minor lips, clitoris, and opening of the vagina

— W —

Western blot: test used to verify positive AIDS virus detected first by the ELISA

Wolffian ducts (WOOL-fee-an): embryonic structures that develop into male sexual and reproductive organs if male hormones are present

— Y —

yeast infection: a type of vaginitis caused by an overgrowth of a fungus normally found in an inactive state in the vagina

— Z —

zona pellucida (ZO-nah pe LOO sa-da): transparent, outer membrane of an ovum

zoophilia (zoo-a-FILL-ee-a): bestiality

Index

Credits/Acknowledgments

Cover design by Charles Vitelli

1. Sexuality and Society
Facing overview—United Nations photo by Jeffrey Foxx.

2. Sexual Biology and Health
Facing overview—Abbott Laboratories. 38—Chart: Earth Surface Graphics. 42—The Dushkin Publishing Group photo by Marcuss Oslander. 58—Illustration by Carol Gillot. 62—Illustration by Marcy Gold.

3. Reproduction
Facing overview—WHO photo.

4. Interpersonal Relationships
Facing overview—United Nations photo by John Isaac.

5. Sexuality Through The Life Cycle
Facing overview—The Dushkin Publishing Group photo by Marcuss Oslander.

6. Old/New Sexual Concerns
Facing overview—New York City Department of Health.

ANNUAL EDITIONS: HUMAN SEXUALITY 90/91

Article Rating Form

We Want Your Advice

Here is an opportunity for you to have direct input into the next revision of this volume. We would like you to rate each of the 59 articles listed below, using the following scale:

1. **Excellent: should definitely be retained**
2. **Above average: should probably be retained**
3. **Below average: should probably be deleted**
4. **Poor: should definitely be deleted**

Your ratings will play a vital part in the next revision. So please mail this prepaid form to us just as soon as you complete it.
Thanks for your help!

Annual Editions revisions depend on two major opinion sources: one is our Advisory Board, listed in the front of this volume, which works with us in scanning the thousands of articles published in the public press each year; the other is you—the person actually using the book. Please help us and the users of the next edition by completing the prepaid article rating form on this page and returning it to us. Thank you.

Rating	Article	Rating	Article
	1. Why We Need Limits		31. Barriers in the Initiation of Intimate Heterosexual Relationships and Strategies for Intervention
	2. Beware of Setting Limits		32. Study Defines Major Sources of Conflict Between Sexes
	3. The Politics of Child Sexual Abuse: Notes From American History		33. How Do You Build Intimacy in an Age of Divorce?
	4. Sex in China		34. Major Mergers
	5. AIDS News, Highlights: Fifth International AIDS Conference: Montreal, June 4–9		35. Sexual Pursuit
	6. The Chemistry of Love		36. Not Tonight, Dear
	7. What Keeps Women "in Their Place"?		37. I Love You, But Can I Ask a Question?
	8. The American Man in Transition		38. Sex in Childhood: Aversion, Abuse, or Right?
	9. Close Encounters		39. Double Vision
	10. The Power of Touch		40. What College Students Want to Know About Sex
	11. Chemistry of Sexual Desire Yields Its Elusive Secrets		41. Masturbatory Behavior in College Youth
	12. Is Orgasm Essential?		42. Sex: Better After 35
	13. Contagious Fortune		43. Good Sex Makes Good Marriages
	14. STDs—Sexually Transitted Diseases		44. What Doctors and Others Need to Know
	15. UTIs: Everything You Need to Know About Urinary Tract Woes		45. Love, Sex, and Aging
	16. The Healthy Male: What's Going On in There?		46. Straight or Gay?
	17. Infertility and the Sexual Health of the Family		47. The Healthy Sexual Development of Gay and Lesbian Adolescents
	18. Demystifying Menopause		48. The Impact of Homophobia on Male Sexual Development
	19. Sharp Rise in Rare Sex-Related Diseases		49. Homosexuality: Who and Why?
	20. Teen-Age Pregnancy: The Case for National Action		50. Shattered Innocence
	21. His Sexuality, Her Reproductive Rights		51. Sexual Harrassment, '80s-Style
	22. Yes, You Can		52. Hidden Rape
	23. Saying No to Motherhood		53. Male Rape: The Hidden Crime
	24. The Crisis in Contraception		54. Patient Guide: How to Use a Condom
	25. Kids and Contraceptives		55. Can You Rely on Condoms?
	26. Vasectomy Update: Effects on Health and Sexuality		56. AIDS and the College Student: The Need for Sex Education
	27. Pill Politics		57. Helping Schools to Cope With AIDS
	28. A Failed Revolution		58. Flirting With AIDS
	29. Voting in Curbs and Confusion		59. The Emerging Strategy to Contain AIDS
	30. Abortion: Right or Wrong?		

(Continued on next page)

ABOUT YOU

Name_____ Date_____

Are you a teacher? ☐ Or student? ☐

Your School Name _____

Department _____

Address _____

City _____ State _____ Zip _____

School Telephone # _____

YOUR COMMENTS ARE IMPORTANT TO US!

Please fill in the following information:

For which course did you use this book? _____

Did you use a text with this Annual Edition? ☐ yes ☐ no

The title of the text? _____

What are your general reactions to the Annual Editions concept?

Have you read any particular articles recently that you think should be included in the next edition?

Are there any articles you feel should be replaced in the next edition? Why?

Are there other areas that you feel would utilize an Annual Edition?

May we contact you for editorial input?

May we quote you from above?

ANNUAL EDITIONS: HUMAN SEXUALITY 90/91

BUSINESS REPLY MAIL

First Class   Permit No. 84   Guilford, CT

Postage will be paid by addressee

The Dushkin Publishing Group, Inc.
Sluice Dock
DPG **Guilford, Connecticut 06437**

No Postage
Necessary
if Mailed
in the
United States